WOVENText

Georgia Tech's

Bedford
Book of
Genres

WOVENText

Georgia Tech's

Bedford Book of Genres

Amy Braziller
Red Rocks Community College

Elizabeth Kleinfeld
Metropolitan State University of Denver

Georgia Tech's Writing and Communication Program
Georgia Institute of Technology

with chapters from

Writer/Designer: A Guide to Making Multimodal Projects
Kristin L. Arola, Jennifer Sheppard, and Cheryl Ball

and

Oral Presentations in the Composition Course: A Brief Guide
Matthew Duncan and Gustav W. Friedrich

BEDFORD / ST. MARTIN'S
Boston ◆ New York

Manufactured in the United States of America.

8   7   6   5   4   3
f   e   d   c   b   a

For information, write: Bedford/St. Martin's, 75 Arlington Street, Boston, MA 02116
(617-399-4000)

ISBN: 978-1-4576-9713-5

Acknowledgments
John Clare. Excerpt, "All nature has a feeling . . . ," from *Selected Poems* by John Clare,
edited by Geoffrey Summerfield. Copyright © 2004 by Eric Robinson. Reproduced with
permission of Curtis Brown Group Ltd., London, on behalf of Eric Robinson.
Roger Ebert. "Review of Ratatouille" by Roger Ebert, from http://www.rogerebert.com
/reviews/ratatouille-2007, August 30, 2007; "Bridesmaids," http://www.rogerebert.com
/reviews/bridesmaids-2011, May 11, 2011; "Harry Potter and the Deathly Hallows: Part 2,"
http://www.rogerebert.com/reviews/harry-potter-and-the-deathly-hallows-part-2-2011,
July 13, 2011. Reprinted by permission of The Ebert Company, Ltd.
Karina Longworth. Syndicated review of "Crazy, Stupid Love" by Karina Longworth from
Miami New Times, July 28, 2011. Copyright © 2011 by Miami New Times. First published
in Miami New Times, a Miami New Times, LLC publication. Reprinted by permission of
Voice Media Group, Inc.
Annie Proulx. "55 Miles to the Gas Pump." Reprinted with the permission of Scribner, a
Division of Simon & Schuster, Inc., from *Close Range: Wyoming Stories* by Annie Proulx.
Copyright © 1999 by Dead Line Ltd. All rights reserved.

The remainder of acknowledgments and copyrights appear on the same page as the text
and art selections they cover; these acknowledgments and copyrights constitute an extension of the copyright page. It is a violation of the law to reproduce these selections by any
means whatsoever without the written permission of the copyright holder.

A STORY . . .

When I walked into my first Georgia Tech class, Composition 101, at 8:00 am on Saturday, 28 September 1963, I expected to learn many things, but I did not expect to develop the foundation that would enable nearly every professional success I was to experience in the following 50 years. Yet that is exactly what happened. Composition 101 (now English 1101) taught me the science and art of good writing and communication: the science of infusing my ideas with structure, logic, and evidence, and the art of composing text that made those ideas engaging and compelling. That duo changed my life.

Professor James Bynum, my instructor, first taught me that good structure begins with good topic sentences. "Your topic sentence for the paper overall and the topic sentence for each paragraph should tell the reader 75 percent of everything she needs to know," said he. I spent hours crafting topic sentences! When I finally felt proficient at this foundational skill, I learned to use logic and evidence to strengthen my assertions, to separate the few significant facts from the trivial many, and to show proper respect for the conventions of grammar, syntax, and usage. Dr. Bynum set a high standard and would brook no deviation: in his class, one misspelling or one error in grammar produced an automatic "F."

Paying homage to the science of structure, logic, evidence, and conventions will produce arguments that are often acceptable, seldom excellent. Powerful, persuasive, excellent writing requires just the right amount of artistry. To produce a persuasive, winning argument, a paper or presentation must engage the audience with ideas that flow gracefully one into the next, must use language that is stylistically compelling and elegant, yet must speak always to the context of the moment, the audience in front of us, and the purpose we seek to achieve. We leave behind the trite, the ordinary, the mundane. Instead, we use language that takes our audience on a journey from where they were to where we want them to be . . . and they don't even know they made the trip.

How lucky you are! Fifty years ago the only communication disciplines we were taught were writing and presenting. And while those two served me well, how I wish I had been exposed to all the possibilities of WOVEN. What a strong tool set you have in front of you. And never forget, be the medium Written or Oral or Visual or Electronic or Non-verbal, the same science and art apply. It's always the same tune, merely played in different keys.

Professors plant the seeds; students grow the crops. I was able to take the seeds planted by Dr. Bynum and turn them into the crops that sustained me over a professional lifetime. I morphed the concepts from Composition 101 into solving complex problems, managing production programs, and marketing innovative solutions to savvy audiences, both military and civilian. I was never the best technician, never the best logistician, never the best manager. But I was always the best writer and the best presenter. The ability to take my commander or my boss or my customers on that journey to where I wanted them to be served me very well. And no matter the problem, the solution set I chose always traced back to Comp 101.

The successes in my career have enabled my wife and me to do some exciting things at Georgia Tech. We endowed a scholarship in honor of Dr. Bynum. I lecture on World War II history and give upper-class symposia on Survival Business Skills. I am proud to be a member of the Ivan Allen College Advisory Board and the Georgia Tech Hill Society. And as you read this, you just might be sitting in a building that has my name on it. Sweet!

So apply yourself. Never underestimate the importance of the writing and communication courses you are taking. You never know where an essay or a presentation may lead. Oh, by the way, I aced the course.

Write well.

Stephen C. Hall, IM '67
Colonel, USAF (Retired)
Senior Fellow, L3 Communications Systems-West (Retired)

Using This Book's Companion Web Sites

This book was custom crafted by taking chapters from different books and combining them with chapters and sections written by Georgia Tech faculty. Two of those books, *The Bedford Book of Genres* and *Writer/Designer*, provide supplementary online content.

In the back of this book are two codes; each code unlocks a companion Web site, one for the site that goes with *The Bedford Book of Genres* and one for the site that goes with *Writer/Designer*. The sites share some similar features: you can create a Macmillan LaunchPad account and use the resources on each site on your own. Your instructors might also create sites for your classes and set up assignments and due dates around content in the sites. If you start using the site on your own, you can easily join an instructor-created site later if you are required to do so. The following general tips will help you get started with the companion Web sites.

Registering your codes and creating a Macmillan student account. You can access the sites in any order you wish, but you must match the corresponding code to each site. You are asked to create a username, enter your name and your email address, and then create a password, all very familiar steps. Use your Georgia Tech email address; school addresses help Macmillan Technical Support troubleshoot problems for you more quickly. After you create your account and register your code at the first site, use the same email address and password at the second site.

Navigating the sites. Each site supports browsing and searching of content, which will be useful if you go to the sites on your own or if you want to use or find an item your instructor hasn't assigned. If your instructor assigns a reading or activity, you'll see that very clearly upon logging in because assignments are foregrounded. You should use the site on your own to better understand the content of your book. Chapters will frequently have a note or comment pointing to one of the Web sites. A comment might say, for example, something like this:

FIGURE 1 ▶
Example of a comment with directions to access online content.

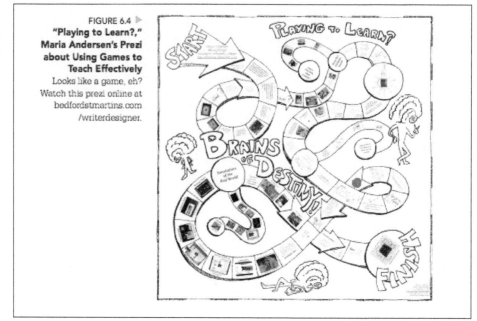

FIGURE 6.4 ▶
"Playing to Learn?,"
Maria Andersen's Prezi
about Using Games to
Teach Effectively
Looks like a game, eh?
Watch this prezi online at
bedfordstmartins.com
/writerdesigner.

When you enter the URL, bedfordstmartins.com/writerdesigner, you will be redirected to the LaunchPad URL your code directions used. After logging in to the site, you can either browse for the content, or you can use the search box to find what you are looking for. The search box is found by clicking the menu item called "Resources." Once you bring up the search box, use either the last name of the author for the item you wish to find or the title of the piece.

Note: Searching for the last name works better in the *Writer/Designer* site and searching for the piece title works better in the *Bedford Book of Genres* site.

FIGURE 2 ▶
The *Writer/Designer* site shows resources being clicked to reveal the search box.

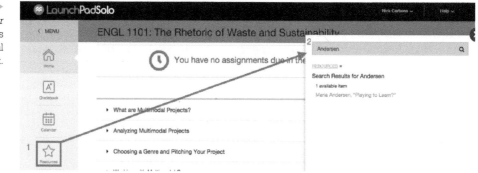

Acknowledgments

This fourth edition of *WOVENText*, a substantial revision to the previous editions, required reimagining what this textbook could do. This new edition reinforces the Writing and Communication Program's vision that communication is based on rhetoric, process, and multimodality.

We would like to thank Lisa Dusenberry for her extraordinary work as the project manager and managing editor from Georgia Tech's Writing and Communication Program (WCP). Her work made this new edition possible: selecting the new foundational textbook content, retooling the table of contents, adding to and extensively revising the existing WCP content, soliciting contributions from WCP faculty, and managing our entire process of development.

We would like to thank the members of the 2013–14 and 2014–15 WCP textbook committees who provided feedback and assistance on this project: Phoebe Bronstein, John Browning, Amanda Golden, Caitlin Kelly, Nicole Lobdell, and Patricia R. Taylor.

We would also like to thank our collaborators at Bedford/St. Martin's who have been committed and invaluable partners in creating this new edition of *WOVENText*: Erica T. Appel, Director of Custom Editorial; Sheila Brewer, Senior Sales Rep; Nick Carbone, Director of Digital Teaching and Learning; Sophia Latorre-Zengierski, Editorial Assistant; and Jane Smith, General Manager for Custom.

WOVENText brings together information from faculty and staff across the Institute, from the Georgia Tech Library to the Communication Center to the Ivan Allen College of Liberal Arts Information Technology Services unit. We thank all of these groups for their contributions and for their support of the students who use this textbook. Below are special thanks to particular individuals who contributed to the content or process of this edition.

**Special thanks to the following people for editorial assistance
for the fourth edition of *WOVENText*:**

John Browning

Rebecca E. Burnett

Lisa Dusenberry

Andy Frazee

Nicole Lobdell

Special thanks to the following contributors for this fourth edition of *WOVENText*:

Sherri Brown

Rebecca E. Burnett

L. Andrew Cooper

Lisa Dusenberry

Peter Fontaine

Stephen C. Hall

Steven Hodges

Jonathan Kotchian

Noah Mass

Malavika Shetty

Britta Spann

Patricia R. Taylor

Elizabeth Wardle

Rebecca Weaver

Special thanks to the following contributors from earlier editions of *WOVENText*:

Jon Bodnar

Ron Broglio

Sherri Brown

Rebecca E. Burnett

L. Andrew Cooper

Shannon Dobranski

Jason Embry

Lori Emerson

Andrew Famigilietti

Jo Anne Harris

Diana Jakacki

Stacy Lavin

Danielle Lawson

Melissa Graham Meeks

Matthew Paproth

Benjamin Robertson

Carol Senf

Malavika Shetty

Nirmal Trivedi

Daniel Vollaro

Robin Wharton

Brief Contents

Contents

The Synergy of Modes and Media in Academic and Professional Communication 43

Understanding Genres 82

Analyzing Multimodal Projects   123

9 Assembling Your Technologies and Your Team 178

10 Oral Presentations, Audience, and Evidence 198

11 Organizing and Developing Oral Presentations 216

14 Informative Genres   323

15 Persuasive Genres   444

16 Considering Communication: Performance, Difference, Language, and Culture   569

19   Process: Evaluating and Choosing Sources   713

20 Process: Integrating and Documenting Sources 776

21 Process: Revising and Delivering Your Project 797

WOVENText

Georgia Tech's

Bedford Book of Genres

PART 1
HOW CAN I BECOME A WOVEN COMMUNICATOR AT GEORGIA TECH?

| 1 | WRITING AND COMMUNICATION AT GEORGIA TECH 2 |

Photo © R. E. Burnett.

HOW CAN I BECOME A WOVEN COMMUNICATOR AT GEORGIA TECH? 💬

CONTENTS

Writing and Communication at Georgia Tech 💬

Welcome to Georgia Tech's Writing and Communication Program. This textbook, *WOVENText*, provides support as you communicate in a range of contexts, including but not limited to your English 1101 and English 1102 classes, your technical communication classes, your senior capstone projects, and your future jobs. *WOVENText* is a guide and supplement to the instruction you will receive in multimodal communication: use it to learn strategies for successful communication and to refresh your memory about conventions for communicating in many modes and media.

What is WOVEN communication?

Georgia Tech's multimodal approach to communication is referred to as WOVEN. The acronym stands for **W**ritten, **O**ral, **V**isual, **E**lectronic, and **N**onverbal communication. Why learn about more than just writing? Although writing is an essential part of effective communication, people communicate using oral, visual, and nonverbal modes as well. They also communicate with electronic/digital media, not just paper.

This textbook provides you with strategies to use various modes in concert with each other. Its six major parts help you address key questions for becoming an effective communicator. These six parts are critical in shaping your communication persona:

» Part 1: How can I become a WOVEN communicator at Georgia Tech?

» Part 2: How can I use WOVEN communication?

» Part 3: How can I create and evaluate multimodal projects?

» Part 4: How can I communicate individually and collaboratively?

» Part 5: How can I use rhetoric to solve communication problems?

» Part 6: How do I use processes for strategic communication?

Along the way, you will learn about multimodal communication while being encouraged to question and challenge various communication strategies. You will view images and also access videos and hyperlinks that extend ideas in the book. You can use this textbook as a reference to review conventions and principles and to seek advice about strategies for communicating effectively.

How is this textbook organized?

This textbook's six parts address important questions about skillful communication. Carefully read the introductory material for each part because it forecasts what each chapter covers, introduces important metacognitive strategies, and helps you develop answers to that part's overall communication question.

The chapters within each part help you learn core concepts, major genres, media, and modes of communication, and work toward helping you develop a nuanced understanding of **rhetoric**, **process**, and **multimodality**—the core tenets of Georgia Tech's Writing and Communication Program. The chapters also include examples of genres that you might encounter in class assignments and in your daily life as a communicator. Most likely your instructor will not create an assignment for every genre you read about, and you may be given assignments using genres that are not discussed in this book. However, you can use all of the examples in this book to develop strategies for approaching new communication problems, modes, media, and genres.

As you read, you will also encounter direct and indirect metacognitive questions and examples in the book's margins that will help you actively learn while you read. These questions ask you to engage in six major areas: remembering, understanding, applying, analyzing, evaluating, and creating. Doing these activities along with your assigned reading will increase your learning and give you a chance to engage more WOVEN modes.

Introduction to Your Course and to This Book GT

The mission of Georgia Tech's Writing and Communication Program is to help students, faculty, and staff across the Institute learn strategies for communicating effectively. The immediate purpose of your course and of this textbook is to help you be more successful as a student at Georgia Tech. The long-range purpose is to help you become a more successful communicator in your personal interactions, in your community, and in your professional life. Why does being a good communicator matter? Having excellent communication strategies is often identified as one of the top qualifications for professionals in virtually every field, including architecture, art, business, engineering, humanities, medicine, politics, science, and social science. More broadly, becoming a good communicator makes your life easier, more interesting, and more fulfilling.

As you start your work in the Writing and Communication Program, you should consider these questions:

» **Why do I have to take a communication course?** The first reason is that it's the law: Georgia mandates that all students meet the requirements for English 1101 and English 1102, which are sometimes referred to together as "first-year composition." The second and much more important reason has to do with the correlation between your personal, academic, and professional success and the ability to communicate effectively. Great innovators must also be excellent communicators to persuade others to endorse new and exciting ideas, products, and procedures.

» **What if I'm already a good communicator?** You can always learn more. Successful people are typically eager to learn ways to be more effective and efficient. Communication strategies are honed over time and improve with each new rhetorical situation you encounter.

» **What if I'm not a very good communicator?** Well, you need to be! And this is the place to learn. If you have been accepted to Georgia Tech, you are definitely capable of extending your competencies to include communication.

» **What kinds of communication can I expect to learn about?** In Writing and Communication Program courses, you will learn about communicating in multiple modes and media (written, oral, visual, electronic, and nonverbal) using rhetorical strategies. You'll use these strategies to think about communication situations and create a variety of artifacts in response to those situations. We use the term "artifact" to designate the full range of multimodal "stuff" you might critique and create: essays and presentations, Web sites and performances, ads and films, and so on. In English 1101 and English 1102, the artifacts you'll critique and create will be multimodal. In English 1101, most of the artifacts you address will be informational (that is, nonfiction); in English 1102, most of the artifacts you address will be literary and often fictional. You will read books, but you will also use digital media, some of which might include blogs, email, Twitter, wikis, Web sites, and YouTube videos. You might give individual and team presentations. Using any or all of these forms of communication, you will learn to analyze text, speech, images, and nonverbal behaviors. You will develop strategies for making strong arguments and for finding compelling supporting evidence. You will learn communication processes that are transferable to many academic, personal, community, and professional situations. You will

Explain what you hope to learn in your multimodal English composition class this semester. #Understand

learn how to be a stronger, more effective team member and leader. And you will learn to recognize that thinking and communicating are inextricably connected. This textbook acts as a guide to help you develop competence and maturity with the many kinds of communication you encounter in English 1101 and English 1102.

Purpose of This Overview

This textbook has been especially designed for students at Georgia Tech. English 1101 and English 1102 rely on this textbook, but you should also keep it as a reference for other courses and professional activities. This overview assembles critical information and resources useful not only for your English courses but for virtually all of your other academic courses. In addition, this information should be useful when you are working as an intern or a co-op student, and it should continue to come in handy when you're a full-time professional.

Why This Book Exists and How You Can Use It

Why is this edition customized, and what do you get out of it? This book is what publishers usually refer to as a "custom edition"—that is, it draws material from faculty members who teach writing and communication at Georgia Tech and from the Georgia Tech Writing and Communication Program's earlier e-book. The other sections of the book come from *The Bedford Book of Genres* by Amy Braziller and Elizabeth Kleinfeld, from *Writer/ Designer: A Guide to Making Multimodal Projects* by Kristin L. Arola, Jennifer Sheppard, and Cheryl E. Ball, and from *Oral Presentations in the Composition Course* by Matthew Duncan and Gustav W. Friedrich. What's the benefit for you? You get the best nationally published materials and the best information from faculty members at Georgia Tech combined into a single book.

Why are some sections marked with the GT icon? The sections of the book marked with **GT** have been written by Georgia Tech faculty members. In a number of these sections, you'll find references to source articles or Web sites that let you track down and further research ideas. Search phrases for these sources will be enclosed in carets (</>), so that you can easily identify them. A textbook customized with information, examples, and discussions from your own professors is more responsive to your needs and interests and, therefore, more relevant to your learning.

Why is some information in textboxes and in the margins? *WOVENText* has textboxes (signaled by a gold box surrounded by blue rules with a blue title above) that include information you will find interesting and useful to supplement the main ideas in the chapter. The information is put in textboxes to separate it from the regular text and make it easy to find. *WOVENText* also has two kinds of marginal information: (1) notes and comments about the text's main ideas and (2) questions you should answer or activities you should complete as you read each chapter to increase your understanding.

Why is the focus on learning strategies rather than practicing correctness? You may not realize it, but you have been learning about language conventions ever since you were very young, even before you went to school. For example, when you were about two or three, you might have said, "Cookie?" In an effort to teach you more about language, your parents might have taught you to ask, "May I have a cookie, please?" In middle school and high school, you had the opportunity to learn conventions of grammar, mechanics, and spelling. A few of you may have also learned conventions of visual and nonverbal communication. *Conventions* are common cultural practices that are often treated as rules; *strategies* tend to focus on heuristics (patterns) and processes. *WOVENText* focuses on strategic knowledge because knowing the strategies increases the likelihood that you can adapt information to new communication situations.

Why is traditional handbook material omitted? Information about language and design conventions is widely available, so it's not included in *WOVENText*. Conventions are important, and you are expected to follow them. However, we didn't want to create yet another textbook with information similar to what's already available in many books and on many Web sites. Whenever you have a question about grammar, mechanics, or spelling, we encourage you to do an Internet search for the term or question and then select an answer/explanation from a reputable site. The *Purdue Online Writing Lab* (Purdue OWL) and *Writing Commons* (peer-reviewed, online open text) are two widely used and highly credible sites, but many other university Web sites and professional Web sites are equally credible.

Compare your previous understanding of rhetoric with Aristotle's definition. #Analyze

Why is the emphasis on rhetoric? *Rhetoric* is an old discipline, dating back to ancient Greece. Over the centuries, the term has sometimes been used in a pejorative way, for example, referring to language used by deceptive politicians in attempts to trick their audiences. However, in Writing and Communication Program courses, you will learn about the widely used classical definition of rhetoric offered by Aristotle in Book I, Chapter 2, of *Rhetoric*, dating from the 4th century BCE. Aristotle defines rhetoric as "the faculty of observing in any given case the available means of persuasion." These available means of persuasion include paying keen attention to factors such as context, content, purpose, audience, argument, genre, organization, design, and visuals — whether you are critiquing or creating written, oral, visual, or nonverbal artifacts.

What are metacognitive questions, and why are they important? Throughout this book, you will encounter direct and indirect **metacognitive questions** to help you with active learning. Metacognition is thinking that controls your cognitive processes (that is, your mental or thinking processes) affecting learning. What are common cognitive activities?

» **Remembering:** Can you recall and define relevant information? Can you remember the 5Ws (who, what, when, where, why)?

» **Understanding:** Can you summarize basic concepts? Can you contrast related ideas?

» **Applying:** Can you plan ways to use information? Can you solve problems?

» **Analyzing:** Can you differentiate similar concepts? Can you infer relationships?

» **Evaluating:** Can you interpret and assess data? Can you justify an argument?

» **Creating:** Can you innovate? Can you create new ideas, processes, and artifacts?

What is Bloom's Taxonomy?

More than 60 years ago, Benjamin Bloom and a group of experts in educational psychology classified levels of intellectual behavior that affected learning. About 20 years ago, a former student of Bloom, Lorin Anderson, updated the original system with the help of a group of experts in cognitive psychology; curriculum and instruction; and educational testing, measurement, and assessment. The revised categories focus on *remembering, understanding, applying, analyzing, evaluating,* and *creating.* The working group emphasized that these six revised categories are relevant to four levels of levels of knowledge: *facts, concepts, procedures,* and *metacognition.* The revised system is used throughout *WOVENText.*

In the introduction to each part of *WOVENText*, you will find a group of direct and indirect metacognitive questions to extend your thinking about the major question posed in that part. The questions encourage you to remember, understand, apply, analyze, evaluate, and create—all critical cognitive activities—as you not only think about facts, concepts, and processes but also consider your own thinking. This reflection is part of what you'll be asked to do throughout *WOVENText.*

Metacognitive Questions to Leverage Your Knowledge

This textbook provides the categories for metacognitive questions—both *direct questions* (e.g., What experience affected your decision?) and *indirect questions* (e.g., Recall an experience that affected your decision). Your goal should be to learn these categories so that you can continue to ask yourself metacognitive questions for the rest of your academic and professional career. Here's the list of the categories and questions for Part 1.

» **REMEMBER:** Recall a communication experience in which you were particularly effective in writing, speaking, designing, or conveying ideas nonverbally. **#Remember**

» **UNDERSTAND:** Based on what you've read so far in Part 1 of this book, contrast your high school experience in a composition class with the approach used here at Georgia Tech. **#Understand**

» **APPLY:** Identify three artifacts for each mode—written, oral, visual, nonverbal—and then identify the modes you most want to strengthen. For example, essays, newspaper editorials, and poems are all examples of writing. Now think of three more examples for writing and three for each of the other modes, and then prioritize the modes you want or need to improve. **#Apply**

» **ANALYZE:** Categorize the aspects of your writing that are strong and effective, and then categorize those that aren't. Look for patterns among your strengths and among your weaknesses. For example, are all your strengths in your use of conventions and your weaknesses in use of rhetorical factors such as adapting to the audience? **#Analyze**

» **EVALUATE:** Communication enables us to address challenging ideas. Do an Internet search for the TED talk "Questions no one knows the answers to." In the video, Chris Anderson poses two big questions: How many universes are there? Why can't we see evidence of alien life? After viewing/listening to the 12-minute video to see how big questions are discussed, identify one big question of your own about which you're especially curious. Then explain why it's both interesting and important. Your ability to express important, abstract thoughts is critical to your academic and professional success. **#Evaluate**

» **CREATE:** What are your strengths as a communicator? Compose a short paragraph that discusses your strengths as a communicator, using at least one concrete example. **#Create**

Making the Transition to Georgia Tech

The transition to college can be exciting and difficult. Students usually live independently and assume more adult responsibilities. Once you turn 18, for example, your parents do not have the legal right to view your grades or have conversations with your professors about your classwork, without your explicit permission. This experience can be simultaneously liberating and daunting. You are now fully responsible for your own performance in your classes, for managing a busy schedule, and for seeking help when you need it. College life is preparation for your professional life, when you—and you alone—will be expected to keep up with your responsibilities and be proactive about handling challenges as they arise.

What's FERPA?
A federal law called the Family Educational Rights and Privacy Act (known as FERPA) protects the privacy of a student's education records. Parents have rights to their child's education records until the child reaches age 18. The rights transfer to the student when he or she reaches the age of 18 or attends a school beyond high school.

In many ways, entering college is like immigrating to a new country, with its own culture and symbols. Pictured here is Tech Tower. For most students and alumni, Tech Tower remains the ever-present symbol of Georgia Tech, a place with its own distinctive culture.

For students entering Georgia Tech's culture from suburban Atlanta, the transition might be straightforward. For first-generation college students from a rural area or for international students, the change may be more challenging. Though the degree of transition varies, all students must adjust to the customary ways of communicating and behaving on a college campus and in the classroom. Your Georgia Tech professors and advisors expect you to complete these four critical actions:

◀ PHOTO
Tech Tower
The Institute has a long history and its own culture—one that you are now adding to as you work toward your degree.
Photo © R. E. Burnett.

1. Read carefully and abide by the course syllabus.

2. Learn actively.

3. Seek help when you need it.

4. Adapt prior knowledge to your new role.

Use your syllabus. Your course syllabus clarifies—from the very beginning of the semester—what your professor expects from you and what you can expect from the course. After you receive a syllabus, take the time to read it slowly and carefully from beginning to end, marking places where you have questions about the course policies, outcomes, and schedule. Even professors who do not spend class time going over every piece of information in the syllabus expect you to read it and abide by its terms. For example, many students neglect to read their professors' attendance policies closely. The temptation—now that you've entered this new land, free of parental oversight—may be to skip classes.

Estimate how many times during the semester you'll check your syllabus. Consider that you need to periodically review it to check class policies for things ranging from attendance to deadlines. #Evaluate

Professors view your presence in the class as essential to your learning, which is why most attendance policies allow only a few absences before your grade is negatively affected. If you miss more than the allotted class time during the course of the semester, you will be in for an unpleasant surprise when you receive your final grade. After you have read the course syllabus carefully, be sure to follow up with your professor if you need anything clarified. Again, you are the only one responsible for keeping up with and managing the multiple responsibilities of your own college life. Your professors expect you to do so and may choose not to provide warnings or reminders beyond those in the syllabus.

Be an active learner. Many college professors in the United States believe that optimal student learning is *active learning*. For this reason, your presence and participation in the classroom are essential to your academic success. While some cultures and fields approach learning as best achieved when professors disseminate information to students, who then memorize it and repeat it back on exams, most of your Georgia Tech professors will also expect you to respond, interrogate, and innovate. In other words, you are expected to think critically. Critical thinking, perhaps the most valuable skill that you will learn in college, is the ability to understand and apply information, develop reasoned and defensible arguments about that information, and offer alternative arguments and solutions.

Imagine your professor has assigned you to write a short paper that creates an argument about the ways in which the following poster conveys its message. To illustrate your critical thinking, you must do more in your paper than simply identify this poster as being made in the United States during World War I. You need to articulate and answer a series of questions: Who created the message? Why is the message being given to the audience? The simple answer is that the U.S. government created the message to tap into Americans' patriotism and to encourage them to support the war effort financially.

In addition to defining the message, you need to **analyze** what elements persuade the poster's viewers to agree with and act on its message. What creative techniques attract the viewers' attention? For example, you might discuss the color scheme, the use of an iconic image (the Statue of Liberty), her humanized form, her gaze, the use of (what was then) the modern technological innovation of the telephone, the repetition of the word *needed*, or the use of alliteration (the repeated consonant sound of *n*). These are all rhetorical strategies used by the poster's artist (Z. P. Nikolaki) to convey his—and the country's—message, and it would be your

This WWI poster would most likely be less effective with a contemporary audience—even though Americans today continue to support the men and women in the military as well as veterans. How could you use the Statue of Liberty to create a contemporary poster supporting U.S. veterans? #Create

◀ POSTER
Z. P. Nikolaki
War propaganda for World War I involved influencing public opinion for what was perceived as the good of the country. *SOURCE: Library of Congress.*

job to explain *why*. How might different people understand the message differently? What values are reflected in (and omitted from) the message? Some viewers might see the poster as war mongering; others might see it as protecting national interests; and still others might see it as a desecration of the iconic symbol of the Statue of Liberty by representing her as a contemporary woman on the phone rather than holding her up as a historic symbol. How might other historical documents or images compare to this one and inform your stance?

Active learners and strong critical thinkers transform their learning experience by engaging with assigned material through outside research and preparation. To add value to your class participation, try exploring images, historical documents, author biographies, or online videos related to your class readings.

Your professors believe that the classroom is a space for *active learning*, for the free and well-reasoned exchange of ideas in multiple modes of communication. In addition to completing written assignments and exams (the *W* in WOVEN), you will also have the opportunity to illustrate your critical thinking skills through class participation and oral presentations (the *O* and *N* in WOVEN) and through the use and creation of visuals such as posters, PowerPoints, and infographics (the *V* in WOVEN). The more adept you become at communicating in written, oral, and visual forms, the more successful you will be, not only in college but also in your personal life, your community activities, and in your professional career.

If speaking up in class makes you uncomfortable or is something you need more experience doing, a useful strategy is to plan beforehand what you intend to say: take careful notes when reading assignments, outline your main ideas, and practice communicating your thoughts in low-stakes settings, such as with friends or in the **Communication Center**. See Part 4 of this book for more about ways to communicate effectively in such contexts.

Seek help. One of the best habits you can develop in college is taking advantage of your professors' regular office hours. Each week professors set aside time dedicated exclusively to working with students outside of class. Every professor posts office hours (indicated on the syllabus and on the course T-Square site or Web site). You can stop by the office, but making an appointment is usually better. During an office meeting, you can get responses to questions you have about class readings and discussions, ask for help with assignments, or just chat about things of interest in the course. Minimally, you should try to visit your professor during office hours for guidance for each major project in the course.

Though college requires much of you, your professors and the Georgia Tech community want you to succeed. If you are ever confused by course material or assignments, overwhelmed by your workload, or tied up in knots because of a conflicting schedule, take advantage of the many resources available to you to work out these problems. Your professor does not want to see you fail or—worse—give in to the temptation to cheat or plagiarize because you feel overwhelmed. *Before the situation becomes dire*, visit your professor during his or her office hours or make an appointment to meet at another time. You should always feel comfortable emailing your professor about class concerns or problems, and expect a response within 24 hours during the workweek. You should not feel that you are intruding; your professors are here to help you do your best work.

Adapt your prior knowledge. Beyond actively using your syllabus, participating in class, and seeking help, you should also consider the following communication-oriented expectations for college writing. Your Georgia Tech faculty members require you to develop new competencies for which you need to adapt your previous knowledge and experience. Specifically, you need to expand the skills you learned in writing five-paragraph essays to college-level writing; attend to correctness and conventions in your grammar, mechanics, and spelling; and build ethos as it relates to your credibility as a communicator.

Writing five-paragraph essays. Many middle school, high school, and college classes assign essays that have an introduction, a three-paragraph body, and a conclusion. Some teachers assign five-paragraph essays as a way for students to answer essay exam questions or briefly describe or analyze topics, but five-paragraph essays are virtually never used in community or workplace communication.

Critics of five-paragraph essays observe that they are formulaic, and the resulting essays are not responsive to important rhetorical factors such as context or audience. You will not be asked to write five-paragraph essays in your English 1101 or English 1102 classes here at Georgia Tech. However, some of the skills you learned while creating five-paragraph essays in junior high school and high school can evolve into strategies useful for multimodal communication at Georgia Tech, in community activities, and in the workplace.

What can you take from your experience learning to write five-paragraph essays? You should carry with you the importance of accurate and well-documented content, global coherence, consistency in tone and voice, and compliance with conventions, such as citing sources correctly. These factors are important, but they're not the only factors important in being an effective communicator. Carefully consider what you already know about communication and use your English 1101 and English 1102 courses to further develop and add nuance to your communication strategies.

Grammar, Mechanics, and Spelling. You'll get farther academically and professionally if you have smart, innovative ideas and present them in ways that make strong,

What strategies did you learn in high school to help you write five-paragraph essays? Which strategies do you think will transfer to creating multimodal artifacts in English 1101 and English 1102? #Remember #Analyze

logical arguments adapted to a particular audience and that respect conventions, typically considered to be grammar, mechanics, and spelling.

Consider an alternative: What if you have smart ideas and credible arguments, but you don't take the time to conform to conventions? For example, what if you violate writing conventions by ignoring expectations for grammar, mechanics, and spelling? After all, should you be expected to do all the work for readers? In practice, can't most readers probably figure out what you mean in spite of occasional typos and other unintentional errors? Wouldn't your time be better spent focusing on the accuracy and depth of content and the sophistication and coherence of the argument? The answer to this question is no.

Here's the position that most workplace professionals take: conventions matter. Certainly, conventions aren't more important than other rhetorical factors, but ignoring conventions sends the message that you are naïve or don't care about communication. In fact, most professionals believe that inattention to grammar, mechanics, and spelling signals a person's inattention to detail more generally; if you don't bother with conventions, what other details have you ignored? Similarly, such inattention signals disrespect for the audience, thinking they're not worth the concern and time needed to use conventions. Also, inattention to conventions signals general sloppiness, indicating that high-quality work isn't part of your approach. By showing you can use conventions appropriately, you fulfill your audience's positive expectations and increase your overall effectiveness. This also allows you to flout certain conventions strategically to create a specific effect; you don't want your audience to assume your intentional break with convention is a careless mistake because you have errors elsewhere.

Ethos. In high school, you learned about ethos, pathos, and logos. You'll learn more about these important rhetorical concepts in your English 1101 and English 1102 courses. One concept particularly emphasized in college is ethos, which is not only

Take a moment to make a list of all the characteristics that you think define good college writing. Then make a list of what you think your instructors' expectations are for good college writing. How does your second list differ from your first? What might account for the differences—and the similarities—between the two lists? #Understand #Analyze

Why do version control and file management matter?

Throughout the semester, you'll be collecting your best and most interesting work to include in your communication portfolio. Part of being able to complete this reflective portfolio necessitates saving copies of your drafts so that you can comment on their development. In order to comment on these drafts, you need to consider a practice common among professionals. They seldom simply write over an old version of a document, replacing it with the new version. Instead, they **save multiple versions** of the document. So, for example, by the time a document such as a rhetorical analysis is completed for a class assignment, your own folder for the assignment could reasonably include RhetAnalysis 11-15-15 ver 1, RhetAnalysis 11-17-15 ver 2, and RhetAnalysis 11-20-15 ver 3. Having these drafts available will be essential to creating your reflective portfolio. (See Chapter 9 for more on version control and file management.)

about the credibility of your sources but also about building your own persona as a communicator. You need to consider that in college you not only write for the professor but also for classmates and even public audiences. For example, if you create a blog post, the professor reads it and so do your classmates; depending on the restrictions of the blog settings, you may also be writing for the public. Another example would be creating a poster to showcase your visual communication competence—to your instructor, to classmates, and also to prospective employers.

Typical Artifacts to Critique and Create

The artifacts you will critique and create in English 1101 and English 1102 reflect all the modes (written, oral, visual, and nonverbal) and both print and digital media. The seven images that follow give you a sense of various categories of artifacts you might critique and create during the semester:

1. Animated video

2. Written document with photos

3. How-to poster

4. Piece of art to invite the public to a discussion

5. Web site celebrating and encouraging sustainability at Georgia Tech

6. 19th-century poem

7. Formal report

Identify artifacts that you're interested in critiquing and in creating. #Apply

In a particular class, you might focus on other modes and media, but these examples represent the range of artifacts you might be asked to critique or create. All English 1101 and English 1102 classes have a topical focus that reflects the disciplinary interests and expertise of the professor. In the examples below, the course focus is on aspects of sustainability.

(1) This short **animated film**, "Bridging Art with Science to Protect Salmon Habitat," is about sustainability. For more information and to view the 3-minute film, search the Internet for <"Bridging Art with Science to Protect Salmon Habitat">; there you'll find a link to "Watch the shallow water habitat animation now." If you were to create a video for your course, you should expect to conduct the research for the project, draft a video treatment (a short document that defines the goals, summarizes the concept, and outlines your approach), create thumbnail sketches of key scenes, write a script (perhaps with collaborators considering whether rhetorical factors have been sufficiently addressed), and then record and edit the video (again, perhaps with collaborators).

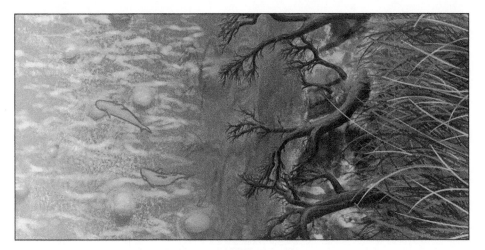

(2) The following **photo** is part of an **article**, "A Deeper Shade of Green: A District Sustainability Plan Encompasses Facilities, Operations, and Instruction." For more information and to view this photo in context, search the Internet for the complete title of the article. (NB: searching for only <A Deeper Shade of Green> will take you to a number of other links for videos and articles about sustainability projects.)

Search the Internet for these abbreviations—or look them up in an online dictionary—to find out what they mean and how to use them, including how to punctuate them in sentences: e.g., i.e., and NB.

School Energy and Recycling Teams (SERTs) are comprised of students, teachers, and administrators at each school. (Photo credit: Montgomery County Public Schools)

If you were to create your own article with illustrations and photos for your course, you should expect to conduct the research for the project, craft a thesis statement, select convincing and credible evidence, write and design two or three (or more) drafts of the article, create and incorporate visuals, edit to consider whether rhetorical factors have been sufficiently addressed, and then proofread.

(3) The following public service **how-to poster** describes a practical way to save water. It appears on a Web site about environmental sustainability as part of the Indian Health Service (IHS), which is responsible for providing federal health services to American Indians and Alaska Natives. For more information and to view this poster in context, search the Internet for <IHS "Fix Your Faucet!">. On the IHS site, you'll also have access to other artifacts, such as formal reports, similar to those you might also critique or create in your course. If you were to create a how-to poster for your course, you should expect to conduct the research for the project, determine steps for the process, consider features such as the dimensions of the poster, write and design multiple drafts of the poster, create and incorporate visuals, follow visual conventions, edit to consider whether rhetorical factors have been sufficiently addressed, and then proofread.

Fix Your Faucet!

- A leaky faucet dripping at a rate of one drip per second can waste more than 3,000 gallons per year. That's the amount of water needed to take more than 180 showers!

- To fix a leaky faucet: Check faucet washers and gaskets for wear, and replace them if necessary.

To learn more about how to fix your faucet, go to:
http://www.epa.gov/watersense/docs/ws_fix aleakfactsheet508.pdf

(4) The following **art** advertises a panel that discusses art and environmental sustainability. If you look closely at the image, you'll see it combines the natural environment (trees and sky) and the human-made environment (crocheted webs). This art is part of an invitation to attend a public panel about art and sustainability, an event sponsored by Seattle's Office of Arts and Cultural Affairs. During your course, you might study art as a way to communicate important ideas. If you were to create a work of art for your course, you should expect to conduct the research for the project, generate an aesthetic vision, sketch the possible variations of your vision, implement the vision, edit to consider whether rhetorical factors have been sufficiently addressed, and then double-check the installation.

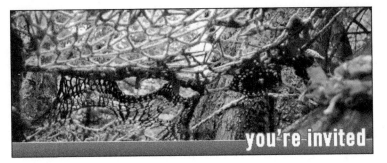

◀ BANNER ART
**Sustainability
Artist Panel
Invitation**
From the Seattle
Office of Arts and
Cultural Affairs
Web site.

(5) The **Web site** for Georgia Tech's Center for Sustainability is part of the Institute's long-term commitment to sustainability. This Web site includes a nearly 5-minute video and defines the center's pillars of business-focused sustainability activities. If you search the Internet for <Georgia Tech Sustainability Scheller>, you will find this site. If you change one word and search for <Georgia Tech Sustainability Stewardship>, you will locate the Web site for the Institute's Office of Environmental Stewardship. If you change a phrase and search for <Georgia Tech Sustainability Institute Planning>, you will be directed to the Web site for the director of the Institute's Office of Environmental Stewardship, which promotes sustainability within and among campus operations, academia, and research. If you were to create a Web site for your course, you should expect to conduct the research for the project, design the front (splash) page and the succeeding pages, map the tabs and links, write multiple drafts of the text, create and incorporate visuals, edit to consider whether rhetorical factors have been sufficiently addressed, and then proofread.

◀ WEB SITE
**Sustainability
at Scheller**
From Georgia Tech's
Scheller College of
Business.

(6) While the preceding examples focus on environmental sustainability in the sense of preservation, a **poem** by the 19th-century English Romantic poet John Clare focuses on the cycle of nature "to pass away / And come again in blooms revivified"—thus, nature is sustained, everlasting like the sun and the moon. Clare is writing in the same period as other English Romantic poets and, like them, focuses on feelings about nature. If you were to write an analysis of Clare's poem, you should expect to read the poem carefully several times and to conduct further research for the project, reading other poems by Clare and about his life, as well as about Romantic poetry more broadly. You would need to write multiple drafts of your analysis, create and incorporate visuals if appropriate, edit to consider whether rhetorical factors have been sufficiently addressed, and then proofread. If you were to write a poem about sustainability, you might think about a particular scene or memory that evokes the feelings and ideas that you want to convey and then think about the words portraying that scene or memory, words with the appropriate sound and feeling. Read your drafts aloud to hear if the poem sounds right, considering its rhythm and other sonic effects like rhyme, alliteration, and assonance. Be willing to revise several—maybe even many—times.

Eternity of Nature
All nature has a feeling: woods, fields, brooks
Are life eternal: and in silence they
Speak happiness beyond the reach of books;
There's nothing mortal in them; their decay
Is the green life of change; to pass away
And come again in blooms revivified.
Its birth was heaven, eternal is its stay,
And with the sun and moon shall still abide
Beneath their day and night and heaven wide.
John Clare (1793–1864)

(From The Poems of John Clare. Edited with an
Introd. by J. W. Tibble. London: Dent, 1935. Print.)[1]

(7) The following **formal report**, *Fathers' Involvement With Their Children: United States, 2006–2010*, focuses on societal and familial sustainability. Here you see the first page of this 21-page report, written by experts at the National Center for Health Statistics, a part of the Centers for Disease Control and Prevention, which is itself part of the U.S. Department of Health and Human Services. If you search the Internet for <"Fathers' Involvement With Their Children">, you'll find a link to the full report. You'll see this example includes many features you'd include in any formal report: title and subtitle, abstract, key words, page numbers, a running head

---

[1] While Tibble's 1935 edited collection names this poem as "Eternity of Nature," it is often called "All Nature Has a Feeling" instead because Clare wrote another poem with a similar title, "The Eternity of Nature."

(at the top of each page), an introduction, level-1 and level-2 headings (sometimes called subheadings), bulleted lists, tables, graphs (called *figures* in the report, a common convention), a conclusion, internal citations, references, appendices, and acknowledgments. If you were to write a formal report for your course, you should expect to conduct the research for the project, create an abstract (and sometimes a table of contents), write multiple drafts, create and incorporate visuals, edit to consider whether rhetorical factors have been sufficiently addressed, and then proofread.

National Health Statistics Reports

Number 71 ■ December 20, 2013

Fathers' Involvement With Their Children: United States, 2006–2010

by Jo Jones, Ph.D., and William D. Mosher, Ph.D., Division of Vital Statistics

Abstract

Objective—This report measures fathers' involvement with their children. Father involvement is measured by how often a man participated in a set of activities in the last 4 weeks with children who were living with him and with children who were living apart from him. Involvement is measured separately for children aged 0–4 years and children aged 5–18 years. Increased involvement of fathers in their children's lives has been associated with a range of positive outcomes for the children.

Methods—The analyses presented in this report are based on a nationally representative sample of 10,403 men aged 15–44 years in the household population of the United States. The father-involvement measures are based on 2,200 fathers of children under age 5—1,790 who live with their children and 410 who live apart from their children—and on 3,166 fathers of children aged 5–18—2,091 who live with their children and 1,075 who live apart from their children.

Results—Statistics are presented on the frequency with which fathers took part in a set of age-specific activities in their children's lives. Differences in percent distributions are found by whether the father lives with or apart from his children, and by his demographic characteristics. In general, fathers living with their children participated in their children's lives to a greater degree than fathers who live apart from their children. Differences in fathers' involvement with their children were also found by the father's age, marital or cohabiting status, education, and Hispanic origin and race.

Keywords: fathers' activities with children • fathers and children • coresidential and noncoresidential children • National Survey of Family Growth

Introduction

Fathers' involvement in their children's lives has been shown to have a positive effect on children and their well-being in many areas (1)—for example, on increasing the chances of academic success (2,3) and in reducing the chances of delinquency and substance abuse (4–6). A literature review found that children whose fathers assumed 40% or more of the family's care tasks had better academic achievement than children whose fathers were less involved (7,8).

In recent decades, fathers who live with their children have become more involved in their children's lives than in previous generations (9,10), although fewer fathers now live with their children because of increases in nonmarital childbearing (9,11–15). The impact of nonmarital childbearing on the presence of fathers is moderated, however, by increases in the proportion of children being born into cohabiting unions (12). For example, Martinez et al. (see Table 12 in reference 12) found that 23% of recent births (those occurring in the 5 years before the interview) to women aged 15–44 in 2006–2010 occurred within cohabiting unions, a significant increase from births to women aged 15–44 in 2002 (14%). Using a national sample of fathers aged 15–44, this report documents how much fathers are involved with their children—both children with whom they live, and children from whom they live apart.

From 1973, when the National Center for Health Statistics (NCHS) first conducted the National Survey of Family Growth (NSFG), to 1995, NSFG measured changes in the factors related

U.S. DEPARTMENT OF HEALTH AND HUMAN SERVICES
Centers for Disease Control and Prevention
National Center for Health Statistics

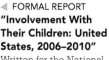

Expectations for College Communication: Standard American English

Australian English, Indian English, African American Vernacular English, Spanglish—these are just some of the many dialects of English spoken in the United States and abroad. Chances are, even if you only speak English, you speak multiple varieties of it. The way you speak to your family members is likely significantly different from the way you speak to an authority figure. Sometimes consciously and sometimes automatically, every time you communicate you vary your vocabulary, your pace, your accent, and your degree of formality. This ability to adjust or shift how you speak—whether in Standard American English, in different dialects, or in different languages—is referred to as **code-switching**. Code-switching is a useful skill, allowing you to communicate to multiple types of audiences in many different kinds of situations.

In American institutions of higher learning and in the professional world, **Standard American English (SAE)** is the accepted dialect. Advancing socially, politically, and financially in the United States is difficult if you cannot communicate in SAE. This is not to say that SAE is a more correct dialect than other versions of English, but rather that it is the dialect of English that is accepted by most people in business, industry, and schools as well as government, nonprofit, and community organizations. People in positions of authority usually expect you to communicate effectively in SAE. SAE is the language of politics, commerce, academia, and even Hollywood. For example, early in her acting career, Georgia-born Julia Roberts received speech training to develop competence beyond her native southern dialect.

Most Americans do not speak perfect SAE at home; however, if SAE is not your first language, then you'll probably require even more effort when you need to switch to it. Your goal should be to develop competence in using SAE and the ability to switch to it seamlessly and effortlessly whenever you need to. The goal is not to make all of your communication conform to the conventions of SAE but to ensure that you can use it whenever it's appropriate, so your audience can understand you.

To follow conventions is to establish yourself as a credible, responsible communicator. In other words, your message—whether you're selling a product, convincing someone to fund your research, or asking for a raise—will likely be better received by your audience if you abide by agreed-upon conventions. Throughout *WOVENText*, we introduce you to many of these conventions. Your job as a skillful communicator is to analyze a particular context, purpose, and audience in order to determine how best to convey your message.

For example, if you are speaking with a group of peers in a very casual setting and want to emphasize how little you saw (or deny that you saw something), saying "I didn't see nothing" instead of "I didn't see anything" might be acceptable. Tech-

Explain what contributes to your ability to speak dialects other than SAE. #Evaluate

Does your family speak one way at home and another way in public settings? Infer the possible reasons. #Analyze

nically, this construction is referred to as a **double negative** and is considered nonstandard English. In some contemporary dialects of English, however, double negatives are acceptable, serving to reinforce a point. How did double negatives become unacceptable in SAE? In the 18th century, certain British grammarians who were especially fond of logic and language decided that two negatives equal a positive. They then declared that double negatives in English are grammatically incorrect, though they had been perfectly acceptable prior to this declaration. Chaucer's classic *Canterbury Tales*, for example, is rife with them. Since double negatives are now nonstandard, however, you must be familiar with this convention in order to wield it appropriately.

Let's consider one more situation that requires a conscious adjustment of your use of English. The following email might be perfectly fine to send to your friend:

> **Subject line:** outta class
> Hey, im not gonna be in class today.

Your friend would get your point and not be put off by the abrupt greeting and typos. However, you would not want to send this email to your professor. College professors expect a certain level of professionalism and respect from their students. For this reason, you ought to abide by appropriate conventions of professional correspondence.

This following revised version of the email begins with a subject line that signals the topic: "Unexpected absence, ENGL 1101-C3, Mary Jane Tripp." The writer includes an appropriate salutation: "Dear Professor Gilligan." Students transitioning from high school may inadvertently rely on Mr. or Ms. as the standard form of address, but keep in mind that most college professors have earned advanced degrees, so they should be addressed as *Professor* or *Dr.* Mary Jane was also sure to write in SAE with no typos or grammatical mistakes and demonstrated respect and responsibility. She included her name at the end, after the complimentary closing of "Sincerely," along with information about which class she is enrolled in. Finally,

Why isn't flouting of conventions a problem when talking with your friends but it might be when talking to your boss? Infer the possible reasons. #Analyze

In what ways is your communication to close friends different from your communication to your professors? #Evaluate

◄ SCREENSHOT
Professional Email
Writing professional emails is an important part of becoming an audience-centered communicator.

she included her email address in her closing to make sure the professor has it. Her professor, who receives many emails over the course of the day, will be much more receptive to Mary Jane's second message than to the first one.

Your ability to determine which conventions should be followed in which situations is essential for your future success. For example, you need to be able to determine when a meme is making a useful and humorous point and when it's just unnecessary and distracting noise.

What is a meme?

Why Correctness Matters

Writing and Communication professors at Georgia Tech are fond of this Internet meme.

Perhaps you have seen it too and have had a good chuckle because, of course, most people would not *hear* that you want to eat Grandma if you uttered the top line; they would hear that you wanted Grandma to sit down and join you for dinner. But pretend for a moment that you silently *read* the top line by itself. You might wonder, if only very briefly, who is eating Grandma.

Complying with communication conventions has consequences. Often, we first meet other people *through writing*. We make impressions through what we write, and certain audiences judge our competence at communication (as well as a number of other personal attributes) by the way we use conventions. This also is true when we speak, especially when we speak in front of people we may not know. In professional settings and academic settings, a lack of correctness can cause a range of negative reactions. Employers will often discard job applications without reading them if they find just one error in grammar, mechanics, or punctuation.

Choose an Internet meme that you find particularly provocative, and explain why you think others will find it interesting or funny or useful. #Understand #Apply

Let's eat Grandma!

Let's eat, Grandma!
PUNCTUATION SAVES LIVES

Consider the case of the Canadian cable company Rogers Communications, where millions of dollars were lost because of a punctuation error. The Canadian telecommunications regulator based its ruling for a lawsuit on a single comma. The dispute centered on the second comma in this sentence:

> This agreement shall be effective from the date it is made and shall continue in force for a period of five (5) years from the date it is made, and thereafter for successive five (5) year terms, unless and until terminated by one year prior notice in writing by either party. —Ian Austen, from "The Comma That Costs 1 Million Dollars (Canadian)," *New York Times* 25 Oct. 2006: C10. *Academic Search Complete*. Web. 4 Oct. 2014.

The *New York Times* reported that "Rogers Communications argue[d] that the agreement [ran] for five years and automatically renew[ed] for another five years, unless a telephone company cancel[ed] the agreement before the start of the final 12 months." The regulator disagreed, ruling that "the comma allowed Bell Aliant to end its five-year agreement with Rogers at any time with notice."

The consequences for lacking correctness can also be personal. You might have seen the Weird Al Yankovic video for his song "Word Crimes" that circulated in July 2014. Both the song and the video work on the emotional level of shaming people who do not use grammar correctly. Weird Al insinuates that people who do not use correct conventions were "raised in a sewer," and they need to "get it together." People who commit "word crimes" are "morons," "mouth-breathers," "lost causes," "incoherent," "spastic," clownish, childish, and shouldn't be allowed to have kids. In short, Weird Al sees errors in grammar, mechanics, and spelling as crimes worthy of violence and insult. While the song is a parody, the parody works because of the truth it's based on: conventions matter.

Although most people you encounter are unlikely to throw insults or objects at you if you commit a "word crime," you may be left out of conversations. All communities, including families, neighborhoods, friendships, and professional and academic communities, use different conventions to converse and to signal membership in that community. Using conventions demonstrates that you belong to that community and that members can trust you. Weird Al's song privileges SAE. It ignores the deep and amazing variety of language practices in this country, but the song does make something clear: know the code.

Explain what dialect you are most comfortable speaking. #Understand

Many of us understand that even monolingual people code-switch between different varieties of the same language on the same day and even in the same conversation. Your goal is not to stop using a variety of codes with your friends, family, and peers, but to use the appropriate conventions (the right "code") in the appropriate context. At school, your work and grades will likely suffer if you submit projects without adhering to SAE conventions. More important, you will not be trusted as a full member of the academic community, and you are less likely to succeed.

Our conventional rules in academia are predicated on a large and diverse mix of learners. Our conventions form a common bond between participants from different backgrounds. In other words, because members of academia come from a broad range of backgrounds, cultures, and languages, we use a language dependent on the codes of Standard American English. Layered on top of SAE is academic jargon that tends to value inquiry, clarity, specificity, knowledge, formality, and the appearance of objectivity. Using such conventions in your classes will help establish you as a credible member of what is sometimes referred to as the "Burkean Parlor" of academia.

Kenneth Burke, in his book *The Philosophy of Literary Form*, writes:

> Imagine that you enter a parlor. You come late. When you arrive, others have long preceded you, and they are engaged in a heated discussion, a discussion too heated for them to pause and tell you exactly what it is about. In fact, the discussion had already begun long before any of them got there, so that no one present is qualified to retrace for you all the steps that had gone before. You listen for a while, until you decide that you have caught the tenor of the argument; then you put in your oar. Someone answers; you answer him; another comes to your defense; another aligns himself against you, to either the embarrassment or gratification of your opponent, depending upon the quality of your ally's assistance. However, the discussion is interminable. The hour grows late, you must depart. And you do depart, with the discussion still vigorously in progress.

By using the appropriate conventions at the appropriate time, you ensure that you can join and continue the conversation. You can, in the words of Burke, "put in your oar." You can be included and valued in the community, and what you say (and write) will be valued too.

Georgia Tech Communication Center 💬

Georgia Tech has many resources on campus to help you become a more effective communicator. The two most important—the ones you should use regularly—are the Georgia Tech Library (which is introduced in Chapter 17) and the Communication Center. Located in Clough Undergraduate Learning Commons 447, the Communication Center promotes excellence in WOVEN communication. The Communication Center enables members of the Georgia Tech community to have greater success in their academic and workplace careers, as well as in their civic and community lives.

At the Communication Center, you'll find trained professional and peer tutors who can help you with everything from multimodal projects to graduate school applications; from engineering and science reports to team presentations; from storyboards for videos to poster designs; from grant proposals to job cover letters and resumes. The Communication Center's tutors can assist you with a project at any stage in the process, from initial brainstorming of an idea to a revision of a final draft. In addition, the Communication Center has a suite of multimodal tools, including computers, facilities for practicing and recording presentations, and a 3-D printer, all of which are available for you to use during your tutoring sessions. Note that although tutors will not proofread or edit your work, they can help you become a more proficient editor.

What Communication Center resources are you likely to benefit from using? #Remember

▲ PHOTO
Communication Center Tutoring
During your free and confidential visit, a professional or peer tutor can help you identify ways to improve your multimodal projects. *Photo courtesy of Peter Fontaine.*

▲ PHOTO
Communication Center Tutoring
Tutors work with students at all stages of project development. *Photo courtesy of Peter Fontaine.*

To make an appointment and check the center's hours of operation, please visit http://www.communication center.gatech.edu/

The Communication Center also ensures that your work in a tutoring session remains confidential. Although you are welcome to bring an assignment for a class to the center, tutors do not report your tutoring session to your instructor. The work that you do in the Communication Center is about you. When you attend a tutoring session, you will find a welcoming staff, a helpful group of tutors, and a relaxed atmosphere in which to receive feedback and assistance for all your communication projects.

PART 2
HOW CAN I USE WOVEN COMMUNICATION?

Read This First! GT

Have you ever composed an email or text message, especially one including pictures, emoticons, or colored text? Given a presentation with visual aids? Created an advertisement to sell your used products or find a roommate? Used Skype or Google Hangouts to communicate with friends, family, or professional acquaintances, wildly gesturing to them with your hands or sharing your screen so you can talk them through a document? Created a YouTube video? If you have done any of these things, you have been practicing **multimodal communication**. Nearly all of our communication tasks, whether they are academic, professional, or personal, engage more than one mode of communication at a time. Even seemingly simple written notes engage the visual mode by using the white space, headings, lists, and bullets to help your reader make sense of your text. Choosing among boldface, italicized, or standard font styles when you compose using word-processing software is another subtle way of engaging multiple modes as you communicate. Your English 1101 and English 1102 courses teach you to move beyond accidental multimodality, adopting strategies that deliberately use several modes together to create accessible, usable, and engaging artifacts for your audience.

Multimodal Communication = WOVEN Communication

As you'll recall, WOVEN stands for **W**ritten, **O**ral, **V**isual, **E**lectronic, and **N**onverbal communication. In combination, these modes allow you to accommodate the learning preferences, interests, and abilities or disabilities of your audience. These modes and media also allow you to appeal to and persuade your audience while leveraging the media you use to reach that audience. Below you'll learn more about the synergy of modes that makes your artifacts more compelling.

To answer the question "How can I use multimodal communication?" you must first know *what* is involved in multimodal communication and *why* we use the WOVEN approach at Georgia Tech. Some colleges and universities have writing programs that focus largely on form and correctness in academic essay writing. However, the Georgia Tech Writing and Communication Program focuses on rhetoric, process, and multimodality. Why? Developing your awareness of these three concepts makes you a better communicator, a more sophisticated innovator, and a more focused decision maker who can tackle any task. You will learn much more about rhetoric, process, and multimodality in the following chapters.

Rhetoric. Rhetoric—a discipline going back to Ancient Greece—is the study of the ways that people make what they write, say, or design persuasive for a particular audience in a particular situation. You need to learn about ways you can use

◀ MEMOIR
Marjane Satrapi,
Persepolis
Everett Collection.

rhetorical elements to influence your creation and interpretation of written, oral, visual, and nonverbal communication. Let's look at the movie poster for *Persepolis*, shown above. *Persepolis*, an autobiographical novel told in comic strips, tells *and* shows the story of Marjane Satrapi's coming-of-age experiences during the Islamic Revolution in Iran. The novel explores the tensions between public and private life, among family members, and among individual and spiritual, religious, and political lives. The film adaptation of *Persepolis* was nominated for the Academy Award for Best Animated Feature in 2007. What questions about rhetorical elements might you consider in analyzing the *Persepolis* poster? Here are some questions you might ask—though they are only a few of the possibilities:

> *Rhetorical elements.* Consider these rhetorical elements when communicating: content, context, purpose, audience, argument, evidence, genre, organization, visuals, design, and conventions.

» *Context*: This graphic novel and movie have a huge international audience. Look at the words on the movie poster reproduced in this book: "A triumph. Feisty and funny. Wonderful." Conduct an online image search for <Persepolis poster>. What do you observe about the language on other versions of the poster? What do you believe accounts for the differences among the posters?

» *Audience*: Are viewers' perceptions of the poster art likely to change if they know the movie is based on a graphic novel? Graphic novels have a mixed audience—young adults and adults. How does the poster appeal to both audiences?

» *Design*: What do you think accounts for the fact that the main character in this version of the movie poster is not smoking, when the main character *is* smoking in some other versions of the poster?

» *Conventions*: Language and design conventions of movie posters include the name of the movie, text to attract viewers, text about actors, and the release date. What other conventions do movie posters—and other promotional posters—use? What movie poster conventions are used in the *Persepolis* poster shown here? What design features enable you to identify the conventions, even when a promotional poster is presented in a language other than English?

Process. You need to develop your own effective and efficient **processes** for researching, collaborating, planning, drafting, reviewing, editing, revising, proofreading, and publishing—processes that work for you in various communication situations. You also need to reflect about your processes, so you can determine when they're working and when they need to be fine-tuned. When you're not happy with the way a project turns out, you need to know what processes led to the poor result, so you can change them. Likewise, when you do something well, you need to know what processes led to the positive result, so you can repeat them.

Return for a moment to the *Persepolis* example. You can use this movie poster to prompt additional thinking about process: What changes are needed to transform a graphic novel into a movie? What processes do you think the graphic designer used to create the movie poster? What processes may the designer have used to adapt the poster to different audiences and contexts?

Multimodality. Multimodal communication is at the heart of the ways you communicate in every part of your life. In your academic, community, and professional work, you need to be much more than a capable writer. You are also expected to be a capable speaker, designer, and collaborator—that is, you are expected to be proficient in communication in written, oral, visual, and nonverbal modes. Multimodality is widely used in universities, communities, and workplaces. Minimally, you need to be competent in these areas. Ideally, you should be extraordinarily proficient. Capabilities you should develop include following language and design conventions (grammar and mechanics) that influence both cultural expectations and audience comprehension (see Chapter 16 for discussions about considering assumptions, audience, and access as well as language and dialects). You also need to realize that simply complying with conventions is not enough. You do not want your work to be shallow and superficial, unworthy of you intellectually. Instead, you need to present strong arguments and consider the context, purpose, and audience of your work so that it will have meaning and depth, be intellectually rigorous, be respectful of your audience, and consider the needs of the situation.

Screenwriting involves a long process of research, organization, writing, revision, and editing. Read the introduction to Part 6 of this book for further discussion about screenwriting and one screenwriter's process for researching and composing a script.

Return to the *Persepolis* example and think about connections to multimodality. Consider the "affordances" of various modes and media to convey the story: What other modes could be used to convey the autobiography of the main character? The graphic novel *Persepolis* has already been transformed into an animated movie, but what would have been done differently if it had been made into an audiobook or into a live-action movie? How might you transform a segment of *Persepolis* into a podcast, an illustrated children's book, or a documentary about girls growing up in Iran?

Considerations in using this textbook. In the following chapters, you will learn vocabulary that will help you understand and discuss rhetoric, process, and multi-modality and create smart, credible arguments. It will give you a way to articulate and to reflect on your practices as a communicator, both of which are key strategies for success in English 1101 and English 1102.

WOVENText approaches rhetoric, process, and multimodality in two major ways: by (1) discussing genre and (2) discussing processes for creating multimodal projects.

First, *WOVENText* discusses multimodality by exploring various **genres** and the ways artifacts from those genres are shaped by their rhetorical situation (purpose, audience, rhetorical appeals) and their genre conventions (style, design, sources). The book illustrates ways modes can work together within an artifact and the ways different genres engage different media. In addition, the material from Georgia Tech faculty members shows you how to weave modes together—to use them synergistically.

Genre is a useful system of categorization to help you think about composition, but at Georgia Tech you are then encouraged to **translate**, **transform**, and **transfer** what you learn about each genre into broader strategies for use in other communication tasks (see Chapter 3). For example, Chapter 4 introduces you to the artist's statement, which is then classified as a persuasive genre and explored in depth in Chapter 15. The artist's statement does not solely persuade, however; it also informs and provides narrative, thus defying simple categorization. You can use genre categories as guides rather than strict rules. Pay attention to the ways effective communicators uphold and transgress the boundaries of particular genres and the ways they use WOVEN modes to influence what a genre can do.

Second, *WOVENText* offers a practical approach to creating **multimodal projects**. The terminology helps you articulate ways in which design and multimodality influence the questions about rhetorical situations posed throughout the text. Chapter 9 and all of the chapters in Part 6 of the textbook help you tackle multimodal projects as a thoughtful and reflective communicator who can make strategic decisions to achieve your purpose. These parts of the book refer to **linguistic**,

Affordances are properties of objects, tools, or environments that allow them to be used in particular ways. In multimodal communication, each mode has its own set of affordances. See Chapter 2 for a more detailed discussion.

Select an artifact in one mode (e.g., written, oral, visual, nonverbal) and in one medium (print, digital) that you've created successfully in another course or situation. Identify a way to transform it into another mode or medium. #Remember #Analyze

Linguistic: written and spoken language

Visual: images and design characteristics

Aural: sound

Spatial: physical arrangement

Gestural: body language and movement

Source: Kristin L. Arola, Jennifer Sheppard, and Cheryl E. Ball, Writer/Designer: A Guide to Making Multimodal Projects.

visual, **aural**, **spatial**, and **gestural** modes, drawing attention to the sensory experience of each mode. You can connect these sensory descriptions to written, oral, visual, electronic, and nonverbal communication. For example, the linguistic mode includes written, oral, and visual communication by focusing on word choice, delivery, organization, and coherence of ideas. The visual mode intersects with written, visual, and electronic communication, helping viewers focus on design. The aural mode intersects with oral and electronic communication, emphasizing sound and sound manipulation. The spatial mode intersects with visual communication, emphasizing arrangement, organization, and proximity. The gestural mode intersects with nonverbal communication, primarily concerned with how the movement of the body conveys meaning.

Metacognitive Questions to Leverage Your Knowledge: Rhetoric, Process, and Multimodality.

You can start to answer the following direct and indirect metacognitive questions now, but you'll have much more detailed and credible responses when you finish reading all the chapters in Part 2.

» **REMEMBER:** Decide which rhetorical strategies you most wish to strengthen during this semester. **#Remember**

» **UNDERSTAND:** Explain your current processes—in collaborating, planning, drafting, reviewing, editing, revising, proofreading, and publishing. What kinds of changes would improve them? **#Understand**

» **APPLY:** Select an artifact (such as a graphic novel, movie poster, fairy tale, painting, poem, play, short story, or documentary film). Identify at least three other genres into which it might be transformed—as with the example of *Persepolis* in the preceding discussion. What additional genres are feasible and have likely audiences? **#Apply**

» **ANALYZE:** Examine the Georgia Tech homepage. Infer the major audiences for the site based on the content and design of the page. **#Analyze**

» **EVALUATE:** Compare a story from the *Technique* (the Georgia Tech student newspaper) with an article from a national or international news outlet. How do they differ in their use of rhetoric and modes of communication? **#Evaluate**

» **CREATE:** Select a short story or article that you have read for a class. Create a sketch of a promotional poster (with all the elements of such a poster) that informs viewers about the story or article's purpose. How can you persuade them that it is worth reading? **#Create**

CRITICAL CONCEPTS OF COMMUNICATION GT

CONTENTS

The Writing and Communication Program at Georgia Tech emphasizes three critical concepts: communication is rhetorical, communication involves a process, and communication is multimodal. You probably already know a considerable amount about these concepts, but English 1101 and English 1102 help you build on what you already know by encouraging you to explore your ideas about communication and to use these concepts in ways that focus on their relationships to society, science, and technology. You learn how to use rhetorical strategies in ways that create professional, expert-like communication and to consider variations in both modes and media. This approach provides you with the communication strategies necessary to excel in a 21st-century world.

Critical Concept One: Communication Is Rhetorical GT

Rhetoric is about being persuasive with a well-crafted and specific argument—specific to the context, specific to the purpose, and specific to the audience—using the tools available to you. Whether in Ancient Greece or 21st-century Atlanta, persuasion involves constructing a logical and credible argument to convince an audience that your position or point of view is appropriate. How can you argue persuasively? Since Ancient Greece, three appeals have been considered requirements for a good argument:

» One appeal, **ethos**, is based on your own reputation and credibility as a writer, speaker, or designer.

» A second appeal, **logos**, is based on the logic and coherence of your argument.

» A third appeal, **pathos**, is based on the emotions, beliefs, and values you evoke.

You'll be reminded of these appeals in various ways throughout this textbook. They should become so familiar to you that you automatically think of them whenever you are creating or critiquing a communication artifact.

Some people say that "everything's an argument"! Explain the ways that this is a defensible position. #Understand

These three appeals all work together to support the arguments of your artifacts. An **argument**—a position or stance supported with logically organized, credible, convincing evidence—can be made by individuals as well as groups, in a variety of cultures, modes, and media. An argument needs to persuade; being persuasive is challenging and involves making strategic decisions about rhetorical elements.

Is it an argument?

Consider how frequently communication involves creating an argument, whether implied or explicit. Consider how the following examples are arguments:

- » Stop sign
- » Advertisement
- » Political campaign speech
- » Editorial cartoon
- » Software installation instructions
- » Global warming documentary
- » Broadway performance

- » Fact sheet describing solar panels for residential or commercial buildings
- » Proposal to fund a stem cell research project
- » Technical report analyzing the safety of a new prescription medication

To create successful arguments, you need to ask questions about rhetorical elements (similar to those you explored in relation to *Persepolis* in the introduction to this part of *WOVENText*), beginning with **audience**: Who are my audiences? What prior knowledge does a particular audience have? Knowing who your audiences are and having some sense of each group's prior knowledge enables you to adapt many aspects of your work to serve your audiences' needs. Based on your audience awareness, you might adjust aspects including the nature of the argument, complexity of the content, organization of the information, formality of the diction, types of supporting evidence, and visual design.

Questions about other rhetorical elements are equally important to consider: What are the **contexts** in which readers, listeners, and viewers will use my document (or presentation or visual)? What **purposes** do I have? And what purposes do my audiences have? What **argument** am I making? What's the most compelling **evidence** I can use, given the attitudes and needs of my audiences? What's the most effective way to **organize** the information? What **visuals** will work, given the audiences and purposes? How does the **design** influence the ways that audiences access, understand, and use the information? What **language conventions** should I use? What **visual conventions** should I use? As you write a paper, prepare a presentation, or design a visual—by yourself or with collaborators—you need to ask and answer questions such as these.

Critical Concept Two:
Communication Involves a Process GT

Although all processes are idiosyncratic, most effective processes also have commonalities. You have probably already learned about basic processes (e.g., planning, drafting, revising), but in English 1101 and English 1102 you will explore a broad variety of processes, so that you can decide which ones work best for you when completing various communication tasks. Your goal should be to develop a repertoire of processes from which you can select each time you approach a new situation. This section introduces two of the many considerations affecting your processes: decision making and affordances.

Decision making. All of your processes involve decision making that is either strategic or tactical:

» *Strategic decisions* in communication are important to your overall purpose, so they typically take a long-term, big-picture view of the situation. One strategic decision frequently affects multiple aspects of the situation. For example, changing the audience for an artifact necessarily changes the nature of the argument, the organization of information, the kinds of persuasive examples, and the kinds of visuals you select.

» *Tactical decisions* in communication are short-term decisions that address immediate concerns. Tactical decisions are often localized decisions. Could the topic sentence be clarified? Is "receive" spelled correctly? Does "well-insulated" need a hyphen? Will adding a transitional phrase be sufficient to strengthen the coherence between the paragraphs?

Simply put, in English 1101 and English 1102 you learn to engage in processes that are strategically and tactically sound.

Identify an example of substantive communication you've engaged in during the last month (written, oral, visual, or nonverbal). Identify both a strategic decision and a tactical decision you made related to that communication. #Understand

Affordances. Your instructor will ask you to complete projects that "consider the affordance of the medium." What does this mean? Dr. Janet Murray, an expert in digital media, explains in her blog, *Inventing the Medium*, that **affordance** refers to "functional properties of objects or environments—the properties that allow particular uses. For example, a blackboard affords writing and erasing; a low, flat, supported surface 30 inches square affords sitting."

When you are planning a project, you need to consider (1) *characteristics of the mode* (e.g., written, oral, visual) as well as (2) *affordances of the medium for dissemination* (e.g., book, newspaper, radio, television, or Web site). Each has particular properties and advantages, letting you do certain things easily and effectively. You need to match the particular mode and medium to your rhetorical intentions—that is, the content, context, purpose, and audience of your project.

To help you consider the affordances of a medium for designing digital projects, Dr. Murray developed a planning tool, an **affordances grid** you can sketch as you develop and analyze your digital projects. The grid considers four affordances of digital media—spatial, encyclopedic, procedural, and participatory (each defined in the sample grid)—that are important to consider.

GRID ▶
Digital Affordances Categories
Modified from Janet Murray's blog, *Inventing the Medium*.

Spatial affordances—attention to location and place	*Encyclopedic affordances*—attention to collection(s) of information
Procedural affordances—attention to executable rules, to instructions	*Participatory affordances*—attention to interaction and manipulation of the represented world

You add your own planning notes to the affordances grid to help you determine what categories of affordances you're addressing in your digital project. The affordances may not be mutually exclusive. You can see how the grid works with examples from a digital project about skateboarding. If you wanted to create a Web site about skateboarding, your affordances grid might look like this:

GRID ▶
Sample Completed Affordances Grid
Modified from Janet Murray's blog, *Inventing the Medium*.

Spatial affordances—attention to location and place Planning notes that consider location and space: Include Google map of local skateboard stores. Local, regional, and national skateboarding competitions. Laws against skateboarding in various locations.	*Encyclopedic affordances*—attention to collection(s) of information Planning notes that consider collections of information: Create archive of skateboard designs. Collect safety instructions about skateboarding (parents, professional skateboarders). Identify equipment for different levels of experience and/or expertise.
Procedural affordances—attention to executable rules, to instructions Planning notes that consider rules and instructions: Create site map. Provide site navigation. Define usable menus. Identify usable links.	*Participatory affordances*—attention to interaction and manipulation of the represented world Planning notes that consider interaction and representation: Develop skateboarding blog. Create a Twitter feed. Provide annotated videos that show tricks.

This grid works well when considering the affordances of digital media; other media may have different affordances. Make sure that the medium you select for a project can do what you want it to do. Or, phrased the opposite way, make sure what you create is conveyed in an appropriate medium. Every medium has particular affordances; learn the capabilities of media that intrigue you and also learn the media that will enable you to communicate ideas that matter.

A planning grid is just one way to define affordances and think about the modes and media of your projects. You'll find your projects are more effective and less stressful to create if you institute deliberate planning steps for accomplishing your rhetorical goals when you get to your final draft.

Critical Concept Three: Communication Is Multimodal GT

You may think that the communication courses you take at Georgia Tech are simply variations of the writing courses you've already taken, but writing is just one part of what you need to master. You need to become competent in all modes of communication, not just writing, as you can see in the examples presented below.

▼ GRID
GT Multimodal Communication
Four examples of multimodal communication in action at Georgia Tech.

Courtesy of The Tower Undergraduate Research Journal.	Courtesy of Dr. Jesse Stommel.	Courtesy of Tommy Thompson, photographer, and the Georgia Tech Image Portal.	
The Tower is Georgia Tech's undergraduate research journal. Search <The Tower Georgia Tech> for access to current and back issues.	*Georgia Tech It Gets Better* is a 20-minute YouTube video of interview clips about diversity on campus. Search <Georgia Tech It Gets Better> to watch.	This video with Dr. Hugh Crawford shows the interaction that can happen in writing and literature. Search <Hugh Crawford on Literature at Georgia Tech> at vimeo.com to watch.	Every day, every hour, the Georgia Tech whistle is a nonverbal reminder of the Institute's history and traditions. Search <Georgia Tech whistle living history> to read more.

Whether people are working individually or collaboratively, domestically or internationally, a WOVEN approach emphasizes ways to create and integrate ideas in multiple modes and in multiple media.

» **Modes** are means of *representation*—that is, the manner you choose to express your ideas, whether written, oral, visual, or nonverbal.

» **Media** are means of *dissemination*, whether in a face-to-face presentation, a print document, or a digital artifact.

A WOVEN approach does not isolate or segregate modes and media; instead, it focuses on how these different modes are woven together in our daily lives and in the work world. This section helps you understand more about the individual modes and media. Chapter 3 focuses on the interactions among these modes.

W—You need to be a good writer. Being an excellent writer would be even better. **Written communication** involves creating artifacts that inform, persuade, and/or entertain audiences using alphanumeric characters. As you develop experience as a writer, you will become more and more skillful in using rhetorical elements to help you make informed, strategic decisions about composing for particular purposes and audiences.

Compare the mode, medium, and affordances from these four examples. How do they work together to make an argument about what it means to be part of the Georgia Tech community? #Analyze #Evaluate

Assignments Focusing on *Written Communication*

In written communication, you are expected to conform to conventions of Standard American English. Even if no one says "Check your genre expectations, grammar, mechanics, and spelling," the assumption is that you *always* check, regardless of the mode and medium. Following are typical written activities and assignments you can expect:

» Emails, letters, other correspondence
» Journals, diaries, blogs
» Editorials
» Persuasive and reflective essays
» Analytical essays, reviews
» Academic research papers
» Technical reports
» Proposals
» Instructions
» Narratives in the forms of scripts and short stories

Notice that this list includes documents that can be either print or digital.

Read. The flip side of writing is the receptive competence, reading; you need to be able to interpret and use the texts others write.

A WOVEN approach in no way de-emphasizes the importance of written communication. Instead, WOVEN communication emphasizes the crucial role that writing plays in other modes as well. Digital composing, for example, relies heavily on traditional approaches to writing, but with important differences because writing on a keyboard and reading on a screen are different from writing and reading on paper. Ultimately, a strong foundation in writing is vital to supporting other types of composing, as well as in virtually every career path. Both English 1101 and English 1102 include a variety of written activities and assignments. These courses stress the importance of planning, researching, drafting, organizing, revising, editing, and publishing your writing. As you would in more traditional writing courses, you read in conjunction with writing, using the writing of others both as models and as evidence in your own documents.

"Standard American English" (SAE), a term linguists use, is problematic because North America includes Canada and Mexico. A more accurate term might be "Standard U.S. English." Since the United States is linguistically diverse, what counts as "standard" is open to discussion, though many people use the term "broadcast English." Refer to Chapter 16 for further discussion.

O—You need to be a competent speaker, capable of contributing to conversations and discussions and giving individual and team presentations. Your competence in these areas requires various kinds of collaboration: participating in, facilitating, and sometimes leading groups and teams. **Oral communication** involves creating artifacts to inform, persuade, and entertain audiences using spoken language, which may be transitory (e.g., a face-to-face conversation) or recorded (e.g., a political speech that is videotaped). From telephone conversations to team presentations, oral communication is important in your everyday interactions—in personal relationships, in academic activities, and in the workplace. As with writing, the preparation and practice of oral presentations mean you need to be responsive to rhetorical elements.

Assignments Focusing on *Oral Communication*

Oral communication forces you to think about the dialect you choose to use, which influences audience perceptions of your capability and credibility. These are typical oral activities and assignments you can expect:

>> Everyday conversations
>> Telephone or other distance interaction
>> Recorded messages
>> Public presentations (e.g., conferences, community meetings)
>> Oral instructions and/or demonstrations
>> Interviews
>> Discussions at meetings (face-to-face or distance)
>> Workplace presentations (e.g., weekly status reports, quarterly summaries)
>> Client presentations (e.g., marketing/sales, project progress)
>> Oral arguments (trials), testimony at public hearings, depositions

(For more on assumptions about language and about languages and dialects, see Chapter 16.)

Listen. The flip side of speaking is the receptive competence, listening. You need to be able to actively listen and respond thoughtfully, respectfully, and productively to presentations and in discussions.

Oral presentations, group activities, and class discussions are the most common methods of practicing oral communication in first-year writing and communication courses. Presentations are used both informally, with discussions of responses to daily assignments, and formally, with presentations in front of the class, to help you gain confidence and experience. You may also conduct interviews, create podcasts, shoot videos with audio elements, and record voice-overs for PowerPoints and Prezis.

As part of these oral communication activities, you can strengthen your ability to present information logically and clearly, as well as develop an effective style that may incorporate humor and audience interaction. The conversations you have in class help you learn how to be a productive member of both small and large groups, how to present your positions persuasively, and how to discourage unproductive conflict and encourage productive engagement.

V — You need to be visually competent, which includes planning, designing, and creating individual visuals for documents, Web sites, and presentations as well as designing entire print pages or screens. You need to be able to select and integrate visuals into print and digital artifacts as well as into demonstrations and presentations, making decisions about the balance of visual and verbal information.

View. The flip side of designing is the receptive competence, viewing; you need to be able to watch, interpret, and use a range of visuals — ads, photos, paintings, drawings, videos, films, maps, tables, graphs, charts, diagrams, and signage.

Visual communication uses images to inform, persuade, and entertain audiences. Understanding various ways to interpret and create images is an important part of your first-year writing and communication experience. The same rhetorical concerns that influence your strategic decisions in writing a report or preparing an oral presentation also shape the visuals you create.

Assignments Focusing on *Visual Communication*

Visual communication encourages you to decide which ideas and information are more effectively presented visually. These are typical visual activities and assignments you can expect:

- » Posters
- » Advertisements, both print and digital
- » Flyers/brochures
- » Data displays (e.g., tables, graphs)
- » Charts/diagrams
- » Photographs
- » Drawings
- » Transparencies and PowerPoint presentations
- » Videos (e.g., workplace training, YouTube satires)
- » Web sites

E—You need to be competent in using electronic/digital media as they emerge and evolve, selecting them for various contexts, audiences, and purposes. You can't possibly learn about every issue and every new digital application, but you can learn about new categories and affordances. **Electronic communication** is a rapidly expanding field that encompasses a huge array of practices and possibilities. Consider this list (which is by no means inclusive) and know that each category can be subdivided. Decide what interests you and what will likely be useful to you personally, academically, and professionally.

Transform. A critical aspect of using digital media is taking advantage of the ability to transform—that is, reshape—ideas and information by changing genre, scale, medium, scope, etc. (see Chapter 3). Conduct on online search for <global digital communication> to locate and read a Pew report about international texting and social networking.

- » Mobile technologies
- » Apps and tools
- » Hardware
- » Coding
- » Telecommunications
- » Internet
- » Intranets
- » Organizational strategies (e.g., branding, internal communication)
- » Research (subject of study; method of dissemination)
- » Online publications
- » Social networking and online communities
- » Entertainment (e.g., online gaming, integration of animation and live action)

Assignments Focusing on *Electronic Communication*

> Electronic communication has affordances specific to the digital world, affected by access to and familiarity with technology. These are typical electronic/digital activities and assignments you can expect:
>
> » Email
> » E-resumes
> » Online journals
> » Blogs
> » Web sites
>
> » Multimedia animation
> » Digital slideshows
> » Podcasting and Web videos
> » Videoconferencing
> » Wikis

» Ethics (e.g., manipulation, taboos, stereotypes)

» Accessibility (e.g., digital divide, physical limitations)

» Big data

» Publications (e.g., e-books, journals, newspapers)

» Interactive installations (e.g., iKiosks, art and scence museums)

» Educational options (e.g., MOOCs, LMSs)

Changing the medium changes the message. Electronic communication is a major part of your English 1101 and English 1102 courses in four broad ways:

» Using T-Square, Georgia Tech's electronic course management system

» Using your laptop computer, tablet, and/or smartphone as a communication tool and perhaps also as an object of study

» Learning about electronic communication and its cultural influences

» Using electronic communication as part of your own processes—for example, engaging in online peer editing or electronic publication

N—You need to understand and appropriately use nonverbal communication (e.g., facial expression, eye contact, body language, vocal expression, spatial distances, clothing) in ways that convey your credibility and cultural sensitivity. **Nonverbal communication** comprises any communication that doesn't emphasize words. It may include *kinesics* (gestures and body movements), *oculesics* (eye behavior, such as eye contact), *paralanguage* (vocal information, such as volume, pace, pitch, tone and inflection), *vocalizations* (e.g., "shhhhh" and "uh-huh"), *proxemics* (spaces between people who are interacting), *haptics* (touch), *chronemics* (use, structure, and orientation related to time), posture, and clothing.

The word *medium* is singular, and the word *media* is plural. Thus, you write/say, "medium is . . ." and "media are. . . ." Conduct on online search for <The Medium is STILL the Message—Five Key Ideas> to read more about Marshall McLuhan and his famous (and often misinterpreted) line, "The medium is the message." #Remember #Understand

Assignments Focusing on *Nonverbal Communication*

Nonverbal communication is almost always incorporated as part of other communication tasks. These are typical activities and assignments in which attention to nonverbal communication is especially important:

Oral Presentations

» Radio broadcast, in which case the voice, silence, and sound effects are the primary cues to interpretation

» Oral presentation with no hand gestures or with stylized hand gestures (like 19th-century orators)

Interviews

» Simulated interview (perhaps for a summer internship) showing how body language, movement, and posture can convey your attitude

» Telephone interview with varying pause times to assess changes in audience response

Team or Small-Group Interaction

» Generation of phrases and sentences whose meaning changes dramatically depending on the vocal characteristics (e.g., emphasis, pauses, pacing, tone)

» Small-group interaction with selected people using different kinds of eye contact (e.g., complete avoidance, intense gaze) to assess the response of both speaker(s) and members of the group

Respond. The flip side of engaging in nonverbal communication is the receptive competence, responding; you need to be able to interpret and respond to the nonverbal communication of others.

When you are engaged in teamwork and class discussions you will see nonverbal communication. You should regularly ask yourself how and why you react to certain nonverbal cues, especially in group interaction. Nonverbal communication, which is powerfully influenced by culture, can either reinforce or contradict a verbal or visual message. Some experts believe that people can more easily distort verbal or visual messages than they can nonverbal messages. This textbook presents two models for understanding nonverbal communication: the presentation model (Chapters 10–12) and the performance model (Chapter 16).

The WOVEN approach to communication encourages you to craft effective arguments multimodally with focused attention to and reflection on rhetoric and process. Understanding the roles these three critical concepts play in communication positions you as a strategic communicator. While this chapter serves to outline the key qualities of each mode, the next chapter provides you with examples of WOVEN modes working synergistically to create compelling and purposeful artifacts.

THE SYNERGY OF MODES AND MEDIA IN ACADEMIC AND PROFESSIONAL COMMUNICATION GT

CONTENTS

This chapter was contributed by Dr. Rebecca E. Burnett, Director of Writing and Communication at Georgia Tech, and Dr. L. Andrew Cooper, Assistant Professor at the University of Louisville and former Assistant Director of Writing and Communication at Georgia Tech.

Let's get directly to the point: Can you be successful in academic, professional, personal, and community contexts without multimodal competence? No. Few questions about communication have black-and-white, either/or answers, but this one comes close. Academic courses, internships, and jobs are as dependent on your ability to give oral presentations, to work collaboratively, and to design effective visuals as on your ability to write reports. Personal, professional, and community relationships are as dependent on respectful nonverbal communication as on coherent conversation.

To be a successful multimodal communicator, you need to be able to understand the features and power of each mode separately and also be able to create, analyze, and interpret them synergistically. You need to be actively engaged as a communicator, not only working to master multimodal strategies that enable you to be effective but also understanding that in practice these strategies aren't separable; they're synergistic.

Synergy refers to objects or actions that work together. Simply put, synergy is what results when things interact and explains why the power of the whole is greater than the sum of its separate parts. You should think of effective communication as being synergistic—involving the interaction of written, oral, visual, and nonverbal modes. For example, written communication involves both a productive part (writing) and a receptive part (reading). Writing can be individual or collaborative and can be produced in a print or an electronic document. In the process of writing, writers talk both to themselves and to others, often sketch ideas in preparation for writing, use design elements to influence audience response (from headings and paragraphs to font choices and illustrations), and are affected by the environment in which they work. This short list of some of the synergistic aspects of writing shows that modes don't exist in isolation. Your academic, professional, personal, and community success depends in large part on your competence with all the modes and your recognition that they function synergistically. As a capable communicator, your communication will be multimodal—that is, WOVEN.

Consider the modes of WOVEN communication. Which are your strengths? Which do you need to improve? Which do you prefer? Which do you avoid? #Remember #Understand

As you advance academically at Georgia Tech and later assume professional roles, communication will become increasingly challenging. Professionals in all fields—ranging from architecture to medicine, engineering to management, environmental science to computer science, the military to public policy—are more successful if they are effective communicators who can express their arguments compellingly in multiple modes and media. Effective communicators have strong written, oral, and visual competencies. In addition, with rapidly expanding social networking technologies, multimodal competencies increasingly rely on electronic modes of communication—for example, cell phones, social media, the Internet, and digital video.

In this chapter, you will learn more about factors affecting the synergy of modes and media. The chapter defines communication and addresses issues related to rules and conventions affecting modes and media. To define communication, it considers two questions you might ask about a writing and communication class: Can't I just learn the rules? and What do conventions have to do with rhetoric and multimodality? Once the definition of communication is established, the chapter then discusses multimodal synergy and describes a series of multimodal examples created by students at Georgia Tech. The chapter concludes with a discussion of four important questions:

» Why focus so much on modes other than writing?

» How does multimodal synergy relate to expectations for students?

» How does multimodal synergy enhance intellectual development?

» Why are self-reflection and self-assessment about communication processes and artifacts important?

What Is Communication?

If you ask 100 different people to define communication, you may get nearly 100 variations in their responses. This chapter establishes common ground for your work in English 1101 and English 1102, focusing on what communication is and isn't.

Communication is an area of disciplinary study (in the sense of intellectual inquiry) as well as a dynamic, interpersonal practice (in the sense that communication enables us to interact with others, whether in classrooms, workplaces, homes, or communities). Some people think that this study and practice are about the transmission of information—a one-way process that involves a sender encoding information and a receiver decoding that information. It's not.

▲ SIGN
NO to the Transmission Model of Communication
This sign is a reminder that the transmission model is not a sufficient explanation of the way communication works, whether in written, oral, visual, or nonverbal communication because, in part, context and interaction are omitted. *Courtesy of Georgia Tech's Writing and Communication Program.*

Communication is dynamic and synergistic, involving many factors that go far beyond simple transmission. Consider these basic features of communication:

» Communication is dynamic, involving an interactive process affected by context, intention, and interpretation.

» Communication involves rhetorical elements in interdependent (that is, synergistic) relationships; each rhetorical element (e.g., content, context, purpose, audience, argument, organization, evidence, medium, design, and various kinds of conventions) is affected by others.

» Communication involves writers, readers, speakers, listeners, designers, and viewers, all of whom interact in specific contexts and respond to specific situations.

» Communication has conventions for writing, speaking, designing, and nonverbal behaviors that are culturally determined and change with situation and time.

» Communication isn't just about the words, sounds, or images of a message; it's about the entire communicative situation. For example, specific audiences have idiosyncratic intentions, abilities, expectations, contexts, and experiences, *all* of which affect interpretation.

What about just learning the rules?

Communication is not about learning a single, well-defined set of rules that tells how and how not to communicate in every situation. Learning mechanical rules by themselves, decontextualized and without nuance, doesn't make you a good communicator. It just makes you a good rule follower. In fact, following rules while ignoring cultural differences in language and ignoring the rhetorical elements and their synergy usually results in inadequate, inappropriate, or oversimplified communication.

You can learn *some* rules, but you can't learn *the* rules because a single set of rules governing all communication situations simply doesn't exist. Academic and professional communication involves certain conventions; you've probably learned conventions as the *rules* governing grammar and mechanics. Those conventions constitute what we commonly refer to as Standard American English, which is used in both written and oral communication in most U.S. academic and professional contexts. Standard American English differs from other versions of written and spoken English in the United States. Standard American English also differs from English in Canada, England, Australia, Hong Kong, Singapore, South Africa, and India—to name just some of the places where English is a primary language. (See the textbox for one small example of the way culture influences conventions.)

"Correctness" is cultural.

English language conventions in the United States and the United Kingdom differ. For example, people educated in the United States generally put commas and periods *inside* quotation marks. People educated in the United Kingdom generally put commas and periods *inside* only if the punctuation belongs to the quotation; otherwise, the punctuation is placed *outside*.

U.S. Example: Accessible means "easy to approach, reach, see, understand, or use."

U.K. Example: Accessible means "easy to approach, reach, see, understand, or use".

In the United States, you need to know the conventions of Standard American English because they help U.S. academic and professional audiences not only understand your ideas but also perceive you as someone who is capable of performing appropriately in U.S. academic and professional contexts. In other words, when you're in the United States, following U.S. conventions contributes to your professional ethos, which gives you authority and credibility as a communicator. The authority and credibility associated with a strong professional ethos are powerful. You can use your versatility as a communicator to bring people's attention to the issues that matter to you most; by demonstrating your mastery of language conventions, you can more easily persuade your audiences to understand—and adopt—your point of view. (See Chapter 16 for more on the conventions of Standard American English.)

Learning about common academic and professional conventions for communication can make you a competent and powerful communicator in many situations, but it won't prepare you for all situations. For example, if you're tweeting about your favorite TV show, you won't write formal academic prose that follows all the conventions of Standard American English. The conventions that govern social spaces like Twitter differ from those that govern most academic and professional contexts. Good communicators know how to adapt to different contexts, recognizing and using the conventions that best enable them to share their ideas and build productive relationships. Although no single set of rules governs all communication situations, you can learn conventions associated with different contexts, cultures, and countries and use them strategically to represent yourself favorably in a variety of situations.

What do conventions have to do with rhetoric and multimodality?

Learning about rhetorical elements—such as context, purpose, and audience—helps you to analyze communication situations and choose the conventions and styles that fit them best. Understanding rhetorical principles is the key to adaptive strategies that define successful communicators. A strong rhetorical foundation allows you to adapt to different conventions within a mode. For example, understanding the needs of different audiences helps a scientist giving oral presentations to choose precise scientific terminology for an audience of professional experts or to choose a more general vocabulary for an audience of nonexperts.

A strong rhetorical foundation also allows you to adapt to the conventions of different modes and media. For example, an architect creating print plans for a new building might use shading and other conventions that suggest three-dimensionality in a static image. The same architect creating plans on a computer might use software that not only allows people to see a three-dimensional view by rotating a dynamic image but also enables viewers to step into a three-dimensional representation to see the building from the inside. The conventions of print and digital media allow for different representations of the same ideas. A competent communicator analyzes the context, purpose, and audience of the communication to determine which type of representation—and thus which modes and media—will be most effective.

With this background to help you think about modes and media in academic and professional communication, let's return to the topic of multimodal synergy. To understand why multimodal synergy enhances communication, we first need to extend our definition of multimodality and then look at several examples.

What Is Multimodal Synergy? GT

Medium—"technologies of *dissemination*, such as printed book, CD-ROM, or computer application" —C. Jewitt (184)

Mode—"organized, regular means of *representation* and communication, such as still image, gesture, posture, and speech, music, writing, or new configurations of the elements of these"—C. Jewitt (184)

According to researcher and theorist Gunther Kress, "[C]ommunication is always and inevitably multimodal" ("Gains and Losses" 5). Multimodality is so important, Kress explains, that "it is no longer possible to understand language and its uses without understanding the effect of all modes of communication that are co-present in any text" ("Multimodality" 337). Colleagues of Kress, including Carey Jewitt, explain that communication includes "all meaning-making systems" (Jewitt et al. 5).

We use the term *multimodality* to describe communication that occurs in different forms, or modes, and through different media. Understanding the differences is not always easy because the terms *mode* and *medium* are sometimes used in ways that overlap. For example, writing is a form in which you can represent your ideas, but it is also a means through which you can share your ideas with others. Writing is a mode that gives form to your ideas, while printed pages and Web pages are media through which you might choose to share ideas.

The overlap between modes and media is not simply a matter of fuzzy thinking or imprecise terminology. If a mode is a form and a medium is the means, the two quite naturally go hand in hand: writing as a mode (the combination of symbols, generally alphanumeric characters, and spaces to form units of meaning such as words and sentences) doesn't exist until you put it into a medium (such as the paper or Web page on which the combined symbols appear). Similarly, a mode is rarely discrete. For the sake of analysis, we can distinguish written communication from visual communication by defining the former as the combination of alphanumeric symbols that make meaning for readers and the latter as the use of images that also make meaning by appealing to the eye.

This distinction between mode and medium allows us to think about a printed word as something with characteristics that differ from a primarily visual artifact, such as a photograph. Such thinking is useful because examining the ways in which printed words and photographs make meaning differently can help us to understand how to use words and photographs more effectively. In another sense, though, the distinction between a word and an image is artificial because a word is also an image. It makes meaning by appealing to the eye. The three examples of "word" that follow demonstrate ways in which a word is an image.

1.WORD   2. *word*   3. *Word*

Courtesy of Georgia Tech's Writing and Communication Program.

The numerals and alphabetic representation of "word" are in the written mode; they are combinations of symbols that form units of meaning—the word "word"—but the differences in typographic style, size, and upper- and lowercase font emphasize various ways in which these words are also images. The first "word," which appears in a common, professional-looking font (Times New Roman) and all capital letters, might convey the ordinariness and perhaps the authority of the word "word." The second "word," which appears in a script font intended to mimic handwriting (Mistral) in an italic style and in all lowercase letters, might convey the idea that a word can be informal and difficult to control. The third "word," which appears in a fancier script font (Vivaldi) and in upper- and lowercase letters, might convey the idea that a word can be elegant and formal.

A word is both alphabetic and visual. Since one characteristic of a written word is that it corresponds to certain sounds, it can also be oral. A word can appear on a Web site, so it can also be electronic. Finally, the way a word looks might give you cues about gestures you could make while speaking it: for example, you might use a dramatic flourish of your hands as you speak a word written like version 1; you might bend over and whisper as you speak a word written like version 2; and you might put on airs and use a snooty accent while saying version 3. A word, therefore, can be completely WOVEN: written, oral, visual, electronic, and nonverbal.

Since synergy happens when things work together productively, the term **multimodal synergy** describes the ways in which modes and media coexist and interact within any instance of communication. The word *synergy* was first used in the English language in the mid-17th century, and the meaning has remained relatively stable, as you can see in the textbox explaining the etymology of the word.

Etymology of "synergy"

synergy: "1650s, 'cooperation,' from Modern Latin *synergia*, from Greek *synergia* 'joint work, a working together, cooperation; assistance, help,' from *synergos* 'working together,' related to *synergein* 'work together, help another in work,' from *syn-* 'together' (see **syn-**) + *ergon* 'work' (see *organ*). Meaning 'combined activities of a group' is from 1847; sense of 'advanced effectiveness as a result of cooperation' is from 1957."

SOURCE: *Online Etymology Dictionary.*

Whether you are analyzing or creating an artifact such as an advertisement that superimposes words on a photograph or a Web site that integrates text, sound, and images on a screen, you should consider the ways in which modes and media work synergistically to inform and persuade your target audiences.

What Are Examples of Multimodality? GT

Modes are inextricably linked, but we separate them for analytical purposes—that is, when we want to identify the critical components and to investigate the relationships among them. The examples in this section illustrate that while a mode may be dominant in a particular artifact, it rarely functions alone. In the following examples, one mode may be perceived as dominant, but others are nonetheless present in various ways.

Written Communication

The following screen capture of a Web site focuses on a written communication, an award-winning essay written by Leah Randall for her English 1101 class at Georgia Tech, taught by Dr. Matt Paproth. You can read most of the first page of Leah's essay, "I Don't Like the Beatles (And You Can't Make Me): How a movie changed my mind—sort of."

Leah's essay uses the written mode, but calling it mere "writing" ignores the many other aspects of this artifact. For instance, the essay itself is posted on a Web site, and a photograph is on the first page (one of four photos in Leah's essay). Clearly, this first-person essay is more than just writing, and knowing some of the details shows the multimodality. The marginal callouts identify some of the rhetorical and multimodal aspects of Leah's essay.

I Don't Like the Beatles (And You Can't Make Me): How a movie changed my mind - sort of.

User Rating: ●●●●● / 17

Poor ○ ○ ○ ○ ● Best | Rate

WRITTEN BY LEAH RANDALL
MONDAY, 24 NOVEMBER 2008

I hate The Beatles.

There. I said it. And damn it, I'm not ashamed.

Although there's a bit more to it than the simple statement that I'm sure caught your attention. The reality of the situation is that it has very little to do with their actual collected works, though I've never particularly enjoyed their music. This dislike for the Beatles is less about the music and more for the institution of the Beatles – and it's not even their fault.

As a pre-teen, I went through my typical listening-to-Oldies phase, eschewing Britney and Christina for Journey, Boston, and Billy Joel. At the same time, my older sister was discovering and fostering a love for the Beatles; she and her friends spent hours upon hours listening to the boys from Liverpool while I grumpily turned up my own stereo to tune it out. I suppose that's where it began; my choice of other groups over the Beatles elicited the strangest reactions, ones I was unable to comprehend. Every time I have uttered the phrase "I hate the Beatles" (along with many less and more severe versions, depending on my level of annoyance that day), I have been met with a reliable reaction of slack-jawed incredulity and disdain. And why? What is it about this group that garners such devotion?

And so there's the foundation for my dislike – a fairly flimsy and immature basis for what grew to be a passionate dislike for the group. At the core, my dislike is really fueled by this pre-teen rebellion that has followed me around. The dislike has grown everytime someone told me in no uncertain terms that I *can't* dislike the Beatles (at the word can't, the preteen still inside of me stamps her foot and cries out 'you're not the boss of me!') and has morphed into disdain for being told what to do. To make matters worse, thea rgument in favor of the Beatles is usually the same: "they're the Beatles!" As a twelve year old, this made little sense to me. At twenty, this still

Movie Headlines

» I Don't Like the Beatles (And You Can't Make Me): How a movie changed my mind - sort of.

» Children of Men Original Soundtrack Review

» South Boston Vigilantes: An Analysis of Troy Duffy's The Boondock Saints

» No Really, Feel Free to Sing Along – Dr. Horrible's Sing-Along Blog

» Review: Kill Bill Vol. 1

» Review: Garden State

» The Disney Institution: A Look at the Morals and Views Perpetuated by Disney

» It Only Takes a Moment: An Analysis of Disney and Pixar's Wall-E

» Pregnant Pauses

» Raise It Up: A Second Look at the Music of August Rush

» Journeying Into Better Movie Competence Through Music

» Defying Mainstream Conventions: Analyzing No Country for Old Men

» Review: Requiem for a Dream

» Review: Signs

» Review: Fight Club

◀ WEB ESSAY
Essay by Leah Randall for her English 1101 class. Leah's essay appears on a Web site that her English 1101 team designed and developed as one of its class projects. This site not only has depth and breadth, but as this screen capture from the site shows, it has the design features of a professional Web site. *Courtesy of Leah Randall.*

Letters refer to specific places on the screen capture.

A. **Context.** Leah's essay appears on a Web site that her English 1101 team designed and developed as one of its class projects.

B. **Oral.** The essay itself has no sound, but Leah acknowledges the oral culture she's writing about and creates a strong sense of orality by her first-person narrative, use of direct quotations, and descriptions of music.

C. **Written.** Leah presents an engaging narrative within which she embeds her argument.

D. **Visual (Images).** The essay includes four photographs that are linked to and illustrate points in the essay.

E. **Nonverbal.** Photographs in the essay are of people whose body language and facial expressions reinforce the arguments Leah makes.

F. **Visual (Design).** The essay appears on a well-designed Web site, so it's easy to find, easy to access, and easy to navigate. Design features identify it as a Web site article.

G. **Electronic.** Leah's English 1101 team uses its Web site to "explore the important relationships between music and other media: books, television shows, video games, and movies." The site incorporates conventional features—for example, user ratings and menu lists.

Oral Communication

The next example focuses on oral communication: a formal team presentation in a technical communication class at Georgia Tech, taught by Dr. Dan Vollaro. The photo that follows shows Taylor Kopacka speaking to an audience that includes both adults and children. She is presenting the billboards that her team designed for its client, the director of a nonprofit organization, Read Aloud Chattanooga, whose goal is to promote regular reading to very young children to encourage child-hood literacy. The audience consists of the class members, the client (the director of a nonprofit organization), several Georgia Tech administrators, and a number of invited guests, both adults and children.

◀ PHOTO

Taylor Kopacka presenting to her team's client and a large invited audience.
A technical communication course team designed billboards for its client, the director of a nonprofit organization, Read Aloud Chattanooga. *Photo © R. E. Burnett.*

Letters refer to specific places on the screen capture.

A. **Oral.** Taylor Kopacka presents her team's recommendations for bill-boards to promote early reading. The presentation involves lots of coordina-tion to showcase prepared materials as well as to respond to audience questions.

B. **Context.** Taylor Kopacka is one of the team members presenting a semester-long project to a large, diverse audience.

The next group of photos adds some critical details about the multimodality of the presentation given by Taylor and her teammates.

◄ PHOTO

Taylor Kopacka and Arman Nayabasadri presenting details of their team's recommendations to the client, audience, and press. Students needed to anticipate audience questions and to handle the added pressure of having press coverage. *Photos © R. E. Burnett.*

Letters refer to specific places on the images.

A. **Visual (Images).** Students created small-scale mock-ups of the billboards as well as Power-Point slides that include the billboards' designs. The presentation uses high-recognition images such as illustrations from the Curious George children's books.

B. **Electronic.** The PowerPoint slide summarizes the project's process and provides examples.

C. **Written.** PowerPoint slides and handouts provide textual information the audience can refer to during and after the presentation.

D. **Visual (Design).** The presentation is about billboard design. The team members use billboard mock-ups as primary visuals, which emphasizes their confidence in their work and illustrates their main points.

E. **Nonverbal.** Taylor's presentation is animated—even lively. She is comfortable using appropriate gestures, making eye contact, and moving around in her presentation space.

F. **Context.** Taylor and one of her teammates, Arman Nayabasadri, work together. The crew of professional photographers and videographers are quiet and efficient, but they certainly affect the context.

What Are Examples of Multimodality?   53

Visual Communication

Most people communicate more visually than they do verbally—especially when you consider that visual information includes not only images of all kinds (e.g., drawings, maps, photographs, screen captures, and videos) but also the graphic design and page/screen layout of the text they create. Occasionally, visuals appear alone—perhaps one stark and dramatic image that enables viewers to create meaning without accompanying text. More frequently, though, visual information is synergistically integrated with textual information. The poster "Sadako: A Woman's Wrath" was created by Julian Foster for his English 1102 class, "Monsters of Technology," taught by Dr. Andrew Cooper. Julian's 2′ × 3′ poster, placed on an easel, was presented in a poster session during which many students displayed and talked about their posters to other classmates and invited guests.

Julian's poster demonstrates a number of strong elements of design and illustrates the integration of text, design, and images, making it a clear example of multimodality. The English 1102 assignment asked students to analyze a film monster of their choice and present that analysis on a poster. This poster focuses on the film *The Ring* (2002), which is about an adolescent girl who is murdered and takes her revenge on the world through a videotape that kills anyone who watches it. For his poster, Julian chose Sadako, the central female figure in *The Ring*, created a visual representation of her by selecting screenshots from the film as well as from Web sites discussing the film, and identified details that reveal this particular monster's cultural significance.

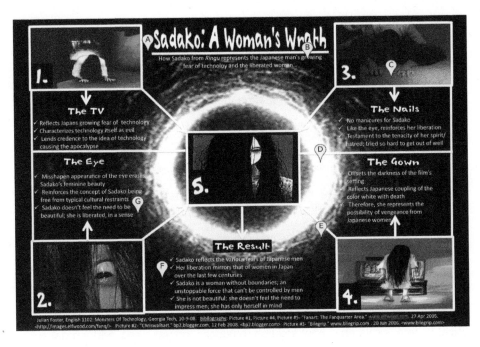

Letters refer to specific places on the screen capture.

A. **Context.** Julian's 2′ × 3′ poster, placed on an easel, is presented in a poster session during which many students display and talk about their posters to other classmates and invited guests.

B. **Oral.** The poster has no sound, but Julian prepared comments for a two- to three-minute explanation of his work to people at the poster session. He was also prepared to answer their questions.

C. **Nonverbal.** During his prepared remarks as well as in his responses to questions, Julian conveys professionalism and confidence by his facial expressions, eye contact, body language, attire, and tone of voice.

D. **Visual (Images).** Julian uses stills of Sadako from the film as well as drawings he found on Web sites. The image sources are cited at the bottom of the poster.

E. **Visual (Design).** Julian uses a three-column design with a radial center as the culmination. Because he uses a counterintuitive organization, he helps his audience navigate by including numerals to signal the order.

F. **Electronic.** Julian uses PowerPoint to create his poster, but if he needed a more complex design layout he would have selected a more robust design software such as Adobe InDesign.

G. **Written.** Julian presents key elements in the film that characterize Sadako as a monster. The text and images are equally important in this poster.

Electronic Communication

Wikipedia defines a wiki as "a Web site that uses wiki software, allowing the easy creation and editing of any number of interlinked Web pages, using a simplified markup language. Wikis are often used to create collaborative Web sites and to power community Web sites." *Wikipedia* identifies three characteristics of a wiki, paraphrased here:

» All users can edit any page or create new pages.

» Page links promote meaningful topic associations between different pages.

» Visitors to the wiki are involved in an ongoing process of creation and collaboration that constantly changes the Web site landscape.

You will learn more about composing with wikis in Chapter 14.

The following wiki example comes from a semester-long assignment in English 1102 that focuses on Thomas Friedman's book *Hot, Flat, and Crowded* (2008). Dr. Melissa Graham Meeks, the course instructor, summarizes the book's key point, saying that it "situates environmental issues within the larger economic and political sphere, explaining how science, business, government, and journalism intersect productively and otherwise." Her students built a collaborative online encyclopedia (like *Wikipedia*) in which they were the primary authors and editors. Dr. Meeks described some of the actions that characterize and enhance the wiki. These actions were often initiated by one student in her class but frequently developed by a group of students:

» Pinpoint many of the locations Friedman mentions in his book via Google map

» Use an index to identify how the entries match the chapters in Friedman's book

» Create a "random page" generator (a common feature on most wikis)

» Organize files to be accessible

» Create usable navigation

» Design an appropriate front page

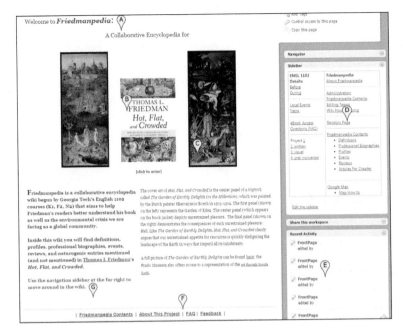

Letters refer to specific places on the screen capture.

A. **Oral.** Orality occurs during the planning and writing. Note the heading identifying the project as a "Collaborative Encyclopedia."

B. **Context.** From the beginning users know that this Web site is about Thomas Friedman's book *Hot, Flat, and Crowded.*

C. **Visual (Images).** Students use the triptych images from Hieronymus Bosch's *The Garden of Earthly Delights* and Thomas L. Friedman's book cover to reinforce the connection with Friedman's book.

D. **Written.** While many parts of the *Friedmanpedia* are collaborative, students also wrote and edited individual documents, listed in the *Friedmanpedia* Contents.

E. **Context** and **Electronic.** Users recognize that the navigation, sidebar, and activity information classify this site as a wiki.

F. **Electronic.** Users are told to "click to enter" the site, are reminded to use the navigation bar, and have links to Content, About This Project, FAQs, and Feedback.

G. **Context** and **Visual (Design).** Students use a three-panel design (like the triptych of *The Garden of Earthly Delights*) to create a cultural context.

Nonverbal Communication

As you have learned elsewhere in this textbook, nonverbal communication encompasses much of what is *not* written, oral, or visual. Nonverbal communication doesn't emphasize words or images; instead, it focuses on factors such as kinesics, oculesics, paralanguage, vocalizations, proxemics, haptics, and chronemics, posture, and clothing (see selected definitions in the textbox).

Types of Nonverbal Communication

The following key terms are useful for discussing nonverbal communication:

Chronemics: the study of time, including perceptions, structure, and reactions to time

Haptics: the study of the sense of touch, being touched, and tactile sensations

Kinesics: the study of body language, including movement, gesture, and facial expression

Oculesics: the study of eye contact, including direction, directness, and duration of gaze

Paralanguage: the nonphonemic elements of oral communication, including pitch, volume, inflection, intonation, pace, and nonphonemic sounds (like "um")

Proxemics: the study of physical distances between and among people

These nonverbal factors are always situated in some context, and they are nearly always associated with some kind of conversation, collaboration, or presentation. Let's look at two images of people in different rhetorical situations and see what their nonverbal communication conveys. The following image shows an English 1101 class. Even though you're viewing a static image of a dynamic situation, you can infer quite a lot from the nonverbal cues in the photograph.

PHOTO ▶
Students working on laptops.
These English 1101 students are performing an in-class review of their projects. *Photo © R. E. Burnett.*

» Consider the key elements of nonverbal communication—kinesics, oculesics, paralanguage, vocalizations, proxemics, haptics, and chronemics, posture, and clothing. What kinds of nonverbal information can you see in the photograph?

» What can you infer about the atmosphere of the class? What leads you to this inference?

» What role does technology play in the class?

When people talk with each other, they typically use language—usually oral language and sometimes visual language such as American Sign Language—but meaning is shaped by far more than the words in language. For example, when we're engaged in conversation, we have facial expressions that contribute to meaning, we gesture to emphasize points, we sit (or stand) at certain distances that match the situation, and we use a particular tone of voice with meaningful inflection and pauses. The photograph that follows shows Dr. Paulette Richards and Dr. Daniel Vollaro engaged in a conversation. They have offices near each other at Georgia Tech and share professional interests in teaching literature, culture, and communication, including technical communication, with a special focus on technology.

◀ PHOTO
Faculty conversation.
The photo shows a conversation between two faculty members, Dr. Paulette Richards and Dr. Daniel Vollaro, who are lively, attentive, and engaged. *Photo © R. E. Burnett.*

» Consider the key elements of nonverbal communication—kinesics, oculesics, paralanguage, vocalizations, proxemics, haptics, and chronemics, posture, and clothing. Which ones can you comment on based on this photograph?

» What nonverbal cues inform you about Dr. Richards and Dr. Vollaro as colleagues and collaborators?

» What kind of information does the space they're in give you?

» What role does technology play in the conversation?

Explicit Synergy

In the preceding examples, you've seen written, oral, visual, electronic, and non-verbal communication, each as the dominant but not exclusive mode. The final series of examples begins with a front page that presents a series of student projects completed in Dr. Crystal Lake's English 1102 class. Each of the student projects was a part of the Web site pictured in the screen capture that follows; each project was accessed by clicking on one of the colored cells. These projects—including the Nexus project featured here—include student-created Web pages that integrate written and visual modes and student-created videos that integrate written, visual, oral, and nonverbal modes. Let's examine a few of the pages from one of the projects, the Nexus project, the pale blue site in the upper left-hand corner of the Web site.

COURSE WEB SITE ▶
Front page of projects from an English 1102 course focusing on utopias and dystopias. Created by students in Dr. Crystal Lake's English 1102 course.

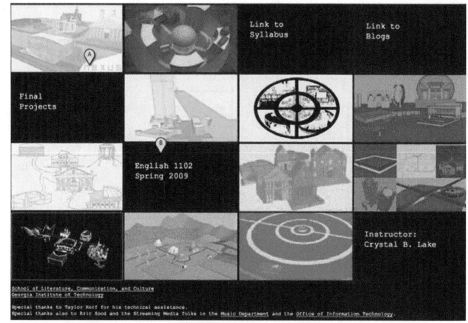

Letters refer to specific places on the screen capture.

A. **Visual (Design).** Each cell of this matrix links to some aspect of the course, "Utopias and Dystopias: The Politics of the Architectural Imagination" (e.g., course description, syllabus, course blog, instructor bio) or to student team projects completed in the course. The next several screen captures are from the Nexus project, designed and developed by one of the English 1102 teams in Dr. Lake's class.

B. **Context.** Because of the information accessible from this front page, users have no difficulty understanding the context for the final projects presented on the site for this English 1102 class. This cell provides a composite link to the course syllabus, blogs, and team projects. Alternatively, users can access any of these elements separately.

The first page of the Nexus Web site that follows introduces the Nexus project ("What is Nexus?") and identifies the site's components: map, design, video, bios, purpose, and sources. This site contextualizes and explores various examples of written, oral, visual, electronic, and nonverbal communication created by students on the Nexus team.

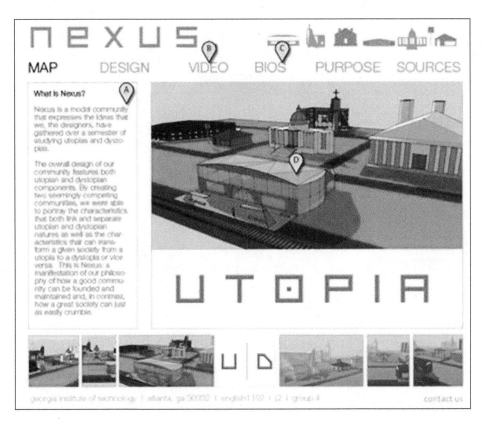

Letters refer to specific places on the screen capture.

A. **Written.** The Nexus team explains its purpose and the overall design, which is to illustrate ways that utopian and dystopian communities function, noting that utopian societies can be created and great societies can crumble.

B. **Multimodal.** The navigation menu shows users the options they have—to access information about the design of each featured site, to view a video about these sites, to learn about the individuals on this team, to learn about the overall purpose of the project, and to find sources that the team used.

C. **Context.** The clickable icons help situate the team's work by providing links to six featured sites in the community: train station, church, textile mill, library, city hall, and coffee house.

D. **Visual (Images).** The Web site provides images of each featured site from different perspectives. Both the primary images and the thumbnail images below them are clickable, allowing users to access more information and switch from site to site.

WEB SITE ▶
Design page of the Nexus project Web site.
Created by students in Dr. Crystal Lake's English 1102 course.

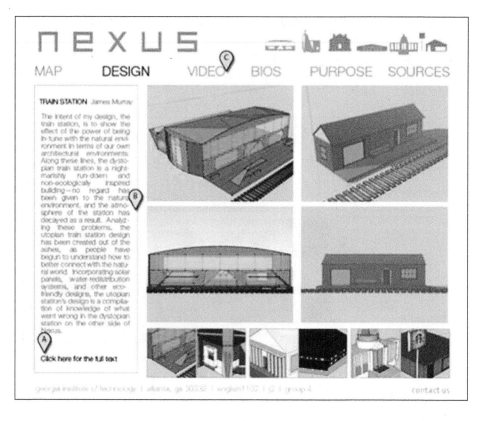

Letters refer to specific places on the screen capture.

A. **Electronic.** The flexibility of the Web site gives users the option of reading the introduction about the train station and stopping or clicking to read a more detailed discussion, including a Works Cited list.

B. **Written.** Each architectural structure created by the Nexus team is explained in detail. This is the description for the train station.

C. **Oral and Visual.** The Nexus team created a six-and-a-half-minute video that highlights each architectural feature and provides an oral commentary by its designer.

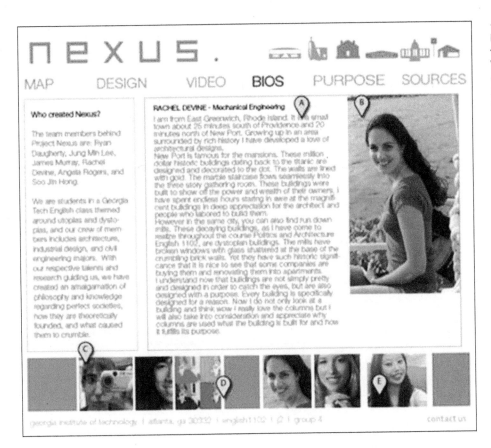

◀ WEB SITE
Biography page of the Nexus project Web site.
Created by students in Dr. Crystal Lake's English 1102 course.

Letters refer to specific places on the screen capture.

A. **Written.** Each Nexus team member provides a bio, presenting background and commentary about his or her approach to the project. Since these students are members of a team, their individual bios are contextualized by the information in the "Who created Nexus?" column to the left.

B. **Visual (Image).** The large image accompanies the written bio, conveying some of the spirit and personality of each team member.

C. **Nonverbal.** The photograph chosen by each team member presents a strong sense of self through body language and eye contact.

D. **Electronic.** Each image is clickable, so users can quickly learn more about each team member.

E. **Context.** The photographs of each team member, when viewed collectively, provide a visual overview of the Nexus team, immediately displaying age, gender, and ethnicity.

WEB SITE ▶
**Purpose page of
the Nexus project
Web site.**
Created by students
in Dr. Crystal Lake's
English 1102 course.

NEXUS.

MAP   DESIGN   VIDEO   BIOS   **PURPOSE**   SOURCES

Why was Nexus created?

It is our hope that all who come across our work, Project Nexus, will better understand the ways in which utopias crumble into dystopias and dystopias can be renovated into utopias. It is our goal, furthermore, to give the people of the world a philosophical model in the hopes that they will use it to **A** our world.

The purpose behind our design for this model community is not to showcase a perfect place to live; instead, we have created 6 utopian buildings and 6 dystopian buildings, each with the potential to transition or transform into its counterpart depending on changing conditions.

In short, Nexus showcases the things that can go wrong in our architecture and our society, as well as how we can use this knowledge to create a better society in the future.

Our "Politics and Architecture **C** Blog page:

http://politicsandarchitecture124.blogspot.com/

Mission Statement for Project Nexus **B**

The fundamental premise of our community, first and foremost, revolves around the central theme that we have explored and researched this semester—the fashion in which utopias often dematerialize over time and become dystopian in nature, or, in contrast, how dystopias can be analyzed and reformatted to create a utopia out of the ashes, as well as the ways in which this tends to happen. The overall purpose of this focal point is to relay the philosophical and political views which we have cultured while reading utopian and dystopian novels, including Cormac McCarthy's *The Road*, Sarah Scott's *A Description of Millenium Hall*, Henry Neville's *The Isle of Pines*, and H.G. Wells's *The Time Machine*. Primary views which we would like to convey and bring into discussion are the questions of whether or not utopias can indeed exist, how such a "perfect" society would be founded and proliferated, whether a population can be considered utopian for some and dystopian at the same time for others, and what commonly causes utopias to transition to dystopias or vice versa.

Upon reading the aforementioned books and many other stories, we began to challenge the concept of a utopia in its most fundamental principles. Specifically, we initiated a series of discussions over whether a utopia must satisfy all needs and desires of an entire population, or if instead perhaps there could exist a "personal utopia," such as that of George Pines. On what is later called the Isle of Pines in the story, George's every desire is fulfilled in his intimate

Letters refer to specific places on the screen capture.

A. **Visual, Design.** The site displays the students' awareness of design features that affect user reaction as well as usability—for example, headings, font variations, boldface, navigation, ragged right margins (rather than full justification), and subtle rules (lines) to divide sections.

B. **Written.** The Nexus team wrote several documents, some individually and some collaboratively. Their collective mission statement highlights the purpose of the project and the Web site and also incorporates a clear sense of the reading, thinking, and collaborating that team members did in preparation for their writing.

C. **Context, Written, Electronic.** The link to the class blog extends the types of writing, extends the audience, and gives students a forum for discussion.

D. **Context.** The link makes clear that the Nexus team's work is based on external sources, available for users to check.

Why Focus So Much on Modes Other Than Writing? GT

By emphasizing multimodal synergy, Georgia Tech's Writing and Communication Program is not trying to de-emphasize the importance of writing or to add more items to your list of things to study. Rather, you are being asked to study the elements that coexist and interact with writing. Multimodal synergy isn't about learning more; it's about learning better.

Why not just focus on writing?

Not all colleges and universities teach multimodal communication as part of their core requirements. In fact, Georgia Tech's Writing and Communication Program was once called simply the Writing Program, and though classes sometimes included digital media and other forms of communication beyond alphabetic text on printed pages, writing still dominated the objectives and outcomes for students' learning. Why? The answer is deceptively simple: historically, the ability to write well has long been considered the hallmark of an educated person. This idea is problematic for two reasons: first, the notion of writing "well" suggests absolute definitions of good and bad writing, and second, the notion of an "educated" person suggests that a person simply is or isn't educated. This thinking involves binaries; that is, it reduces multiple possibilities into paired options such as good/bad and is/isn't, and in doing so it oversimplifies both writing and education.

As other sections of this textbook demonstrate, writing is rhetorical, and thus it depends on variable elements such as audience and context. What's appropriate for one audience in one context could be entirely inappropriate for another audience in another context, so communicators can't be certain of writing well in every situation simply because they are successful in a college writing program.

Binary formulations about writing and education do more than oversimplify the rhetorical dimensions of communication: they imply hierarchies of value that are inextricable from economic class and other aspects of cultural identity. Judgments about appropriate and inappropriate writing (what some people might even call "good writing" and "bad writing") are, in a sense, matters of taste; and, as sociologist Pierre Bourdieu argues in his seminal study *Distinction*, "taste classifies, and it classifies the classifier," and thus it can "fulfill a social function of legitimating social differences" (6–7). In other words, when you judge something to be good or bad (or appropriate or inappropriate), you reveal something about your own education while you imply that a certain type of education (probably yours) is intrinsically better than others. Georgia Tech's own president, shown in the photo the follows, spoke with English 1101 students about the complexity of planning an education for the 21st century, one that moves students well beyond binary formulations.

For example, if you judge a piece of writing that violates grammatical conventions to be bad, you reveal what you have learned about grammatical conventions. Opportunities for learning are not equal for everyone. If you learned about grammatical conventions in high school or college, then you had the privilege of attending high school or college instead of having to work full-time for your own or others' sustenance. Knowledge about art, literature, communication, and other areas of study are a kind of cultural capital, associated with social status, and as Bourdieu claims, some forms of cultural capital "can only be acquired by means of a sort of withdrawal from economic necessity" (53–54). When someone judges a person as "educated" because she or he writes "well," then the judge's claim, intentional or not, reflects on that person's economic background. The judgment classifies the person whose writing it judges, and in doing so, it classifies the judge as the sort of person who has enough cultural capital to make such a judgment. Thus, the judge's taste differentiates people with economic access to education from people who lack such access.

How do the power and privilege of communication contribute to cultural capital?

Reading and writing alphabetic text have a particularly strong historical association with cultural capital. In an autobiographical account of his life as a slave in the United States in the 19th century, Frederick Douglass writes about how he learned that "it was unlawful, as well as unsafe, to teach a slave to read" from a slave owner who explained that a slave "should know nothing but to obey his master—to do as he is told to do." As Douglass learned to read and write, he gained knowledge and power—and thus he defied the constraints of his social station. The connection Douglass makes between this sort of knowledge and political power marks alphabetic text as *a*—and perhaps *the*—privileged form of communication. To paraphrase an old adage, pens and keyboards, not swords and guns, have the might to make and break nations.

If reading and writing have such a privileged relationship to culture and power, students, parents, teachers, and legislators might have good reason to contend that writing is the most important mode and that it should therefore be the primary, if not the sole, focus of communication instruction in college. While in many situations writing might be the most powerful and appropriate form of communication, the question "Is writing the most important mode?" demands a binary yes/no answer, and the answer is rarely that simple. The importance of writing is, like everything else related to communication, highly contextual. Instead of trying to judge one mode as

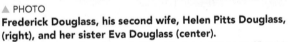

▲ PHOTO
Frederick Douglass, his second wife, Helen Pitts Douglass, (right), and her sister Eva Douglass (center).
Douglass was an American abolitionist whose first book, *Narrative of the Life of Frederick Douglass, an American Slave*, was published in 1845. *National Park Service (FRDO 3912).*

better or more important than the others, successful communicators will assess when, why, and how one mode might be the most powerful or appropriate while considering how that mode's interactions with other modes will affect it. Georgia Tech emphasizes multimodality in part because a communicator cannot fully understand or effectively use writing or any other mode without understanding how that mode relates to others within a given rhetorical situation.

Scientific communication provides many instructive examples about the ways in which combinations of modes and media create historic successes and failures. One obvious example of a scientist whose success depends in part on his competence as a communicator is Stephen Hawking. Beyond his articles for peer scientists, Hawking writes books and creates films and television specials for general audiences (including children). Hawking has been able not only to help his ideas gain traction but also to gain enormous popularity—including being the subject of the 2014 film *The Theory of Everything*.

However, writing isn't the only form of communication competence that successful science requires. One of the most notorious incidents in the history of scientific debates about the possibility of cold fusion does not stem from a piece of writing but from public speaking. When Stanley Pons and Martin Fleischmann announced at a press conference on March 23, 1989, that they had achieved cold fusion, they started more than two decades of public outrage and condemnation, and their work became a synonym for junk science. Simply put, accuracy and credibility are critical aspects of good communication. Recently, cold fusion is getting a second look by scientists, reenergizing the debate. Of course, a piece of writing is rarely purely written, and a press conference is never purely oral: you can find graphs and pictures in Hawking's academic works, you can see the colorful images alongside the text in Hawking's children's books, you can see Pons and Fleischmann's infamous press conference on YouTube, and you can see and hear a 2009 story about the recent investigations related to cold fusion on the television program *60 Minutes*.

Modes Influence Argumentation

What do you agree with and disagree with in the following quotation? #Evaluate

"From the emergence of alphabetic writing as a portable, durable, and replicable means for the preservation of knowledge, to the development of typography and mass literacy, and to the early and mid-20th-century emergence of cinema, radio, and television, shifts in dominant modes of information at once tend to generate moral, intellectual, and institutional panic and critique, as well as powerful evangelical discourses about their capacity to revolutionize thinking, everyday life, and, of course, the practices of education."

SOURCE: Carmen Luke, "Pedagogy, Connectivity, Multimodality, and Interdisciplinarity"

Writing certainly remains important, and thus in your communication classes at Georgia Tech you will be expected to write a great deal—and to write well. Nevertheless, most writing today occurs on computers, and like the scientific examples just cited, most professional communication today requires communicators to use writing in conjunction with other modes in order to share their ideas and perform successfully in their jobs. The emphasis on multimodality in English 1101 and 1102 affirms writing's importance and seeks to enhance your cultural maneuverability by teaching you to communicate using the modes and media that define contemporary society.

How Does Multimodal Synergy Relate to Expectations for Students? GT

The synergy of modes and media is similar to the synergy that occurs in learning and memory. Think about the sorts of cues that might help you to remember a film you saw a long time ago. If you saw the line "You're gonna need a bigger boat" in print, you might not think of a particular film title. If you saw the line in print and heard someone read it aloud, you still might not get it. If you saw and heard the line and also viewed a drawing of the related animal, your chances of thinking of the film's title are better.

If you saw and heard the line, saw a picture, and heard the repeating notes from John Williams's famous soundtrack, you'd be very, very likely to think of the film

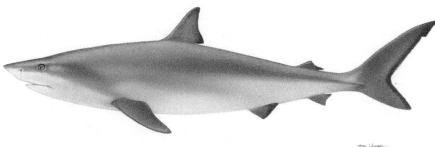

Jaws (1975). Exposure to ideas expressed in different modes and media gives you multiple ways to recall and analyze those ideas.

How does multimodality help learning?

Learning and memory are more likely to be successful when multiple modes and media are involved, but combinations of modes and media won't affect everyone the same way. Some people believe they learn better by reading, while others believe they learn better by hearing, by seeing, or by movement and tactile engagement. However, you should not conflate personal preferences and abilities with a singular learning style.

Cognitive psychologists suggest that such individual preferences and abilities don't neatly add up to a learning style. Instead, virtually everyone can learn new information, whether the meaning is presented in a visual, auditory, or kinesthetic manner. While many people prefer learning through visual, auditory, or tactile means, their personal preferences and abilities don't impede their learning but rather strengthen it.

Your chances of learning increase when you recognize that your abilities across modes (written, oral, visual, nonverbal/kinesthetic) can enhance your learning and your recall as well as your use of new ideas and processes. Your own multimodal communication allows you greater power as a learner. For example, encountering the same idea in different modes/forms is likely to improve your learning because each version (or iteration) of the idea can reinforce the others. When a professor lectures about the concepts you've read about in a textbook, the oral communication reinforces the written communication. When you draw a diagram that uses arrows to show how pictured objects relate to one another and then write a paragraph that explains what the arrows between the objects mean, your combination of visuals with alphabetic text increases your chances of recalling the relationships you represent.

Though research is unlikely to uncover a single best way to accommodate all approaches to learning, a survey of research about multimodality conducted by the

Conduct an online search for the Cisco report, "Multimodal Learning Through Media: What the Research Says." Read about the myths and then learn about what is affecting your own learning. #Understand

Metiri Group for Cisco Systems indicates that "students engaged in learning that incorporates multimodal designs, on average, outperform students who learn using traditional approaches with single modes." By increasing your competence in multiple modes and media, you increase your chances of understanding the unfamiliar and sometimes difficult concepts you encounter in college.

The communication courses you take at Georgia Tech allow you to gain experience with different modes and media. Given time to reflect about these modes and media, you should be able to develop insight about ways to take advantage of them to increase your learning. This insight should help you to learn more and to learn faster, making you not only a better communicator but also a better student.

How does multimodality encourage translation, transformation, and transference?

The notion that a single idea can be expressed in different modes and media requires some exploration. As media scholar Marshall McLuhan famously proclaimed, "the medium is the message." You can't separate form from content. If you look back to page 49 in this chapter to see the display of *word* in three different typefaces, where the appearance of the word changes what it expresses, the ideas are inseparable from the shapes they take. However, you can represent a single idea through different modes and media, using those modes and media strategically to increase your audiences' understanding of the idea. The *content* of the sentence "A word is both written and visual" and the *visual* depiction of that idea exist simultaneously. The content and its visual depiction demonstrate that modes coexist and interact. To reinforce the coexistence and interaction (that is, the synergy), consider how your reaction to the content of this book would be affected if the visual representation were transformed—if fonts were dramatically different and if the color and texture of the paper on which this book is printed were markedly different. In general, considering transformation makes the synergy between written and visual modes clear. Learning more about concepts we call *translation*, *transformation*, and *transference* will help you understand more about multimodality.

Translation involves adapting information for a new audience. In the workplace, translation might involve adapting information in a medical journal to a mass-market newspaper. In English 1101 or English 1102, you might translate information you have collected in a face-to-face interview with a musician, artist, performer, scientist, or engineer by simplifying the language so it makes sense to the general reader.

Translation is rhetorical—whether you are translating text designed for English readers to one for an audience of Japanese readers or translating a visual designed for experts in aerospace engineering to one for nonexperts watching CNN. You consider the rhetorical situation and preferences of your new audience—contextual influences, conceptual sophistication, vocabulary, responsiveness to various kinds of evidence, familiarity with different kinds of visuals, preferences in design, appropriateness of mode and medium for the purpose, and so on. Imagine, for example, that you have interviewed a biomechanical engineer who has invented a new kind of prosthesis. For a short article in an annual report, you need to translate the engineer's discussion of materials and mechanics into a description that an audience without an engineering background can understand.

Transformation involves changing and reshaping ideas or information. These examples provide some sense of the nature of transformation:

» Changing genre (e.g., moving a print brochure to information on a Web site)

» Changing scale (e.g., from a postage stamp to a poster)

» Changing medium (e.g., from a live demonstration to a video)

» Changing scope (e.g., from a lengthy manual to a one-page tip sheet)

» Changing color palette (e.g., from a four-color to a sepia-tone photograph)

» Changing pacing (e.g., from a self-paced to an automated PowerPoint)

When you transform an idea from a representation in one mode or medium to a representation in another mode or medium, you consider how the transformation affects rhetorical elements. How does the transformation affect your audience? How does it reflect your purpose? How does it change the organization of your ideas?

Consider the challenge of helping people to understand concepts and practices foreign to their experience and culture. For example, how can a museum in South Africa help foreign visitors understand the horrors of apartheid—legally enforced racial segregation? One way is to reproduce the passes (shown in the accompanying photos of a museum exhibit) that black South Africans needed in order to go anywhere outside the black settlements.

In the exhibit about apartheid (legal in South Africa from 1948 to 1994), the museum transformed a pass from its original dimensions (about the size of a modern passport) to a dramatically large model (nearly 7′ tall). The transformation in

▲ PHOTO
Close-up of a domestic passport.
Oversized reproduction of photo, address, and signature page that all black citizens in South Africa needed to carry with them during apartheid, now displayed as a nearly 7′ tall exhibition in the Kwa Muhle Museum, Durban, South Africa. *Photo © R. E. Burnett.*

▲ PHOTO
Signature page on domestic passport.
Oversized reproduction of the kind of passport that all black citizens in South Africa were required to carry with them during apartheid, now displayed in the Kwa Muhle Museum, Durban, South Africa. *Photo © R. E. Burnett.*

scale reinforced the power differential—official government control that stripped black South Africans of their citizenship, eliminated voting rights, restricted employment, and forced people to relocate to segregated black settlements. A transformed pass was displayed to represent the tremendous control it wielded. The transformed pass is larger than the 6′ model of a man holding an actual pass.

Transference involves applying communication strategies from one context to another. The ability to transfer strategies is one of the most important skills you can learn in college; literally, you are transferring your learning from one situation to another. Gaining enough familiarity with a concept or strategy to help you in a single situation doesn't do you much good in the long run (though it may help you pass a quiz the next day). What's important is long-term learning—the ability to generalize from one situation to another.

The greater the similarity in the two situations, the closer the proximity in time, and the greater the relevance you see from one situation to another, the more likely you are to transfer your learning. So, when in week three of an English course you learn that evaluating sources involves assessing credibility, relevancy, currency, and reliability, you're likely to use these criteria not only in the paper you write in week four but also in the history paper you write in week five. You may be less likely to use these criteria in an engineering report you write in week 14. Why? Even though all three disciplines (English, history, and engineering) require evaluating sources, you may see English and engineering as dissimilar, have forgotten what you temporarily learned 10 weeks ago, and consider the work you do in English to be irrelevant to the work you do in engineering. The problem might be compounded by the fact that your engineering professor knows that you were supposed to learn about evaluation in English classes, sees the similarity, proximity, and relevance to your engineering assignment, and expects you to transfer the learning without direct instruction. If you have actually learned about evaluating sources, however, you should be able to transfer the knowledge from one situation to another. For learning to be transferrable, you must be able to adapt your prior knowledge to new situations.

One productive way to increase transference is to increase your use of verbal and visual metaphors, which help you compare dissimilar or unfamiliar concepts, processes, or objects. By identifying similarities, you can develop new ways of thinking, transferring what you know to help you think about unfamiliar concepts, processes, or objects in new ways. Metaphors can help you carry over or transfer meaning from one situation to another.

Transference has additional practical value for you. In your study and practice of communication, both in communication classes and in other classes, jobs, or situations where you are expected to communicate effectively, you will be engaged in two broad kinds of learning, both of which involve transference:

Etymology of "metaphor"

metaphor: "late 15c., from Middle French *metaphore* (Old French *metafore*, 13c.), and directly from Latin *metaphora*, from Greek *metaphora* 'a transfer,' especially of the sense of one word to a different word, literally 'a carrying over,' from *metapherein* 'transfer, carry over; change, alter; to use a word in a strange sense,' from *meta-* 'over, across' (see *meta-*) + *pherein* 'to carry, bear' (see *infer*)."

SOURCE: *Online Etymology Dictionary.*

» **Learning to communicate** involves developing effective ways to share ideas. You should expect to transfer what you learn in communication classes to all other communication you do in academic, workplace, personal, and community situations. You can see the value of transferring strategies such as making arguments, adapting to various audiences, selecting and organizing evidence, respecting different cultures, and designing effective pages and screens.

» **Communicating to learn** involves using communication in order to understand new and sometimes difficult concepts. Specifically, you can use communicating to learn strategies that include writing definitions and descriptions, creating comparison tables, listing arguments and counterarguments, diagramming key components, synthesizing opposing views, summarizing specifications, categorizing kinds of evidence, and graphing changes over time.

How Does Multimodal Synergy Enhance Intellectual Development? GT

The ways you think about and use modes and media influence your intellectual development. This section focuses on cognition and representation, encouraging what is often called *metacognition*—that is, thinking about thinking, a kind of self-awareness about your own thinking processes that enables you to monitor and change these processes in productive ways. The metacognitive questions in the margins of this textbook are just one way it prompts reflective thinking and action regarding composing and multimodal synergy. Metacognition helps you consider ways to use modes and media to represent various ideas, processes, and objects.

How does multimodality affect cognition?

The term *cognition* refers to mental processes involved in thinking—which includes activities such as knowing, understanding, remembering, questioning, analyzing, evaluating, using, and solving problems. When we think, we respond to

Try to think of a communication situation that only involves one mode—for example, only writing (with no elements of design) or only orality (with no nonverbal cues). Examples are difficult to think of because nearly all communication situations involve more than one mode. #Understand

Thoughtfully select and name three of the colors represented in the color chart below. See if others can accurately match your color names with the actual colors. The names you selected aren't arbitrary, so what makes the task difficult? #Understand #Apply

multimodal cues, but because we have individual approaches to learning, we respond to and often prefer one mode over another. For example, when you're learning new information, do you prefer to read about it or watch a video? Do you prefer a hands-on activity that lets you try out the new idea or process? Do you prefer observing a face-to-face demonstration or listening to a podcast? Your preference for one mode or another doesn't make you a better or worse thinker or learner (see the discussion of learning styles earlier in the chapter), but it influences the ways in which you may choose to learn and communicate. Unless you have specific learning disabilities, you can learn in all modes, so you need to be at least competent in creating and interpreting all modes. Personal and professional success is more likely to come if you are excellent rather than merely competent.

Regardless of the mode, and no matter how good you are in engineering, math, and science, most theorists believe that thinking requires language. The classic example is based on a theory offered more than 50 years ago by linguist Benjamin Whorf, who speculated that language determines the way we think. Even though most linguists think Whorf's position is extreme, they nonetheless agree that language lets us name, recall, investigate, and build on abstractions (e.g., feelings), phenomena (e.g., color), objects (e.g., the Hubble telescope), events (e.g., a soccer game), and processes (e.g., splicing a gene). Being good with language (written, oral, and nonverbal) is a strong influence on your ability as a thinker. The better you are with language, the more productive you will be as a thinker and doer.

But language alone, even if you're very good at it, isn't enough for effective communication and thinking. Many people also think in images—that is, they engage in visual thinking. Consider a simple example: words help us differentiate "teal" and "sage," but images do an even better job. Notice the bar that presents 12 colors on a continuum of color. While most of us have the physiological ability to perceive the differences in these colors, we do not have consistent language for naming these colors.

CHART ▶
Color continuum chart for green.
SOURCE: "Full Greens," MyPantone Web Site.

What is the relationship between epistemology and visual thinking?
Epistemology is the study of the nature of knowledge, including its origin, nature, methods, and limits. Epistemology is especially concerned with ways of knowing and concentrates on questions related to thinking such as these:

» What is knowledge?

» How is knowledge acquired?

» Where does knowledge come from?

» What are the limits of knowledge?

» How does experience affect knowledge?

» How do we know what we know?

» Why do we know what we know?

» How can knowledge be tested?

Does visual thinking have epistemological functions or are visuals simply a way of defining and illustrating points already made in language? Visual thinking—defined to include visual imagination as well as perception of various kinds of images (drawings, videos, photographs, diagrams, symbols), and mental operations related to these images—is common in engineering, medicine, and the sciences and has been called "omnipresent in mathematics" (Giaquinto). If visual thinking is important to these disciplines, does it do more than provide a support function for language? Can visual thinking function (without language) as a means of knowing, understanding, remembering, questioning, analyzing, evaluating, using, and solving problems? Is visual thinking critical for creating multimodal artifacts?

Many researchers would answer yes to the above questions. For example, for more than 50 years, Rudolph Arnheim has claimed that visual thinking is central to our cognition. In a lengthy excerpt from an interview, he explained his position:

> [S]ensory knowledge, upon which all our experience is based, creates the possibilities of language. Our only access to reality is sensory experience, that is, sight or hearing or touch. And sensory experience is always more than mere seeing or touching. It also includes mental images and knowledge based on experience. All of that makes up our view of the world. In my opinion, "visual thinking" means that visual perception consists above all in the development of forms, of "perceptual terms," and thereby fulfills the conditions of the intellectual formation of concepts; it has the ability, by means of these forms, to give a valid interpretation of experience. Language, on the other hand, is in itself without form; one cannot think in words, since words cannot contain an object. Language is instructed by sensory perception. It codifies the given knowledge through sensory experience. This doesn't mean that language isn't tremendously significant for thought, for all of human development. Human existence is unimaginable without language. I am only stressing that language is an instrument of that which we have gained through perception, in that it confirms and preserves the concepts it forms. We encourage you to consider visual thinking as having enormous epistemological value. (Grundmann and Arnheim)

Reread Rudolf Arnheim's statement about visual thinking and language. Do you agree? Disagree? What aspects of your experience influence your position? #Evaluate

The debate about whether language or visuals form the basis for thinking is less important than recognizing that both language and visuals influence the way you represent ideas, processes, and objects; both are critical to your ability to create, interpret, and use multimodal artifacts.

How does multimodality affect representation?

The term *representation* refers to the way that you think about and instantiate an idea, process, or object. Several broad categories can influence your representation of a particular idea, process, or object:

» The nature of the idea, object, or process itself, information that is usually considered verifiable

» Your perceptions that influence your interpretations of verifiable information

» Sociocultural factors about context or situation in which the idea, process, or object you're representing will be used, including beliefs, customs, or behaviors typical in a particular group or population

» Your selection of information to represent, based on your sense of appropriateness for the audience and purpose

» The nature of modes and media you choose to represent the idea, object, or process

» Your selection of modes and media as well as your competence in using them

These categories interact synergistically to result in what is often called a "mental model," or your own internal representation, that is made into a multimodal artifact. As a successful student, you need to become competent in developing mental models—that is, visualizing the representation. Your mental model can be adjusted as you reflect on it to more accurately represent the idea, process, or object and to capture the details you consider appropriate for the audience and purpose.

Imagine you're interested in maps as objects people can use more easily and conveniently than big, printed paper maps that can be folded and refolded multiple times but are inconvenient to use if you're walking the streets in an unfamiliar city, trying to find a particular place. You can create a mental model of the kind of map you'd like to use. You can imagine the information this new kind of map would need to display, the symbols or icons that it would use (ones that are easy to see and interpret), the reactions people would have to seeing you use this new kind of map, and so on. Your mental model could also include ideas about the modes and media of the map: Is it entirely visual? Does it have words or symbols or both? Does it talk to you? Can you talk to it? Does it work wherever you are—regardless of location or weather? Does it create a path for you to follow? Does it require training to use, or is it intuitive? You can easily add or discard information in your mental model, responding to the context and sociocultural situation.

Your mental model can be represented multimodally. The success of your representation depends, in part, on your mastery of the "grammar" of the modes you select. As Gunther Kress and Theo van Leeuwen explain, "All modes have grammars" (1). Part of your responsibility is to learn those grammars—the concepts and the conventions—and use them productively. For example, to make your mental model of a map into an actual artifact, you may need to learn some of the concepts and vocabulary of maps. Some of the terms may be familiar (bearing, coordinates, or elevation) while other map terms may be less familiar (azimuth, gradicule, or plat). (For additional map terms, simply do an Internet search for <map terms> or <map glossary> or <cartography terms>.) All of them will help you consider ways to instantiate your mental model.

Your representation cannot be thought of simply as factual reporting, even if all of the features you describe can be verified as accurate. This is because the concept, process, or object you represent in various modes and media exists in a context, so, as psychologist Lev Vygotsky's work makes clear, you need to make sure that your representation reflects the context. When you consider the concept, process, or object in context, you can develop alternative views that need to be examined. During the "talking to yourself" phase, you consider and discard, consider and reshape, and consider and formulate your representation. For example, in making your mental model into an actual, usable map, you need to consider a range of contextual factors such as these: How much time will you have to refer to a map? How will the light affect your ability to see the map? Will you be using the map while you're standing still or walking?

Why Are Self-Reflection and Self-Assessment about Communication Processes and Artifacts Important? GT

You shouldn't be surprised if your instructors ask you to reflect about your communication processes as well as about the artifacts you create. In general, reflection means deliberate consideration or careful analysis and contemplation of a particular subject. Historically, reflection has taken a number of forms, but the definition has remained relatively stable. Many people take time every day or every week to reflect on their activities; they consider what they've done, how they could have done it differently, and why they did it in a particular way.

In Chapter 7 you will read about the importance of showcasing your work in a carefully curated portfolio that includes reflective comments about your processes and products. In this section, your book discusses the merits of reflection itself as a common practice and as a part of the composing process. Reflection has great potential to help you improve your work, both the processes and the products.

Etymology of "reflection"

reflection: "late 14c., reflexion, in reference to surfaces throwing back light or heat, from Late Latin reflexionem (nominative reflexio) 'a reflection,' literally 'a bending back,' noun of action from past participle stem of Latin reflectere 'to bend back, bend backwards, turn away,' from re- 'back' (see re-) + flectere 'to bend' (see flexible). Of the mind, from 1670s. Meaning 'remark made after turning back one's thought on some subject' is from 1640s. Spelling with -ct- recorded from late 14c., established 18c., by influence of the verb."

SOURCE: Online Etymology Dictionary.

The best reason for engaging in reflection is that it is a metacognitive function that enables and reinforces transference. Reflection is the best way to increase the likelihood that what you learn in one activity or assignment transfers to other activities and assignments. You can generate reflective comments—jotted in a journal, written on your laptop, or recorded on a digital recorder—during your work on a project.

The questions below can help as you compose reflections. These questions are not intended to be exhaustive or mutually exclusive. They're representative of the kinds of questions you can generate. The overlap among the questions demonstrates that although the composing process has identifiable parts, the process itself is multifaceted, synergistic, and recursive. You certainly should not feel compelled to answer all of the questions. Rather, pick and choose ones that you believe can help you increase your facility in all modes and media because your reflection is an opportunity for you to consider their synergy.

Reflective Questions

» What is my purpose in this reflection?

» Who is my audience for the reflection?

» What argument am I making?

» How can I organize my reflection?

» What kinds of evidence are appropriate and persuasive (quotations from my journal, quotations from my artifact)?

» How much attention do I need to give to language and design conventions?

Role

» What can you say about your work as a writer, speaker, or designer in completing this assignment?

» How have your own experiences and biases affected the way you engaged in the process and affected the way you selected the modes and media for the artifacts?

» How have your social circumstances (e.g., race, sexual orientation, socioeconomic class, gender, religious preference) affected your artifact?

Multimodality and Media

» What might happen to the artifact you've created if you changed the mode? If you changed the medium?

» In what ways are the modes and media in your own work synergistic?

» How did you creatively and productively use conventions in each mode?

Collaboration

» In a collaborative project, what was your role and how well did you carry it out?

» What would your teammates say about your reliability, contributions, attitude, cooperation, and quality of work?

» Based on your most recent collaborative project, what collaborative strategies can you improve? What leadership strategies can you improve? What support strategies can you improve?

Performance

» What's your favorite aspect of the design of your visual artifact (Web site, brochure, poster, PowerPoint, etc.)? Why?

» What's your favorite sentence in the entire paper or oral presentation? Why?

» What are three of the best aspects of the assignment you just completed? What makes them so good?

Development

» What parts of your project would you make sure not to repeat in the future? What would you absolutely want to do again?

» What would you have done differently if you had more time or greater access to software or other tools?

» How did your views of the work change or stay the same? To support your position, quote from the reflective comments you wrote during the project.

Learning

» What did you learn that wasn't part of the official assignment?

» What did you learn in doing this assignment that surprised you?

» What have you learned that you can carry to the next communication task?

Consider how you want to present your reflection—as a journal largely or exclusively for yourself, as email to reviewers of your draft, as a memo largely for your instructor, as a prefatory or concluding commentary for the audience, as a blog entry commenting about your own processes or style, as an entry in a class discussion board about developing communication competencies, or in some other form (O'Neill).

What is assessment, and why is it important?

Assessment matters because it lets you know what works and what doesn't in a particular process and for a particular artifact. In Chapter 7, you will learn more about the assessment practices and rubric used by the Writing and Communication Program. However, the best assessment you can get is the complete and conscientious assessment you learn to do for yourself. Experts in disciplinary and professional arenas are able to seek feedback from others, but they also conduct rigorous, thorough self-assessment. They are often their own toughest critics.

Who else can assess your multimodal work?

» Your instructor is an invaluable critic. Seek feedback. Listen carefully and take notes during conferences. Read your instructor's written remarks. Ask questions about what you don't understand. Follow up by checking in your textbook for further explanations.

» Your peers are also invaluable critics. Although they usually make very different remarks than your instructor, they are a good audience. When a peer identifies problems, for example, in logic, evidence, or coherence, you should pay attention.

» Your friends outside of class may be willing to review your work. Provide them with the assignment sheet and the assessment criteria so they can make useful remarks.

» If you are doing a service-learning or client-based project, your client may well be able to provide feedback. Be specific in indicating what you want the person to review. You usually shouldn't ask a client to proofread, but a client can provide invaluable insight about aspects of your argument that are (or aren't) persuasive.

What tools can you use to assess your own work and progress? Your instructor will give you assessment criteria (probably a list or a rubric) for each assignment. While the criteria separate various rhetorical elements and modes for purposes of assessment, you know that in practice these elements are inseparable. For example, you can discuss "audience" as a separate rhetorical element in a paper you write or a Web site you develop, but in practice audience cannot be separated from the organization you use, the argument you make, the examples you select, or the visuals you incorporate. While the separation is artificial, you can think of the separate elements as a way to gain greater understanding about what feeds the synergy of the final product.

References

Arnheim, Rudolph. *Visual Thinking*. Berkeley: U of California P, 1969. Print.

Bourdieu, Pierre. *Distinction: A Social Critique of the Judgement of Taste*. Trans. Richard Nice. London: Routledge, 1984 (1979). Print.

Douglass, Frederick. *Narrative of the Life of Frederick Douglass, An American Slave*, Chapter 7. Project Gutenberg, 1845. Web. 2009.

Giaquinto, Marcus. *Visual Thinking in Mathematics: An Epistemological Study*. London: Oxford UP, 2007. Print.

Grundmann, Uta, and Rudolf Arnheim. "The Intelligence of Vision: An Interview with Rudolf Arnheim." *Cabinet* 2 (2001). Web. 2009, rev. 2015.

Jewitt, Carey. "Multimodality and New Communication Technologies." Ed. Phillip Levine and Ron Scollon. *Discourse and Technology: Multimodal Discourse Analysis*. Washington, DC: Georgetown UP, 2004. 184–95. Print.

Jewitt, Carey, Gunther Kress, Jon Ogborn, and Charalampos Tsatsarelis. "Exploring Learning through Visual, Actional, and Linguistic Communication: The Multimodal Environment of a Science Classroom." *Educational Review* 53.1 (2001): 5–18. Print.

Kress, Gunther. "Gains and Losses: New Forms of Texts, Knowledge, and Learning." *Computers and Composition*, 22 (2005): 5-22. Web. 2009, rev. 2015.

Kress, Gunther. "Multimodality: Challenges to Thinking About Language." *TESOL Quarterly*, 34.2 (2000), 337–40. Web. 2009, rev. 2015.

Kress, Gunther. "Rhetorics of the Science Classroom: A Multimodal Approach." *Multimodal Teaching and Learning: The Rhetorics of the Science Classroom*. New York: Continuum, 2001. Print.

Kress, Gunther, and Theo van Leeuwen. *Reading Images: The Grammar of Visual Design*. London: Routledge, 2006. Print.

Luke, Carmen. "Pedagogy, Connectivity, Multimodality, and Interdisciplinarity" *Reading Research Quarterly*, 38.3 (2003): 397–403. Web. 2009, rev. 2015.

"Metaphor." *Online Etymology Dictionary*. 2001–2015. Web. 2009, rev. 2015.

Metiri Group. *Multimodal Learning Through Media: What the Research Says*. Cisco Systems. 2008. Web. 2009.

O'Neill, Peggy. "Reflection and Self-Assessment: Resisting Ritualistic Discourse." *The Writing Instructor* (2002). Web. 2009, rev. 2015.

"Reflection." *Online Etymology Dictionary*. 2001–2015. Web. 2009, rev. 2015.

"Synergy." *Online Etymology Dictionary*. 2001–2015. Web. 2009, rev. 2015.

"Wiki." *Wikipedia*. 2015. Web. 2009, rev. 2015.

4 UNDERSTANDING GENRES

MEMOIR ▶
Marjane Satrapi,
Persepolis
Everett Collection.

What is a *genre*, anyway? A *genre* is a composition's kind, category, or sort. Genres give us a way to categorize or describe types of compositions. For example, a song is a musical composition—but individual songs fall into specific genre categories, including punk, rap, R&B, soul, indie, and death metal.

Why bother thinking about genres? Because they represent possibilities. We wrote this book to acknowledge that in college and beyond there are *way* more genres available to us besides the five-paragraph essay or the traditional term paper. As respectable and time-honored as those genres are, there are a whole lot of other options out there. We wrote this book to help you understand and create in a variety of genres—and we invite you to produce works that matter to you and enjoy doing so. As an added bonus, paying attention to genre will make you a better writer and artist. Why? Because you'll be focused on the needs of your audiences and your own purposes as a composer.

What do you need to know about genres? First, genres change according to the ways people use them. Before digital composing, writers who wanted to record their thoughts wrote with a pen in a journal or diary, in a physical notebook. Then blogs were created.

Second, genres are flexible: They overlap and don't fall neatly into the categories and primary purposes we've outlined in this book. For example, we present graphic memoirs in Chapter 13, "Narrative Genres," but this genre could also work in Chapter 15, "Persuasive Genres." That's because while memoirists tell the stories of their own lives, they also persuade readers to empathize with them and to see the world in a certain way. Remember that as a writer, you define your use of a genre based on your purposes and audiences, and you can do more than one thing at a time. Your ad can do more than persuade; your literacy narrative can do more than tell a story.

What do you already know about genres? Think for a minute about the different genres you compose in each day. As a student, you write research papers and presentations; these are two examples of academic genres. In each case, you know what is expected of you as a writer, because you understand certain features of the genre. You know that to write a research

What kinds of composing have you done so far as a student? What are some of the features that define the works you've composed? #Remember

▼ BLOG
The Dragonfly Woman Blog. *Christine L. Goforth.*

For an Index of Sources & Contexts for material referenced in this chapter, visit **bedfordstmartins.com /bookofgenres**.

What do you already know about advertising? What qualities make an ad successful? #Remember #Analyze

paper, you must gather and interpret a variety of reliable sources and cite them in a specific way.

In other situations, you choose your own genre to compose in, depending on what you want to say, who you want to say it to, and how you want to say it. Your choice of genre also depends on your own skills and interests, as well as the materials available to you. For example, your band is playing next week and you need to advertise the event. Your purpose is to persuade your potential audience to come to your show. You might choose to present your ad as a poster. Depending on your supplies and desired effect, you could create a handmade poster to tape up at school or design one on your computer to post on Facebook. Alternatively, you might choose to advertise by creating and posting a short music video.

One of the best ways to become a better writer/composer is to read like one—to pay attention to what other writers/composers do, how and why they work in a particular genre, and how they make that genre work for them.

Let's look at an example from history. Annie L. Burton (ca. 1858–unknown) was born a slave and as an adult decided

PHOTO ▶
Annie L. Burton
Author of the memoir *Memories of Childhood's Slavery Days* (1909). *Images courtesy of Documenting the American South, The University of North Carolina at Chapel Hill Libraries.*

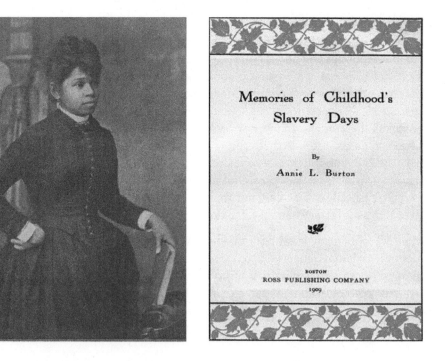

Memories of Childhood's Slavery Days

By
Annie L. Burton

BOSTON
ROSS PUBLISHING COMPANY
1909

to write about her experiences; her 1909 memoir is titled *Memories of Childhood's Slavery Days*. Why did she choose to write a memoir instead of poetry or editorials or technical manuals? Most likely, Burton chose the memoir because it was a popular genre in her day that allowed her to tell the story she wanted to tell, suited her interests and skills, and reached the audience she wanted to reach. Maybe if she had been trained in music, she would have written operas, or if she had been born a little later, she would have told her story as a documentary film.

> Our clothes were little homespun cotton slips, with short sleeves. I never knew what shoes were until I got big enough to earn them myself. If a slave man and woman wished to marry, a party would be arranged some Saturday night among the slaves. The marriage ceremony consisted of the pair jumping over a stick. If no children were born within a year or so, the wife was sold. At New Year's, if there was any debt or mortgage on the plantation, the extra slaves were taken to Clayton and sold at the court house. In this way families were separated.
>
> **—Annie L. Burton**

What we do know is that Burton wrote a memoir (a genre), specifically one that detailed her life as a slave. In her memoir, Burton wrote in the first person, portrayed real people, described settings, conveyed conflict, and told stories from her own life. These elements are features of the memoir genre and of any autobiography. Burton's purpose as a memoirist would have been to inform readers about what life as a slave—and later as a free person—was like; another purpose might have been to connect with women readers about what it was like to be a woman and a slave; yet another might have been to engage the imagination of readers. Her audience would have been literate former slaves and white readers, most likely in the North because her book was published in Boston. Her current readers might include students, scholars, and historians who want to read a firsthand account of slave life.

Do you read memoirs? What other observations can you make about the memoir as a genre?
#Remember
#Understand

The Rhetorical Situation

What is *rhetoric*? *Rhetoric* refers to the ability to communicate effectively and with a purpose. So what is a *rhetorical situation*? It's the context in which you create a composition. To put it simply, as a writer, you have a specific purpose and an audience. You need to know what you want to say; you also need to know your readers' expectations and accommodate them in some way. For example, when you write a review of a restaurant on yelp.com, you know that Yelp readers want to know your opinion of the meal; they also expect specific details about the individual dishes, service, and ambience you experienced.

Purpose: Why are you composing?

Every time you write—or compose anything, in any genre—you do so for a reason. In this book, we've identified three main purposes for composing:

» To present a narrative / to tell a story (Chapter 13)

» To inform (Chapter 14)

» To persuade (Chapter 15)

There are many reasons to write and sometimes these reasons overlap. As writers, we often have several purposes for creating a single text. Let's look at a possible example. Let's assume that you love farmers' markets and want to establish one in your town.

Your purpose   You want to start up a weekly local farmers' market. To make this happen, you need to (1) present your idea to others and (2) persuade them that it's worth acting upon. You expect that some people will object.

Your rhetorical situation   In this context, you have more than one purpose. In order to persuade others, you need to explain your idea, say what's great about it, provide supporting statistics, and tell a persuasive story about how a similar plan succeeded in a neighboring town. You also have more than one audience. Some people will agree with you 100 per-

---

CHECKLIST **Composing with a Purpose**

As you begin to compose, ask yourself:

☐ Why am I writing? What do I want to communicate? And to whom?

☐ What do I want my audience to believe or do after reading my composition?

☐ Is what I'm communicating objectionable or controversial to anyone? If so, how will I address this?

☐ If I'm telling a story, why is it significant, and how will I make it compelling?

☐ If I'm sharing information, why is it important, and how will I communicate its authority?

☐ If I'm trying to persuade others, what are the best ways to do so, for my particular readers?

cent; others won't be so sure; still others, maybe grocery store owners or city planners, will reject your idea altogether.

Your plan and genre choice   After considering your purpose and audience, you decide to write an editorial on your local newspaper's blog. You also plan to present your idea in person at the next town meeting.

As you begin writing your editorial, you may shift your purpose slightly—away from simply proposing and arguing for your plan—and toward focusing on the success of neighboring towns' farmers' markets and how they benefited local grocery stores. This will boost your persuasiveness with your resistant grocery store owners.

However, you may decide that rather than an editorial or a presentation, some other genre might better serve your purpose. For example, you may find that the best way to establish a farmers' market is to take a more personal approach by writing a letter to the mayor. You might also survey local citizens to see whether they'd like the opportunity to buy produce from local farmers. The point here is to see how your purpose affects your choice of genre, and how you can work in your genre to impact your audience.

Audience: Who are you composing for?

Every time you compose, you do so for an audience. Audiences are made up of people—and people can be easily bored, pressed for time, or generally disinterested. You need to grab their attention and keep it.

Let's look at an example: Imagine you are traveling across the country and want to tell stories of your adventures (your purpose) to your friends, family, and even strangers interested in travel (your audience). You decide that the best way to reach your audience is to create a blog where you can write about your experiences, show maps and photos, and connect to other social media sites. That is what the world-traveling blogger who calls himself Giladhiz decided to do (see p. 88).

Giladhiz clearly understands his audience and wants them to stick with him. To this end, he:

>> Provides a photo of himself and an "About the Author" section so that readers can make a personal connection with him.

What genres have you written in today? Why? And who were your audiences? #Remember

---

CHECKLIST **Composing for an Audience**

As you begin to compose, ask yourself:

☐   Who is my audience in terms of demographics? Are they mostly male or mostly female? What is their age range? Where do they live? What do they like? Do they have particular religious beliefs? Are they from a particular social class? Are they of a particular race or ethnic background?

☐   What is my audience's stake in the issue I'm presenting? Do they care? Why or why not?

☐   What does my audience value? Will my message be in line with—or contradictory to—their values? How can I present my message so that my audience will consider it? And perhaps even be persuaded by it?

☐   What level of education does my audience have? What kind of language will best reach them?

The Rhetorical Situation   87

» Addresses his readers directly: "So, dear friends and accidental surfers, allow me to begin with the reasons that brought me to plan and go on that trip."

» Writes in a casual, readable, and humorous style, meant to hook his readers and keep them interested in his ongoing adventures.

INFORMATIVE ▶
TRAVEL BLOG
Blogger Giladhiz
From *Gilad Is Doing South America*. Gilad H.

When you write, do you think of who will read your writing? When you compose a song, a video, or even a status update, do you think of who will experience what you've created? #Remember

---

Prologue - The beginning

Giladhiz's Profile ▸ About this blog ▸ Entry from Herzlia

Trip Start
Oct 12, 2010

Trip End
Jun 15, 2011

▣ Herzlia, Israel
Monday, October 11, 2010

👍 Like   ▣ One person likes this. Be the first of your friends.

Prologue - The beginning.

This really isn't an interesting part of my journey... This part is meant for those of you who wish to know me a little bit better, for some friends who hasn't been in close touch with me lately and for others who just happen to have too much free time and nothing better to do at the moment.

Map Options

Where I stayed
Home
Herzlia hotels

Mellow excitement

If you were about to embark on a 7 months journey around South America, rafting through rapid rivers, exploring the jungle, diving with sharks, climbing icy mountains, dancing (or watching other people dance) at the famous Brazilian carnival and partying wildly at night – how would that make you feel?
I assume "mellow" would not be one of the ways to describe your feelings. And yet, I'm pretty convinced that this is how I feel at the moment.

But I jump ahead... first of all – thank you all for navigating your browsers to my Blog. If you've read all the way down to this line – I assume you're the "reader" kind of person rather than the "browser" type who's looking for anchor words or just looking at the pretty pictures... so from now on I'll consider my writing as a kind of a monologue, knowing that there's someone out there who actually listens to me babble.

So, dear friends and accidental surfers, allow me to begin with the reasons that brought me to plan and go on that trip.

Reason #1
Coincidence

I still have no idea how it happened. One day I was in a middle of a long term relationship (3 year), living in a rented apartment in Ramat Gan, working at a place I'd rather not mention – while studying for my MBA degree.
The next day I found myself alone, mourning the loss of a dead-end relationship (which ended like a train crash – unexpected derailing and crashing into the mountain side instead of going through a dark tunnel). And on the next day – I graduated my MBA, giving me even more free time for myself, alone. Lo and behold – at the very next day I decided to dump my promising career and quit, surprising many of my colleagues who were convinced I would reach a high position in my organization, as I was a highly valued (and well rewarded) employee.
Hmm...

Just chilling...

About the Author
Giladhiz ▣

✉ Send a message
♡ Add as favorite
✉ Get email updates
➕ Turn blog into a book
➕ Share
🔊 RSS

About this Blog

Gilad is doing South America

● Start your own travel blog

» Structures his post with subheadings to guide readers, and provides options for navigating content and for e-mailing or connecting by social media.

Rhetorical Appeals: Ethos, pathos, and logos

Whether your purpose is to tell a story, report information, or persuade, you need to get your audience on board. Even when persuasion is not your primary goal, it is always part of what you're doing, no matter what. We persuade our audiences by using what are called rhetorical appeals. There are three types of these, and they are often used in combination:

» *Ethos* is the credibility, authority, and trustworthiness the writer/composer conveys to the audience.

» *Pathos* is an appeal to an audience's emotions or values.

» *Logos* is the logic and connection of facts and evidence to the point being made.

As a writer/composer, you get to decide which appeals to use, depending on your audience, purposes, and choice of genre. For example:

» You're creating a memoir or an encyclopedia entry; you need to get readers to see you as an expert and accept your information as credible. In this case, you rely on *ethos*.

» You're creating an ad to persuade your audience to buy a product (especially something without tangible benefits, such as potato chips or a vacation package). In this case, you might appeal to their emotions and desires, relying on *pathos*.

» You're writing an editorial or an argumentative essay; you need to get your readers to agree with your conclusions. In this case, you might take them logically through the different elements of the arguments you're analyzing, relying on *logos*.

Modes & Media

What is a *mode*? What does it have to do with *media*? *Mode* is how a composition is experienced by readers/viewers/listeners.

For much of this book, we work with three main modes: written, visual, and oral/audio.

Media is the delivery mechanism of the composition, including the following:

» Print

» Digital

» Face-to-face

A particular mode can be delivered in multiple media; for example, an audio essay could be recorded either on an old-fashioned tape recorder or digitally. We've broken out the modes and media of some of the genres in this chapter.

NARRATIVE GENRES	Mode	Medium
MEMOIR Marjane Satrapi, *Persepolis* (p. 82)	**WRITTEN AND VISUAL**	**PRINT AND FILM**
MEMOIR Annie L. Burton, *Memories of Childhood's Slavery Days* (p. 84)	**WRITTEN**	**PRINT**
TRAVEL BLOG Giladhiz, *Gilad Is Doing South America* (p. 88)	**WRITTEN AND VISUAL**	**DIGITAL**
ARTIST'S STATEMENT Kristen LaCroix, *Prescription for Change* (p. 111)	**WRITTEN (BUT ACCOMPANIES A COLLAGE/SCULPTURE**	**DIGITAL**

Genre Conventions

Do you want to be a great writer or composer? If so, you need to know something about the genre you're composing in; you need to know its basic qualities and agreed-upon rules, and you need to be familiar with some examples. As Scott McCloud shows in his book *Understanding Comics*, writers and artists who work on comics use visual images and text to convey ideas, balloons to indicate dialogue, and simple but dynamic drawings and design to hold the reader's attention. Let's say you want to tell a story and you want to convey it graphically. You don't need to be McCloud or Picasso or Art Spiegelman, but you do need to understand how artists, graphic novelists, and memoirists work with visuals and text to tell stories. It helps to have some familiarity with the genre (read a few examples!) and perhaps have one example in mind as a model. Or let's say you want to draw an annotated map of your neighborhood. It would help to know some of the established conventions of mapmakers, such as using color to represent specific geography, or symbols to identify features or places. If your blog posts give your opinions on the editorials published on *Slate* or *The Huffington Post*, for example, you will have more authority if you link directly to the material you're responding to. Hyperlinking is a convention of the blog genre.

How much do you need to know? Keep an open mind as you choose genres to compose in. Consider collaborating with classmates who have more detailed knowledge of the genres that you're less familiar with. Often students in our writing

◀ COMIC
Scott McCloud
From his book
*Understanding Comics:
The Invisible Art.*
HarperCollins.

classes will discuss and figure out together the conventions of specific genres and media (e.g., video or PowerPoint) and go from there. Other times they keep it simple but thoughtful, creating scrapbooks, print-based texts, or audio essays.

Elements of the Genre

In this book, we ask you to pay attention to the main features of a given genre: the specific elements that are common to most examples of the genre. For instance, most press release writers try to be as brief and objective as possible, and aim at answering the questions who, what, why, where, and when. For those reasons, we consider brevity, objectivity, and thoroughness to be elements of the press release genre. (For an example, see Paul Henderson's press release on p. 96 about the Wall Arch collapse.)

Style

Style refers to the particular ways we communicate. In this book, we pay attention to the techniques that individual writers use—and to what extent these techniques reflect the style of others composing in the same genre. We look at how much detail writers include, and how precise that detail is. We listen for tone (seriousness, humor, etc.) and voice (the presence of the author) and analyze how these qualities affect the overall composition. How a writer uses sources is part of style, as well. A writer who has cultivated a serious, academic style will probably use serious, academic sources as evidence. On the other hand, a writer with a more casual, chatty style might depend more on conversations with friends for evidence.

As a writer, you use style when you compose. The trick is to make sure that the style you're using is appropriate to your purpose and accessible and persuasive to your audience. For example, the writer and traveler Giladhiz uses a particular style on his blog. Because he is interested in attracting "accidental surfers" to his blog—that is, people who stumble upon his blog accidentally—he takes a casual and funny approach to his travels rather than a serious, scholarly tone. A serious, scholarly tone would probably appeal to an audience interested in the economics or politics of his travels, but because Giladhiz's purpose is to share his quirky, funny adventures, his casual, humorous style makes more sense.

Design

Design describes the visual features of a composition, including the use of headings, format, color, and illustration. Design is aesthetic but also functional. As we discuss throughout the book, the design features you and other writers choose can play an important role in the level of success in achieving purposes and reaching audiences. Take a look at how Giladhiz uses images in his blog. Maps show readers exactly where this traveler is, and the photos of Giladhiz help readers connect with him personally. Giladhiz's photos documenting his travels let readers see what he saw. Because one of his purposes is to allow others to share in his travels vicariously, the photos are particularly important.

Sources

Sources are the people, conversations, documents, books, journal articles, movies, and other works that we refer to for facts, perspectives, and models as we compose. For example, sources Giladhiz drew on for his travel blog (see p. 88) include Google Maps, the people he meets, and tourist information, such as brochures from historical sites. In this book, we consider sources because sources shape what writers create.

When you compose in certain genres, such as academic and research essays, you need to document the sources you refer to. In other cases, such as novels, comics, and music lyrics, while you've read and used sources, you're not required to document them formally. Whether or not sources need to be documented depends on the rhetorical situation. Sources referred to in a research essay aimed at academic readers should be documented because readers will want to know where ideas and information came from; the purposes of song lyrics are different, though. Listeners of a song aren't listening for information, so the sources of information are less important. Throughout the book we look at the conventions of specific genres in this regard, and in Chapter 20, we provide guidelines for using sources.

In order to compose in different genres, you first should be able to identify them, see how other writers use them to achieve purposes and reach audiences, and learn some of the basic features so you can experiment.

How might the use of sources help boost—or undermine—your ethos as a composer? #Analyze

CHECKLIST: Identifying Genres
Are you looking at a particular composition and wondering what genre it is? Keep the following questions in mind.

☐ **Purpose.** Is the author telling a story? (See Chapter 13, "Narrative Genres.") Is the author reporting information? (See Chapter 14, "Informative Genres.") Is the author persuading? (See Chapter 15, "Persuasive Genres.") Is the writer telling a story, reporting, writing creatively, and persuading all at the same time? Don't worry. Sometimes purposes for writing/composing—and the genres we use—overlap.

☐ **Audience.** Who seems to be the author's primary audience? Secondary audience? How do you know? Why do you think someone would read (view, listen to, etc.) the text? How does the author capture and sustain audience attention?

☐ **Rhetorical appeals.** How does the author use the rhetorical appeals—ethos, pathos, and logos—to reach his or her audience? How does the author convey credibility? What kinds of evidence does the author offer to support the point of the piece?

☐ **Modes & media.** What choices has the writer made about mode? If multiple modes are used, how do they interact with each other? For example, if the piece includes both visuals and writing, is meaning conveyed by both the visuals and the writing, or does one mode convey more meaning than the other? What choices has the writer made about media? How do the writer's choices about modes and media reflect his or her purposes and audiences?

☐ **Elements of the genre.** What do you know about this genre already? What are some of the typical features of this genre? How is the content organized? How does the author use words, images, or other media to convey a purpose and reach an audience?

☐ **Style.** What is the author's tone? How would you describe the language of the piece? How much detail does the author use?

☐ **Design.** What does the composition look (sound, feel, smell, etc.) like? How do words and visuals and other media work together in the genre, physically? How would you describe the format of the composition? Would the format change if the mode were changed? For example, if a newspaper editorial moves from a print medium to an online medium, what changes occur in the genre?

☐ **Sources.** What sources does the author draw on for research? How do you know? How does the author incorporate and give credit to sources? Is there documentation? Hyperlinking?

CASE STUDY:
ONE EVENT, TWO GENRES

Arch Collapse at a National Park

In this case study, two writers report on a single event. One writes a press release, the other a blog post.

The event: In August 2008, a rock formation in Utah's famous Arches National Park collapses.

The writers:

» **Paul Henderson**, a ranger at the park who also wrote press releases

» **Shaan Hurley**, a blogger and fan of the park who had hiked and photographed it

The compositions:

» "Wall Arch Collapses," a press release by Paul Henderson

» "The Wall Arch Collapses in Arches National Park," a blog post by Shaan Hurley

As you'll see, Henderson and Hurley provide much of the same information about the arch collapse, but they write in different genres, and with different purposes and audiences in mind. The notes in the margins of each piece explain their rhetorical situations and how they work within the conventions of the press release and the blog post.

Think of a current issue. How is the issue covered in different genres—for example, in a news report, an editorial, a documentary, and a comic strip? #Understand

Guided Reading: Press Release ▼

Paul Henderson

Wall Arch Collapses

At the time of the collapse, Paul Henderson was chief of Interpretation and Visitor Services for Arches National Park, which is managed by the National Park Service, part of the U.S. Department of the Interior. When the arch collapsed, Henderson was interviewed by news outlets, including MSNBC, which also quoted from the press release on page 96.

(Images on page 96 courtesy of National Park Service.)

What is the composer, Paul Henderson, doing?

THE RHETORICAL SITUATION

Purpose
Audience
Rhetorical appeals
Modes & media

see page 97

How do I know this is a press release?

THE GENRE'S CONVENTIONS

Elements of the genre
Style
Design
Sources

see page 97

Arches | National Park Utah

Wall Arch Collapses

Date: August 8, 2008
Contact: Paul Henderson, 435-719-2140

Subscribe | What is RSS

Wall Arch, located along the popular Devils Garden Trail at Arches National Park collapsed sometime during the night of August 4, 2008. Rock has continued to fall from the arms of the remaining portion of the arch necessitating the closure of the Devils Garden Trail just beyond Landscape Arch.

On August 7, 2008, representatives from both the National Park Service Geologic Resources Division and the Utah Geological Survey visited the site and noted obvious stress fractures in the remaining formation. Rock debris has completely blocked this section of the trail. The closure will remain in effect until visitor safety issues can be resolved.

First reported and named by Lewis T. McKinney in 1948, Wall Arch was a free standing arch in the Slickrock member of the Entrada sandstone. The opening beneath the span was 71-feet wide and 33-1/2 feet high. It ranked 12th in size among the over 2,000 known arches in the park.

All arches are but temporary features and all will eventually succumb to the forces of gravity and erosion. While the geologic forces that created the arches are still very much underway, in human terms it's rare to observe such dramatic changes.

No one has reported observing the arch collapse and there were no visitor injuries.

THE RHETORICAL SITUATION

Purpose

Henderson, who works for the National Park Service, a government agency, writes **to inform** readers about the collapse. He reports that there were no injuries and that the area is temporarily closed. He reassures readers that the event is normal, that arches are temporary and "eventually succumb to the forces of gravity and erosion."

Audience

Henderson's readers want an **official statement** from park management, rather than one by an outside observer. Readers are mainly members of news organizations—but also park patrons, including hikers and nature photographers, looking for details.

Rhetorical appeals

For Henderson and other press release writers, **ethos** is crucial. Readers need to trust the authority of the writer and his information, especially because Henderson represents a government agency.

Henderson establishes **logos** by presenting information in a sensible order, beginning with the event and ending with its effects.

Modes & media

Henderson **uses text to inform and visuals to show the effect** of the collapse. His press release was posted digitally on the National Park Service's site and was probably also distributed by e-mail to various news organizations.

THE GENRE'S CONVENTIONS

Elements of the genre

Addresses who, what, when, where, why, and how. Henderson does so as follows:
Who = readers who care about the environment and park
What = the arch collapse
When = 8/4/08
Where = specific location of the collapse
Why = gravity and erosion
How = falling debris

Is brief and timely. Like most press releases, this is concisely worded, just a few paragraphs long. Henderson wrote it just four days after the event.

Begins with most important content. Henderson begins with the most crucial information and follows it with significant details.

Includes contact info for media. Henderson wants readers, especially the news media (the target audience for press releases), to be able to get in touch.

Style

Conveys an objective tone. Henderson doesn't give his opinion; he also writes in the neutral third person.

Is clear, direct writing. Henderson provides facts simply and details concisely (e.g., "Rock debris has completely blocked this section of the trail").

Design

Presents a simple, clean layout. Henderson uses a standard press release design, with a headline to summarize and get attention, a dateline, and contact information. There are just two images to support the text.

The Web page itself includes the name of the park, an image, and a menu bar for easy navigation.

Sources

Draws on official information. Henderson uses facts from the National Park Service and from the Utah Geological Survey, which he credits in the body of his press release.

Guided Reading: Blog Post ▼

Shaan Hurley

The Wall Arch Collapses in Arches National Park

Blogger Shaan Hurley has a background in mechanical design and works in the field of technology. *All Things Autodesk & Technology* is Hurley's personal blog; he also posts on Twitter. He posted the following entry in August 2008. *(Image courtesy of Shaan Hurley at Autodesk.)*

All Things Autodesk & Technology

Shaan Hurley
Autodesk Technologist for the Office of the CTO

The Wall Arch Collapses in Arches National Park

Almost one year ago to the week I was in the beautiful and world famous Arches National Park which is little more than 4 hours drive from my home in Utah. Just this week perhaps Tuesday one of the famous sandstone arches fell, Wall Arch is now Wall Pile. While Wall Arch was not the most spectacular or stunning, it was a beautiful arch.

Arches are formed by an ever changing nature and erosion and leave us with only a small window of geological time in which to marvel at the arches before they succumb to gravity. Who knows, perhaps another arch was born that we have not seen in the past year as well. Last year while I was photographing many of the arches and absolutely enjoying the natural beauty and silence in between the tourist buses,

I hiked back to Landscape arch which itself had suffered a partial collapse in 1991. Since it was so hot that day and I figured I would get back there again soon I did not hike the remaining quarter mile to photograph Wall Arch by the Devils Garden. Now I will not have the opportunity to photograph Wall Arch except the remnants on the ground. It is another example of how things you take for granted may disappear.

If you ever have the chance to Visit the Moab Utah region or Southern Utah you should do so as it is beyond words and one of the reasons I know call this state home. This is photography heaven for color and so many varied landscape and rare geography. One of the other things I love about the area is the history of the Fremont people from thousands of years ago leaving their art on the rock walls and then last but not least Green River Utah having the worlds best watermelon when hiking in 100+ deg F. weather. If you are ever in Utah let me know as I am always happy to get an excuse to head to Moab and love showing the hidden gems beyond the tourist trails.

Here are a couple of my photos from the hike back on August 4th 2007 in Arches National Park. I still have hundreds of photos yet to publish, It may sound odd for someone to see some sense of loss in what to some may just be a sandstone structure born of erosion but if you have ever been there in the silence and the vibrant glow of red at twilight you would understand the magic of the area. This is natures art and landscape at it's finest.

http://www.flickr.com/photos/btl/

Never take for granted who or what you can see today, you may not have the opportunity tomorrow.

Have a great weekend,

Shaan

What is the composer, Shaan Hurley, doing?

THE RHETORICAL SITUATION

Purpose
Audience
Rhetorical appeals
Modes & media

see page 99

How do I know this is a blog post?

THE GENRE'S CONVENTIONS

Elements of the genre
Style
Design
Sources

see page 99

Purpose

Hurley has a few reasons for writing: **to inform** readers about the collapse, **to share** his own experiences and photos of the park, and **to persuade** readers to enjoy nature now, rather than later, when the opportunity may not exist. He writes: "Now I will not have the opportunity to photograph Wall Arch except the remnants on the ground. It is another example of how things you take for granted may disappear."

Audience

His readers are fans of the park, other hikers and photographers, and even potential park visitors. His readers are looking for a **personal take** (rather than an official statement) on the arch collapse.

Rhetorical appeals

Because Hurley's main goal is to urge readers to seize an opportunity, he relies largely on **pathos** to appeal to emotion. Notice how he describes the beauty and "magic" of the park.

He also establishes **ethos**, or his authority to write on this topic, by sharing his firsthand experiences and photos of the park.

Modes & media

Hurley **uses text and visuals to inform**. His blog is digital and embedded with hyperlinks that bring readers to additional information. Readers can also share the link so others can read Hurley's post.

Elements of the genre

Presents brief, visual, hyperlinked content. Like most effective blog posts, Hurley's is just a few paragraphs long, visually interesting, and embedded with links that offer more information without adding length.

Written in short paragraphs. Hurley's concise, chunked text keeps digital readers interested.

Includes relevant photos. Hurley's images provide context, attract readers, and offer his perspective on the event.

Provides an "about" page and a comments area (not shown here). Hurley gives biographical information and a space for readers to offer feedback and share their own views on the park.

Style

Conveys a conversational voice/tone. Hurley, like many bloggers, offers his own reflections and is present in his writing. He writes in the first person, addressing readers directly.

Design

Clear layout; user-friendly navigation. Like other blogs, Hurley's is designed so users can easily find additional content; they can also access his page on flickr.com.

Sources

Draws on official and firsthand information. Hurley credits the National Park Service for some of the photos; he also draws on his own experience (his trip of 2007) and external sources such as *Wikipedia*.

Questions: Analyzing Paul Henderson's press release and Shaan Hurley's blog post

1. Purpose. Reread Henderson's press release and Hurley's blog post. What are the writers' purposes? How can you tell? How do these purposes differ? How might they overlap?

2. Audience. Who do you imagine is the primary reader for Henderson's press release? For Hurley's blog post? Explain.

3. Rhetorical appeals. How effective are Henderson and Hurley in using ethos, pathos, or logos to reach their audiences? Which appeals do they rely on most effectively, and why?

4. Rhetorical appeals. Consider how hyperlinks, photos, and other information can contribute to a composer's ethos. Why do you think Hurley used the National Park Service as a source for information and images? How did this choice affect his ethos?

5. Modes & media. Both Henderson and Hurley use a combination of text and visuals. If you were to add audio or video to either piece, what would you add? What meaning or information would the audio or video add?

6. Elements of the genre. As a reader interested in the arch collapse, would you be likely to consult a press release? A blog? Both? Neither? Explain. To what extent is genre important? And in what contexts? When might it not matter?

7. Elements of the genre. What are the most significant differences between the press release and blog post as genres? Based on these examples, what conventions of these genres can you identify? How do these conventions affect what the writers say and how they convey it?

8. Style. Analyze the language Henderson and Hurley use. What do their words and tone suggest about their different purposes and audiences?

9. Design. How does the design of each piece enable readers to quickly find information they want or need?

10. Design. Look again at the photos included in the blog post and press release. What purposes do they serve in each? How effectively do the authors use them?

11. Sources. How does Hurley use the National Park Service's press release as a source? How does that source contribute to his success in achieving his purpose and reaching his audience?

For examples of **informative genres,** see Chapter 14.

STUDENT CASE STUDY:
ONE TOPIC, MULTIPLE GENRES

Kristen LaCroix's Project on Drug Advertising

Let's look at a project by student writer Kristen LaCroix. Kristen is a former student of Liz Kleinfeld (coauthor of this textbook); Kristen was enrolled in Liz's composition class at Red Rocks Community College.

Kristen reflects on what she's doing now:

> Following my time at Red Rocks, I attended Colorado State University and graduated in the summer of 2010 with a degree in biological sciences. I am an intern with the Rocky Mountain Raptor Program and volunteering at the Denver Aquarium to pursue a career working with exotic wildlife. I hope to end up working as a medical director of a sanctuary or rehabilitation clinic for exotic animals.

Kristen reflects on her project:

> Looking back at this project, I remember wanting to choose a topic that I could find a lot of information on—I also wanted to be able to conduct interviews with experts. My grandfather worked in the pharmaceutical industry, and it's an area that has always interested me. It's a topic I care about and could easily take a stance on, largely because of my grandfather's experience. I found that the most challenging portion of this project was connecting all of the information together and getting it to flow. This project ultimately got me to see that there are lots of ways to present information and to persuade other people about your ideas.

Kristen created her project in response to an assignment Liz gave the class. Liz asked students to:

» Research a specific issue or topic of interest to them.

» Present an argument about that topic to their audience (their primary audience would be Liz and the rest of the class).

◀ STUDENT AUTHOR PHOTO
Kristen LaCroix
Kristen LaCroix.

>> Choose three genres to compose in, being sure to pick those that would work well for their topics and arguments.

>> Persuade their audience to agree with their perspective—and/or to take action on the issue.

Students were also asked to submit the following with their genre pieces:

>> An Author's/Artist's Statement for each piece, in which they explain their rhetorical choices and include an MLA-style Works Cited list

>> An Introduction to the project that states the overall objective and unifies the genre pieces into a whole

What issues are most important to you? How do you figure out which issues make the best topics for research and writing projects? #Apply #Evaluate

Researching a Topic

Kristen thought she'd like to write about the pharmaceutical industry because her grandfather had spent his career in that field and his stories about it fascinated her. She had no idea how she would focus her topic, so she started by doing some research. In addition to interviewing her grandfather, she also began her research

PEER-REVIEWED ▶
JOURNAL ARTICLE
Julie M. Donohue, PhD, et al.
From *The New England Journal of Medicine (NEJM).* Courtesy of the New England Journal of Medicine.

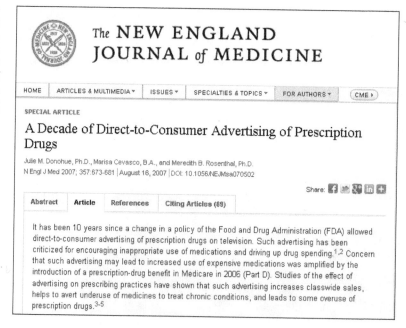

The NEW ENGLAND JOURNAL of MEDICINE

HOME | ARTICLES & MULTIMEDIA ▾ | ISSUES ▾ | SPECIALTIES & TOPICS ▾ | FOR AUTHORS ▾ | (CME ▸)

SPECIAL ARTICLE

A Decade of Direct-to-Consumer Advertising of Prescription Drugs

Julie M. Donohue, Ph.D., Marisa Cevasco, B.A., and Meredith B. Rosenthal, Ph.D.
N Engl J Med 2007; 357:673-681 | August 16, 2007 | DOI: 10.1056/NEJMsa070502

Share: [icons]

| Abstract | **Article** | References | Citing Articles (89) |

It has been 10 years since a change in a policy of the Food and Drug Administration (FDA) allowed direct-to-consumer advertising of prescription drugs on television. Such advertising has been criticized for encouraging inappropriate use of medications and driving up drug spending.[1,2] Concern that such advertising may lead to increased use of expensive medications was amplified by the introduction of a prescription-drug benefit in Medicare in 2006 (Part D). Studies of the effect of advertising on prescribing practices have shown that such advertising increases classwide sales, helps to avert underuse of medicines to treat chronic conditions, and leads to some overuse of prescription drugs.[3-5]

with some copies of *Health* magazine and *Good Housekeeping,* which contained ads and articles related to the drug industry, geared toward a general audience. As her research deepened, she looked into more scholarly professional resources, too, such as an article (by Julie M. Donohue, PhD, et al.) on advertising prescription drugs from *The New England Journal of Medicine* (*NEJM*). (For guidelines on research and working with sources, see Chapter 17, "Process: Exploring Topics and Creating a Research Proposal," Chapter 19, "Process: Evaluating and Choosing Sources," and Chapter 20, "Process: Integrating and Documenting Sources.")

Choosing a Topic

Kristen reflected on the conversations she'd had with her grandfather and the articles she'd read in *Health, NEJM,* and other periodicals. She was particularly struck by the number of direct-to-consumer drug ads she'd found in *Health* magazine and at the Food and Drug Administration Web site. She did more research and found that this type of advertising by drug companies is pervasive in popular magazines and media. Kristen felt these ads might also be dangerous and decided to explore further.

Determining a Purpose

As she focused her topic and conducted more research, Kristen was further persuaded that direct-to-consumer drug ads could be harmful. She decided that she would use her project to persuade others as well. With this purpose in mind, she thought about her audience of classmates. They might not be aware of the extent of direct-to-consumer drug ads; she realized that she would first need to inform her readers of the ads' pervasiveness before she could build her main argument about their possible impact on consumers.

Considering Audience

In order to connect with her audience, Kristen knew she needed to first consider what her potential readers might already know and think about pharmaceutical companies and the ads they produced. She figured her classmates were probably a lot like her: interested in staying healthy and somewhat ignorant about how drug companies market their products and spend their money. She knew they would not want to read a dry report about advertising trends, so she began thinking about genres that might grab and hold their attention.

Who are the main audiences for the compositions you create as a student? Your classmates? Instructor? Anyone with an Internet connection? How do you negotiate and appeal to your audiences? #Understand #Apply

Using Rhetorical Appeals

Kristen knew that she would need to use ethos, pathos, and logos to her advantage in order to persuade her audience. She could establish her ethos as an author by taking her subject seriously and by drawing upon authoritative sources. She could appeal to her readers' pathos by including sad stories of consumers who suffered or even died as the result of the aggressive marketing of a drug. And while she didn't want to bog down her audience with excessive detail, she did want to provide major facts about how drug companies advertise—and the figures related to the money they make as a result. This information, presented in an order that made sense and accompanied by an Author's Statement explaining her choices, would appeal to her readers' sense of logos.

Choosing a Genre(s)

Taking into account her purpose, audience, and the ways she planned to persuade her audience, Kristen decided to create a series of compositions:

A collage/sculpture   Kristen created a giant capsule and covered it with a collage of prescription drug ads pulled from *Health* magazine and *Good Housekeeping*. She thought this creative and visual genre would get her classmates' attention and give them a sense of the hefty volume of direct-to-consumer ads created by drug companies. Kristen hoped that once readers saw in a visually graphic way exactly how many direct-to-consumer ads by drug companies appeared in two mainstream magazines, they would be persuaded that there was a problem. Kristen chose drug ads for her collage that appeal to the emotions (pathos) of her readers through scary stories of untreated illness; the ads also feature statistics, which appeal to readers'

ARTIFACT ▶
Kristen LaCroix
Pill capsule collage/
sculpture. *This and
all images on pages
106–111 courtesy of
Kristen LaCroix.*

sense of logic (logos) and draw on the authority (ethos) of doctors. She also used the capsule in a creative and functional way—as a container for her other genre pieces, described below.

A biographical profile   Kristen wrote a profile of her grandfather, Charles, who worked in the pharmaceutical industry. She used this genre as a way to convey facts and information about the drug industry. She thought that this information, coming through her grandfather's perspective, would be more interesting to her audience than if she presented it in a different genre, such as a report. She hoped that because her grandfather worked in the pharmaceutical industry, his observations about how it had changed over time would help persuade readers to question some industry practices. Kristen used her profile of her grandfather—which is based on her own primary research and his recollections—to appeal to readers' sense of logic (logos) and draw on her grandfather's authority (ethos) as a professional in the field.

LaCroix 7

Charles

He appeared weathered with thousands of memories and emotions; consequently, he sat serenely in his chair inhaling the calm air around him. This skillful man, Charles Fortin, had cared for and supported three beautiful daughters and an amazing wife. Charles presented himself with pride due mainly to his great success during his younger years. However, after retiring from a lifetime spent traveling while working for growing companies, he had suffered greatly through many medical tribulations. His outfit this day, a gray sweat suit, illustrated his need for comfortable settings and less movement. His bulbous glasses encompassed his face, demanding attention. A man of eighty-five years, his movements were gradual and his responses defined tranquility.

Gently, Charles began, "After finishing college, I paid a visit to my student advisor in hopes that I would be able to find a suitable career to support my wife and three-month-old daughter." His statement, coupled with perfect presentation, depicted Charles as the man who worked relentlessly to accomplish his goals. His advisor organized an interview with Lederle Laboratories where Charles was first introduced to the pros and cons of the drug industry. Slightly tipping back his frail head, Charles explained, "I worked for Lederle for fifteen years, promoting their products to doctors and pharmacies around the globe before I switched companies and gained the title of Sales Manager of Pharmaceuticals for all countries except the U.S." Charles paused shortly to collect his thoughts, illustrating his irrefutable abilities as a well-spoken gentleman.

Charles's pale complexion began to glow as he described the fulfillment he gained during his career. His grin spread across his face as he explained that through his profession he was able to help people because he assisted in the distribution of life-saving products to individuals all over the world. Charles's smile defended his movements as he slowly leaned back in the black chair, reminiscing about his past. Inhaling deeply, he continued, "Back in those days, prescriptions were so successful in healing people, they were only used when they were needed."

His face bloomed with frustration as he considered the different advertising campaigns utilized throughout the pharmaceutical industry today. Pausing for a short break, Charles went into the kitchen. He came back with several pills of different colors and sizes, explaining, "Each of these medications I take for many reasons, whether for my heart, arthritis, or my cold, each of these came from my doctor and are the only things stopping the pain that I would be forced to deal with on an everyday basis." His assorted prescriptions all seemed necessary. Charles inhaled deeply while looking down at his medications, revealing the different purposes each pill served. None of the pills, he divulged, were medications he'd asked for after seeing them in advertisements; they'd all been prescribed by his physician. "I wouldn't know what I wanted if I needed medication, that is a decision best left in the hands of a trained professional," he explained.

▲ BIOGRAPHICAL PROFILE
Kristen LaCroix
The first page of her biographical profile of her grandfather, Charles.

▲ PHOTO
Kristen LaCroix's grandmother and grandfather.

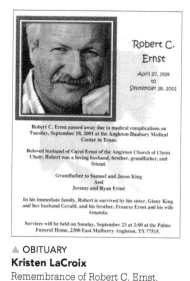

▲ OBITUARY
Kristen LaCroix
Remembrance of Robert C. Ernst.

An obituary   Kristen also created an obituary for a man named Robert C. Ernst, who died from a prescription drug–induced heart attack. She drew on an article that she'd read about Ernst's death, and also listed it in her Works Cited list. Kristen created the obit to help bring home to her audience the life-and-death seriousness of the topic; here she was able to convey facts to inform her readers, and also appeal to her readers' pathos. She thought that once readers learned that prescription drugs themselves can be lethal, they would be persuaded to take the issue seriously. Kristen uses the genre of the obituary to appeal to readers' emotions (pathos) by building sympathy for the man who died and the family left behind.

An Artist's Statement and Introduction   To accompany each of her three compositions (her capsule, profile, and obituary), Kristen also wrote an Artist's Statement in which she explained her rhetorical choices. Kristen's primary audience for these Statements is her instructor, Liz, but she also knew some of her classmates would be interested in knowing more about the decisions she made as she worked on her project. Kristen used a serious tone to convey to Liz that she approached the entire project in a scholarly, serious way (ethos). She also talked methodically about the choices she made, to show that she had thought through her decisions and their consequences (logos). Kristen composed an Introduction that addressed her project as a whole; in it, she discussed how her genre compositions work together to form a unified argument about direct-to-consumer drug advertising—and also prepared her audience to experience her project in a coherent way.

Working with Modes & Media

Have you ever created a project that you wish you'd had more time to complete? What would you have done differently to make your point more effectively, and why? #Remember #Analyze #Evaluate

Kristen was comfortable working in written modes, but she also wanted to use visuals to stimulate her readers' imaginations and keep their attention. Her pill capsule collage/sculpture is the most visual composition she created and the only one that is three-dimensional; Kristen assumed her readers would be seeing it face-to-face (you are seeing it in print because the collage has been photographed and reprinted in this book). She wrote the biographical profile and it appears in print. She also wrote the obituary and included visuals; this piece also appears in print. However, if she'd had more time, she might have included these pieces on a blog or Web site. When considering her audience—her classmates and instructor—Kristen decided to create print pieces that could be passed around and read in class. Kristen composed her Artist's Statements as print documents; however, if she had decided to present her genre pieces digitally on a Web site or blog, she

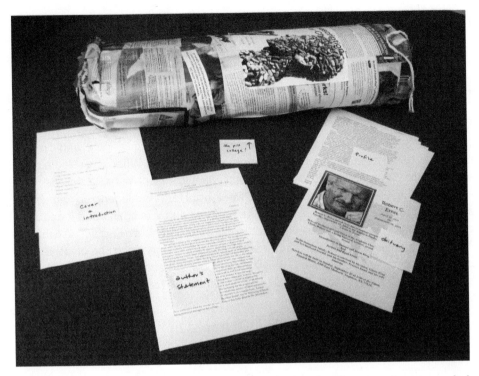

might have chosen to incorporate different media into her Statements, or recorded them as audio or video essays, for example.

Working with Style

Kristen observed the conventions of the genres she chose: She also chose to compose in a style that would be very accessible to her readers. She did not want to bore her readers with technical language, or alienate readers she hoped to persuade. She anticipated that many of her readers might not see direct-to-consumer advertising by pharmaceutical companies as a serious enough problem for them to spend time and energy worrying about. Kristen knew that she had to provide enough details to convince readers to take her argument seriously, but not so many that readers would feel overwhelmed.

Working with Design

To catch her readers' attention, Kristen included visuals (see the obituary) and color (see her collage). Further, while a collage is normally flat and two-dimensional,

Kristen decided to present hers in sculpture form. She also hoped that by composing her collage out of prescription drug ads, she'd spark her audience's curiosity so that they'd want to know more about her project and main point.

Drawing from Sources

Kristen used a variety of sources for her project, including interviews with her grandfather, the advertisements she found in *Good Housekeeping* and *Health* magazine, and several articles from peer-reviewed journals. When she selected her sources, she thought about how her choices would reflect upon her ethos. She wanted to come across as authoritative, thoughtful, and intelligent, so she chose sources that struck her as authoritative, thoughtful, and intelligent. She found articles in journals she knew were respected, such as *The New England Journal of Medicine*. She wrote an Artist's Statement for each genre piece she created, and in those Statements she spoke directly about how the sources she used affected her thinking about her subject. She also provided a Works Cited list with each Statement.

Guided Reading: Collage/Sculpture ▼

Kristen LaCroix (Student)

Prescription for Change:
The Impact of Direct-to-Consumer
Drug Advertising

Following is a photo of Kristen's collage capsule. The annotations on page 110 show how she addressed her rhetorical situation and connected with her audience through the genre she chose.

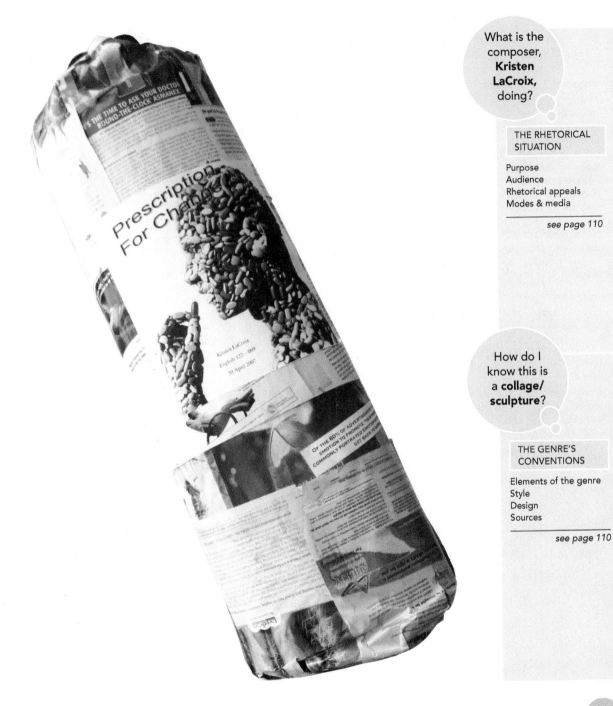

What is the composer, **Kristen LaCroix,** doing?

THE RHETORICAL SITUATION

Purpose
Audience
Rhetorical appeals
Modes & media

see page 110

How do I know this is a **collage/ sculpture**?

THE GENRE'S CONVENTIONS

Elements of the genre
Style
Design
Sources

see page 110

Kristen LaCroix, *Prescription for Change*

LaCroix, *Collage/Sculpture*, *Continued*

THE RHETORICAL SITUATION

Purpose

Kristen's main purpose—for her project as a whole—is **to persuade** her audience that direct-to-consumer ads are potentially dangerous; she must also first inform her audience about the pervasiveness of these ads, which she does by creating this capsule.

Audience

Kristen's instructor and classmates are her primary readers.

Rhetorical appeals

Kristen appeals to **pathos** by presenting viewers with an imaginative object, and to **logos** and **ethos** by providing her sources as part of that sculpture.

Modes & media

Mode = visual
Medium = face-to-face

THE GENRE'S CONVENTIONS

Elements of the genre

As a piece of sculpture, it is **three-dimensional,** and in this case, handmade out of everyday materials.

As a collage, it features **layered texts and images,** which convey a main theme. Color directs attention to different content.

A DIY feel invites viewers to interact with and explore the object.

Style

Kristen conveys a **playful tone, but also makes an argument** with this piece. The numerous ads from two mainstream magazines reinforce her argument that they are pervasive and potentially dangerous. Her title, "Prescription for Change," and the image of the pill-covered face on the cover sheet further telegraph her argument.

Design

While most collages are two-dimensional, Kristen's piece is a **3-D sculpture** made from plastic bottles and **covered with a collage.** The two halves fit together in the middle and open up, capsule-like, to reveal not medicine, but her individual genre pieces.

Sources

Kristen draws on ads from *Good Housekeeping* and *Health* magazine.

Kristen submitted her project with an Author's/Artist's Statement for each genre piece in which she explains and supports the rhetorical choices she made as she created her project. On page 111 is her Statement for the capsule collage/sculpture part of her project. Sometimes an instructor will specify that students write one Author's/Artist's Statement that encompasses an entire project instead of individual Statements for each piece. For this particular class, Liz asked students to provide individual Statements for each genre piece, as well as an Introduction to provide a kind of project-wide Statement.

Guided Reading: Artist's Statement

Kristen LaCroix (Student)

Artist's Statement

Artist's Statement:

How and Why I Created My Collage/Sculpture

It is necessary for all individuals to realize the amount of drug advertisements in all forms of media, to recognize the problem with our current drug industry. I created a collage to allow people to see the immense amount of marketing found merely throughout common magazines. Using only two magazines, I created a collage that couldn't even hold all the full-page advertisements that I found. Furthermore, oddly enough, the two magazines that included such an intense amount of advertising were *Health* and *Good Housekeeping*. The drug advertisements throughout these magazines included anything from sleeping pills to medication to ease the aftereffects of chemotherapy.

The collage displays a few examples of the marketing campaigns for prescription drugs and is in turn the best genre to present the obvious problem. The collage represents a message to simply acknowledge the ways companies advertise in an attempt to gain consumers' trust while marketing a product. A massive amount of pharmaceutical companies' income is turned around to be used for advertising. One CBS News article I found listed the top twenty drugs advertised in 2000. The drug with the largest advertising campaign, Vioxx, had approximately $161 million spent on advertising that year (Lee). Soon thereafter, in 2004, the drug Vioxx was pulled off the market after causing the death of many patients using it. Many prescriptions that are on the collage, such as Flonase and Celebrex, were listed in this article as well. The company that produced the nasal spray Flonase spent $78 million advertising their product in 2000 (Lee). There have been no adverse implications for this drug thus far; nevertheless, similar to several other drugs that are heavily advertised, there are other products available for consumers that are not as pricey and work as well if not even better.

Drug companies create their advertisements to be directed at specific target audiences in an effort to gain the most profit during their campaigns; however, this genre piece is not intended for any specific audience and instead is meant to heighten the awareness of all individuals because we will all at some point be victims of advertising schemes. This genre piece functions as both the packaging for the project and the introduction to the project. It highlights the overwhelming number of advertisements for prescription medications the average person is exposed to on a regular basis. Another way I incorporated information throughout the entire project was by displaying different facts scattered around my collage as well. I believe this helps describe the information being portrayed throughout the collage.

Continues next page

What is the composer, Kristen LaCroix, doing?

THE RHETORICAL SITUATION

Purpose
Audience
Rhetorical appeals
Modes & media

see page 112

How do I know this is an Artist's Statement?

THE GENRE'S CONVENTIONS

Elements of the genre
Style
Design
Sources

see page 113

LaCroix, *Artist's Statement,* Continued

LaCroix 5

Purpose

In her Statement, Kristen **describes the rhetorical choices** she made while creating the collage/sculpture piece of her project. She also **discusses the sources** she drew on.

Audience

Kristen's audience for her collage and Statement is the same as that for the rest of her project: her instructor and classmates.

Rhetorical appeals

Kristen clearly articulates her intentions and shows her credibility (**ethos**) by noting and documenting her sources. She supports her argument logically (**logos**) by drawing on research and providing her sources in her Statement. She informs readers about drug ads, and supports her claims with specific ads.

Modes & media

**Mode = written
Medium = print**

The next step to rising above the pharmaceutical companies' control is to recognize the trend with drugs that are being advertised as well as their current usage. The drug industry defends their promotional advertising, suggesting that it "helps educate consumers of potential conditions and encourages them to see their doctor for diagnosis and treatment" ("Direct-to-Consumer"). However, critics argue that this advertising is primarily emotional and commonly understates the side effects, causing misleading information to be fed to consumers. According to SourceWatch, a report conducted by the U.S. Government Accountability Office in November 2006 explained:

> "Studies we reviewed found that increases in [direct-to-consumer] advertising have contributed to overall increases in spending on both the advertised drug itself and on other drugs that treat the same condition . . . one study of 64 drugs found a median increase in sales of $2.20 for every $1 spent on [direct-to-consumer] advertising" ("Direct-to-Consumer").

Moreover, it was also found that 86% of consumers who had seen promotional advertisements for prescription drugs requested and ultimately received a prescription for the drug they wanted (Graham).

Although this genre piece doesn't directly convey information gathered from the advertisements themselves, different sources pointed out the common characteristics throughout each advertisement. Almost all of the advertisements use the same techniques to persuade the consumer to relate health, well-being, and happiness with the use of the prescription medication. In one analysis, it was found that 67% of advertisements collected used emotional appeals to gain the reader's attention. Of the 60% of advertisements that were using emotion to promote their product, the most commonly portrayed emotion was the aspiration to get back to normal (Woloshin). This is evident in advertisements on the collage in which individuals with allergies run through fields with flowers because they're "Claritin clear" and elderly arthritis sufferers can convey their happiness hugging a child because of Celebrex. Overall, this genre shows the common characteristics of drug advertisements presenting the ways they induce a reader to believe that the answer to their problem lies within being prescribed the medication.

LaCroix, *Artist's Statement,* Continued

LaCroix 6

Works Cited

"Direct-to-Consumer Advertising." *SourceWatch.org.* SourceWatch, 7 Mar. 2007. Web.
19 Apr. 2007. <http://www.sourcewatch.org/
index.php?title=Direct-to-consumer_advertising>.

Graham, John R. "Direct-to-Consumer Pharmaceutical Advertising: What Does
the Literature (Not) Say?" *Health Policy Prescriptions* 3.4 (2005): n. pag.
27 Apr. 2007. <http://www.pacificresearch.org/pub/hpp/2005/hpp_11-5.html>.

Lee, Kent. "Drug Advertising Skyrockets." *CBS News.* CBS News, n.d. Web.
25 Apr. 2007. <http://www.cbsnews.com/2100-204_162-329293.html>.

Woloshin, Steven, Lisa M. Schwartz, and H. Gilbert Welch. "The Value of Benefit Data
in Direct-to-Consumer Drug Ads." *Health Affairs.* Project HOPE, 28 Apr. 2004.
Web. 25 Apr. 2007. <http://content.healthaffairs.org/content/suppl/2004/04/28/
hlthaff.w4.234v1.DC1>.

THE GENRE'S CONVENTIONS

Elements of the genre

Composers use Statements to **explain how and why they created a work.** Kristen explains why she created her collage: to give viewers a sense of the quantity of drug ads in mainstream magazines.

Style

A Statement can be written in different styles: Kristen chose an **academic style and tone.** She makes a case for how she reached her audience through appeals and discusses how she used sources.

Design

Kristen designed this document using **MLA format.**

Sources

Kristen draws on research of a variety of sources. She explains and analyzes her decisions in this Statement. She also documents her sources in a Works Cited list.

Questions: Analyzing Kristen LaCroix's project

1. Purpose. Kristen's overall purpose is to persuade her audience that direct-to-consumer drug ads are dangerous. How persuasive are her individual genre compositions (capsule, profile, obituary, and Artist's Statement)? Explain.

2. Audience. Kristen, who was writing for her instructor and classmates, made some assumptions during her composing process about how to reach them. What are some of her assumptions? And how accurately do you think she assessed her audience?

3. Audience. As a student, do you feel you are included in the audience for these pieces? Why or why not?

4. Rhetorical appeals. How effectively does Kristen work with the appeals of logos, pathos, and ethos? Does she seem to favor one over the others? Explain.

5. Modes & media. Kristen created her biographical profile and obituary in print form; do you think they would be more effective in digital form? Why or why not? How might her pill capsule collage/ sculpture be conveyed digitally? How might she make her compositions more interactive?

6. Elements of the genre. How does Kristen use the conventions of each genre to help her make her point? For example, how does the image of the deceased man make the obituary more powerful? How does the overlapping of images in the collage help to make her point?

7. Style. Kristen wanted to write the biographical profile in a tone that would appeal to her classmates. Did the tone she used appeal to you? Why or why not? And how effective is her use of detail in the obituary? Explain.

8. Design. How does the shape of the collage contribute to its appeal and persuasiveness? Look again at the obituary and think of some related genres. For example, at some memorial services, small brochure-type documents that include memories about the deceased are distributed. How might Kristen's obituary message have changed (or not) if she had chosen a different genre?

9. Sources. After reviewing Kristen's Artist's Statement for her collage/sculpture, are you surprised to see how her sources informed her work? Why or why not?

CHECKLIST: Choosing a Genre Do you need to decide on a genre to compose in? Ask yourself the following questions.

WHAT'S YOUR RHETORICAL SITUATION?

☐ **Purpose.** Is my purpose to tell a story, inform, or persuade? Do I have several purposes, and if so, which is my primary purpose?

☐ **Audience.** How would I describe my primary audience? Whose attention do I want most? Who are the people I want to persuade? Do I have another, secondary audience? How will I entice this audience?

☐ **Rhetorical appeals.** How will I establish my credibility (ethos)? Will appealing to my audience's emotions help me persuade them (pathos)? How might logic (logos) help me convince others?

☐ **Modes & media.** Do I want to work with written words? Will I present my ideas in person, orally? Will I use visuals? How about audio? Does my idea lend itself to video? Do I want my piece to be available digitally or in print? Will I use some combination of these modes and media?

WHAT GENRE CONVENTIONS MATTER?

☐ **Elements of the genre.** How will I structure my composition? What is the best way to combine elements to convey my purpose—and make my case to my audience?

☐ **Style.** Whatever form my composition takes (visual, verbal, etc.), what is the best tone to use to reach my audience? What voice will I use? How present will I be in my composition? What kind of language will I use? What level of detail will I need to convey my purpose?

☐ **Design.** How do I want my composition to look? How will the layout help me achieve my purpose?

☐ **Sources.** What sources will I draw on for my composition? Do I need to conduct interviews? Do I need to research online or in the library? How will I attribute my sources?

PART 3
HOW CAN I CREATE AND EVALUATE MULTIMODAL PROJECTS?

Read This First! GT

So far in this book you have read about the importance of rhetoric, process, and multimodality, and you have developed a sense of what's effective and what isn't. Now, you will explore more precise criteria for evaluating multimodal projects. The goal of learning about evaluation is not to get better grades in English 1101 and English 1102 but to help you develop a lifelong ability to create multimodal artifacts and to accurately assess your own and others' communication. If learning about evaluation helps you improve your course grades, that is an added bonus.

How are creation and evaluation linked? When you create an artifact, it's for a purpose and audience, whether personal, academic, or professional. Knowing evaluation criteria will help you make adjustments to what you're doing as you go along—rather than waiting until the end and expecting someone else to judge your processes and artifacts. As you become a more capable communicator, you should be able to evaluate your own communication.

Evaluation is more challenging in a class because you need to consider what, beyond the artifact itself, comes into play—for example, whether the artifact was created individually or collaboratively, whether you are taking risks in trying a new approach, or whether a great concept didn't work because of a technical malfunction. In evaluating artifacts created in a class, you also need to consider how process should be considered as part of the evaluation of an artifact. For example, is a project (whether in a class or in the workplace) a success if the artifact is excellent but the collaboration was so dysfunctional that, in the end, the team refuses to work together again?

In addition to considering process when you evaluate an artifact, you need to consider the ways in which cultural context can influence evaluation. For example, in exploring concepts of evaluation, think about some of the many artifacts that have evolved from Jane Austin's 1813 novel *Pride and Prejudice*. The book is set in England in an important historical period, shortly after the American and French Revolutions and during the Napoleonic Wars. Take a few minutes to look up Columbia College's Web page "Historical Context for *Pride and Prejudice* by Jane Austen." You will learn that some things written about the book are historical, such as the examinations of war, social class, economics, gender roles, and culture. If you search for <*Pride and Prejudice*> on Google Scholar, you will find thousands of academic articles about the novel and the period. Take a few minutes to do an Internet search for these secondary materials. In addition, you'll also find some of the variations of the novel itself listed in the following textbox. Consider that evaluating a work (whether a novel or a class assignment) requires interpreting and understanding an original work and its variations in a cultural context and assessing its cultural authenticity.

Variations of *Pride and Prejudice*

▶ *Original novel: Pride and Prejudice* is available online in its entirety and available in audio editions as well.

▶ *Movie versions:* Many movies and television series have been created, including versions in 1938, 1940, 1952, 1957, 1958, 1961, 1967, 1980, 1995, 2004, and 2005.

▶ *Ads:* Many types of products depict quotations or visuals, including coffee mugs, posters, beer, condoms, and laser treatments, among others.

▶ *Comic books and graphic novels:* A number of artists and authors have tried to transform *Pride and Prejudice* into this highly visual genre.

▶ *Visuals:* Visuals include numerous line graphs, bar graphs, area graphs, scatter plots, charts, tables, diagrams, flowcharts, pie diagrams, and data mining visuals related to various aspects of the novel (many available through Google images).

▶ *Games:* Board games let you stroll through the Pemberley gardens or attend a ball. Digital select-your-own-adventure games let you define your own paths to happiness and choose your own endings. A *Pride and Prejudice* trivia game pits your knowledge against questions on 300+ trivia cards. Card games require skill in developing character and cunning. Digital games let you earn points toward wedding a spouse.

▶ *Adaptations and sequels of the novel:* Seth Grahame-Smith's parody, *Pride and Prejudice and Zombies* (2009), combines approximately 80 percent from Austen's original text with 20 percent of his own additions. A parody prequel to Grahame-Smith's novel is Steve Hockensmith's *Pride and Prejudice and Zombies: Dawn of the Dreadfuls* (2010), which has received a lot of attention. *Longbourn* (2013) by Jo Baker tells the story from the servants' perspectives. P. D. James's *Death Comes to Pemberley* (2011) is a murder mystery set at Pemberley. The *Lizzie Bennet Diaries* is a multiplatform video blog that won a 2013 Emmy award. *First Impressions* is a Broadway version, first staged in 1959. *Bride and Prejudice* (2004) is a Bollywood version.

▶ *Graphic art:* Examples include book covers, cartoons, postcards, movie posters, and plot summaries.

The reviewers of various versions of *Pride and Prejudice* are often rigorous, sometimes even harsh, in their evaluation of these adaptations. For example, one reviewer deems the Marvel comic version of *Pride and Prejudice* unacceptable, claiming that the novel is very difficult to bring into another medium without sacrificing some critical aspect of plot or character. In their criticism, reviewers often draw on the same criteria you'll be asked to use in self-assessment of your own work, in assessment of the work of your peers, and in the assessment of the work done by people outside the class.

You probably already have experience assessing written artifacts, but you can evaluate other modes as well. In a recent popular press article about book covers for *Pride and Prejudice*, Margaret C. Sullivan discusses the appeal of various covers

Visual Note Taking

We can make meaning through images. As part of your evaluation process, create sketches—visual notes—that capture the main points of what you're trying convey in a particular artifact you've already created. Then ask your reviewers (your classmates) to engage in visual note taking about your artifact, creating notes (what blogger Austin Kleon called "cartoon journalism") to improve their understanding and increase their memory. To get started with visual note taking, check out Claudine Delfin's YouTube video, "Sketcho Frenzy: The Basics of Visual Note-taking" or Craighton Berman's three-part series, "Sketchnotes 101: Visual Thinking." How can visual note taking be considered a kind of evaluation? How might checking comprehension *visually* rather than *verbally* change audience reactions? What are some benefits of using visual note taking to capture the main point of an artifact?

used over several decades. These covers exhibit period-specific and audience-specific features, some of which definitely don't work with a contemporary audience. To see the many covers she discusses, search the Internet for <Jane Austen, Reinvented> and select the 2014 article by Margaret C. Sullivan.

In Sullivan's discussion, she uses many of the concepts you'll read about and use later in this part of the book—emphasis, contrast, organization, alignment, and proximity—critical terms and concepts about design. For instance, Sullivan's examples show us that on some covers, the **emphasis** is on the author, Jane Austen; on other covers, the emphasis is on the title, *Pride and Prejudice*. Emphasis is created by font type, style, size, and placement. The covers show remarkable differences in the ways **contrast** is used; some are nearly monochromatic, others are primarily pastels or dark, saturated colors, and still others display dramatic figure-ground contrast. The sequence or **organization** of the information on the covers is different; sometimes the title and author are at the top, sometimes in the middle, and sometimes at the bottom. On other covers, the title and author are separated. On one cover from the mid-20th century, Sullivan comments on the **alignment** of a series of contrasting woodblock engravings of the book's two main characters. Sullivan notes that the covers are markedly different in the **proximity** of the two main characters—touching each other or not, facing each other or not.

The bolded terminology just discussed will help you use the Writing and Communication Program rubric in Chapter 7. Sometimes your professor may distribute the rubric or a modified version of the rubric intended for a particular assignment. Let's look at ways in which the terms above (emphasis, contrast, organization, alignment, and proximity) might be related to the rubric categories. So, for example, decisions about what to *emphasize* on a book cover are influenced by the intended audience, which is part of **rhetorical awareness**. Similarly, a cover designer's **stance** about the relative importance of the author, title, or publisher influences the *organization* of the key textual elements on the cover. A designer might choose to use visual *contrast* to subtly forecast the **development of ideas** in the novel and, perhaps, hint at their **organization**. A designer will be careful to respect widely held **conventions** in cover design, for example, reflecting emotional closeness between characters by placing them in close *proximity*. Finally, when **designing for the medium**, a designer must consider the ways affordances (such as margins, gutters, page dimensions, and the book's overall trim size) interact with design principles such as *alignment*. These examples are just that—examples; you have many possible ways to relate these terms to the categories in the rubric. Using the rubric to critique and create artifacts is one effective way to help you actively engage in your English 1101 and English 1102 courses.

Metacognitive Questions to Leverage Your Knowledge: Assessment of Multimodal Projects

You can start to answer these direct and indirect metacognitive questions now, but you'll have much more detailed and credible responses when you finish reading all the chapters in Part 3.

» **REMEMBER:** Look ahead to the Writing and Communication rubric in Chapter 7. Recall your best college entrance essay and choose the rubric category in which that essay was most successful. Why? #Remember

» **UNDERSTAND:** Explain how and why the rubric's categories apply equally well to written, oral, and visual artifacts. #Understand

» **APPLY:** During English 1101 and English 1102, you need to become skillful in using the Writing and Communication Program rubric. Use the rubric to evaluate this poster, which shows a skull, a gas pump, a whiskey bottle, and a message against drunk driving. The poster was created in 1937 by the Pennsylvania WPA Federal Art Project. #Apply

» **ANALYZE:** List the elements in the poster and then examine the relationships

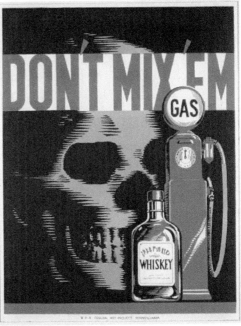

▲ POSTER
Don't Mix 'Em
This 1937 poster was part of the Work Projects Administration (WPA) Federal Art Project. *Library of Congress LC-USZC2-1106.*

among them. How does each element contribute to an argument against drunk driving? **#Analyze**

» **EVALUATE:** Search the Internet for <MADD posters> (Mothers Against Drunk Driving). Select a contemporary drunk driving poster and compare it to the 1937 poster. Contrast the effectiveness of the two posters for 21st-century college students. **#Evaluate**

» **CREATE:** Contemporary MADD posters tend to humanize the risk, especially the cost in lives—a different approach from the 1937 poster. Create a plan to modify either the 1937 poster or a MADD poster to create a more effective argument against drunk driving. **#Create**

5

ANALYZING MULTIMODAL PROJECTS

CONTENTS

Have you ever been walking through town, and one flyer among the hundreds of flyers you see every day stands out so much that you can't help but stop and read it? Have you ever been rushing to leave the house when your favorite song starts playing on the radio, and you have to listen to it before you can leave? Have you ever found a Web site link or online video so exciting or funny that you have to immediately share it with your friends? These multimodal texts are captivating—they capture your attention and encourage you to interact with them and share them. Chances are the multimodal texts that caught and held your attention are the ones that used the most effective design choices. These are the kinds of texts we want you to build. In this chapter you will learn how to analyze multimodal texts to discover how effective design choices are made for different texts in different situations.

Writer/designers have a wide variety of options for creating an effective text. What makes a text effective depends on a number of factors: What is the author's reason

FIGURE 5.1 ▶
An Effective Multimodal Flyer
This flyer on a school bulletin board caught Cheryl's attention. It was printed in color and in landscape orientation on 11" x 17" paper.

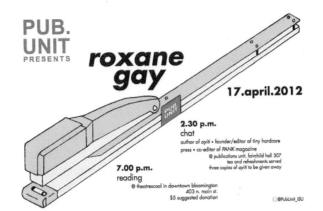

for creating the text? What audience is the author trying to reach? In what place, time, or situation is the text being created? Analyzing these factors will help you understand the projects of other writer/designers and will help you create your own multimodal texts (a task we'll take on in Chapter 6).

Analyzing Design Choices

Let's examine how an author's design choices support the rhetorical situation by using as an example the Web site for Washington State University. As we look more closely at the types of choices a designer makes, we focus on five key design concepts: **emphasis**, **contrast**, **organization**, **alignment**, and **proximity**. These terms aren't the only ones you could use to talk about choices—you may come up with some terms on your own or in collaboration with your colleagues—but to give you a start, we describe how these five design concepts are enacted through a variety of design choices. We call your attention to how these choices connect with the rhetorical situation described above, and we ask you to think about how such choices are or are not effective in this particular rhetorical situation.

Visit **bedfordstmartins.com/writerdesigner** to see an interactive version of our design choices analysis.

Emphasis

In speech or writing, emphasis means stressing a word or a group of words to give it more importance. In visual texts, it means the same thing; emphasis gives certain elements greater importance, significance, or stress than other elements in the text, which can guide your reading of the text as a whole.

The three photos shown in Figure 5.2 are given primary visual emphasis on the WSU home page from 2010. Simply put, they stand out. By emphasizing something bright, colorful, and positive (a smiling man, a picturesque wheat field, and a marching trombone from the WSU marching band), the author conveys the feeling of a happy and productive environment where people are filled with school spirit. Given that one of the purposes of the home page is to positively brand the university, this use of emphasis is an effective design choice.

Contrast

Contrast is the difference between elements, where the combination of those elements makes one element stand out from another. Contrast can be determined by comparing elements in a text. Color, size, placement, shape, and content can all be used to create contrast in a text. Contrast plays a large role in emphasis, in that the most contrasted element often appears to be the most emphasized.

◀ FIGURE 5.2
The Front Page of the Washington State University Web Site (October 2010)

Notice how the WSU home page takes advantage of white space—a design technique that subtly employs contrast by leaving more of the background of the page (which usually lacks any elements other than a color or graphic) empty, making everything else on the page "pop." Thus, the page is not too busy, and the audience can easily find what they're looking for, be it donors looking for ways to give to WSU, a student searching for a professor's email address, or the parents of a potential student looking to learn more about the school's reputation.

Organization

Organization is the way in which elements are arranged to form a coherent unit or functioning whole. You can talk about an organization of people, which puts people into a hierarchy depending on their job title and department, or about organizing your clothes, which might involve sorting by color and type of garment. You can also talk about organizing an essay, which involves arranging your ideas so as to make the strongest argument possible. Or you can talk about organizing the multimodal elements of a Web site to support the purpose of the text.

The WSU home page is organized into four rows of information (**see Fig. 5.3**). The first row is a crimson-colored rectangle that includes an index and a search bar. The second row includes the WSU logo, links to the Web sites for the various WSU campuses, and Quick Links. The third row, the one most emphasized, includes the three photos and the main topic links (About, Admission, Academics, Research,

FIGURE 5.3 ▶
**Organization of the
WSU Web Site**
This graphic repre-
sents the four blocks
of information on the
WSU Web site.

Services, and WSU Life). The final row includes a News link as well as links specific to particular audiences (future students, parents, alumni and friends, current students, faculty and staff). If we consider the purpose of this Web site as well as its audience, this organization appears to be effective in many ways.

Alignment

Alignment literally means how things line up. A composition that uses alignment to best effect controls how our eyes move across a text. Even if we're working with a text that is all words, every piece of it should be deliberately placed. A centered alignment—an easy and popular choice—causes our eyes to move around the space with less determination, as we move from the end of one line and search for the beginning of the next one. A justified alignment stretches the content so that it is evenly distributed across a row; thus the left and right margins remain consistent. This is a popular choice for newspapers because it can make a large amount of text appear neat and orderly. A strong left alignment gives us something to follow visually—even elements that contrast in size can demonstrate coherence through a single alignment. A strong right alignment creates a hard edge that connects disparate elements. Grouping things in a clear and interesting way can be useful.

Remember that we described the WSU home page as being organized into four rows. Notice how each row aligns with the other rows. The crimson-colored row at top runs from the left to the right margin, yet the linguistic content of this row is right aligned. The remaining three rows are justified and run from the left margin of the photo bar to the right margin of the photo bar. The only exception is the row of links center-aligned beneath the photos, yet these links appear cohesive because they are encased in the photo row itself (notice the white rectangle that encompasses both the pictures and this row of links). The justified alignment makes the page feel clean, crisp, and easy to use, which is important to an audience looking for easy-to-find information.

Proximity

Proximity means closeness in space. In a visual text, it refers to how close elements (or groupings of elements) are placed to each other and what relationships are built as a result of that spacing. The relationships created by the spacing between elements help readers understand the text, in part because readers might already be familiar with similar designs of other texts. Proximity can apply to any kind of element in a visual text, including words and images, or to elements of an audio text, such as repeating rhythms or the verses and chorus.

As described in the organization analysis, there are four major groups of written links in the WSU home page. An audience member might be looking for information specific to a campus or to an audience, so it makes sense that the author chose to place the items in each group close together; the words' close proximity to one another suggests a close relationship, whereas the groups themselves are placed farther apart. This design choice helps to make the page more usable.

Process

Visit your favorite Web site. Take note of the design choices that stand out to you, paying attention to the following:

▶ What elements does the design of the Web site emphasize? The logo? A certain picture? The navigation bar?

▶ Notice the organization of elements on the page. What comes first? What comes last? Why do you think the designer chose this order?

▶ How is contrast used on the page? Does the use of contrast help to emphasize certain elements? Does the use of contrast create a certain feeling? (Consider how certain colors can be used to encourage certain emotional responses.)

▶ What elements are aligned on the page? Does this alignment help you navigate the page? Does it cause your eye to travel in a certain direction on the page? Why might the designer have made this choice?

▶ How are elements positioned in relation to one another? Why do you think the designers of this page put certain elements in close proximity to one another while placing others farther apart?

Writing and Designing Rhetorically

We began this chapter by discussing the rhetorical situation and then moved on to the design choices. However, we can also work the other way around—starting with an analysis of the design choices so as to understand the rhetorical situation. Don't be surprised if analyzing a text's design (as we asked you to do in the Process! activity on page 37) causes you to go back and say more about the audience, purpose, context, and genre of the text. Examining design choices helps us learn more about the rhetorical situation. Doing a rhetorical analysis isn't always a linear or formal process, as the WSU case study shows—we could have written a lot more about the design choices or the rhetorical situation of the WSU home page.

Keep in mind that using rhetorical analysis to understand a text may result in a favorable opinion of the text but may also illuminate various problems—the rhetorical analysis may help explain why the text has that "wow" factor, or why it doesn't. For instance, consider if, instead of providing a few welcoming photos and easy-to-find links, the WSU home page were designed like an essay in a word-processing document. This primarily linguistic mode of design would be appropriate for an essay but would not be appropriate for the audience, purpose, context, or genre expectations of a Web site in 2014; thus, a Web page with this design would most likely be seen as a failure.

write/design assignment

Rhetorical Analysis of Multimodal Texts

Find three examples of multimodal texts that come from similar genres (e.g., university Web sites, talking cat videos, newspaper ads). If you already know what genre you're expected to produce for a class, project, or client, choose three texts from that genre. Perform a rhetorical analysis of the texts, whereby you describe each text's author, purpose, audience, genre, and context, and explain how different design choices are used to meet the demands of the rhetorical situation. When describing design choices, begin with the terms from this chapter: emphasis, contrast, organization, alignment, and proximity. However, you may realize other terms are necessary to fully describe the texts.

6 SELECTING AND PROPOSING PROJECTS

CONTENTS

One of the best ways to begin thinking about a multimodal project is to see *what* has already been said about a topic you are interested in (or have been assigned) as well as *how* other authors have designed their texts on that topic. For instance, you may want to create a text about how students use technology to enhance their learning experience. Before getting started, you'll need to know what's already been said about that topic—an exploratory process that's similar to what you'd do when writing a research paper. Researching your topic is the *what* part of the equation (in other words, figuring out *what* you want to say). We'll talk more about doing research to figure out the *what* of your multimodal project in Chapter 20.

While you're researching your topic, you'll also need to explore *how* other authors are presenting that topic. What combinations of communicative modes do you see in other authors' texts about your topic? What design choices are they making? What genres are they using? Unless your teacher or client has assigned you a specific genre to work within, you'll want to research multiple genres in multiple media outlets—both academic (probably texts you'd find in your university library) and popular (texts you'd find on Web sites such as YouTube or in bookstores, trade magazines like *Good Housekeeping* or *Wired*, personal blogs, brochures in doctors' office waiting rooms, ads on the sides of buses, etc.). You'll see a different combination of modes and different design choices in each of these texts, depending on the rhetorical goals of the publisher and the author's rhetorical situation.

When examining the *how* of your topic, you'll need to ask yourself:

» How do other authors present your topic?

» Which of their texts seems to address its rhetorical situation most effectively?

In this chapter, we'll talk about how you can answer these questions by performing a rhetorical analysis on a sample set of texts about your topic (such as the front and

FIGURE 6.1 ▶
***Seasonal and Savory*, A Food Blog by Angela Buchanan**
This genre of food writing features step-by-step pictures and instructions.

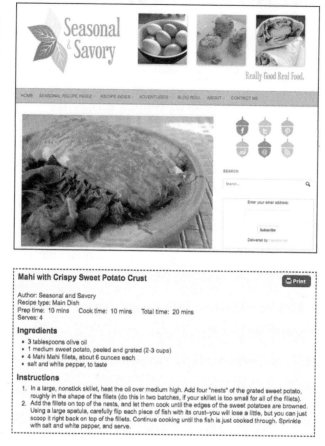

back of a recipe card contrasted in Figures 6.1 and 6.2), and then how you can use that information to decide which kind of text *you* want to compose given your own rhetorical situation.

Exploring the *What* and the *How*

Although we've referred to the *what* (the content of your text) and the *how* (the form your text takes) as separate things, it isn't actually possible to separate what you want to say from how you will say it. Your topic and your design are closely connected, which is why this book is called *Writer/Designer*. You can't be just a writer or just a designer; you're always both.

For instance, even if you're just posting an update to Twitter, you have to consider what you will say, how you will say it given who will see it, the context (the time of day, the event about which you're posting, etc.), and the ways that Twitter allows you to post supplementary information such as links or photos. Additionally, the design of Twitter's user interface restricts the choices you can make as you craft your tweet; for example, you can't post anything longer than 140 characters.

> **Cheryl E. Ball** @s2ceball　　　　　　　　　now
> What you say cannot be divorced from how you say it. It's the same with all multimodal texts. #WriterDesigner
> Expand

Let's look at an example to see more clearly how content and form are dependent on one another and on the rhetorical situation. Here are two texts that discuss the topic of video games and learning:

1. A scholarly book called *What Video Games Have to Teach Us about Learning and Literacy* by James Paul Gee, in which the author, drawing on lots of other scholarly research, argues that video games help promote literacy because they offer complicated, interactive narratives that game players have to learn to navigate

2. A prezi (an interactive, online, multimedia presentation application) called "Playing to Learn?" by Maria Andersen, in which she argues that using games in the classroom is an effective teaching tool because it engages students' brains in different ways and keeps them interested in learning tough topics (like math, which she teaches)

So, the *what* is that these two scholar-teachers agree that games are good pedagogical tools. And they give lots of scholarly and popular examples as to why games are good for us. In making our own project, we could cite either of these texts to support our own argument about games. Citing sources is something you probably have some experience with already (plus we'll talk more about it in the next chapter), so for now we want to focus on *how* these authors make their arguments.

On the one hand, Gee has written a scholarly book, although it's written in a style that's easier to read than most scholarly books. But he still relies on the genre conventions of scholarly books (like prose, citations, and formal language) to connect with his audience. There are visual modes used in his book—a few tables—but the text consists mostly of words formatted in a way that we're used to seeing in scholarly (or even popular) books. That is to say, his book looks pretty much like every other book in that genre (see **Fig. 6.3**).

▼ FIGURE 6.3
A Page from James Paul Gee's What Video Games Have to Teach Us about Learning and Literacy
Looks like a book, eh?

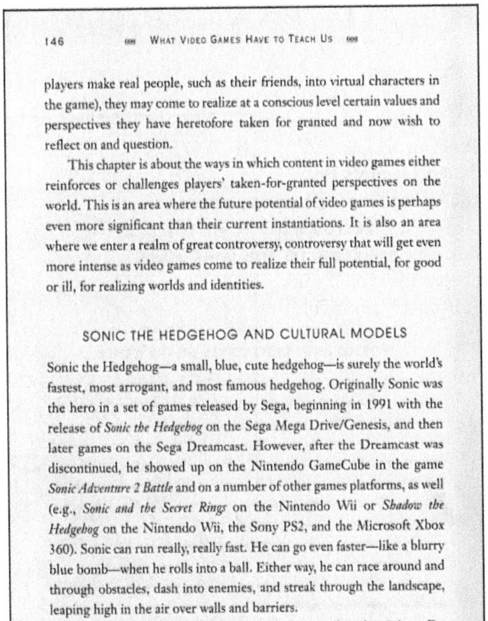

146　　　**WHAT VIDEO GAMES HAVE TO TEACH US**

players make real people, such as their friends, into virtual characters in the game), they may come to realize at a conscious level certain values and perspectives they have heretofore taken for granted and now wish to reflect on and question.

This chapter is about the ways in which content in video games either reinforces or challenges players' taken-for-granted perspectives on the world. This is an area where the future potential of video games is perhaps even more significant than their current instantiations. It is also an area where we enter a realm of great controversy, controversy that will get even more intense as video games come to realize their full potential, for good or ill, for realizing worlds and identities.

SONIC THE HEDGEHOG AND CULTURAL MODELS

Sonic the Hedgehog—a small, blue, cute hedgehog—is surely the world's fastest, most arrogant, and most famous hedgehog. Originally Sonic was the hero in a set of games released by Sega, beginning in 1991 with the release of *Sonic the Hedgehog* on the Sega Mega Drive/Genesis, and then later games on the Sega Dreamcast. However, after the Dreamcast was discontinued, he showed up on the Nintendo GameCube in the game *Sonic Adventure 2 Battle* and on a number of other games platforms, as well (e.g., *Sonic and the Secret Rings* on the Nintendo Wii or *Shadow the Hedgehog* on the Nintendo Wii, the Sony PS2, and the Microsoft Xbox 360). Sonic can run really, really fast. He can go even faster—like a blurry blue bomb—when he rolls into a ball. Either way, he can race around and through obstacles, dash into enemies, and streak through the landscape, leaping high in the air over walls and barriers.

The back story for *Sonic Adventure 2 Battle* is that the sinister Dr. Eggman, while searching the remnants of his grandfather's laboratory, uncovers a dark form of his arch-nemesis, Sonic, namely a black hedgehog named Shadow. Together the two conspire to unleash the Eclipse Cannon, a weapon of mass destruction. The government, unable to tell the blue Sonic from the dark Shadow (they look alike) arrests Sonic for

Andersen, on the other hand, has chosen to present the same topic using a much different design: a media-rich, interactive prezi on the Web site Prezi.com. She also includes citations and examples, just like Gee does, although hers are usually much more brief because of the design conventions afforded by the Prezi interface. (We'll talk more in Chapter 9 about the impact of technological choices on designing multimodal projects.) However, unlike Gee, Andersen makes her argument about how games promote learning by designing her text to *look like* a game (see **Fig. 6.4**), which adds visual, spatial, and gestural meaning to her linguistic text. Andersen doesn't have to present as much linear, written information as Gee does to get a similar point across because she has the visual, spatial, and gestural design of the text do some of that work better than the linguistic could do. Thus, *how* Gee and Andersen present their topics is as important as *what* they want readers to get from their texts.

Process

Given the rhetorical situations for Gee's and Andersen's texts, why do you think they chose to use the modes that they did? Do you think Andersen could have effectively made her point through a scholarly written article? Do you think Gee would have been more successful if he had used an interactive visual mode instead of the book?

Gee's and Andersen's works are different, despite their similar topics, because they are written for different audiences and purposes. Gee's purpose is to reach an audience of public readers who are interested in games and reading practices; he also wants to reach academics who study literacy and gaming. Andersen's purpose is to use the multimodal and interactive affordances of a prezi,

FIGURE 6.4 ▶
**"Playing to Learn?,"
Maria Andersen's Prezi
about Using Games to
Teach Effectively**
Looks like a game, eh?
Watch this prezi online at
bedfordstmartins.com
/writerdesigner.

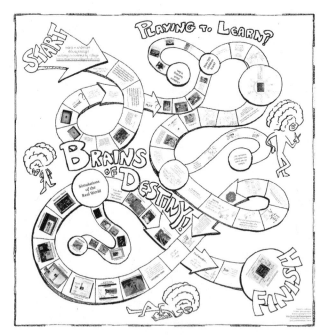

Researching Your Project Idea

To narrow your topic idea and help you think about ways to design your multimodal project, use the following steps:

1. Find and read eight to ten texts on your topic, across a range of media.

2. List the arguments, points, or key ideas those texts offer about your topic. This is the *what*. For instance, in the examples above, both Gee and Andersen chose to focus on how teaching games improves students' learning. That's a key idea within the topic of games.

3. Next, list the genres, modes, and multimodal design choices (think about WOVEN and the design choices discussed in Chapter 5—emphasis, contrast, organization, alignment, and proximity) that the texts use. This is the *how*.

4. Analyze how the *what* relates to the *how* (using rhetorical analysis—context, author, purpose, audience, and genre), and decide which texts seem the most successful given their rhetorical situations.

5. Identify which themes in those successful texts most inspire you to do further research. (If a key idea seems to be missing from the list you compiled in step 2, that might also be a good place to do more research.) Shorten your list of themes down to one or two ideas.

---

which helps her create a gamelike experience, to persuade teachers that games can engage students' brains by keeping them interested in learning tough topics. One text is meant for solitary, in-depth reading, while the other could be presented to a group of people (since Prezi is a presentation tool) in a shorter amount of time. One text is not better than the other, in this case, because they serve different rhetorical situations.

Genre Conventions

You now have several new pieces of information to help you start building your own multimodal project: a few ideas for a suitable topic or theme; a list of texts that you can potentially cite or that at least will inform the purpose of your project; and a list of multimodal texts that were successful in other rhetorical situations, which you could use as models when choosing your own project design.

One final thing we have to do before you start designing is to take a closer look at how authors know to choose particular kinds of texts or genres to work with in particular rhetorical situations (see **Fig. 6.5** for an example of matching genre to rhetorical approach). We talked a bit about genres and genre conventions in Chapter 4, but here we're going to go into more depth about analyzing the genres of multimodal texts and figuring out how genre conventions work. If you learn to analyze the conventions of multimodal genres, you can apply that analytical skill

FIGURE 6.5 ▶
Panel from *Understanding Rhetoric*, by Elizabeth Losh, Jonathan Alexander, Kevin Cannon, and Zander Cannon
This panel talks about comics while using the genre conventions of a comic.

to any kind of text you come across, and you will add more design choices to your rhetorical knowledge every time you compose a text for a new rhetorical situation.

In exploring your topic, you may have noticed that some of the texts used similar design choices in similar rhetorical situations. For example, if you analyzed breast cancer pamphlets, you probably found that almost all of them featured a pink ribbon and a script-like font. These are genre conventions that authors and readers use to make meaning within a rhetorical situation. It's important to analyze how these conventions are used within texts because genre conventions are a good starting place when designing a similar text for a similar rhetorical situation. They help us understand what audiences expect from particular kinds of texts in particular kinds of situations. For example, if you're making a breast cancer awareness brochure, do you need to use the pink ribbon in order to be taken seriously? And do you have good reasons to break with this genre convention?

Here's a different example: music. What are the conventions of songs that can be classified under the genres of rock, pop, jazz, classical, rap, disco, or country? Some classical music, with its soothing stringed instruments or mellow piano solos, might help relax or calm us, while disco's quick, pulsing beats and high-hat taps might energize us enough to dance. A site like Musicovery (http://musicovery.com/) color-codes musical genres and suggests certain genres depending on the listener's mood, which he or she can pick through an interactive mood tool (see **Fig. 6.6**). These tools—and our brains—rely on pattern recognition to classify musical genres. That pattern recognition is based on genre conventions. And while not every song within a particular genre uses the exact same conventions, being

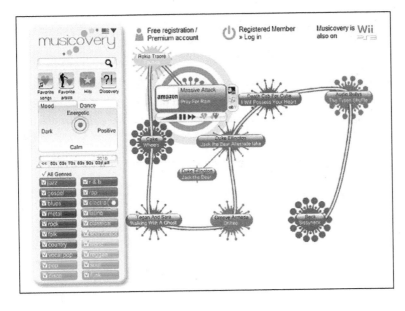

able to recognize the patterns can help us distinguish one song, and genre, from another.

What If the Genre Is Unclear?

When researching texts for your multimodal project, you may come across a text whose genre is unclear. If you don't know the genre of a text, remember that genres are created based on other genres and on social circumstances and rhetorical situations that we're familiar with. That is, if you don't know the genre, ask yourself what the text *reminds* you of. Then maybe ask a few of your friends and your teacher the same question. Collectively, you'll be able to identify a genre that most closely fits the kind you want to study further. Also, texts sometimes mash up multiple genres. For example, when social networking sites (like Twitter) were first created, they asked users to "microblog" in 140 characters or less, whereas blog posts are typically much longer than that. The term *microblog* shows that when status updates were new, they were compared most closely in genre to blogs. So if you encounter a text whose genre is new to you, see what other genres the text relates to and consider studying those as well.

Process

Pick a text, any text—it may be your favorite song, your office space, a restaurant, or your favorite movie. What mood does it put you in? What patterns does it have? How is it structured? Are the answers to these questions related? Consider other texts or artifacts in the same genre: Do they make you feel the same way? Do they have similar patterns or structures?

Case Study Looking at Genre Conventions

Here's how we might compare Andersen's gaming prezi with two other prezis about the same topic (see **Figs. 6.7 and 6.8**). We can use this exercise to figure out what genre conventions authors of prezis have come to use and have used successfully.

FIGURE 6.7 ▶
Visual Outline for Edmond Chang's "Gaming Writing: Teaching (with) Video Games"
Watch this prezi online at bedfordstmartins .com/writerdesigner.

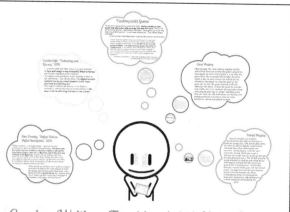

FIGURE 6.8 ▶
Visual Outline for William Maelia's "Using Web-Based Games to Support 21st Century Learning"
Watch this prezi online at bedfordstmartins .com/writerdesigner.

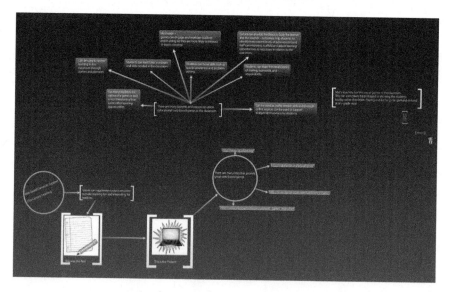

The Prezi software is based on our genre knowledge of other presentation tools (like Keynote and PowerPoint, which are in turn based on our knowledge of poster presentations). However, Prezi is also significantly different from other presentation software in that it allows readers to create zooming and animation features that are very difficult, if not impossible, to use in other presentation tools. For this reason, you will rarely run across a PowerPoint presentation that you're expected to interpret without any help from the author (e.g., notes posted online from a class lecture are still intended to go *with* the face-to-face lecture), whereas with Prezi you are more likely to run across presentations that stand on their own. Thus, that similarity across Prezi becomes one possible genre convention, as noted in the table on page 138 (under "Does the text stand alone?"). We could list many more "Prezi Genre Conventions" in the table, but we'll leave it at these, just to give you an idea of how you might come up with your own comparative list. For example, based on the number of readers who have "liked" each of the Prezis in the table, we might be able to judge the Prezis' relative success, although such an evaluation doesn't do justice to some of the successful qualities within the two Prezis that have zero likes so far. The more stand-alone the Prezi is, the more successful it seems to be.

Of course, if you are required to create a presentation for your multimodal project and you know that the rhetorical situation requires you to deliver it personally, perhaps your presentation will still be successful even if your Prezi doesn't stand alone. You just have to figure out *which* conventions are needed to make the text interesting and useful for your audience. For instance, the three Prezis analyzed here use the standard linear navigation path, which allows readers to click on the right arrow to navigate to the next node of information, as opposed to the readers skipping nodes or the authors placing information outside of the path for readers to discover on their own. The latter types of navigation would be more appropriate for readers to play with in a stand-alone piece than in a public presentation. The navigation path that your presentation uses is a design decision you have to make based on your rhetorical situation.

PREZI GENRE CONVENTIONS			
Prezis	Andersen's "Playing to Learn?"	Chang's "Gaming Writing: Teaching (with) Video Games"	Maelia's "Using Web-Based Games to Support 21st Century Learning"
URL (for reference)	http://prezi.com/rj_b-gw3u8xl/	http://prezi.com/ai6wnm0l_j1l/	http://prezi.com/yiknhf2wapi_/
Background color	White	White	Blue
Navigation	Left and right arrows	Left and right arrows	Left and right arrows
Use of words	Uses titles, quotes, and explanatory text	Uses titles, quotes, and explanatory text	Uses titles and explanatory text
Levels of zoom and rotation	Zooms in on key elements; rotation follows game board path	Zooms in on frame; no rotation	Mostly uses same level of zoom throughout (with a few variances); minimal rotation
Author	Bio and contact info in Prezi	Contact info in Prezi	No information in Prezi
Use of images	Images supplement the written text	Images convey an example	Very few images are used, and mostly for shock value
Path points	120	14	20
Does the text stand alone?	Yes	Yes	Yes
Use/purpose of navigational path	Path is designed around a background illustration that corresponds to the argument; great "bigger picture" view	Path revolves around central figure; "bigger picture" conveyed through thought bubbles	Path is based on mind-mapping concept, but not all nodes are related; some "bigger picture" purpose
Citations	Yes	Yes	No (but there is a resource list)
Number of reader likes	More than 1,900	0	0
Use of video/ animation	Yes (15)	0	0

In the previous Write/Design assignment (p. 133), we asked you to come up with a topic idea for your multimodal project. You also came up with a list of multimodal texts related to that topic that you thought were successful. In this assignment, you'll build on that work to learn how to analyze genres and use that knowledge in your own project.

1. Go back to the list of successful multimodal texts you made in the previous assignment and pick one that you think best fulfills the author's purposes for that rhetorical situation. Do some research to find two or three more texts in that genre (they do not have to be on the same topic, although they might be). If several genres seem particularly appealing and successful, research them all.

2. Analyze the examples in this genre or genres and make a list of similarities and differences. These might relate to design choices such as layout, navigation, and multimodal elements, as well as to what each of those choices accomplishes within the text. You may also list rhetorical choices such as audience, purpose, context, historical period, etc. Refer back to Part 2 for a sampling of rhetorical and design choices that you might use. Also, see the Case Study on pages 136–37 for an example of how to create this list.

3. What design elements are similar? Do they look similar or function in a similar way across most of the examples? If so, you have a genre convention. Make a short list of all the conventions for that particular genre, which you should keep as a handy checklist when designing your own multimodal project in that same genre. (You'll also use it later in this book.)

Conceptualizing Your Project

Now that you have a better idea about the expected genre conventions and sources for your multimodal project, you are ready to put the *what* and the *how* together. You've already done a lot of preparatory work, so you can begin designing something on screen or paper, so you can start to see how the pieces might fit together and get feedback from your instructor or client. Actually getting started can be a little intimidating, but we're going to give you two ways to begin conceptualizing your project: *representation* and *association*.

Representation

If you have writer/designer's block, try brainstorming some ways you could represent your topic idea using different modes. If you're creating a text about eating habits in different cultures, maybe your text could look like a plate with different kinds of food on it. Your goal is to find a way of representing your topic that adds meaning to your text. This is called a *guiding metaphor*. Maria Andersen created a guiding metaphor for her Prezi that we saw earlier in this chapter: she used an illustration of a game board to represent her argument that games promote learning. The guiding metaphor adds meaning to her argument by actually showing, through visual, spatial, and gestural modes, how games can promote learning.

Representations don't have to be visual. For instance, if you're working on an audio text, ask yourself whether your sound effects should exactly mirror the content of your narrative—should the cat meow like a typical cat in your piece? Or does the cat represent something else—a lion, a specter, a guardian angel—that might suggest a different sound effect?

Association

▼ FIGURE 6.9
Movie Poster by Elyse Canfield
Kristin's student, Elyse, made this movie poster after brainstorming the best ways to visually link to her film projects on a portfolio Web site.

If you're having trouble coming up with something that *represents* your idea, try brainstorming things that are *associated* with your idea instead. This strategy can be helpful if the representations you're coming up with seem too literal or too specific (for example, if you're writing about love and the only representation you can come up with is a heart). Authors use associations all the time in everyday texts; how often have you seen Mickey Mouse's ears used to mean the Disney Company, for example, or heard the term "9/11" used to refer to the terrorist attacks in the United States on September 11, 2001?

For instance, Elyse (a student of Kristin's) wanted to work on a Web-based portfolio that showcased her photography and videography skills. While she had little trouble composing the photo pages, she wanted to find a unique way to link to her short films. With Kristin, she brainstormed the various genres, such as trailers, through which filmmakers showcase their films. But Elyse didn't have time to make a trailer for each of her short films (given the rhetorical situation of the assignment). She realized that movie posters would work better, since in a single glance a reader associates a movie poster as a stand-in to advertise a full-length movie. Elyse searched the Web for movie posters and began to compose posters for her films following the genre conventions (see **Fig. 6.9** for one example). Each poster linked to the film in her portfolio.

A big part of designing is to experiment with ways of combining content and form. This means that there isn't one perfect way to begin and it's perfectly OK (and normal) for your first ideas to need adjustment. Experimentation is natural. Coming up with several ideas as you conceptualize your project is a good strategy, because sometimes your first idea might be too literal or clichéd, or

Process

Using pens, crayons, pencils, and paper—or a software program, if you prefer—brainstorm some ideas for your project's overall design; use one of the design suggestions listed above, if appropriate, or one of your own. Your designs don't need to be elaborate—in fact, they *shouldn't* be elaborate at this stage. They might just be flow charts or line drawings.

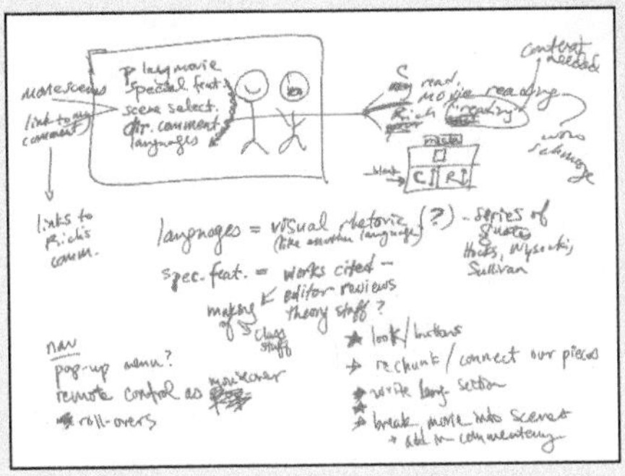

◀ FIGURE 6.10
Cheryl's Visual Design Brainstorming
This crude drawing that Cheryl made visualizes the basic design of a collaborative webtext that she worked on and that was later published in an online journal.

it just may not be what you want. Once you have a general idea of your overall design, you can also use trial and error to flesh out some of the details. While the trial-and-error process can often take a long time initially, it makes for good practice in analyzing multiple modes in relationship to one another. Plus, the more you practice putting modes together and analyzing how they affect readers, the more quickly you'll be able to design your next multimodal project.

When you have a design in mind, record it quickly—maybe on paper, or with a video camera or voice recorder. It's not about how well you can draw or act but about getting the idea down in visual and spatial (not linguistic) form. Colored pencils or crayons are useful here if color is a significant part of the visual design. And although some authors are more adept at creating these visualizations on their computers, we find that most authors are more comfortable with using pen and paper because it's less of an initial commitment and provides a quicker way to brainstorm.

Pitching Your Project

No single approach or kind of text will work in all situations for all audiences. Knowing how to perform rhetorical analyses and looking closely for genre conventions will help you figure out how to write or design any kind of text in any future writing situation, but you also need to look for guidance from others. By explaining your project idea to your teacher, boss, or client before you really get started, you can be better assured that you're on the right track as you create a text for a particular rhetorical situation.

FIGURE 6.11 ▶
Matt Wendling's Pitch
Visit bedfordstmartins
.com/writerdesigner
to watch Matt's
video pitch.

A **pitch** is a short presentation that explains how the *what* and the *how* of your idea might come together in the final project. It's a means of convincing audience members who have some stake in what you are proposing that you know what you're talking about and can take on the project at hand. (Pitches are sometimes called elevator speeches, drawing on the idea of a writer who is on an elevator with a publisher and has only four floors to convince the publisher to accept his or her book proposal.) Once an idea you've pitched is approved, you can start fleshing out the form and content of the project. In the next few chapters, then, we'll offer some practical suggestions for pulling all the rhetorical, generic, multimodal, and technological parts of your project together. In the meantime, the next assignment asks you to prepare a pitch for your stakeholders, clients, or teacher.

Stakeholders, Clients, Teachers, Audience— Who ARE All These People?!

Like the terms *writer*, *designer*, *author*, and *composer*—meaning the person or people who create texts, in this case YOU—the terms we use for the readers or recipients of those texts are multiple and may include *stakeholders*, *teachers*, *clients*, or *audiences*. We tend to use these terms interchangeably, but only because they are often dependent on the rhetorical situation for your text. Stakeholders, for instance, might refer to people from the community or from an organization on campus that you are working for or with, and each of these potential groups will have a different stake in your project. But stakeholders and clients may not be the primary audience for a project.

As one example, Cheryl has worked on projects funded by the National Endowment for the Humanities (an agency of the US government that supports humanities-based projects by providing federal grants to researchers), but the primary audience for those projects was other scholar-teachers. So, NEH is a stakeholder and expects certain kinds of reporting on such projects in exchange for funding, but the scholar-teacher communities in which we work are also stakeholders.

The term you use to refer to your multiple audiences will depend on the rhetorical situation. The important thing is to gather input from as many stakeholders as possible throughout the composition process. By pitching your project ideas early on, you can get a better sense of how to proceed. You should discuss the details of this rhetorical situation with your stakeholders before you embark on your pitch.

The Pitch

Put together a pitch for your stakeholders. When planning your pitch, make sure you have these details about your project:

» What is the rhetorical situation for your multimodal project (as opposed to your pitch)?
» What genre will you use for your project?
» What is your topic? How will you convey your topic to your pitch audience? How much do they need to know at this point in the project, and what will you tell them to hook their interest? (How much more research do you need to do?)
» How will you design your project in relation to your topic? How is the design appropriate to your project's rhetorical situation?
» What do you need to know or learn so that you can complete your project? (In other words, how do you convince your teacher or client that you are able to complete this project in the time frame given for this multimodal assignment?)

You'll also need to think about designing the pitch itself:

» What is the rhetorical situation of your pitch?
» What genre of pitch does the rhetorical situation require (live presentation, stand-alone presentation, paper handouts, a formal written proposal)?
» What are the genre conventions you will use to pitch your project?
» Are there other requirements for your pitch, such as a time limit, a specific technology, or a dress code?

Keep in mind that at this point you have not completed a ton of research into the topic or designs, so you will have room for change. This is the same basic process used in writing essays; as you research and write more on an essay topic, the topic might become more concrete, or it might change direction, etc. In the case of a multimodal project, a change in topic or a refinement of your argument due to additional research might result in a rethinking of the project's genre and design — it's no longer as easy as cutting and pasting words into a different order. So you should expect some level of contingency in your project idea as your work progresses.

ASSIGNMENTS, PROJECTS, AND ASSESSMENT GT

What Is the WOVEN Rubric? GT

The Writing and Communication Program at Georgia Tech teaches WOVEN communication (see Chapter 2). To help you learn about and use WOVEN communication, not only in your writing and communication courses but also in your other courses and in your workplace and community activities, you have access to an important tool. This tool is a **rubric** (a matrix) that characterizes communication in six important areas (see pp. 146–147). The top row of the rubric presents a continuum with six broad levels of competence, from *basic* (learning literacy competence) to *exemplary* (demonstrating consistent professional-level excellence). The left-hand column presents six rhetorical categories that are particularly important to achieving effective communication. You can self-assess your own work using this rubric, checking your own competence in each category to determine how you compare with all communicators (not just those in college classes), from people who have limited literacy to those who win Pulitzer Prizes and Nobel Prizes for their writing. Don't be surprised if your self-assessment shows that your competence varies from category to category, depending on the kind of artifact, including its mode and medium.

The rubric will also be used by your professors and peers to assess your work in English 1101 and English 1102. Your professors may often customize the rubric for an assignment in order to focus on specific rows or columns. In those situations, your energy and emphasis should reflect the selected categories in the rubric, so that you develop the particular competencies targeted in the assignment.

How Does the Rubric Affect My Grades?

The Writing and Communication Program rubric helps you identify your overall communication performance, giving you a holistic sense of how you compare to other people (from those with limited literacy to those with expertise). This **macro view** of your performance is based on examining your performance over a period of time.

Your professor will also use the rubric for assessing specific artifacts you create in response to class assignments. Feedback on an assignment-specific version of the rubric gives you information you can use to improve your performance on the particular assignment (if a revision is permitted) and provides information you can use to improve your performance on the next assignment. The assignment-specific rubric gives you a **micro view** of your performance on a specific assignment.

Because they are neither complete novices nor expert practitioners, most student communicators fall in the middle ranges of the WOVEN rubric. You might earn a B or an A on an artifact for class, indicating that you are advanced in your performance for that specific class assignment. However, an A on a first-year college assignment does not mean you are in the same category as expert communicators. The rubric provides you with overall feedback about what you are doing well and what you can do to improve. If you adequately meet expectations, then you will probably earn a C or perhaps a B. If you exceed expectations, you will probably earn an A or a B. Earning a D or an F reflects a failure to meet expectations. If you want more feedback about your performance or your grade, you should make an appointment with your instructor to discuss your progress.

Building Your Communication Portfolio

A **portfolio** is an archive of related work that is curated; that is, the items are collected, selected, framed, arranged, and discussed for particular purposes. Throughout your career, you may be asked to create many types of portfolios—ones related to work projects, periods of time, professional expertise, professional growth/performance, and so on. In English 1101 and English 1102, you will be asked to create one important type—a **reflective portfolio**—that will give you both experience in building a portfolio and a framework for extending this one and for later creating other types as well. Understanding the context and purpose of a portfolio helps you best showcase your own capabilities. When you hear people talk about portfolios or ask you for a portfolio, you should ask for clarification: "What kind of portfolio are you talking about?" or "What kind of portfolio are you looking for?" or "How will you use the portfolio?"

	Basic	Beginning	Developing
Rhetorical Awareness Response to situation, including purpose, audience, register, and context	Overlooks two or more aspects of the situation or assignment and, thus, does not fulfill the task	Overlooks at least one aspect of the situation or assignment and, thus, compromises effectiveness	Attempts to respond to all aspects of the situation or assignment, but the attempt is incomplete
Stance Argument, importance, and implications (the "so what" factor)	Involves an unspecified or confusing argument; importance is not evident	Makes an overly general argument; importance is difficult to discern or not appropriate to the rhetorical situation	Makes a simplistic or implicit argument, or makes multiple arguments that have no clear connection to one another; gestures toward importance, but does not fully develop it
Development of Ideas Evidence, analysis, and substance	Omits necessary evidence for claims requiring support; lacks analysis of major pieces of evidence; content is not substantive	Uses weak or contradictory evidence for claims requiring support; does not account for important evidence that could support or disprove the argument	Provides minimal evidence necessary to support each point; attempted analysis is not sufficient to prove the argument
Organization Structure and coherence, including elements such as introductions, conclusions, and logical connections between points	Lacks unity in constituent parts; fails to create coherence among constituent parts; contains major argumentative holes or fallacies	Uses insufficient unifying statements; uses few effective connections; some logical moves necessary to prove the argument are absent	Uses some effective unifying claims, but a few are unclear; inconsistently makes connections between points and the argument; employs simplistic organization
Conventions Expectations for grammar, mechanics, style, and citation	Involves errors that risk making the overall message distorted or incomprehensible	Involves a major pattern of errors	Involves some distracting errors
Design for Medium Features that use affordances of the genre to enhance factors such as usability and comprehensibility	Lacks features necessary or significant for the genre; uses features that conflict with or ignore the argument	Omits some important features; distracting inconsistencies in features; uses features that don't support the argument	Uses features that support the argument, but some match imprecisely with content; involves minor omissions or inconsistencies

▲ RUBRIC
**Writing and
Communication
Program Rubric**

Competent	Mature	Exemplary
Addresses the situation or assignment in a complete but perfunctory or predictable way	Addresses the situation or assignment completely, with unexpected insight	Addresses the situation or assignment in a sophisticated manner that could advance professional discourse on the topic
Makes an explicit and straightforward argument that does not oversimplify the problem or question; explores at least one implication of the argument in depth	Makes a complex, unified argument that clearly articulates a position or stance; explores multiple implications of the argument	Offers an inventive, expert-like argument that clearly articulates a sophisticated position/stance; explores multiple implications of the argument in a compelling manner
Provides substantive evidence and analysis; supports the argument and all related claims in predictable ways	Fully support the argument and all related claims; always pairs evidence with compelling analysis	Provides evidence and analysis that are precise, nuanced, fullyw developed, and work together to enhance the argument
States unifying claims with supporting points that relate clearly to the overall argument and employs an effective but mechanical scheme	Asserts and sustains a claim that develops logically and progressively; adapts typical organizational schemes for the context; achieves substantive coherence	Artifact is organized to achieve maximum coherence and momentum; connections are sophisticated and complex when required
Meets expectations, with minor errors	Meets expectations in a virtually flawless manner	Exceeds expectations and manipulates conventions to advance the argument
Supports the argument with features that are generally suited to genre and content	Promotes engagement and supports the argument with features that efficiently use affordances	Persuades with careful, seamless integration of features and content and with innovative use of affordances

Beyond the reflective portfolio you'll complete for this class, you should develop and regularly update a **professional communication portfolio** that demonstrates your competence as a communicator in your field—your performance as a writer, speaker, designer, and collaborator. As part of your professional development, this portfolio can showcase your accomplishments in communication, including work selected from this course, a technical communication course, and other courses (as well as internships, co-ops, summer jobs, and study abroad programs). Instructors and advisers can help you to select and assess artifacts that show your development as a communicator.

Why do self-assessing and showcasing accomplishments in communication matter?

Self-assessment is an important skill, enabling you to identify your strengths and determine areas for improvement. Historically, critical self-appraisal has been a common practice among professionals—from artists to scientists, athletes to musicians, and architects to engineers. Self-assessment requires seeing yourself and your capabilities honestly. Take a quick look at these visual self-assessments—self-portraits by famous artists that each believed captured their essences. Your self-assessment of your communication competence will be similarly distinctive.

▲ SELF-PORTRAITS
Self-portraits painted by Judith Leyster (1630), Rembrandt van Rijn (1630), Paul Gauguin (1889), and Vincent van Gogh (1889). Notice the contrasting styles even though two of the paintings were produced in 1630 and the other two were produced in 1889. *Courtesy National Gallery of Art, Washington.*

Advancing in your career often depends on your ability to self-assess your capabilities and performance. Your self-assessment in English 1101 and English 1102 will focus on your communication competence, using the Writing and Communication Program rubric presented earlier in this chapter. Self-assessment for your English 1101 and English 1102 reflective portfolio involves three critical components:

1. Selecting, identifying, and analyzing your best multimodal artifacts

2. Reflecting on how you developed those artifacts from early to final drafts, what you were trying to accomplish, and whether you achieved these goals

3. Presenting your work and reflection to demonstrate your achievement for yourself, your instructor, and other outside audiences, including potential employers

The ultimate purpose of developing a portfolio is to transfer what you learn from one assignment to the next assignment, from one course to the next course, and from your courses to your career.

How does a reflective communication portfolio help to transfer learning?

The reflections about your processes and artifacts that give your portfolio coherence are perhaps even more important than the artifacts themselves. Reflecting on your work prompts you to identify patterns in your performance and to consider the ways in which these patterns might apply to your future communication. Identifying patterns helps you to see your strengths, which you can develop further, as well as areas you can concentrate on improving.

For example, when you reflect on designing a research poster, you might notice that you have a tendency to omit subheadings that could help viewers to understand your argument. Identifying this tendency necessarily encourages you to focus on subheadings when you revise any poster—or perhaps any other type of artifact. Thus, reflection enables you to transfer what you learned during the specific poster assignment to situations you are likely to encounter both in the classroom and in the workplace.

English 1101 and English 1102 require you to create a reflective portfolio of multimodal works and reflective essays at the end of each semester; some of these items might later become part of your overall professional communication portfolio. You may also choose to continue developing your portfolio in other classes, in your internships and co-ops, and in your other campus and community activities. Pursuing self-assessment while maintaining an organized record of your work in your reflective portfolio creates a resource that you can easily draw from to build your professional portfolio, sharing your accomplishments and advancing your career.

What is the English 1101 or 1102 portfolio and how does it enhance my education?

At Georgia Tech all students in English 1101 and English 1102 are required to submit multimodal portfolios that reflect their work in each course. The end-of-semester portfolio is in lieu of a final exam for the course. You should design it as a culminating, representative, and reflective example of your overall performance in the course. The portfolio should demonstrate that you have met these stated competencies:

Rhetoric	• Consider the rhetorical situation, specifically the relationships between context, audience, composer, and argument
Process	• Draft, revise, and edit • Offer and receive feedback on work in progress • Reflect on the composing process and performance
Argument	• Craft a purposeful stance on an issue • Demonstrate critical thinking • Persuasively organize ideas
Research	• Find and use credible evidence in support of a stance and in rebuttal to counterarguments
Attribution	• Borrow and cite ideas, words, images, and so on from other composers skillfully, ethically, and appropriately
Conventions	• Demonstrate appropriate use of genre, language, punctuation, style, and citation to suit the audience
Modes and Media	• Integrate multiple modes and media in communication (written, oral, visual, electronic, nonverbal) ethically and skillfully • Select an appropriate medium for delivery of the argument

Thus, the portfolio serves two purposes for your learning:

1. It enables you to document the ways in which your efforts meet the stated course goals.

2. It requires you to reflect on your learning during the semester, which research indicates will improve your ability to transfer these skills to other situations.

During the semester, you will spend some time working on your portfolio (the amount of time varies from professor to professor). At the end of the semester, you will write a self-review essay and select evidence from the artifacts you have produced in this course; then, you will describe and make an argument about the ways in which each artifact demonstrates your ability to apply the concepts and skills taught in this course. The directions for submitting the portfolio may be slightly different for each class, so students should follow the instructions given by their professor. However, each successful portfolio will contain these items:

1. A **1,200- to 1,800-word self-review essay** that introduces and analyzes the portfolio

2. A series of **short-answer reflections** that address questions about each individual artifact

3. **Three to four artifacts** that, taken together, best reflect your work and development in the course

Throughout the semester, you'll be collecting your best and most interesting work to include in your communication portfolio. Part of being able to complete a reflective portfolio necessitates saving copies of your drafts so that you can comment on your development. In order to comment on these drafts, you need to consider a practice common among professionals. They seldom write over an old version of a document, replacing it with the new version. Instead, they **save multiple versions** of the document. So, for example, by the time a document such as an OpEd column is completed for a class assignment, your own folder for the assignment could reasonably include OpEd 9-15-15 ver 1, OpEd 9-17-15 ver 2, and OpEd 9-20-15 ver 3. Versions of various projects you complete are likely to include visuals (such as graphs, photos, or videos) and sound (such as voice-overs, music tracks, or podcasts). Having this archive of materials will be essential to creating your reflective portfolio. (See Chapter 9 for more on version control and file management.)

The artifacts in your portfolio must together address all of the following requirements:

Requirements	Details
At least one artifact must emphasize **written communication** through extended prose in **Standard American English**.	**Written** texts rely chiefly on printed words, typography, and layout. Examples include essays, reports, proposals, blog posts, or Web site content.
At least one artifact must emphasize **oral/nonverbal communication**.	**Oral/Nonverbal** texts involve spoken words, sound effects (including vocal effects or music), the body, spacing, or timing. Examples include speeches, presentations, podcasts, or performances. **If students do not have recorded oral/nonverbal artifacts** (for example, they did a class presentation or performance that was not recorded), they may submit a detailed description of the oral and nonverbal components of the presentation/performance along with a script, handout, and/or PowerPoint/Prezi that accompanied the presentation.
At least one artifact must reflect **intentional visual design**.	**Visual** texts foreground image and design. Examples include pamphlets, posters, presentation aids, videos, visual art, Web sites, or reports/essays with intentional design.
At least one artifact must reflect **electronic communication**.	**Electronic texts** leverage interactive features of digital media and combine several modes. Examples include Web sites, wiki pages, blogs, Twitter feeds, electronic games, video, or audio.
At least one artifact must reflect a **substantial revision process**.	The revision process must be exemplified through **process documents**, the most common of which will be multiple drafts. In cases of electronic or visual artifacts, these might be photographs or screenshots of early iterations. Other options include brainstorming notes, outlines, proposals, drafts with peer-review letters, draft cover letters, video reflections, and so on.

Preventing Assignment Stress GT

Keeping up with lectures, homework, assignments, and projects for four or more classes across various disciplines can sometimes feel overwhelming. Following these tips offered by current juniors and seniors can help you reduce assignment stress.

Start early. Many Georgia Tech students are in the habit of completing assignments at the last minute. Although this strategy may have worked for assignments in high school, it's not a good idea now. As a college student you now have added stress—taking harder classes, getting accustomed to new surroundings, juggling lectures and labs, and so on. By starting assignments early, you leave yourself time to revise and edit, ensuring your ideas are expressed clearly and correctly. The result will be increased insight, creativity, and accuracy, and higher grades.

Talk to your professors. Professors are not mind readers. When you are struggling with a class, your professor may not realize it until you have already submitted an assignment and earned a poor grade. The best way to prevent this from happening is to talk to your professor. If you regularly communicate with your professors, they will become your allies in helping you learn as much as possible and earn grades that reflect your best performance.

Plan your ideas. You can plan assignments in many ways. Some students outline key ideas or arguments they want to make. Others put key ideas on index cards—in sentences or paragraphs—and then treat the cards like a puzzle, arranging and rearranging them to find relationships among the ideas. Still others create idea maps and brainstorm as key parts of planning. Whatever method works best for you, plan—in your mind and on paper—before writing and designing. The lack of a plan will likely result in a paper, presentation, or visual that lacks consistency and coherence, thus reducing the accessibility, comprehensibility, and usability of your work. You will then create a product that doesn't reflect your abilities and receive a grade that may disappoint you.

Use available campus resources. Georgia Tech has many offices, groups, and organizations that can assist you. Academic services include the Communication Center in the Clough Undergraduate Learning Center, the Multimedia Studio in the library, the subject and media librarians, and 1-to-1 Tutoring. Services for health and wellness (emotional and physical) include Stamps Health Services and the Counseling Center. Advocacy offices that will support you include the Dean of Students' office, the LGBTQIA Resource Center, and the Women's Resource Center. All of these services can help you manage your work-life balance. You can reduce your stress by planning, varying, and balancing your academic and extracurricular activities. If you need a way to get started, visit the Student Affairs Web site to explore ways to get involved on campus. Using available campus resources will give you a more well-rounded and rewarding college experience.

Proofread carefully before submitting. The simplest way to improve the quality of your work and increase the likelihood of good grades is to proofread. Proofreading is a *critical* part of an assignment; it shows you care about the credibility and quality of your work. Because you spend so much time on your assignments, you can become too close to your work; over time, you may stop seeing what you actually wrote and instead see what you intended to write. Ask classmates, roommates, or friends to exchange proofreading responsibilities with you so that you read their work and they read yours. A fresh pair of eyes can often spot mistakes in grammar, mechanics, spelling, and style. Even so, make sure to proofread your work more than once before turning it in. This will result in higher-quality work that reflects your capabilities.

As you become accustomed to self-assessment of and reflection about your work, the categories in the Writing and Communication Program rubric will become part of your process. You'll find your confidence increasing and your performance improving. Ultimately, you'll transfer and generalize what you learn in English 1101 and English 1102 to other communication situations.

PART 4

HOW CAN I COMMUNICATE INDIVIDUALLY AND COLLABORATIVELY?

Read This First! GT

Collaboration probably began for you when you were young, perhaps as young as the elementary school children in the photo below. In elementary school, you may have learned strategies to engage in cooperative and small-group learning activities and to work on creative problem solving. Now that you're in college, you will build on these elementary strategies and learn new ones that work in academic, community, and workplace situations.

You can work independently—unless the task will be better completed collaboratively. How can you decide? If a task meets one of these criteria, completing it collaboratively may be a good idea: (1) comprises a wide-ranging problem, (2) addresses a complicated issue, (3) benefits from multiple perspectives, (4) requires diverse areas of expertise, or (5) involves a process that requires two or more people.

In English 1101 and English 1102, you will often work with classmates on tasks such as collaborative planning, team project development, and peer review. *Collaborative planning* enables two or more individual writers, coauthors, or team members to interrogate each other about rhetorical elements as they plan and draft artifacts. *Project development* teams (ranging from small to huge groups) commit to a common goal and an interactive process to complete a task. *Peer editing* involves two or more people who offer evaluative comments about the quality of the other's work, usually focusing on the ways rhetorical elements are addressed. You can address all of these collaborative activities in face-to-face meetings or at a distance using tools such as Google Drive or Dropbox. More important than the technology, however, is your engagement in the collaboration; without your commitment, enthusiasm, and follow-through, your collaborative activities are more likely to be painful than productive.

PHOTO ▶
Backyard Collaboration
Four children playing together in a dirt pile. *Cade Martin/Centers for Disease Control and Prevention.*

What's the *least* effective approach to collaboration? Get together, divide up the work, and then combine it into a single artifact the night before it's due. What's the *most* effective approach? That's nearly impossible to say without knowing the specific group and task. In general, you want to leverage the strengths of your group's members. Effective collaborators acknowledge that working together takes time and may involve disagreements that need to be resolved. If you spend time figuring out what your group members do well and invite each person's individual opinions, you're very likely to increase the quality of your interaction and the quality of the product.

You've probably done a lot of group work, collaborative work, and teamwork, but too often the process may have simply involved a teacher putting you in a group or on a team and telling you to accomplish the task. In contrast, in English 1101 and English 1102, you'll have an opportunity to learn and practice a variety of strategies that will enable you to become a skillful collaborator and leader. One of the primary strategies involves consistently checking that you and your collaborators are attending to rhetorical elements that affect the way your multimodal artifact is designed and developed.

CHECKLIST: Questions Collaborators Can Ask Each Other about Rhetorical Elements

Use this checklist to help you work with your collaborators. Your goal is to ask each other about a range of rhetorical elements, including content, context, purpose, argument, audience, organization, evidence, and design for medium. Frequently, saying your ideas aloud is more useful than just thinking about them. Talking about your plans is usually a highly productive part of planning.

☐ **CONTENT:** What information must be included in the artifact? What should be added (or omitted)? What will the audiences expect to be included in the artifact?

☐ **CONTEXT:** When, where, and how will this artifact be used? How can contextual factors (time, place, use) influence audience reactions to the artifact?

☐ **PURPOSE:** What is the primary purpose of the artifact? The secondary purpose? How receptive are the audiences to the purpose(s)?

☐ **ARGUMENT:** What is your primary argument? What arguments will the audiences think you're making? What are the audiences likely to accept or reject in your argument and its supporting evidence?

☐ **AUDIENCE:** Who are the intended audiences? What are the expectations of the audiences?

☐ **ORGANIZATION:** What is the conventional organization of information for this artifact? In what ways are you complying with or flouting conventions of, for example, language, genre, and/or design?

☐ **DESIGN FOR MEDIUM:** What are design conventions for this artifact? What design conventions will influence the audiences? How can you use the design conventions to strengthen your argument?

Awareness of your individual and collaborative processes increases the likelihood that your group or team will be successful. Why? Such awareness may identify problems (procedural, affective, or substantive) that influence the interaction. You should try to reflect about your processes to increase the effectiveness of the group or team.

Metacognitive Questions to Leverage Your Knowledge: Collaboration

You can start to answer these metacognitive questions now, but you'll have much more detailed and credible responses when you finish reading all the chapters in Part 4.

» **REMEMBER:** What strategies have you used in previous collaborations to manage your projects? **#Remember**

» **UNDERSTAND:** How can working with collaborators extend possible ways to interpret a problem? **#Understand**

» **APPLY:** How can consulting with your collaborators help you identify additional ways to solve the problem? **#Apply**

» **ANALYZE:** How can collaborators impede the rapid completion of a task? What are the benefits/disadvantages of impeding the speed of completion? **#Analyze**

» **EVALUATE:** How does working with collaborators influence the way(s) your course of action is justified? **#Evaluate**

» **CREATE:** How can you work with your collaborators/teammates to create more innovative solutions? Plan a project process to generate new patterns and solutions. **#Create**

COLLABORATING COOPERATIVELY: TIPS FOR TERRIFIC TEAM PROJECTS GT

Most jobs require you to collaborate in order to complete assigned tasks. Sometimes collaborators read and write print and digital documents; at other times, collaborators critique and create various kinds of videos or podcasts. Collaborators typically listen and speak as well as view and design in face-to-face and distance interactions. The large amount of collaborative interaction that's expected in the workplace is a surprise to many recent college graduates.

Collaborative behaviors are not intuitive nor are they consistent from culture to culture. Rather, they are learned. You can improve your collaborative interaction by learning more about the nature of collaboration, the types of conflict that might occur during a collaborative project, and the strategies that help group members deal with these conflicts. Simply understanding these concepts is not enough, however. To become a good collaborator, you need to put your knowledge into practice by participating in collaborative interactions and then reflecting on these interactions.

As you read this discussion, you will first learn about various types of conflict that occur in collaborative interactions; you will then examine a number of strategies and techniques that effective collaborators use to help diminish destructive conflict and promote productive conflict. Periodically in the discussion, you will be asked to reflect about your ideas and recall your own experiences.

This chapter has been adapted from an article written by Dr. Rebecca E. Burnett, Director of Writing and Communication at Georgia Tech, and Dr. Elizabeth Wardle, Chair for the Department of Writing and Rhetoric at the University of Central Florida.

Types of Conflict GT

The following discussion about conflict should help you strengthen your own collaborative interaction. Keep in mind that types of conflicts—and the behaviors recommended for avoiding or provoking them—are culture specific. This means that you might inadvertently misinterpret someone's actions or reactions if that person is from a different culture.

Procedural Conflict

In a collaborative interaction, procedures involve what gets done, how things get done, who is doing what, who (if anyone) is in charge, and how the schedule is constructed. **Procedural conflict** involves disagreements about the way work is done.

If left unresolved, procedural conflicts can damage or even destroy a team. Unresolved procedural conflicts can result in teams that are unorganized and unprepared as well as team members who are disappointed—and even angry—with one another. Procedural conflicts can occur when people don't take time to discuss factors such as these:

<table>
<tr><td>» Individual responsibilities</td><td>» Leadership</td></tr>
<tr><td>» Schedule for completing tasks</td><td>» Conflict resolution</td></tr>
<tr><td>» Pace of work</td><td>» Expectations of quality</td></tr>
<tr><td>» Time and duration of work</td><td>» Work style</td></tr>
<tr><td>» Assessment of individual performance</td><td></td></tr>
</table>

How can your team or group avoid damage caused by procedural conflict? Successful collaboration begins when—before meeting together—collaborators have individually thought about and prepared a preliminary plan that includes their views about the factors in the bulleted list above. Then, during the initial group meeting, all members of the team can compare and talk about their own preliminary plans. Usually, during this initial discussion, group members find that each member of the team has differing ideas about the project. If team members are open to an active and honest exchange with one another about areas of agreement and disagreement, they can create a shared vision of the project. Neglecting to have a preliminary discussion at the very beginning of a collaborative project can have several harmful results:

» Preventing work from being done, so a team or group is never functional

» Causing a team to limp along, never quite meshing smoothly

Determine what factors do not need to be discussed at the beginning of a collaborative project, either because everyone already agrees or because the questions might make you (and others) uncomfortable. Then identify procedural factors you believe are essential to discuss because agreeing about them will make interaction more productive. #Evaluate

» Acting like a time bomb, waiting to explode and derail a group when some seemingly small procedural problem arises

Addressing procedural issues up front is essential to team success.

Affective Conflict

Affect deals with a person's feelings and emotions that are, of course, strongly influenced by personal beliefs. Seen positively, these are values; seen negatively, they are prejudices. **Affective conflict** involves disagreements caused by people's personal beliefs—their values and prejudices. These conflicts occur when people disagree about things that matter a great deal to them but about which others may disagree just as strongly. For example, affective conflicts can occur when people allow factors such as these to negatively influence their interactions:

» Politics	» Race
» Gender	» Religion
» Sexual orientation	» Nationality
» Age	» Cultural prejudices
» Class	» Personal prejudices

These factors can cause ugly and detrimental affective conflict simply because they matter so much to people—and often rightly so. However, in order to work as a team, all members need to realize that their individual views about politics or religion are not necessarily shared and that trying to persuade others to change their views on these matters is not productive. But restraining yourself from trying to convert others to your views is not enough: team members must also choose not to act on any prejudices they feel toward group members who may be different from them in some way. If all team members do not come to understand these two important points early on, they may engage in conflict that can destroy their team's ability to be effective and productive.

How can your team or group avoid the damage of affective conflict? First, you need to conduct an honest self-assessment of your own values and prejudices. In order for you to work on a project cooperatively, you need to manage your prejudices, and in order to do that you need to acknowledge them—at least to yourself. This is often difficult because what most of us see as our "views" others may see as our "prejudices"; most of us don't like admitting that we ever feel any prejudices. But the reality is, if you feel dislike or express bias toward people because of their political or religious views, their race, their country of origin, their sexual orientation, their age, their culture—even for things as small as their taste in music—then what you are feeling is prejudice. You need not disclose your prejudices to others.

Formulate a personal plan to help ensure that you are fair and thoughtful in your collaborative interactions on a team, reducing or eliminating the negative influence of affective conflict. #Create

However, in order to engage in a positive and constructive team project, each member of the team has to be *self-aware* about his or her prejudices and exhibit *self-control* over those prejudices.

Neglecting to manage your prejudices can result in affective conflict and damage the relationships necessary for productive collaboration. Affective conflict can emerge from arguments about these value-related factors or from unspoken negative judgments about your collaborators based on differences in race, religion, culture, and so on. Whatever the source of the conflict, if it is not managed it is sure to be a destructive influence on your team's productivity. If the conflict becomes an overriding concern, it can destroy interpersonal relationships and take important time away from substantive, project-related issues.

Substantive Conflict

Substance, as discussed here, deals with the concepts and ideas of a project, the information as well as the rhetorical factors that influence the way information is presented and interpreted. **Substantive conflict** involves disagreements caused by differing perceptions about concepts and ideas important to the outcome of a project. Numerous studies show that groups engaging in substantive conflict almost always produce better products, projects, and presentations than groups that don't engage in substantive conflict.

Put another way, substantive conflicts are fervent discussions—which sometimes sound like disagreements—about major issues that affect the quality of the final product. For example, substantive conflict might take the form of a disagreement about the solution to a problem you are addressing in a proposal or about which source information is more reliable. When rational people engage in substantive conflict, the result is usually synergistic interaction that provokes different (and often better) ideas than any individual would come up with alone. Unlike procedural conflict and affective conflict, which are almost always destructive, substantive conflict is almost always productive. The value of the substantive conflict is determined by the relevance and importance of the topic under discussion—in other words, the more important the topic is to the outcome of the project itself, the more valuable the substantive conflict.

In order to produce a high-quality team project, you need to devote time to important questions that may lead to substantive conflict. This is mostly likely to happen when all team members actively participate. For example, engaged team members usually respond to other people's suggestions) by asking questions such as, "Why do you like this particular idea?" or "Why do you think that suggestion is better than the one John made earlier?" You have many ways to be engaged and ensure that your group discussions address substantive issues. Try some of these:

» Don't ask only yes or no questions. Explain your idea and then ask, "What is your response to this?" or "What other ways can you think of to solve this problem?"

» Don't give only yes or no answers. If someone makes a suggestion, respond to it by explaining your reaction, not by simply saying, "Okay, that's fine."

» Ask people to explain further if you don't understand them or disagree with them.

» Give reasons for your suggestions and responses. Don't simply say you like an idea; say *why* you like it.

» Be open to other people's suggestions. Engage in active listening, where you demonstrate your attention and understanding of your team members' opinions.

» Find ways to incorporate different people's suggestions so that your project represents the ideas of more than one person.

You might be wondering what makes a topic substantive. Generally, anything that influences the outcome of a project might be considered substantive. However, some substantive conflicts are more worthwhile than others, and some groups may be better able to engage in substantive conflict about a particular issue. For example, your team may spend a lot of time discussing what font works better in a document. This issue matters, but you cannot engage in substantive conflict about it unless the collaborators on your team have the expertise to discuss the matter productively. In other words, arguing about font preferences when you can only base your comments on personal preference is not productive (for example, telling the group to use another font "just because I like it" is not useful). If, however, the collaborators can argue that one font is more appropriate for a specific audience than another font (for example, one can be more easily read than another by limited literacy adults or visually impaired children) or if they can argue that a particular font creates a desired image (for example, the font **Chalkduster**, though not very legible, creates the impression of an open, playful document), then your team can engage in fruitful substantive conflict.

Explain why substantive conflict is likely to increase the quality of a group or team's processes and products. #Understand

---

The key to engaging in substantive conflict is to ask yourself three questions at every turn:

1. What expertise do we have to discuss this issue in a substantive way?

2. Why is this an important issue to spend time discussing?

3. How will devoting time to this issue result in a better project?

Practical Strategies for Promoting Substantive Conflict GT

Three important strategies—making collective decisions about procedural issues, especially regarding different roles and responsibilities; being sensitive to cultural differences; and making strategic verbal moves—can help you focus on substantive conflict to increase the likelihood of a high-quality product.

Strategy 1: Making Collective Decisions about Roles and Responsibilities

At the beginning of a project, you need to make sure that everyone on the team understands and agrees about important procedural issues, especially regarding roles and responsibilities. With this understanding, team members can then give their attention to substantive issues. As we mentioned earlier, asking all members of the team to write their understanding of the project and their vision for the way procedural matters will be handled is quite useful. In their reflective plan, individual team members should address some specific questions:

» What are the tasks we need to accomplish?

» What approaches or strategies will we use to accomplish these tasks?

» What is our timeline for completing these tasks?

» What roles need to be filled?

» Who is most qualified to fill these roles? What are the implications of having both men and women in these various roles?

» What qualifies someone to be a team leader? What are the ramifications of selecting various people as team leader?

» Who will be our team leader? Facilitator?

» Where will we work? When? For how long?

» How will we resolve disagreements?

» What will happen if group members do not fulfill their responsibilities?

Before the first meeting, have all team members write their answers to these questions in the form of a memo to the team. At the first meeting, each team member can read his or her individual memo aloud, and others can compare that person's response to his or her own. After each person has read, the team then needs to collectively decide on ways to deal with each of these questions. This first meeting will probably focus largely on procedural issues—and that's okay; this time will be well spent if it prevents the group from wasting time later on procedural conflict.

Strategy 2: Being Sensitive to Cultural Differences

Team interaction can be complex, even difficult, when people on a team come from different cultures. Multicultural collaboration would be difficult enough if "multicultural" simply referred to people from various countries. However, "multicultural" refers additionally to cultural differences that may be the result of geography, ethnicity, race, dialect, education, sociopolitical views, and so on. If you and your team members are not sensitive to cultural differences, you are likely to engage in unproductive affective conflict.

A number of cultural issues often affect a team's ability to collaborate effectively. Consider the following as only a few of the possible cultural factors you need to learn to manage during collaboration:

> **National cultures:** Are members of your team from different countries? Do team members have different perceptions of time than you do? Do these people have different senses of personal space—proxemics? Do they have different expectations of interpersonal interaction? Do they have different ways of determining priorities? If so, how do these issues affect your team interaction—and how can you turn these differences into something productive, rather than destructive?

> **Racial and ethnic cultures:** If you have team members of different races or ethnicities, you need to ask yourself how people from different racial and/ or ethnic backgrounds interpret history or current events in ways that might influence on-the-job attitudes or actions. Have they had different educational and employment opportunities than you? If so, how might these differences influence your team interaction? Whether you are a member of the majority or the minority racial or ethnic group on a team, you should be sensitive to the perceptions and experiences of those who are different from you.

> **Religious cultures:** You probably won't know the religious beliefs of your coworkers, but you can assume that their on-the-job decisions are affected by personal and/or spiritual beliefs, whatever they may be. You should consider what links people who observe different religions see between their religious beliefs and their workplace decisions and actions. You need to be respectful of other people's religious choices and make sure that religious differences do not derail your project.

> **Gender:** The structure of teams, leadership styles and functions, team roles, and cultural biases can all be influenced by gender. Team members should be aware of different styles that might be a result of gender differences. These styles are especially important if you are working in areas that have typically been managed by one gender more than another. For example, engineering has typically been a male-dominated field, and women working on engineering teams could potentially feel that leadership styles and team structure are not

Analyze cultural aspects of yourself that might influence team members as they react or respond to your interactions with them. #Analyze

conducive to their ability to participate. You cannot undo years of prejudice while working on one project, but you can be sensitive to it and not perpetuate problems or stereotypes.

» **Class cultures:** People who appear to share the same ethnicity, religion, and nationality may come from different economic classes. The values and habits of different economic classes often influence the way members of those classes express themselves and deal with those in authority. If other members of your team are reacting to conflict in ways that seem unusual to you, you might consider that often members of different classes are taught to react to conflict differently.

Multicultural teams are potentially polyvocal—that is, the team is a productive mélange of views and voices. However, team members may have to go out of their way to privilege minority voices—making room in conversation for alternative views and perspectives they might find uncomfortable, reseeing options from a different perspective.

So how do you make sure that affective conflicts about cultural differences do not interfere with the substantive conflict you want to encourage with your collaborators? Here are some guidelines that might help. Regardless of the specific affective topic (for example, nationality, ethnicity, gender, religion), the ways of managing it to encourage substantive conflict are often similar.

» **Humor:** Avoid telling jokes that depend for their humor on ridiculing some person or group to which you do not belong.

» **Imitation:** Avoid assuming an accent or expressing stereotypical attitudes or behaviors that mock members of groups to which you do not belong.

» **Assumptions:** Avoid acting on your unvoiced assumptions about how others will behave based on their beliefs or group membership. This means that you should not expect people to behave in certain ways simply because they are a Bosnian, a Native American, a Mormon, a woman, or a billionaire.

» **Conversion:** Avoid trying to convert people to think or behave like you do about affective issues since such efforts detract from substantive issues.

Ignoring affective problems increases the likelihood of silencing team members. Someone will sit in a group, listening to an ethnic joke or a sexist stereotype or a racial slur and think, "I'm not going to open my mouth and make myself vulnerable to this ridicule" or "I'm not going to contribute to a project that marginalizes me as a person" or "I simply don't want to work with people who act (or think or talk) like this." If you want your team to be productive and truly collaborative, not acting on your own prejudices is not enough; you must also discourage your team members from acting on theirs.

Strategy 3: Making Strategic Verbal Moves during Work Sessions

Certain verbal moves are strategic—that is, they are concrete actions that contribute directly to the overall goal. In this case, the goal is promoting substantive conflict, and you can do this by focusing on rhetorical elements, prompting your team members, contributing information to your team members, challenging your team members, directing your team members, and acknowledging your team members' contributions.

Focusing on rhetorical elements: The substance isn't all about content, although content certainly plays a part in any good project. Most experienced writers and collaborators center their substantive conflict around rhetorical elements—that is, they ask themselves and each other questions about the following issues even more than they ask about content.

» **Context:** What's the situation? What's the occasion? How will the document be used?

» **Purpose:** What are the goals? What are the objectives?

» **Audience:** Who are the audiences? What do they need? Expect?

» **Organization:** How is the document's information arranged? Sequenced?

» **Development:** What kind of support is used? Examples? Statistical data?

» **Visuals:** What kinds of visuals are appropriate: tables, graphs, charts, diagrams, drawings, maps, screen captures, photographs?

» **Design:** What's the design grid? What typographic decisions need to be made?

» **Language Conventions:** What conventions of mechanics and grammar should be observed?

» **Usability:** How has the usability of the document been assessed?

Prompting team members: Substantive conflict involves a conversation, so you need to show that you're listening and also prompt others to respond to you so that all collaborators are engaged. Prompts include *back-channeling cues* ("Uh-huh"), *neutral comments* ("I see"), *acknowledgments* ("Yes, I understand your point"), *reinforcing comments and encouragement* ("Tell me more"), *reminders* ("Is that what you meant before?"), and *questions about rhetorical elements* ("Why will the audience respond to that argument?").

Contributing information to team members: Substantive conflict can't occur if team members don't contribute information. Information varies in form and content but can include facts, observations, and suggestions in the form of summaries,

What is your favorite conversational prompt—similar to one here or another that is entirely different? Generate a list of additional prompts you'd be comfortable using, so you have more ways to respond to collaborators. #Remember #Create syntheses, or reflections about the group, task, or text. Contributing information ensures that team members take responsibility for themselves and each other, thus lessening the possibility of freeloading, a common frustration in collaborative projects. You can promote substantive conflict by contributing new information: "That might work, but have you considered what [expert X] says about [topic Y] in last week's issue of [authoritative journal Z]?"

Challenging team members to engage in substantive conflict involves asking critical questions, suggesting alternatives, and arguing opposing views. These are typical examples:

What are other examples of these three ways to challenge a team member? What typical phrases do you use to express disagreement with your collaborators? Create a list of phrases to give yourself more latitude in expressing disagreement. #Remember #Create

» Critical question: "What do you think the audience is most likely to respond to in this current argument?" or "How can I change the opening hook to attract a broader audience?"

» Alternative: "I think we should use a different example." or "Let's try incorporating maps and photos rather than just drawings and graphs."

» Opposing view: "This histogram is ineffective; not only is it the wrong kind of data display, but the calculations are incorrect." or "I believe our approach to the analysis is incorrect."

Directing team members involves encouraging them to modify plans and/or text by adding, changing, or deleting what they've done. This verbal move often creates conflict—and your responsibility is to make that conflict substantive rather than affective (you want to build on team members' views rather than criticizing them *for* their views). This verbal move should be used sparingly and with diplomacy: being aggressive or insulting during collaboration is rarely productive. If you need to direct team members, do so specifically and carefully. Directives that produce productive substantive conflict typically include a rationale. Telling others to do something is insufficient; instead, you must also tell them *why* they should do it. Some examples of effective directives include phrases such as, "You should reorganize these three points in order of importance if you want the reader to recognize their relative importance" or "Because the reader might be confused, I think we should try another way of explaining this" or "I think we should use a different example because we already have a similar version of this one earlier in the article."

What typical phrases do you use to express agreement and praise for good work by your collaborators? Create a list of phrases to give yourself more latitude in expressing support and agreement. #Remember #Create

Acknowledging team members: Substantive conflict isn't about attacking your collaborators; it's a friendly—though often lively and strongly opinionated— negotiation about ideas and issues. In order for teams to work well, members must acknowledge and appreciate what their collaborators have contributed. Directives and challenges will be better received if they are coupled with acknowledgments such as "That's a convincing argument you're making" or "You've done some really good work so far."

Managing the Conflict in Your Collaboration

You have probably gained some new knowledge about conflict. For example, you have learned that conflict is not always a bad thing; in fact, substantive conflict is likely to improve the quality of team interaction and, thus, the quality of the artifacts a team creates.

You have also learned some practical strategies that team members can engage in so that they avoid unproductive conflict and spend more time on substantive issues. Even with this new knowledge, however, you will find that being good at collaboration takes practice.

Now you'll be able to put your knowledge into action. Using what you have learned, consider the following brief case studies. Take a leadership role in your teams, since you now know more than most people about being a productive team member. Put your knowledge to use, share it with members of your team, and engage your team members in discussions to help them grow to be successful collaborators.

Could This Collaborative Project Have Been Saved? GT

One way to learn more about being an effective team member is to reflect about the experiences of others. To prompt discussion about effective collaboration, in the following examples you will read about the experiences of team members who faced very different challenges in their interactions.

» Mariah, a PR manager who worked on a group project for one of her classes

» William, a proposal writer who worked on a group project for one of his classes

» Maggie, a newly hired technical communicator who copyedited a document for a project manager in another department

» Lloyd, a contract writer who developed online training materials and an accompanying reference manual

» Lynn, a social worker who was the lead (that is, the coordinator) for a project to implement new procedures for adoption cases

All of these five people are real, not fictive (although their names have been changed for the sake of privacy). Each of them contributed one of the following scenarios that describes the roles and responsibilities as well as frustrations they experienced in their classroom and workplace teams. As you read these scenarios, put yourself in the shoes of these collaborators:

» Explore possible reasons for the problems their teams faced **#Analyze**

» Recommend solutions for managing these problems **#Evaluate**

» Discuss the ways each of them actually dealt with their problems **#Understand**

These problems are typical of those you are likely to encounter in your own class-room and workplace experiences. As you complete this activity, remember the three types of conflict (procedural, affective, and substantive), and be sure to review the strategies just discussed for dealing with conflict.

The Case of the Wimpy Writer: Mariah's Story

Collaboration can sometimes be a problem for a very simple reason: one of the col-laborators doesn't have the courage to speak up about an issue that, in the end, has major repercussions. In the Case of the Wimpy Writer, Mariah knew from the beginning of the project that one of the group's procedural decisions was a bad one—one that would decrease the group's effectiveness and increase the amount of time needed to complete the work. As you read Mariah's story, you will be asked to consider ways in which reluctant or shy collaborators can be encouraged to voice dissenting opinions.

What are several possible reasons for the problems Mariah's team is facing? **#Analyze**

How does the inequity in status between the participants contribute to the affective conflict? **#Understand**

Mariah's Story

I was involved in a difficult collaborative writing project in a cross-listed class that included both undergraduate and graduate students. Our group project assignment was to locate a set of poorly written instructions and revise them. We were also required to write rhetorical analyses of both the original and revised instructions and to test the revised instructions and include the test results with the assignment. I worked with three other women on this project: two of them were graduate students, and one was an undergraduate—like I was. I felt intimidated by the graduate students and convinced myself they knew a lot more than I knew. We experienced several different types of conflict during this project. The primary conflicts I experienced stemmed from my lack of self-confidence.

The Conflict. A specific conflict in this project that caused me to experience frustration and annoyance was our choice of meeting location. In the beginning stages of our project, one of the graduate students suggested that we hold all of our team meetings at the food court in the Student Union (we had agreed to work on parts of the project in pairs and come together in these meetings as a full team of four).

I was very much against meeting at the food court because I did not view it as a location where we would be able to be productive. If we met there, I thought our meetings would be reduced to status reports of the work we had accomplished in our pairs. I felt we should meet at someone's house, at a computer lab, or in the multimedia studio where we could be more productive.

What solutions do you recommend for manag-ing these problems? **#Create**

On two different occasions, I mentioned my hesitancy to meet at the food court. Because of my lack of self-confidence, I did not make these comments as directly as I normally would have, and they were brushed off by my collaborators. I never made an attempt to push the issue because I was hesitant to voice my opinion strongly.

I believe this conflict changed the outcome of our project by making it take much longer than any of us had anticipated. Our meetings at the food court did, as I anticipated, become status reports rather than productive, hands-on sessions, and I felt they greatly extended the duration of the project. In these meetings, we talked about changes that needed to be made and discussed issues that were unclear, but none of the changes were made during the meetings. By the time we were finally ready to turn in our project, our patience was short and tensions were high. If I had taken a stronger stand about my concerns regarding our meeting location then the other project members would not have ignored me.

I selected this particular conflict to talk about because I learned a valuable lesson from it: do not keep quiet about issues that you feel strongly about in collaborative projects. If I had taken a stronger stand about my concerns with our meeting location then the project would not have dragged on so long, and we all would have had a more positive experience working together.

How could team members have decreased the procedural conflict and, thus, increased the likelihood that Mariah would have felt more comfortable to express her reservations strongly? #Apply #Evaluate

> **STOP!** Before you read the rest of Mariah's story, stop and suggest what you would have done if you were Mariah. Then speculate about what you think actually happened and how things were resolved. **#Create**
>
> Finish reading Mariah's story to see if your speculations are on target.

The Resolution. We did not manage to solve this particular conflict because I never pushed the issue about changing our meeting location. We continued to work in pairs and come together as a team at the food court for our meetings. At these meetings, we found that we had too many opinions and ideas about the work we had done in pairs and ways it could be changed or improved. At our last food court meeting, one of my collaborators expressed her frustration about how long the project was taking when she said, "I don't want to change another stinking word in this. All I'm doing is cleaning this up." Although we still managed to receive an A on our project, our collaborative experience was certainly not a pleasant one.

The Case of the Controlling Collaborator: William's Story

Collaboration can be a problem if one of the collaborators acts on an overwhelming need to maintain control of the project. Team members who refuse to engage in a cooperative project and instead act as if it's a solo endeavor block the team's ability to interact collaboratively and, thus, do not take advantage of the strengths of other members of the team. As you read the Case of the Controlling Collaborator, you will be asked to suggest ways in which the team either could have prevented the problem from occurring by making better procedural decisions or could have wrested the project away from the controller sooner.

What are several possible reasons for the problems William's team is facing? **#Analyze**

What solutions do you recommend for managing these problems? **#Create**

How do you assess the way the print team actually handled the problem? **#Evaluate**

What would you have done in their situation? **#Apply**

William's Story

Our 12-person team was assigned two major projects: one was to create a Web site listing the names of all of our department's graduates, their educational backgrounds, their accomplishments, and their current employment. For the second project we were asked to create a "flashy" booklet that could be sent out to students interested in applying to our program.

During our first meeting, we quickly split into two teams. We did not know each other very well yet, so these teams were picked in a pretty arbitrary way: whoever wanted to create the Web site went to that team, and the others joined the print document team. We also decided that since this was a "team project," we should not appoint any leaders.

I was on the print document team. The print document moved along quickly and easily. The team members worked well together and were pleased with our progress. We assumed that the Web site team was coming along just as well as we were, but we did not bother to check. Every time we spoke with a team member on a casual basis, he or she would say, "Oh, we're fine. Bob has the data and is working on coding it." Since most of us were not Web designers, we thought that meant things were going well.

The Conflict. With two weeks left until the project was due, we decided both teams should meet together. When we did, we realized the Web site team had accomplished nothing. We had gathered the data they were using. They had nothing done beyond copying what we had given them. To top it off, Bob, the person the Web site team was relying on to get things done, did not come to this meeting. To make a long story short, after several more frantic meetings, we figured out that Bob really did not know how to code very well. The project was due in only one week. To top it off, he finally told us that the parts of the project he *had* worked on had gotten "lost"—and he wanted to know if any of us had them! Bob refused to hand over any of the work he had done and never came to the team meetings.

The Web site team seemed content to sit and hope that Bob would pull through. Our team, however, was not content to do this, since every person in the course was going to receive the same grade for this team project. What should we have done? Should one of us have confronted Bob? Should all of us have confronted the Web team? How could we have salvaged the project with only one week left?

STOP! Before you read the rest of William's story, make a list of what you think went wrong in this project. What would you have done to resolve this problem? **#Create**

How could the team have either prevented the problem from occurring or wrested the project away from the controller sooner? **#Analyze**

The Resolution. The solution wasn't a pretty one, but it worked. Several members of the print team confronted the other members of the Web site team and told them that they *must* get Bob to hand over his work. Then they needed to find a way to complete the project themselves within the next week. By this point the Web site team was frantic, so they agreed. Bob never handed over any of the project in his possession, and the Web site team had to start over from scratch. They turned in the project a few weeks late, but they did get it done.

During this project, we made serious mistakes in neglecting procedural issues. We needed a fuller understanding of each person's strengths and weaknesses before we divided into teams. All the "leader" types ended up on one team, while all the "laid-back" types ended up on the other team. We also mistakenly understood *team* to mean "leaderless." We should have appointed one leader for the entire project, as well as a leader for each team. We also mistakenly thought that each group could function in isolation from the other and waited too long to talk about our progress and compare notes.

The Case of the Angry Administrator: Maggie's Story

Workplace collaborations frequently involve working with people who may not be as well informed about the organization's standards (which might include policies, guidelines, and procedures) as you are. Those who are not as informed as they should be often tend to blame their coworkers for their own inadequacy, resulting in affective conflict that, at best, can be demoralizing and, at worst, can derail the project. As you read the Case of the Angry Administrator, you will be asked to consider what other avenues Maggie, the technical communicator/editor, might have used to educate and placate the administrator who was unhappy to find she had not been apprised of the company's most current standards.

Maggie's Story

The collaborative documentation project was a white paper profiling a new software product. The collaborators—including associates from software development, project management, documentation, and marketing/sales—had no formal project meetings, and the project manager worked for a different software development department than we usually work with. Most of the work was via email and on Google Drive.

I received a draft of the white paper as an email attachment from the project manager via my team leader. My role was to copyedit and proofread the white paper and return it to the project manager.

The Conflict. The fact that the project manager did not have the most current company-standard style guidelines and document templates turned out to be a major problem. As I was editing the document, I quickly realized that virtually none of the company standards/guidelines for formatting had been applied.

What do you see as other contributing causes to the problem? **#Understand**

What other avenues did Maggie have in dealing professionally with the administrator? **#Create**

What are several possible reasons for the problems Maggie faces? #Analyze

What solutions do you recommend for managing her problems? #Create

I called the project manager to discuss this. I asked her if she wanted me to implement the current formatting styles to the document or to pass it on to the marketing department without the changes. The project manager was not aware of many of the new styles and standards, and she expressed frustration and hostility. I sensed that she was very angry and annoyed with me *and* the project. She wanted to know *exactly* what needed to be changed. She mentioned that she should have already received the latest style and formatting information and did not appreciate being left out of the loop.

As a relatively new employee, I was not even aware of who *was* in the loop. I described some of the document's problems and invited her to stop by and look at a hard copy. She then came to my work area, so that I could show her some of the style issues. Again, the project manager seemed hostile and annoyed. However, I felt that I was being completely honest and professional in my project role. I asked her how she would like to see the changes and in what form she would like the edited document to be returned. She requested it to be sent as an email attachment, using Track Changes.

> **STOP!** Before you read the rest of Maggie's story, suggest what you would have done if you were Maggie. Then speculate about what you think actually happened and how things were resolved. **#Create**
>
> Finish reading Maggie's story to see if your speculations are on target.

The Resolution. I sent the project manager the template and two versions of the edited document: one with the template (standard formatting) applied, and one without. This is the text of the email I sent:

> I'm sending you two formats of the white paper: the first with only copyedits and the second with both copyedits and formatting changes. The second is formatted for duplex; you can change it to simplex if necessary. The white paper doesn't fit the standards the company had for software manuals/guides, so I adjusted certain parts (for example, headers and TOC) to comply with the guidelines.
>
> I am also sending you a link to the product terminology database (work in progress), in case you don't have the most current version. I am also sending you the GUI template along with the new covers, graphics, and anything else you should need. John Hoi is the template administrator; he has offered to answer any questions you may have about the template functions.
>
> Please call or email if you have any questions.
> Maggie Weisner
> X12345

I did not get any reply or feedback from the project manager. However, she did contact my team leader to complain that she had found two errors in my copyediting and that maybe I did not know how to do a copyedit. My team leader assured her (and me) that the errors were not substantive, and I did know how to copyedit. The complaint seemed petty and unrelated to the primary conflict.

I don't think that much, if any, of the conflict was resolved. I assume that the project manager was able to incorporate my editing and formatting changes via the email attachments. I assume that the project manager will use the template and standard guidelines for future projects. My team leader assured me that I fulfilled my role correctly and professionally. He mentioned that some of the people that I will be working with might be hostile, and most of them won't offer feedback. The most important thing for a writer/editor is to complete the requested task accurately and as scheduled, leaving as little room as possible for miscommunication.

How do you assess the way Maggie actually handled the problem? #Evaluate

What would you have done in her situation? #Create

The Case of the Reprehensible Reviewer: Lloyd's Case

Many classroom and workplace projects have a formal review cycle built into the schedule. Collaboration on major projects often extends beyond the immediate and primary team to include the people doing these reviews. These reviewers are typically professionals who have no direct link to the project at hand, but they do have the expertise to comment in substantive ways. An often-unstated assumption when material is sent to a reviewer is that the reviewer will treat the material confidentially. In the Case of the Reprehensible Reviewer, the reviewer violated this assumption. As you read the details of this story, you will be asked to suggest ways that the primary author might have handled the situation differently—or even prevented it, had he anticipated it.

Lloyd's Story

A couple of years ago a colleague and I were writing computer exercises to accompany a training manual. We had completed the actual exercises and had drafted a seven-page introductory statement, the purpose of which was to try to persuade reluctant teachers to consider using computers in their classrooms.

To persuade our audience, we'd taken some of the arguments people commonly make against using computers in the classroom ("computers are inherently evil," "they are inherently gendered and will further gender my classroom," "I'm resistant because I don't know how to use all the new software") and tried to gently contradict them. We decided to seek some outside reviewers to learn if our intro was on the mark, so I asked a colleague at another university to do a peer review; when he agreed, I emailed him the intro.

The Conflict. Several days later, I received an email from the colleague that began "I hope you don't mind. . . ." He said that he'd found himself "incredulous" at our introduction and had therefore taken it upon himself to email portions of it to an online discussion list that almost 3,000 technical writers subscribe to, to see what they

What are several possible reasons for the problems Lloyd is facing? #Create

Should Lloyd have anticipated the reviewer's behavior? #Analyze

How else could Lloyd have handled the situation? #Evaluate

What solutions do you recommend for managing Lloyd's problems? #Create

What would you have done in his situation? #Evaluate

thought. I quickly logged on to the list and found *myself* incredulous: he'd cut our intro significantly, sending out only the arguments that we refuted, making it seem that *we* were making those arguments. For the next several days, we were publicly (if anonymously—he had left off our names) excoriated on the list for being "out of touch ivory-tower academics."

> **STOP!** Before you read the rest of Lloyd's story, suggest what you would have done if you were Lloyd. Then speculate about what you think actually happened and how things were resolved. **#Create**
>
> Finish reading Lloyd's story to see if your speculations are on target.

The Resolution. I called my colleague at home, because I was angry at what I saw as a violation of our collaboration and of the very notion of peer review, which is normally designed to take place *outside* the public gaze. He defended his actions, and I hung up still angry, although not before asking him to at some point send us *constructive* feedback on our introduction. He never sent any.

The Case of the Doddering Director: Lynn's Case

Collaborative projects, particularly ones in government agencies, are constrained in many important ways by state and federal regulations. In the Case of the Doddering Director, you will read about a project in a state social service agency that had a federal mandate to use technology that the old-fashioned director was completely opposed to. The lead for this project tried a number of conciliatory strategies to help the director understand the role of technology and agree to its use on this project, including setting up a meeting with one of the state's attorneys who explained the legal mandate to the section director.

What are several possible reasons for the problems Lynn's team is facing? #Create

What solutions do you recommend for managing these problems? #Create

Lynn's Story

I inherited the position of lead for a project to develop the method for implementing the procedures for adoption cases into the existing computer program used by field staff. I was working with a joint committee of social workers and technical people.

The Conflict. Numerous conflicts existed from the inception of the project, prior to my coming on board. The section director from Central Office was unwilling to find compromises and seemed completely closed to the use of appropriate technology even though this is a federal requirement and would improve record keeping. During a lengthy stalemate, some unwieldy interim procedures were eventually agreed upon and implemented. I took over at this point. The conflict was not immediately obvious to me; I took some weeks to figure out the problem by talking individually to various people on the committee. The animosity appeared to be between the technical and social work staffs, even though some on the technical side had previously been social workers (myself included).

The committee continued to meet but no resolution could be reached. The two sides showed some improvement in relationships, which seemed to be the result of my background that acted as bridge building. Some of the social work staff had been my central office contacts while I was working in the field up to a year prior to working with this committee. I made the time to work with some of these people on the actual program so they would become more familiar and comfortable with the technology.

I continued discussing the situation with my superior, who finally called a meeting, at which he, his superior, and an attorney were all present to interpret the federal requirement. The idea was to clarify the conflict and refer it up the hierarchy for resolution by the cabinet director. For unknown reasons, no resolution was reached. The technical staff proceeded working on the specific data fields required for federal reporting and were able to complete them. However, the process for field workers to enter this data remained complicated and unwieldy.

> **STOP!** Before you read the rest of Lynn's story, stop reading and suggest what you would have done if you were Lynn. Then speculate about what you think actually happened, how things were resolved. **#Create**
>
> Finish reading Lynn's story to see if your speculations are on target.

The Resolution. About nine months after I took over, the section director retired. The new director is more open to complying with federal requirements and was committed to finding solutions. We are now working together without the tension of unresolved conflict and are well on the way to an agreeable solution.

How do you assess the way Lynn actually handled the problem? **#Evaluate**

What would you have done in her situation? **#Create**

If you were the lead on this project, what additional attempts at resolution might you have tried—ones that wouldn't alienate the director or other members of the team? **#Create**

Acknowledgments: This article evolved from research by Rebecca E. Burnett, published in *Making Thinking Visible: Writing, Collaborative Planning, and Classroom Inquiry* (NCTE, 1994), in *Professional Communication: The Social Perspective* (Sage, 1993), and in *Hearing Ourselves Think: Cognitive Research in the College Writing Classroom* (Oxford UP, 1993). We thank the following people for their insights about classroom and workplace collaboration. Their observations provided useful details for the scenarios presented here: Mary Carey, David Clark, Sharon Wiederanders, and several other anonymous contributors. —Rebecca E. Burnett and Elizabeth Wardle

ASSEMBLING YOUR TECHNOLOGIES AND YOUR TEAM

CONTENTS

By this point you have an idea of the *what* and the *how* of your project, and you've found some sources that can help you get started. Now you need to think about the practical steps you will take to start building your project. This chapter covers some possibilities for designing multimodal projects, asks you to consider the affordances of various technologies, and encourages you to think about the best practices for working in groups and sharing your assets as you proceed. In this chapter, we'll show you how to put together a technology review, a group contract, a project proposal, and a style guide. These documents will help you focus your efforts as you proceed with your multimodal project.

How Do I Make a Multimodal Text?

When it comes to building a multimodal project, there are hundreds of technology options to choose from. Any number of technologies may work best for your *current* project, but next month you might be working on a completely different project that needs a totally different piece of technology, so we can't just say "Use Dreamweaver!" or "Learn Movie Maker!" Instead, we're going to show you how to *learn how to learn* which technologies might be most useful for you in any given writing situation.

To figure out which technology is best suited to your multimodal project, you need to know what technologies are available. The short list of technologies on page 179 can be used to create or edit different media. The list includes some of the most common and most often used applications, but plenty of other software is available, and more is developed all the time. (This list may be outdated, as technologies change rapidly, but searching for some of these programs might help you find other, more up-to-date ones.)

Technology Choices for Multimodal Authoring

I need to design . . .	I can use . . .
Video	Windows Movie Maker, iMovie, Final Cut Express, Final Cut Pro, Avid, Adobe Premiere, Sony Vegas
Audio	Audacity, GarageBand, Logic Pro, Peak, Pro Tools
Images	GIMP, Adobe Photoshop, Adobe Illustrator, Picasa, Adobe Fireworks, Corel Painter, Adobe Lightroom, CorelDRAW, Microsoft Paint
Web Site	Adobe Dreamweaver, KompoZer, text editors
Blog	Blogger, WordPress, Weebly, Moveable Type, TypePad
Pages/Posters	Publisher, Adobe InDesign, most word-processing programs, construction paper, stencils, printer, scissors, ruler, etc.
Animation	Xtranormal, Blender, Adobe Flash, Comic Life
Slide Show	PowerPoint, Keynote, Prezi, Microsoft Photo Story, Google Docs Presentations
Screen Captures	Snapz Pro X, Camtasia, Snagit, Screencast-O-Matic, Jing
Micro- and Multimedia Blogs	Tumblr, Twitter, Storify, Pinterest, Jaiku

Remember that your multimodal project doesn't have to be digital. Many of the technology examples listed in the table above require screen-based presentations of your multimodal project, but that type of presentation may not be what you need. Perhaps you'll be delivering your multimodal project on posterboard at a meeting, or as a printed brochure, or as a flyer hung on the town bulletin board. However, even if you're planning to deliver your project on paper or in person, you may still need to gather digital assets and use digital technologies to produce it; for example, you may want to use InDesign to create a printed brochure.

When choosing a technology, you should also consider how people will actually view or use your final project. If you create a video, for example, you might choose to distribute it on a site like YouTube or on a DVD. We'll talk about distribution options in more detail in Chapter 21.

Case Study Assessing Technological Affordances

Ariel was asked to compose a genre analysis Web site. She knew she wanted to compose a Web-based comic, but she wasn't sure which Web editor would be the best choice. Ariel had never done any Web design before, so she had to carefully think through what would work best for her given her project, her timeline, and her learning style.

Ariel knew she wanted to create a very simple Web site so that the comic itself would be the visual focus on the page. Someone reading a print-based comic can usually see many panels at once, but Ariel felt that her comic would be more effective if the user could see only one panel at a time. Because of this, she decided her Web page needed to have a slide show embedded in it. She also wanted to learn a bit more about coding in HTML, but she was hesitant to code from scratch since she had never done it before and had only a limited amount of time in which to get the project done. Given that she wanted a simple page and an embedded slide show and was willing to play around with code, she decided to search for a free HTML template that she could modify.

Ariel downloaded a template from freecsstemplates.org (see **Fig. 9.1**) and began playing with the code, using the basics that Kristin provided and tutorials she found online. She edited the colors and headers to her liking and then inserted her comic into the slide show. Ariel knew a little about HTML and was willing to learn a bit more, but she wasn't confident about starting from scratch; thus the template was the best choice for her. While she was worried about the template looking a bit bland, the design of the comic itself gave her site visual interest.

FIGURE 9.1 ▶
Free CSS Template
Ariel used this free HTML template from http://www.freecsstemplates .org/preview/throughout. Ariel's final version of her site deleted the bottom section of the template.

The purpose of the comic varies, also, depending on the author. For some it is for money, others for fame, most of them it's for fun, and then I assume the pressure to keep it going starts coming in from a growing audience, which we discussed what that is in the last panel. It might make a difference to say that all are also publishing books of their comics, PHD runs in a school newspaper (or a few), and both the authors of GWS and QC are "professional webcomic artists", meaning they make a living off their comics. Obviously they are popular comics, but how do they do it?

◀ FIGURE 9.2
A Panel from Ariel's Comic, Drawn in Microsoft Paint
See Ariel's final Web site at bedfordstmartins.com /writerdesigner.

Choosing an image editor for drawing her comics was significantly easier. Ariel knew she wanted a crude, hand-drawn look similar to that found in Hyperbole and a Half. Microsoft Paint, the program used by Allie Brosh to draw Hyperbole, would achieve the rhetorical effect Ariel was looking for and was easy for her to use, and she already had it on her home computer.

Organizing and Sharing Assets

If you're working in a group, or even if you're working alone but across multiple computers in a lab, at work, or at home, you'll need to find a good way to share your multimodal assets. Using a USB flash drive or an external hard drive can work in some cases—except when you lose it, forget to bring it with you, drop it, or try to save files on it that are too big. Online storage sites are a great alternative. These sites allow you to register (sometimes for free) and save files remotely on their Internet servers so that you can access the files from any other computer, smartphone, or netbook connected to the Internet. These sites are usually password protected, so you can back up your private files online (although the sites do come with security risks, so don't upload all your banking information!), and you can share project-based folders with anyone you are collaborating with.

No matter what type of sharing system you use, it's good practice to name and organize your files and folders clearly. Doing so will help you find items and keep track of which assets you've already edited, and it will also help other users collaborate, edit, or revise your project later, whether or not you're there. In this section you'll find some tips for naming, organizing, and sharing your assets. These tips are specific to certain kinds of media files. For instance, avoiding spaces and punctuation in filenames is useful when producing multimodal projects in certain kinds of technological systems (Web sites, audio files, etc.) but not as important with other types of systems (presentation software like Prezi or blogging platforms like

Technology Review

Based on your project idea, review the table on page 179 and choose a set of programs that you think might be the best match for your project's needs. (Depending on your project, you may need several different kinds of programs, such as a photo editor, an audio editor, and a Web editor.) Create a chart for each technology or program you want to explore. In the left column of each chart, list the questions below.

» What does this tool do? What is its purpose? (Is it an HTML editor, a sound editor, a social media application, or something else?) What kinds of texts are usually made using this technology?

» Is the tool platform-specific (Mac/PC/Linux), or is it only available online?

» Do you have access to this software? Do you already own a copy, is it installed on computers in labs you have access to, or is it available as a free download or on a trial basis for a long-enough period of time for you to complete your project?

» How does the program work? (This is not meant to be a huge tutorial; just note the basic compositional or editorial features.)

» How steep is the learning curve, and will you have the time and resources to learn enough about the technology to complete your project? What are some tutorial sites or videos that seem effective for learning the basics?

» What do you need to do before you can start designing in the technology? (Do you collect assets elsewhere and import them into the program, or do you "record" directly into it?) Do you need additional technologies, like an external video camera or audio recorder, to make this tool function the way it's supposed to?

» What are the benefits of using this particular technology for the genre of your multimodal project? What are the drawbacks? What does the technology do or not do that will affect how you compose a text in your chosen genre? What file formats does it import and export?

As you research a particular technology, jot down your answer to each question in the right column of the corresponding chart. Compare your answers about the different technologies to help you choose the technology that will best suit your needs. If none are suitable, pick another subset of programs and begin your research process again. Then, based on the affordances you've listed in your chart, choose which program (or set) you will explore further to complete your multimodal project.

WordPress). Although following a standard set of guidelines will ensure that your final project will work across all software and media types, you do have some flexibility in managing your assets depending on the genre, technology, and media you're using or producing.

Categorize Your Files Appropriately

Creating folders will help you keep your assets organized and will help you find them again when you need them, just as keeping your clothes organized in a dresser or on shelves makes it easier to dress yourself in the morning. Most effective folder structures are arranged in a hierarchy, with the broadest categories at the top and with the categories getting progressively more detailed as they go down. Follow these suggestions for using a folder structure to keep your assets organized:

» **Keep all of your project files in one place.** Some software programs require you to keep the files in a specific location. Research the requirements of your chosen software program and follow its instructions.

» **Create a folder structure** that will be easy to maintain throughout the design and revision process.

» **Name your files and folders** according to what they *are* and what they *do*. If you're using multiple images, sound clips, and videos, you might create three folders called *images*, *sound*, and *video*. (See the discussion of naming conventions in the following section.)

» **Create a separate folder for editable files** that won't go in the final project (we call these *working files*).

Use Good Naming Conventions

Certain types of technologies, such as the Web, rely on exact characters to find files. For example, if you save an .html page as "PuP-Pies.html," you will find it in a Web browser only by typing the exact filename—i.e., *not* "Puppies.html" or "puPPies.html." If you can't remember whether you capitalized the first (or second or third) letter, then you won't be able to find your file. Here are some best practices for naming files:

» **Use all lowercase letters in file-names.** If you know that you use all lowercase letters without exception, then you'll know to (1) name the file "puppies.html" and (2) look for "puppies.html" in your Web browser.

» **Use hyphens (-) or underscores (_) instead of spaces.** Web browsers and some multimedia editing programs can't read spaces, and/or they will translate them to a "%20" symbol (which nobody can understand), so it's best to avoid spaces entirely (as in the filename "student-interviews10-11.mov").

▼ FIGURE 9.3
Be Careful When Naming Something "Final"

"FINAL".doc

FINAL.doc!

FINAL_rev.2.doc

FINAL_rev.6.COMMENTS.doc

FINAL_rev.8.comments5.CORRECTIONS.doc

FINAL_rev.18.comments7.corrections9.MORE.30.doc

FINAL_rev.22.comments49.corrections.10.#@$%WHYDIDICOMETOGRADSCHOOL?????.doc

WWW.PHDCOMICS.COM

» **Be brief and informative.** Instead of naming an image "red_butterfly_on_ fence_in_spring.jpg," consider using "red_butterfly.jpg" as the filename. Or simply call it "butterfly.jpg" if this is your only image of a butterfly.

Use Version Control

You will likely compile multiple versions of your assets throughout your project. For instance, you'll need to crop that audio track from two minutes to ten seconds. If you are exchanging files or using an online, shared repository such as Dropbox, using version control is especially important, so that you don't accidentally save over a revised version, causing you to lose new work.

» **If you plan to include dates in your filenames, decide as a group what date format you will use.** Will it be MM_DD_YYYY (for example, "clip1_10_23_2011.mov") or MM_DD_YY? Dates in filenames are OK, but everyone on your team needs to use them in a consistent manner.

» **Use an online version control system**—Git, Subversion, Mercurial, etc. (some of them are free)—that automatically assigns versions to your project files. Using these can be a little more complicated than just naming a file, but they will ensure that there is no confusion among versions, particularly if you are collaborating on different stages of a project. They also provide cloud-based backups of your work.

write/design assignment

Creating a Style Guide

A style guide is a set of agreed-upon standards that a group uses to write, design, and edit documents. Search the Web for "information architecture guides," "file-naming conventions," and "version control" to get a sense of what information you might include in your style guide. Discuss with your project team the best way to organize and share your assets, based on the best practices you have found through your research. Your style guide should include plans for naming, storing, and sharing assets as well as a brief description of why your group has chosen to follow this particular style, based on the technologies you plan to use and the kinds of assets you found in this chapter's other assignments. (Refer back to your technology review from earlier in this chapter and your source list from Chapter 4. You can use this style guide in writing your proposal, which we'll discuss next, and in creating documentation for your clients, which we'll discuss in Chapter 21.)

Proposing to Get It All Done

By this point, you have done a lot of work to brainstorm, pitch, and research the content and design of your project and to consider the best practices for collaborating. Now it's time to pull all that information together and map out in detail what you plan to do and how you plan to get there. It's time to write your proposal.

A **proposal** describes what you define as the scope of a project and how it will be completed. A proposal is a common and important document used to get suggestions and feedback on your detailed plan from an instructor, a boss, a stakeholder, or a client and to gain approval for moving forward with your project. Putting together your proposal will also be helpful as you move forward with designing and building your project; it's a chance to make sure that you have a solid plan, that you have all the materials you'll need, that you know how to use the tools you want to use (or have a good plan for learning how to use them), and that you have a realistic schedule for getting everything done.

Proposals can take many forms, such as business plans, cover letters for job applications, workshop and fellowship applications, conference proposals, grant applications, and even party invitations. Different genres of proposals have their own conventions, so when you're asked to put together a proposal for a particular situation, always research what kind of proposal will be appropriate and what sorts of information you'll need to include.

Whatever the genre of your proposal, however, here's some information that you should think about including:

» **Introduction/summary.** Give an overview of what your project is about, how you will approach it, what genre you will use, and how that genre fits the rhetorical situation.

» **Project plan.** Explain in detail how you plan on designing the project to support your argument; be sure to describe which technologies you will use, how you will gain access to or create media assets, and how you will integrate your research.

» **Justification.** Discuss why your proposed design is appropriate and effective for making your argument. (Your genre conventions checklist on page 138 in Chapter 6 will be helpful here.)

» **Roles and responsibilities, if you're working with a group.** Identify which group members are responsible for which project activities. If you have a group contract, consider attaching it to the proposal.

» **Timeline.** Give a detailed work plan of how and when you will complete all of the project's components, including a breakdown of your tasks at each stage of the project:

    » doing further research

    » preparing a storyboard or mock-up (discussed in Chapter 18, p. 704)

    » creating an asset list (discussed in Chapter 20, p. 784)

    » preparing a rough cut or draft (discussed in Chapter 17)

FIGURE 9.4 ▶

**Example of a
Timeline**

This is an example
of a detailed timeline
from Project Bamboo,
a consortium that
builds technology
infrastructure for
humanities scholars.

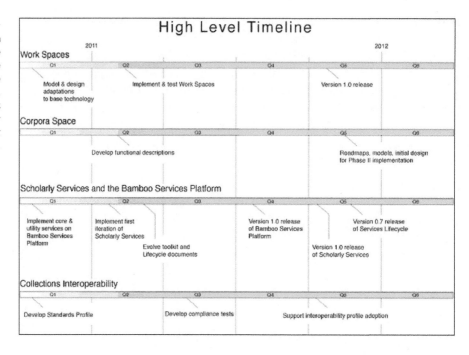

» revising and editing your final project (discussed in Chapter 21)

» delivering your project (discussed in Chapter 21)

You'll notice that this list includes information about parts of the writing and designing process that you have yet to complete! If you haven't yet started drafting your project, how do you know how it's going to work? Well, you'll make an educated guess and leave yourself some space to adjust. Even the best-laid plans require adjustment once you get into the thick of developing them. Build time into your schedule to account for problems and readjustments, and be open to feedback on your plan.

Once you've completed your proposal and gotten feedback on it, you are ready to begin the drafting process by creating a storyboard or mock-up of your project. We'll help you to do that in Chapter 18.

write/design assignment

Project Proposal

Write a proposal for your project that provides the basic information listed in the section above. Once your proposal is complete, get feedback from your instructor, classmates, stakeholders, and/or intended audience members. Use these responses to make refinements to your plan and to revise your ideas where necessary.

Managing Expectations for Digital and Team Projects GT

One of the exciting aspects of developing digital projects—especially those using audiovisual, gaming, and visualization platforms—is letting your imagination run wild in ways that it might not with more traditional print-based assignments. However, the challenge of digital projects is tempering your creative ambitions in light of your schedule and abilities.

As you plan a multimodal project, especially one that involves a group of your classmates, you should complete these steps:

1. Work as a group to identify individual strengths related to the project and determine ways work can be equitably distributed among group members (e.g., who has editing software installed on his or her computer? Who has experience running a video camera?). One group member should take on the role of project manager to keep everyone organized and ensure that all milestones are met. This practice works for all project work, but it is particularly valuable when you are working with an electronic platform that might not be familiar to everyone in the group.

2. Look carefully at the assignment milestones and due dates. Examine them in conjunction with your calendar; if you identify a date on which several assignments are due in a number of classes (a lab is due or an exam is scheduled), make sure that you leave yourself enough time to accomplish everything. Remember that professors are not always able or willing to give extensions. If your group is relying on you to complete your part of a project, you want to be sure you can manage their expectations of your participation.

Identify any steps of the project planning process that will be difficult for you. Then, identify steps you will easily accomplish. #Analyze

3. Consider the platform or platforms with which you are working. Keep some basic rules of thumb in mind. For example, one minute of edited video can require more than an hour of filming and many more hours of editing time. Programming even a simple video game demands a lot of execution time, even from group members who are familiar with programming.

4. Build time into your schedule for peer learning. You may be a whiz at podcast production, but the other members of your group may be interested in learning how to use the software as well. Share what you learn across the group so that everyone's knowledge is improved.

5. Work with your instructor throughout the project development process to be certain that the work you are doing aligns with the learning objectives and that you are meeting self-imposed and instructor-identified milestones. Performing periodic assessments like these increases the likelihood that your project will be both complete and successful.

When experimenting with media applications, especially those with which you and your classmates are not experts, concentrate on using the software to create a unique and effective message rather than a glitzy product. Manage your own expectations as well as those of your fellow group members and your instructor. Creating a shorter work (especially with audio, video, or computer programming) that is polished and speaks directly to the learning outcomes for the assignment is better than creating an unfinished longer piece because you ran into unexpected obstacles and out of time.

Composing with Teams in Digital Environments

Online collaboration tools have made working in groups to complete class assignments much simpler. Now you can meet with your classmates in Google Hangouts to brainstorm ideas during a video chat and then simultaneously write and edit a document in Google Docs, all without leaving your dorm room. Other collaborative tools like Dropbox, which allows you to upload and download documents, and Zotero, which allows you to form collaborative groups for research and source organization, facilitate working together remotely or together in the classroom. However, working in a group in an electronic environment can be very different from working independently and can pose some unique challenges. To work effectively with your peers on electronic and online projects, remember to consider the following guidelines:

» Establish a protocol for communicating with your group members at the first meeting. You might all agree that email is the preferred way to keep in touch or that using text messages or Facebook is easier. Make sure to choose a method that all group members have access to and are comfortable with. Many software applications are device or platform specific. Whichever method you choose, be sure to set up clear guidelines about how you will communicate and define what constitutes a timely response.

» Similarly, at your first meeting you should also establish what electronic tools or platforms you prefer to use for your collaborative work. Rather than having everyone share individual documents via email, set up a Google Drive folder to which everyone can contribute (to do this, you need to have a Google account). You can agree to work on the document asynchronously (on your own time) or synchronously (by setting a time to meet "in" the document). If you work on the document at the same time, you will be able to see each other editing the document, and you can chat about the process in the sidebar chat room. If you are working in a different environment — for example, if you are creating a Web site or a blog — you should ensure that everyone has editorial access to the site and can work on it independently; then you might choose to have everyone track additions and modifications in an editable document (Google Drive) or wiki. At the same time, you should all also decide how you will connect to discuss your progress on the project. Face-to-face meetings are often preferable and more effective, but when that is not possible you might choose to chat on T-Square or Facebook, have a conference in Skype, or video chat in Google Hangouts.

» As you set goals and assign tasks, decide as a group where you will save drafts and how you will name documents (come up with a consistent file-naming system), how you will keep track of edits, and who will be responsible for turning in deliverables. The strategies for implementing naming conventions and version control, listed earlier in this chapter, will help you make these decisions.

» When you are working together in a digital environment, remember to pay attention to the basic rules of *netiquette*. Always communicate with your group members *as if* you were in the same room. Remember that sometimes tone and nonverbal aspects of communication can get lost in online communication. Be sure to keep track of the work you have done and save multiple drafts. If you are editing someone else's work, save a backup of the original first, in case any of the group members disagree with the changes you have made. Using Track Changes in a Word document or editing text in a wiki allows you to keep track of the document's history.

Revising with Teams

Giving and receiving feedback is a collaborative process, even for individual projects. On an individual project, you should give and receive feedback from others about how well your artifact meets your goals and the project assessment criteria. Testing your work with a colleague or friend is a great way to make sure your communication is clear and effective, and critiquing what other people have produced can give you ideas to improve your own projects. However, many of the projects assigned in any of your Georgia Tech courses will be team-based projects. Team projects afford you even more opportunities to create and receive feedback during every stage of your project's development. Whether each team member has a specific role or the team works collectively, feedback is essential to meeting your project goals; use your team as a built-in peer review group, providing one another with feedback and advice throughout the project. In a team project, you should gather feedback from and give feedback to individual team members at multiple stages including brainstorming, drafting, and final polishing. You should also work collectively as a team to give feedback to and receive feedback from other teams to refine your team's overall project. Soliciting internal feedback from your team members and external feedback from other teams helps you revise to make sure your final artifacts are cohesive and unified.

While these strategies for revising team projects can be adapted to giving and receiving feedback on individual projects, you will find more strategies for drafting, peer review, and revision of individual projects in Chapter 21.

▲ PHOTO
Agency for Toxic Substances and Disease Registry (ATSDR) Town Hall Meeting
Your group's dynamics influence the quality of your projects. For example, group members can help each other to understand multiple points of view represented in source materials. Working with a group increases the likelihood that you'll consider a broad range of rhetorical factors such as context, purpose, and audience. *Cade Martin/Centers for Disease Control and Prevention.*

Although feedback is an essential part of any collaborative process, critiquing or revising a teammate's work can be difficult. You don't want to offend or upset a classmate, but your grade may be partially dependent on the work of others, so you have a stake in the final result.

This section offers strategies not only for developing an atmosphere in which to share feedback with teammates but also for learning to accept feedback professionally, gracefully, and gratefully. Recall the cases of collaborative interactions that went awry, discussed in Chapter 8. One of your goals should be to develop collaborative strategies that prevent such problems from occurring or that resolve them quickly and effectively if they do occur.

When team members feel comfortable critiquing and revising one another's work, the team draws on everyone's strengths and insights, producing a superior product. Developing a strong revision process and a team culture in which constructive critique is welcomed and encouraged allows your team to focus on what is best for the project without worrying about hurt feelings or who "owns" a particular section of the project.

Historical Collaborative Revision

Did you ever consider that important historical artifacts were at one point living documents—drafts that were revised over and over? Look up the U.S. Declaration of Independence to remind yourself of the language. Then do an Internet search for <original rough draught of the Declaration of Independence> (with the original spelling!). Your search should locate the Library of Congress reconstruction of Thomas Jefferson's initial draft compiled by Professor Julian Boyd. The draft shows the text before it was revised with feedback from other members of the committee and Congress. Consider how comparing the original manuscript to the final version illustrates the collaborative process of feedback and revision, showing many places where words and phrases were changed. The document underwent a dramatic revision of its language.

HISTORICAL DOCUMENT ▶
Thomas Jefferson

A living document, this "original Rough draught" of Jefferson's work shows the many levels of changes that Congress and committee members asked for before accepting and supporting the Declaration of Independence. Each small change in language has an effect on our current legal system and legal education. *Library of Congress.*

Developing a Culture in Which Constructive Feedback Is Encouraged

The dynamics of your team greatly influence the effectiveness of the feedback that you give and receive. In the workplace, you will often be called on, both in person and electronically, to engage in semi-public critique of others' work. Developing strategies for giving feedback can make you a sought-after colleague; graciously accepting and implementing feedback can make you a desired teammate. However, before you can create effective, focused feedback you need to intentionally create an atmosphere within your team that allows feedback to be both given and received; you must be brave enough to be critical about the work of others and brave enough to accept feedback yourself without becoming defensive. Keep in mind that being brave does not mean acting without tact, thoughtfulness, and sensitivity.

Here are four steps your team can follow to develop a culture in which constructive feedback is encouraged:

1. *Build revision and feedback into the task schedule.* Creating a task schedule that includes time to comment on or revise one another's work not only

Before making a plan to complete your project and decisions about software and tools your group will use, read Part 6 of this textbook to ensure you've thought through each stage of your process—topic brainstorming, planning, researching, drafting, reviewing, revising, editing, and so on.

Recall an unsuc-
cessful or stressful
group project. How
did the feedback
process (or lack of
one) affect the out-
come? #Remember
#Evaluate

encourages team members to give feedback but also helps them accept feedback as part of the necessary work that goes into a successful collaborative
document. If writers know that other team members are required to provide
suggestions for change (or are required to make revisions), they do not take
these suggestions or revisions personally. Scheduling revision and feedback
into the task schedule creates a team culture in which constructive feedback
is simply part of completing the project, not a negative reflection on anybody's
work.

List ways your team
might establish and
enforce guidelines
for revision. Then,
compare them to
identify the most
effective ones.
#Identify #Evaluate

2. *Decide on a revision process and follow it.* This chapter describes two basic
models for revision: feedback and direct revision. Many teams use a combination of these two methods. For instance, a team might use feedback at
the beginning of a project to provide global suggestions for a writer and then
switch to direct revision at the end. After considering the advantages and disadvantages of these methods, your team should decide how to handle revision
at various stages of the project and create a task schedule that reflects this
decision.

What software tools
have you already
used for collabora-
tive projects? List
each program's
advantages and
disadvantages to
help you select your
tools. #Remember
#Create

3. *Use writing software that keeps a history of revisions.* This chapter describes
three software tools that help with collaborative authoring by tracking all the
changes made to a document. These tools allow one team member to revise
another member's work while still preserving the original copy. They also make
it easy to undo revisions that the team disagrees with and to offer provisional
changes that can easily be reversed. The team can use the software to compare
different versions of a document and to discuss the pros and cons of individual
changes.

Team contracts
help members
define appropriate
behavior. Define ele-
ments of feedback
etiquette that lead
to effective team
projects. #Under-
stand #Evaluate

4. *Include a statement about the importance of revision and feedback in the team
contract.* Once your team decides on a revision process, you can note this in a
team contract along with a statement acknowledging that the team agrees that
providing honest and constructive feedback is essential to a quality project and
that all team members agree to provide thorough feedback on one another's
work to the best of their abilities.

Before You Start: Ground Rules for Revision When writers submit work
to teammates for direct revision or comments, they should first take a moment to
clarify the state of the draft and the goals for revision. Initially, you should tell the
reviewer(s) the state of your draft. Simply put, where are you in the overall process?
Do you see the draft as nearly final, needing only minor editing and polishing?
Or is it very rough, needing major reorganization and content changes? Have you
submitted a draft missing major sections, with plans to add those sections later?
Whenever you hand off a draft to others for comment or revision, you should provide a brief statement summarizing the state of the draft and outlining the types of

changes you believe the draft needs. This explanation helps teammates gauge their feedback. For instance, if a teammate believes that a draft needs major changes but you see it as close to finished, that teammate should expect some resistance and, therefore, should provide detailed justification for the proposed changes.

Second, you need to clarify the goals of the revision or feedback. If the draft is very rough, sentence-level editing would be a waste of time because entire sections may be deleted or entirely changed during the revision process. If the project is nearing the final deadline, seeking or offering major suggestions or revisions may be inappropriate. Taking a moment up front to agree on the goals for your feedback can help your team use its time more effectively. Reviewers and coauthors need to make sure that they understand the goals of the project as a whole before they respond to the writer. Thus, before responding to or revising a draft, teammates should take time to review the assignment instructions to ascertain what the final product should look like.

CHECKLIST: Giving Feedback during the Initial, Rough Stage

Use this checklist to help you develop your feedback once you've clarified that this is the rough draft and your goals are to identify global changes.

- ☐ **Begin with praise.** In your discussion with the writer, note one or two things that this draft does really well—even if all you can say is that the draft does a good job getting some ideas on the table.
- ☐ **Identify/fix oversights.** Look for parts of the text that do not meet the assignment requirements or do not match what the group decided on.
- ☐ **Suggest/add new material.** What else could be included that would strengthen this draft?
- ☐ **Note/revise misleading or inaccurate information.** Look for places where the information included is presented in a misleading way or is simply wrong.
- ☐ **Suggest/implement alternative organizations.** Do you think the organization could be improved? Would you recommend reordering some of the sections? Or creating new headings to make the material easier to skim? Should the recommendations be in a bulleted list rather than in paragraph form? Should any tables be reorganized to better communicate the data's message?
- ☐ **Identify/resolve inconsistencies in content and argument.** Look for inconsistencies in the information and arguments included. You can address inconsistencies in formatting or vocabulary in later drafts.

Providing Effective Feedback   If you have been assigned to provide written feedback to a teammate or directly revise a draft a teammate has prepared, you should take time to provide thoughtful suggestions. You don't have to be certain about every suggestion you propose. After all, other people are commenting as well, and the team can decide later which suggestions are good ones. However, you should be constructively critical of the draft. This constructive criticism is key to creating a strong final project and is a major part of teamwork.

Before you provide feedback or make revisions on a draft for a class assignment, make sure you completely understand the project's requirements:

» **Review the assignment instruction sheet.** Make a checklist of the criteria for the assignment. Then read the draft and compare it against this checklist.

» **Check against the grading rubric.** If the instructor has distributed a grading rubric (a sheet that lists the evaluation criteria for the assignment), carefully check your team's document against this rubric to make sure that all the criteria are met.

» **Review the team contract.** Make sure you understand the main goals that the team has set forth in the contract.

Because writers often have difficulty seeing shortcomings in their own writing, someone other than the original writer(s) needs to check the artifact for completeness and accuracy. Artifacts always benefit from having a fresh set of eyes review them.

Once you understand the project's requirements and have reviewed the draft, you are ready to give feedback or implement revisions. Depending on how far along the project is, you can use the checklist preceding this section for initial rough drafts or the one following for polished drafts to develop professional, responsible feedback for others.

CHECKLIST: Giving Feedback during the Final, Polished Stage

☐ **Begin with praise.** Note one or two things in this draft that are improvements over the previous draft.

☐ **Identify/fix oversights.** Look for parts of the text that do not meet the assignment requirements or do not match what the group decided on.

☐ **Note/revise misleading or inaccurate information.** Look for places where the information included is presented in a misleading way or is simply wrong.

☐ **Identify/resolve inconsistencies in content, organization, vocabulary, and formatting.** Look for inconsistencies not only in the arguments and information included but also in the organization, vocabulary, and format. Does the heading style change from one part of the document to another? Does the document use inconsistent terminology for the same idea? Does the document have any unexpected changes in the font or formatting?

☐ **Suggest/implement alternative formatting.** Do you think a different type of graph or table should be used? Would you recommend a different heading style or different font throughout?

☐ **Correct grammar and style.** Fix grammatical errors, wordy sentences, or awkward phrases.

Responding to Feedback and Making Good Revisions When you are given a group assignment, you will probably receive an explanation of how the group component will be graded. Some instructors will assign the same grade to everyone involved in the project; others may assign grades based on the final product and factor in each student's individual contribution/participation. Especially when all team members will receive the same grade, you need to take time to review, edit, and revise all elements of the project to ensure that the quality is consistent throughout the work; remember, you will all be responsible for the mistakes that any one group member makes.

As a group, you might want to establish how you will review and assess each other's work; for example, using the Review feature in Microsoft Word is effective for written documents. One tactic is to use a *peer review session* to look for problems or omissions in your project: ask a classmate to review your work and give feedback in written or oral form. If you will be graded both on the project as a whole and on your individual contribution/ participation, be sure to ask your group members to evaluate your individual work as well. Doing this evaluation midway through the project gives you time to improve your performance if necessary.

What approach is your instructor using to evaluate your collaborative projects for this course? #Understand

What nonverbal cues is the woman in the red sweater jacket using to show she's paying attention? How does she make her collaborator feel valued? #Analyze

▲ PHOTO
Agency for Toxic Substances and Disease Registry (ATSDR) Town Hall Meeting
You've seen these individuals in a visual earlier in this chapter working as a single group to solve a problem. Now they're working in pairs (often called dyads). Notice the nonverbal communication each person is displaying. Nonverbal cues foster an environment that invites discussion and constructive criticism among group members. *Cade Martin/Centers for Disease Control and Prevention.*

When you collaborate on a group project, you should also consider how each group member will be credited and to whom the project belongs as a piece of intellectual property. In most classes, collaborative work will belong to the group as a whole, but sometimes individual members may wish to divide up the work and claim ownership of their respective sections. You may choose to identify the authors/ creators of each part of the project on the artifact itself (for example, in an "About" page on a Web site or blog).

The ability to accept feedback represents a high level of professionalism that, as a student, you may not yet have had the opportunity to develop. A few situations might make giving or receiving feedback remarkably uncomfortable:

1. *You ask for feedback and really need it, but the reviewer gives you inappropriate feedback (e.g., too vague, inaccurate, or impossible to implement in the available time).* Consider following up with the reviewer to ask the person to provide details to support the generalizations. If that doesn't work, find another reviewer to provide a second opinion.

2. *Part way through a project that you've spent a great deal of time on you get feedback recommending a major overhaul.* You're devastated by the feedback—and resistant to the advice. Instead, consider how the audience for the project will react if you don't implement the recommended revisions. Be grateful that you have a reviewer who is sufficiently invested in your project's success to provide substantive feedback, even if it's advice you don't want to hear.

3. *You've spent a good deal of time providing detailed feedback, and the author does not appreciate it.* You send your feedback to the author, who rejects it and throws a temper tantrum. Unfortunately, the reality is that not everyone behaves professionally; however, you should always strive to be professional and mature, regardless of the actions of your collaborators or colleagues. If you need to respond to the author after the tantrum, make sure *your* response is professional.

4. *You encounter people who are unkind in their feedback.* You'll need to work with them, but you can model appropriate professional behavior and not respond as they do. The following techniques can help you accept feedback to improve your work for the intended audience rather than react emotionally, based on your connection to the piece as its author:

   » **Count to 10.** Before responding to feedback, give yourself a chance to recover from your initial reaction.

   » **Ask the person why he or she made this suggestion.** You may find that you and the other person agree more than you originally thought or that the person misunderstood or misinterpreted something.

Refer back to Chapter 8 to review various kinds of conflict that might productively or unproductively affect feedback you give or receive.

» **Understand criticism.** Before accepting or rejecting feedback, repeat back the criticism, the rationale, and the proposed solution (if presented), and then ask the person to confirm that you understood him or her correctly.

» **Receive comments by email.** If you have trouble accepting feedback in face-to-face situations, ask group members to use email to give their comments and suggestions. This gives you a chance to react to these suggestions in private and gives you time to tone down your initial reactions.

Responding to feedback may be one of the most difficult parts of working on a team. When your teammates offer feedback or revisions, do not respond defensively. If someone notes a problem, assume that some sort of problem exists—even if that person has mislabeled the problem or presented an incorrect solution. Do not reject any feedback until you have considered it from all angles.

Becoming a more capable collaborator requires you to develop several characteristics that are not immediately obvious: awareness of the constraints that might exist because of time and/or personality; familiarity with and ability to use digital tools; ability to give and receive productive feedback; and ability to use a workable process and to create and stick with a workable schedule. Set yourself the goal of becoming the teammate everyone respects and appreciates. Accomplish this goal by carefully and thoughtfully managing your individual and team projects. Establish clear group guidelines and be graceful, grateful, and professional as you work with others to transform your project development processes from an anxious mess to a confident, collected build to project success. Don't overlook assembling, managing, and critiquing your technologies and your team as critical components of any composing process.

10 ORAL PRESENTATIONS, AUDIENCE, AND EVIDENCE

CONTENTS

Analyzing Your Audience

Public speaking audiences base their expectations on many factors, which include internal as well as external ones. Audience members' existing beliefs and values, their knowledge (or lack of knowledge) about the speaker or topic, events happening in the outside world, and even the time of day or comfort of the speaking room all influence an audience's expectations. You need to know about these expectations in order to fulfill or deal with them. For every speaking situation, therefore, it is important to ask these questions:

» Why are members of the audience here?

» What are they expecting to hear in this kind of situation?

» What expectations do they have about me?

» What are they expecting to hear from me on this topic?

» What features of the environment (both internal to the speaking room and external to it) might affect audience expectations?

» In what ways will it benefit my presentation or argument to fulfill the audience's expectations?

» In what ways will it benefit my presentation or argument to violate these expectations? (For example, if your audience expects to be bored by a dry and lifeless presentation, how can you confront their expectations?)

NMAfA Docent James Brown, Jr., with Preschoolers

This docent modifies his presentation style to fit his audience of preschoolers. He uses physical actions and a puppet friend to engage child visitors with the art of Africa at National Museum of African Art (NMAfA). *Smithsonian Institution Archives, Image 2003-19519.*

How do you determine the beliefs, attitudes, values, experiences, and needs of an audience? One way to begin is to classify the audience in terms of its cohesiveness or togetherness. You can group audiences into five types: selected, concerted, passive, pedestrian, or organized.[1] Whatever its type, any audience will also have an existing attitude toward your position or topic—hostile, sympathetic, or neutral. In the following sections, we look first at the five types of audiences and then at audience attitudes.

Types of Audiences

The Selected Audience and the Concerted Audience   In a selected audience, the speaker and audience share a common and known purpose, but they do not necessarily agree on the best way to achieve their shared goals. As Democrats or Republicans gather at their convention, for example, they agree, in general, on what will help get their party's candidates elected. Nevertheless, as they work on the party platform, many disagreements arise concerning the best approach to take on issues like the economy or defense policy. Thus, your first task when addressing a selected audience is to channel any shared motives into a direction you have planned and developed.

The concerted audience is a subset of a selected audience and is therefore quite similar to it. Its members share a need to achieve some end and are usually positively disposed toward the speaker and the topic. They are inclined to do what the speaker suggests, but they still need to be convinced. When members of the Republican Party meet to put together a party platform, they are a selected audience—they have a common goal. But different wings of the party are likely to have different concerns about what should be included in the platform—each wing is a

---

[1]Harry L. Hollingsworth, *The Psychology of the Audience* (New York: American Book, 1935).

concerted audience. Your task when addressing a concerted audience is to capitalize on the audience's predisposition to accept your ideas.

Selected and concerted audiences are not common in a classroom setting, but it may be to your advantage to consider treating your classmates as one of these types of audiences. Ideally, all students at a university or college should share some goals and values. In particular, everyone is there to learn and grow. While this may seem idealistic, you should work from this basic assumption that your audience is invested in learning. The more you invest in your topic and your presentation, the more likely it is that your peers will be engaged and respond to your message.

The Passive Audience   In a classroom setting, you are most likely to encounter a passive audience. The passive audience is a group that is already gathered to hear the speaker, but its motivation level is low. When you speak in class, for example, an attendance requirement guarantees you the presence of an audience; it does not guarantee, however, that your audience will be interested in everything (or anything!) you have to say. Any time you address a passive audience, your first goal is to gain their attention. Then, your main task is to sustain and direct listeners' interest.

One way to sustain the interest of a passive audience is to treat them the way you might treat a selected or concerted audience. By speaking as if your audience shares your purpose, you change not only your expectations about the audience, but also their potential responses to your message or argument. Making a presentation to a class is a type of performance. You can shape an audience's response to your message by treating them as if they are already allies (as with a concerted audience). If the demeanor of your presentation positions your audience as sympathetic, but acknowledges a need to allay fears or address concerns (as with a selected audience), even the harshest critics may respond more favorably. But a skilled public speaker never assumes too much about an audience. While this tactic may work more successfully in a first-year composition class, a careful and practiced speaker will treat each presentation separately and analyze each audience carefully.

The Pedestrian Audience and the Organized Audience   The least cohesive group is the pedestrian audience—people who have no obvious connection with either the speaker or one another. For example, a fundamentalist preacher might stand on a busy street corner and attempt to attract a pedestrian audience (literally) by vividly describing people's sins and their need for salvation. Most of us are familiar with how such an audience reacts. At the other end of the spectrum is the organized audience. Organized audiences are completely devoted to the speaker and to the speaker's purpose. Some religious and political groups fall into this category, as do audiences who have committed themselves to a noncontroversial cause, such as honoring basketball star Allen Iverson on his birthday. Thus,

Audience Characteristics and Strategies

	Characteristics	Examples	Strategies
Selected	• Speaker and audience share a common and known purpose • Speaker and audience do not necessarily agree on best way to achieve shared goals	• Political party convention attendees • Students attending a campus meeting to discuss a specific problem	• Channel any shared motives into a planned and developed direction • Treat as sympathetic, but acknowledge need to calm fears or address concerns
Concerted	• Subset of a *selected* audience • Members share a need to achieve some end • Usually positively disposed toward the speaker and the topic • Inclined to do what the speaker suggests, but still need to be convinced	• A faction within a political party • A division within a company • Members of a campus club or organization	• Treat as if already allies • Capitalize on expected willingness to accept your ideas
Passive	• Already gathered to hear the speaker • Motivation level is low	• Your classmates • Office staff	• Capture their attention • Sustain and direct interest • Consider treating as *selected* or *concerted* (see above)
Pedestrian	• No obvious connection with either the speaker or one another • Least cohesive group	• Passersby on a street corner • People on the subway	• Work to attract the audience • Entertain them • Invite controversy
Organized	• Completely devoted to the speaker and to the speaker's purpose • Most cohesive group	• Some religious groups • Fan clubs	• Focus less on informing and persuading • Celebrate with them

informing and persuading organized audiences is typically less important than celebrating with them. An extreme such as the pedestrian or organized audience is unlikely in a classroom situation. Your audience is most likely to be passive, and in ideal situations, the audience may be selected or concerted.

Audience Attitudes

Identifying the type of audience you are facing is an important component of audience analysis, but it is only the first step. You also need to discover your audience's attitude toward and knowledge about your topic:

» A *hostile* audience is resistant to your message.

» A *sympathetic* audience probably already agrees with many of the points you are making, or at least is willing to listen to your position.

» A *neutral* audience does not have strong feelings one way or another.

▲ PHOTO
Agency for Toxic Substances and Disease Registry (ATSDR) Town Hall Meeting
At town hall meetings such as this, speakers must be prepared to interact directly with their audiences. Knowing the audience's attitudes toward your topic is essential to an effective interaction. *Cade Martin/Centers for Disease Control and Prevention.*

Not every member of an audience need share the same disposition, but the prevailing attitude of the audience is important to identify and acknowledge. The degree to which your audience is hostile, sympathetic, or neutral to your message can have a dramatic effect on how you deliver it.

The audience's attitude is sometimes difficult to predict, but often depends on the level of controversy surrounding your topic. You may have to assess the audience as you make the presentation and meet their reactions with your own counterresponses. Keep in mind that the audience's attitude toward your message is independent of what type of audience they are. For example, your class may be a passive audience, but they may also be hostile to your message. They just may not care to voice those differing perspectives. A passive audience may also be sympathetic, which may greatly decrease the dynamic feedback they offer. And a pedestrian audience is not always going to be neutral. Usually, any audience is made up of a mixture of hostile, sympathetic, and neutral members. Small clusters of any faction, though, may influence your presentation.

Hostile Audiences Although hostile audiences are not necessarily angry with the speaker or throwing rotten tomatoes, they do begin the presentation with a bias against the message of the speaker. Hostile audiences often offer feedback with their body language, for example, by looking away from the speaker, sitting with their arms crossed, or scowling and shaking their heads. Facing a hostile audience is challenging, but it also provides a potential source of energy for your presentation. The tension between the audience and your message can invigorate your delivery. A hostile audience is likely to pay more attention to your presentation, if only to scrutinize every detail and pick apart your arguments. Do not let the hostility of the audience members shake your delivery style; do not let any hostile audience members derail your train of thought or lead you off on unrelated tangents. Be prepared to answer a number of questions.

Sympathetic Audiences   Sympathetic audiences agree with at least the main idea of the presentation. Their opinions may still differ from that expressed in your presentation, but they are willing to listen to and consider your message with open minds. The fact that the audience is sympathetic may not be the most beneficial situation, though, for a dynamic or rousing presentation. If the audience is so sympathetic that they already know the details you are presenting or they feel that what you are arguing is a foregone conclusion, then you may find them becoming hostile, not to your message, but to the situation. They may feel that you are "preaching to the choir" and question your choice of subject. They may also become (or remain) passive. If you know in advance that the audience is sympathetic, do not rely on their body language or feedback to drive your delivery. Instead, keep them engaged through interesting new insights, dynamic body language and verbal delivery, and challenging explorations of the merits of the opposing arguments.

Neutral Audiences   Many audiences are neutral to your message. They may have no previous knowledge about your topic or have no firm opinions about the subject matter. The neutral audience is possibly the most interesting group to address because the substance of your presentation is likely to help sway their opinions one way or another. The next time you address this audience about the same subject matter, they may have shifted from neutral to sympathetic. Many of the challenges faced in dealing with a passive audience are also present with a neutral audience. Your main tasks are to gain the neutral audience's attention and to sustain their interest.

Communication Barriers

Communication barriers are problems that prevent you from getting your message across or that prevent your audience from responding in the way you hope. Listed on the next page are eight of the most common communication barriers that speakers encounter.[2] Most of these barriers arise from extremes and are resolved by seeking balance and compromise.

---

[2] R. P. Hart, *Lecturing as Communication*, unpublished manuscript, Purdue University, Purdue Research Foundation, 1975.

BARRIERS THAT INVOLVE CONTENT	BARRIERS THAT INVOLVE AUDIENCE AND DELIVERY
» Too much or too little information	» Level of feedback from the audience
» Information is fact-heavy or opinion-heavy	» Pace of presentation
» Information is too concrete or too abstract	» Chronology and logical organization
» Information is too general or too specific	» Intensity of speaker's delivery

Barriers That Involve Content   Your choices of information to include in an oral presentation may elicit the following communication barriers.

» **Too much information.** "Information overload" produces frustration as an audience feels buried by an avalanche of information and stops listening. You must analyze, filter, and succinctly and precisely deliver information in order for it to become useful knowledge. Your audience is attempting to analyze and filter that same information based on what you say and how you say it.

EXPLAIN SPECIALIZED LANGUAGE: Technical jargon and acronyms (mp3, AAC, RIAA, MPAA, 802.11b, IEEE 1394, etc.) are often confusing. Handouts or visual aids are useful for defining terms and abbreviations.

AVOID UNNECESSARY DETAILS: When giving a 5-minute presentation on copyright and media licensing, do not spend most of your time citing Senate propositions and House bills by number and date. Instead, give a broad overview with general terms and a handout with links and citations for more information to make your point more effectively.

» **Too little information.** Be aware of your audience's level of expertise and present enough information to challenge the average member. If you do not have enough information, you risk boring or insulting your audience. It is unlikely that you will complete the requirements of the assignment if you have too little information. But be careful not to confuse clarity and precision with having too little information. Seek a balance between "overload" and "skimming the surface."

DEFINE NEW TERMS: Take time when introducing each new term in context. Again, handouts are useful, as are projected presentations (PowerPoint, overheads, etc.). If the terms are not new for your audience, move more quickly through the material.

STAY FOCUSED: If your task is to compare and contrast the features of several blog service providers, spend only one paragraph in your paper, and one slide in your software or overhead presentation, defining a blog as a "web log" or online journal. Make the majority of the paper or presentation about the various service providers, not the uses of blogs, especially in a course about online communication.

» **Information is too factual or too inferential.** Ideal speakers are neither fact-spewing computers nor rambling philosophers. Rather, they know how to extend their listeners' knowledge by blending hard data and intelligent speculation. Most audiences want enough facts to support your inferences and enough inferences to answer the question "So what?" about the facts.

> MAKE FACTS EASY TO DIGEST: Consider placing numerical or statistical facts in a chart or graph. Audiences respond better to visualized information, especially when confronted with many numbers and figures.

> USE SOUND LOGIC: Do not fall into the trap of logical fallacies. Does your data really support what you are saying, or is it just conveniently similar to your own opinion? (For more about providing logical evidence, see p. 214.)

» **Information is too concrete or too abstract.** Curious, searching audiences demand that speakers satisfy their needs for both concrete and abstract information. If you carefully mix and match concrete and abstract material, you should be able to satisfy both of these audience demands.

> INTERPRET FACTS: Facts and figures are concrete. If you recite only fact after fact, your audience will grow bored or, worse, confused. You need to provide some analysis and interpretation of the facts for your audience.

> SUPPORT OPINIONS: Ideas, analyses, and interpretations tend to be abstract. If you offer only ideas and opinions, but have no concrete evidence to support your claims, an audience may find you untrustworthy or doubt your conclusions.

» **Information is too general or too specific.** By carefully and consciously moving from the general to the specific and back again, the speaker can introduce variety and improve the audience's chances of seeing both the forest and the trees.

> EXAMPLE: An article about assessing the reliability of an online encyclopedia offers a *general* statement that the task of checking facts and accuracy in an encyclopedia is too huge to do exhaustively or consistently. Not every article can be double and triple checked, so statistical and representative tests are used to verify reliability. The article then goes on to provide a *specific* example, noting that biographical information about Revolutionary War figure Alexander Hamilton offers a useful representative test due to conflicting information about his date of birth.[3]

---

[3]Robert McHenry, "The Faith-Based Encyclopedia," *Tech Central Station* 15 Nov. 2004, 3 May 2005 <http://www.techcentralstation.com/111504A.html>.

Barriers That Involve Audience and Delivery Four additional barriers to communication involve the circumstances of the presentation and the speaker's style in organizing and delivering the presentation.

» **Audience provides too much or too little feedback.** Because a presentation is primarily a one-way transmission of information, the speaker must find ways to assess whether the audience understands the content of the presentation. You can use a variety of techniques to obtain feedback from your audience—for example, you can watch the reactions of one or two representative members of an audience, or you can pause periodically to invite the audience to ask questions. Of course, if you focus too much on one or two members of an audience, you may lose the focus of your message. On the other hand, too much feedback or too many questions from the audience can disrupt the flow of your presentation or take up valuable time that you need to present your message. You need to balance getting feedback from the audience while keeping your presentation on course.

» **Information is presented too rapidly or too slowly.** Research suggests that "normal conversational delivery" is the best pace for covering material clearly and efficiently. If you talk too quickly or too slowly or do not allow enough time for the audience to absorb your major points, the audience will not be able to understand and retain as much information. Keep in mind that someone reading your paper can backtrack and reread complex points; someone listening to your presentation cannot.

» **Information is presented too soon or too late.** Fortunately, with careful preparation and the knowledge of a few elementary principles of organization, the "too soon/too late" problem is easily solved. For example, by remembering that listeners find it easier to move from the simple to the complex, from the concrete to the abstract, and from the immediate to the anticipated, you can often avoid moving into material

◄ PHOTO
Ellen Glassman
As a volunteer docent at the National Museum of American Art, artist and former high-school art teacher Ellen Glassman gives tours that depend on the feedback from her audience of students.
Smithsonian Institution Archives, Image 2004-10332.

too quickly. Similarly, by knowing that listeners have a need for pattern, chronology, and completeness, you are reminded that information must be "packaged" and organized for an audience to be able to absorb and retain it. (For more about organizing your presentation, see Chapter 11.)

» **Information is presented with too much or too little intensity.** If you get overly involved in the material you are presenting, the audience may feel you are more concerned about preaching or performing than you are about sharing information. On the other hand, if you merely go through the motions without conveying any interest in your topic, the audience will probably share your lack of enthusiasm.

By analyzing your audience and determining their attitudes and expectations, you will be better prepared to overcome potential communication barriers when you deliver your presentation. In the next section, you will learn more about choosing the information and evidence that will be most useful and convincing to your specific audience.

Adapting Your Ideas and Evidence

In your composition class, written assignments come with specific requirements, one of which may be to present your paper's information orally. Although writing and speaking are related and interdependent, your work is not finished when your paper is written. You may not have time to orally present all of the details in your paper. You need to identify the main ideas that will best help you accomplish the purpose of your presentation and the key evidence that will lead the audience members to accept what you tell them. Remember that you are *presenting* your ideas and scholarship, not *reading* the paper in its entirety.

If you have already written the paper, use the topic sentences of your paragraphs to help you identify main ideas to cover in your presentation. (If you did not create an outline before writing your paper, it's a good idea to do so now.) If you have more than three to five main points to cover in your presentation, consider ways to combine or synthesize the ones that are similar. You also need to decide which pieces of evidence from your paper will be most convincing to your audience of listeners.

Listening and Learning

Your oral presentation probably will present information to your audience that they do not know or that they have only a passing familiarity with. You want them to listen to you and internalize the information you provide. In other words, you want them to learn. You should keep in mind that your presentation is facilitating the audience as they learn new information. The following points may help you relate more effectively to your audience.

DRAWING ▶
The United States Senate, A.D. 1850
Senator Henry Clay speaking about the
Compromise of 1850 in the Old Senate
Chamber. Getting your audience to listen is
a critical part of being an effective presenter.
Keep in mind that individual members of
your audience will respond to different
techniques and appeals based on prior
knowledge and experience as well as on
the immediate circumstances (ambient
light, heat, distracting noise, etc.).
*SOURCE: P. F. Rothermel (artist),
R. Whitechurch (engraver); c1855.*

» *Individuals have different motivations for learning.* Although "What's in it for me?" and "There might be something of value that I can use" may reflect the bottom-line motivation of audience members, each person has a different motivator. Thus, it is important to build your message on audience analysis.

» *Learning is an individual activity.* The accumulation of knowledge, skills, and attitudes is an experience that occurs within and is activated by the learner. Although you can set the stage and do much to orchestrate a climate conducive to learning, learning is still an internal process.

» *Audience members have prior experiences.* The more you incorporate an audience's life experiences into the construction of a message, the more the audience will retain and use the information provided.

» *Learning results from stimulation to the senses.* An audience member learns better when you appeal to multiple senses. Learners learn best by doing. As Confucius stated it: "I hear and I forget; I see and I remember; I do and I understand."

Choosing Forms of Support

Within a learning framework, then, what specific verbal and nonverbal forms of support can you use to make it easier for the audience to retain and accept your message? Consider the following five forms of support: explanation, examples, statistics, testimony, and visual aids.

Explanation   Explanation is the act or process of making something plain or comprehensible. Providing a definition is one mode of explanation. This alternative can take a variety of forms.

» *Providing a dictionary definition.* Defining typically involves placing the item to be defined in a category and then explaining the features that distinguish the item from all other members of the category—for example, "*Primary* is a word that means 'first in time, order, or importance.'"

» *Using synonyms and/or antonyms.* Synonyms are words with approximately the same meaning—for example, "*Mawkish* as an adjective indicates that someone or something is sentimental, maudlin, or gushy." Antonyms are words that have opposite meanings.

» *Using comparisons and contrasts.* Comparisons show listeners the similarities between something unfamiliar and something familiar. Contrasts emphasize the differences between two things.

» *Defining by etymology (word origin) and history.* For example, "*Pedagogy*, a term used to describe the art and science of teaching children, is derived from the Greek words *paid* meaning 'child,' and *agogus*, meaning 'leader of.'"

» *Providing an operational definition.* An operational definition defines a process by describing the steps involved in that process—for example, "To create calligraphy, you begin with a wide-nibbed pen . . ."

To be effective, explanations must be framed within the experiences of the audience and should not be too long or abstract. You may have explanations in your paper that work well for your presentation as they are. For those that don't, adapt them for listeners—for example, turn a written operational definition into a live demonstration that shows the process to your audience.

Examples   Examples serve as illustrations, models, or instances of what is being explained. An example can be either developed in detail (an illustration) or presented in abbreviated, undeveloped fashion (a specific instance). An illustration—an extended example presented in narrative form—can be either hypothetical (a story that could but did not happen) or factual (a story that did happen). For example, a presenter might involve the listeners in a hypothetical illustration by suggesting, "Imagine yourself getting ready to give an oral presentation. You reach into your bag for the manuscript that you carefully prepared over the course of the past week. It isn't there! You madly search through everything in the bag." Whether hypothetical or factual, an illustration should be relevant and appropriate to the audience, typical rather than exceptional, and vivid and impressive in detail.

A specific instance is an undeveloped or condensed example. It requires listeners to recognize the names, events, or situations in the instance. A presenter, for example, who uses "President Dewey" as a specific instance of the dangers of poor sampling techniques when engaged in public opinion polling must know in advance that the audience will understand that Thomas Dewey was Harry Truman's Republican opponent who was mistakenly announced as the winner in the 1948 presidential election. Otherwise, this example will not make the point clear and vivid and, in fact, probably will confuse or distract the audience.

You may have specific instances in your paper that you can develop further into illustrations so that your audience can get involved and relate to what you are saying. Likewise, you may have illustrations in your paper that you want to mention but not take time to develop in full detail. You could reduce some of those illustrations to specific instances.

Statistics   Statistics describe the end result of collecting, organizing, and interpreting numerical data. They are often presented in graph or table form. Statistics are especially useful when reducing large masses of information to more specific categories, as in the following example accompanied by a bar graph.

» Adults who start smoking in their early teens are less likely to quit by age 30 than those who start later. Of those who start after the age of 16, 13.6 percent quit by age 30. But only 9.6 percent of those who start at the ages of 14–15 and 4.4 percent of those who start before age 14 quit by age 30.

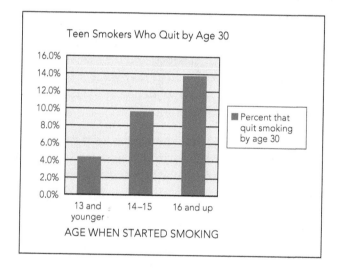

Statistics are also useful for emphasizing the largeness or smallness of something, as in the following example.

» Adults spend an average of 16 times as many hours selecting clothes—145.6 hours a year—as on planning for retirement—9.1 hours a year.

And finally, statistics can describe indications of trends—where we've been and where we're going. The following example describes a trend and summarizes the information in a table.

» According to a 1996 survey of 800 newspapers and magazines, 25 percent distributed at least part of their publications electronically. Another 31 percent intended to do so within 2 years; 19 percent intended to do so within 5 years; and 23 percent had no plans to do so.

ELECTRONIC DISTRIBUTION OF NEWSPAPERS AND MAGAZINES IN 1996

Already doing it (at least partially)	25%
Within 2 years	31%
Within 5 years	19%
No plans	23%

When using statistics, you should be aware of two basic concerns:

1. Are the statistics accurate and unbiased?

2. Are the statistics clear and meaningful?

To address the first issue, you need to answer such questions as these: Are the statistical techniques appropriate, and are they appropriately used? Do the statistics cover enough cases and a sufficient length of time? Although you may not have the expertise to answer such questions, you can ask about the credibility of the source of the statistics. Do you have any reason to believe that the person or group from whom you got the statistics might be biased? Are these statistics consistent with other things you know about the situation?

Addressing the second issue involves more pragmatic considerations: Can you translate difficult-to-comprehend numbers into more immediately understandable terms? How in the smoking example, for instance, might you make the difference between 4.4 percent and 13.6 percent more vivid? How can you provide an adequate context for the data? Is it useful in the electronic publishing example, for instance, to put together both newspapers and magazines when exploring use of electronic publication? Is the comparison between planning for retirement and selecting clothing a fair one? Would a graph or visual aid clarify the data and statistical trends? Supplementing a verbal presentation with visual aids can greatly increase the audience's comprehension and retention.

If conducted with rigor and proper scientific methodology, statistical research offers useful analysis of trends and potential outcomes. Be certain, though, that you properly cite the source of your statistics and do not rely on "they say" or "experts report." Also, be sure to give the context and scope of the study you cite. One danger of using statistics is the tendency to oversimplify the complexity of the critical question asked in the research study and to downplay the limiting factors that impact the outcomes. For example, a research study may find a statistical link between members of a specific cultural background and left-handedness, but if the study was limited to a test group of art school students, you should be sure to mention that the test group was in art school. You should not assume that the study's findings apply to members of the same cultural group who are interested in engineering or mathematics.

Testimony   Testimony involves using a credible person's statement to lend weight and authority to aspects of your presentation. For this to happen, the person being cited must be qualified; that is, the testimony must come from a person who is an expert on this topic and free of bias and self-interest. Just as important as actual credentials is the perception the audience has of the source of the testimony. Is the individual known to the audience? If not, you will need to tell the audience why the individual is a good authority. If known, is the person accepted by the audience as both knowledgeable and unbiased on the topic? In short, to lend support to a message, the testimony of a source must both be actually credible and be perceived as credible.

For example, recent articles on technology Web sites have debated the value of the online reference site Wikipedia.org. One such article, "The Faith-Based Encyclopedia," critiques not only the reliability of the data in Wikipedia entries, but also the entire notion of accountability within a free online reference written and edited completely by unpaid volunteers. Though the author of the article, Robert McHenry, is an expert on encyclopedias, his bias against the Wikipedia may perhaps be explained (or complicated) by his former position as editor-in-chief of the print edition of *Encyclopaedia Britannica*. Another related article, "Why Wikipedia Must Jettison Its Anti-Elitism," which appeared on the news Web site Kuro5hin. org, appears to be more even-handed in its critique of the Wikipedia; however, the article was written by L. Sanger, one of the founders of the Wikipedia, whose disagreements over how to run the Wikipedia "forked" the project in a new direction into another project called Nupedia. Though Sanger is a reliable source of information about Wikipedia due to his early involvement, his personal reasons for leaving may color and tarnish his objectivity about the subject. Appropriately objective information is found in a third article by technology writer Edward W. Felten, who has no ties to either Britannica or Wikipedia. Together, the three articles offer a number of informed perspectives, but Felten's piece is in many ways more compelling, even though he has no experience in reference writing or editing, either online or in print.

Visual Aids   Visual aids are primarily used to enhance the clarity and credibility of your message. They can also help you control your own nervousness by providing a safety net in an uncertain situation, reminding you of the structure of your presentation and the important points you want to make. Obtaining these advantages requires skill in selecting appropriate aids and using them well.

Choosing Forms of Proof

What motivates the audience to accept your claim about a fact, value, problem, or policy? Since the time of the ancient Greek philosopher Aristotle, forms of proof have been organized into three categories. Aristotle called them *pathos* (motivational proof based on the drives, values, or aspirations of the audience), *ethos* (ethical proof based on the credibility of the source of the message), and *logos* (logical proof based on evidence, such as statistics and examples).

Motivational Proof or *Pathos*   At the heart of persuasion is the ability to adapt a message to the feelings, needs, and values of an audience. People want and need to interact with others and belong to social groups. They need to feel worthy and to be recognized for their merits. Most, if they have their most basic needs met, develop a desire to grow and achieve their full potential. As you speak, make clear the ways in which your message answers or addresses these needs for the audience. Pathos often involves relating to the audience on a visceral, emotional level. Empathy, which means identifying with and understanding another person's feelings, motivations, or circumstances, shares the same root as *pathos*. If you recognize and anticipate the ways your words will resonate with your audience, you can tie your argument to the emotions you evoke.

In his famous speech, President John F. Kennedy urged Americans to "[a]sk not what your country can do for you. Ask what you can do for your country." By appealing to the traditional work ethic in the American tradition, President Kennedy tapped into an emotional wellspring within the hearts and minds of the public. By using the feelings of responsibility, duty, and even a hint of shame in his stern command that Americans not ask but instead give, Kennedy tied his message to deep, personal feelings in his audience.

Ethical Proof or *Ethos*   The persuasiveness of a message is commonly assumed to be influenced by the person who delivers it. For example, in social conversations, you may drop the names of respectable sources even as you pass along rumors and gossip. Source credibility—an audience's perception of the speaker separate from the speaker's intent or purpose—is an important factor in whether listeners accept the message. The ethos of a speaker takes into consideration both public reputation and personal standards of conduct. The external evidence of a person's ethical and consistent behavior is one part of ethos. Another is the person's actual behav-

▲ PHOTO
East Africa Training Project (EATP) Session in South Sudan
Your visual aid selection depends on your access to resources as well as your audience's needs. Visual reinforcement helps your audience retain your message and engage with your presentation's organization. *SOURCE: Steve Stewart (photographer), Centers for Disease Control and Prevention 2012.*

ior, no matter who is watching or what the perceptions of others are. Audiences are confident in a speaker who is known for her deeds, actions, accomplishments, and positions—the letter of the law and evidence of compliance. Speakers gain confidence in themselves by relying on their own morals, responsibilities, and values—the spirit of the law and thoughtful compliance no matter what the repercussions.

Logical Proof or *Logos* *Logos* is one root of any word ending in -*logy*. In Greek, it means "word," but it has come to mean "science," "study," or "theory." *Logical* also comes from *logos*. Appeals to logos involve logical, scientific evidence. We described five verbal and nonverbal devices that you can use to help an audience understand and accept your message: explanations, examples, statistics, testimony, and visual aids. Three of these devices (examples, statistics, and testimony) are especially useful as evidence—that is, information used as logical proof by a speaker. Evidence increases the persuasiveness of a message.[1] As you might expect, highly credible evidence sources are more persuasive than less credible ones. High-quality evidence is especially effective if the audience is unfamiliar with the subject and if the evidence is from multiple sources. Outdated evidence and evidence already familiar to the audience are not as highly persuasive.

To be persuasive, you should use multiple types of evidence. Although research does not suggest that one form of evidence is superior to the others, there is some indication that examples may have greater impact than statistical evidence, perhaps because they create vivid images in the minds of receivers.

Not all sources of information are of equal value, but how can you decide which are more credible than others? In order to evaluate sources, whether you are presenting or listening to a persuasive message, consider the following criteria: Is the source reliable? Recent? Complete? Accurate?[2]

The reliability test holds that sources should be objective and competent. Be skeptical of sources who might have something to gain from promoting a particular point of view. Sources should be in a position to know about the subject at hand, and they should be competent to judge or comment on the specific issue, item, or idea. Strive for the most up-to-date information possible. To meet the completeness criterion, evidence should be based on as many sources as possible. Having multiple sources lets you test the evidence for accuracy. Accurate information is redundant and verifiable. In other words, a variety of sources should present similar information. You should be skeptical of the aberrant figure or idea.

---

[1]John C. Reinard, "The Empirical Study of the Persuasive Effects of Evidence: The Status After Fifty Years of Research," *Human Communication Research* 15 (1988): 3–59.

[2]Patricia Bradley Andrews, *Basic Public Speaking* (New York: Harper & Row, 1985).

As you choose which ideas and forms of support to include in your presentation, keep in mind that combining different forms of support and forms of proof is often effective. For example, presenting only statistics can result in a dry presentation; presenting only emotional testimony from individuals with no logical evidence can result in an unconvincing presentation. Include in your presentation the same variety of forms of support and proof as in your paper. Balance in both will produce the most persuasive argument possible.

Manipulating Conventions for Evidence and Proof

Effective oral presentations do more than focus on the oral mode; they integrate many modes of WOVEN communication to engage with audiences. Strategic selection of and balance among modes is key to informative and persuasive presentations. How might you adapt basic strategies for oral presentations to multimodal composing? Consider specifically the strategies presented in this chapter and in Chapters 11 and 12, which you're about to read.

Although college students most often think of oral presentations as "stand-and-deliver" class presentations (often called platform presentations), you'll be expected to deliver or participate in many forms of academic and professional presentations. The most effective presentations combine the genres in this book (narrative, informative, persuasive) along with conventions for visual aids, organization, and nonverbal performance to engage an audience. One example of a narrative performance that also uses informative and persuasive strategies is "The 4 a.m. Mystery."

Conduct an Internet search for <Rives The 4 a.m. Mystery> and watch performance artist and poet John Rives's eight-minute TED talk about his experience researching the hour of 4 a.m. and its cultural meaning. While Rives's presentation is meant to be humorous rather than academically rigorous, he uses many of the conventions for proof and support explained in this chapter.

Once you have watched the video, analyze the presentation and evaluate it based on your course rubric and the qualities of oral presentations described in this chapter.

» *Rhetorical awareness:* How does Rives's presentation engage the audience and provide context for his topic?
» *Stance:* Does Rives make his stance clear? What evidence leads you to this conclusion?
» *Development of ideas:* How do Rives's ideas build over the course of the presentation? How effective is the evidence he presents? What forms of proof and support does he use or parody?
» *Organization:* Is Rives's presentation effectively organized? How does he create continuity from beginning to end?
» *Conventions:* What communication conventions does Rives follow well? What conventions could he refine?
» *Design for medium:* How does Rives use the mode of oral presentation and the medium/genre of Ted talks to support his message?

ORGANIZING AND DEVELOPING ORAL PRESENTATIONS

Organizing Your Presentation

Once you have your statement of purpose, your thesis, and your supporting details, you need to reorganize the ideas in your paper so they are most effective when you make your presentation. When an audience reads a paper, they have the advantages of written text: They can move at their own speed, reread confusing or complicated passages, and look up new vocabulary. In an oral presentation, the audience has few of these options. As a speaker, you have several advantages, however. You can accentuate certain points by altering your tone, volume, or speed, and by gesturing, making eye contact, and using body language. The key task is determining how to translate what you wrote in your paper into a clear, coherent, and effective oral presentation. An outline visually displays the main points and subpoints of your presentation (as well as the support for those points) in a way that helps you develop the presentation.

Creating an Outline

A good strategy for beginning to organize your oral presentation is to turn your paper into a complete sentence outline. Once you have developed such an outline, you may find it useful to reduce it to a topic outline or speaker's outline, which uses brief phrases and keywords in place of sentences. Often presentations do not allow enough time to cover every detail found in the paper. As you outline and organize your presentation, hit all the main points and use examples only sparingly if time is an issue. You may want to include more examples and details in a handout, but speak about only two or three during the presentation.

An outline generally includes several main points (I, II, III, etc.) and at least two subpoints (A, B, etc.) that develop each of the main points. Further subpoints are included for supporting material such as examples, testimony, statistics, and illustrations. In this way, an outline alternates numbers and letters in clearly identifiable columns and can accommodate as many levels of headings as you need. The following example shows a portion of an outline for a presentation on the merits of a popular online encyclopedia:

I. Are free online resources like Wikipedia equal to traditional purchased, print encyclopedias?
    A. What is Wikipedia?
        1. definition of *wiki*
        2. mission statement of Wikipedia.org
    B. What value does online encyclopedia offer?
        1. easy access
        2. current information
        3. multiple volunteer authors
    C. What potential problems?
        1. volunteer status of authors
        2. instability/constant changes
        3. ease of access for uneducated writers and users
            a. writing not of consistent quality
            b. readers not analytical enough
            c. might not be problem, but advantage
II. Wikipedia's reliability . . .

Although the type of labeling used in the above outline is the most common, another popular style is legal-style or decimal-number labeling. The next portion of the sample outline is shown in this style:

2. Wikipedia's reliability
    2.1. Edward W. Felten Sept. 2004 "spot check" of Wikipedia[1]
        2.1.1. checked entries on 6 topics he was well-versed in
        2.1.2. on advice of colleague, checked Britannica online entries same items

---

[1]Edward W. Felten, "Wikipedia vs. Britannica Smackdown," *Freedom to Tinker* 7 Sept. 2004, 3 May 2005 <http://www.freedom-to-tinker.com/archives/000675.html>.

2.2. Sanger, Wikipedia co-founder, on Kuro5hin[2]

    2.2.1. first problem is not how reliable but public's perception of reliability

    2.2.2. acknowledges Wikipedia not reliable for specialized topics, and better sources exist

        2.2.2.1. *Stanford Encyclopedia of Philosophy*

        2.2.2.2. *Internet Encyclopedia of Philosophy*

2.3. Robert McHenry, former editor-in-chief of *Encyclopaedia Britannica*[3]

    2.3.1. explains fact checking in encyclopedias is similar to Felten's approach

    2.3.2. statistical and representative tests are used . . .

Headings at a particular level of an outline should be of equal importance and written using parallel structure. In the first example, the main points, indicated by roman numerals, are the main divisions of the presentation and are of equal importance. The subpoints (A, B, and C) also designate equally important divisions of the main point to which they refer. The outline has two or more elements at any level; that is, there are two or more main points, two or more subpoints under any main point, and two or more levels of support. This is normally the case because a topic is not "divided" unless it has at least two parts. If you wish to make only one subpoint, do not show it on the outline as a subpoint but include it as part of the main point.

Choosing an Organizational Pattern

When adapting a paper for an oral presentation, you may need to rearrange the organization of information. What represents a logical progression of ideas in a paper may leave your listeners confused since, unlike readers, they cannot reread passages or look back to important points that preceded. For a presentation, it is often better to provide an overview at the outset, clearly stating which points you intend to cover. Doing so gives your audience a frame of reference that helps them follow and understand your points as you speak. It is sometimes best to cover the most important points first, both because the audience is still fresh and because you have limited time. Alternatively, if you're covering only a few points, you might want to build up to the most important idea so that it remains fresh in the audience's minds after you finish speaking. During your presentation your audience will also rely on you to occasionally summarize or remind them of what you've already covered. The structure of your paper offers a good starting point for organ-

---

[2]L. Sanger, "Why Wikipedia Must Jettison Its Anti-Elitism," *Kuro5hin: Technology and Culture, from the Trenches*, 31 Dec. 2004, 3 May 2005 <http://www.kuro5hin.org/story/2004/12/30/142458/25>.

[3]Robert McHenry, "The Faith-Based Encyclopedia," *Tech Central Station*, 15 Nov. 2004, 3 May 2005 <http://www.techcentralstation.com/111504A.html>.

izing your ideas and indeed may be the best structure for your presentation as well. But don't be afraid to experiment with a different pattern of organization for your presentation.

Although you can organize ideas in many ways, the following six organizational patterns are common: chronological, topical, spatial or geographical, cause-effect, problem-solution, and compare and contrast. You will likely already have used at least one of these organizational patterns in your paper.

Chronological Pattern   When using the chronological pattern, you organize your main points in a time-related sequence: that is, forward (or backward) in a systematic fashion. You might, for example, focus on the past, present, and future of digital recording technology. When describing a process step by step, you are also using a chronological pattern. The following terms make good transitions in a chronological pattern:

first . . .	next . . .	afterwards . . .
to begin . . .	before you continue . . .	eventually . . .
at the outset . . .	when that is completed . . .	finally . . .

Topical Pattern   Also known as a categorical pattern, the topical pattern organizes the main points as parallel elements of the topic itself. Perhaps the most common way of organizing a presentation, the topical pattern is useful when describing components of persons, places, things, or processes. A secondary concern when selecting this approach is the sequencing of topics. Depending on the circumstances, this is often best handled in ascending or descending order—that is, according to the relative importance, familiarity, or complexity of the topics. The example that follows begins with a specific question about a particular online resource and progresses to more complex questions about the reliability of online resources in general.

I. Are free online resources like Wikipedia equal to traditional purchased, print encyclopedias?

II. Wikipedia's reliability is a question of both real and perceived accuracy.

III. Can some solution be achieved, or are critics just complaining without offering to help?

IV. Is the question of reliability in online resources really a problem? Why?

Spatial or Geographical Pattern   The spatial or geographical pattern arranges main points in terms of their physical proximity to or direction from each other (north to south, east to west, bottom to top, left to right, near to far, outside to inside, and so on). It is most useful when explaining objects, places, or scenes in terms of their component parts.

Cause-Effect Pattern   With the cause-effect pattern, you attempt to organize the message around cause-to-effect or effect-to-cause relationships. That is, you might move from a discussion of the origins or causes of a phenomenon, say increases in the cost of fuel, to the eventual results or effects, such as increases in the cost of airplane tickets. Or, you could move from a description of present conditions (effects) to an identification and description of apparent causes. The choice of strategy is often based on which element—cause or effect—is more familiar to the intended audience. The cause-effect pattern of organization is especially useful when your purpose is to achieve understanding or agreement, rather than action, from the recipients of a message.

Problem-Solution Pattern   The problem-solution pattern involves dramatizing an obstacle and then narrowing alternative remedies to the one that you recommend. Thus, the main points of a message are organized to show that (1) there is a problem that requires a change in attitude, belief, or behavior; (2) a number of possible solutions might solve this problem; and (3) your solution is the one that will most effectively and efficiently provide a remedy. Topics that lend themselves to this organizational pattern include a wide range of business, social, economic, and political problems for which you can propose a workable solution. The problem-solution pattern of organization is especially useful when the purpose of a message is to generate audience action.

Compare and Contrast Pattern   One of the most common assignments (and most commonly misunderstood assignments) is a comparison paper or compare and contrast paper. Comparing is the act of identifying similarities, the characteristics shared by two or more distinct items or topics. Contrasting is identifying differences, the characteristics not shared by those items or topics. If your instructor assigns this type of presentation, be sure you understand whether you are supposed to compare only, contrast only, or both. Ask questions if you are unsure.

Patterns of Organization

Chronological organization

I want my audience to know that building a new student center on campus is a complex process.

- Gain approval of board of trustees
- Garner community support
- Raise additional funds
- Work with architects, engineers, consultants, and contractors
- Anticipate and solve problems caused by construction

Patterns of Organization
Topical organization
I want my audience to know that there are three major issues for the college to consider before deciding whether to build a new student center.
• The cost of the project
• The short-term problems associated with the project
• The potential long-term benefits of the project
Spatial organization
I want my audience to know that the proposed student center will have four main areas.
• Café
• Game room
• Computer lab
• Club offices
Cause-effect organization
I want my audience to know that campuses with good student centers have a better sense of community among the student body.
• *Cause:* Good student center
• *Effect:* Greater sense of community
Problem-solution organization
I want my audience to know that a problem associated with building a new student center is lack of funds for the project, and that the problem can be solved by using more effective fundraising techniques.
• *Problem:* Lack of funds
• *Solution:* Better fundraising techniques
• *Advantage:* Increased income for the project
Comparison organization
I want my audience to know that the new student center and the existing athletic center will be similar in three ways.
• Open to all students
• Appeals to incoming applicants
• Provides work-study job opportunities for students
Contrast organization
I want my audience to know that the new student center and the existing athletic center will be different in two ways.
• *Student center:* Open to students only; no classes meet there
• *Athletic center:* Open for paid public use during certain hours; some required courses meet there

Writers and speakers rarely use only one structure in the course of a paper or oral presentation. Effective speakers tend to use more complex combinations of several patterns to develop each main point of an oral presentation, as illustrated in the following partial outline.

There are three major issues for the college to consider before deciding whether to build a new student center on campus:

I. The cost-effectiveness of the project	TOPICAL
A. Not enough money in the current budget to fund the project	PROBLEM-SOLUTION
B. Enough funds can be attained through better fundraising techniques	
1. Special campaign to target recent alumni	TOPICAL
2. Joint fundraising efforts with clubs and other student organizations on campus	
II. The short-term problems associated with the project	TOPICAL
A. An unsightly construction site	PROBLEM-SOLUTION
B. Detours and traffic flow problems along the main campus road	
C. Potential security risks	
III. The potential long-term benefits of the project . . .	TOPICAL

Once you have determined the overall pattern of organization for your presentation, examine each main point in your outline. On the basis of each point, choose appropriate subpatterns for developing your ideas. If ideas fall naturally into a particular pattern of organization, do not force them into some other pattern; develop whatever combination of patterns works best for your ideas and achieves your purpose.

Developing Effective Introductions, Transitions, and Conclusions

Composing a paper (at least a good paper!), is a process, one in which you discover new ideas, and new ways to organize your ideas, as you write. After writing a first draft, for example, you may find that your thesis statement isn't as clear or as narrowly focused as you intended. Or perhaps you decide that your thesis statement needs stronger supporting points. You may find too that your conclusion needs to be summarized or restated. Writers who compose strong and persuasive papers regularly use all of these strategies.

Another part of the composing process involves choosing words and transitions. All the information in your paper needs connective words and phrases that link your points together into one cohesive and coherent argument. Rethinking their word choices during writing of second drafts is common among strong writers.

All of the composition principles true for writing papers are also true for making oral presentations. You need to write an introduction and a conclusion, and tie the sections of your presentation together with transitions.

The Introduction

When you give an oral presentation outside of class, the setting or the person introducing you may have already provided an overview of your message. Your audience may be so fired up about the topic that motivating them to listen to you is not necessary. Maybe your credibility as a speaker on the topic is so high that it does not require additional development. For most of your presentations in class, however, this is not the case. To compensate, you need to provide an overview of your message, motivate your audience to pay attention, and establish your credibility as a speaker on the topic.

Your introduction often is the most important part of the presentation. You must be clear, concise, and efficient when beginning your presentation in order to keep your audience's attention and prepare them for your message. Writing your introduction last, after you have written the rest of your paper or presentation, is often a good strategy because doing so gives you the opportunity to prepare your audience for all the main points you will cover. Keep in mind that your audience cannot refer back to your introduction in the same way they can when reading a paper. Refer back to your main points at strategic times throughout your presentation.

When you get up to speak, your audience probably has questions: What will this presentation be like? Will I like and trust this speaker? What will I get out of listening to this presentation? A good introduction answers these and other important questions. Dedicate about 5 to 10 percent of your speaking time to answering questions like these about your intent, the audience's relationship to both you and to the material, and the importance of this presentation to their lives or ways of thinking.

Although there is no guaranteed approach to making your intentions clear, consider explicitly stating the topic, thesis, title, or purpose. Previewing the structure of the message ("The three points I will develop are . . .") may be another useful plan. You may also want to explain why you narrowed the topic down from something more complex or involved.

A good way to motivate your audience to listen is to link your topic and thesis to their lives. Showing how the topic has, does, or will affect the audience's past, present, or future will help gain their interest and investment. You may also succeed in gaining the interest of your audience by demonstrating how the topic is linked to a basic need or goal, of either people in general or this audience specifically. Make the audience feel important through your introduction; show the audience how important they are in your details and supporting information.

Of course, you need to motivate your audience and build your credibility throughout your presentation, not only in your introduction. Many of the ways to build credibility are similar to those you use in writing a paper; however, when you are speaking in front of an audience, you are also communicating your credibility and trustworthiness through your body language and your ability to connect with the audience. Strategies for building credibility include the following.

» Cite highly credible individuals and reliable sources.

  » "Robert McHenry, former editor-in-chief of *Encyclopaedia Britannica*, has written . . ."

  » "In a speech from his hospital bed, Ambassador Morris B. Abram, a lawyer, educator, civil rights activist, and diplomat, has said that 'the question of treatment . . . should be based not on the length of time from birth but on the length of time from death.'"[1]

» Place your topic in historical context.

  » "Since the advent of digital music technology, especially the CD in the 1980s and the mp3 in the 1990s, . . ."

  » "Before the advent of the World Wide Web, this discussion would not have made sense. In fact, even as recently as 2000, the topic of a publicly edited free encyclopedia would have sounded more like a dream than reality to most people."

» Describe your personal acquaintance with the topic.

  » "I was an early adopter of Napster, and after legal problems changed their business model, I switched to Morpheus and KaZaa."

  » "My parents both have living wills, and I, myself, am an organ donor, as you can see by this symbol on my driver's license."

» Entertain alternative points of view to show that you are speaking from a balanced perspective.

» Be sure your body language supports what you claim to think and feel about your topic.

---

[1] Morris B. Abram, "Some Views on Ethics and Later Life," *Controversies in Ethics in Long-Term Care*, ed. Ellen Olson, Eileen R. Chichin, and Leslie S. Libow (New York: Springer, 1995): 146.

» Be gracious and polite with your audience, even if they seem hostile to your message.

» Use relevant humor, if appropriate, to demonstrate that both you and your listeners laugh at the same things.

The introduction to your presentation need not accomplish all of these goals. However, many opening strategies can function in multiple ways, allowing you to state your topic, establish a connection with the audience, and begin to demonstrate your credibility. For example, a story or an analogy can do all three of those things—"The reason I am so impassioned about end-of-life care is readily summed up in this story about my grandmother. . . ." Humor can both emphasize your motivation for making the presentation and help develop a better relationship between you and the audience. The best advice is to make your introduction as brief as possible while fulfilling the audience's expectations concerning what you want to do, how you relate to them, and why you feel the way you do about the topic.

Language Choices

When you begin to think through how best to convey the main ideas of a message, it is imperative that you examine your word and language choices; the best choices make your message relevant, clear, and unbiased for audience members. Here are some guidelines that can help you achieve this goal for your oral presentation.

» **Public language should be personal.** Don't borrow someone else's vocabulary. Use language that you can use easily. Never use a word in an oral presentation that you haven't said out loud previously. Practice pronouncing a new word until you make it yours.

» **Public language should be fitting.** Listen carefully to the language patterns of your listeners before you speak to them. Adjust the formality of your language to fit the situation. Resist the temptation to use a pet phrase just because you like it. Don't be flip with a serious topic or melodramatic with a light one.

  » APPROPRIATE WORD CHOICE FOR A RESIDENCE HALL FLOOR MEETING: "So we have to stop leaving a mess in the bathroom, know what I'm saying? You can't be leaving surprises for the janitors, you feel me?"

  » MORE APPROPRIATE LANGUAGE FOR A CLASS PRESENTATION: "The defacement of public property on campus is the responsibility of the entire campus community, as I am sure you will agree."

» **Public language should be strategic.** If you're dealing with touchy topics or hostile listeners, try out several different ways of phrasing a volatile idea in order to achieve the right tone. Don't depend on the inspiration of the moment to guide your language choice. Think in advance about what you're going to say and how you're going to say it. Compare the tone of the following three examples.

» "The ROTC needs to get off campus now."

» "The college needs to expel the recruiters immediately."

» "While the military offers a number of benefits to recruits as far as job placement and tuition support, perhaps the time has come for the administration of this university to examine its policies regarding on-campus recruiting."

» **Public language should be oral.** Except in certain rare circumstances, do not read your presentation; instead, make your presentation in an expository fashion. An oral presentation is meant for the ear, not the eye. Listen to the words and phrases you intend to use. Put "catch phrases" in your outline rather than long, elaborate sentences. Use your voice and body to signal irony and rhetorical questions and to emphasize important points. And practice reading your presentation at least several times, ideally with a friend or family member as a test audience.

» **Public language should be precise.** If you're talking about bulldozers, don't call them *earth-moving vehicles*. As in a paper, avoid unnecessary jargon and define all technical terms for your listeners. Try to avoid vague generalities; instead, use concrete and specific language when providing descriptions.

» **Public language should be simple.** Readers have an easier time understanding complicated sentences than listeners do. When speaking, use simple sentences as often as possible, and use five-syllable words sparingly.

» **Public language should be unaffected.** Don't seek to have your listeners remember your language. Don't get carried away with metaphors; a single simple image is always superior to several complex ones. Don't invent "cute" phrases. Euphemistic language often sounds ludicrous or evasive (for example, referring to firing employees as *downsizing*).[2]

Transitions

Transitions guide an audience through your presentation. They are signs that tell the audience where you are, where you are going, and where you have been. Thus, they need to be overt, clear, and frequent. You might, for example, preview the structure of the message toward the end of the introduction ("Today, I will talk about five behaviors that characterize effective leaders. They are . . ."). Overt tac-

---

[2]Robert P. Hart, Gustav W. Friedrich, Barry Brummet, *Public Communication*, 2nd ed. (New York: Harper & Row, 1983): 170–171.

tics like this ground your message for the audience and maintain the context of the information.

Informative presentations benefit from direct and overt descriptions and lists. Persuasive arguments may also benefit from such directness, but more subtle transitions are often more useful and reveal a greater degree of sophistication. Sometimes it is enough to put the elements of your presentation in the proper order and then allow your audience to arrive at the same conclusions without you telling them what comes next. Be sure, though, that you move from point to point in a logical fashion, and that you occasionally remind your audience of the thesis, topic, or main idea.

As the presentation proceeds, you can use internal previews and summaries to review a main point and anticipate the next one ("Having described why leaders need to challenge the process, let's turn now to the need to inspire a shared vision"). Sequential terms like *First . . . , Next . . . , And finally . . .* help tie points together. Too-frequent use of these types of transitions, however, can make your presentation sound clinical or sterile, like a user manual or cookbook.

Occasional use of coordinating conjunctions (such as *and*, *but*, and *or*), correlative conjunctions (such as *either . . . or, not only . . . but also*) and similar grammatical constructions often alleviates the "step-by-step" feel. Use *further* or *furthermore* to enhance certain points and build on previous information. *Again* can accomplish a similar goal. A semicolon (in the written outline) followed by *however* can introduce another perspective and reveal the depth of your research and the degree of your objectivity. Be certain that you use these constructions correctly, and don't overuse the same one. Starting every sentence with *"However . . ."* or *"Though . . ."* quickly grows boring. Check your writing guide or handbook for advice on making smooth transitions in your paper; many of the same techniques work well in a presentation. Remember, however, that you need to summarize and even repeat points more frequently in speaking than in writing.

The Conclusion

A conclusion typically summarizes the main points of the presentation and reinforces the importance of the message by demonstrating its potential impact. An effective way to accomplish this is by using the conclusion to elaborate on an example, illustration, or quotation that was used in the introduction. The conclusion might include a final summary that revisits your transitions ("I've talked today about five behaviors that characterize effective leaders. Effective leaders . . .").

The introduction and conclusion of your presentation act as a frame or set of bookends for your message. As you write the conclusion, consider your introduction carefully. Has your presentation covered all the material you mention in your introduction? Is your thesis statement or main idea supported by the details in the presentation? If you have a rough outline but have not written the details of the presentation, try writing your conclusion first. The conclusion then becomes a target toward which you aim as you compose the presentation. You may want to write more than one conclusion. The one you decide *not* to use as a conclusion may be a good model for your introduction.

PRACTICE, DELIVERY, AND EVALUATION FOR ORAL PRESENTATIONS

CONTENTS

Practicing, Polishing, and Delivering the Presentation

Good speakers thoroughly plan both the content of their presentations and their style of delivery. Although it is fundamental to have a clear and logical message to present, that message must be presented effectively. Otherwise, the only person who will understand and accept it is the speaker. Once you have prepared an effective message, you must develop effective strategies to deliver it. Your mode of speaking and your voice, body language, and comfort level all have a significant effect on your audience.

Modes of Speaking

Presentations involve any of four modes of speaking: impromptu, extemporaneous, scripted, or memorized.

Impromptu Speaking   Impromptu speaking is done on the spur of the moment without any formal preparation. By definition, this kind of speaking is not the kind you will be doing if you are preparing an oral presentation for class. But you are likely to be called on to do this type of speaking in other situations, for example, in a classroom setting in which the teacher asks you to summarize and give your opinion of the most recent reading assignment, or in a committee meeting in which you have special expertise on the topic at hand. You cannot prepare your exact words in advance, but you can anticipate the situation and prepare your ideas. When you are asked to answer a question or describe something on the spur of the moment, do the following.

» Quickly identify why you are speaking (for example, to supply needed information, to urge action, to clarify an issue, to provide humor).

  » "In order to defend the position that online reference works such as Wikipedia are sometimes more useful than traditional encyclopedias . . ."

  » "What are the real issues at the heart of the debate over Digital Rights Management and downloading music? I will offer a brief list of concerns . . ."

» Use an organizational strategy (for example, chronological, cause-effect, problem-solution).

  » "Before the early days of the movie industry, film piracy was usually a matter of theft and copying the actual film stock . . . The development of the VCR in the 1970s changed the way the film industry thought about piracy . . . Recent technology like TiVo and the DVD have once again changed perspectives about copyright infringement . . ."

» Grab the audience's attention and relate the core of your message in your introduction.

  » "I get angry every time I pay $10 to see a film at a movie theater and have to sit through a public service announcement warning me not to copy and trade movies because I will put all the members of the film crew out of work. Maybe you have felt this way, too. We paid for this movie! Why are they preaching at us?"

» Speak briefly. If you ramble on, the audience will miss your point.

» When in doubt, summarize. A quick review often restores your perspective and gets you back on track.

  » "I have explained Mr. Sanger's involvement in creating the Wikipedia. I have also detailed Mr. McHenry's former employment with *Encyclopaedia Britannica*. These roles are significant because . . ."

  » "So, licensing is a complicated issue. As I said originally, the owners of copyrighted material and the companies that distribute that material are often working from a different perspective than we, the customers, are. While we believe that we own a song or movie, as I have discussed, they believe that they have only licensed a copy of the performance or film for us to use in our homes. You can see why copying and playing those performances is such a complex subject . . ."

» Finish up with a brief summary stating the outcomes of accepting your message.

» "If you want to see better quality free resources, you will have to be conscientious, both as a reader and as a writer. Rather than complaining like Robert McHenry about problems with online resources, we need to read them carefully. Analysis is the most important skill we can learn and use in the current age of information technology. When we see problems, it is up to us to make changes and take part—to give back. I hope what I have said today will make two things clear—that information is not true just because we see it in print, whether online or in a book, and that we have a responsibility to double-check and help correct the information we find online."

» Whatever you do, don't apologize—for your lack of preparation, your lack of information, or your lack of ability as a speaker.

Extemporaneous Speaking Extemporaneous speaking is characterized by advance preparation of ideas and supporting material, with the precise wording to be composed at the moment of speaking. As a result, no matter how many times the presentation is delivered, the expression of the ideas is never exactly the same. Extemporaneous speaking has a number of important advantages.

» It allows the speaker to adapt to unforeseen situations (for example, by adding a reference to something that occurred in the setting and adding or deleting an argument based on audience response).

» It promotes a more personal relationship between the speaker and the audience.

» It leads, with experience, to a superior delivery—greater earnestness, greater sincerity, and greater power.

◀ PHOTO
Agency for Toxic Substances and Disease Registry (ATSDR) Town Hall Meeting
This speaker uses a visual aid during his town hall meeting presentation. Speakers at these events must be both credible and approachable, striking a balance between formal and informal—a type of extemporaneous speaking. *Cade Martin/Centers for Disease Control and Prevention.*

Because of these advantages, extemporaneous speaking is the preferred mode of speaking for most situations. Extemporaneous speakers construct a detailed outline and reduce it to a speaker's outline. (For more about outlining, see Chapter 11.) Using the speaker's outline, the speaker rehearses the presentation in front of a mirror, an audio- or video-recorder, and/or helpful friends. During the presentation, the speaker watches the audience for clues about how they are receiving the message and modifies the presentation based on that feedback.

Scripted Speaking   Although extemporaneous is the preferred mode of delivery for most situations, some occasions require you to write out a speech word for word and read the resulting document to the audience. Situations that require or encourage scripted speaking are those for which precision of expression is crucial. When the president of the United States makes a major policy statement on an important issue, he wants to be sure that the wording of the statement will not be misunderstood. Thus, he (or a speech writer) is likely to write out that statement and read it. Scripted speaking is also encouraged in situations that require precise timing (for example, a 2-minute speech written for inclusion in a political commercial).

Preparing a scripted presentation involves the same process as preparing an extemporaneous presentation. That is, you start with a detailed outline, reduce it to a speaker's outline, and rehearse from this outline. (For more about outlining, see Chapter 11.) Once you have experimented with a conversational style for presenting the message, write it down word for word and then rehearse and rewrite, rehearse and rewrite. Once in final form, the scripted presentation is prepared for easy reading—that is, put in a format and type size that are easy to read and marked appropriately to indicate any special emphases. The following example shows an excerpt from a scripted presentation.

» "If you want to see better quality free resources, you will have to be conscientious, [*pause*] both as a reader and as a writer. Rather than complaining about problems with online resources, we need to read them carefully. Analysis is the most <u>important</u> skill we can learn and use in the current age of information technology. When <u>we see problems</u>, it is up to <u>us</u> to make changes and take part—[*pause*] to give back. I hope what I have said today will make two things clear—[*pause*] that information is not true just because we see it in print, whether online or in a book, [*pause*] and that we have a responsibility to <u>double-check</u> and <u>help correct</u> the information we find online."

When presenting a scripted oral presentation, you attempt to establish a level of contact with the audience that approaches that of the extemporaneous mode, including steady eye contact and a conversational style of delivery.

Memorized Speaking   Memorized speaking adds one step to a scripted presentation: After writing out the manuscript, you memorize the presentation and then deliver it from memory rather than reading it. In many situations, speakers combine these two approaches: They read parts of the manuscript and deliver other parts of the message from memory in an extemporaneous fashion. In some situations, however, speakers make the extra effort of memorizing the whole document, especially for ceremonial speeches such as tributes and eulogies. When speakers make a special effort to memorize a presentation, they also make a special effort to deliver it using a style of delivery that is as close to an extemporaneous style of delivery as possible. Such a style is best developed by observing the skills of effective speakers, learning to evaluate your own delivery, and practicing to improve your skills.

Voice and Body Language

Once you have chosen a mode of delivery, you next need to consider how to use delivery to focus attention on the message and not on you. This means delivering the message in a conversational style that the audience can both hear and understand. Chapter 10 covers the following potential barriers to effective communication with your audience:

» The amount of information you include

» The type of information you include

» The level of feedback from the audience

» The pace of the presentation

» Organization and timing

» The intensity with which you present the information

As you practice your presentation, you need to consider two other factors that affect the audience—your vocal delivery and your body language.

Whether you are speaking extemporaneously or from a script, speak loudly enough, slowly enough, and clearly enough for the audience members at the back of the room to hear and understand you. If you have the opportunity to practice your presentation in the room where you will be presenting, ask a friend to sit at the back of the room to test whether you are speaking loudly enough. Nervousness may tempt you to rush through your presentation, and you may end up speaking faster than you think you do. Slow down and pause between major points so that your audience has time to absorb what you're saying. Take care to pronounce your words clearly and to speak in a natural, conversational style. Finally, avoid using distracting filler words such as *uh*, *um*, *like*, and *you know*. A brief pause is often

more effective for helping you get your thoughts together without distracting the audience.

Your audience will be watching you as well as listening to you, of course, so use body language to your advantage. Natural, conversational gestures help you emphasize important ideas or direct the audience's attention to key visuals. Making eye contact with the audience is extremely important—doing so helps them feel a connection to you and your message, and it also helps you to monitor your audience's reaction. By making eye contact, you'll be able to tell whether the audience is paying close attention and whether they understand your message. Don't be afraid to move around as you speak—movement can help the audience stay focused on you—but avoid pacing back and forth or fidgeting, as these activities will distract them.

Dealing with Stage Fright

Another potential barrier to effective delivery is your level of anxiety about speaking in front of a group. Many people experience stage fright when asked to speak in front of a group, regardless of whether they are habitually nervous about communicating with others or they generally feel comfortable communicating.

Stage fright is most often a situational attack of anxiety that depends on factors such as

» the size of your audience;

» how well you know the people you are talking with;

» how well you know your subject;

» the status of the individuals you are talking with.

For example, you may feel relaxed when talking with a friend about a movie you saw the previous evening, but feel a sudden surge of panic when asked to describe your reaction to that same movie for a professor and your classmates in an English class. Or you may feel comfortable offering a lengthy response to a question from the professor during class, but feel extremely nervous about getting up in front of the class to give an oral presentation on that same topic.

To overcome nervousness before or during a presentation, try the following.

» **Develop a constructive attitude toward fear and anxiety.** Instead of wondering how you will get rid of these common emotions, ask yourself how you can use them. Individuals need tension—feelings of excitement and challenge—to increase their thinking ability and powers of concentration. Realize that everyone who speaks publicly experiences some apprehension and fear before speaking and that, in fact, some measure of anxiety is necessary for you to do your best. If you have ever participated in sports, this may sound familiar. Let the adrenaline energize your performance by using all that pent-up energy like fuel. Being nervous is similar to being excited, so channel your nervousness into a positive energy.

» **Grab every opportunity to practice and gain experience.** Whether you are snowboarding, building a Web site, or speaking in front of a group, knowledge of the requirements is likely to increase your comfort level. For example, you naturally will be more comfortable the tenth time you've gone scuba diving than the first time. Seek out opportunities to practice and gain experience. Sometimes this will be easier around people you know, but for some, it is easier to perform for an anonymous audience. Because you will be making your presentation in class, where you may know many but not all of your classmates, practice in both types of situations.

» **Prepare thoroughly for each presentation.** If you are worried about what you will say, how you will say it, *and* what the outcome will be, you certainly will be more anxious than if your *only* concern is about the outcome. Prepare. Rehearse. Be thorough. Then, when you rise to speak, you will be able to concentrate on the outcome. Control all the things you can control *before* the day of the presentation.

» **Concentrate on communicating with your audience.** Ask yourself, "How do I know that these individuals are hearing and understanding what I'm saying?" If, as you speak, you work hard to observe the reactions of your audience and to adapt to them, you will be much too busy to worry about your anxiety or fear.

» **Remember that your listeners want you to succeed.** Your listeners are just like you—friendly people. Just as they want to succeed when they get up to speak, they want you to do well when you speak. Even if you do make a slip, they will understand and forgive you! Not even the best speakers perform flawlessly every single time they speak. Do not hold yourself to an unreasonable standard, and remember that others are not holding you to that standard.

» **Keep in mind that it will be over more quickly than you expect.** You have prepared for days or weeks, but the presentation will be over in only a few minutes.

Polishing the Presentation

One of the best ways to alleviate nervousness and to be sure you are well prepared is to polish your presentation through rehearsal. It's best to have your presentation ready several days to a week in advance to allow time to practice several times in front of a mirror or your friends. Assuming that you intend to speak extemporaneously, use the first few rehearsals to test various phrasings of your ideas. As you start to feel comfortable with the flow of your presentation, begin to work on time. Most classroom assignments will give you a time limit or a range (say 3 to 5 minutes).

Develop your presentation with the middle of the range in mind. That is, if the range is 3 to 5 minutes, develop a presentation that requires 3 to 4 minutes to deliver during practice. When you make the actual presentation, you may find that because of audience reaction, impromptu remarks, and so on, the presentation takes longer than it did during rehearsal. You may also find, though, that you speak more quickly during the presentation than you did during practice. Pace yourself.

As the day of the actual presentation approaches, try to practice in the classroom where you will speak. This will add to your comfort level and allow you to anticipate the unexpected. This is especially important if you are using unfamiliar equipment, such as a microphone, presentation software, an overhead projector, or an LCD projector.

If you are extremely nervous or feel unsure about your ability to give a presentation, be proactive; address the problem early and directly. But keep in mind that you do have sources of support. Seek help from campus resources, such as the writing center or your instructor during office hours. Seek help well in advance of the due date. The night before the presentation is due is usually too late. Some of the advice in this chapter may not seem practical, but keep in mind that in most cases you will have at least a week, and often two or three, to complete an assignment. Don't forget that the instructor's goal is to help you learn and grow, and he or she understands that you may be nervous about presenting.

Evaluating Presentations

In addition to your role as a presenter, you have another important role as an audience member for your classmates' presentations. You may be asked to evaluate their work, to offer suggestions for improvement, or even to demonstrate your understanding of the information they share. The following checklist will help you identify strengths and weaknesses in a presentation, both in the content and the speaker's delivery. As a student and a listener, you probably assess many of these strengths and weaknesses subconsciously. Being aware of the following components of a presentation (or paper) can change your mode of listening to one that is more active and critical.

At first, listening critically may seem like hard work, but as time goes on you will become comfortable and confident in this new style of listening. Paying attention to all of the items on this list is not easy or even advised. Instead, pay attention to the items that you already tend to notice and feel confident about evaluating. Pick a few other areas to concentrate on each time you hear a new speaker. Eventually, you will build better listening and analysis skills. A final recommendation: During a presentation, *make* (not *take*) notes. Writing every word the speaker says is never a good idea, but making comments in the margins of a handout or keeping a bulleted list or outline to trigger memories is very helpful, especially if you want to ask questions later.

Checklist for Evaluating a Presentation

The Speaker's Delivery   While the topic and the content are the most important parts of any presentation, the speaker has an incredible impact on the success of any presentation. The point is not to critique the speaker's every word or gesture; instead, note the places where the speaker's poise, demeanor, and performance help or hurt the presentation's message.

- ☐ **Voice**
  - ☐ Can you understand the speaker?
  - ☐ Is the speaker loud enough (but not too loud)?

- ☐ **Pace**
  - ☐ Is the speaker's pace comfortable, not too fast or too slow?
  - ☐ Does the speaker take time to allow for questions or repeat complex or confusing concepts?

- ☐ **Nervousness**
  - ☐ Does the speaker seem relaxed and comfortable?
  - ☐ Does the speaker avoid most meaningless filler words such as *uh* or *um*? (Do not nitpick, but is the number of *ums* distracting?)

☐ **Engagement with the audience**

    ☐ Does the speaker avoid simply reading his or her paper?

    ☐ Does the speaker make eye contact?

    ☐ Is the speaker aware of the audience's responses or reactions?

    ☐ Has the speaker adapted the material well for the audience?

☐ **Use of visual aids**

    ☐ Do the visual aids help you understand the speaker's message?

    ☐ Are the visual aids well designed and free of distracting or confusing elements?

    ☐ Does the speaker direct your attention to key points or visuals? Does the speaker adequately explain their significance?

Content and Coherence   Coherence refers to the degree to which all the parts and details in a paper or presentation work together toward the statement of purpose and thesis. If a presentation lacks coherence, it will seem to ramble all over and go off on tangents, not really making one clear point. A strong thesis and attention to coherence will make for a much stronger presentation.

☐ **Thesis**

    ☐ Is the thesis clearly expressed?

    ☐ Does the thesis make sense? Can you restate it in your own words?

    ☐ Is there only one apparent thesis or purpose?

    ☐ Do all of the main ideas go together?

☐ **Language choices**

    ☐ Does the speaker avoid using jargon?

    ☐ Does the speaker define key terms and unfamiliar words?

    ☐ Does the speaker address the audience using an appropriate and effective tone?

☐ **Transitions**

    ☐ Does the speaker clearly and smoothly link ideas and sections of the presentation?

    ☐ Are transitional words and phrases used correctly? For example, sometimes speakers overuse or misuse certain conjunctive adverbs in an attempt to sound more formal or "educated." The most common of these adverbs have very specific implications, as follows:

        • *therefore* = because of what I just said

        • *however* = in spite of what I just said

        • *furthermore* = in addition to what I just said

☐ **Support**

    ☐ Does the speaker's support for his or her thesis make sense?

    ☐ Are examples and evidence appropriate and credible? Do they mean what the speaker says they mean?

    ☐ Do the examples and evidence support the speaker's claim(s)? Do you come to a similar conclusion based on these examples? Has the speaker mentioned other possible conclusions?

Argument and Persuasion

☐ **Does the speaker avoid logical fallacies? Does the speaker**

    » offer only two options or solutions, when many more really may exist? (*false dilemma*)

    » assume that an event that follows another event happens *because* of the first, even though this may not be true? (*post hoc ergo propter hoc*, "after this, therefore because of this")

    » suggest that one decision will lead to more bad outcomes, even though there is very little evidence supporting this suggestion? For example, "if we legalize drugs, then everyone will have access to drugs all the time, and we will become a nation of drug addicts." (*slippery slope*)

    » claim that something is true simply because most people believe that it is true? "Ninety-five percent of people surveyed believe that the sun does, in fact, revolve around the earth." (*popularity*)

    » use other fallacies like these? (Books and Web sites about argument list many other fallacies. Consult your instructor if you have trouble understanding the occasionally complex definitions of some fallacies.)

☐ **Does the speaker seem credible and convincing?**

☐ **Do you agree with the speaker? Did the presentation make you change your opinion? Why or why not?**

☐ **Even if you disagree with the speaker, does the speaker adequately explain and defend his or her position?**

Thinking Critically about Your Own Presentation

The checklist above is a good guide for evaluating your own presentation too. One problem many people face when evaluating their own work is being too close to the material and too invested in the paper or the argument. A good way to evaluate your work critically is to distance yourself from it for a while. If possible, record yourself practicing the presentation, either on audio or video. Then spend a day or two (or longer if you have the time) not working on the project. When you return to the paper or presentation, read, view, or listen to the entire piece. Pretend that you are an audience member and use the above checklists to evaluate your own work. Do not be afraid to play devil's advocate and take an opposing view or to adopt a hostile attitude toward the presentation's message; however, rather than attacking all your own thoughts, ideas, and statements, instead be fair and tough. Envision how you would defend your ideas and statements to an audience member making the same kinds of critical comments and asking similarly probing questions. If you can, rework your project to anticipate and address these issues before making your presentation.

PART 5
HOW CAN I USE RHETORIC TO SOLVE COMMUNICATION PROBLEMS?

Read This First! GT

At Georgia Tech this year and for the next several years, you'll hear a lot about *sustainability* and ways to *create sustainable communities*. You'll have an opportunity to critique institutional, local, regional, national, and global problems related to sustainability and also to create ways to address those problems, especially at the community level.

The U.S. Environmental Protection Agency (EPA) defines *sustainability* this way:

> Sustainability is based on a simple principle: Everything that we need for our survival and well-being depends, either directly or indirectly, on our natural environment. Sustainability creates and maintains the conditions under which humans and nature can exist in productive harmony, that permit fulfilling the social, economic and other requirements of present and future generations. Sustainability is important to making sure that we have and will continue to have, the water, materials, and resources to protect human health and our environment.[1]

Not addressing sustainability is often classified as a risk. Some would even classify it as a "wicked risk," a problem that is part of an enormously large system and so complicated (e.g., scientifically, socially, politically, economically, and/or environmentally) that successfully solving one aspect of the problem creates new problems elsewhere in the system.

Why all this attention to sustainability? Sustainability—and the ability to apply research about it in various communities—is the subject for the new Georgia Tech Quality Enhancement Plan (QEP), called "Serve•Learn•Sustain." Like many other colleges and universities, every 10 years, Georgia Tech asks people across the Institute to create a QEP for student learning. The QEP is based on Georgia Tech's own assessment of its institutional mission and needs as defined in the Institute's strategic plan.

In English 1101 and English 1102, you'll learn that an important initial step in investigating a problem is identifying critical concepts and locating a range of perspectives about them. Consider these two additional definitions of sustainability and then compare them to the EPA's definition of sustainability.

> *A widely cited definition of sustainable development*: "meets the needs of the present without compromising the ability of future generations to meet their own needs."[2]

---

[1] From *What Is Sustainability?* United States Environmental Protection Agency.

[2] From *Our Common Future*, a 1987 report (often referred to as the Brundtland report) prepared by the World Commission on Environment and Development (Oxford UP).

Definition used by Georgia Tech as part of its QEP: "Transforming our ways of living to maximize the chances that environmental and social conditions will indefinitely support human security, well being, and health."[3]

A report describing Georgia Tech's new QEP explains that "this definition was chosen because it is explicit not only about environmental considerations but also community-level social considerations such as human security, well-being, and health, considerations that provide a practical and meaningful context for our students." Throughout your years at Georgia Tech, you'll have an opportunity to put this definition into practice.

Perform an image search for the many variations of <Venn diagram sustainability>. Now repeat the same search at least twice, each time adding a keyword representing a different field of study. Select two distinctive diagrams and explain how the profession appears to affect the subcategories. #Understand

Faculty Leading Georgia Tech's QEP Initiative

Two Georgia Tech professors spearheaded the recent campus-wide effort to create a new QEP for Georgia Tech: Dr. Beril Toktay (professor and Brady Family Chair in the Scheller College of Business) and Dr. Ellen Zegura (professor of computer science in the College of Computing). You'll hear a lot from them if you read the campus newspaper and newsfeeds. Here's what they said in a newspaper article about the new QEP:

» Dr. Beril Toktay: "This QEP will enhance foundational classroom instruction and curricular opportunities [for Georgia Tech students]. It will focus on the establishment of experiential and contextual learning opportunities that emphasize connections between the real world and subject matter, such as project- and problem-based learning, service learning, entrepreneurial opportunities, internships, and co-ops. We look forward to developing a set of external partnerships to achieve this."

» Dr. Ellen Zegura: "A successful QEP will result in Georgia Tech graduates who have a deep understanding of the societal impacts of economic value creation and the needs of communities they live and work in. This depth of understanding will not be attained when it is sought as an 'add-on.' Rather, the interdependence of economic and societal value must be integrated as part of our students' core education, and our students must be challenged to work on relevant problems that cut across disciplinary boundaries."

Both Dr. Toktay and Dr. Zegura believe English 1101 and English 1102 are good places to explore sustainability in our communities, learn about sustainability in our broader culture, suggest innovative solutions to sustainability problems, and communicate about the problems and possible solutions in a range of multimodal artifacts.

Source: "QEP to Focus on Sustainability, Community," *A Strategic Vision for Georgia Tech*, March 30, 2014.

---

[3]From A. J. McMichael, C. D. Butler, and C. Folke, "New Visions for Addressing Sustainability," *Science*, 2003: 302, 1919–1920.

Knowing more about the QEP helps you understand more about the way Georgia Tech works on Institute-wide initiatives and helps you generalize to ways other big organizations work. Each succeeding QEP at Georgia Tech identifies a significant, Institute-wide issue that focuses on student learning outcomes and the environment to support those outcomes. Georgia Tech provides sufficient resources to initiate, implement, sustain, complete, and assess the QEP. Georgia Tech is held accountable for its QEP by the Southern Association of Colleges and Schools Commission on Colleges (SACSCOC), which accredits Georgia Tech.

QEP proposals are specialized documents that use all three genre categories introduced in this textbook: narration, information, and persuasion. The QEP process also includes other modes, such as formal presentations. Many universities adapt information about their QEPs into videos that are available on YouTube.

Learning about complicated topics such as sustainability and sustainable communities by focusing on only one or two genres or methods of inquiry results in a distorted view; such a narrow approach creates an incomplete picture of the interrelated problems of "wicked" risks. For example, a business report about return on investment may neglect the important human cost of a corporate decision. This human element explains why considering sustainability in relation to community makes good sense.

In Part 5 of this textbook, you are introduced to a useful system for identifying categories of genre that help you develop and apply strategies to address many communication problems you'll encounter. You will learn about three broad categories:

» *Narrative genres* (e.g., short stories, fairy tales, memoirs, novels, dramatic films) are invaluable as you explore human joys, anxieties, and fears and as you consider the intangible pleasures and costs of change and innovation.

» *Informative genres* (e.g., technical reports, encyclopedia entries, graphs, tables, charts, maps, infographics, news articles, journal articles, documentary films) use verifiable information from credible sources that may inform and influence your decision making.

» *Persuasive genres* (e.g., advertising, op-ed pieces, editorials, researched arguments, author and artist statements, visual arguments, oral presentations) try to convince you to change your beliefs, attitudes, and behaviors.

While these genre categories help you, your classmates, and your instructors critique and create various artifacts, they are not mutually exclusive categories. Rhetorically responsive artifacts often use traits from multiple genres. A movie poster created by students in English 1101 informs the audience, but it also suggests a

Ford Pintos had a fatal defect. Ford used cost/benefit analysis to decide to pay damage claims rather than to repair the problem. Do an Internet search for <Ford Pinto Mother Jones> to read the Pulitzer Prize–winning article with the details and assess whether Ford's reasoning was sustainable. #Evaluate

narrative to which the audience can relate and has several layers of persuasion at work (e.g., come see the movie, take a stand about the importance of bees, recognize that bees affect sustainability). In this example, the poster is promoting a documentary film that has screenwriters, fact checkers, videographers, film editors, subject experts, script supervisors, and continuity editors, among many film professionals, all working to make sure the film is accurate and well-researched (informative). They also make sure the film has a story (narrative) and is intellectually and emotionally compelling (persuasive).

During some classes in English 1101 and English 1102, you'll explore other issues that contribute to or are influenced by sustainability and sustainable communities. Classes in writing and communication are an appropriate place to explore this

Recall a short story (narrative genre), a podcast or radio segment (informative genre), and an advertisement (persuasive genre). Explain how each artifact not only uses the conventions of its categorical genre but also incorporates strategies of the other genre categories.
#Remember
#Understand
#Evaluate

important topic, which has for many decades (even centuries) intrigued scientists and poets, children's authors and moviemakers, business entrepreneurs and journalists. What's so intriguing? We need to consider the balance of our natural world and our human-made world. We need to consider the cost of innovation—not just the economic cost but the cost to the natural world.

Even when you were a child, sustainability was probably part of your everyday world, and the focus was often on the ways human communities were affected—from recycling cans and bottles to reading Dr. Seuss's *Lorax*, Rudyard Kipling's *The Jungle Book*, or Ray Bradbury's "There Will Come Soft Rains." Children and adults loved the Lorax, many flocking to the 2012 film, which a reviewer in *Nature* called a "parody of a misanthropic ecologist."[4] *The Jungle Book*, originally published in 1894, has been adapted into comic books, animated and live-action films, cartoons and anime, plays, and radio shows; all promote a sense of people's affection for and connections with the natural world. Bradbury's sci-fi story, named after Sara Teasdale's poem, "There Will Come Soft Rains," is set in a postapocalyptic world in which humans are gone but much of the natural world continues; adaptations of the story abound in comic books, radio, puppet shows, and games. Such works of fiction encourage readers to think about people's relationships with the natural world and ways to develop and maintain sustainable communities.

Frankenstein has been adapted into many genres: comic books, films, plays, and TV shows. What versions have you read or seen? #Remember

More recently in your high school and college literature classes, you've perhaps read about sustainability and communities from other perspectives. For example, the novel *Frankenstein, or the Modern Prometheus*, written by Mary Shelley and first published in 1818, explores various aspects of the power of nature and its danger when humans try to pervert it. A later exploration of the relationship between people and nature, *Walden* (first published in 1854), was written by Henry David Thoreau based on his reflection about more than two years of living in a cabin on the edge of Walden Pond. Both *Frankenstein* and *Walden* provide philosophical perspectives that provoke us to think about how our actions (and inactions) can change the nature of our communities.

The importance of sustainability and community, and the power of narratives to tell related stories, extends beyond the 19th century, as the next two examples illustrate. The well-respected British newspaper the *Guardian* recently published an article that called for not more Hollywood blockbuster stories but, instead, stories about sustaining life on a natural and human scale. The article noted that many people "crave a different kind of social, business and political leadership that is

---

[4]Emma Marris, "In retrospect: The Lorax," *Nature*, 476 (2011): 148–49.

more focused on helping us find new and healthier stories than on propping up the old ones."[5] In another article, the *Guardian* notes,

> Stories have real power, and which ones we choose to tell ourselves matters. . . . As small and large businesses wrestle with the transformative demands of living and embodying sustainability in practice, the words, stories and metaphors they use to stay focused and motivated are crucial.[6]

Sustainability and community aren't just touted in newspapers. The *Harvard Business Review* annually summarizes "some of the latest stories about the big environmental and social pressures on business and the ways some innovative companies are dealing with them."[7] What's important? Attention to sustainability in ways that inform, tell a story about the human role and scale, and persuade.

Attention to creating sustainable communities isn't just an international or national concern; it shows up at Georgia Tech in a remarkable number of ways.

» The Georgia Tech Science Fiction Collection is one of Georgia Tech's unique research resources, including more than 11,000 cataloged science fiction novels, anthologies, monographs, journals, and films—all of which you can access in the library. Science fiction often creates compelling stories about creating sustainable communities, as it contrasts utopian and dystopian cultures.

» Many research projects at Georgia Tech focus on various aspects of creating sustainable communities. Professor Carl DiSalvo—in the School of Literature, Media, and Communication—directs the Public Design Workshop. This research studio focuses on engaging with the public about issues of science and technology, specifically the design of digital communication infrastructures to support social interaction. For example, working together with undergraduate and graduate students, the studio created a Web-based visualization tool to chart an urban farm's yield over time. Research like this provides urban farmers with evidence to make more effective arguments for increased public support.

» Recycling is ubiquitous on the Georgia Tech campus. Bins are everywhere, and the systems to inform, share success stories, and persuade are easily

To learn more about the science fiction archive at Georgia Tech, go to the library archives to check the description of what's available and learn ways to access these sci-fi materials. You can search the collection online by going to the "Research Tools" link on the library's homepage and selecting "Archives," then "GT Science Fiction."

[5]Geoff Mead, "Sustainability Needs New Narrative between Catastrophe and Utopia," *The Guardian*, April 30, 2014, Web.

[6]Ed Gillespie, "Sustainable Storytelling Is a Powerful Tool That Communicates Vision," *The Guardian*, January 28, 2013, Web.

[7]Andrew Winston, "10 Sustainable Business Stories Too Important to Miss," *Harvard Business Review*, December 17, 2013, Web.

accessible. The recycling Web site includes "did you know" tips to engage and educate site visitors.

» Georgia Tech's Center for Business Strategies for Sustainability (CBSS) in the Scheller College of Business is designed as a hub for business-focused sustainability activities across campus, involving students, research entities, and industry.

» Georgia Tech's Brook Byers Institute for Sustainable Systems (BBISS) contributes to and supports campus research, education, service, and operations, especially efforts focusing on the intersections of leadership, communication, decision making, and development related to sustainability.

What other LEED-certified buildings are on campus? What enables a building to be certified? #Understand

» New and renovated buildings on Georgia Tech's campus use LEED (Leadership in Energy & Environmental Design) standards. Architects and contractors as well as building owners, managers, and residents are encouraged to be environmentally responsible and use resources efficiently in order to create sustainable communities. The Clough Undergraduate Learning Commons, Old CE, and the Stephen C. Hall Building are all LEED-certified buildings.

Metacognitive Questions to Leverage Your Knowledge: Sustainability, Sustainable Communities, and Problem Solving with Communication

You can start to answer these metacognitive questions now, but you'll have much more detailed and credible responses when you finish reading all the chapters in Part 5.

» **REMEMBER:** What previous knowledge do you have about sustainability and creating sustainable communities? What kinds of information shape your opinions about the relationships among humans, nature, and technology? #Remember

» **UNDERSTAND:** Part 5 introduces three genre categories: narrative, informative, and persuasive. Compare them and then decide which is most compelling for you in influencing your beliefs about sustainability and creating sustainable communities. #Understand

» **APPLY:** Using an artifact about sustainability or about creating sustainable communities that you've encountered recently, identify the conventions that enable you to categorize it as a particular genre. #Apply

» **ANALYZE:** Using the artifact you selected for Apply (on the previous page), infer how the conventions it uses make its argument more effective for its intended audience(s). **#Analyze**

» **EVALUATE:** Assess the messages from recycling initiatives across campus. How effective are they in getting students to recycle? **#Evaluate**

» **CREATE:** Propose a campaign to increase engagement in the QEP—Serve•Learn•Sustain—on campus. Use multiple genres as part of your creative approach. **#Create**

13 NARRATIVE GENRES

CONTENTS

FAIRY TALE ▶
Gustave Doré
Illustration from "Le Petit Chaperon Rouge."

e For e-Pages content, visit **bedfordstmartins .com/bookofgenres.**

We share stories every day: on the bus, in the checkout line, at home. We experience them through social media, memoirs (p. 269), history books, comics, movies, and the evening news. We remember them from the fairy tales of childhood. Constructing narratives is a universal impulse; stories help us make sense of our lives and connect with others. Regardless of the specific genres our stories take—and whether they're fact or fiction, comedies or tragedies, or something in between— they generally include real people or made-up characters, a setting, a conflict, and action.

In your composition course, you may be asked to write a literacy narrative: a story about how you learned to read and write. But there are other, less formal ways to share stories. For example, even a single page from a photo album or scrapbook, such as the one below, suggests part of the story of someone's life. Enikö DeLisle, a blogger in Edgartown, Massachusetts, created an online scrapbook page dedicated to the story of Peter Farkas and Edith Nanay.

For an Index of Sources & Contexts for material referenced in this chapter, see **bedfordstmartins .com/bookofgenres.**

◀ SCRAPBOOK PAGE
Enikö DeLisle, "Peter and Edith"
The caption for this couple, Peter Farkas, and Edith Nanay, reads: "Like the story of the country mouse and the city mouse, Peter and Edith were from very different worlds, brought together by fate and circumstance—Or was it destiny? They met at a photographer friend's studio on the day this photo was taken of Edith at age 20—it was love at 1st sight." Above the photos of Peter and Edith are images of their parents. *Enikö DeLisle Design.*

Creating narratives goes back to ancient times: Early aboriginal people painted cave walls with symbols and pictures of animals to convey meaning. Ancient Greeks told stories of gods and heroes, and Native Americans created and passed down legends to warn about tricksters and celebrate heroes. Today's oral histories function similarly, preserving stories that might otherwise be forgotten. For example, the StoryCorps project, archived at the Library of Congress, records the life stories of everyday people.

ORAL HISTORY ▶
StoryCorps project
StoryCorps.

▼ OBITUARY
Elizabeth A. Niles
From the National Archives and Records Administration. *Old Records Division Reference File, Record Group 94, Records of the Adjutant General's Office, National Archives.*

Woman Who Fought In Civil War Beside Hubby Dies, Aged Ninety-Two

RARITAN, N.J., Oct. 4.—Mrs. Elizabeth A. Niles, 92, who, with close-cropped hair and a uniform, concealed her sex and is said to have fought beside her husband through the civil war is dead here today, aged ninety-two.

The war call found the couple on their honeymoon. The husband, Martin Niles, joined the ranks of the Fourth New Jersey Infantry, and when the regiment left Elizabeth Niles marched beside him. She fought through many engagements, it is said, and was mustered out, her sex undiscovered. Her husband died several years after the war.

Another narrative genre is the obituary. Sound morbid? Check out the obituaries shown here for Elizabeth A. Niles and Harvey Phillips (on p. 259). Don't these sound like people you wish you'd met? Writers of obituaries, sometimes the deceased himself or herself (some people write them well in advance), sometimes a friend or family member, tell the story of the deceased through key biographical details. A related genre, the eulogy, is a speech delivered at the funeral or memorial, usually written by friends or family members. Through eulogies, writers share stories about the deceased's life, character, and accomplishments. Even an epitaph, the inscription on a gravestone, can tell a story about a life.

The Rhetorical Situation

There are a lot of ways to tell a story—and countless genres for telling them. However, as a composer you always make specific rhetorical choices. These choices have to do with your purpose and audience, the strategies you use to reach your readers, the media you create in, the style and design of your story, and the sources you draw on to create it.

For coverage of **fairy tales** and a sample tale, see **bedfordstmartins.com/bookofgenres**.

Purpose: Why tell stories?

As we worked on this book, we always began our sessions with an exchange of stories about what happened during the course of the day. It helped us reconnect. Our students do this before class, talking about what happened in other classes or at their jobs; no doubt, they do the same at home.

We also use narrative genres to chronicle events. A story may be just a few sentences or it may be epically long, such as *The Odyssey* or *War and Peace*. A story can be true (such as an autobiography) or it can be made up (such as a short story, novel, or other work of fiction). Some stories change history, such as the *Narrative of the Life of Frederick Douglass, an American Slave, Written by Himself.* Douglass's autobiography, which he published in 1845 while living in the North as an escaped slave, helped spark the abolitionist movement in the United States.

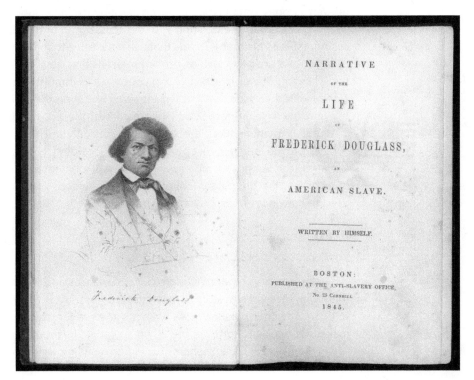

◀ MEMOIR
Frederick Douglass (1818–1895)
Narrative frontispiece and title page. *Newberry Library, Chicago, Illinois, USA / The Bridgeman Art Library.*

We also use stories to entertain—and instruct. For example, while most well-known fairy tales are pretty good reads, they were actually created to teach children some kind of lesson. Following is the text of "The Shepherd's Boy and the Wolf," commonly known as "The Boy Who Cried Wolf." This fable is attributed to Aesop (ca. 620–564 BCE), a (possibly mythical) storyteller who lived in Ancient Greece. Note the final line, which explicitly states the moral of the story.

FABLE ▶
Aesop
"The Shepherd's Boy and the Wolf," from the digital collections of the University of Virginia Library.

UNIVERSITY *of* VIRGINIA LIBRARY

The Shepherd's Boy and the Wolf

A SHEPHERD-BOY, who watched a flock of sheep near a village, brought out the villagers three or four times by crying out, "Wolf! Wolf!" and when his neighbors came to help him, laughed at them for their pains. The Wolf, however, did truly come at last. The Shepherd-boy, now really alarmed, shouted in an agony of terror: "Pray, do come and help me; the Wolf is killing the sheep"; but no one paid any heed to his cries, nor rendered any assistance. The Wolf, having no cause of fear, at his leisure lacerated or destroyed the whole flock.

There is no believing a liar, even when he speaks the truth.

Have you ever read a story and wondered about its authenticity? How much does a story's validity have to do with its author? Can you think of examples of an author (or speaker) who seems unreliable?
#Remember
#Evaluate

Why else do we tell stories? To persuade others—or even to sell something. For example, in a job interview, you might tell relevant stories about your previous experience that show you're qualified for the position you're discussing. In terms of selling, think of the many TV ads that use a narrative to make a case about a product, such as car commercials that go something like this: A well-dressed young couple walks through the woods with their kids and golden retriever, and then they all pile into their shiny new SUV. The creators of the ad, hired by the SUV manufacturer, are selling you not only the shiny vehicle but an entire conceptual package including luxury, romance, the American dream, and even environmentalism. In this case, the brief story (couple, kids, dog, woods, car) is used to convince you to buy a large automobile.

Audience: How do we get others to connect with our stories?

We write stories in order to explore our experiences and share them with others. For a story to resonate, readers must be able to connect with it personally. As writers, we strive for ways to make that happen. For example, in his memoir, *Dreams from My Father*, Barack Obama shares his experiences growing up as a black American and the struggles he faced as he traced his origins, something many readers can relate to. He tells his story through a series of anecdotes that read like a conversation, beginning with how he heard of his father's death. By beginning with such a universal situation and using an informal tone, Obama gets readers invested in his story. Alison Bechdel's *Fun Home* (p. 282) is a graphic memoir about her family's sometimes comedic, sometimes tragic dysfunction. To reach her audience, she tells a series of stories through images and text written in the first person. She uses humor and her strong writer's voice to invite readers into her story.

There are many reasons for sharing stories—and many ways of reaching readers or listeners. For example, Erna Anolik tells of her experience at Auschwitz through the University of Southern California's Shoah Foundation. Anolik appeals directly to her audience by appearing on video. (To view her testimony, select "Camps" from the topics menu at Shoah.) ▼

◀ ORAL HISTORY/ TESTIMONIAL
Erna Anolik
"On Surviving a Concentration Camp," from the Shoah Foundation. *Image of Erna Anolik, "On the Topic of Camps," provided by the USC Shoah Foundation— The Institute for Visual History and Education, http://sfi.usc.edu/.*

What are the stories that make up your life? What are your earliest memories? How did you learn to read and write? #Remember #Understand

Rhetorical Appeals: How do we use ethos, logos, and pathos to tell stories?

Whether your favorite narrative genre is the Facebook status line or the memoir, you'll be most effective if you tap into the rhetorical appeals: ethos, logos, and pathos.

▲ VIDEO MEMOIR
Amy Braziller
From *Writing the Music Train*.

Ethos—How you, as an author or composer, are perceived by your audience is crucial when you tell a story. For example, if you write an autobiography, deliver a eulogy, or share an oral history, your readers and listeners assume that what you are telling them is true, that the stories have actually taken place. If you create a photo essay, such as the one included in this chapter (p. 293), your viewers assume that you have accurately depicted real events. If you create a work of fiction (a short story, a novel, etc.), your ethos as an author is also important. Readers want to trust that you're going to tell them an interesting, worthwhile story, perhaps with a solid, interesting plot and relatable characters they can care about.

In her video memoir, *Writing the Music Train*, Amy documents her days as a punk rocker. She presents herself as a writer who was stunted by a teacher's comments on her early writing; she tells how she succeeded as a writer by composing songs and lyrics in a punk rock band. Here, Amy establishes her ethos as a memoirist by presenting original lyrics, a piece of writing "corrected" by her teacher, and a series of punk-inspired self-portraits.

Logos—The logic you use as an author or composer is also significant when you tell a story. For example, a short story, even if it is not told chronologically, usually follows a pattern in which the plot and characters unfold in a logical manner to the reader.

Pathos—Your appeal to readers' emotions can go a long way in bringing your story home. For example, when you write a memoir, you identify a moment in your life that has emotional significance, and convey it in a way that gets readers to identify emotionally with that experience.

The Tyler Clementi Foundation was created in memory of Tyler Clementi, a Rutgers University student who was bullied for being gay and who ultimately committed suicide in 2010. The language on the page titled "Tyler's Story" reflects love, pride, and grief. The foundation briefly described at the bottom of the screen was created in Tyler's honor and to provide anti-bullying resources for gay teens.

Modes & Media: What are the best choices? How will they affect your story?

A story's *mode* is how the story is communicated—text, audio, video, or a combination of these modes. A story's *medium* can be print, digital, or face-to-face.

NARRATIVE GENRES	Mode	Medium
MEMOIR Frederick Douglass, *Narrative of the Life of Frederick Douglass* (p. 253)	WRITTEN	PRINT
FABLE Aesop, "The Shepherd's Boy and the Wolf" (p. 254)	WRITTEN	DIGITAL
ORAL HISTORY/TESTIMONIAL Erna Anolik, "On Surviving a Concentration Camp" (p. 255)	VISUAL AND AUDIO	DIGITAL

The Genre's Conventions

Elements of the Genre: What do all stories have in common?

Writers rely on certain techniques and conventions to tell a story. You might start with a premise and think about how to convey the story in terms of exposition (the basic information you need to share), tension, rising action, conflict, climax, and resolution (also known as plot, if you're writing creatively). You need to think about your viewpoint, tone, and voice as a storyteller, and the ways they will affect your reader or listener. You also need to make sure the people involved (or characters, if you're writing creatively) are as interesting and dynamic as possible. Use every sentence to move your story forward to its resolution.

Style: How does it contribute to your story?

What is your individual style? Individual writers use different styles, have different voices, and include different kinds of details. The following paragraph is by the fiction author Junot Díaz. This is his character Yunior speaking in a short story called "Fiesta, 1980." Pay attention to how he works with the short story genre.

EXCERPT FROM A SHORT STORY

Mami's youngest sister—my Tia Yrma—finally made it to the United States that year. She and Tio Miguel got themselves an apartment in the Bronx, off the Grand Concourse, and everybody decided that we should have a party. Actually, my dad decided, but everybody—meaning Mami, Tia Yrma, Tio Miguel, and their neighbors—thought it a dope idea. On the Friday of the party Papi got back from work around six. Right on time. We were all dressed by then, which was a smart move on our part. If Papi had walked in and caught us lounging around in our underwear, man, he would have kicked our asses something serious.

—**Junot Díaz,** from "Fiesta, 1980" (*Drown*)

Díaz uses style and voice to convey a narrator who is young and hip within the context of 1980. His narrator, Yunior—who Díaz has acknowledged in interviews is an alter ego—uses language such as "dope idea" and "man, he would have kicked our asses something serious." He creates a narrator who is observant, who has an eye for detail. Díaz writes from the first-person (I) point of view, inviting readers to identify with his main character/narrator. He hints at a conflict between the narrator and his father; Díaz uses the technique of foreshadowing to suggest a future struggle, telling readers that the father's response to laziness ("lounging around in our underwear") would have been to "have kicked our asses." Díaz assures us, as readers, that we'll get the whole story: His choices contribute to his ethos as an author, and to the ethos of his narrator as a central character and storyteller.

What stories (or other kind of writing) have you read that have a strong, memorable "voice"—whether in terms of the author or a character? How does voice affect your experience as a reader? #Apply #Evaluate

Design: What is the best format for your story?

How we design a narrative contributes to our readers' experience. The obituary shown here for Harvey Phillips, for example, was designed by editors and designers at *The New York Times*, who made careful decisions about what to emphasize through images, typeface, and interactive features. The photo of Harvey Phillips playing the tuba reinforces his career as "Titan of the Tuba." The large font size used for the title and the second color used for the hyperlinks add emphasis, making essential information clear to the reader. Hyperlinks in the obituary connect readers to related content. For example, the phrase "to play carols and other festive fare" links to a YouTube video of Harvey Phillips playing at Rockefeller Center's skating rink in 2008. Clearly, the editors and designers anticipated that readers might want to see and hear one of Phillips's performances, and so they added that link and presented it in the first paragraph.

Sources: What information should you draw on to tell stories?

When we tell or write stories, we often draw on our own experiences. For example, Liz may tell a story about something funny that happened to her this morning, in which case her own life is the source. In other situations, we draw on other sources. Take, for example, the obituary of Elizabeth A. Niles (p. 252). The author interviewed Niles's family to learn details about her life and death. Another example is Amy's video memoir (p. 256); sources she used include photographs, video recordings of her musical performances, and a poster from the club where she performed. Other works, such as fairy tales (see "The Shepherd's Boy and the Wolf," p. 254, and "Little Red Riding Hood," in the e-Pages for this chapter), movies such as *Star Wars*, and books such as *The Lord of the Rings*, draw on tales and legends of the past, including Greek mythology, European folklore, and Icelandic epic poetry. (*For more on short stories, see the short story section on p. 299.)

Music

Harvey Phillips, a Titan of the Tuba, Dies at 80
By DANIEL J. WAKIN
Published: October 24, 2010

The tuba players mass by the hundreds every year on the Rockefeller Center ice-skating rink to play carols and other festive fare, a holiday ritual now ingrained in the consciousness of New York.

The tradition began in 1974, the brainchild of Harvey Phillips, a musician called the Heifetz of the tuba. In his time he was the instrument's chief evangelist, the inspirer of a vast solo repertory, a mentor to generations of players and, more simply, Mr. Tuba.

Most tuba players agree that if their unwieldy instrument has shed any of the bad associations that have clung to it — orchestral clown, herald of grim news, poorly respected back-bencher best when not noticed, good for little more than the "oom" in the oom-pah-pah — it is largely thanks to Mr. Phillips's efforts. He waged a lifelong campaign to improve the tuba's image.

▲ OBITUARY
Daniel J. Wakin
"Harvey Phillips, a Titan of the Tuba, Dies at 80." *From The New York Times, October 24, 2010 © 2010 The New York Times. All rights reserved.*

LITERACY NARRATIVES

A literacy narrative tells a story of remembering. In this sense, it is similar to the memoir (p. 269) and the graphic memoir (p. 279). Like memoirists, when the writers of literacy narratives tell their own stories, they relate events and also analyze how these events have shaped their identities. However, there is an important difference between the memoir and the literacy narrative: The writers of literacy narratives tell a story specifically about how they learned to read and/or write.

You may be familiar with literacy narratives already; many memoirs include sections about how the author learned to read or write or important moments in the development of their literacy. Examples include Jimmy Santiago Baca's *Working in the Dark* and Eudora Welty's *One Writer's Beginnings*. Other memoirs focus more on the development of the author's literacy, such as Stephen King's *On Writing* and Anne Lamott's *Bird by Bird*. Sometimes memoirists will use the story of the development of their reading and writing as a context in which other stories are woven, as Azar Nafisi does in *Reading Lolita in Tehran: A Memoir in Books*, in which she tells the story of a secret women's book group in Iran and how the books they read reflected and affected the lives of the women in the group.

What was the first book (or sentence or word) you read? What was the context? Where were you, and who was present? What was the experience like for you?

Analyzing Literacy Narratives: What to Look For

THE RHETORICAL SITUATION

Purpose   People write literacy narratives because their formative experiences with reading and writing are important to them; they want to share their stories with others, especially if their literacy histories involve obstacles or challenges. Some may also want to make an argument about the importance of literacy.

Audience   Literacy narratives are often written in composition classes and other college courses. Instructors assign this genre to help students understand what influences their speaking, reading, and writing. In this case, a writer's main audience is his or her instructor and classmates. Outside of the classroom, writers create literacy narratives to help educators, librarians, and other people involved in literacy fields better understand how literacy practices and histories manifest themselves in people's lives. (For examples of narratives in various media—text, audio, and video—see the Digital Archive of Literacy Narratives at Ohio State University.)

Literacy narratives are often published for a wider, popular audience; they may appear in a magazine or journal, or as part of a larger collection of essays, as is the case for the narrative that appears later in this section (the excerpt from Richard Rodriguez's *Hunger of Memory* on p. 263).

Rhetorical appeals   Writers of literacy narratives use direct language and real details from their lives to establish credibility (ethos). They also make logical connections (logos) between their narratives and the larger issues of literacy; oftentimes, these authors write to emphasize and argue about the importance of literacy, which makes the use of logos especially important.

Modes & media   Many writers of literacy narratives use the traditional essay or book form; for example, Helen Keller includes her memoir of learning to understand Braille in her autobiography, *The Story of My Life*. Other literacy narratives appear on the Internet as blog entries or YouTube videos or are presented in online archives.

THE GENRE'S CONVENTIONS

Elements of the genre   Literacy narratives can take the form of memoirs, in which writers reflect on moments in their lives that show how reading and writing have affected their experiences and sense of self. Authors of literacy narratives convey their experiences, framing their interactions with the world in terms of reading and writing. They also use personal anecdotes and autobiographical details to re-create their experiences for the reader.

Like memoirs, most literacy narratives are written in the first person. Authors of literacy narratives tell stories not just for the sake of recounting events; rather, their goal is for the narrative to culminate in a larger idea or theme that drives the essay. Writers also use literary elements such as setting, character development, dialogue, vivid descriptions and details, symbols, and metaphors.

Style   Authors use detail to re-create their literacy experiences for readers. For example, in her literacy narrative, Helen Keller shows readers, through specific examples, what it was like to be a blind and deaf child:

EXCERPT FROM A LITERACY NARRATIVE
My aunt made me a big doll out of towels. It was the most comical, shapeless thing, this improvised doll, with no nose, mouth, ears or eyes—nothing that even the imagination of a child could convert into a face. Curiously enough, the absence of eyes struck me more than all the other defects put together. I pointed this out to everybody with provoking

persistency, but no one seemed equal to the task of providing the doll with eyes. A bright idea, however, shot into my mind, and the problem was solved. I tumbled off the seat and searched under it until I found my aunt's cape, which was trimmed with large beads. I pulled two beads off and indicated to her that I wanted her to sew them on my doll. She raised my hand to her eyes in a questioning way, and I nodded energetically. The beads were sewed in the right place and I could not contain myself for joy.

—**Helen Keller,** from *The Story of My Life*

Most authors of this genre take literacy seriously, which is why they want to write about it and share their experiences with readers; however, each author of a literacy narrative conveys his or her story in a unique voice. Keller's voice emphasizes that in many ways she was just like any other child, playing with dolls, for example. Her matter-of-fact tone helps readers identify with and understand her childhood experiences.

Design   The literacy narrative usually takes an essay format: It has an introduction, body paragraphs, and a conclusion. However, literacy narratives can take different forms, including audio essay and documentary. In their written form, literacy narratives use typography to emphasize certain points or language.

Sources   Like print and graphic memoirs, literacy narratives seldom cite outside sources, because the source of information is almost always just the writer's memories of his or her own life.

Think of the stories, memoirs, and other narratives you've read, viewed, or listened to in your life. What details stand out from these stories? How do they affect the ways you think about and remember each story? #Understand

Richard Rodriguez

From Hunger of Memory: The Education of Richard Rodriguez

Richard Rodriguez's *Hunger of Memory* is a collection of autobiographical essays. In the following excerpt, which he calls a memoir, and which is also a literacy narrative (see how genres overlap!), Rodriguez focuses on the power of language as he explores his childhood experiences in a bilingual world. Rodriguez relates the struggles he faced living in between a Spanish-speaking world and an English-speaking world.

The notes in the margins point out Rodriguez's goals as a writer and his strategies for connecting with his readers. They also show how he works with the genre's conventions to tell a compelling story about literacy. *(Excerpt on pp. 264–65 reprinted by permission of David R. Godine, Publisher, Inc. Copyright © 1982 by Richard Rodriguez.)*

◀ BOOK COVER
Richard Rodriguez on the cover of his autobiography.
Used by permission of Bantam Books, a division of Random House, Inc. Any third party use of this material, outside of this production, is prohibited. Interested parties must apply directly to Random House, Inc., for permission.

What is the composer, **Richard Rodriguez**, doing?

THE RHETORICAL SITUATION

Purpose
Audience
Rhetorical appeals
Modes & media

see page 265

How do I know this is a **literacy narrative**?

THE GENRE'S CONVENTIONS

Elements of the genre
Style
Design
Sources

see page 266

Richard Rodriguez
From *Hunger of Memory*

Three months. Five. Half a year passed. Unsmiling, ever watchful, my teachers noted my silence. They began to connect my behavior with the difficult progress my older sister and brother were making. Until one Saturday morning three nuns arrived at the house to talk to our parents. Stiffly, they sat on the blue living room sofa. From the doorway of another room, spying the visitors, I noted the incongruity—the clash of two worlds, the faces and voices of school intruding upon the familiar setting of home. I overheard one voice gently wondering, "Do your children speak only Spanish at home, Mrs. Rodriguez?" While another voice added, "That Richard especially seems so timid and shy."

That Rich-heard!

With great tact the visitors continued, "Is it possible for you and your husband to encourage your children to practice their English when they are home?" Of course, my parents complied. What would they not do for their children's well-being? And how could they have questioned the Church's authority which those women represented? In an instant, they agreed to give up the language (the sounds) that had revealed and accentuated our family's closeness. The moment after the visitors left, the change was observed. "*Ahora*, speak to us *en inglés*," my father and mother united to tell us.

At first, it seemed a kind of game. After dinner each night, the family gathered to practice "our" English. (It was still then *inglés*, a language foreign to us, so we felt drawn as strangers to it.) Laughing, we would try to define words we could not pronounce. We played with strange English sounds, often over-anglicizing our pronunciations. And we filled the smiling gaps of our sentences with familiar

Rodriguez, From *Hunger of Memory*, *Continued*

Spanish sounds. But that was cheating, somebody shouted. Everyone laughed. In school, meanwhile, like my brother and sister, I was required to attend a daily tutoring session. I needed a full year of special attention. I also needed my teachers to keep my attention from straying in class by calling out, Rich-heard—their English voices slowly prying loose my ties to my other name, its three notes, Ri-car-do. Most of all I needed to hear my mother and father speak to me in a moment of seriousness in broken—suddenly heart-breaking—English. The scene was inevitable: One Saturday morning I entered the kitchen where my parents were talking in Spanish. I did not realize that they were talking in Spanish, however, until at the moment they saw me, I heard their voices change to speak English. Those gringo sounds they uttered startled me. Pushed me away. In that moment of trivial misunderstanding and profound insight, I felt my throat twisted by unsounded grief. I turned quickly and left the room. But I had no place to escape to with Spanish. (The spell was broken.) My brother and sisters were speaking English in another part of the house.

Again and again in the days following, increasingly angry, I was obliged to hear my mother and father: "*Speak to us en inglés*" (*Speak*). Only then did I determine to learn classroom English. Weeks afterward, it happened: One day in school I raised my hand to volunteer an answer. I spoke out in a loud voice. And I did not think it remarkable when the entire class understood. That day, I moved very far from the disadvantaged child I had been only days earlier. The belief, the calming assurance that I belonged in public, had at last taken hold.

THE RHETORICAL SITUATION

Purpose

Rodriguez aims to share the story of how he came to speak both English and Spanish.

Audience

The author knows his primary readers care about language and identity. They are bilingual or native English speakers interested in themes of education, family, and coming-of-age.

Rhetorical appeals

Rodriguez begins with a brief story about his parents being willing to do anything for their children, an appeal to **pathos**. The teachers' connecting of Rodriguez's behavior to his lack of English is an example of **logos**.

(Continued on p. 266)

Rodriguez, From *Hunger of Memory*, *Continued*

THE RHETORICAL SITUATION

Modes & media

Mode = written This literacy narrative is written. Because Rodriguez's topic is language, his choice to convey his story in written words makes sense. If he were to adapt this narrative using digital technology, he might embed audio so his readers could hear what he experienced.

Medium = print Rodriguez's book is intended to be read in hard-copy format or as an e-book. In either case, it's intended to be read from beginning to end, one page at a time, unlike online literacy narratives, which can be read in a non-linear fashion.

THE GENRE'S CONVENTIONS

Elements of the genre

This is an **autobiographical account about literacy.** Rodriguez shares childhood experiences of learning to speak, read, and write.

He uses **anecdotes** to advance a central idea; e.g., with the brief, personal story in paragraph 1, Rodriguez prepares readers for his ideas about language and identity, and his argument about bilingual education.

He writes in the **first person** and **describes settings** to connect readers with his experience. He contrasts his home setting with his classroom (where he is an outsider) to emphasize the difference in his private and public encounters with literacy.

Style

Rodriguez **uses rich detail** to re-create his experience for readers. Because his essay centers on how he hears language, he focuses on bringing the dialogue alive and uses **phonetic spelling** so that readers hear exactly what he hears.

His **tone and voice reflect his personality and speech.** He quotes the nuns to emphasize how they enunciate and "Americanize" words.

Design

Rodriguez uses italics to highlight Spanish and English words, and also to emphasize certain passages and sounds (*"That Rich-heard!"*).

Sources

Rodriguez does not cite outside sources because he is the source of his story.

Questions: Analyzing Rodriguez's literacy narrative

1. Purpose. Rodriguez not only tells a story about his experiences with language but also makes an argument regarding bilingual education. What is his argument? How persuasive is he?

2. Purpose. Reread the final paragraph of the essay. Why do you think Rodriguez chose to conclude this way?

3. Audience. What techniques does Rodriguez use to connect with his audience? Is an audience that has experienced bilingual education his target audience? Why or why not?

4. Rhetorical appeals. How does Rodriguez develop his ethos as someone who speaks about education with authority? How does his phonetic spelling of "Rich-heard" contribute to the pathos of the piece?

5. Modes & media. Imagine Rodriguez's literacy narrative as a digital text online. Which words of the excerpt could be linked to other Web sites? For example, perhaps the word "Rich-heard" could be linked to a YouTube video in which someone says the name as Rodriguez's family would say it; this might emphasize how strange the Americanized pronunciation sounded to Rodriguez.

6. Elements of the genre. What are some similarities between Rodriguez's literacy narrative and memoirs that you may be familiar with (e.g., see Dave Eggers's memoir on p. 273)?

7. Style. Given that writers of literacy narratives tell stories about how they learned to speak, read, or write, why might many of them include dialogue? What role does dialogue play in Rodriguez's literacy narrative?

8. Style. Rodriguez includes some Spanish words in his narrative. How do the Spanish words contribute to the essay's effect?

9. Design. Rodriguez italicizes bits of dialogue. What do you think is his purpose for doing so?

10. Sources. The source for this literacy narrative excerpt is Rodriguez's own memory. Do you think a narrative written by one of the nuns would differ significantly from Rodriguez's? Why or why not?

Drafting a Literacy Narrative

CHECKLIST: Drafting a Literacy Narrative

Thinking of writing about how you learned to speak, read, and write? Ask yourself the following questions.

WHAT'S MY RHETORICAL SITUATION?

☐ **Purpose.** What specific moment in my life as a reader or writer do I want to write about? Why? What questions do I have about that moment? How might I interpret that moment? What insights do I want to share with others? How did that moment shape me as a reader or writer?

☐ **Audience.** How would I describe my readers? Why will my experience with reading or writing matter to my readers? What do I want them to get out of my story? And how will I reach them?

☐ **Rhetorical appeals.** How will I establish my authority as a writer? How reliable will I be as a narrator? To what extent will I appeal to my readers' emotions? To what extent will I rely on logic to support my interpretations of my experiences?

☐ **Modes & media.** Do I want readers to experience my story in written, audio, or visual form? Do I want my literacy narrative to be print, electronic, or presented face-to-face?

WHAT GENRE CONVENTIONS MATTER?

☐ **Elements of the genre.** I'm writing about my own life: How will I keep my writing true and accurate? How much will I disclose about myself (and others) in my literacy memoir? Will I write in the first person? What anecdotes will I use to tell the story of myself as a reader or writer, and why? Also, what literary elements might I use? For example, will I use dialogue (as Rodriguez does) or a metaphor to help readers compare my experience to something else?

☐ **Style.** What tone will I take in my writing? Will my literacy narrative be serious or funny? Academic or down-to-earth? What kind of language will I use? How much detail will I include?

☐ **Design.** What format will my literacy narrative take? Do I want to compose a standard literacy narrative, focusing on words, or do I want to create a graphic literacy narrative that includes illustrations?

☐ **Sources.** What memories will I draw on? Will I need to check my story with others from my life, or will I rely on my own recollections and interpretations?

PRACTICE Want to experiment? Draft your own literacy narrative.

Do some freewriting about an early memory of reading or speaking and how that early event shaped your attitudes and experiences with language. Draft a narrative in which you tell the story of your early experience; be sure to make specific points about how that experience shaped you as a reader, writer, and/or speaker. Include anecdotes, details, and quotations from conversations, as Rodriguez does.

MEMOIRS

The word *memoir* comes from the Old French *memoire* and Latin *memoria*, both meaning "memory." A memoir is a written (or graphic, film-based, etc.) and true account about one's own life and experience. Often, memoirists' works focus on a specific and significant moment in their lives—one that has specific meaning and importance.

A memoir is like a personal essay, except that memoirists tend to focus on looking at their past, asking questions, analyzing, and attempting to make sense of their lives. Memoirists also tend to use literary techniques, including dialogue. Some memoirs are funny, like David Sedaris's *Me Talk Pretty One Day*, which includes essays about his life as an American in France. Other memoirs are more serious, such as Joan Didion's *The Year of Magical Thinking*, about her loss of her husband and daughter, and Frank McCourt's *Angela's Ashes*, about his impoverished childhood in Ireland.

Some memoirists are famous; some are infamous. For example, former president Bill Clinton, in his memoir, *My Life*, discusses his two presidential terms with a focus on his successes and failures, as well as the life that brought him to the White House, and even his intimate life, including his affair with an intern. In the category of infamous, French art thief Stéphane Breitwieser wrote a memoir, *Confessions of an Art Thief*, about how he stole a billion dollars' worth of art. Another infamous example is author James Frey, who came under fire for fabricating his struggles with addiction in *A Million Little Pieces,* a book that he and his publisher originally presented as a memoir.

> What moment(s) in your life would you most want to write about in a memoir? Why? #Remember #Evaluate

Analyzing Memoirs: What to Look For

THE RHETORICAL SITUATION

Purpose Memoirists share their stories because they believe they can offer insights to others, as does Mitch Albom in his memoir, *Tuesdays with Morrie*, in which he writes about how people develop values. Memoirists write because they want to share lessons learned in difficult times, as Isabel Allende does in *Paula*, her memoir of watching her adult daughter die. Sometimes they write because they want to explain themselves, or "tell their side of the story," as rapper Eminem's mother, Debbie Nelson, does in her memoir, *My Son Marshall, My Son Eminem*. Many memoirists (like Sedaris) also aim to entertain their readers, but for most, the goal is to share their experiences.

Audience   Memoirists (such as Albom and Allende, mentioned above) often write for a wide readership and publish their works in books and magazines such as *The New Yorker* and *O: The Oprah Magazine*. Some write for popular audiences (such as Nelson, especially). However, some write for narrower audiences, such as fans of poetry: Donald Hall, in his memoir *The Best Day the Worst Day*, writes about his life with poet Jane Kenyon. This book appeals to Liz, for example, because she is a fan of both of these poets and is interested in learning about them as writers and partners too. Memoirists can offer insights and information about what they are most famous for (in Hall's case, poetry).

How would you describe your life—in six words? *SMITH* magazine invites you to publish your mini-memoir at its site. #Apply

Rhetorical appeals   To earn their readers' trust, memoirists must be reliable narrators of their own stories. They develop their ethos through the anecdotes they share but also through the language and tone they use. Isabel Allende, in another memoir, entitled *Aphrodite: A Memoir of the Senses*, uses sophisticated yet playful language to establish herself as—you guessed it—sophisticated and playful: "I repent of my diets, the delicious dishes rejected out of vanity, as much as I lament the opportunities for making love that I let go by because of pressing tasks or puritanical virtue." Sensationalist or overly dramatic language, such as the use of many superlatives (*biggest, grandest, smartest*) or an overreliance on exclamation points (*I was so scared!!*) could compromise the ethos of the memoirist.

Modes & media   Traditionally, memoirs are written in book or essay form. A memoir will sometimes include photos of the memoirist to supplement the text, giving the reader a visual image to associate with an anecdote or bit of personal history. Memoirs are occasionally adapted into films or television movies, as in the case of *Persepolis*, Marjane Satrapi's graphic memoir, which was made into an animated film in 2007.

THE GENRE'S CONVENTIONS

Elements of the genre   Because memoirs are based on writers' memories, most are naturally written in the first person. Memoirs feel intimate not only because of their first-person perspective but because their authors reveal personal thoughts and feelings to the reader. Self-disclosure, the sharing of emotion, personal ideas, facts, and other information, invites readers into a bond with the author, drawing them into a shared sense of trust.

Memoirists use many of the same techniques fiction writers use, such as dialogue, vivid descriptions of settings, imagery, and metaphor. Instead of inventing *characters*, memoirists include other real people in their work. For example, in David Sedaris's memoirs, his boyfriend Hugh is a frequent presence, as are members of Sedaris's family.

Memoirists present anecdotes to illustrate specific moments or points. An anecdote is usually just a few sentences long and is usually amusing rather than sad, such as this anecdote from Donald Hall's *The Best Day the Worst Day*:

> One morning when I tried to start the Plymouth, it barely turned over and wouldn't catch. I was puzzled until I checked the thermometer on the porch. It was minus twenty-one degrees—and I had not noticed: New Hampshire's cold is drier than Michigan's and less painful.

Memoirs are true, or at least represent the truth as the author honestly remembers it. Sometimes others who have a stake in the stories in someone else's memoir challenge the accuracy of those stories. For example, some of Frank McCourt's neighbors from his hometown in Ireland have different memories of the degree of misery McCourt suffered. McCourt writes in his memoir *Angela's Ashes*:

> People everywhere brag and whimper about the woes of their early years, but nothing can compare with the Irish version: the poverty; the shiftless loquacious alcoholic father; the pious defeated mother moaning by the fire; pompous priests; bullying schoolmasters; the English and the terrible things they did to us for 800 long years.
>
> Above all—we were wet.

But is *Angela's Ashes* a totally factual story? asks *Los Angeles Times* writer Tim Rutten, upon McCourt's death. Rutten explores the answer:

> [S]ome outraged Limerick residents insisted not, and the local newspaper dredged up old photos of Frank and [McCourt's brother] Malachy well dressed and their long-suffering mother sleek and fed. Still, if the McCourt family misery was neither as unrelieved nor as perfect as the author recalled it, his account "was no less true for all of that."

How "true" or accurate a memoir is has to do with the nature of memory; memory is subjective and imperfect. Memory, and how we write about it, also has to do with our personalities, our sense of others—and of justice and injustice, our hopes and wishes. As readers and writers, we need to take these factors into account when we approach the memoir. However, there is a big difference between lapses and other imperfections of the memory—and the purposeful invention of things that never happened. In extreme cases, when an author's work is more fiction than truth, the memoirist loses all credibility (see the discussion of James Frey on p. 269).

Style　Memoirists use a lot of detail to tell their stories. In fact, Bill Clinton's memoir was criticized for being too richly detailed. (One Amazon.com review asks, "Do we really need to know the name of his childhood barber?")

Memoirists also use a great range of tones to tell a story. For example, even Frank McCourt's memoir about misery is not without wit and charm ("Above all—we were wet"). The style of a memoir can vary considerably depending on who the author is. Bill Clinton, known as charismatic and talkative as governor of Arkansas and president of the United States, comes across as charming and garrulous in his memoir. His vocabulary reflects his worldliness and education, and his sentences are often long and detailed. Consider the first sentence in Clinton's *My Life*:

> Early on the morning of August 19, 1946, I was born under a clear sky after a violent summer storm to a widowed mother in the Julia Chester Hospital in Hope, a town of about six thousand in southwest Arkansas, thirty-three miles east of the Texas border at Texarkana.

At forty-nine words long, this sentence is three times the length of the average written sentence. A much shorter but very powerful sentence begins Isabel Allende's memoir *Paula*:

> Listen, Paula.

These words instantly indicate that the memoir is part letter to Paula, Allende's dying daughter.

Design　Most memoirs are print texts published in book form (however, see also "Graphic Memoirs," p. 279). Although the text-based memoir focuses on words (not images), some memoirs feature a gallery of photos and documents from the writer's life. The book cover usually presents a flattering photo of the writer. For example, on the cover of his memoir, Bill Clinton does not look beleaguered (as he may have felt during the Whitewater hearings or impeachment proceedings of his second term); rather, he is smiling and looks healthy and at ease.

Sources　Most memoirs are based on personal observation and experience. For this reason, memoirists seldom cite outside sources. However, if someone were to write a memoir of a group or an organization, that person would, no doubt, draw on historical documents, interviews, and other sources of information.

Dave Eggers

From A Heartbreaking Work of Staggering Genius

The following excerpt is from Dave Eggers's memoir, *A Heartbreaking Work of Staggering Genius*. In it, Eggers tells the true story of how, at the age of twenty-two, he became the guardian fully responsible for raising his younger brother after both his parents died within a few weeks of each other. This excerpt is from the beginning of the book, when his mother is dying. Eggers has since made a name for himself as an author and editor, writing several highly praised novels and running McSweeney's, an independent publisher. Eggers also cofounded 826 Valencia, a literacy tutoring center for kids.

Annotations in the margins of the excerpt on pages 274–75 show the choices Eggers made in terms of his purpose, sense of audience, and use of rhetorical appeals. You'll also see notes on how this work reflects the conventions of the memoir genre—in terms of its real-life content and specific techniques. *(Excerpt on pp. 274–75 reprinted with the permission of Simon & Schuster, Inc.)*

PHOTO ▶
Dave Eggers
Courtesy of
McSweeney's
Publishing.

What is the composer, **Dave Eggers**, doing?

THE RHETORICAL SITUATION

Purpose
Audience
Rhetorical appeals
Modes & media

see page 275

How do I know this is a **memoir**?

THE GENRE'S CONVENTIONS

Elements of the genre
Style
Design
Sources

see page 275

Dave Eggers
From *A Heartbreaking Work of Staggering Genius*

I am holding the nose. As the nose bleeds and we try to stop it, we watch TV. On the TV an accountant from Denver is trying to climb up a wall before a bodybuilder named Striker catches him and pulls him off the wall. The other segments of the show can be tense—there is an obstacle course segment, where the contestants are racing against each other and also the clock, and another segment where they hit each other with sponge-ended paddles, both of which can be extremely exciting, especially if the contest is a close one, evenly matched and with much at stake—but this part, with the wall climbing, is too disturbing. The idea of the accountant being chased while climbing a wall . . . no one wants to be chased while climbing a wall, chased by anything, by people, hands grabbing at their ankles as they reach for the bell at the top. Striker wants to grab and pull the accountant down—he lunges every so often at the accountant's legs—all he needs is a good grip, a lunge and a grip and a good yank—and if Striker and his hands do that before the accountant gets to ring the bell . . . it's a horrible part of the show. The accountant climbs quickly, feverishly, nailing foothold after foothold, and for a second it looks like he'll make it, because Striker is so far below, two people-lengths easily, but then the accountant pauses. He cannot see his next move. The next grip is too far to reach from where he is. So then he actually *backs up*, goes down a notch to set out on a different path and when he steps down it is unbearable, the suspense. The accountant steps down and then starts up the left side of the wall, but suddenly Striker is there, out of nowhere—*he wasn't even in the screen!*—and he has the accountant's leg, at the calf, and he yanks and it's over. The accountant flies from the wall (attached by rope of course)

Eggers, From *A Heartbreaking Work of Staggering Genius,* Continued

and descends slowly to the floor. It's terrible. I won't watch this show again.

Mom prefers the show where three young women sit on a pastel-colored couch and recount blind dates that they have all enjoyed or suffered through with the same man. For months, Beth and Mom have watched the show, every night. Sometimes the show's participants have had sex with one another, but use funny words to describe it. And there is the funny host with the big nose and the black curly hair. He is a funny man, and has fun with the show, keeps everything buoyant. At the end of the show, the bachelor picks one of the three with whom he wants to go on another date. The host then does something pretty incredible: even though he's already paid for the three dates previously described, and even though he has nothing to gain from doing anything more, *he still gives the bachelor and bachelorette money for their next date.*

Mom watches it every night; it's the only thing she can watch without falling asleep, which she does a lot, dozing on and off during the day. But she does not sleep at night.

"Of course you sleep at night," I say.

"I don't," she says.

THE RHETORICAL SITUATION

Purpose
As a memoirist, Eggers's overall purpose is to tell a story about his life. In this case, the story is also about the lives of his family members.

Audience
Eggers's audience is adults who appreciate creative, innovative, and literary memoirs.

Rhetorical appeals
Eggers establishes his **ethos** as an author, writing directly to readers and setting up the story of his mother's illness. He details the chase scene on TV, building tension and appealing to the **pathos** (emotions) of his readers, inviting us to identify with his experience.

(Continued on p. 276)

THE GENRE'S CONVENTIONS

Elements of the genre

Is written in first person ("I am holding . . .").

Is a true story about the writer's real life. The narrative represents Eggers's memory of this time in his life; however, his sister Beth objected to this account because Dave did not portray her as an equal parent to their brother Toph, though she claims to have been.

Mentions actual people in the writer's life.
Here Eggers writes about his mother and mentions his sister Beth; elsewhere he writes about his younger brother, Toph; other siblings; friends; and acquaintances.

(Continued on p. 276)

Eggers, From *A Heartbreaking Work of Staggering Genius,* Continued

THE RHETORICAL SITUATION

Modes & media

Mode = written

Author Dave Eggers probably assumed that his readers would be adults reading his memoir alone to themselves because that is the conventional way that books are read. Although some memoirs include photographs of the author, Eggers did not include any images beyond artwork for the cover.

Medium = print *A Heartbreaking Work of Staggering Genius* is available in print and as an audiobook. It is presented here in print, and the assumption is that you will read it linearly, that is, from beginning to end. (Though in this case, you might be noticing the annotations in the margins as well.)

THE GENRE'S CONVENTIONS

Includes a personal anecdote. In this case, it's a serious one about his mother's illness, and which shows itself one night in front of the TV.

Is written using literary techniques, including dialogue ("Of course you sleep at night.").

Style

Eggers's style and tone convey his personality. "There is an obstacle course segment, where the contestants are racing against each other and also the clock, and another segment where they hit each other with sponge-ended paddles, both of which can be extremely exciting," for example, indicates his wry wit.

The writing is rich in details. Instead of simply saying he is watching a physical contest on TV, he specifies, "On the TV an accountant from Denver is trying to climb up a wall before a bodybuilder named Striker catches him and pulls him off the wall."

Design

Text with little white space between paragraphs.

Sources

No footnotes or Works Cited list. The main source for the memoir is Eggers's life.

Questions: Analyzing Eggers's memoir

1. Purpose. Why might Eggers give so much detail about the shows he is watching on television?

2. Audience. Why would someone want to read Eggers's story, which is, in part, about his mother dying of cancer?

3. Audience. In this excerpt from his memoir, how does Eggers develop a sense of intimacy with his readers?

4. Rhetorical appeals. Most memoirists are themselves their main source of information. Based on this excerpt, are you convinced that Eggers has established his ethos? Is he a reliable narrator? Why or why not?

5. Modes & media. If you were in charge of selecting an actor to read the audio version of this book, whom would you select, and why?

6. Elements of the genre. Considering how fallible human memory is, how much accuracy do you expect in a memoir? Do you have higher or lower expectations of accuracy for autobiographies or histories? Why? And how does creativity figure into the memoir as a genre?

7. Style. Eggers wrote his memoir in the first person. Imagine that he rewrote this excerpt in the third person (*"Dave is holding his mother's nose. As the nose bleeds and they try to stop it, they watch TV."*). How would you read the memoir differently?

8. Style. Based on the excerpt from *A Heartbreaking Work of Staggering Genius*, what is your impression of Eggers's personality? Which details in the excerpt lead you to feel this way?

9. Design. In this brief excerpt, Eggers uses a long, unbroken paragraph: What do you think this text style indicates about the tone and style of the book?

10. Sources. Because Eggers himself is the main source of the book, the story he tells is told from his perspective. His sister, Beth, claimed that he inflated his role in raising their little brother, Toph. Might anything in this excerpt be seen differently by someone who was there?

Drafting a Memoir

CHECKLIST: Drafting a Memoir Thinking of composing a memoir?
Ask yourself the following questions.

WHAT'S MY RHETORICAL SITUATION?

☐ **Purpose.** What specific moment in my life do I want to write about? Why? What questions do I have about that moment? How might I interpret that moment? What insights do I want to share with others?

☐ **Audience.** How would I describe my potential readers? Why will my memoir matter to them? What do I want them to get out of it? And how will I reach them?

☐ **Rhetorical appeals.** How will I establish my authority as a writer? How reliable will I be as a narrator? To what extent will I appeal to readers' emotions? How will I use logic to support my interpretations?

☐ **Modes & media.** Do I want readers to experience my story in written, audio, or visual form? Do I want my memoir to be print, electronic, or presented face-to-face?

WHAT GENRE CONVENTIONS MATTER?

☐ **Elements of the genre.** As a person writing about my own life, how will I keep my writing true and accurate? How much will I disclose about myself (and others) in my memoir? Will I write in the first person? What anecdotes will I use, and why? Also, what literary elements might I use? For example, will I use dialogue?

☐ **Style.** What tone will I take in my writing? Will my memoir be funny? Serious? Tragic? What kind of language will I use? How much detail will I provide?

☐ **Design.** What format will my memoir take? Will I compose a print memoir—and if so, will I include photographs and other images? Or will I compose a graphic memoir or other type of memoir?

☐ **Sources.** What memories will I draw on? Will I need to check my story with others from my life, or will I rely on my own recollections and interpretations?

PRACTICE Want to experiment? Draft your own memoir.

Think about a key event in your life. Draft a few paragraphs in which you begin telling the story of the event in the first person. Use specific details and language so that your readers will feel like they were there. Consider how you want your readers to feel as they read your draft: Do you want them to laugh, cry, be outraged, or something else?

GRAPHIC MEMOIRS

The graphic memoir is a memoir told through text and images, usually drawings. Sometimes a graphic memoir uses more words than images, but usually it's the other way around. If you are interested in composing any kind of memoir (whether it's in graphic or comic book form, or a film, for example), we suggest that you read the "Memoirs" section of this chapter (p. 269).

The graphic memoirist Alison Bechdel (p. 282) has described her process in interviews: First she writes her text; then she inks the images. Other graphic memoirists use different techniques, foregrounding the images in the panels and writing the text in later. You may already be familiar with graphic memoirs, a genre first made popular by Art Spiegelman's *Maus*, a graphic memoir about surviving the Holocaust. Graphic narratives now have a place as respected literary texts: They're the focus of college courses; they've won Pulitzer Prizes; and they've inspired successful movies including *A History of Violence* and *Sin City*.

> What are your favorite graphic memoirs or novels? What aspects of the story are most memorable? Why? #Remember #Analyze

Analyzing Graphic Memoirs: What to Look For

THE RHETORICAL SITUATION

Purpose   Like other memoirists, graphic memoirists tell the story of (or a story from) a writer's life. Using such literary devices as character (in this case, real people rather than fictional ones), dialogue, and setting, graphic memoirists connect their readers with their work. Graphic memoirs, which look something like extended comic strips, focus on transporting the reader to a world that is very different from everyday reality. Sometimes a graphic narrative, such as Marjane Satrapi's *Persepolis*, discloses elements of a culture—Satrapi's life growing up in Iran and later as an expatriate— showing readers a world that may be outside their own experience.

Audience   Graphic memoirists know that their audiences want a look into someone else's life, as told by that person. Graphic memoirists know their audiences are particularly drawn toward the visual, and perhaps grew up reading comic books, or really like illustrated texts or alternative narrative forms.

As graphic memoirs are becoming more popular in academic settings, with instructors assigning them as part of their reading lists—or as an alternative to the print memoir in composition classes—more students are creating and reading them.

Rhetorical appeals   The play between visuals and text helps graphic memoirists emphasize certain aspects of the narrative to readers. Because memoirists want their readers to empathize with their experiences, they often use appeals to emotion to draw readers into their world. For example, when a story is meant to elicit shock, the shape of the letters and the use of bold graphics, along with the expressions on the character's face, can guide the reader's emotional response, emphasizing pathos. In a graphic memoir, ethos is a central concern, because the audience must trust that the writer is accurately representing experience and events.

Modes & media   Graphic memoirs usually take print form but are sometimes digitized for the Web. Graphic memoirs and novels are often adapted for film, reimagined as animated stories, as is the case with *Persepolis*.

THE GENRE'S CONVENTIONS

Elements of the genre   Like all memoirs, the graphic memoir has a real-life plot that revolves around a series of events, or a storyline. The storyline hinges on a central conflict driven by real people who function as characters do in fiction. The central conflict of Marjane Satrapi's *Persepolis*, for example, is her (and her family's) struggle to survive the Iranian Revolution (of 1979, also known as the Islamic Revolution); at that time, the country's monarchy was overthrown and Iran became an Islamic republic with an increasingly repressive government.

To tell their stories, graphic memoirists use words—usually organized into short, simple sentences—that provide dialogue and move the plot along toward the conflict and its resolution. The visuals (usually inked drawings) move the plot, too, but also assist in creating the setting, atmosphere, and emotion of the memoir.

The written content of the graphic memoir often appears in boxes or in sentences interspersed among the visuals. Dialogue is usually placed in a bubble or box linked to the character's mouth. Most graphic composers do not present words and sentences in traditional paragraphs. The advantage is that by isolating a sentence in a box, the author creates a snapshot of a moment, or of a series of moments, adding to the power of the story. Further, though the graphic narrative may not provide traditional transitions between ideas and scenes, some transitional expressions help the visual memoirist move from one idea to the next. For example, the words "only four months earlier" show a jump back in time.

Just as in comic strips, the visuals of a graphic memoir do a lot to relate the story and reinforce aspects of the written narrative. The visuals, which can focus in on a detail and pan out like a movie camera, for example, emphasize certain moments

Consider Art Spiegelman's graphic memoir *Maus*, which is a Holocaust narrative (the story of Spiegelman's father). To what extent is the graphic memoir an appropriate genre for dealing with traumatic experiences? #Evaluate

and allow readers to see what is happening. See the "Design" section below for more on how drawings function in a graphic memoir.

Style   The reader's experience depends on the written and visual style of the graphic memoirist—how much (and what kind of) detail and specific techniques he or she uses, and the quality of the visual story's voice and tone.

Tone and voice. Graphic memoirists communicate the tone of their stories and their voices as storytellers through word choice, diction, visuals, and the choice of typeface and other graphics. For example, if a character is feeling exasperated, the writer might choose a font (such as **Impact**) to illustrate that mood.

Detail. Depending on their target audience, graphic memoirists may use intricate, almost lifelike detail, as in Bechdel's *Fun Home* (p. 282). Other times, graphic memoirists might take a more cartoon/superhero approach, such as that of DC Comics' *Watchmen*. Typically, graphic memoirists limit their reliance on text, using it primarily to keep the plot moving. Sentences in a given panel tend to be short, without much embellishment. In Satrapi's *Persepolis*, the narrative detail is written in a journalistic style, giving readers a sense of watching a revolution unfold.

Design   Like comic strips, graphic memoirs are organized into visual panels, usually squares or rectangles that essentially freeze a moment in its own individual space. Like all graphic composers, graphic memoirists make choices about where to place panels, how large to make them, and what words from the written narrative to emphasize. They also decide how and where to place figures and objects within a panel, in order to direct the reader. The size of one object next to another (scale), the direction an object is facing in relation to the page, and the cutting off of part of an object in a frame are all careful choices that create meaning for readers.

Other design choices include whether to use a font, real handwriting or lettering, or a font that mimics handwriting. Many graphic composers use block lettering, boldface, and italics when they want to show emphasis, and use different graphical styles when needed (such as `Courier` or other distinctive fonts). Graphic memoirists also need to make decisions about the style, shape, and size of boxes, balloons, or other word-framing devices. Sometimes they assign specific shapes for specific speakers in the story. They also make choices about white space from panel to panel, and within a frame of text. White space is used for aesthetic reasons, but also to call attention to certain parts of the text, to provide a visual pause, or to represent the absence of something or someone.

Sources   See "Memoirs" (p. 269).

TIME MAGAZINE'S #1 BOOK OF THE YEAR
NATIONAL BOOK CRITICS CIRCLE AWARD FINALIST

"A splendid autobiography . . . refreshingly open and generous."
— *Entertainment Weekly*

ALISON BECHDEL

▲ BOOK COVER
& AUTHOR PHOTO ▶
Alison Bechdel
*Fun Home: A Family
Tragicomic.* Author
photo: Liza Cowan.

Alison Bechdel

From Fun Home: A Family Tragicomic

Alison Bechdel gained notoriety in the comics scene in 1983 with her syndicated strip *Dykes to Watch Out For.* In her comic strip, Bechdel combined political commentary with the daily lives of mostly lesbian characters, narrating their love affairs, breakups, and adventures as attendees at such lesbian festivals as the Michigan Womyn's Music Festival.

After years of working on this comic strip, Bechdel wrote a graphic memoir, *Fun Home: A Family Tragicomic,* published in 2006. In *Fun Home*, she tells the story of growing up with a closeted father who ran a funeral parlor and taught English. In this work, Bechdel conveys the importance of her father in her life. The section that we've excerpted is from the book's first chapter. In it, Bechdel's own coming-out story is overshadowed by the death of her father.

As a graphic memoirist, Bechdel makes plenty of decisions about her purposes and ways to draw in her readers. She also works with many of the conventions of the graphic narrative, while using a style that is all her own. The annotations in the margins of the work draw your attention to these choices, inviting you to think critically about their impact on you as a reader and composer. *(All images and cover: From FUN HOME: A FAMILY TRAGICOMIC by Alison Bechdel. Copyright © 2006. Reprinted by permission of Houghton Mifflin Harcourt Publishing Company. All rights reserved.)*

Bechdel, From *Fun Home*, *Continued*

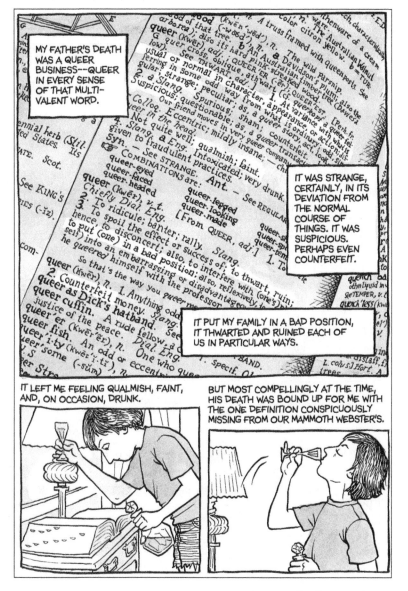

Continues next page

What is the composer, **Alison Bechdel**, doing?

THE RHETORICAL SITUATION

Purpose
Audience
Rhetorical appeals
Modes & media

see page 284

How do I know this is a **graphic memoir**?

THE GENRE'S CONVENTIONS

Elements of the genre
Style
Design
Sources

see page 285

Bechdel, From *Fun Home*, *Continued*

THE RHETORICAL SITUATION

Purpose

Bechdel's goal is to tell a story about her life, which includes childhood, coming out, and coming to terms with her father's identity and death.

Audience

Bechdel knows her readers enjoy memoirs and are especially drawn to comics and graphic novels. They are also interested in the coming-of-age and sexual identity themes in *Fun Home*.

Rhetorical appeals

Bechdel appeals to readers' emotions (**pathos**) by showing how her father's "queer death" caused her to feel "qualmish, faint, and, on occasion, drunk." The author uses events from her life to establish her **ethos**. Announcing "I am a lesbian" helps establish her ethos in what is partly a coming-out story.

(Continued on p. 286)

Bechdel, From *Fun Home*, *Continued*

(Continued on p. 286.)

Bechdel, From *Fun Home*, *Continued*

THE RHETORICAL SITUATION

Modes & media
Mode = written and visual Bechdel uses both the written and visual texts to communicate her story about coming out. Bechdel's use of visuals—such as when she mails a letter to her parents or talks on the phone with her mother—shows readers how Bechdel wants us to view her at that moment.

Medium = print
Just like traditional memoirs, graphic memoirs are available in both print and digital media. Bookstores, these days, have sections devoted to graphic novels, where you can also find graphic memoirs such as Bechdel's. Digital graphic novels and memoirs are also often created online. Web sites such as Comic Master allow you to create your own short graphic novel/memoir online using their free software.

THE GENRE'S CONVENTIONS

The visuals don't just represent the text—they highlight specific aspects and create emphasis. E.g., Bechdel presents the dictionary definition of the word *queer*. By blowing up the dictionary page, she shows her narrator-self coming to grips with ways to read her father's identity and death.
The visuals move the action along by showing it. E.g., we know Bechdel mails the letter not because the text says so, but because she shows herself licking the envelope and putting it in the mailbox.

Bechdel's **drawings take up more space than her words**; her words convey the weight of the narrative while the images convey the emotion.
Text is not presented in paragraphs. E.g., the isolated sentences in the top frame create a snapshot of moments. Combined, they would create a traditional paragraph but would have a very different effect.

Style
Bechdel uses **diction and word choice** to portray an educated, articulate character. E.g., she says she "imagined my confession as an emancipation. . . ."
The distance Bechdel's narrative voice has from her story gives the reader a lens through which she sees her past from an adult perspective. E.g., when she tells how others responded to her coming-out letter, she states, "The news was not received as well as I had hoped."

Design
Bechdel's text font mimics handwriting and she uses bold, italics, and other type effects to convey emotion.

She also **varies her layout**; e.g., some panels are parallel to each other, while others are not aligned evenly.
The **shapes of frames** around the text indicate what is thought, spoken, or narrated. Different shapes indicate who is speaking. In the bottom right frame, the mother's dialogue appears in a jagged box that comes out of the phone.
Bechdel uses **graphical style** to approximate reality. E.g., when the narrator types out, "I am a lesbian," Bechdel switches to Courier to approximate typing. On the third page shown here, Bechdel uses a lot of **white space** to call attention to the text and to represent the absence of her father.

Sources
Bechdel's source is her own memory, so there are no citations to outside materials.

Questions: Analyzing Bechdel's graphic memoir

1. Purpose. What parallels does Bechdel draw between her father's homosexuality and her own coming out?

2. Audience. Based on the short excerpt, who would you say is the audience for this graphic memoir? Why?

3. Rhetorical appeals. How do the visuals emphasize the main character's emotional state?

4. Modes & media. What different elements of the plot do the text and visuals emphasize?

5. Elements of the genre. Are there any places where the visuals and words seem to contradict each other or seem to be in tension with each other? If so, why do you think there is a contradiction or tension?

6. Elements of the genre. How much time is covered in the pages shown? How does Bechdel show the passage of time?

7. Elements of the genre. Only three pages of the graphic memoir are represented here. Even though these pages are a small snapshot of the book, what sense do you get of Bechdel as the narrator of her own story? How do the different graphic elements, combined with words, give you that sense of her?

8. Style. How would you describe the level of detail Bechdel uses in her visuals? In her text? Does the level of detail serve different purposes? If so, how?

9. Design. Sometimes Bechdel chooses to sandwich the narrative text between the visual panels. Other times, she places the narrative text within its own box. What reasons might she have for this? Are the narrative pieces that are in a box more significant? Why?

10. Sources. The main source for the graphic memoir is Alison Bechdel's life and experience. How does this influence your reading of the work?

Drafting a Graphic Memoir

CHECKLIST: Drafting a Graphic Memoir Thinking of composing a graphic memoir? Ask yourself the following questions.

WHAT'S MY RHETORICAL SITUATION?

☐ **Purpose.** What specific moment in my life do I want to write about? Why? What questions do I have about that moment? How might I interpret that moment? What insights do I want to share with others? How would visuals illustrate the moment and make my experience more tangible for my reader?

☐ **Audience.** Who are my potential readers? Why will my memoir matter to them? What do I want them to get out of it? How old are they and how will I reach them? How will I use visuals to do that?

☐ **Rhetorical appeals.** How will I establish my authority as a writer? How reliable will I be as a narrator? To what extent will I appeal to my readers' emotions? How might I use logic?

☐ **Modes & media.** Do I want to create my story first with graphics or text? What aspects will I represent visually, and what aspects will I represent in written form? Would my graphic memoir be appropriate to translate into a film? Do I want to create my story using ink on paper or using a digital program?

WHAT GENRE CONVENTIONS MATTER?

☐ **Elements of the genre.** How will I keep my writing true and accurate? How much will I disclose about myself (and others) in my graphic memoir? Will I write in the first person? What anecdotes will I use to tell my story, and why? How will I visually represent my characters? Will they be true to life or exaggerated? How will I balance the narrative with dialogue?

☐ **Style.** What tone will I take in my writing? Will my graphic memoir be funny? Serious? Tragic? What kind of language will I use? How much detail will I provide? How will I use the visuals to convey my tone?

☐ **Design.** What fonts will I use? How might I use shapes of boxes to indicate specific character voices? Will I vary the shapes of my panels?

☐ **Sources.** What specific memories will I draw on? Will I need to check my story with others from my life, or will I rely on my own recollections and interpretations? Will I need to research historical and cultural events related to the time period of my story?

PRACTICE Want to experiment? Draft and sketch out your own graphic memoir.

Identify a pivotal moment in your life. Sketch out a few panels of a graphic memoir that convey the moment and its importance. Think about how you want the key people who participated in the event to come across to readers and how you can convey those characteristics with visual details. Think about what you want to convey through dialogue and what you want to convey through internal reflection.

PHOTO ESSAYS

A photo essay is a group of photos that tells a unified story or makes a unified argument. Some photo essayists provide supplementary text or brief captions for their images; others choose to present the images without words. Some photo essayists are journalists whose purpose is to convey a news or human interest story or offer commentary on an event. The photo essays published by *Mother Jones* about the aftermath of the 2010 earthquake in Haiti and a piece on how Ikea has partnered with UNICEF in a program to encourage reading in Albania are examples of works by photo essayists using images and text to provide information and even make an argument.

◄ PHOTO ESSAY STILL
UNICEF
"Ikea Partners for Reading in Albania."
© UNICEF/NYHQ2008-0133/Giacomo Pirozzi.

Photo essays can also be viewed as works of art that express ideas and evoke emotional responses in the viewer. You can find them online, in galleries and museums, and also in magazines such as *Life*, *Time*, and *National Geographic*. Photo essayists generally aim to make a particular point or argument; some make specific social commentaries. For example, photographer Walker Evans (1903–75) and writer James Agee (1909–55) collaborated on a book-length photo essay about the hardships of tenant farmers in the American South in the 1930s. *Let Us Now Praise Famous Men* is a very word-heavy photo essay.

TEXT FROM PHOTO ESSAY
During July and August 1936 Walker Evans and I were traveling in the middle south of this nation, and were engaged in what, even from the first, has seemed to me rather a curious piece of work. It was our business to prepare, for a New York magazine, an article on cotton tenantry in the United States, in the form of a photographic and verbal record

PHOTO FROM ▶
PHOTO ESSAY
Walker Evans
"Lily Rogers Fields."
This photo appeared
in *Let Us Now Praise
Famous Men*. Shown
here is Lily Rogers
Fields, the wife of
sharecropper Bud
Fields, and their
two children. Evans
took this photo in
1936 in Hale County,
Alabama. *Library of
Congress*.

of the daily living and environment of an average white family of tenant farmers. We had
first to find and to live with such a family; and that was the object of our traveling.

—**James Agee,** from *Let Us Now Praise Famous Men*

Other photo essays involve fewer words, such as many of the photo essays available online at the *Time* magazine site. See, for example, the photo essay titled "Famous Couples."

Analyzing Photo Essays: What to Look For

THE RHETORICAL SITUATION

Purpose Photo essayists have two main goals: to tell a story and/or to make a point. Usually their work is focused on a specific theme. For example, the Agee and Evans photo essay collaboration (p. 289) focuses on the experiences of sharecroppers in the South, and in doing so, asks the viewer to look at the relationship of those who are privileged (those who read the book) and those who are less fortunate (the subjects of the book). Photo essayists usually seek to evoke an emotional response in the viewer. For example, the creators of the *Time* essay on famous couples emphasize the endurance of love in relationships by showing celebrity couples enjoying a happy moment.

Audience   Photo essayists know that their audiences are drawn to visual storytelling—and to the issues and themes of their works, which may be social and cultural, journalistic, and/or artistic. For example, photo essayist and documentarian Brenda Ann Kenneally, creator of an ongoing project called "Upstate Girls," aims her work at those interested in her intimate look at working-class women and their families. Norbert Wu targets his essay "Life beneath Antarctic Ice" at an audience interested in nature.

Rhetorical appeals   Depending on their subject matter and composition, photo essayists may emphasize logos, pathos, or ethos to make their point. For instance, Andrew Testa's disturbing photo essays of Bangladeshi women who were scarred by acid for refusing to accept marriage proposals emphasize pathos by showing the women's scars close up; ethos is also important because viewers must trust that Testa has not used lighting or perspective to distort reality.

Modes & media   While photo essayists usually combine visuals with some written text, some also incorporate bits of audio, such as in *The New York Times* photo essay "One in 8 Million," which highlights the lives of ordinary New Yorkers. Photo essays can be print based, but also offered digitally, as is *Let Us Now Praise Famous Men;* or they can be created mainly for online publication, such as *Time* magazine's photo essays.

When might it be more appropriate to create a photo essay rather than a written essay? To what extent do your purpose, audience, and subject affect your choice of whether to create in a visual mode? #Evaluate

THE GENRE'S CONVENTIONS

Elements of the genre   A photo essay can be used to tell a simple story, but the genre is often used to persuade viewers to sympathize with a point of view or to take a specific action. For example, through "Upstate Girls," Brenda Ann Kenneally, hopes that viewers connect with the subjects' struggles and triumphs.

Some photo essayists include captions to provide context; others include more text, with a 50:50 text-to-image ratio, such as in Suzanne Merkelson's "Keeping Up with the Qaddafis," published online in March 2011 in *Foreign Policy*. In this piece, Merkelson accompanies each photo with at least one paragraph of text.

Photo essayists make rhetorical choices about their purpose and audience, and they choose images carefully, in the same way a writer chooses words, paragraphs, and structure. The photo essayist chooses each image with the viewer's intellectual, emotional, or other responses in mind. Similarly, a photo essay can be structured much like any persuasive essay. For example, the introductory images, which function like a written essay's introduction, need to establish the subject matter and further the purposes of the piece—to push the narrative or argument forward.

Photo essayists use some techniques that narrative essayists, storytellers, and persuasive writers do (pp. 257–58 and 437). That is, they select and sequence their content in a way that will spark their readers' interest, keep them reading/viewing, and ultimately convince them of a particular point of view. Initial images may serve as an introduction, while those that follow may build in terms of intensity to support the argument the photo essayist wants to make. (See "Design," below.)

Style

Detail. Most photo essayists do not provide much detail in the text of their essays. For example, most captions give just enough information for readers to understand the story behind (and location of) the related photo. The photos themselves can show varying degrees of detail—in some cases, capturing one element up close, such as a person's face; in others, showing a panoramic view of a landscape.

Tone. Photo essayists choose images that reflect the mood they want to convey. For example, a photo essayist who wants to stir readers to take action in response to an environmental disaster such as an oil spill might feature an image of someone rescuing and rehabilitating an oil-soaked bird.

Design   A good photo essayist usually presents a variety of images (from different perspectives) and arranges the images in an order that builds emotion, furthers an argument, or advances a story. For example, a photo essayist who wants to tell a story might sequence the images from one event to the next, much like a narrative essayist would. In other cases, the photo essayist might not choose a linear progression, but might instead order images for maximum impact, especially when presenting an argument.

Sources   Photo essays always involve primary research, as the photographer is always witnessing the subject of the photos firsthand. Brenda Ann Kenneally's photo essay on working-class women, for example, is entirely informed by Kenneally's interviews with the women she photographed. Sometimes secondary research must be conducted as well, to fill in historical details or other information.

Eros Hoagland

From "Life in the Googleplex"

Time, a weekly news and current events magazine, often features photo essays related to world events. The magazine commissioned and published in February 2006 an online photo essay titled "Life in the Googleplex." Presented as a slide show, the essay was created by photojournalist Eros Hoagland of Redux Pictures. Hoagland, who began his career reporting on the fallout of El Salvador's civil war, is also interested in showing the subtleties of place, something he clearly brought to the Googleplex project. Given the range of his subject matter, the quality of his work, and the publications he calls his clients (including *The New York Times* and *Newsweek*), Hoagland, like *Time* magazine, has some good ethos.

▲ AUTHOR PHOTO &
▼ PHOTO ESSAY
Eros Hoagland
From his profile at Redux, and the "Life in the Googleplex" slide show online at *Time*.

His purpose in creating "Life in the Googleplex" was to give readers an inside look at what it's like to work at Google. By highlighting gadgets and leisure opportunities, Hoagland suggests that employees do serious work but also have plenty of time to play. Further, by showing the human side (and human faces) of Google, Hoagland establishes that the company is more than a search engine.

The annotations in the margins point out the decisions that Hoagland made, perhaps with the input of editors at *Time*, including the purpose of the piece, the perceived audience, and the genre conventions applied. *(All images on pp. 293–96: Eros Hoagland/Redux Pictures.)*

What is the composer, Eros Hoagland, doing?

THE RHETORICAL SITUATION

Purpose
Audience
Rhetorical appeals
Modes & media

see page 295

How do I know this is a photo essay?

THE GENRE'S CONVENTIONS

Elements of the genre
Style
Design
Sources

see page 295

Hoagland, *From "Life in the Googleplex,"* Continued

Photos: Life in the Googleplex 1 of 12 ◄ BACK NEXT ►

EROS HOAGLAND / REDUX FOR TIME

◄ BACK NEXT ►

BE YOURSELF
Desktop gizmos and lava lamps express Google's laid-back ethos.

• In Search of The Real Google

Continues next page

Hoagland, *From "Life in the Googleplex,"* *Continued*

Photos: Life in the Googleplex   2 of 12   ◀ BACK   NEXT ▶

OPEN 24 hrs

TECH STOP

EROS HOAGLAND / REDUX FOR TIME

◀ BACK   NEXT ▶

ASK THE HELP DESK
Laptop on the fritz? Google keeps experts on site to fix computers and other digital gadgets.

• In Search of The Real Google

Continues next page

THE RHETORICAL SITUATION

Purpose
Hoagland (perhaps with the help of *Time* editors) set out to illustrate how a high-tech work environment, such as Google, can be filled with creativity and fun.

Audience
The audience for the photo essay is *Time* magazine readers, Google fans, and people interested in cultural trends related to technology and the workplace.

Rhetorical appeals
Hoagland uses **logos** to appeal to readers by building a logical case about how a creative work environment inspires workers' creativity. He establishes the essay's **ethos** by using photos of Google workers.

Modes & media
Mode = written and visual
Hoagland's primary goal was to visually portray a typical workday at Google.

(Continued on p. 296.)

THE GENRE'S CONVENTIONS

Elements of the genre
Is comprised mainly of photos, with some text.
Is focused on a topic, in this case, specifically workers' play and leisure time at Google's offices.
Tells a story, in this case, about a typical workday at Google.
Makes an argument, in this case that Google's workers are productive and inspired by creativity and recreation.

Includes captions that explain the photos. For example, the caption with the first image reads, "Be Yourself." Without it, viewers could assume the message is that the office is crowded and cluttered rather than supportive of individuality and expression.

Style
Use of the present tense reinforces the "this is happening now" feel of the piece.

Hoagland, *From "Life in the Googleplex,"* Continued

Adding written
details tells a more
complete story;
it also provides a
commentary about
what is taking place,
to persuade viewers
that the workplace
atmosphere is
pleasant.

Medium = digital
Although *Time*
publishes photo
essays in their print
edition, "Life in the
Googleplex" was
published digitally
at *Time*'s Web site.
Publishing this essay
online is especially
appropriate because
Google is a digital
company; further,
the advantages of
publishing online
are obvious. As long
as viewers have an
Internet connection,
they can see and
share the essay; if
it were only in print
form, they would
need to locate a copy
of that edition of the
magazine.

Photos: Life in the Googleplex　　3 of 12　◀ BACK　　NEXT ▶

EROS HOAGLAND / REDUX FOR TIME

◀ BACK　　NEXT ▶

GOOGLER WITH GOGGLES
A lifeguard sits on duty as an employee works out in one of two swim-in-place pools at
Google's headquarters.

• In Search of The Real Google

THE GENRE'S CONVENTIONS

A **playful tone** emphasizes that Google is a
fun place to work. For example, the swimmer
is referred to as a "Googler with Goggles."

Design
The variety of the photos suggests the
breadth of activities that can take place in
the Googleplex. Elements of the text are
highlighted by typeface choice and color.

Captions consistently appear below the
photos and each caption has a pithy heading.

Sources
Hoagland conducted primary research—
spending time at Google, following around
employees, trying to capture the elements of
a typical day and different aspects of work
and play.

Questions: Analyzing Hoagland's photo essay

1. Purpose. What is the unifying message of the three photos shown? Explain in one sentence.

2. Purpose. Do the photos tend to focus more on people or objects? Why do you think Hoagland chose that emphasis?

3. Audience. What techniques did Hoagland use so that viewers would see the playful nature of working at Google?

4. Rhetorical appeals. Based on the three photos shown, what is your impression of the ethos of Hoagland and the *Time* editors he most likely worked with?

5. Modes & media. If the photos had no captions, what assumptions might you make about life at Google? Do some images fully convey the message without the text? Where and how? Why is this essay best viewed digitally, rather than in print?

6. Elements of the genre. In "Life in the Googleplex," do the photos illustrate the captions or do the captions describe the photos? Explain your answer.

7. Elements of the genre. View the entire "Googleplex" slide show. Now that you've seen the whole thing, would you say that this essay is primarily telling a story or making an argument? Why?

8. Style. How does the tone and voice of the writing emphasize the working environment at Google? How does the selection and presentation of photographs contribute to that tone? Use specific examples to illustrate your answer.

9. Design. View the entire "Googleplex" slide show again. Pay attention to how Hoagland and *Time* ordered the images. How might a different ordering of images affect the narrative? How do Hoagland and *Time* use organization of the images to build logic?

10. Sources. The photos were taken by Eros Hoagland, a professional photographer commissioned by *Time* magazine (Hoagland is the source of the images). Do you think someone working at Google would choose to highlight different aspects of working there? How?

Sketching Out a Photo Essay

CHECKLIST: Sketching Out a Photo Essay Thinking of composing a photo essay? Ask yourself the following questions.

WHAT'S MY RHETORICAL SITUATION?

☐ **Purpose.** What is my story, and why do I want to tell it? Or do I want to do more than tell a story? If so, what main point or argument do I want to make, and why?

☐ **Audience.** Who are my readers/viewers that I want to attract to my photo essay? Why will my photo essay matter to them? What do I want them to get out of it? And how will I reach them?

☐ **Rhetorical appeals.** How will I use ethos, pathos, and logos to reach my audience? How will I establish my authority as a photographer and writer? Will I rely more on pathos or logos? How will my photos and text work together to appeal to my readers' sense of ethos, pathos, and/or logos?

☐ **Modes & media.** Do I want to present my photo essay in hard-copy format, as in a photo album; or electronically, as on a Web site; or in some other way? How will these choices impact how my viewers experience my photo essay? For example, would it be better to present it online or as a collection of large photos matted and framed on the wall?

WHAT GENRE CONVENTIONS MATTER?

☐ **Elements of the genre.** I know that the best photo essays tell a story but also put forth some type of argument. For example, in his "Googleplex" essay, Eros Hoagland asks viewers to see Google as a successful company in part because the workplace itself encourages creativity. How does this compare to what I want to do? What argument will I make in my photo essay—and how will I do it?

☐ **Style.** What tone do I want to strike? Playful, like in "Life in the Googleplex"? Or more serious, like in Kenneally's photo essay?

☐ **Design.** What order will I arrange the photos in, and how will the order affect how my viewers understand my story?

☐ **Sources.** Where will I need to go to take my photos? Will I want to photograph individuals and their possessions? Or perhaps historical sites? Will I need to request special permission to do so?

PRACTICE Want to experiment? Draft your own photo essay.

Just as Hoagland and *Time* convey a sense of work life at Google in their photo essay, you might want to do something similar. What do you have to say about your own workplace, campus, or residence? Brainstorm about how people at one or more of those locations feel about that place; then take three to five photos of the place that convey that feeling. Your draft photo essay should offer some kind of commentary on the place you've chosen as your subject; it should not simply show it. Add brief captions similar to the ones in the "Googleplex" essay that help tell a story and offer perspective.

SHORT STORIES

A short story is a work of fiction, that is, a nonfactual work of the imagination. Short stories are briefer than novels and often focus on a central theme. You can read them in magazines such as *The New Yorker*, in literary journals such as *Ploughshares*, and on blogs; they are also published as collections in book form. (For more information on literary journals, see the list published by *Poets & Writers*.) Fiction authors—whether they're writing a novel or a short story, serious literature or a bodice-ripping romance—generally use specific elements, such as plot, characters, and setting, to tell a story.

If you've taken an introduction to fiction course, you have probably read classic stories such as "A Good Man Is Hard to Find" by Flannery O'Connor or "A Rose for Emily" by William Faulkner, or more contemporary works such as "Brownies" by ZZ Packer or one of the stories from Jhumpa Lahiri's collection *Interpreter of Maladies*. Whether you are a reader, an aspiring writer, or both, the following guidelines will help you look at short fiction with a critical eye, examine the conventions and rhetorical contexts of the genre, and experiment a little with your own work of narrative fiction.

Analyzing Short Stories: What to Look For

THE RHETORICAL SITUATION

Purpose   Fiction writers often write stories to entertain, but many also write to share insights into the human condition. For example, Edgar Allan Poe, in the "The Tell-Tale Heart," looks into the world of a paranoid madman. Amy Tan, in her short stories about Chinese Americans, shares perspectives on what it's like to live in the United States when one's cultural and familial heritage clashes dramatically with everyday life.

Among the goals of short story writers is to offer a compelling narrative about memorable characters—characters that invite readers to identify with them or that challenge readers' assumptions. To achieve these goals, authors work with a variety of literary techniques. (For more on these, see "Style.") Some fiction writers (such as the late David Foster Wallace) play around with the form, using alternative techniques and styles, with the purpose of creating experimental literary art. Whatever short story writers' purposes are, they must achieve them within a limited page count.

Audience   Authors may aim their work at a broad, popular audience looking for fun and escape, such as Stephen King does, or at a narrower audience of literary readers, such as Alice Munro or Sherman Alexie do, or at audiences along that spectrum. Some fiction authors (such as J. M. Coetzee or Ralph Ellison) write (or in Ellison's case, wrote) for audiences looking for intellectual stimulation and depth. Other authors who embrace various subgenres of fiction—such as horror (Stephen King), fantasy (J. R. R. Tolkien), sci-fi (Ray Bradbury), romance (Jackie Collins), and mysteries (Agatha Christie)—aim(ed) to connect with readers who want entertainment. These authors follow certain established formulas for writing fiction; it's what their readers want and expect.

Rhetorical appeals   Most fiction authors connect to their readers primarily through pathos. Because they want readers to understand and sympathize with (or, sometimes, loathe) their story's protagonist, they need readers to see things from that character's point of view. They need readers to form an emotional connection to that character. Edgar Allan Poe accomplishes this, for example, in "The Tell-Tale Heart," partly by telling the story in the first person. This allows his readers to experience the unfolding drama of a murder at the same time that the protagonist does.

Modes & media   Short stories usually appear in print form in collections of short stories or literary journals. Occasionally, a short story is reimagined as a film, as was the case with *Minority Report*, based on a Philip K. Dick story, and *Brokeback Mountain*, based on an Annie Proulx story. In retelling these stories as feature films, the filmmakers had to invent backstories for the characters and create new material to flesh out moments that are not mentioned in the stories.

THE GENRE'S CONVENTIONS

Elements of the genre

Plot. Short stories are structured around a few main elements, one of which is a plot. The plot is the series of events that shape the action of the narrative. The plot in Poe's "The Tell-Tale Heart," for instance (spoiler alert!), involves the narrator caring for the old man, becoming disturbed by the old man's eye, murdering the old man, defending his sanity to the police officers who arrive to investigate, and finally, being discovered as the murderer.

Characters and conflict. The plot involves the story's characters and revolves around a central conflict or struggle that drives the plot and builds it toward a climax, ultimately resolving in some way by the end of the story. The main character (protagonist) in "The Tell-Tale Heart" is the one telling the story (the narrator). Sometimes the conflict is internal, between a character's sense of right and wrong, for example; other times the conflict is external, between a character and

Do you read formula fiction, such as romances or mysteries? What do you like about these stories? What rhetorical choices do the romance and mystery authors make in terms of character, plot, depth, and style? #Understand #Analyze

an outside force, such as another character, or a tornado or political upheaval. The narrator's conflict in "The Tell-Tale Heart" is between his desire to be seen as sane and the fact that he murdered an old man because the old man's eyeball bothered him. The story's characters, the people in the story, are inventions of the author.

Setting, symbolism, and theme. Fiction authors also provide a setting (the time, place, and atmosphere in which the story takes place), use symbolism (the use of a person, object, image, word, or action that has a range of meaning beyond the literal), and convey a theme (the story's central meaning or main idea).

Narrator. Every work of fiction is told by a narrator, and from a specific point of view. For example, if a story is narrated by a particular character and told from an "*I*" point of view, it is described as *first person*. One example of a work with a first-person narrator is James Baldwin's "Sonny's Blues," told by the main character, Sonny's brother.) Most stories are told from a *third-person* point of view (from the *he, she, it,* or *they* point of view) because this is the most flexible type of narration. Very few works are told from the unwieldy *you* point of view, but some examples include Lorrie Moore's "How to Become a Writer," and Dennis Lehane's "Until Gwen." Some works of fiction shift points of view, depending on the type of narrator the author uses, and through which character's consciousness the author wants readers to receive the story (such as Jill McCorkle's story, "Magic Words").

Many first-time novelists write in the first person; that is, their narrators speak from the I point of view. Why do you think this may be? #Analyze

Style

Detail. Fiction writers use detail to enrich their plots, provide a setting, convey believable characters, and bring their stories to life for readers. This sentence, from Shirley Jackson's "The Lottery," gives a sense of the relationships between men and women in the town where the story takes place and creates for readers a visual image of the women:

> The women, wearing faded house dresses and sweaters, came shortly after their menfolk.

Techniques. Authors use dialogue, vivid descriptions of the story's location, metaphor, simile, imagery, and other techniques to engage readers' imaginations. Dialogue is conversation between characters, as in this passage from Ernest Hemingway's "The Short Happy Life of Francis Macomber":

> "Here's to the lion," he said. "I can't ever thank you for what you did."
> Margaret, his wife, looked away from him and back to Wilson.
> "Let's not talk about the lion," she said.
> Wilson looked over at her without smiling and now she smiled at him.
> "It's been a very strange day," she said. "Hadn't you ought to put your hat on even under the canvas at noon? You told me that, you know."
> "Might put it on," said Wilson.
> "You know you have a very red face, Mr. Wilson," she told him and smiled again.

Authors use metaphors and similes to show comparisons, so that readers can understand something in terms of another thing, as in Sherwood Anderson's story "Hands":

> In the dense blotch of light beneath the table, the kneeling figure looked like a priest engaged in some service of his church. The nervous expressive fingers, flashing in and out of the light, might well have been mistaken for the fingers of the devotee going swiftly through decade after decade of his rosary.

Imagery refers to sensory details that put a mental picture (or sound or smell or taste or tactile sensation) in a reader's mind, as this passage from Isabel Allende's "Clarisa" does:

> Clarisa was born before the city had electricity, she lived to see television coverage of the first astronaut levitating on the moon, and she died of amazement when the Pope came for a visit and was met in the street by homosexuals dressed up as nuns.

Tone and voice. The writer's persona comes through in the voice (often specifically through the voice of the narrator). The voice is the personality the reader hears; in the sentence above from Isabel Allende's "Clarisa," the voice we hear is whimsical. The tone is the attitude that comes through in the writing. We could describe the tone of Hemingway's narrator in "The Short Happy Life of Francis Macomber" as detached.

Design

Print. Most short stories are published in collections in book form, in magazines (hard copies or online) that feature short fiction along with articles, or in literary journals. In all of these, the central focus is the words themselves.

Length. Short stories can be as short as a single paragraph or as long as thirty or forty pages. Most short stories can be read in one sitting, although of course, there's no standard definition for "one sitting." Extremely short stories are called "flash fiction."

Form. Short stories are written in prose form, meaning sentences organized into paragraphs.

Sources   Sometimes fiction writers need to conduct research to make their stories realistic. A story set in the past would probably require the author to research the time period. An author writing about a character who is a scientist might need to do research to find out what a typical workday for a scientist is like.

Annie Proulx

55 Miles to the Gas Pump

In the following short-short story, Annie Proulx provides a complete narrative with a beginning, middle, and end—and all in just three brief paragraphs. "55 Miles to the Gas Pump" first appeared in her collection titled *Close Range*: Wyoming Stories, where "Brokeback Mountain," the story made into an Academy Award–winning film, also appears. Proulx is a journalist and fiction author whose novel *The Shipping News* won the Pulitzer Prize for fiction in 1993; her stories have also won awards, including the O. Henry Prize for short fiction.

In the margins of Proulx's story, we've provided some notes for reading the story in terms of conventions of fiction, such as elements of style and design, as well as the author's purpose, audience, use of rhetorical appeals, and choice of mode and medium. (Annie Proulx, excerpt from *Close Range: Wyoming Stories* by Annie Proulx. Copyright © 1999 by Dead Line Ltd. All rights reserved. Reprinted with the permission of Scribner, a Division of Simon & Schuster, Inc.)

◀ AUTHOR PHOTO
Annie Proulx
Toby Talbot/Associated Press.

What is the composer, **Annie Proulx**, doing?

THE RHETORICAL SITUATION

Purpose
Audience
Rhetorical appeals
Modes & media

Purpose

Proulx's main purpose (arguably) is to entertain readers and get them looking under the surface. She also offers insights into marriage, Western rural life, mental health, serial killing, and suicide.

Audience

Proulx's main audience is made up of readers who tend toward literary works and horror, and who also appreciate her dark sense of humor.

Rhetorical appeals

Proulx appeals to readers' logic **(logos)** by referring to a newspaper headline and letting readers make the connection between the headline and what Mrs. Croom finds. Proulx appeals to readers' **pathos** by including gruesome details about how the bodies have decayed.

Modes & media

Mode = written
Proulx's story is clearly meant to be read in just a few minutes. It is unlikely that a reader would read the story aloud, although it is certainly possible, and with the right orator, the story's creep factor could be increased significantly.

Medium = digital
The story originally appeared in print format in a collection of Proulx's stories, but can also be found online, posted on a blog. While the story's appearance on a blog that is not authored by Proulx calls into question whether copyright infringement has occurred, it also enables readers to post comments and reactions to the story, allowing for potential interaction among readers.

Rancher Croom in handmade boots and filthy hat, that walleyed cattleman, stray hairs like curling fiddle string ends, that warm-handed, quick-foot dancer on splintery boards or down the cellar stairs to a rack of bottles of his own strange beer, yeasty, cloudy, bursting out in garlands of foam, Rancher Croom at night galloping drunk over the dark plain, turning off at a place he knows to arrive at a canyon brink where he dismounts and looks down on tumbled rock, waits, then steps out, parting the air with his last roar, sleeves surging up windmill arms, jeans riding over boot tops, but before he hits he rises again to the top of the cliff like a cork in a bucket of milk.

Mrs. Croom on the roof with a saw cutting a hole into the attic where she has not been for twelve years thanks to old Croom's padlocks and warnings, whets to her desire, and the sweat flies as she exchanges the saw for a chisel and hammer until a ragged slab of peak is free and she can see inside: just as she thought: the corpses of Mr. Croom's paramours—she recognizes them from their photographs in the paper: MISSING WOMAN— some desiccated as jerky and much the same color, some moldy from lying beneath roof leaks, and all of them used hard, covered with tarry handprints, the marks of boot heels, some bright blue with the remnants of paint used on the shutters years ago, one wrapped in newspaper nipple to knee.

When you live a long way out you make your own fun.

How do I know this is a **short story**?

THE GENRE'S CONVENTIONS

Elements of the genre
Style
Design
Sources

Elements of the genre

Tells a story using plot, characters, conflict, setting, and point of view.

Provides a **plot**. In this case, Proulx writes about a woman, who, suspicious of her husband's time away from home, breaks into the attic and makes a grim discovery.

Focuses action on two central **characters**: Mr. and Mrs. Croom.

Reveals a **conflict** between the two characters: Mr. Croom wants to keep his murders secret, but Mrs. Croom becomes suspicious.

Provides a **setting**—probably the West: Croom is a rancher; also, the words "cattleman" and "dark plain" suggest the West.

Is told through a **point of view**—through a **narrator** who is not a character (through the third person). However, the final line is an editorial comment; the narrator is not neutral or unbiased.

Style

Detail. Proulx uses specific details to evoke character, mood, and setting. For example, Mr. Croom's "stray hairs like curling fiddle string ends" give a sense that his hair (and his character) is coarse and unruly. What Mrs. Croom sees in the attic is especially gruesome: Some bodies are described as "dessicated as jerky" and others as "moldy from lying beneath roof leaks."

Techniques. Proulx chooses not to use dialogue in this story. The first sentence contains a simile: "stray hairs like curling fiddle string ends." One example of imagery in the story is the gory description of what Mrs. Croom sees when she looks inside the attic.

Tone and voice. The voice of the narrator is detached and unemotional, and the tone is distant. The narrator does not seem particularly moved or disturbed by the grisly scenario.

Design

Print. The story is meant to be read linearly from beginning to end.

Length. The entire story is three paragraphs long and the final paragraph is a mere sentence; yet, there is a clear beginning, middle, and end, as well as plot, characters, and conflict.

Form. The final paragraph of Proulx's story is just one sentence long, which calls attention to it.

Sources

There are no sources cited or overtly referenced, although Proulx's knowledge of the West informs her choice of details and her descriptions of the Crooms.

Questions: Analyzing Proulx's short story

1. Purpose. Why has Proulx structured the story with back-to-back narratives by the two characters? How does this help her convey her purpose? What would change if she intermingled the narratives?

2. Audience. How does Proulx's story appeal to a reader with a twisted sense of humor?

3. Rhetorical appeals. Proulx is often labeled a western writer. How does she establish her ethos as a western writer in the story?

4. Rhetorical appeals. What details does Proulx use to make her readers feel the horror of the crime committed?

5. Modes & media. If you were to record Proulx's story to be listened to, would you have a male or female narrate the story? Why?

6. Elements of the genre. What is the function of the story's final line? Is it meant to be read ironically? Is it a commentary on life in the West?

7. Style. How does the title "55 Miles to the Gas Pump" fit the story's content? How does it shape your understanding of the story?

8. Style. Based on Proulx's use of language and sentence structure, how would you characterize the tone of her story? How does her tone contribute to the overall effect of her story?

9. Style. What details shape your understanding of the history of the Crooms' marriage? Which details about the characters shape your understanding of them as people? For example, what do Rancher Croom's handmade boots tell you about his personality?

10. Design. What does Proulx gain by keeping her story just a few paragraphs long? What is the effect of designing the story so that it ends with a one-sentence paragraph?

11. Sources. How is Proulx's familiarity with westerners, such as ranchers, evident in the short story?

Drafting a Short Story

CHECKLIST: Drafting a Short Story
Thinking of drafting a short story? Ask yourself the following questions.

WHAT'S MY RHETORICAL SITUATION?

☐ **Purpose.** What is my story, and why do I want to tell it?

☐ **Audience** Who are my readers? What is the main message I want to deliver? How will I reach readers and make my story matter to them?

☐ **Rhetorical appeals.** How will I use ethos, pathos, and logos to tell my story and reach my audience? How will I establish my authority as a writer? To what extent will I appeal to my readers' emotions? Do I want my story to elicit laughter, horror, sadness? What role, if any, will logic play in my story?

☐ **Modes & media.** Will I compose my short story in written, audio, or visual form? Do I want to present my story in print, electronically, or face-to-face?

WHAT GENRE CONVENTIONS MATTER?

☐ **Elements of the genre.** How will I structure my plot? Who are my characters? What is going to happen to them? What is my story's setting? Who will narrate my story, and how? What is the central conflict of my story?

☐ **Style.** What tone will I take in my writing? Will my story be funny? Serious? Tragic? What kind of language will I use to emphasize my approach? How much detail will I include?

☐ **Design.** What format will my story take? Will I include elements other than prose with my story (visuals, etc.)? If so, what kind? And for what key scenes? Why?

☐ **Sources.** What source, if any, will I draw on for my story? What about that source interests me? How will my fictional story depart from the source story? That is, what will I invent? Do I want to base my story on a news article I've read? If so, how will I fictionalize it?

PRACTICE
Want to experiment? Draft your own short story based on a news article.

Find a local news article and imagine what kinds of events might have led up to or followed the incident reported. Draft a very short story, similar in length to Proulx's story, about what you have imagined. Your draft needs to convey a sense of place and time (setting) and the people involved (characters). Keep in mind notions of purpose, audience, and rhetorical appeals as you draft.

DRAMATIC FILMS

Lots of kinds of films—action, adventure, comedy, crime, historical, horror, musicals, science fiction, war, and westerns—are widely available. (See also "Documentary films," in the e-pages for Chapter 3.) What these types of films have in common is that they all tell a story. For the purposes of this chapter, we are going to focus on dramatic films. Filmmakers who work in this genre dramatic film tells imaginative (fictional) stories featuring realistic characters grappling with emotional conflict—or gripping stories (fictionalized) based on real-life events. Unlike most action films, which rely on physical stunts and fast pacing, a dramatic film tends to tell its story through the development of character. Like fiction writers, dramatic filmmakers use plot, setting, characters, and dialogue to tell a story; however, they have additional tools at their disposal, including sound, vision, motion, lighting, and framing of shots.

If you've been to a movie theater lately or watched a film online or on TV, you have probably watched a dramatic film. Most Hollywood films that are not action movies are dramatic feature films. Some examples of popular dramatic films are *The Shawshank Redemption, Brokeback Mountain,* and *Fight Club* (all fictional), and *The King's Speech* and *127 Hours* (which are fictionalized versions of the stories of real people). Whether you are a film buff, a casual viewer, or a director-in-the-making, the following information will help you look at this genre more closely, become familiar with the conventions and rhetorical decisions involved, and even try your hand as a filmmaker.

Analyzing Dramatic Films: What to Look For

THE RHETORICAL SITUATION

Purpose   The dramatic filmmaker's purpose is to tell a story that entertains and reveals something about human experience. Some filmmakers, such as Danny Boyle, focus on stories in which characters engage in some kind of struggle and seek to overcome obstacles. For example, his film *Slumdog Millionaire* focuses on the violence and dire poverty that a fictional character named Jamal and other "slumdogs" face growing up in the poorest neighborhoods of Mumbai, India.

Dramatic filmmakers tell stories in some of the same ways that fiction writers do. They tell a good story by creating realistic characters and situations, and by using the tools at their disposal—camera angles, sound, props, costuming, and lighting—to shape viewers' experiences.

Audience   Like fiction writers, dramatic filmmakers create works for a variety of audiences—from broad, popular audiences to narrower, more critical audiences, and all points in between. The success of mainstream filmmakers (such as Steven Spielberg) who aim to create blockbuster films for the widest possible audience is measured by public response (or the Academy of Motion Picture Arts and Sciences) and rewarded with nominations and awards. The success of filmmakers with different purposes, smaller budgets, and stories that will appeal to select or even cult audiences (such as John Waters) is measured by the response and recognition of that smaller audience—which might include independent film critics, film scholars, attendees of specialty film festivals, and other niche filmmakers. As is true for fiction, there are many subgenres of dramatic films, including comedies, romances, and crime. Popular filmmakers can do much to influence their viewers because films can have far-reaching cultural effects; for example, Francis Ford Coppola's *The Godfather* gave several generations of Americans a dramatic story about the inner workings of a crime family—a fictional story that shaped popular ideas about the Mafia.

Rhetorical appeal   Because dramatic filmmakers aim to reveal something about human experience, they use pathos to help viewers connect emotionally to the story being told on the screen. For example, in *The King's Speech*, when King George VI (played by Colin Firth) is finally able to give a speech without fumbling and stuttering, viewers are meant to feel the same sense of relief and celebration that the king's audience experiences; collectively, viewers and characters exhale. Filmmakers also need to establish ethos in dramatic films—they need to establish their ethos as composers and also the ethos of their stories, especially if the film is based on real events or people. They can further reinforce ethos, for example, by using costumes, music, and props that reflect the time period represented and the mood they wished to create.

Modes & media   Dramatic films bring together audio and visual modes of communication. The audio includes the dialogue of the characters, the background sounds, and the musical soundtrack. The visual aspect of the film is achieved through framing, perspective, and lighting. Movies are often either in a film reel format or a digital format.

Which films (mainstream or independent) have most resonated with you? Have you ever rewatched a favorite film? How has your viewing experience changed over time? Why? #Remember #Analyze

---

THE GENRE'S CONVENTIONS

Elements of the genre

Story arc. The story arc (or plot) of a dramatic film is similar in structure to that of a play (or even of a short story). In the exposition, the filmmaker sets up the story, introducing characters, setting, time, and the beginnings of the conflict. This is followed by the rising action, in which the filmmaker develops the conflict (often introducing subconflicts) and moves the film toward the climax, or turning point, of the story. From the climax, the filmmaker moves the story toward a conclusion (falling action to denouement) in which the conflict moves toward resolution and a conclusion. In Frank Capra's *It's a Wonderful Life*, James Stewart plays George Bailey, who on Christmas Eve, discovers that his company, the Bailey Building and Loan bank, is destined for doom and his future is threatened by the possibility of bank fraud. He ends up (spoiler alert!) crashing his car, and after getting drunk, walks toward a bridge, intending to end his life; there he is saved by Clarence, an angel, who takes him on a tour of what his town, Bedford Falls, and its inhabitants would have experienced if George had never been born. Watching this wakes George up and he realizes that he wants to remain alive and rescue the town from its impending doom.

Music. Dramatic filmmakers use music to create tension and to influence viewers' emotional response. In Francis Ford Coppola's *Apocalypse Now*, a key war scene shows helicopters approaching a village while Richard Wagner's "Ride of the Valkyries" plays loudly in the background to emphasize the tension and destruction that is about to occur. In horror movies such as *Psycho*, the soundtrack amplifies the violence taking place on screen and can be as memorable and unsettling as the visuals.

Acting/performance. How effectively an actor portrays a character narrows the distance between the imagined film and the reality of the situation the film portrays. For example, in the closing emotional scene of *Brokeback Mountain*, the actor Heath Ledger, who plays Ennis Del Mar, stands before his open closet, revealing to the viewer a postcard of the mountain and two shirts (Ennis's shirt covering Jack's shirt). At this moment, the viewer feels Ennis's pain and loss.

Do you have a favorite movie soundtrack? If so, do you like the music because of its role in the film—or perhaps because you like the artist or the way the songs work outside of the film, as a collection? #Remember #Understand

Style

Screenplay/script. Filmmakers create screenplays that include both the dialogue (what the characters say) and the action (what the characters are doing and what else is happening in the background). A shooting script will also include specific techniques, such as shot instructions (INT. LIVING ROOM) or transitions between film shots (DISSOLVE TO).

Dialogue. Filmmakers create dialogue that will develop characters, advance the plot, and illustrate conflict. Dialogue can establish a character's level of education, economic status, and his or her relationship to other characters and to the story itself. The use of idiomatic expressions and vocabulary can also reinforce the film's geographic location and historical period.

Design

Shots. Camera angles orient viewers toward what the filmmaker wants them to see—and allow them to see it from the perspective that is most appropriate for the scene and story. If the filmmaker uses a high-angle shot, viewers get the sense of being onlookers; if he or she uses an eye-level shot, viewers are invited into the story—into the eye of the character. Filmmakers choose and vary long shots and close-ups, depending on the purpose behind a given scene and the ways they want the audience to experience it.

Costumes. In a dramatic film, costumes make characters more realistic. In Danny Boyle's *Slumdog Millionaire*, characters are dressed to look like they live in the slums; their dirty, ripped clothes emphasize their impoverished conditions. In *The Godfather*, mob characters are dressed in expensive black suits, showing their social and professional status and access to money.

Lighting. Lighting dramatizes certain events in a film. For example, in *Slumdog Millionaire*, the scene of Jamal's interrogation is lit starkly to emphasize the tension of the moment.

Sound effects. Like lighting, sound creates mood and emphasis. For example, a filmmaker might build tension and hint at disaster with a slow rumble or sudden clap of thunder. Another way to do this is with a musical soundtrack—think of the notes that accompany the shark as it circles its victims in *Jaws*, or the effects such as the heavy reverb of Darth Vader or cheerful chirps of R2D2 in Star Wars.

Sets/props. Sets re-create the reality of the film's setting. If a filmmaker wants the viewers to believe that the film takes place in a quaint European village, he or she will either shoot the movie in a specific village or on a set that approximates that village. For example, in *Slumdog Millionaire*, the set of the game show in the movie looks just like the set of the actual program *Who Wants to Be a Millionaire*.

Sources   Filmmakers attribute their sources in the credits. If the film is based on an original screenplay, the screenwriter is credited. If the film is based on a previously written book, the author is credited. Also, the place where the film is shot is usually listed in the credits, along with the names of the actors and actresses, film crew, and the music and songs (and their creators) used throughout the film.

Guided Reading: Dramatic Film

George A. Romero & John A. Russo

Scene from Night of the Living Dead

The 1968 horror film *Night of the Living Dead* was directed by George A. Romero and co-written by Romero and John A. Russo. The two had recently founded (and funded with some friends) a small independent film production company called Image Ten. Their first full-length release, shot on a micro-budget ($114,000) and gruesome to the extreme for its time, *Night of the Living Dead* became a cult classic and predecessor to *Dawn of the Dead* (1978), and the less-than-successful *Day of the Dead* (1985). In *Night*, a group of citizens in rural Pennsylvania take refuge in a farmhouse and fight for their lives against a mob of flesh-hungry "undead." Amid the gore and chaos, the original zombie apocalypse film is born. At first, *Night* was dismissed or railed against by critics—*Variety* magazine deemed

What is the director, **George A. Romero**, doing?

THE RHETORICAL SITUATION

Purpose
Audience
Rhetorical appeals
Modes & media

Purpose

The filmmakers' main purpose is to entertain—and scare and gross out—their viewers. They tell a simple and bleak horror story, set in rural Pennsylvania, in which a group of people are devoured by zombies. Another purpose may be to offer social commentary on life in the United States in the 1960s (the film was released in 1968 against the backdrop of the Vietnam War and the civil rights movement). For example, the zombies might be read as signifying cultural fears of death and outsiders or "otherness."

Audience

Romero and Russo geared the movie toward a general audience,

(Continued on p. 314)

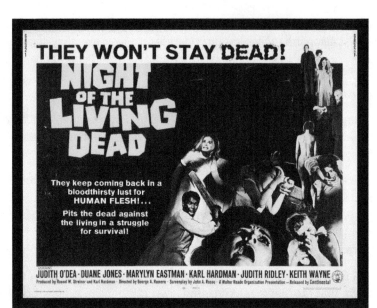

◄ The promotional poster for *Night of the Living Dead* (1968). Courtesy of Wikimedia Commons.

it "an unrelieved orgy of sadism" and Roger Ebert was outraged that children were allowed to see it—but is now considered one of the best horror films and B movies of all time. Dave Kerr of *Chicago Reader* wrote in 2007: "Over its short, furious course, the picture violates so many strong taboos—cannibalism, incest, necrophilia—that it leaves audiences giddy and hysterical." Others say that, whether Romero or Russo intended it or not, many viewers read the film as social commentary on life in America. For example, given the racial climate in 1968, the casting of a black actor as the lead

▲ From *Night of the Living Dead*. Clip courtesy of Movieclips.com.

(Duane Jones as Ben) was a notable choice. (See Matt Thompson's editorial for NPR, "Why Black Heroes Make Zombie Stories More Interesting.")

In the following section we look at one scene from *Night of the Living Dead* called "Safe House." But you may want to look at other clips or view the entire film online at the Internet Archive.

For more context, see reviews at MoMA and the Internet Movie Database.

From the Shooting Script of *Night of the Living Dead*

"Safe House" Scene

Barbara finds that she is in the kitchen of the old house. She gropes through a door and into a large living room . . . no sign of life. Her impulse is to cry for help, but again she stops herself for fear of being heard by the man outside. She darts back to the kitchen, rummages through drawers in a kitchen cabinet, and finds the silverware. She chooses a large steak knife and, grasping it tightly, goes to listen at the door again. All is quiet. She goes back in to the living room.

Beyond it is an alcove that contains the front entrance to the house. She rushes to the front door and makes sure it is locked. Cautiously, she pushes back a corner of the curtain to see outside. The view overlooks an expansive lawn, large shadowy pine trees, and the service station across the road.

There is no sign of the attacker. Suddenly, there is noise from outside: the pounding and rattling of a door. Barbara drops the curtain edge and stiffens. More sounds. She hurries to a side window. Across the lawn, the man is pounding at the door to the garage. She watches, her eyes wide with fear. The man struggles with the door, then looks about and picks up something and smashes at it. In panic, Barbara pulls away from the window.

Across the room is a telephone. She rushes to it and picks up the receiver . . . dial tone . . . she frantically dials the operator . . . some Buzzes and clicks . . . then . . .

Continues next page

How do I know this is a **dramatic film**?

THE GENRE'S CONVENTIONS

Elements of the genre
Style
Design
Sources

Elements of the genre

Characters. Some characters, such as the hero Ben (played by actor Duane Jones) are portrayed in a more realistic and dimensional way than others. For example, Barbara (played by actor Judith O'Dea), arguably, is portrayed as a stereotypically powerless female, while Harry Cooper (played by actor Karl Hadman) is portrayed with little depth, as selfish and unheroic.

Plot. The drama focuses on a basic conflict: the undead cannibals versus the living humans holed up in the farmhouse. The living struggle to survive as the ghouls try to break into the house to eat them. There are also

(Continued on p. 315)

George A. Romero & John A. Russo, Scenes from *Night of the Living Dead*   313

From the Shooting Script of *Night of the Living Dead* Continued

particularly (according to interviews) drive-in theatergoers. In 1968, many viewers were shocked by the gore and some complained it was upsetting to children (the film was not rated). Now considered a classic—it's one of the most downloaded movies on the Internet—this grainy black-and-white film attracts a wide audience including horror buffs, film students, and social critics.

Rhetorical appeals

Romero and Russo establish a gritty kind of ethos through many of their editorial and technical choices, including their use of black-and-white film, shaky camera work, and a stark landscape in which to set their story. While the film may be seen as technically amateurish, this very

(Continued on p. 316)

TELEPHONE OPERATOR RECORDING (V.O.)

I'm sorry . . . our lines are busy . . . would you hold the line please . . . I'm sorry . . . our lines are . . .

She quickly depresses the receiver buttons . . . lets them up and dials again . . . long pause . . . she can hear sounds from the gas station.

TELEPHONE OPERATOR (V.O.)

I'm sorry . . . our lines . . .

She depresses the buttons again . . . dials 411 for information . . . another long pause . . . then the rasp of a busy signal. The noises from the service station have stopped. She listens for a moment . . . she shudders with fear . . . notices a telephone directory in a stand near the phone. Frantically, her fingers search to pages for the emergency numbers . . . the police. She dials shakily, but before she has dialed the last numbers the rapines of the busy signal comes over the receiver. She depresses the buttons again . . . footsteps . . . she puts the phone down and rushes to another window. A figure is crossing the lawn, coming toward the house. It is a different figure, a different man. She runs to the door and peers out through the curtains again. The man still walks toward the house. A shadow darkens a strip of window at the left of the door. Its abruptness startles her. She peels back a corner of the curtain and sees the back of the first attacker not ten feet away, facing the man who is approaching. The attacker moves toward the new man. Barbara freezes against the door, and glances down at her knife . . . she looks back out at the two men.

They join each other under the dark, hanging trees, and stand looking back toward the cemetery. From inside the house, Barbara squints, trying to see. Finally, the attacker moves back across the road, in the direction of the cemetery. The other man approaches the house, seeks the shadows of a tree, and stops . . . in an attitude of stolid watching . . . Barbara stares,

From the Shooting Script of *Night of the Living Dead* Continued

but can see little. She lunges toward the phone again . . . dials the operator . . . the same recorded message. She barely stops herself from slamming down the receiver.

Then suddenly a distant sound . . . an approaching car. She scampers to the window and looks out. The road seems empty. But after a moment a faint light appears, bouncing and rapidly approaching . . . a car coming up the road. Barbara reaches for the doorknob, edges the door open very slightly. The light spills dimly over the area. There, under the great tree in the lawn, is the silhouette of the second man. Barbara shudders . . . she is afraid to make her break for the approaching car.

The figure appears to be sitting, quite still, it's head and shoulders slumped over . . . it seems to be looking right at the house. The car speeds by . . . Barbara just stares at the figure. She cannot run. She closes the door and backs into the shadows of the house.

She turns to see all around her. The large dreary rooms are very quiet, cast in shadow . . . she spies a stairway . . . runs toward it still carrying the knife and starts up the stairs. The camera is level with her eye, and picks up her view of the stairs as she runs up . . . panting and frantic she climbs, her hand grazing the banister . . . still at her eye level, The camera starts to pick up the top of the stairway . . . the floor of the second landing . . . A brief glimpse of something on the floor there . . . she continues to climb . . . the floor of the landing . . . zoom in . . . toward camera, the hand of . . . A corpse.

Barbara stops . . . the corpse is almost skeletal with its flesh ripped from it, and it lies at the end of a trail of blood. Screaming in absolute horror, Barbara almost falls down the stairs. She is gagging . . . she breaks for the door, unlocks it, and flings herself out into the night, completely unmindful of consequences . . . she is bathed in light . . . two headlights are

Continues next page

THE GENRE'S CONVENTIONS

conflicts among the living—particularly between Ben and Harry Cooper—as they clash over how to fight and where in the house to take shelter as they await rescue. Interestingly, the story ends differently in the final film, departing from the original conclusion of the shooting script.

Music. As illustrated in the "Safe House" scene, the soundtrack to the film is used to build tension and emphasize the horror. For example, a grating, high-pitched sound begins at the moment Barbara discovers the body on the landing and gets higher as it goes on for many seconds, until the end of the scene, when Ben and Barbara make it back into the kitchen and safely, for the moment, behind the closed door.

Acting/performance. In order to get the audience on the hero

(Continued on p. 317)

quality contributes
to its impact.
The filmmakers
also appeal to
viewers' pathos by
tapping into primal
human fears and
creating suspense
as the characters
barricaded in
the farmhouse
try to escape the
slow-moving
but persistent
cannibalistic
undead; Romero
called them "ghouls."
For example, in the
"Safe House" scene,
an unsteady camera
follows Barbara as
she discovers she
is cut off from help
(the phone is dead)
and that not only
have ghouls been in
the house, they are
headed toward it
again.

Modes & media

**Mode = audio
and visual.** The
filmmakers combine
audio (dialogue,
music, and sound)
and visuals to tell
their story. Music
and sound effects are
crucial to this film in
terms of reinforcing

(Continued on p. 318)

From the Shooting Script of *Night of the Living Dead* Continued

*screeching toward camera . . . the sounds of a vehicle stop-
ping. Barbara covers her face with her arms. Someone rushes
toward her.*

MAN
Are you one of 'em?

*She stares, frozen. A man stands in front of her. He is large
and crude, in coveralls and tattered work shirt. He looks very
strong, and perhaps a little stupid. Behind him is an old, battered pick-up truck, which he has driven right up onto the
lawn of the house. He holds a large jack-handle in his hand,
and stands there panting. Behind him, the man at the tree still
stands.*

Barbara is still frozen . . .

MAN (The man shouts again)
Are you one of 'em? I seen 'em look like you . . .

*The man at the tree moves forward . . . Barbara screams and
steps back . . . the truck driver spins to face the other man.
The other man stops in his tracks. The truck driver backs pro-
tectively toward the girl, while the other stands, just watching.
Finally, the truck driver seizes Barbara's wrist and pulls her
into the house, slamming the door behind them.*

*Barbara falls back against a wall. The truck driver locks the
door and throws the bolt. He is breathing hard. He turns
to look at the girl. She brings the knife up in a defensive
gesture . . .*

TRUCK DRIVER (Soothingly, in a drawl, almost as he
would address a scared rabbit)
All right . . . It's awright now . . .

THE GENRE'S CONVENTIONS

Ben's side, actor Duane Jones must convince viewers that his character is real and deserves their empathy. He must also convince them to have confidence in his actions. In the "Safe House" scene, actor Judith O'Dea's main job is to convince viewers of her terror.

Style

Dialogue. In the shooting script for the film, the dialogue is formatted in a specific way, indented, with characters' names capitalized and centered over the dialogue spoken. In the "Safe House" scene, more than a dozen paragraphs describe the action, but only a few lines of dialogue toward the end describe Barbara's encounter with Ben. In the final film, this scene doesn't include any dialogue at all. It is documented that Romero and Russo revised the script as they shot the film. For this scene, they must have decided on set that it was more effective to let the action, music, and sound effects convey this part of the story.

Action. In the shooting script, the action is indicated in paragraph form, aligned on the left margin of the pages. In this scene, the action in the script begins when Barbara enters the farmhouse, and closes when Ben arrives indoors. As noted above, the writers revised the script as they shot the film. The final film varies from the shooting script in a number of ways, not only in the action and (lack of) dialogue this scene, but in the plot, in the ultimate conclusion of which character survives the undead.

Camera shots. Typically a shooting script includes camera shots, provided with scene numbers and directions, usually in all capital letters. In this particular script, camera shots are included in the action paragraphs.

Camera work in the "Safe House" scene includes (from p. 14 of the shooting script): "The camera starts to pick up the top of the stairway . . . the floor of the second landing . . . a brief glimpse of something on the floor there . . . she continues to climb . . . the floor of the landing . . . zoom in . . . toward camera, the hand of . . . a corpse."

Design

Cinematography. Camera angles emphasize point of view. For example, in the "Safe House" scene, a long shot shows Barbara as she enters the living room, but the camera closes in on her and the horrors she discovers in the house (the animal trophies, the dead phone, the corpse).

Sound. The shooting script includes directions for sound in the action paragraphs. For example: "There is no sign of the attacker. Suddenly, there is a noise from outside: the pounding and rattling of a door."

Setting. The settings for this film are realistic: the location a farmhouse in rural Pennsylvania. The film is shot outdoors in the natural landscape, and inside the house; the interior scenes are shot in a way meant to make viewers feel trapped and claustrophobic.

Props are indicated in the script. For example, in this scene, the script notes the steak knife that Barbara finds in the kitchen, and the phone that she tries to use in the living room.

Sources

George A. Romero and John A. Russo co-wrote the script for this horror fiction film. While the work is the product of their imaginations, Romero has cited an earlier novel—Richard Matheson's 1954 *I Am Legend*, which was adapted for film—as inspiration for the story.

THE RHETORICAL SITUATION

emotion. In the scene "Safe House," deep thunder rumbles as Barbara tiptoes into the living room. The camera suddenly cuts to the animal trophies hanging on the wall as the music crescendos in classic horror-movie style; this moment is a warm-up for the real scare that awaits Barbara on the second floor landing.

Medium = film. As a medium, film can be used as the basis for new compositions, such as mash-ups and film trailers, and can be shared as video in any digital environment. A quick Google search reveals plenty of *Night of the Living Dead* mash-ups and remixes on the Internet, including a music video and a repurposing of a scene to critique recent U.S. wars.

Questions: Analyzing Romero & Russo's film

1. Purpose. Based on the "Safe House" scene, what is your take on Romero and Russo's story about zombies and humans? Why might they have chosen to set their horror story in rural Pennsylvania, rather than in, say, New York City? How do the house and landscape function in the story?

2. Audience. How does the film portray human responses to fear? In the "Safe House" scene, what details pull you in as a viewer? Why?

3. Rhetorical appeals. How do Romero and Russo establish their ethos in the "Safe House" scene (in addition to the suggestions included in the annotations)? And how do they connect with viewers' pathos? What specific choices contribute most to conveying horror? Why do you think so?

4. Modes & media. In the "Safe House" scene, what are some moments where the audio and visuals come together to make the viewer root for (or perhaps disconnect from) Barbara? Ben? The ghouls?

5. Elements of the genre. Based on this scene, how much dimension does Barbara have as a character? What are the challenges that actor Judith O'Dea faced in performing the character, especially in a horror movie? How does she handle these challenges? If you were directing this scene, what, if anything, would you change about the portrayal and actions of Barbara?

6. Elements of the genre. What happens, plot-wise, in the "Safe House" scene? How do the filmmakers use it to move the story forward? Is the scene effective in this regard? Why or why not?

7. Style. How do the action, camera angles, and lack of dialogue (or monologue) contribute to the "Safe House" scene? Compare the clip to the shooting script. How closely does the final clip follow the script? Why might the filmmakers have gone "off script"? Do you agree with their choices? Why or why not?

8. Design. How do the sound effects and music contribute to the suspense of the scene? How effective is the presentation of the outside world (the yard) versus the inside world (the house)? Of the dead versus the living? What props did you notice? How important are they to the scene?

9. Source. Romero and Russo cite another horror story and movie, *I Am Legend* (1954), as an inspiration for *Night of the Living Dead* (1968). Based on what you may know of the horror genre, are there other films that can be seen as forerunners to *Night of the Living Dead*? Do you see *Night of the Living Dead* an original and/or groundbreaking work? Why or why not?

Drafting / Sketching Out a Dramatic Film

CHECKLIST: Drafting/Sketching Out a Dramatic Film Thinking of drafting a script for a dramatic film? Ask yourself the following questions.

WHAT'S MY RHETORICAL SITUATION?

☐ **Purpose.** What is the story I want to dramatize in the film, and why do I want to tell it?

☐ **Audience.** How would I describe my intended viewers? Who do I want to see my film? Why should/will my story matter to my viewers? What do I want them to get out of it? And how will I reach them?

☐ **Rhetorical appeals.** How will I use ethos, pathos, and logos to tell my story and reach my audience? How will I establish my authority as a screenwriter? To what extent will I appeal to my audience's emotions? What role, if any, will logic play in my story?

☐ **Modes & media.** How can I use visuals to benefit my story? How about audio?

WHAT GENRE CONVENTIONS MATTER?

☐ **Elements of the genre.** How will I structure my plot? Who are my characters? What is going to happen to them? What is my story's setting? Who will tell my story, and how? What is the central conflict of my story?

☐ **Style.** How will my camera shots emphasize the story's conflict? How will I weave action in with dialogue to advance my story—and emphasize emotion?

☐ **Design.** How will I use camera angles to tell my story? What kinds of sound will I use? How will I use music in my scenes? What props will I use to emphasize the story and setting?

☐ **Sources.** What source, if any, will I draw on for my film? Will I base my screenplay on an existing work of fiction? Will I base it on a work of nonfiction, such as a memoir? In what ways will my film depart from any source I might use?

PRACTICE Want to experiment? Shoot your own film adaptation.

The creators of *Night of the Living Dead* use every scene to advance their plot (a story of humans suffering as they are attacked by the undead) toward its tragic conclusion (the death of humans). Think of an existing narrative that you like that tells a tragic story and adapt it into a horror film that follows the basic plot structure of *Night of the Living Dead* (or other dramatic film of your choice). Begin by sketching out a synopsis of the plot, the main conflicts, basic qualities of the main characters, setting, and techniques you'd like to use to tell the story. Shoot a video of a one or more of the most important scenes. As you do so, keep your audience in mind and pay attention to the decisions you make in terms of rhetorical appeals.

Using Twitter GT

Twitter is a social networking tool that allows users to post 140-character observations, questions, and links. Twitter accounts can be public (anyone can read the tweets) or private (you give people permission to "follow" you). As a Twitter user, you can follow other users, which means that you will see their tweets appear in your Twitter feed.

You can also send a private (140-character) message to someone you follow on Twitter. Your Twitter "address" is a username preceded by the @ symbol, for example, @GeorgePBurdell. You can reply to other people's tweets by prefacing your tweet with the person's address, or simply by hitting Reply within the Twitter interface. If you want to reference or "tag" someone in your tweet, simply include the person's Twitter address in your tweet with the @ symbol; the person will be notified that you mentioned him or her. To copy and repost another person's tweet, you can begin your tweet with RT ("retweet") and then paste in the user's Twitter name and the original message. If you modify or shorten the original post, be sure to indicate that something is omitted by using ellipses (. . .) and by marking the tweet with MT ("modified tweet"). Within a tweet, you can include links (URLs) and pictures.

> Georgia Tech Library retweeted
>
> **GA Tech ISSS** @GATechISSS · Oct 22
>
> Communication Ethics: Avoiding Plagiarism workshop tomorrow from 11-12:30. More info & registration at b.gatech.edu/1sVuym6.
>
> 1

Tweeting as a Course Assignment

A conversation on a particular topic can be tagged with a hash tag—a pound sign (#) followed by a name or acronym (e.g., #ENG1101). By searching for the hash tag, you can follow all the tweets pertaining to a particular conversation. Some instructors ask students to tweet during class discussions to create a backchannel (i.e., a separate conversation going on in the background). Other instructors use Twitter to allow students to comment on student presentations as they are happening or to participate in a silent discussion during a movie viewing. Similarly, Twitter can be used outside of class for asynchronous discussion. By following the hash tag, you can tweet your ideas about the course reading and respond on your own time to the tweets of your classmates.

When you are tweeting, concision is key. You can use abbreviations, but be sure not to lose the clarity of your comment. Check with your instructor to find out if correct grammar and conventional punctuation are necessary for your class-related tweets.

Twitter can be an exciting venue for following ongoing conversations among friends and people who share similar interests. However, keep in mind the guidelines for thinking about audience and voice (if your account is public, anyone can see your tweets), privacy, and attribution.

Use a tool called Storify as a visual way to create stories using your tweets, Facebook updates, pictures, and other information from social media. You create a story on a timeline by importing content from social media. Create an account at Storify, which guides you through the process to create a story in text and pictures that you can update as events and comments unfold. #Create

14 INFORMATIVE GENRES

CONTENTS

e For e-Pages content, visit bedfordstmartins.com/bookofgenres.

◀ CHART/INFOGRAPHIC

For an Index of Sources & Contexts for material referenced in this chapter, see the e-Pages at **bedfordstmartins.com /bookofgenres**.

Information is everywhere, all the time: online, on your phone, in e-mail, on social networking sites, on TV, and on radio. It's on billboards, road signs, and menus. But not all information is equal: Some is reliable; some is not. How do we make sense of it all? The trick is to (1) figure out which *sources* of information are the best, and (2) analyze, use, and share that information according to your needs as a reader or writer.

In daily life, you draw on a variety of sources for information. When you don't know the meaning of a word, you might go to *Dictionary.com*.

DICTIONARY ENTRY ▶
Dictionary.com
"Vertiginous."
© *Dictionary.com, LLC vertiginous. Dictionary .com. Collins English Dictionary—Complete & Unabridged 10th Edition. HarperCollins Publishers, http:// dictionary.reference .com/browse/ vertiginous.*

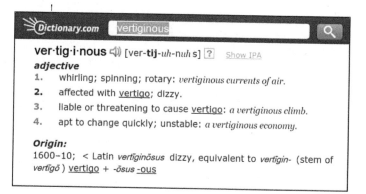

How else do you use sources? A few more scenarios:

» You're curious about Prohibition after watching a movie set in the 1920s, so you check out the History Channel site, a trusted encyclopedia, or a PBS documentary for a better sense of that period.

» You want to plant tomatoes on your back porch, so you consult a reference book or online guide by the American Horticultural Society on varieties that grow best in your region.

» You want to avoid the flu, so you read the U.S. Department of Health and Human Services' latest recommendations online or stop in at your pharmacy for information about the flu vaccine.

» You need to create a presentation using software you don't know how to use, so you refer to a Microsoft PowerPoint tutorial or ask an experienced colleague for a quick lesson.

How do you deal with the information you encounter online every day? How do you know what's fact and what's not? #Apply #Analyze

» There's something wrong with your car and you don't know what the flashing light on your dashboard means, so you flip through your owner's manual or call a knowledgeable mechanic.

In each of these cases, you've found convenient but also authoritative sources.

Authoritative sources of information   Here's another scenario. Let's say you want to prepare for a disaster. You do a quick search on YouTube, and turn up a video by a guy in a gas mask who is part of a survivalist fringe group living in a desert bunker. His instructions in the video are rambling, confusing, and possibly paranoid (to take the example to an extreme). Though the video may be riveting, this is a poor source of information because the author lacks credibility (or ethos) and logic (logos). A better, if less colorful, source would be a government organization such as Homeland Security, FEMA (Federal Emergency Management Agency), or the American Red Cross. These are considered excellent sources of information because these organizations are long established and made up of experts. The material they publish is researched, written, and reviewed by authorities in the field of emergency preparation; approved by the government; and tested out in actual emergencies. For example, Homeland Security's "Preventing Terrorism" advice has been vetted by a major government organization (see p. 326).

Author bias   No author is purely objective, including Homeland Security. Personal viewpoints, inclinations, and prejudices can creep into any communication, whether it's a recipe or a government document. Bias can show up in the language that writers use. For example, Homeland Security's use of the terms *Counterterrorism* and *Border Security* indicate a specific point of view. No matter its source, information is never 100 percent unbiased.

Bias can also be apparent in the tone a writer uses. Let's say an article appears in your local newspaper about a family lost during a snowmobiling trip. You might expect the reporter to simply present the facts of what happened. However, after reading closely, you see the reporter's opinion has subtly found its way onto the page: The family's lack of preparation and

▼ PHOTO
John W. Gertz
"Man Wearing Gas Mask Using Cell Phone." Beware of information from unreliable sources. *John W. Gertz/Corbis.*

Official website of the Department of Homeland Security

Homeland Security

Home   Topics   How Do I?   Get Involved   News   About DHS

Preventing Terrorism

Preventing Terrorism Overview
Protecting the American people from terrorist threats is the reason the Department of Homeland Security was created, and remains our highest priority.

Biological Security
We protect the nation's health security by providing early detection and early warning of bioterrorist attacks.

Chemical Security
Some chemical facilities possess materials that could be stolen and used to make weapons. A successful attack on certain high-risk facilities could cause a significant number of deaths and injuries.

Countering Violent Extremism
The threat posed by violent extremism is neither constrained by international borders nor limited to any single ideology.

Critical Infrastructure Security
Critical infrastructure is the physical and cyber systems and assets so vital to the United States that their incapacity or destruction would have a debilitating impact on our physical or economic security or public health or safety.

Explosives
DHS works to enhance the nation's counter-IED capabilities and reduce the threat of explosive attack against critical infrastructure, the private sector, and federal, state, local, tribal, and territorial entities.

If You See Something, Say Something
A program to raise public awareness of indicators of terrorism and terrorism-related crime, and to emphasize the importance of reporting suspicious activity to the proper state and local law enforcement authorities.

NTAS

National Terrorism Advisory System
NTAS alerts communicate information about terrorist threats by providing timely, detailed information to the public, government agencies, first responders, public sector organizations, airports and other transportation hubs.

When was the last time you noticed a sign in an airport, train station, or bus stop? Make a point to examine one and ask yourself: Who created the sign? Whose point of view does it convey? What assumptions does it convey about travelers?
#Remember
#Analyze

ignorance about avalanche safety influenced the writer and affected his or her tone and the use (or omission) of details. On the other hand, imagine that the reporter thinks the family did the best they could have—they were as prepared as possible, but no one could have survived that avalanche. In that case, the writer would use a more sympathetic tone.

Even a nutritional label reflects the biases, assumptions, and values of its authors. For example, the creators of the label here assume that calories and fat are more important than other nutritional information, and so calories, calories from fat, and total fat grams are presented first. Protein, vitamins, and minerals appear toward the bottom of the chart. The author, in this case, is a government organization, the National Heart, Lung, and Blood Institute (NHLBI) at the National Institutes of Health.

Presenting information is not a neutral activity. All writing has a persuasive quality, and informative writing is no exception. This is not a bad thing, just something to keep in mind as you read and compose.

◀ LABEL
National Institutes of Health
Standard U.S. food label.

The Rhetorical Situation

Purpose: Why share information?

When we write to inform, we share facts and details with our readers. One type of informative writing is instructions. If you've ever purchased a piece of furniture that required assembly, you've probably worked with a set of instructions. The instructions were likely designed by an engineer or technical writer with two goals: (1) to help you put together parts of an object, and (2) to persuade and assure you that through simple language and design that the task would be easy.

Sharing information, according to *Merriam-Webster*, is sharing "knowledge obtained from investigation, study, or instruction." A set of instructions certainly gives information "obtained from investigation": Most instructions undergo usability testing and are revised for clarity and accuracy before publication.

Another example of informative writing is the informational brochure. You've probably seen these at your doctor's or dentist's office—brochures about how to control asthma or whiten your teeth. Consider the teeth-whitening brochure: It may provide facts about various methods; however, it might also offer reasons for whitening, pricing information, and a photo of an attractive model with sparkling-white teeth. Is the material in the brochure presented *only* to inform, or is there another motive at work? Could the brochure creators also be trying to convince you to whiten your teeth?

What instructions have you referred to lately? How helpful were they? Were they written for someone like you? How could you tell? #Evaluate

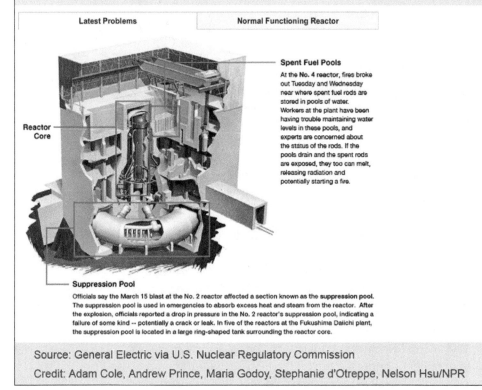

SPECIAL SERIES

the science of japan's nuclear crisis

Explainer: What Are Spent Fuel Rods?

by JOE PALCA

March 15, 2011   2:28 PM

Inside The Nuclear Reactors

Latest Problems	Normal Functioning Reactor

Reactor
Core

Spent Fuel Pools

At the No. 4 reactor, fires broke
out Tuesday and Wednesday
near where spent fuel rods are
stored in pools of water.
Workers at the plant have been
having trouble maintaining water
levels in these pools, and
experts are concerned about
the status of the rods. If the
pools drain and the spent rods
are exposed, they too can melt,
releasing radiation and
potentially starting a fire.

Suppression Pool

Officials say the March 15 blast at the No. 2 reactor affected a section known as the suppression pool.
The suppression pool is used in emergencies to absorb excess heat and steam from the reactor. After
the explosion, officials reported a drop in pressure in the No. 2 reactor's suppression pool, indicating a
failure of some kind -- potentially a crack or leak. In five of the reactors at the Fukushima Daiichi plant,
the suppression pool is located in a large ring-shaped tank surrounding the reactor core.

Source: General Electric via U.S. Nuclear Regulatory Commission

Credit: Adam Cole, Andrew Prince, Maria Godoy, Stephanie d'Otreppe, Nelson Hsu/NPR

When you read informative genres, keep an eye out for what
else is going on. An author of a scientific report, for example,
may present facts, but as a way to influence you to share an
opinion or take an action.

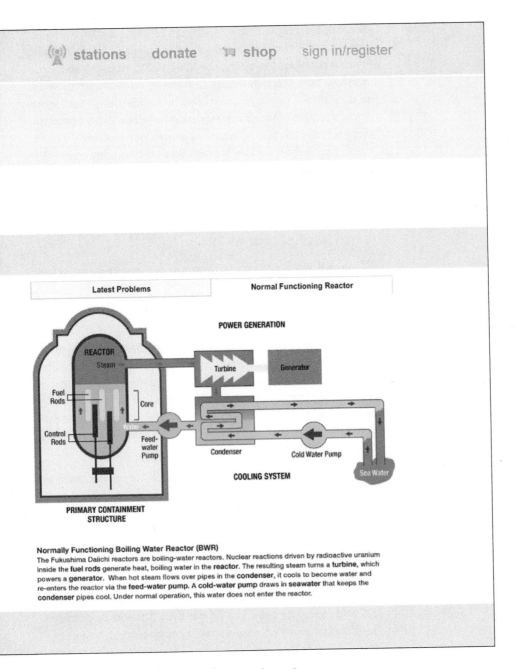

Latest Problems | Normal Functioning Reactor

POWER GENERATION

Normally Functioning Boiling Water Reactor (BWR)
The Fukushima Daiichi reactors are boiling-water reactors. Nuclear reactions driven by radioactive uranium inside the **fuel rods** generate heat, boiling water in the **reactor**. The resulting steam turns a **turbine**, which powers a **generator**. When hot steam flows over pipes in the **condenser**, it cools to become water and re-enters the reactor via the **feed-water pump**. A **cold-water pump** draws in seawater that keeps the **condenser** pipes cool. Under normal operation, this water does not enter the reactor.

Audience: How do we inform others?

As writers, we need to know our audiences—who they are and what they want. For example, in the piece above an "Explainer" feature created for National Public Radio, writer

Joe Palca, along with the illustrators listed below the images, provides the facts of a recent news event (Japan's nuclear reactor problems following the March 2011 tsunami) and visuals that show the differences between a normally functioning reactor and a damaged one. The NPR writer and illustrators know that most of their readers are not nuclear experts and do not want tons of text or technical jargon; general readers want clear information (in "lay terms") so they can understand the basics of a complex system.

Rhetorical Appeals: How do we use ethos, logos, and pathos to inform?

When we write to inform, how do we get our audiences invested? Whether you're composing a research paper, fact sheet, or flowchart, you will use the rhetorical appeals: ethos, logos, and pathos.

Ethos—how you, as an author, are perceived by your audience—is extremely important when reporting information. You must draw on reliable sources of information in your research and convey that knowledge as authoritatively and as neutrally as possible. If your audience thinks you are unreliable, or that you have some unstated motive, then you will not have established your ethos.

The article on page 331 was written by Mireya Navarro, an environmental reporter for *The New York Times*. In her article, "E.P.A. Rejects City Timeline on PCBs," she covers the facts about the ways the Environmental Protection Agency is putting pressure on New York City public schools to speed up their plan to replace toxic and potentially hazardous fluorescent light fixtures. Navarro establishes her ethos by stating facts, quoting from authoritative sources, and keeping her tone neutral and her writing as free of her own opinion as possible. Further, her position as a writer for a renowned newspaper contributes to her ethos, as does her profile, which notes her experience and links to her other articles about the environment.

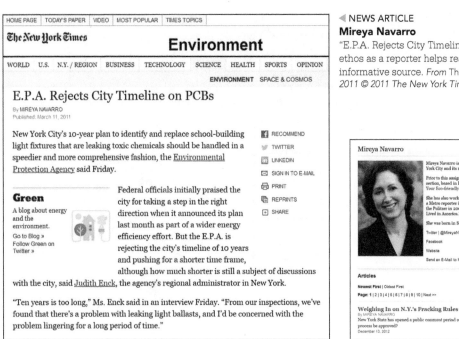

Inside the news article image:

HOME PAGE | TODAY'S PAPER | VIDEO | MOST POPULAR | TIMES TOPICS

The New York Times

Environment

WORLD   U.S.   N.Y. / REGION   BUSINESS   TECHNOLOGY   SCIENCE   HEALTH   SPORTS   OPINION

ENVIRONMENT   SPACE & COSMOS

E.P.A. Rejects City Timeline on PCBs

By MIREYA NAVARRO
Published: March 11, 2011

New York City's 10-year plan to identify and replace school-building light fixtures that are leaking toxic chemicals should be handled in a speedier and more comprehensive fashion, the Environmental Protection Agency said Friday.

Green

A blog about energy and the environment.
Go to Blog »
Follow Green on Twitter »

Federal officials initially praised the city for taking a step in the right direction when it announced its plan last month as part of a wider energy efficiency effort. But the E.P.A. is rejecting the city's timeline of 10 years and pushing for a shorter time frame, although how much shorter is still a subject of discussions with the city, said Judith Enck, the agency's regional administrator in New York.

"Ten years is too long," Ms. Enck said in an interview Friday. "From our inspections, we've found that there's a problem with leaking light ballasts, and I'd be concerned with the problem lingering for a long period of time."

RECOMMEND
TWITTER
LINKEDIN
SIGN IN TO E-MAIL
PRINT
REPRINTS
SHARE

Mireya Navarro

Mireya Navarro is an environmental writer for The Times focusing on New York City and its region.

Prior to this assignment she was a correspondent with the Sunday Styles section, based in Los Angeles, where she wrote "Green Wedding: Planning Your Eco-friendly Celebration."

She has also worked as Miami Bureau chief for the National section and as a Metro reporter in New York. She was part of the writing team that won the Pulitzer in 2001 for national reporting for the series "How Race is Lived in America."

She was born in San Juan, P.R. She lives with her husband in Manhattan.

Twitter | @MireyaNYT
Facebook
Website
Send an E-Mail to Mireya Navarro

Articles
Newest First | Oldest First
Page: 1 | 2 | 3 | 4 | 5 | 6 | 7 | 8 | 9 | 10 | Next >>

Weighing In on N.Y.'s Fracking Rules
By MIREYA NAVARRO
New York State has opened a public comment period on the impact of hydraulic fracturing. Will the gas drilling process be approved?
December 13, 2012

Logos—or your use of logic as an author—is also significant. "How to" or instructional genres, such as recipes, make heavy use of logos. When cooks create recipes, they direct the reader in what to do, in a specific order. Chopping ingredients, mixing them, and cooking them must be presented to readers as logical steps. In the example on page 332, the chef, Lora Guillotte of *Saucie.com*, presents her recipe for Louisiana Pork Chops in a logical manner, listing the ingredients and measures clearly, outlining the steps, and illustrating them with helpful images.

Pathos—your appeal to your readers' emotions—is generally not a priority when you're writing to inform. On the other hand, if you want to inform but also persuade your readers, you can appeal to their emotions. For example, in the *Saucie .com* recipe for Louisiana Pork Chops, the author appeals to readers' pathos by suggesting that like her, they are busy preparing for holidays, and therefore want an uncomplicated

RECIPE ▶
Lora Guillotte
"Louisiana Pork
Chops," *Saucie.com*.
Guillotte's instructions
are clear and logical.
Lora Guillotte.

RECIPE PHOTOS ▶
Lora Guillotte
"Louisiana Pork
Chops." These images
show the final steps in
cooking: the pleasures
of plating and eating.
They reflect the
chef's sense of humor,
which she uses as a
rhetorical strategy to
draw readers in.
Lora Guillotte.

recipe. Lora also posts two final images under her recipe that reflect her sense of humor and show that she enjoyed her own "fine" creation. Use your judgment about when to use humor when writing to inform; generally it is appropriate for less formal informational genres, but you also have to consider this in terms of your specific purposes and audiences.

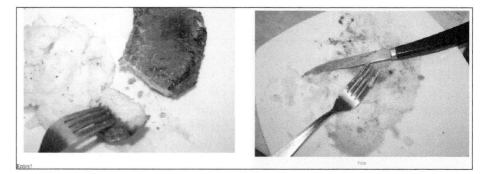

Modes & Media: How can they help you inform?

A composition's *mode* is how the content itself is communicated—whether in writing, by voice, through images, through sounds, or in some combination. A composition's *medium* is the final form or mechanism that it's delivered in, such as print, digital, or face-to-face. Following is a breakdown of the modes and media of some of the compositions presented in this chapter:

INFORMATIVE GENRES	Mode	Medium
ILLUSTRATION, ONLINE Harvard School of Public Health, "Food Pyramid" (p. 357)	**VISUAL**	**DIGITAL**
INSTRUCTIONS, ONLINE Homeland Security, "Preventing Terrorism" (p. 326)	**WRITTEN**	**DIGITAL**
DICTIONARY ENTRY, ONLINE *Dictionary.com*, "vertiginous" (p. 324)	**WRITTEN AND AUDIO**	**DIGITAL**
RECIPE, ONLINE Lora Guillotte, "Louisiana Pork Chops" (p. 332)	**WRITTEN AND VISUAL**	**DIGITAL**
INSTRUCTIONS, ONLINE Ann Pizer, "Downward Facing Dog" (p. 335)	**WRITTEN, VISUAL, AND VIDEO**	**DIGITAL**

A Word about Modes

Visuals are crucial when we're learning something new, such as the pork chop recipe (p. 332) and the yoga pose (p. 335), which is provided in three modes—through text, an image, and video. For the yoga pose, without the visual, readers would need much more text to understand what they should be doing. Even better is the video, which shows viewers all the steps required to achieve the pose.

The pork chop recipe also benefits from accompanying visuals. When people are cooking, they usually want text that describes the ingredients they need and steps they need to follow—as well as images of what the food should look like as they prepare it, and when it's done. Still images might be best in this case. While a video might show a reader how the actual steps are performed, it's difficult to cook and watch a video at the same time.

Think about your favorite ads or commercials (or even the ones you find most annoying). Do you find yourself identifying with the people featured in them? Why or why not? #Analyze

Audio is also useful in certain situations. For example, *Dictionary.com* presents information about the word *vertiginous* in two modes—as text (for readers and writers), and as an audio file (for speakers) so users of the site can learn the correct pronunciation of the word.

The Genre's Conventions

Elements of the Genre: What does all informative writing have in common?

Two essential qualities of the best informative writing are accuracy and clarity. Whether you are writing a news report in which you provide straight facts, or are creating a set of instructions in which you detail the steps for performing a certain task, you need to be accurate, clear, and direct. Informative writing should also be presented in an order that will make sense to readers. For example, when providing instructions, it's a good idea to present information in small, digestible units—and to move from simple to complex.

Let's examine the choices Ann Pizer makes in her instructions for doing a yoga pose, shown on page 335. In this example, Pizer starts with basic information about a yoga pose known as "downward facing dog," including the benefits of the pose. She then breaks it down into a series of numbered tasks; each step represents a single move, so that viewers can take their time. The order of the steps is very important too. While an experienced yogi may go into the pose in what appears to be one fluid motion, a new practitioner needs to consciously move each body part into place and do so in a particular order to avoid injury. Because alignment is important in yoga, Pizer carefully specifies how body parts should line up, as in step 1, where she notes that the wrists should be "underneath the shoulders" and the knees should be "underneath the hips." Barry Stone's photo of a woman in the pose shows readers how wrists and knees should be aligned. Pizer follows her directions with notes tailored for beginners and more advanced practitioners to allow for some customization of the directions.

What informative texts have you read today? Think of street signs, recipes, product labels, news articles, and course assignments. What traits do they share? How do these texts function to inform you? #Remember #Analyze

About.com Yoga
Health ›

🏠 Yoga | Yoga Styles | Beginners | Poses & Workouts

Downward Facing Dog - Adho Mukha Svanasana
By Ann Pizer, About.com Guide *Updated October 06, 2012*

About.com Health's Disease and Condition content is reviewed by our Medical Review Board

See More About: beginning poses   standing poses   downward facing dog

Also known as: Downward Dog, Down Dog

Type of pose: Standing, Mild Inversion, Resting

Benefits: Stretches and strengthens the whole body. Can help relieve back pain.

Downward facing dog is done many times during most yoga classes. It is a transitional pose, a resting pose and a great strengthener in its

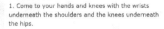

Downward Facing Dog - Adho Mukha Svanasana
© Barry Stone

own right. It may be the first yoga pose you encounter as you begin a yoga practice.

Ann Pizer
Yoga Guide
• Sign up for My Newsletter
• Headlines • Forum

Instructions:

1. Come to your hands and knees with the wrists underneath the shoulders and the knees underneath the hips.

2. Curl the toes under and push back raising the hips and straightening the legs.

Related Video

How to Do Downward Facing Dog

3. Spread the fingers and ground down from the forearms into the fingertips.

4. Outwardly rotate the upper arms broadening the collarbones.

5. Let the head hang, move the shoulder blades away from the ears towards the hips.

6. Engage the quadriceps strongly to take the weight off the arms, making this a resting pose.

7. Rotate the thighs inward, keep the tail high and sink your heels towards the floor.

8. Check that the distance between your hands and feet is correct by coming forward to a plank position. The distance between the hands and feet should be the same in these two poses. Do not step the feet toward the hands in Down Dog in order the get the heels to the floor. This will happen eventually as the muscles lengthen.

Beginners: Try bending your knees, coming up onto the balls of your feet, bringing the belly to rest on the thighs and the sit bones up high. Then sink your heels, straightening the legs keeping the high upward rotation of the sit bones. Also try bending the arms slightly out to the side, drawing the chest towards the thighs. Then restraighten the arms.

Advanced: If you are very flexible, try not to let the rib cage sink towards the floor creating a sinking spine. Draw the ribs in to maintain a flat back. Try holding the pose for five minutes, placing a block under your head for support.

▲ INSTRUCTIONS
Ann Pizer
"Downward Facing Dog," About.com: Yoga. © 2012 Ann Pizer About.com. Reprinted with permission.

Style: How does it help you inform?

When you're writing to inform, you should present content in a style that's accessible to your audience. You'll also want to consider the voice and tone you will use. Is a strong writer's presence appropriate for your composition, or should you be more neutral? And how much detail will you need to provide to get your ideas across? For most informative genres, you will probably use a neutral tone to convey information. Because your primary goal is to inform your readers about something, you'll probably want to avoid wild flourishes of language. For example, in the pork chop recipe, the writer instructs readers to "mix spices together"; she does not say "merge all the aromatic flavors of world cuisines." Attention to detail is also crucial in genres that inform. For example, in step 8 of Ann Pizer's yoga pose instructions, she gives enough detail so beginners understand how the pose will change for them over time as they become more practiced.

Design: What is the best format for informing?

Design helps readers (and viewers, listeners, etc.) navigate information. In the instructions below, the designers at Tieknots.org show readers where to begin, what steps to follow, and where to end. The number next to each step shows readers where they are in the process. The simple design and limited detail allow readers to focus in on each move. Further, the design is scaled so that it can fit on a business card, making the instructions both concise and portable.

INSTRUCTIONS ▶
"How to Tie a Tie."
Who needs words when a clear "how to" diagram can do the trick? *Shutterstock*.

What colors grab your attention? Do these colors change depending on what you're looking at? For example, what colors might attract your attention in a textbook design, or an advertisement, or online instructions? #Understand

Sources: What research should you draw on to inform your readers?

When you write to inform, you need to be informed yourself: You need to draw on the best sources possible (see "Authoritative sources of information," p. 325). For example, journalist Mireya Navarro, author of "E.P.A. Rejects City Timeline on PCBs" (p. 331), interviews EPA administrator Judith Enck for her article. We can assume that Enck is an expert in her field and a reliable source. To take another example, imagine that it's an election year, and you're creating a chart about voting trends. You might use information from the U.S. Census Bureau.

ENCYCLOPEDIA ENTRIES

Collecting facts has been a human pursuit for a long time. In the first century CE, a Roman author, naturalist, and military man named Pliny the Elder tried to record everything known about the natural world in his thirty-seven-volume *Naturalis Historia*, the world's first encyclopedia-like document. (You can read it at the Perseus Digital Library, in English or the original Latin.)

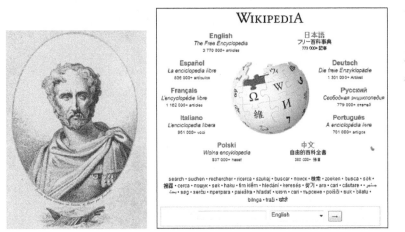

◀ PORTRAIT & WIKI ENCYCLOPEDIA
Pliny the Elder and Wikipedia
What would Pliny say about *Wikipedia*? *Pliny the Elder: Library of Congress. Wikipedia homepage: Courtesy of Wikimedia Foundation, Inc. All rights reserved.*

Pliny, like all encyclopedists, aimed to provide what was known about a specific or general topic in a way that worked best for his target audience. The *Encyclopaedia Britannica* is a source of general information on many topics; it's geared toward readers who want to gain a broad understanding of a given subject. More specialized encyclopedias, such as *The Encyclopedia of Women's History in America* by Kathryn Cullen-DuPont, may cover topics in more depth, assuming readers already have some understanding of the topic.

Encyclopedias share several characteristics:

» They serve as a general (or sometimes specialized) reference.

» They provide information that is considered true (meaning it is agreed upon by experts on the topic).

» They are compilations and syntheses of what others have said, rather than original research (that is, they are tertiary sources).

» They are organized into individual articles that are well researched and written by content experts, typically people with an academic degree related to the subject they're writing about.

How often do you refer to encyclopedias? What are the benefits—and limitations—of using an encyclopedia as a source? #Evaluate

Analyzing Encyclopedia Entries: What to Look For

Purpose Encyclopedists provide an overview of a subject so that readers can gain a general understanding of it. For example, here is how editors of *The Columbia Encyclopedia* describe their reference book (accessed at *Encyclopedia.com*):

▼ ENCYCLOPEDIA
ENTRY
***Gale Encyclopedia
of Medicine***
Via Encyclopedia.com,
"Psychosis." *From*
Gale Encyclopedia
of Medicine V4,3E.
© 2006 Gale, a part
of Cengage Learning,
Inc. Reproduced by
permission. www.
cengage.com/
permissions.

Encyclopedias available in our online research library

The Columbia Encyclopedia (Sixth Edition): An authoritative, English-language dictionary containing more than 51,000 topics, The Columbia Encyclopedia provides trusted facts and information you can count on. Because more than 200 editors and academic advisors strive for depth and accuracy in each edition of the oldest, most venerable English-language encyclopedia in the world, this encyclopedia's topics are thorough and clear.

◄ ONLINE
ENCYCLOPEDIA
***Columbia
Encyclopedia***
Reproduced by
permission. www.cengage
.com/permissions.

Other encyclopedias are more specialized; they tend to be aimed at readers interested in a particular field. The *Gale Encyclopedia of Medicine* is an example of a specialized resource. Below is the entry for "Psychosis," written by Paula Ford-Martin and Rebecca Frey.

International Encyclopedia...	Gale Encyclopedia of...	The Oxford Companion to the...	Gale Encyclopedia of Psychology	Further reading

Psychosis

Gale Encyclopedia of Medicine. 3rd ed. | 2006 | Ford-Martin, Paula; Frey, Rebecca | Copyright

Psychosis
Definition
Psychosis is a symptom or feature of mental illness typically characterized by radical changes in personality, impaired functioning, and a distorted or nonexistent sense of objective reality.

Description
Patients suffering from psychosis have impaired reality testing; that is, they are unable to distinguish personal subjective experience from the reality of the external world. They experience **hallucinations** and/or **delusions** that they believe are real, and may behave and communicate in an inappropriate and incoherent fashion. Psychosis may appear as a symptom of a number of mental disorders, including mood and **personality disorders.** It is also the defining feature of **schizophrenia,** schizophreniform disorder, **schizoaffective disorder,** delusional disorder, and the psychotic disorders (i.e., brief psychotic disorder, shared psychotic disorder, psychotic disorder due to a general medical condition, and substance-induced psychotic disorder).

Causes and symptoms
Psychosis may be caused by the interaction of biological and psychosocial factors depending on the disorder in which it presents; psychosis can also be caused by purely social factors, with no biological component.

Biological factors that are regarded as contributing to the development of psychosis include genetic abnormalities and substance use. With regard to chromosomal abnormalities, studies indicate that 30% of patients diagnosed with a psychotic disorder have a microdeletion at chromosome 22q11. Another group of researchers has identified the gene G72/G30 at chromosome 13q33.2 as a susceptibility gene for child-hood-onset schizophrenia and psychosis not otherwise specified.

With regard to **substance abuse**, several different research groups reported in 2004 that cannabis (**marijuana**) use is a risk factor for the onset of psychosis.

Migration is a social factor that influences people's susceptibility to psychotic disorders. Psychiatrists in Europe have noted the increasing rate of schizophrenia and other psychotic disorders among immigrants to almost all Western European countries. Black immigrants from Africa or the Caribbean appear to be especially vulnerable. The stresses involved in migration include family breakup, the need to adjust to living in large urban areas, and social inequalities in the new country.

Audience Encyclopedists know that their primary audience is general readers looking for a reliable but quick snapshot of a topic. For example, writers for the online encyclopedia *MedlinePlus* know their readers are mainly nonprofessionals consulting *Medline* for basic information about symptoms, causes, and treatment. The writers know they must be accurate and fairly brief; they can link to additional resources with more in-depth information. On the other hand, encyclopedists who write for more specialized reference works aimed at specific professional audiences, such as *Medpedia*—an open resource geared toward doctors and associated with major medical schools including Harvard and Stanford—provide a deeper level of information in their entries.

A Word about *Wikipedia*

Wikipedia is the most popular reference site on the Internet. As an encyclopedia, *Wikipedia* has all the features of that genre, with one important exception: Instead of entries being written by scholars, entries can be written by anyone. Indeed, that's what the *wiki* part of the name means: A wiki is a Web site that can be edited by users. *Wikipedia* is open-access, meaning almost all of its entries can be edited by anyone who registers with the site.

Because anyone can edit an entry, many people have concerns about the reliability of the information found on *Wikipedia*. However, others argue that because anyone who finds an error can correct it, *Wikipedia* is actually as reliable as any other reference source. In fact, a 2005 study by the science journal *Nature* found that *Wikipedia* entries had no more errors than entries in *Encyclopaedia Britannica*.

Tip: Most entries on *Wikipedia* include a list of (often linked) sources drawn on by the entry authors. These sources are often worth checking out, so even if you (or your instructor) decide that *Wikipedia* is not an appropriate source for your research, you might find an entry's reference list useful.

Rhetorical appeals   Encyclopedists appeal to readers through ethos—as content experts presenting accurate information. In turn, readers can assume that an encyclopedia entry is authoritative and trustworthy. Encyclopedists also appeal through logos, presenting content in a logical manner, often moving from general to more specific information. Writers begin an entry by defining the topic and often then break it out into subtopics, bringing up associated terms, people, and places. You can see this at work in the "Psychosis" entry from the *Gale Encyclopedia of Medicine* (p. 343). Further, in an online encyclopedia, keywords and subtopics are hyperlinked, which contributes to the logos of the entry.

Modes & media   Encyclopedia entries are written texts that can appear in print or digital formats. Before the digital age, a family would purchase an entire set of print encyclopedias; now a family would more commonly purchase an encyclopedia on DVD, or to use free online resources such as *Encyclopedia.com* or *Wikipedia*.

What are your thoughts on digital encyclopedias—specifically on open-source reference works such as *Wikipedia*? How do you use these sources? And to what extent do you consider them trustworthy? #Understand #Evaluate

Elements of the genre

Well researched and accurate. Entries are completely fact based. Encyclopedists gather, scrutinize, and synthesize information from many reliable sources to create an entry on a given topic. They convey proven information as objectively as possible (without the interference of opinion).

Written by experts. Most encyclopedias enlist professionals who have a deep level of knowledge on the topic of the entry to be written. This can also be true of wiki-platform encyclopedias that have a peer-review policy.

Clear. Encyclopedists provide basic information in a direct and straightforward manner.

Brief. Entries are not exhaustive; rather, they are intended as jumping-off points for further research. While some entries can be relatively long—for example, the complete entry on "Global Warming" from *Encyclopaedia Britannica* (p. 344) prints out at thirty-four pages long—they are still extremely short compared with the length of a book on the subject. The top three books on global warming at this moment—*Climate of Extremes* by Patrick J. Michaels and Robert Balling Jr., *Climate of Corruption* by Larry Bell, and *Climate Change* by Edmond A. Mathez—average 303 pages long.

Style

Just enough detail. Encyclopedists provide just enough detail to inform general readers. However, in a given entry, they mention related topics, concepts, and keywords that readers may want to pursue with further research. For example, *Wikipedia*'s "Motivation" entry (approximately seven printed pages) includes a one-paragraph summary of self-determination theory as well as links to a separate entry on that topic, one of the developers of the theory, and the topic of intrinsic motivation (see p. 341).

In contrast, Daniel H. Pink's book on motivation, *Drive: The Surprising Truth about What Motivates Us*, offers a deeper level of information on the theory, devoting five pages to who originally posed it, how it's been applied, and how it's held up through cultural and societal changes.

Precise language/word choice. Encyclopedists are specific and exact writers. For example, the *Wikipedia* entry on "Motivation" refers not just to "researchers" but

Self-determination theory [edit]

Self-determination theory, developed by Edward Deci and Richard Ryan, focuses on the importance of intrinsic motivation in driving human behavior. Like Maslow's hierarchical theory and others that built on it, SDT posits a natural tendency toward growth and development. Unlike these other theories, however, SDT does not include any sort of "autopilot" for achievement, but instead requires active encouragement from the environment. The primary factors that encourage motivation and development are autonomy, competence feedback, and relatedness.

to three specific researchers: Deci, Ryan, and Maslow. Imagine how you might question the authority of a reference work if the writers used ambiguous terms and generalizations, rather than specifics.

Encyclopedists often use formal, academic language to bolster their authority and emphasize their seriousness. That means they avoid contractions, slang, and abbreviated forms such as "info" for "information."

Use of the third person and a serious tone. Encyclopedists write in the third person, which reinforces their ethos and reminds readers that the entries are based on shared knowledge amongst an expert group, not just the perspective of one person. They use a serious tone to project credibility (ethos) to readers. If you were creating an encyclopedia entry, you probably wouldn't write it in the sarcastic tone of Jon Stewart, for example. Although the information in an entry might be informative *and* funny, using humor as a rhetorical strategy in an encyclopedia entry might undermine your authority and trustworthiness as an encyclopedist.

Design

Accessible. Encyclopedia entries need to be designed so that readers can quickly identify and use information on a particular page. Hard-copy reference works often use descriptive headers or footers so readers can navigate easily.

▲ *WIKIPEDIA* ENTRY
Wikipedia
"Motivation." Shown here is the "self-determination theory" section of the main entry, "Motivation." The writers of this entry use clear language and specifically name the researchers who developed self-determination theory. *Courtesy of Wikimedia Foundation, Inc. All rights reserved.*

Consistent. Encyclopedias and other reference works follow a consistent format. In a dictionary, for example, each entry might begin with the name of the entry, followed by the part of speech, followed by a phonetic spelling. Every entry in the dictionary would follow that format.

Clearly titled. The name or title of the entry is in large, bold letters at the top of the entry, in order to clearly indicate the topic. In the case of a longer entry, the repetition of the title words orients the reader back to the original search term.

Hyperlinked to other entries (in online editions). The use of hyperlinks in an entry allows encyclopedists to provide more information without lengthening the entry itself. These links identify terminology (see "Just enough detail" above) and provide additional search terms to assist readers in narrowing their investigation of a broad subject. For example, the *Gale Encyclopedia of Medicine* entry on "Psychosis" (p. 343) connects that topic with schizophrenia and other specific disorders, helping narrow the broad initial term. As a researcher, you might then go to *EBSCOhost* or another rich database to explore the connection between psychosis and schizophrenia.

When you refer to an encyclopedia entry, do you think about the people who composed it? About their expertise? Their biases? To what extent do these factors affect your trust in the source itself? #Remember #Evaluate

Sources

Variation in attribution of sources. Encyclopedia entries may not contain any documentation attributing the information to particular sources. While this might appear to be plagiarism, it is not. Encyclopedia entries are usually composed by experts in the field; therefore, the encyclopedists have firsthand knowledge of the information through their extensive research background.

Encyclopaedia Britannica entries, for example, are written and overseen by an editorial board of advisors. Board members often include Nobel Prize winners, scholars, and scientists who are well-known in their respective fields.

On the other hand, *Wikipedia* entries and many other encyclopedia entries do include footnotes as well as extensive reference lists. For example, here is the bibliography section of the entry for "Psychosis" by Paula Ford-Martin and Rebecca Frey, from the *Gale Encyclopedia of Medicine*:

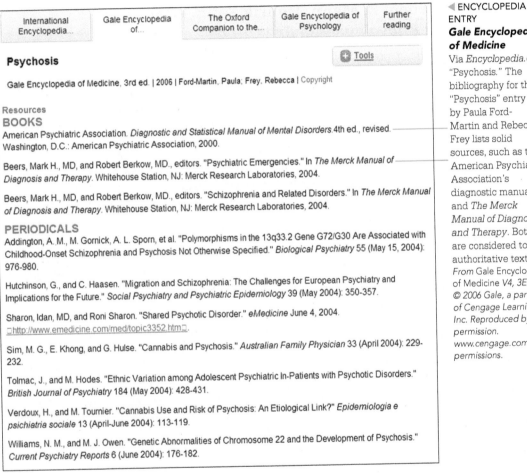

International Encyclopedia...	Gale Encyclopedia of...	The Oxford Companion to the...	Gale Encyclopedia of Psychology	Further reading

Psychosis

⊕ Tools

Gale Encyclopedia of Medicine, 3rd ed. | 2006 | Ford-Martin, Paula; Frey, Rebecca | Copyright

Resources

BOOKS

American Psychiatric Association. *Diagnostic and Statistical Manual of Mental Disorders.*4th ed., revised. Washington, D.C.: American Psychiatric Association, 2000.

Beers, Mark H., MD, and Robert Berkow, MD., editors. "Psychiatric Emergencies." In *The Merck Manual of Diagnosis and Therapy*. Whitehouse Station, NJ: Merck Research Laboratories, 2004.

Beers, Mark H., MD, and Robert Berkow, MD., editors. "Schizophrenia and Related Disorders." In *The Merck Manual of Diagnosis and Therapy*. Whitehouse Station, NJ: Merck Research Laboratories, 2004.

PERIODICALS

Addington, A. M., M. Gornick, A. L. Sporn, et al. "Polymorphisms in the 13q33.2 Gene G72/G30 Are Associated with Childhood-Onset Schizophrenia and Psychosis Not Otherwise Specified." *Biological Psychiatry* 55 (May 15, 2004): 976-980.

Hutchinson, G., and C. Haasen. "Migration and Schizophrenia: The Challenges for European Psychiatry and Implications for the Future." *Social Psychiatry and Psychiatric Epidemiology* 39 (May 2004): 350-357.

Sharon, Idan, MD, and Roni Sharon. "Shared Psychotic Disorder." *eMedicine* June 4, 2004. ☐http://www.emedicine.com/med/topic3352.htm☐.

Sim, M. G., E. Khong, and G. Hulse. "Cannabis and Psychosis." *Australian Family Physician* 33 (April 2004): 229-232.

Tolmac, J., and M. Hodes. "Ethnic Variation among Adolescent Psychiatric In-Patients with Psychotic Disorders." *British Journal of Psychiatry* 184 (May 2004): 428-431.

Verdoux, H., and M. Tournier. "Cannabis Use and Risk of Psychosis: An Etiological Link?" *Epidemiologia e psichiatria sociale* 13 (April-June 2004): 113-119.

Williams, N. M., and M. J. Owen. "Genetic Abnormalities of Chromosome 22 and the Development of Psychosis." *Current Psychiatry Reports* 6 (June 2004): 176-182.

◀ ENCYCLOPEDIA ENTRY
Gale Encyclopedia of Medicine
Via *Encyclopedia.com*, "Psychosis." The bibliography for the "Psychosis" entry by Paula Ford-Martin and Rebecca Frey lists solid sources, such as the American Psychiatric Association's diagnostic manual and *The Merck Manual of Diagnosis and Therapy*. Both are considered to be authoritative texts. *From* Gale Encyclopedia of Medicine *V4, 3E.* © 2006 Gale, a part of Cengage Learning, Inc. Reproduced by permission. www.cengage.com/permissions.

Michael E. Mann, Henrik Selin, et al., for *Encyclopaedia Britannica*

Global Warming

Visit the *Britannica* site to see the presentation of advertising in the entry. How does the presence of ads affect your reading of this entry? To what extent do ads affect *Britannica's* ethos? #Apply #Evaluate

Encyclopaedia Britannica has been publishing for nearly 250 years, giving it a level of credibility and authority that other, newer encyclopedia brands can't compete with. This status is further bolstered by the fame of some of its recent contributors, who include Albert Einstein, Marie Curie, Sigmund Freud, and Carl Sagan.

The primary contributors for the entry below on "Global Warming" are Michael E. Mann and Henrik Selin. Mann is a professor of meteorology at Pennsylvania State University and the director of the Earth System Science Center. He has published many journal articles and received numerous awards for his research. Selin is a professor in the international relations department at Boston University and an affiliated researcher at the Center for Climate Science and Policy Research at Linköping University in Sweden. He has authored books, book chapters, and articles on energy and climate. These authors and *Encyclopaedia Britannica* have some serious ethos.

The following example from the online edition of *Britannica* is typical of an entry in a general encyclopedia. Note: Reprinted here are short excerpts from the much longer entry for "Global Warming." *(Illustrations on pages 344–49: Reprinted with permission from* Encyclopaedia Britannica, © 2012 by Encyclopaedia Britannica Inc.)

ENCYCLOPEDIA ▶
PAGE
Encyclopaedia
Britannica
Editorial Board
of Advisors. An
encyclopedia entry
is only as good as its
writers and editors.
Britannica has
bragging rights to
some authoritative
contributors, including
Albert Einstein and
Marie Curie. *Reprinted*
with permission
from Encyclopaedia
Britannica, © 2012
by Encyclopaedia
Britannica, Inc.

ENCYCLOPÆDIA Britannica

About the Editorial Board

Current Members
Wendy Doniger
Richard Fishman
Benjamin M. Friedman
Leslie H. Gelb
David Gelernter
Murray Gell-Mann
Vartan Gregorian
Lord Sutherland of Houndwood
Lord Weidenfeld of Chelsea

Recent Members
Rosalia Artaega
David Baltimore
Nicholas Carr
Zaha Hadid

The Encyclopædia Britannica Editorial Board of Advisors

For any organization that aspires to take all human knowledge, organize it, summarize it, and publish it in a form that people find useful, the challenges and opportunities have never been greater than they are today. The volume of information is exploding, the world is shrinking, and digital media are changing the way we read, think, and learn.

To meet these challenges and opportunities, Britannica has done what we have always done throughout our 240-year history: sought the very best minds in the world to help us.

In the past, they had names like Albert Einstein, Sigmund Freud, Marie Curie, Bertrand Russell, T.H. Huxley, and George Bernard Shaw, all of whom were Britannica contributors in their day.

Today they are the men and women of Britannica's Editorial Board of Advisors—the Nobel laureates and Pulitzer Prize winners, the leading scholars, writers, artists, public servants, and activists who are at the top of their fields. They meet regularly to share ideas, to debate, and to argue, in a unique collegium whose purpose is to understand today's world so that the resulting encyclopedia can be the best there is. We are proud to be associated with these exceptional people, and we are deeply grateful for their contributions, not only to our own publishing objectives but to the larger cause of promoting knowledge in the world today.

ENCYCLOPÆDIA
Britannica
Facts matter

Search Articles

global warming

Contributors

Primary Contributors

Michael E. Mann

Henrik Selin

Other Contributors

The Editors of *Encyclopaedia Britannica*

Heather Campbell

Swati Chopra

Darshana Das

John Higgins

Gloria Lotha

J. E. Luebering

Richard Pallardy

Dutta Promeet

John P. Rafferty

Marco Sampaolo

Veenu Setia

Gaurav Shukla

Shiveta Singh

What are the composers, **Mann, Selin, et al.**, doing?

THE RHETORICAL SITUATION

Purpose
Audience
Rhetorical appeals
Modes & media

see page 346

How do I know this is an **encyclopedia entry**?

THE GENRE'S CONVENTIONS

Elements of the genre
Style
Design
Sources

see page 346

Michael E. Mann, Henrik Selin, et al., for *Encyclopaedia Britannica, Global Warming*

THE RHETORICAL SITUATION

Purpose

Authors Mann and Selin (and other contributors) write to inform readers with facts and uncontested ideas. While they acknowledge a debate around the term ("A vigorous debate is in progress. . . . "), their purpose is not to express opinions or persuade. Their writing is businesslike and factual.

THE GENRE'S CONVENTIONS

Elements of the genre

Gives an overview of the topic, providing established facts (e.g., facts about temperature and gases).

Serves as a starting point for further research; introduces related concepts (e.g., the political debate on global warming), but does not get into detail.

(Continued on p. 348.)

ENCYCLOPÆDIA Britannica
Facts matter

Search Articles

global warming, the phenomenon of increasing average air temperatures near the surface of Earth over the past one to two centuries. Since the mid-20th century, climate scientists have gathered detailed observations of various weather phenomena (such as temperature, precipitation, and storms) and of related influences on climate (such as ocean currents and the atmosphere's chemical composition). These data indicate that Earth's climate has changed over almost every conceivable timescale since the beginning of geologic time and that, since at least the beginning of the Industrial Revolution, the influence of human activities has been deeply woven into the very fabric of climate change.

Giving voice to a growing conviction of most of the scientific community, the Intergovernmental Panel on Climate Change (IPCC) reported that the 20th century saw an increase in global average surface temperature of approximately 0.6 °C (1.1 °F). The IPCC went on to state that most of the warming observed over the second half of the 20th century could be attributed to human activities, and it predicted that by the end of the 21st century the average surface temperature would increase by another 1.8 to 4.0 °C (3.2 to 7.2 °F), depending on a range of possible scenarios. Many climate scientists agree that significant economic and ecological damage would result if global average temperatures rose by more than 2 °C [3.6 °F] in such a short time. Such damage might include increased extinction of many plant and animal species, shifts in patterns of agriculture, and rising sea levels. The IPCC reported that the global average sea level rose by some 17 cm (6.7 inches) during the 20th century, that sea levels rose faster in the second half of that century than in the first half, and that—again depending on a wide range of possible scenarios. Many climate scientists agree that significant economic and ecological damage would result if global average temperatures rose by more than 2 °C [3.6 °F] in such a short time. Such damage might include increased extinction of many plant and animal species, shifts in patterns of agriculture, and rising sea levels. The IPCC reported that the global average sea level rose by some 17 cm (6.7 inches) during the 20th century, that sea levels rose faster in the second half of that century than in the first half, and that—again depending on a wide range of scenarios—the global average sea level could rise by another 18 to 59 cm (7 to 23 inches) by the end of the 21st century. Furthermore, he IPCC reported that average snow cover in the Northern Hemisphere declined by 4 percent, or 1.5 million square km (580,000 square miles), between 1920 niles), between 1920 and 2005.

The scenarios referred to above depend mainly on future concentrations of certain trace gases, called greenhouse gases, that have been injected into the lower atmosphere in increasing amounts through the burning of fossil fuels for industry, transportation, and residential uses. Modern global warming is the result of an increase in magnitude of the so-called greenhouse effect, a warming of Earth's surface and lower atmosphere caused by the presence of water vapour, carbon dioxide, methane, and other greenhouse gases. Of all these gases, carbon dioxide is the most important, both for its role in the greenhouse effect and for its role in the human economy. It has been estimated that, at the beginning of the industrial age in the mid-18th century, carbon dioxide concentrations in the atmosphere were roughly 280 parts per million (ppm). By the end of the 20th century, carbon dioxide concentrations had reached 369 ppm (possibly the highest concentrations in at least 650,000 years), and, if fossil fuels continue to be burned at current rates, they are projected

ENCYCLOPÆDIA Britannica
Facts matter

Search Articles

to reach 560 ppm by the mid-21st century—essentially, a doubling of carbon dioxide concentrations in 300 years. It has been calculated that an increase of this magnitude alone (that is, not accounting for possible effects of other greenhouse gases) would be responsible for adding 2 to 5 °C (3.6 to 9 °F) to the global average surface temperatures that existed at the beginning of the industrial age.

A vigorous debate is in progress over the extent and seriousness of rising surface temperatures, the effects of past and future warming on human life, and the need for action to reduce future warming and deal with its consequences. This article provides an overview of the scientific background and public policy debate related to the subject of global warming. It considers the causes of rising near-surface air temperatures, the influencing factors, the process of climate research and forecasting, the possible ecological and social impacts of rising temperatures, and the public policy developments since the mid-20th century.

Climatic variation since the last glaciation

 Global warming is related to the more general phenomenon of climate change, which refers to changes in the totality of attributes that define climate. In addition to changes in air temperature, climate change involves changes to precipitation patterns, winds, ocean currents, and other measures of Earth's climate. Normally, climate change can be viewed as the combination of various natural forces occurring over diverse timescales. Since the advent of human civilization, climate change has involved an "anthropogenic," or exclusively human caused, element, and this anthropogenic element has become more important in the industrial period of the past two centuries. The term *global warming* is used specifically to refer to any warming of near-surface air during the past two centuries that can be traced to anthropogenic causes.

To define the concepts of global warming and climate change properly, it is first necessary to recognize that the climate of Earth has varied across many timescales, ranging from an individual human life span to billions of years. This variable climate history is typically classified in terms of "regimes" or "epochs." For instance, the Pleistocene glacial epoch (about 2,600,000 to 11,700 years ago) was marked by substantial variations in the global extent of glaciers and ice sheets. These variations took place on timescales of tens to hundreds of millennia and ere driven by changes in the distribution of solar radiation across Earth's surface. The distribution of solar radiation is known as the insolation pattern, and it is strongly affected by the geometry of Earth's orbit around the Sun and by the orientation, or tilt, of Earth's axis relative to the direct rays of the Sun.

Worldwide, the most recent glacial period, or ice age, culminated about 21,000 years ago in what is often called the Last Glacial Maximum. During this time, continental ice sheets extended well into the middle latitude regions of Europe and North America, reaching as far south as present-day London and New York City. Global annual mean temperature appears to have been about 4–5 °C (7–9 °F) colder than in the mid-20th century. It is important to remember that these figures are a global average. In fact, during the height of this last ice age, Earth's climate was characterized by greater cooling at higher latitudes (that is, toward the poles) and relatively little cooling over large parts of the tropical oceans (near the Equator). This glacial interval terminated abruptly about 11,700 years ago and was followed by the subsequent relatively ice-free period known as the Holocene Epoch. The modern period of Earth's history is conventionally defined as residing within...

Continues next page

Michael E. Mann, Henrik Selin, et al., for *Encyclopaedia Britannica, Global Warming*

THE RHETORICAL SITUATION

Audience
The audience for *Britannica* and this entry is readers who want an overview on a topic, in this case global warming. Readers are most likely from a general rather than an expert audience. They may use this entry as a jumping-off point for further research.

Rhetorical appeals
Mann and Selin establish their **ethos** as experts through their clear writing, authoritative tone, and bibliography of sources. Readers can also click on their names to see their qualifications to write on this topic.

The other contributors are "content editors" that *Britannica* uses for their subject knowledge and analytical abilities, to ensure the accuracy and currency of the article.

(Continued on p. 349.)

Is well researched. The authors are experts and they provide additional reliable sources.

Style

The authors are **precise**, summarizing a seventy-four-page report into one paragraph.

The authors use **specific language**, referring to "carbon dioxide" rather than "certain gases."

The **tone is neutral and the voice is professional**; the entry is written in the **third person**.

Design

The entry has a clear title and an organized layout. The entry is hyperlinked to other *Britannica* entries. Includes images, charts, graphs, videos, and other content to illustrate key concepts. In the online entry, the text is interspersed with ads, which have been cut here.

(Continued on p. 350.)

ENCYCLOPÆDIA Britannica
Facts matter

Search Articles

Bibliography

Documentaries

Of the several productions describing the scientific concepts behind the global warming phenomenon, *An Inconvenient Truth* (2006), produced by LAURIE DAVID, LAWRENCE BENDER, and SCOTT Z. BURNS and narrated by ALBERT GORE, JR., is the most lauded. A feature placing special emphasis on solutions that reduce carbon dioxide production is *Global Warming: What You Need to Know* (2006), produced by the Discovery Channel, the BBC, and NBC News Productions and narrated by TOM BROKAW. Other noted documentaries on global warming include two originally aired on PBS-TV: *What's Up with the Weather?* (2007), produced by JON PALFREMAN; and *Global Warming: The Signs and the Science* (2005), produced by DAVID KENNARD and narrated by ALANIS MORISSETTE.

Michael E. Mann

Scientific Background

An excellent general overview of the factors governing Earth's climate over all timescales is presented in WILLIAM RUDDIMAN, *Earth's Climate: Past and Future* (2000). In addition, RICHARD C.J. SOMERVILLE, *The Forgiving Air: Understanding Environmental Change* (1996, reissued 1998), is a readable introduction to the science of climate and global environmental change. JOHN HOUGHTON, *Global Warming: The Complete Briefing* (1997), also offers an accessible treatment of the science of climate change as well as a discussion of the policy and ethical overtones of climate change as an issue confronting society. SPENCER WEART, *Discovery of Global Warming* (2003), provides a reasoned account of the history of climate change science.

A number of books present thoughtful discussions of global warming as an environmental and societal issue. Still prescient is an early account provided in BILL MCKIBBEN, *The End of Nature* (1989). Other good treatments include STEPHEN SCHNEIDER, *Laboratory Earth* (2001); ALBERT GORE, *An Inconvenient Truth* (2006); ELIZABETH KOLBERT, *Field Notes from a Catastrophe* (2006); EUGENE LINDEN, *The Winds of Change* (2006); TIM FLANNERY, *The Weather Makers* (2006); and MIKE HULME, *Why We Disagree About Climate Change: Understanding Controversy, Inaction and Opportunity* (2009). An excellent exposition for younger readers is found in ANDREW REVKIN, *The North Pole Was Here* (2007).

Public Policy Background

STEPHEN H. SCHNEIDER, ARMIN ROSENCRANZ, and JOHN O. NILES (eds.), *Climate Change Policy: A Survey* (2002), is a primer on various aspects of the policy debate that explains alternatives for dealing with climate change. A broad analysis of the climate change debate is imparted in ANDREW E. DESSLER and EDWARD A. PARSON, *The Science and Politics of Global Climate Change: A Guide to the Debate* (2006). A summary of the quantitative aspects of greenhouse gas emissions designed to assist stakeholders and policy makers is provided in KEVIN A. BAUMERT, TIMOTHY HERZOG, and JONATHAN PERSHING, *Navigating the Numbers: Greenhouse Gas Data and International Climate Policy* (2005).

ENCYCLOPÆDIA
Britannica
Facts matter

Search Articles

A somewhat more technical introduction to the science of climate change is provided in DAVID ARCHER, *Global Warming: Understanding the Forecast* (2006). More advanced treatments of the science of global warming and climate change are included in INTERGOVERNMENTAL PANEL ON CLIMATE CHANGE: WORKING GROUP I, *Climate Change 2007: The Physical Science Basis: Summary for Policymakers: Fourth Assessment Report* (2007); and INTERGOVERNMENTAL PANEL ON CLIMATE CHANGE: WORKING GROUP II, *Climate Change 2007: Climate Change Impacts, Adaptations, and Vulnerability: Fourth Assessment Report* (2007). Possible solutions to the challenges of global warming and climate change are detailed in INTERGOVERNMENTAL PANEL ON CLIMATE CHANGE: WORKING GROUP III, *Climate Change 2007: Mitigation of Climate Change: Fourth Assessment Report* (2007).

JOHN T. HOUGHTON, *Global Warming: The Complete Briefing*, 3rd ed. (2004), offers a perspective on climate change from one of the leading participants in the IPCC process. DANIEL SAREWITZ and ROGER PIELKE, JR., "Breaking the Global-Warming Gridlock," *The Atlantic Monthly*, 286(1):55–64 (2000), presents an alternative view on how to make progress on climate policy by focusing on reducing vulnerability to climate impacts.

Thoughtful discussions of the politics underlying the issue of climate change are provided in ROSS GELBSPAN, *Boiling Point* (2004); MARK LYNAS, *High Tide* (2004); and ROSS GELBSPAN, *The Heat Is On* (1998). The social justice implications involved in adapting the human population to changing climatic conditions are presented in W. NEIL ADGER et al. (eds.), *Fairness in Adaptation to Climate Change* (2006).

Henrik Selin

THE RHETORICAL SITUATION

Mann and Selin appeal to readers' sense of **logos** (logic) by presenting the information in an accessible way; further, they provide specific data in relation to the topic, such as temperatures.

Modes & media

Mode = written and visual The authors convey information in words, but also with charts and graphs. For example, they use a chart to explain temperature changes, and a video to illustrate greenhouse gases, showing how fossil fuels get released into the environment. These modes, along with animations, show readers the impact of pollutants on the environment.

Medium = digital There are pros and cons to providing information digitally. The pros are the many options for providing information. Digital encyclopedias also allow readers to connect through social media. For example, in the *Britannica* "Global Warming" entry, a share button allows readers to share the

link on such sites as Twitter, Facebook, and LinkedIn, and to add the link to a social bookmarking site such as del.icio.us or Google. The cons are the ads. Because the entry is part of the free online resources *Britannica* provides, it is surrounded by ads. A printed encyclopedia would not include ads.

THE GENRE'S
CONVENTIONS

Sources

Mann and Selin,
who themselves
are sources of
information, do not
provide footnotes,
in-text citations, or
a Works Cited list,
but they do provide
a bibliography and
a list of links to
external sites that
connect readers to
other sources that
they recommend as
authoritative.

ENCYCLOPÆDIA
Britannica
Facts matter

Search Articles

Websites

External Websites

- Common Questions About Climate Change - United Nations Environment Programme - World Meteorological Organization
- StopGlobalWarming.org
- A Paleo Perspective on Global Warming
  Discussion on paleoclimate research and global warming, and other issues regarding climate variability and change.
- U. S. Enviornmental Protection Agency - Global Warming
  Educational information on global warming and climate change, from the U.S. Environmental Protection Agency. Includes a primer on the greenhouse effect and recent trends in global climate; a glossary of climate change terms; material on the potential global warming impacts on health, water resources, and different ecosystems; and notes on local, national, and global actions to reduce climate change. Offers the contents of the quarterly newsletter "Inside the Greenhouse," a presentation on the impacts of climate change, and an inventory of U.S. emissions of carbon dioxide, methane, nitrous oxide, and other greenhouse gases.
- Environmental Education For Kids - Global Warming is Hot Stuff!
- Fact Monster - Global Warming
- How Stuff Works - Science - Global Warming
- NeoK12 - Educational Videos, Lessons and Games - Global Warming
- Science and Society - Global Warming
- National Geographic - Environment - What Is Global Warming?
- Think Quest - Global Warming
- National Aeronautics and Space Administration - Global Warming
- PBS Online - Savage Seas
- The Electronic Universe - Greenhouse Effect
- The Official Site of "An Inconvenient Truth"
- How Stuff Works - Science - How Does Global Warming Affect Hunting Season?
- How Stuff Works - Science - How Will Global Warming Affect Autumn?
- How Stuff Works - Science - Is Global Warming Destroying Mount Everest?
- How Stuff Works - Science - The Top 10 Worst Effects of Global Warming

Questions: Analyzing *Britannica*'s encyclopedia entry

1. Purpose. Although the topic of global warming is somewhat controversial, encyclopedists aim to inform—to take a neutral stance rather than try to persuade. What are some of the strategies the authors of the "Global Warming" entry use in order to avoid taking a position?

2. Audience. Who do you imagine is most likely to look up "global warming" in an on-line encyclopedia: a student, a businessperson, a teacher, or a scientist? What do you imagine his or her purpose might be?

3. Rhetorical appeals. Read an entry on a topic of your choice in *Wikipedia* and then read an entry on the same topic in another online encyclopedia. Compare the authors' techniques in the two entries. Do you notice them using similar methods to develop their ethos? What differences do you notice? Which entry sounds more authoritative, in your opinion? Why?

4. Modes & media. In what modes and media have you used encyclopedias? Do you have a preference for one mode or medium over another? Why?

5. Elements of the genre. As pointed out in the "Global Warming" annotations, encyclopedia entries serve as starting points for research. After reading the entry, what questions do you have about the topic? What are you curious about that you might want to research through other, more in-depth sources?

6. Elements of the genre. An encyclopedia entry about global warming is briefer than a book on the topic. As you read the *Britannica* entry excerpt, did you find information you wished had been expanded upon? Why?

7. Style. Notice the neutral, third-person voice. How might your reading of this entry be different if the authors had written it in the first person?

8. Design. The entry is consistently formatted and designed so readers stay oriented. How important is it to you that information be easy to find in a reference work? Why? Can you think of examples of reference works that are not well designed?

9. Sources. In the *Britannica* entry, the authors rarely use attribution phrases such as "according to." How does this affect your reading of the entry? How might your experience as a reader be different if the entry were peppered with parenthetical notes and attribution phrases?

Michael E. Mann, Henrik Selin, et al., for *Encyclopaedia Britannica, Global Warming*   351

Drafting an Encyclopedia Entry

CHECKLIST: Drafting an Encyclopedia Entry
Thinking of drafting an encyclopedia entry? Ask yourself the following questions.

WHAT'S MY RHETORICAL SITUATION?

☐ **Purpose.** What specific topic do I want to write about? Which subtopics do I want to write about? How will I define my topic and subtopics? Writing an entry about "fashion" implies that I will cover fashion over the course of history. Writing about "street fashion," however, significantly narrows the time period I would need to cover.

☐ **Audience.** Who are my readers? How many of them are experts on my topic? Nonexperts who have a mild interest in my topic? What questions will they expect my entry to answer? Are there technical terms I may need to define (or hyperlink to definitions)? What kinds of examples will my readers relate to?

☐ **Rhetorical appeals.** How will I establish my authority as a writer? What kinds of vocabulary, diction, and examples will I use to convey authority?

☐ **Modes & media.** Do I want readers to experience my entry in print or digital format? Do I want to include images or videos?

WHAT GENRE CONVENTIONS MATTER?

☐ **Elements of the genre.** To keep my entry relatively brief, I will need to summarize other, longer works on the topic. Which works will I summarize? How will I make sure my writing is extremely precise? What terms might I need to carefully define?

☐ **Style.** How much do I want to develop my discussion of the topic? An entry geared toward a general audience (as in *Wikipedia*) will be less developed than one geared toward experts (as in *Medpedia*). Should I outline all the topics and subtopics I plan to cover? Then I can consider whether I'm over- or underdeveloping any of the subtopics, given who I imagine my audience to be.

☐ **Design.** How can I use titles and subtitles to make my entry easy to access for readers? If I create a digital entry, how will I use hyperlinks to direct readers to other entries?

☐ **Sources.** In addition to a list of sources, will I want to include a list of "additional resources" for readers who want to do their own research?

PRACTICE
Want to experiment? Draft your own encyclopedia entry.

Are you an expert on a particular subject? Choose one that you're well versed in, and draft an encyclopedia entry on that topic based on what you already know and what you can learn by doing some research (that does not involve *Wikipedia* or any encyclopedia). Remember to include only facts and information that are largely uncontested by others who are well versed in the subject. You may want to include visual features to illustrate key concepts.

Composing with Wikis GT

According to Wikipedia, a **wiki** is a Web site with

> a web application [that] allows people to add, modify, or delete content in collaboration with others. In a typical wiki, text is written using a simplified markup language (known as "wiki markup") or a rich-text editor. While a wiki is a type of content management system, it differs from a blog or most other such systems in that the content is created without any defined owner or leader, and wikis have little implicit structure, allowing structure to emerge according to the needs of the users.

Wikis are a popular way to gather and organize encyclopedia entries and create accessible databases of knowledge and interconnected material. Many wiki applications are available, including MediaWiki (the software upon which Wikipedia is based), TWiki, Foswiki, Tiki, and XWiki, to name but a few. Furthermore, content-management systems (CMS) and learning-management systems (LMS) such as T-Square often have wiki functionality within their interfaces.

Wikis are sometimes assigned in courses to help students think more flexibly about multimodal and collaborative communication. In many ways, composing a wiki entry is like using a word processor: you will need to learn some formatting commands. The difference is in how your work meshes with the work of others. If you are assigned to create a wiki or add to a wiki, here are steps you should consider to successfully produce it—planning; drafting; reviewing, revising, editing; and submitting; each step in the process is detailed below.

> What types of wikis have you encountered? What communities do you belong to that have their own wikis (fandoms, knowledge communities, campus/local/national/international groups, etc.)? What do these wikis allow these communities to accomplish? #Understand #Evaluate

Planning

Once you have received the wiki assignment, review the goals and objectives as defined by your instructor. Ask yourself these questions:

» What type of work does the instructor expect me to complete in the wiki?

» What is the subject of my contribution?

» How do I want to organize and compose this work?

» Where does the idea of collaboration come into play with this work: am I linking to other students' wiki pages or are we writing in the same space?

» How will my independent contributions to the wiki be recognized as distinct from the group contributions?

Remember that *before* you start drafting the assignment, you are responsible for making sure you understand the wiki interface and ways to format, enter, and save text. Consider creating a "sandbox" page so that you and your classmates can experiment with the form and see the various ways it functions before you start drafting your assignment.

Drafting

We focus on MediaWiki (http://www.mediawiki.org/) in this section, but you might choose any other wiki software and apply the same principles. As with any composition, every communicator develops work using a different process. Two that work extremely well in a wiki environment are freewriting and skeleton building. When you *freewrite*, you compose your wiki page as a block of text, drafting your approach to the subject and then editing and organizing it once you feel you have all of your information on the screen. Alternatively, before composing your text, you might consider building a framework, the *skeleton* for your wiki page. With this approach, you can organize the flow of information (chronologically or thematically), identify where you will want to embed images to reinforce your arguments, and determine how you might want to link your work to that of your classmates or to other Internet sources. Either approach allows you to shape and hone your work to make it particularly effective in the wiki environment.

Reviewing, Revising, and Editing

As you write and refine your draft, be sure to frequently click the "Save page" button at the bottom of the screen, so that you don't lose any of your work. Each time you save your work, you record a version of your text in the wiki database. In MediaWiki, you'll see three tabs at the top of your editing screen: "Read," "Edit," and "View History." "View History" allows you to go back and view a log of all saved versions of the wiki page. This log includes the username of each contributor to the page and a time stamp, and allows you to click to a version. This log is not only useful in terms of managing your editorial process but is also particularly valuable when you and several of your classmates are collaborating on a wiki page: you can see which classmate contributed to the page and in what way.

As you revise and add to the content on your wiki page, think about the visual nature of the environment. The rhetorical appeal and design for the medium of wikis are often more in line with an encyclopedia entry than a traditional expository

What are the benefits of using either *freewriting* or *skeleton building* in creating a wiki? #Analyze essay. Your instructor, though, may ask you to take another rhetorical approach, depending on what sort of wiki you are building in class. An effective wiki entry should include the following elements:

» A brief **summary** of your subject, including pertinent information such as dates and important associations or accomplishments

» A **table of contents** that provides a top-line navigational system to help the audience understand how you've organized your content

» Carefully structured **sections** that give in-depth information supported by properly cited sources

» Appropriate **images** placed on the page in balanced fashion, to help guide the audience through the body of your page

» **Footnotes** and a **list of sources** at the bottom of the page, which demonstrate to your audience that you have done your research about this subject. Remember also that a list of sources helps your audience members to pursue their own interest in the subject.

Drafting and revising a wiki page offers flexibility in the process unavailable with word-processing software and other platforms such as blogs. Experiment with the elements in the preceding list to make your wiki page a confident and authoritative representation of your approach to the subject.

Submitting

When you select a medium that requires you to use specific software or online services, you should always have a plan for extracting, publishing, or saving your work. You should design your submission plan *before* starting work on a project to avoid costly time revising your work should you find out that you cannot submit it as required. For example, if you decide to create a wiki for your course projects, make sure the instructor will accept a link to the finished project and that your instructor has any access credentials necessary to view the wiki (username, password, link, etc.).

Unlike other forms of word processing, wikis as a genre have no formal publication process. They are, by design, living documents—meant to be developed and refined over time, and, in the case of sources like Wikipedia, the editorial process is designed to be never ending, a democratic and limitless collaborative process. For the purposes of your course, however, time limits are associated with your work. Your instructor will identify milestones and deadlines that can be reviewed via the "View History"/time stamp feature discussed previously. This form of submission is in some ways reminiscent of the "pencils down" experience when you took standardized tests in high school. Your grade or grades for this assignment may be linked to a deadline in a much more specific way than other writing forms.

CHARTS/INFOGRAPHICS

As writers, students, and professionals, we create charts—or any type of info-graphic, such as tables, graphs, and diagrams—to present information simply and visually. Anyone can create a chart, especially with software such as Microsoft Excel or shareware such as iCharts.

Analyzing Charts/Infographics: What to Look For

Purpose   Writers create charts to give a snapshot of complex information—and to draw attention to relationships among the items presented. If you are creating a chart, you might want to keep it simple. An effective way of achieving your pur-pose through an infographic is to create a chart with x- and y-axes.

When might you create a chart? Let's say you're thinking about majoring in engi-neering, but you're not sure which branch would be most lucrative. Because you are an excellent but rather obsessive student, you decide that the best way to represent this information is to create a bar chart (also known as a bar graph). In the PayScale example on page 358, the x-axis represents the range of salaries (in dollars); the y-axis represents the range of types of engineering. In this format, the data—which is clearly labeled—is easy to understand. Clearly, petroleum engineering majors have the high-est earning potential, at least as of 2012, when PayScale created the graph. Note that in digital form, the graph links to PayScale's full methodology for creating it.

Another reason to create a chart is to use it as a persuasive tool. A chart showing that incomes rise as education levels rise can be used to persuade lawmakers to invest more money in education, for example.

Audience   Graph creators know that their readers want information in a concise, easy-to-read format. They know readers might consult their chart for data that will help them make a decision, as in the salaries graph. To take another example, someone creating a chart that compares test scores of students admitted to graduate schools knows that readers are probably students choosing graduate schools to apply to.

▲ CHART
The x and y axes.

CHART/INFOGRAPHIC ▶

Harvard University Food Pyramid. © 2008 Harvard University. For more information about The Healthy Eating Pyramid, please see The Nutrition Source, Department of Nutrition, Harvard School of Public Health, http://www.thenutritionsource.org, and Eat, Drink, and Be Healthy, by Walter C. Willett, M.D., and Patrick J. Skerrett (2005), Free Press/Simon & Schuster Inc.

BAR GRAPH ▶
PayScale, Inc.
"Majors That Pay You Back." The left column (or *y* axis) lists specific majors; the bottom row (or *x* axis) shows salaries, making this chart clear and effective. Petroleum engineering, anyone? *PayScale.com.*

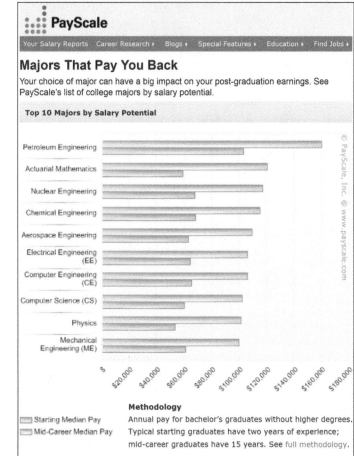

What types of information are best presented visually? Do you prefer certain types of infographics (pie charts, graphs, etc.) that you prefer over others? Why? #Understand #Evaluate

Rhetorical appeals   Chart authors need to establish ethos by conducting research and presenting correct information in their infographics, in order to gain readers' confidence in the content. They can also appeal to audiences through logos, by using logical organization and smart, digestible design. In the example on page 359, job seeker Christopher Perkins appeals to readers' logic and pathos (in this case, through humor) by reimagining how to connect with his potential readers/employers with a visual resume.

Modes & media   Chart authors use visuals and text to share data. Often the visual content dominates and text is used mainly for labels. In terms of media, charts are communicated in print and digitally. Digital charts have the benefit of including hyperlinks to the chart's sources of information (as in the PayScale chart on engineering salaries above).

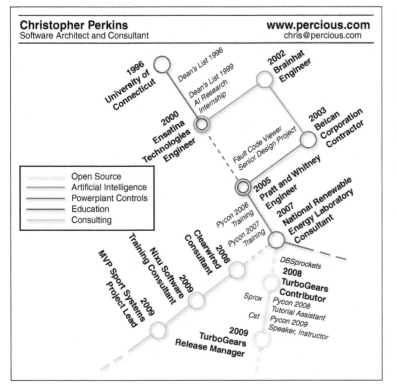

Christopher Perkins
Software Architect and Consultant

www.percious.com
chris@percious.com

◄ RESUME
Christopher Perkins
Resume designed as a subway map. Perkins takes a chance by presenting his employment history this way, but chances are good that his potential employers (software companies) may value his creative visual thinking and humor.
Courtesy of Christopher Perkins.

THE GENRE'S CONVENTIONS

Elements of the genre   Chart makers compose works that are:

Based on facts/data. The information that writers present in charts is based on research that the writer draws on (such as existing statistics from a government Web site), or collects personally (through primary research such as interviews).

Precise; clearly labeled and titled. Chart makers provide specific values for each item they address and show readers exactly how items relate to each other. Chart makers choose titles that define the scope of the chart's content, convey purpose, or summarize their findings. For example, the chart on page 362 is titled "Why Does a Salad Cost More Than a Big Mac?" Within the chart, labels further clarify. For example, in a chart with *x*- and *y*-axes, both axes are labeled so readers/viewers know if numerical amounts are billions or thousands.

Have you ever seen a resume or other business document presented in a way that surprised you? What was it? Was it as informative as the more conventional version would have been? #Evaluate

Illustrated with symbols that convey information. Visual devices such as bars, lines, and sections or slices (of a pie chart) represent specific values and convey data clearly. Writers need to decide which type of chart works best for the information they're presenting. For example, line charts are best used when time is involved, because they can show trends over the course of a particular period.

Supplemented with a key or footnotes when needed. Chart makers sometimes provide a key (or legend) to let readers know what certain features of the visual mean. A key for a map defines each symbol; for example, tents might represent campgrounds. Footnotes connect readers to the sources of the chart's information.

Style　Chart makers make careful choices about style, including:

When it comes to charts, what is the happy medium between providing too many details and not enough? #Understand

What details to present. Most chart makers don't include much detail; they usually provide a clear visual accompanied by brief text. The goal of chart writers is to make it easy for readers to absorb data quickly. Too much detail, especially for a general audience, might make it difficult for readers to see what's most important. However, if your audience is a group of specialists in a particular field who would like detail, then more in-depth data would be appropriate.

What techniques, tone, and voice to use. The best charts use simple, direct language, and the less the better. Chart makers use text judiciously, to provide a title, convey facts, label axes, and concisely explain symbols and colors in accompanying keys or legends. Their tone is neutral and objective.

Design　When chart makers lay out their work, they keep the following in mind:

Simple is best. The whole point is to make information accessible and digestible.

Color is key. Chart makers use color and shading to separate and highlight different pieces of information.

The parts need to be arranged logically/spatially. Chart makers lay out information and visuals in a way that shows readers what is most important to glean. In charts where there are multiple elements, or even multiple visuals that form one infographic, designers add white space between the elements to show separation, or place the elements near each other to show connections.

Sources　Charts are based on composers' knowledge or research. Readers assume that the chart maker is presenting reliable data based on specific sources. Many charts include a source or list of sources, which adds to their credibility and authority.

Guided Reading: Chart/Infographic ⊽

Physicians Committee for Responsible Medicine

Why Does a Salad Cost More Than a Big Mac?

The Physicians Committee for Responsible Medicine (PCRM) is a nonprofit organization focused on promoting nutrition and good health. The editors at PCRM created the chart on page 362 to compare the cost of a salad with that of a Big Mac, and to determine why a salad is more expensive. PCRM's choice of a pyramid allows them to make an easy-to-digest comparison of data; it also brings to mind the food pyramid chart created by the U.S. Department of Agriculture, whose purpose is to direct people to eat healthier diets. (See the new and old pyramids online at *The Washington Post*.) *(Illustration on page 122: Courtesy of Physicians Committee for Responsible Medicine.)*

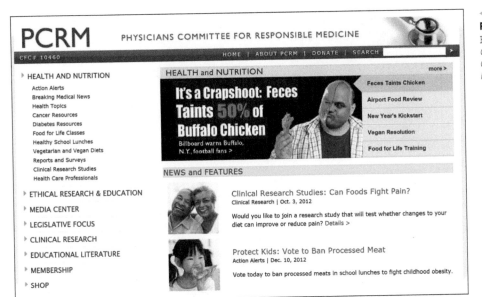

◀ WEB SITE
PCRM
Homepage.
Courtesy of Physicians Committee for Responsible Medicine.

What is **PCRM**,
the composer
of the chart,
doing?

THE RHETORICAL
SITUATION

Purpose
Audience
Rhetorical appeals
Modes & media

see page 363

How do I
know this is a
chart?

THE GENRE'S
CONVENTIONS

Elements of the genre
Style
Design
Sources

see page 363

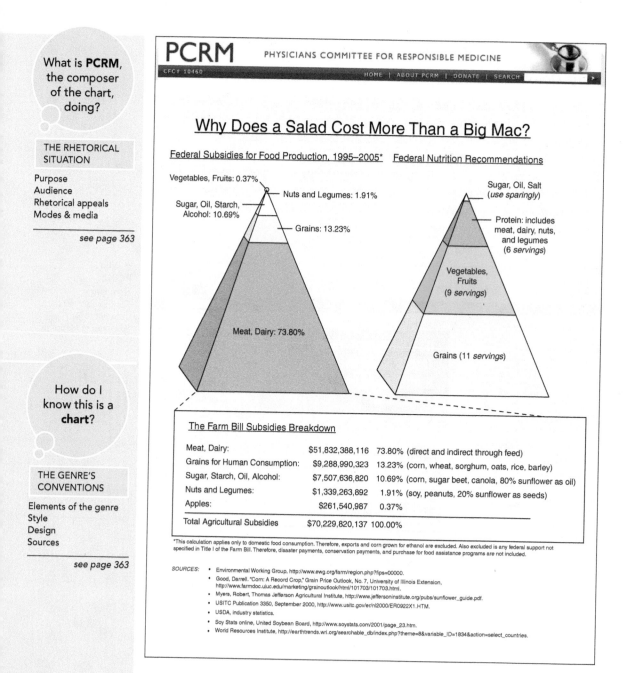

PCRM
CFC# 10460

PHYSICIANS COMMITTEE FOR RESPONSIBLE MEDICINE

HOME | ABOUT PCRM | DONATE | SEARCH

Why Does a Salad Cost More Than a Big Mac?

Federal Subsidies for Food Production, 1995–2005*   Federal Nutrition Recommendations

Vegetables, Fruits: 0.37%

Nuts and Legumes: 1.91%

Sugar, Oil, Starch,
Alcohol: 10.69%

Grains: 13.23%

Meat, Dairy: 73.80%

Sugar, Oil, Salt
(*use sparingly*)

Protein: includes
meat, dairy, nuts,
and legumes
(6 *servings*)

Vegetables,
Fruits
(9 *servings*)

Grains (11 *servings*)

The Farm Bill Subsidies Breakdown

Meat, Dairy:	$51,832,388,116	73.80% (direct and indirect through feed)
Grains for Human Consumption:	$9,288,990,323	13.23% (corn, wheat, sorghum, oats, rice, barley)
Sugar, Starch, Oil, Alcohol:	$7,507,636,820	10.69% (corn, sugar beet, canola, 80% sunflower as oil)
Nuts and Legumes:	$1,339,263,892	1.91% (soy, peanuts, 20% sunflower as seeds)
Apples:	$261,540,987	0.37%
Total Agricultural Subsidies	$70,229,820,137	100.00%

*This calculation applies only to domestic food consumption. Therefore, exports and corn grown for ethanol are excluded. Also excluded is any federal support not specified in Title I of the Farm Bill. Therefore, disaster payments, conservation payments, and purchase for food assistance programs are not included.

SOURCES:
• Environmental Working Group, http://www.ewg.org/farm/region.php?fips=00000.
• Good, Darrell. "Corn: A Record Crop," Grain Price Outlook, No. 7, University of Illinois Extension, http://www.farmdoc.uiuc.edu/marketing/grainoutlook/html/101703/101703.html.
• Myers, Robert, Thomas Jefferson Agricultural Institute, http://www.jeffersoninstitute.org/pubs/sunflower_guide.pdf.
• USITC Publication 3350, September 2000, http://www.usitc.gov/er/nl2000/ER0922X1.HTM.
• USDA, industry statistics.
• Soy Stats online, United Soybean Board, http://www.soystats.com/2001/page_23.htm.
• World Resources Institute, http://earthtrends.wri.org/searchable_db/index.php?theme=8&variable_ID=1834&action=select_countries.

Purpose

PCRM's purpose is to present complex information in a simple, digestible format. They also seek to persuade readers of a problem in terms of foods the U.S. government subsidizes (left pyramid) versus the foods Americans should be eating (right pyramid).

Audience

Readers of this infographic want facts, and they want them efficiently presented. They may be general readers, healthcare professionals, lawmakers, voters, or anyone with a specific interest in food subsidies, nutrition, and government.

Rhetorical appeals

The authors establish their **ethos** by identifying themselves as physicians, and therefore as health and nutrition experts. They further support that ethos with the precision of the information, their choice of sources, and the careful citing of sources.

The authors use logic (**logos**) by presenting the data in the pyramid charts, and also in the table below.

Modes & media

Mode = written and visual The editors at PCRM use a combination of visuals and text to convey information and make an argument about federal subsidies and nutritional costs levied on consumers. At the top of the chart, they rely on the visual, juxtaposing two food pyramids (one of federal subsidies and one of nutrition recommendations). Below the food subsidies pyramid is a table that breaks down exact dollar amounts. Combining the table, graphic, and sources (at the bottom) provides rich information, boosting the persuasive power of the piece.

Medium = digital This information is geared toward a general online audience (anyone searching online for nutritional information, or even the cost of a Big Mac, might find this chart). If PCRM created the chart to be published in their own newsletter, the audience would be limited to physicians or other healthcare professionals. Though this infographic isn't interactive, many online charts like this are, allowing audiences to plug in certain information; can you imagine how the PCRM chart might be made interactive?

Elements of the genre

Based on data. The PCRM authors draw on seven sources, including the USDA.

Precise. Percentages and numbers of items are precise (down to the decimal point); e.g., vegetables and fruits are listed as .37%, rather than rounded up to .4%.

Clearly titled. The words in the title convey the main point of the chart.

Clearly labeled. The labels clarify what each item is and its specific value (e.g., labels convey that grains make up 13.23% of subsidies).

Uses symbols. The two pyramids represent items and values related to federal subsidies versus those related to federal nutrition recommendations.

Style

Minimal detail is used—but enough to make the information clear and authoritative. The two pyramids convey the essence of the information; the text provides concise information about subsidies.

PCRM's tone is **objective.** All information is presented as fact.

Design

Color indicates the separation of categories (e.g., vegetables and fruits are green in the right-hand pyramid). Leader lines make clear how text and visuals relate. Information below the visuals is provided in list form and as a bulleted list for easy reading.

Sources

PCRM's research draws on seven sources, which are listed at the bottom of the chart.

Questions: Analyzing PCRM's chart/infographic

1. Purpose. How do the PCRM editors inform their readers about why a salad costs more than a Big Mac? To what extent are they presenting an argument?

2. Audience. Describe the audience that PCRM targets with this infographic. Is the target audience consumers? People interested in economics? Dieters? Vegetarians? Provide support for your answer.

3. Rhetorical appeals. One way the PCRM editors establish ethos is by listing the sources they used. How else is ethos established?

4. Modes & media. What are the advantages of making the chart available digitally? How might the PCRM editors revise the chart to take better advantage of a digital medium?

5. Elements of the genre. How does the title of the chart help shape the way you understand the information presented? Describe the tone of the title. To what extent does it reflect the conventions of the genre?

6. Elements of the genre. The chart has two visuals. What is the impact of the side-by-side presentation of these visuals?

7. Style. Describe the level of detail in this chart. Why do you think the PCRM editors chose to add another layer of detail with the table underneath the first graphic?

8. Design. How does the use of color relate to the information presented in the chart?

9. Design. Why is a pyramid an appropriate chart for presenting this information? What would be different if the PCRM editors had used a bar chart or a pie chart?

10. Sources. Why do you think the PCRM editors omitted any data from McDonald's in the chart?

Drafting a Chart/Infographic

CHECKLIST: Drafting a Chart/Infographic
Thinking of creating a chart or other infographic? Ask yourself the following questions.

WHAT'S MY RHETORICAL SITUATION?

☐ **Purpose.** What financial experience that I've encountered might be interesting to represent in a chart? Why? Do I want to look at it from a personal angle or a more global perspective? What are all the considerations I need to take into account to represent the data that correspond to that experience?

☐ **Audience.** Who are my readers? Why should/will my chart matter to them? What do I want them to get out of it? And how will I reach them? Does my audience consist of general readers or specialists in the field? What level of detail will my chart need?

☐ **Rhetorical appeals.** How will I establish my authority and reliability as a writer? How will I convey my information so my readers believe my data? To what extent will I rely on logic to support my interpretations? How will I organize the information to convey the logic?

☐ **Modes & media.** Do I want readers to experience my chart primarily as a visual? How much text will accompany my chart? Do I want readers to access my chart digitally or in print? Why?

WHAT GENRE CONVENTIONS MATTER?

☐ **Elements of the genre.** What types of data will I use to create my chart? Will I use colors or symbols in the chart? How will I represent those in my legend? Have I used sources based on research? Will I use footnotes to attribute those sources? Do I want my title to indicate my ultimate findings or present a question?

☐ **Style.** How will I keep my tone objective? What level of detail will I include in my chart?

☐ **Design.** How do I want to organize my chart spatially? Are there multiple visuals? Does each visual have accompanying text? Are colors appropriate for my chart? If so, what colors will help me convey my information? Is a bar chart or a line graph better for conveying my information?

☐ **Sources.** Is my chart based on my own knowledge or do I need to do research to gather data and statistics? How many sources do I need to draw on in order to present the information effectively?

PRACTICE
Want to experiment? Draft your own chart or other infographic.

Think about how you spent time over the last week: doing homework, attending class, working, socializing, sleeping, eating, exercising, and so on. Then choose a visual way to represent this information, taking into account your data, what you want to convey and why, how you can best establish your ethos—and also your choices of text, images, color, and design.

MAPS

When was the last time you referred to a map? How helpful was it? How might you have improved the map? #Remember #Evaluate

Maps might be the oldest form of nonverbal communication. Humans mapped the stars on cave walls ten thousand years ago; by 2200 BCE, Babylonians had created maps on clay tablets, making them somewhat portable. Fast-forward to the Renaissance, when, thanks to the printing press, maps were reproduced for a larger audience. Maps began to reflect a global view during the age of exploration in the fifteenth and sixteenth centuries, when Columbus and others made their voyages. The invention of the compass and telescope made maps more accurate, and now, thanks to geographical information technology and satellites, maps are more exact than ever before.

In its simplest form, a map is a spatial representation of a place. Maps are very precise, noting, for example, not simply that a route is a highway, but that it is an interstate. Further, real-time maps on GPS (global positioning systems) and smartphones also indicate the amount of traffic on a given road.

Maps are available in a variety of media. The American Automobile Association (AAA) produces foldout print maps for road trips, and travel books and sites such as Lonely Planet provide maps for travel destinations. We can get them by GPS, on our smartphones, and through popular sites such as Google Maps, Bing Maps, and Mapquest, while Google Earth can give you an aerial map of your location—taken from live satellite images—at any moment.

Analyzing Maps: What to Look For

THE RHETORICAL SITUATION

Purpose   The purpose of the mapmaker is to visually represent an area—so readers can figure out the best route and driving distances between different points, understand the topography of a region, and see geographical landmarks and bodies of water. Maps can also provide a historical record, such as Ptolemy's world map created in the second century, or a cultural or political record, such as the contemporary election map. (See also the map collection at the Library of Congress.)

What features do you think mapmakers think are most important when designing a map for a general audience? #Understand

Audience   Mapmakers know that people mainly use maps to find the best route from one location to another, especially hikers who use topographical maps to discover trails. The creators of Google Earth maps imagined that educators might want to use the maps and "layers," which include additional information about the places mapped, such as weather patterns and historical events, in their teaching. Makers of online interactive maps consider the needs of travelers; for example, just

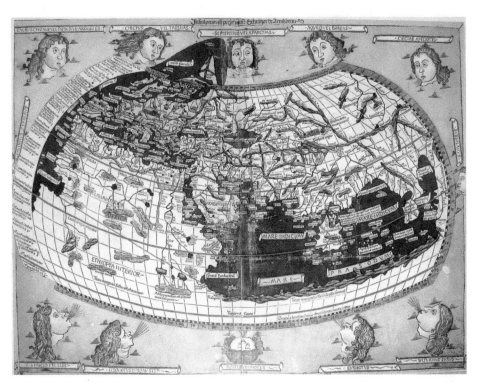

◄ MAP
Hey, where's the U.S. of A.?
A sixteenth-century world map, based on the work of mathematician and astronomer Claudius Ptolemaeus, a.k.a. Ptolemy (ca. 100–170 AD).

☞ **Attention, mappers!**

Keep in mind that maps do not have to represent real places. You can create a map to address concepts, ideas, and opinions—and to metaphorically illustrate dreams, memories, imaginary places, and personal geographies. Really, you can map just about anything.

Take a look at Kim Rae Nugent's "RAEvN LAND" map. Unlike a logically organized, fact-based map, Nugent's map is imaginative. Her ethos comes from her expertise in her own life; she also appeals to viewers through pathos (e.g., creativity and humor).

---

recently, Amy was trying to find a hotel for a vacation in Florida and used an online map to determine how close the hotel was to the beach.

Rhetorical appeals   Mapmakers rely mainly on ethos (authority) and logos (logic) to reach their readers. When you use a map, you trust that it accurately re-creates the topography of an area. However, if something happens to shake your trust—say you realize that your map mistakenly shows two parallel streets as intersecting, or you realize that your GPS doesn't recognize streets that you're passing—you would probably lose faith in the authority of your map (or your GPS's source) and find an alternative. Good mapmakers follow certain conventions to appeal to users' logos. For example, for a print map, they might use the same color and symbol to represent all hospitals or parks, and use variations in font size to indicate the size of a city; in an e-map, they might use an icon to indicate that more information can be viewed by hovering your cursor over the icon.

Modes & media   Mapmakers generally use visuals and text to communicate, although GPS apps and devices also add audio. The visual aspects of the map, including colors and symbols, represent streets, rivers, and other geographical features. Often, color and text will work together; for example, a mapmaker might use bands of color with a text label to indicate the elevations of individual mountains in a mountain range. Makers of digital maps often add animation, as in the case of

Analyzing Maps: What to Look For

MAP ▶
Kim Rae Nugent
"RAEvN LAND" map
represents the artist's
personal landscape.
Kim Rae Nugent.

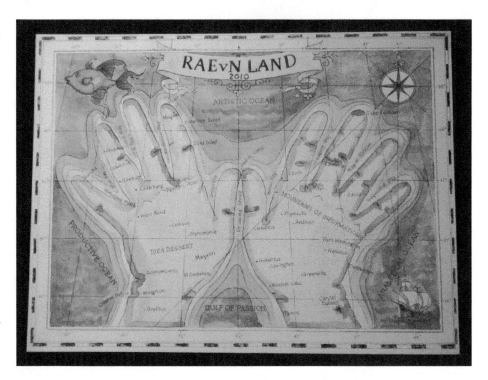

Do you have a
preference for
using print maps or
digital maps? Are
there advantages
to using one over
the other? What are
they? #Understand
#Evaluate

maps on smartphones that feature a color icon that shows you exactly where you are on the map, and moves on the map as you move. Mapmakers use text to label specific items, such as the names of cities and other landmarks, and to identify elements in the map's legend or key. Maps can be printed or digital. Many digital maps are interactive, such as the maps on Google Earth, in which users can add different "layers" to maps of the world to highlight specific aspects, such as weather, trees, or street views.

THE GENRE'S CONVENTIONS

Elements of the genre

Based on solid data. The information presented in maps is based on careful survey-ing of land, or, as in Google Maps, on satellite photos.

Precise. Maps indicate distances and sizes accurately.

Clearly titled. Map titles are usually straightforward and specific. Aside from func-tion-specific titles such as "BurgerMap," maps can also be titled according to their location.

Clearly labeled. Labels help readers understand what is being presented. Digital maps have labels for streets, bridges, and places of interest, such as museums and parks. When the map is interactive and digital, users can also choose to have it show hotels, subway stations, and other features of interest.

Correctly oriented. Mapmakers usually orient objects so that north is up or at the top of the page or screen, south is down or at the bottom of the page or screen, east is right, and west is left.

Clarified through symbols and a legend (or key). Mapmakers use many visual cues to help readers grasp information quickly. They use conventional symbols, such as an image of an evergreen tree to indicate a park, a large capital *H* to indicate a hospital, and an image of a tent to indicate a campground. Mapmakers usually include a legend that tells the reader exactly what each symbol and color stands for.

Style

Detail. Mapmakers generally use minimal written detail, preferring to use clear visuals with very little text to convey information. Lots of text will slow down map users, while visual cues, such as color and symbols, can be understood quickly.

Techniques. Mapmakers use simple, direct language and also title their works as straightforwardly as possible so the map's purpose is obvious to readers.

Tone and voice. Mapmakers use a neutral, objective tone to convey information without analysis, interpretation, or judgment.

Design

Varying type and feature sizes. The relative sizes of cities and other areas are indicated on a map by the type size: The name of larger cities and towns are shown in larger type sizes. Drivers using maps may be interested in the relative sizes of streets, for example, when choosing an efficient route.

Scale. Map users (especially when driving) need to see the distance between one place and another. Mapmakers include scales so that users can measure these distances; scales are usually provided in inches/feet/yards and miles/kilometers.

Direction. While most maps are oriented with north at the top or twelve o'clock position, it is still necessary to have a marker to show exactly where north is.

Colors. Mapmakers use a universal set of colors, such as brown for a landmass, green for vegetation (forests, parks, etc.), and blue for water.

Highway markers. Mapmakers use particular shapes, lines, and colors to indicate highways. For example, in the United States, the National Highway System mandates that interstate highways (e.g., I-44) be indicated with a blue shield with a red strip at the top, with a large number in white at the center of the shield. State highway shields have their own unique set of conventions for each state.

Zoomability and interactivity. Digital maps allow users to zoom in or zoom out to see more or less detail. "BurgerMap" is a digital map that allows users to zoom and interact with the content in different ways.

Sources   Traditional mapmakers generally rely on land surveys for information about the territory being mapped. Creators of topographical maps often rely on surveys from the U.S. Geological Survey (USGS). Google Maps are based on satellite images. Some mapmakers credit their sources; some do not. Some indicate trademarks or copyright information. For example, maps at Nationalatlas.gov credit both the USGS and the National Atlas of the United States.

Guided Reading: Map ▼

Chris Peterson

BurgerMap: Alaska Burgers: Kriner's Diner

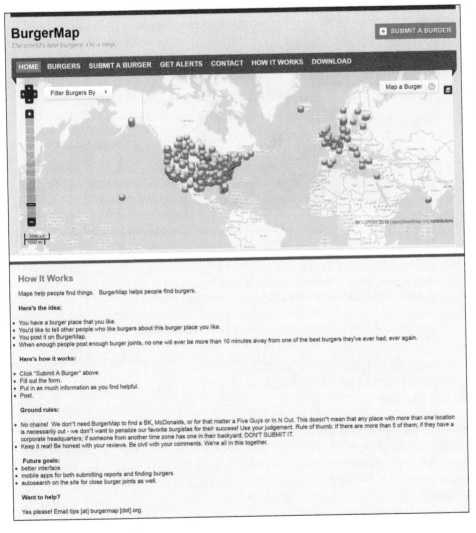

BurgerMap
The world's best burgers. On a map.

⊕ SUBMIT A BURGER

HOME   BURGERS   SUBMIT A BURGER   GET ALERTS   CONTACT   HOW IT WORKS   DOWNLOAD

Filter Burgers By ▸

Map a Burger ⊚

©CCBYSA 2010 OpenStreetMap.org contributors

2000 km
1000 mi

How It Works

Maps help people find things.   BurgerMap helps people find burgers.

Here's the idea:

- You have a burger place that you like.
- You'd like to tell other people who like burgers about this burger place you like.
- You post it on BurgerMap.
- When enough people post enough burger joints, no one will ever be more than 10 minutes away from one of the best burgers they've ever had, ever again.

Here's how it works:

- Click "Submit A Burger" above.
- Fill out the form.
- Put in as much information as you find helpful.
- Post.

Ground rules:

- No chains! We don''t need BurgerMap to find a BK, McDonalds, or for that matter a Five Guys or In N Out. This doesn''t mean that any place with more than one location is necessarily out - we don''t want to penalize our favorite burgistas for their success! Use your judgement. Rule of thumb: If there are more than 5 of them; if they have a corporate headquarters; if someone from another time zone has one in their backyard; DON'T SUBMIT IT.
- Keep it real! Be honest with your reviews. Be civil with your comments. We're all in this together.

Future goals:
- better interface
- mobile apps for both submitting reports and finding burgers
- autosearch on the site for close burger joints as well.

Want to help?

Yes please! Email tips [at] burgermap [dot] org.

Attention, mappers!

Learn more about OpenStreetMap— how it works and who contributes to and edits the map—from the OpenStreetMap site.

HOME | SUBMIT A BURGER | GET ALERTS | CONTACT | PRODUCED BY PETEY   POWERED BY THE Ushahidi PLATFORM

Chris Peterson

Home   Projects   Papers   Media   Blog   Contact

My name is Chris Peterson. I make and study things. A lot of them have to do with the Internet.

I'm presently on leave from my administrative position in web communications at MIT as a full time graduate student in the Comparative Media Studies program, where I work with the Center for Civic Media on a variety of projects.

I'm also on the board of the National Coalition Against Censorship, a Fellow at the National Center for Technology and Dispute Resolution, and a former research assistant at the Berkman Center for Internet and Society at Harvard Law School. In these capacities I spend a lot of time reading and writing and thinking about the Internet and how it impacts the way we all communicate and experience our lives. That's much of what you'll find here.

I also spend a lot of time reading about politics and policies, eating hamburgers, and trying to escape Boston for the New Hampshire woods whence I came. I'm allergic to cats and cat macros. I like kind people, *Archer*, and bouldering. Against all odds, frequent disgruntlement, and my better judgment, I am still a cautious optimist about the Internet and the world. I think.

The following example is a typical interactive map. The BurgerMap site states its purpose simply: "The world's best burgers. On a map." The site was created and is hosted by Chris Peterson, a graduate student. He writes: "Maps help people find things. BurgerMap helps people find burgers." To render the map below, we looked at the full-screen version of the BurgerMap, and clicked to focus on Alaska. Kriner's Diner in Anchorage was among other burger spots identified and reviewed by BurgerMap users.

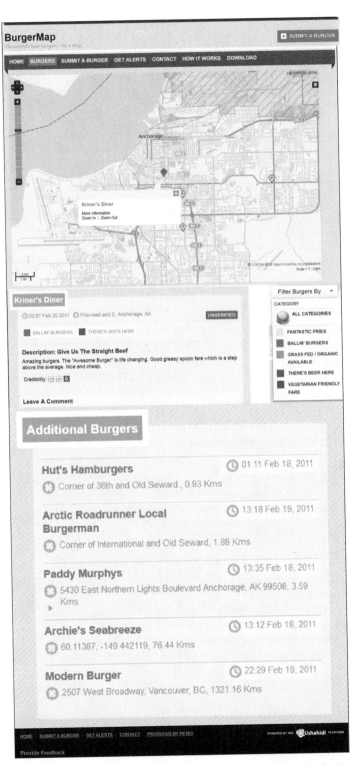

What are
the composers
of **BurgerMap**
doing?

THE RHETORICAL
SITUATION

Purpose
Audience
Rhetorical appeal
Modes & media

Purpose

Chris Peterson,
creator of
BurgerMap, seeks
to gather and show
the "world's best
burgers" through an
interactive map that
users contribute to.
Viewers can move
around the map,
search, and filter
their search areas
in order to find what
they're looking for.

Audience

The primary
audience is people
who enjoy burgers
and travel.

Rhetorical appeals

Peterson establishes
ethos by presenting
rules for contributors
to follow, and
by crediting
OpenStreetMap
as his source map.
Peterson and his
contributors (the
world-traveling
burger lovers who
submit reviews)
also appeals to
readers' sense of
logos by using

Chris Peterson, *BurgerMap: Alaska Burgers: Kriner's Diner*

clear categories of information; they appeal to pathos through humor, as in when Peterson writes: "Keep it real! Be honest with your reviews. Be civil with your comments. We're all in this together."

Modes & Media

Mode = visual and written

This map conveys information about burger joints around the world through visual and textual elements. Without visuals, the map would simply be a list of city, place, and road names; the visuals give those names geographical and spatial relevance. Without text, we wouldn't be able to find streets or other locations. Because this map is interactive, we can navigate by clicking to zoom in to specific locations and information, and even contribute our own burger reviews and photos.

Medium = digital

Because this map is digital, anyone with an Internet connection can access it. Users can highlight different information, depending on their needs.

How do I know this is a map?

Elements of the genre
Style
Design Sources

Elements of the genre

Based on data

that comes from satellite images, and from users adding information.

Precise.

The map is accurate in its representations; for example, when you zoom in, you can see that Kriner's Diner is on the corner of West Fireweed Lane and C Street in Anchorage, Alaska.

Clearly titled.

The title says exactly what the map is/shows; conveniently it is also the title of the site (BurgerMap.org).

Clearly labeled

streets and landscape features.

Orientation

follows the convention of north at the top.

Uses symbols.

For example, the highway name is presented in an oval.

Use of a legend/key.

Because the mapmakers use conventional symbols and colors, they don't provide a key. However, one interactive feature allows readers to show and highlight different locations on BurgerMap.

Style

The writing is brief, simple, and direct. E.g., Kriner's Diner (and other burger vendors) are labeled, but for more information, users need to click on the name of the restaurant.

Design

Colors indicate specific things. For example, the system of icons is color coded, and indicates, for example, whether a burger joint has "fantastic fries" or beer or "vegetarian friendly fare."

Sources

In the lower right of the map is the notice of the Creative Commons license ("CCBYSA") and also a link to OpenStreetMap, the free worldwide map used as a basis for the BurgerMap.

Questions: Analyzing WorldView's map

1. Purpose. What was mapmaker Chris Peterson's main goal in creating "BurgerMap"? What different types of information does the map present? What does it leave out? Does all the information contribute to the same purpose? How might the interactive feature of this map affect the mapmaker's purposes)? Explain.

2. Audience. If you didn't know where to find delicious hamburgers around the world, what could you learn from the map? How does the map convey this information to you?

3. Rhetorical appeals. How does the consistent use of map conventions appeal to your senses of ethos and logos?

4. Modes & media. Go to BurgerMap.org and click to focus on specific locations. What do you learn from this view that you weren't able to learn from the site homepage?

5. Elements of the genre. Have you ever seen a symbol on a map that you couldn't make sense of? Or is there a symbol you'd like to see? (For example, parents of small children might like to see symbols indicating facilities that are "family friendly" and have diapering stations.)

6. Style. When you use maps, how do you use the text content? Can you think of an example of a map that was difficult to use because of how it was labeled?

7. Design. "BurgerMap" is a digital map, so we've focused on conventions for digital maps. However, can you think of conventions associated with print maps that differ?

8. Design. Maps are sometimes seen as artwork. Aside from the attractive color combinations, why might a person consider a map art?

9. Sources. We expect maps to be accurate. What are some repercussions of a mapmaker relying on inaccurate data sources?

Drafting/Sketching Out a Map

CHECKLIST: Drafting/Sketching Out a Map
Thinking of drafting a map? Ask yourself the following questions.

WHAT'S MY RHETORICAL SITUATION?

☐ **Purpose.** What is my goal in creating a map? Maps usually inform people about a particular aspect of a place: the roads, the terrain, the restaurants and tourist attractions, the immigration patterns, and so on. Some maps, such as "RAEvN LAND" by Kim Rae Nugent, convey a personal, imaginary world. What do I want my map to do? Inform people? Make a statement? Express an opinion? Illustrate a fantasy world? Something else? How do I think people will use the information I give them?

☐ **Audience.** Who will use my map? What will they need to know? What will they want to know? What is interesting about the area I am mapping, but probably a distraction from the point of view of my audience?

☐ **Rhetorical appeals.** How will I establish my authority as a mapmaker? How will I convince my readers that my map is reliable? I need to use a consistent scale to appeal to readers' sense of logos.

☐ **Modes & media.** Will readers use my map in print form or digitally? If digitally, will they expect an audio component?

WHAT GENRE CONVENTIONS MATTER?

☐ **Elements of the genre.** How can I use labels, symbols, color, and a title to quickly and efficiently convey information to my readers?

☐ **Style.** How will I keep my tone neutral and objective? What level of detail will I include in my map?

☐ **Design.** What colors do I want to use for my map? What symbols do I want to use? Will readers instantly associate my symbols with whatever they represent?

☐ **Sources.** Do I need to do any research to find out about relative populations (to determine font size of places), distances, or anything else?

PRACTICE   Want to experiment? Draft your own map.

A group of students visiting from abroad is about to visit your campus for a week. The students have asked for a campus map so that they can figure out how to get around. Your task is to create a map that illustrates academic areas, student service areas, cool hangouts, places to avoid after dark, places to study, and so on. Draft a map that will assist the students. If you'd like to take a different approach for a map, check out the site Fun Maps USA.

Mapping and Data Visualization GT

The increased accessibility of electronic tools means that you now have a number of creative options for completing assignments. If an assignment asks you to analyze, argue, critique, or research, two innovative ways to present your work are data visualization and mapping. Creating a visualization or map allows you to use visual rhetoric, design principles, and multimodal communication to effectively communicate your ideas.

Mapping

Mapping is a way of visualizing geospatial data. Different tools and platforms exist that allow a user either to create a map or to add data to a preexisting map.

Creating a map.   Google Maps simplifies the process of creating a customized map by dropping pins and adding data to existing map and satellite images. Simply go to "My maps" from the Google Maps homepage and follow the tutorial to create your map. You can also use Google Earth to create a more sophisticated map with customizable layers (including historical map data), 3-D features like buildings and historical landmarks, and fly-through views. If you want to add 3-D buildings to your project, you can use Trimble SketchUp to create and add them to your map.

Watch the TED talk by Lalitesh Katragadda, "Making Maps to Fight Disaster," about the ways local communities help themselves by connecting data to maps. Why do "maps matter"? How might mapping support sustainability and sustainable communities? #Understand #Apply

◀ SCREENSHOT
Custom Google Maps
Google Maps lets you create a custom map. You can use the place descriptions to give information or to transform your map into a persuasive argument. *Courtesy of Google Maps.*

Customizing a map. Other mapping tools allow you to add various kinds of data to existing maps. Twittervision, for example, allows you to map tweets in real time, and Esri's Mapping for Everyone allows you to create customized maps and then share them online. If you plan to create a map, perform an Internet search to find free and easy-to-use mapping tools as well as video tutorials that will help you translate and transform your data.

Data Visualization Tools

From graphs to pie charts and Venn diagrams, visualizations are a common way to present scientific and mathematical data. However, other types of projects can also benefit from data visualization, including more traditional composition and research assignments. Before you begin using these tools, however, be sure to verify that you have your instructor's permission, that you fulfill the requirements of the assignment, and that you conduct rigorous and responsible research.

An overview of some easy data visualization tools and techniques follows.

Numerical data. You can use Excel or Google Charts to develop graphs and charts that can then be imported into image manipulation software and combined with other elements to create a cohesive artifact. A simple way to transform traditional graphs and charts into a usable visualization such as an infographic is to use PowerPoint (or more advanced software such as Adobe InDesign) to create an electronic poster (see "Creating Electronic Posters" in Chapter 15). You might also choose an online service such as Easel.ly or Piktochart, which include tools for making posters and infographics from your data visualizations.

Watch Erez Lieberman Aiden and Jean-Baptiste Michel's TED talk "What We Learned from 5 Million Books," in which they discuss using Ngrams to search for and correlate words and ideas in a database of five million books from across centuries. #Understand

Plan for Publishing

Make sure you have a plan for publishing your visualization from the program you select. Some online programs will not let you download your artifact for free or require you to make your work publicly available. Ask your instructor to identify acceptable file formats or modes of submission before proceeding.

Textual data. For analyzing and visualizing data extracted from texts, online tools like Wordle and Google Ngrams allow users to run keyword searches and search for patterns and frequencies. The resulting data can be presented in a variety of formats. Similarly, Visual Thesaurus allows you to visualize the meanings, synonyms, and "family tree" of a word.

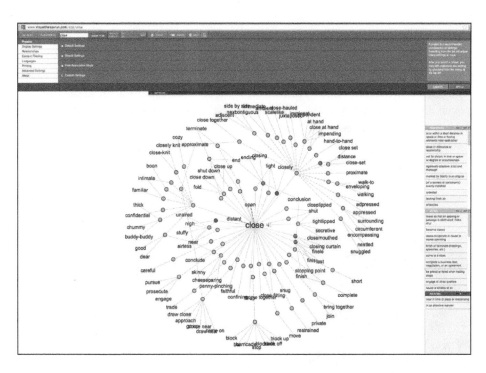

Narrative or research data. For visualizing narratives or research, Prezi can serve as a dynamic data visualization tool. You can add text, images, audio, and videos and then create a "path" that leads the viewer through the content and zooms in on particular items. By adding your data to Prezi, you can create an innovative visualization of your research findings.

The first newspapers were handwritten pages that reported on economic and social issues in Europe in the 1400s. The first successful English-language paper was *The Weekly Newes*, established in the 1620s; a little later, *The London Gazette* became the official newspaper of Great Britain (1666). In 1704, a bookseller and postmaster named John Campbell kicked off newspapers in America with *The Boston News-Letter*, an effort that was followed up more successfully in 1728 by Benjamin Franklin, who published *The Pennsylvania Gazette*, a paper considered to be *The New York Times* of the eighteenth century.

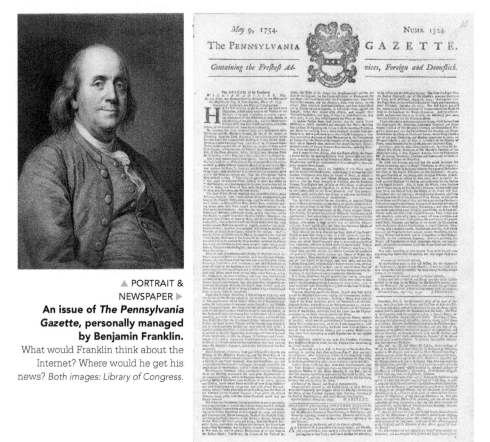

▲ PORTRAIT &
NEWSPAPER ▶
An issue of *The Pennsylvania Gazette*, personally managed by Benjamin Franklin.
What would Franklin think about the Internet? Where would he get his news? *Both images: Library of Congress.*

Today, most cities have at least one local daily newspaper; Chicago, for example, has the *Chicago Sun-Times* and the *Chicago Tribune*. Daily newspapers are divided into sections on world, domestic, and local news; sports; business; science; health;

obituaries; and weather. Many have sections dedicated to editorials/opinions, food, travel, education, entertainment, and fashion, along with advice columns, comics, puzzles, and horoscopes. Smaller communities and organizations also publish newspapers on topics of interest to more specific audiences (such as the Boston area's *Wicked Local*, a consortium of local/community newspapers). Many publications are available online and include links to related stories and topics, as well as social media features that allow readers to post reactions to published stories.

Before the Internet, major newspapers were published once or twice a day. However, now that readers can check news headlines and follow stories online throughout the day, they expect constant updates. News reporting and publishing is now a 24/7 occupation; this makes us all better-informed citizens, but it also means that news agencies focused on breaking news are more vulnerable to misreporting and error. (For example, in 2011, in their zeal to break and update the story of the shooting of Arizona congresswoman Gabrielle Giffords, several news agencies reported that she was shot dead, though she survived the shooting. See the *Columbia Journalism Review*.)

While newspapers publish many kinds of writing—persuasive editorials, letters to the editor, advice columns, ads—at their core are factual news articles written by reporters. Reporters research their writing: They gather information for a story by conducting interviews, serving as eyewitnesses (reporting from the scene, for example), checking public records, and working with library and online sources. News journalists need to be able to back up the accuracy of their writing with facts from several reliable sources.

In news articles, writers present facts. In editorials, they present opinions. That said, the line between fact and opinion can blur, especially on broadcast news programs. Can you think of examples where a news report feels too much like an opinion piece? If so, how do you account for this? #Understand #Analyze

Analyzing News Articles: What to Look For

THE RHETORICAL SITUATION

Purpose   Journalists research and write news articles to inform readers of facts and events. Their purpose is to present verifiable and fair accounts of issues and happenings, and to do so while adhering to ethical standards, such as those outlined by the Society of Professional Journalists.

Among the largest news providers are CNN, ABC, MSNBC, Fox News, the Associated Press, *The New York Times*, and *The Washington Post*. (For more news providers, see "Modes & media" below.) Depending on a news organization's size and scope, it might cover a range of world, national, and perhaps local news, and specific subject areas such as business, culture, science, and entertainment. Like any organization, each news provider has its own policies, agenda, and built-in biases. That said, ideally, the news articles that they publish or air are as fact based and objective as possible.

Keep in mind that news articles can appear in the context of other genres. In an online newspaper, for example, a news article might appear near an advertisement or an editorial or other opinion piece. It's a good practice to clarify for yourself what is informative fact-based reporting and what is editorial writing (see also Chapter 15).

Audience   Journalists who write news articles know readers want to be informed about world events and issues, and to be kept up-to-date, especially online. They know that some readers will scan the first few paragraphs to get the main idea, so they need to include the most important material up front. Some readers who are especially interested—personally or professionally—in a given topic, however, will read for depth. They will read the entire article and also turn to related articles. Journalists keep that audience in mind as well.

Rhetorical appeals   Journalists use ethos and logos to reach their audiences. A news publisher's reputation for "getting the story right" is crucial, as are the reputations of reporters associated with the publisher. If a reporter's credibility is seriously tarnished, his or her career in journalism will quickly end. In 2003, for example, promising *New York Times* reporter Jayson Blair was fired for plagiarizing parts of several news reports he had written. The *Times* called it "a low point in the 152-year history of the newspaper" and apologized profusely to its readers.

There is debate, both within the news industry itself and among readers and commentators, of what constitutes "news." The impact of reality television, which is cheaper to produce than dramas or news programs, is a factor, as is the mainstream appeal of celebrity and reality-star gossip. Whatever your opinion of the entertainment news published by *Gawker*, *TMZ*, and others, it's clear that the writers and editors at these organizations know how to appeal to their readers' pathos (emotions) with sensational headlines and stories about affairs, addictions, and arrests.

Modes & media   News articles can take many forms. Here, we're highlighting written news articles, because text can appear in print or digital formats. With the rise of digital news sites such as *The Huffington Post*, many print newspapers have moved online (see also "Purpose" on p. 381). Most traditional print newspapers have companion Web sites; for example, you can read many of the same stories in both the print and online versions of *The New York Times*, the *Wall Street Journal, The Washington Post*, and the *Los Angeles Times*, although some online content requires a subscription. The advantages of the online news article are that it can be updated instantly, can link to related articles and sources, and can be accompanied by video. Online publications also allow readers to post comments, making these sources much more interactive than print newspapers.

Traditional news outlets, such as those just mentioned, are not the only sources of news reports. News reports also commonly appear in news magazines, such as *Time, Newsweek/The Daily Beast, Slate, Salon*, and *Harper's*, and on blogs. Some news blogs, such as *This Just In*, are associated with a particular news outlet, in this case CNN. Others, such as the *Renewable Energy Law Blog*, report on news relevant to their readers; in the case of the *Renewable Energy Law Blog*, readers are clients and potential clients of the law firm that hosts the blog. In still other news blogs, writers report or comment on news, but they're not affiliated with a news outlet. Rather, these are individual blogs, such as *Not a Sheep, Jezebel*, and *Buzzfeed*, where bloggers present news snippets and then comment on them.

In addition to appearing in print and in digital formats, news stories can also take the form of audio and video reports. National Public Radio covers all the top stories that print and digital news outlets cover, but they of course do it in audio form. Many digital news outlets, such as MSNBC, also make videos of news coverage available online.

THE GENRE'S CONVENTIONS

Elements of the genre
Well researched and fact-checked. As discussed above, the authority (or ethos) of the reporter, publisher, and content is crucial. Writers must be scrupulous in their research and fact-checking. A rule of thumb in journalism is to verify a report with at least three reliable sources. When an error is discovered in an article, journalists

and publishers are usually quick to make a correction and apologize. For example, CNET News, a technology publication affiliated with CBS News, states their corrections policy on their Web site.

Corrections

CNET strives to meet the highest standards for accuracy and completeness in our editorial coverage; it is our policy to always correct errors when they occur and to notify readers of changes to our content. We classify editorial changes as *corrections, clarifications,* or *updates.*
• A correction rights a factual error.
• A clarification adjusts statements that were not factually incorrect but may have been unclear or misleading.
• An update revises content with information not available when the story was originally published.
To report possible errors in content, please email our editorial department. Include the URL of the page where the error occurs. Our editors will review all reports of errors to determine if a correction is warranted.

Please note: This page pertains to text corrections and factual errors on existing editorial product reviews only. For help with pricing errors, CNET Download.com descriptions, broken links, passwords, and registration, please visit CNET Customer Help Center.

Usually aimed at a broad audience. Most newspapers, news magazines, and news sites have a very broad readership with varying degrees of education, so the level of vocabulary in a news article must be appropriate for all. Most are written with a vocabulary considered to be ninth or tenth grade. *The New York Times*, however, is written at a twelfth-grade level of vocabulary and comprehension.

Opens with a concise summary in a lead paragraph. Most journalists begin their news articles with a paragraph that states the most important aspects of their story and grabs the reader's attention. In the rest of the article, reporters elaborate on what was presented in the opening paragraph. Because many readers skim rather than read a full article, the content of the lead paragraph is especially important.

Think of the sources where you get your news. How would you characterize the writing? The vocabulary level? How do a journalist's style and word choice contribute to your reading experience? #Analyze

Presents information in order of importance. Paragraphs that follow the lead and make up the body of the article provide details and supporting evidence from sources. Paragraphs closer to the beginning of the story provide details that are more important in understanding the essence of the story; those closer to the end, however, provide information that is less essential, given that some readers may not read the whole article to the end.

As explained in the "Style" section below, news journalists tend to structure their articles with an overview of the important information at the beginning, so readers can get information quickly.

Includes quotations. Journalists often quote sources directly to add flavor to their articles and to maintain the feel of "just the facts, ma'am." No one can accuse a reporter of misinterpreting what someone said if the reporter includes direct quotations.

Written in short paragraphs. Journalists often write in short paragraphs because they're easier to read than long ones. They're also easier on the eyes, especially considering the formats news articles are generally published in—either in narrow columns in print newspapers or online.

Style

Neutral tone/absence of personal opinion. The goal of writing a news article is to report information. It's appropriate for news journalists to use a serious and fairly formal tone in their writing; of course, "formal" doesn't have to mean dry. It's also appropriate for journalists to refrain from editorializing, unless they are writing an editorial or hosting an opinion column, for example.

Objective, third-person voice. An objective stance conveys the cut-and-dry, fact-based nature of news articles. News journalists also use precise language in order to clearly communicate facts and details, and use the third person (*he/she/they*) rather than the first person (*I/we*).

Just enough detail for the general reader. Journalists use specific details to support their generalizations. In the annotated article by Nicholas Wade (p. 391), you'll notice that the writer is very specific about how cats lap water. However, Wade gives only the level of detail that a general reader can understand. For example, he explains that "the cat darts its tongue, curving the upper side downward so that the tip lightly touches the surface of the water. The tongue is then pulled upward at high speed, drawing a column of water behind it." A general reader can grasp this level of detail easily. A scientist or veterinarian may want more detail, but that level of detail would only be appropriate for a specialized audience of scientists or veterinarians.

Design

Attention-grabbing title/headline. The title of a news article is called a headline. It is usually presented in much larger or bolder type than the story itself, and is brief and descriptive. Headlines are used to attract readers and are sometimes provocative; see, for example, the front page of the *New York Post*, a paper that is notorious for its over-the-top headlines. Compare that to the longer, more serious headline used by the BBC News on page 386.

Usually reporters write in the third person (*he/she/they*) because it is a neutral way to present facts. However, sometimes they use the first person (*I/we*). How might a journalist's use of *I* affect your reading of an article? What strategies might that writer use to persuade you that he or she is being objective? #Analyze #Evaluate

▲ NEWSPAPER
New York Post Front Page
When it comes to unrestrained headlines, the *Post* rarely disappoints. *From the* New York Post © *4/15/1983 NYP Holdings, Inc. All rights reserved.*

Byline. A byline is the presentation of the author's name, usually below the headline and above the text of the article. Sometimes the byline notes that the author is a correspondent or staff writer. Below, BBC News correspondent James Reynolds is credited for his report from Cairo.

NEWS ARTICLE ▶
James Reynolds
Byline at BBC News (bbc.co.uk). Reynolds, who has been with the BBC since 1996, is the group's Tehran Correspondent. Note also the headline for Reynolds's report: descriptive and serious. Compare it to the *Post* headline on page 389.

BBC

NEWS MIDDLE EAST

News   Sport   Weather   Capital   Culture   Autos   TV   Radio   More...   Search

Home   US & Canada   Latin America   UK   Africa   Asia   Europe   Mid-East   Business   Health   Sci/Environment   Tech   Entertainment   Video

14 August 2013 Last updated at 06:51 ET

65   Share

Egypt unrest: BBC witnesses Cairo raid on pro-Morsi camps

Latest | Live page | In Pictures | Q&A   At the scene   'Ready to die' | World re

By James Reynolds
BBC News, Cairo

The BBC's James Reynolds near the Rabaa al-Adawiya mosque encampment, says the air is thick with smoke from burning tyres

At four o'clock in the morning, at one of the entrances to the Rabaa al-Adawiya mosque encampment, a dozen guards stood behind a row of sandbags.

The men carried sticks and wore small gas masks around their necks. Some leaned back against the sandbags. Beyond the barricade, I could just make out the heads of a group of men standing for pre-dawn prayers. No-one appeared to want to leave.

Serif typeface. A serif font has a very small flare at the stroke ends and corners of letters, while a sans serif font lacks these strokes. Print articles are often presented in serif fonts (such as in the print edition of *The New York Times*), while sans serif fonts, such as those used by BBC News (below) are a good choice for the readability of digital content. Compare a serif **A** to a sans serif **A**.

Use of columns or chunking. News sites such as the BBC's (see below) present articles in chunked sections that have their own headings. Digital content may be presented in multiple columns or on different sections of the grid with various ways to navigate the content. Print newspapers are limited to columns of no more than fifty-two characters wide.

Images: photos, graphs, and multimedia components. Many news articles, especially breaking news on a Web site, or a front-page story in a print paper, are con-

◄ NEWS SITE
BBC News
The layout chosen by the editors and designers at the BBC presents content in a clean, streamlined format. The consistent sans serif font for text and headings, the three-column grid, the chunking of text, and the use of images contribute to the readability and modern aesthetic.

textualized with photos, charts, graphs, and, in the case of the online source, video and other multimedia. This is true of the BBC News site (p. 386), where the main story (of August 14, 2013, about Egypt) features prominently and leads readers to plenty of related content and live video. A piece with a video or audio component usually includes an arrow icon or other visual element to indicate this; sometimes the video or audio itself is the news story.

News publishers use visual and multimedia to grab readers' attention, provide context, and enrich the content of print articles. For example, the article on page 389 reports on the civil-union ceremonies that took place after Colorado's civil-union law went into effect. The article features a large photo; a few paragraphs down are links to related stories. The featured photo and photo gallery give readers context for the event.

Headers, footers, and tabs. Designers of online news sites provide tabs and navigational menus and search boxes to keep readers oriented. The designers use repeated design features to reinforce the agency's identity. For example, a print newspaper's title appears on every page and in other elements, and titles, headers, and footers (which include the date and section, for example) help readers find what they need on the page.

Use of color. Online news sites include color images and video. Designers also use color typographically to direct attention toward particular content. Blue is used for hyperlinks (which turn a different color once you select them), red is sometimes used for breaking news headlines, and gray shading is sometimes used to orient readers as to their location within the content. Images and videos are shown in full color. Print newspapers, which are published on a thin paper called newsprint, are printed in black ink (such as *The New York Times*) or in color (such as *USA Today*).

Sources News reports are based on eyewitness accounts, authoritative published documents, interviews, and records. Most journalists indicate their sources within their news articles, using attribution phrases such as "according to" and linking directly to their sources. In his article on how cats drink, *New York Times* reporter Nicholas Wade writes:

> Cats, both big and little, are so much classier, according to new research by Pedro M. Reis and Roman Stocker of the Massachusetts Institute of Technology, joined by Sunghwan Jung of the Virginia Polytechnic Institute and Jeffrey M. Aristoff of Princeton. Writing in the Thursday issue of Science, the four engineers report. . . .

Wade makes it clear that the information he draws on is a researched article from the journal *Science* and from the four researchers he names. Journalists, unlike the authors of peer-reviewed journal articles (p. 397), do not use academic documentation styles such as MLA or APA. Because news journalism is a popular genre and not a scholarly genre, it has a different set of conventions for documenting sources, such as the phrasing that Wade uses on page 391. In news journalism, the thinking is that the reader doesn't need the same level of detail about sources that scholarly audiences need. That said, online news providers and journalists can boost their ethos by linking to their sources.

Nicholas Wade

For Cats, a Big Gulp with a Touch of the Tongue

The New York Times, which has been publishing since 1851, is considered highly accurate and is regarded as one of the most authoritative newspapers available. Its Web site and print circulation make it one of the most widely read newspapers in the world. It has won over one hundred Pulitzer Prizes, the most prestigious reporting award given. Nicholas Wade is a science reporter for *The New York Times*. He has written several science books, including 2009's *The Faith Instinct*, about the scientific basis of religious faith. The following article appeared in the Science section of the *Times*; the online version includes links to sources, infographics, and video that support the text. *(Text and images on pp. 392–93, From* The New York Times, *November 11, 2010 © 2010* The New York Times. *All rights reserved.)*

▲ AUTHOR PHOTO
Nicholas Wade
New York Times reporter. *Nicholas Wade.com, Naum Kazhdan/The New York Times/Redux.*

What is the composer, **Nicholas Wade**, doing?

THE RHETORICAL SITUATION

Purpose
Audience
Rhetorical appeals
Modes & media

see page 393

How do I know this is a **newspaper article**?

THE GENRE'S CONVENTIONS

Elements of the genre
Style
Design
Sources

see page 394

The New York Times

Science

For Cats, a Big Gulp With a Touch of the Tongue

By NICHOLAS WADE
Published: November 11, 2010

It has taken four highly qualified engineers and a bunch of integral equations to figure it out, but we now know how cats drink. The answer is: very elegantly, and not at all the way you might suppose.

Enlarge This Image

Pedro Reis
Cutta Cutta, who inspired the study, belongs to a researcher at M.I.T.

Multimedia

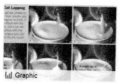

Graphic
A Study of Cat Lapping

Connect With Us on Social Media
@nytimesscience on Twitter.
· Science Reporters and Editors on Twitter

Like the science desk on Facebook.

Cats lap water so fast that the human eye cannot follow what is happening, which is why the trick had apparently escaped attention until now. With the use of high-speed photography, the neatness of the feline solution has been captured.

The act of drinking may seem like no big deal for anyone who can fully close his mouth to create suction, as people can. But the various species that cannot do so — and that includes most adult carnivores — must resort to some other mechanism.

Dog owners are familiar with the unseemly lapping noises that ensue when their thirsty pet meets a bowl of water.

The dog is thrusting its tongue into the water, forming a crude cup with it and hauling the liquid back into the muzzle.

Cats, both big and little, are so much classier, according to new research by Pedro M. Reis and Roman Stocker of the Massachusetts Institute of Technology, joined by Sunghwan Jung of the Virginia Polytechnic Institute and Jeffrey M. Aristoff of Princeton.

Writing in the Thursday issue of Science, the four engineers report that the cat's lapping method depends on its instinctive ability to calculate the point at which gravitational force would overcome inertia and cause the water to fall.

What happens is that the cat darts its tongue, curving the upper side downward so that the tip lightly touches the surface of the water.

The tongue is then pulled upward at high speed, drawing a column of water behind it.

Continues next page

RECOMMEND
TWITTER
LINKEDIN
SIGN IN TO E-MAIL
PRINT
REPRINTS
SHARE

The New York Times

VIDEO »   More Video | Multimedia »

PLAY

SCIENCE
How Cats Lap
The Biomechanics of Feline Water Uptake

Just at the moment that gravity finally overcomes the rush of the water and starts to pull the column down — snap! The cat's jaws have closed over the jet of water and swallowed it.

The cat laps four times a second — too fast for the human eye to see anything but a blur — and its tongue moves at a speed of one meter per second.

Being engineers, the cat-lapping team next tested its findings with a machine that mimicked a cat's tongue, using a glass disk at the end of a piston to serve as the tip. After calculating things like the Froude number and the aspect ratio, they were able to figure out how fast a cat should lap to get the greatest amount of water into its mouth. The cats, it turns out, were way ahead of them — they lap at just that speed.

To the scientific mind, the next obvious question is whether bigger cats should lap at different speeds.

The engineers worked out a formula: the lapping frequency should be the weight of the cat species, raised to the power of minus one-sixth and multiplied by 4.6. They then made friends with a curator at Zoo New England, the nonprofit group that operates the Franklin Park Zoo in Boston and the Stone Zoo in Stoneham, Mass., who let them videotape his big cats. Lions, leopards, jaguars and ocelots turned out to lap at the speeds predicted by the engineers.

The animal who inspired this exercise of the engineer's art is a black cat named Cutta Cutta, who belongs to Dr. Stocker and his family. Cutta Cutta's name comes from the word for "many stars" in Jawoyn, a language of the Australian aborigines.

Dr. Stocker's day job at M.I.T. is applying physics to biological problems, like how plankton move in the ocean. "Three and a half years ago, I was watching Cutta Cutta lap over breakfast," Dr. Stocker said. Naturally, he wondered what hydrodynamic problems the cat might be solving. He consulted Dr. Reis, an expert in fluid mechanics, and the study was under way.

At first, Dr. Stocker and his colleagues assumed that the raspy hairs on a cat's tongue, so useful for grooming, must also be involved in drawing water into its mouth. But the tip of the tongue, which is smooth, turned out to be all that was needed.

The project required no financing. The robot that mimicked the cat's tongue was built for an experiment on the International Space Station, and the engineers simply borrowed it from a neighboring lab.

THE RHETORICAL SITUATION

Purpose
As a science news reporter, Wade's purpose as author of this article is to explain recent findings about how cats drink.

Audience
Wade's audience includes general news readers, online readers, Times fans, animal lovers, and science enthusiasts.

Also, as a science journalist, Wade may have his own following, so some readers may be his fans.

Rhetorical appeals
Wade appeals to readers' sense of ethos through specific references to the work of four scientists who published an article in the journal Science.

He appeals to pathos by using humor, especially at the start of the article. He begins with a tongue-in-cheek statement: "It has taken four highly qualified engineers and a bunch of integral equations to figure it out."

Nicholas Wade, *For Cats, a Big Gulp with a Touch of the Tongue*

THE RHETORICAL SITUATION

He also appeals to readers' sense of logic (**logos**) by beginning with general statements about cats drinking water and then continuing with more specific details.

Modes & media

Mode = written, visual, and video
Wade shares most information in words, but the photos of Cutta Cutta and the video illustrate his most important points (note: scroll down to the video box on the *Times* page). Some news sites, such as *The Huffington Post*, present articles as videos that are introduced by a small amount of text.

Medium = digital
Wade's article was published at *The New York Times* online and also in print. Among the advantages of the digital version of the article are the addition of video and the links to other information, including the researched article that was Wade's source.

THE GENRE'S CONVENTIONS

Elements of the genre

Well researched and accurate. Wade read a research report in *Science* and talked to the scientists who wrote it. He found out how the research was inspired, funded, and conducted.

Opens with a lead paragraph that sets up the article's subject: "[W]e now know how cats drink."

Presents information in order of importance. Wade begins with the researchers' findings: They discovered how cats drink, something previously unknown. "Cats lap water so fast that the human eye cannot follow what is happening, which is why the trick had apparently escaped attention until now."

Wade ends with information on how the research was funded, something fewer readers will be interested in.

Includes quotations to personalize the experience or information for the reader. The quote from Dr. Stocker shows what inspired his research: "Three and a half years ago, I was watching Cutta Cutta lap over breakfast."

Short paragraphs hold readers' attention.

Style

Neutral/no opinions. Wade doesn't indicate his personal opinion about how cats drink.

Objective, third-person voice. Wade reports what researchers

discovered, leaving himself out of the article. E.g., though he may be a dog owner himself, instead of writing "My dog," he writes "Dog owners are familiar" with the sounds dogs make when they drink.

Just enough detail for the general reader. Wade relates relevant details precisely, such as the formula used to calculate the drinking speed of cats: "The lapping frequency should be the weight of the cat species, raised to the power of minus one-sixth and multiplied by 4.6."

Design

Appealing headline. The title interests readers and conveys the gist of the article in a few words. Also,

the page presents the newspaper's title, the name of the section, and the date of publication.

Byline. Wade's name (rather than "staff writer") appears under the headline, which adds to his ethos.

Friendly typeface. *The New York Times* online uses a clean Georgia serif font designed specifically for easy screen reading.

Columns and chunking. The *Times* divides its Web page into columns—in this case the content and images are in one area; advertising (not shown here) is on the right.

Images and multimedia. A photo of Cutta Cutta gives readers a visual of the cat that inspired

the research, and a series of photos shows how cats drink. A video features the researchers explaining why they decided to study cats drinking.

Sources

Sources are acknowledged. Wade and the *Times* use hyperlinks to acknowledge sources. The names of the four engineers who wrote the report on cats are linked so readers can learn more about them. Linking to sources further conveys Wade's reliability and objectivity.

Questions: Analyzing Wade's news article

1. Purpose. What is Wade's main purpose in writing this article? What are some of his secondary purposes? Identify passages in the article where these purposes are apparent.

2. Purpose. Notice how Wade uses a slightly humorous title for his science- and research-based article. Why does he do this?

3. Audience. How does Wade appeal to people who are not cat lovers?

4. Rhetorical appeals. The online version of Wade's article includes hyperlinks that connect readers with additional information, including a researched article in *Science* and the biographical profiles of the scientists who wrote it, which contributes to the ethos of Wade and his article. How else does Wade convey a sense of ethos?

5. Rhetorical appeals. Cats and kittens can be extremely cute and there are many online videos devoted to celebrating how adorable they can be. How does Wade approach the subject from a different angle? Are there any spots where Wade emphasizes their cuteness? If so, where— and to what end?

6. Modes & media. Do you read news primarily online or do you read print newspapers? Why?

7. Elements of the genre. How does the lead paragraph set the stage for the rest of the article?

8. Style. How does Wade convey scientific information in a way that a general audience can understand? If possible, watch the video embedded in the article. How does its content connect with Wade's article? What stylistic differences, if any, do you see between Wade's writing and the voice-over of the video?

9. Design. Notice that the images and video are neatly lined up on the left side of the article rather than interspersed within the article where they are mentioned. Why did the designers at *The New York Times* lay it out this way?

10. Sources. Make a list of all the sources Nicholas Wade consulted while writing this article. Are there any sources that surprise you? How can you categorize the sources? Are they primary? Secondary? Tertiary? (See Chapter 19.)

Drafting a News Article

CHECKLIST: Drafting a News Article
Thinking of drafting a news article? Ask yourself the following questions.

WHAT'S MY RHETORICAL SITUATION?

☐ **Purpose.** What newsworthy event or issue do I want to report? Of all the people involved with the story, which person will be my focus? How can I bring the story and people to life for my readers?

☐ **Audience.** Who will read my article? How carefully will they read it? Why will they read it? What will they do with the information?

☐ **Rhetorical appeals.** How will I establish my authority as a writer? How will I logically connect ideas and details? How will I make sure that my use of pathos does not undercut my ethos?

☐ **Modes & media.** Will readers experience my article in print form or online? Do I want to include images or videos?

WHAT GENRE CONVENTIONS MATTER?

☐ **Elements of the genre.** Which information is important enough to my readers that I should present it first? Which information is interesting but not as important?

☐ **Style.** How will I keep my tone objective and neutral? What level of detail will I include in my article?

☐ **Design.** How will I use headers and footers, titles, headlines, tabs, and other design features to keep my readers oriented? Will my article appear online? If so, what information will I hyperlink? How might I embed photos or videos into the layout?

☐ **Sources.** How much research will I need to do to compose this article? Are there people I'll need to talk to? Where will I need to go? Will I need to locate documents or records in a library or online?

PRACTICE
Want to experiment? Draft your own news article.

Think of an event or issue on your campus that you'd like to report on. Who are the people associated with the event or issue? Arrange to interview at least two of those involved so you can include their voices and perspectives in your article. How will you quote them? What quotes will do the most to bring your article to life? Next, draft a short article for an online newspaper that conveys the big picture of the topic, as well as relevant details that will interest your readers. Be sure to create a catchy headline and to hyperlink to any sources you use (including the people you interview).

PEER-REVIEWED JOURNAL ARTICLES

As a student, you've probably written a research paper or two. When you write research papers in the academic setting, your purpose is to investigate a specific topic, usually by examining what others have already said about it. You begin by drawing on a variety of sources, for example, articles from *EBSCOhost*. The articles from these journals are secondary sources. Once you've gathered your sources, you don't merely report what you've found: You also synthesize, compare, and analyze what has been said. You incorporate the voices of your sources in a systematic way, using quotations, citing sources in the body of your paper (or other composition), and listing them at the end. For some assignments, you might also respond to the sources you've researched by presenting and supporting your own argument. Like most writing, researched writing can also be persuasive. (For more on researched writing, see Chapter 17. For more on persuasive writing, see Chapter 15.)

What is the purpose of peer-reviewing? What makes a text authentically peer-reviewed? #Understand

Research papers do exist outside of the classroom, but they're not usually called "research papers"—and they are usually informed by primary research (that is, research conducted by the writer himself or herself). These papers may be called "articles," "professional researched reports," "scholarly journal articles," or "peer-reviewed journal articles." When we say a work has been "peer-reviewed," we mean that it has been read, critiqued, and approved by other experts/scholars.

Authors of peer-reviewed articles are scholars; they are recognized by other scholars as experts on the subject they're writing about. Many scholars are employed as professors at colleges and universities; others work in research laboratories. Research laboratories can be associated with universities, medical facilities (such as the Mayo Clinic), the government (such as the U.S. Naval Research Laboratory), for-profit organizations (such as Pfizer and other pharmaceutical companies), or nonprofit organizations (such as the Pew Research Center). Research laboratories and centers are sometimes referred to as "think tanks."

The organizations that publish peer-reviewed articles usually do so for a professional audience (rather than general readers). Two examples include *Nature*, a weekly science journal, and the Web site of the American Psychological Association, which compiles scholarly articles. Peer-reviewed articles are often presented at academic conferences, usually to audiences of peers and other experts on the subject.

Should a wiki—where content is read and edited by peers—be considered a peer-reviewed source in the same way that a scholarly journal is? Why or why not? #Evaluate

In these forums, scholars must cite their sources rigorously; a charge of plagiarism can easily end an academic career. The readers of peer-reviewed journal articles are usually other experts in a given field, but might sometimes include more general readers, such as students or other nonexpert readers interested in the topics covered.

Analyzing Peer-Reviewed Journal Articles: What to Look For

THE RHETORICAL SITUATION

Purpose   Scholars write articles for peer-reviewed journals in order to share their research results with others in the same field. Sometimes scholarly writers present groundbreaking new research, such as a new drug or an alternative energy source. Other times, they present more subtle findings, such as a different way of looking at existing data.

Another purpose of scholarly writers is to persuade readers to see things the way they do. For example, when presenting data, a scholar may want to argue for his or her own particular interpretation of the data. Most scholarly articles are meant to both inform and persuade.

What scholarly
journals are related
to your major?
To what extent
do you relate to
them as a reader?
#Understand

Audience   Authors of scholarly articles usually write for a fairly narrow primary audience that includes researchers, professors, and other scholars who want to stay up-to-date in their fields. However, they also have secondary audiences in mind. For example, as a student, you might refer to a scholarly journal article as a source for a research paper. Peer-reviewed journals exist in every academic field, including the sciences, humanities, and social sciences. For example, Amy and Liz both read academic journals such as *College Composition and Communication*, which focuses on teaching and composition; they use *CCC's* journal articles to deepen their own understanding of writing and teaching research. Another example, this one in science, is ▼ *Nature*, the most widely read journal of its kind. For academics needing to keep abreast of major stories in the sciences, reading *Nature* is crucial, as it keeps them informed about new discoveries, developments, and research by other professionals.

ONLINE JOURNAL ▶
***Nature* Homepage**
Nature is cited by
more scientists than
any other science
journal. *Macmillan.*

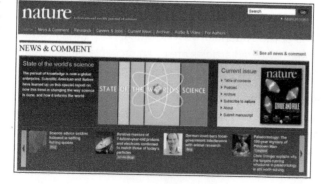

Rhetorical appeals Scholars who write articles for peer-reviewed journals need to establish ethos by describing their research methods, explaining what data they collected and how they analyzed that information, and discussing their findings and conclusions in detail. They must also cite sources appropriately, taking into account the findings of others. And, because logic is important to scholarship and the writers' audience, writers must appeal to logos by building arguments that rest on tightly organized pieces of evidence and scrupulously researched data. Scholars must keep in mind that their readers will need to be convinced of the legitimacy of their research methods, the accuracy of their data collection, and the logic of their data analysis.

Modes & media Scholarly articles are text based and may include visuals such as charts, graphs, and images to support and illustrate points. Journals are available in print and, increasingly, online; many articles that originate in print-based journals are available through subscription databases such as *EBSCOhost*, *JSTOR*, and *Project MUSE*. A few scholarly journals are only available digitally.

THE GENRE'S CONVENTIONS

Elements of the genre
Based on original research—or research of another expert or peer. In a peer-reviewed journal article, scholars usually write about their own original research.

» First, they identify a question that needs to be answered (such as "How does living near a nuclear reactor affect birthrates?").

» Next, they design an experiment or research plan that will allow that question to be studied (for example, identifying nuclear reactors, collecting data on birthrates in the surrounding communities over time, interviewing obstetricians who practice in the surrounding communities, etc.).

» Then, they perform the research, analyze the data gathered in the research, and offer their interpretations in writing. Authors usually refer to related research by other scholars to contextualize their own work.

Reviewed by others in the field for accuracy and reliability. Scholarly articles are written by scholars, for scholars. During a process known as "peer review," other experts in the field review the article to check for clarity and style, but even more important, to make sure the research conducted is a legitimate means of measuring or studying the subject of the article. Peer reviewers might question, for instance, the validity of studying birthrates near nuclear reactors by merely interviewing people who live in the community. They would probably want more rigorous, objective data, such as hospital records documenting pregnancies, fertility rates, and births.

Is thesis-driven. Scholarly authors write to make a point about the research they've conducted—a point that usually has both informative and persuasive elements to it. For example, if an author's point is "drugs X, Y, and Z alleviate symptoms of condition A," she will go on to inform readers of how she drew that conclusion (how she conducted the research and analyzed the data) and will also—if the article is well researched and written—persuade readers that the drugs discussed in the article should be prescribed more often.

Attributes sources/work of others. Scholars who write articles for peer-reviewed journals summarize, paraphrase, and quote from their sources. When writers use other sources (outside of their own original research), they properly document the work/voices of others through in-text citations and Works Cited lists.

Synthesizes sources. Like a student writing a research paper, scholars must synthesize their sources in journal articles. That is, they pull together information across multiple sources to make their points.

Uses formal and precise language. Scholarly writers use formal language to convey the seriousness of their ideas and research. They also use precise language to communicate complex information accurately and in detail. In a scientific research study, the difference between .1 and .01 can be crucial.

Style

Descriptive title. The title of a scholarly article needs to make clear what the article is about. In scientific fields, the more descriptive the better, such as "Hospital Mortality, Length of Stay, and Preventable Complications among Critically Ill Patients before and after Tele-ICU Reengineering of Critical Care Processes" (from *JAMA*). In the humanities, titles often have two parts: an imaginative or creative phrase, followed by a colon, and then a more descriptive phrase, such as "Black, White, and Blue: Racial Politics in B. B. King's Music from the 1960s" (an article by Ulrich Adelt, from *The Journal of Popular Culture*).

Strong, authoritative voice and tone. Authors of scholarly journal articles tend to use an authoritative voice and tone in their scholarly writing, which helps establish their ethos. For example, in "Status Struggles: Network Centrality and Gender Segregation in Same- and Cross-Gender Aggression," an article in *American*

Why do authors of scholarly articles tend to use long, descriptive titles? What are the benefits and drawbacks of such titles? #Understand #Evaluate

Sociological Review, authors Robert Faris and Diane Felmlee begin their article in a way that reinforces their expertise and authority:

> Aggression is commonplace in U.S. schools: bullying and other forms of proactive aggression adversely affect 30 percent, or 5.7 million, American youth each school year (Nansel et al. 2001). The National Education Association (1995) estimates that each weekday, 160,000 students skip school to avoid being bullied. This aggression has important consequences. Being victimized by bullies positively relates to a host of mental health problems, including depression (Baldry 2004), anxiety (Sharp, Thompson, and Arora 2000), and suicidal ideation (Carney 2000). —**Robert Faris and Diane Felmlee,** from "Status Struggles: Network Centrality and Gender Segregation in Same- and Cross-Gender Aggression," *American Sociological Review*, February 2011

Use of detail. Authors of scholarly articles use specific details to develop complex ideas. They also use details as evidence to back up their assertions. For example, in the article discussed above, Faris and Felmlee support general statements ("Aggression is commonplace in U.S. schools") with examples and evidence (bullying "affect[s] 30 percent, or 5.7 million, American youth each school year").

Design

Subheadings. Many peer-reviewed journal articles are divided into sections by subheadings that make a long, complex article accessible. Subheadings also signal to the reader when the writer is about to turn his or her focus to another example or another aspect of the topic.

Images. Many scholarly articles include images, such as photos, charts, and illustrations, to convey complex information visually. Those that are published digitally can include hyperlinks to sources and other materials.

Sources

Types of sources used. Scholarly writers must use sources that are authoritative and are appropriate to the topic and approach they've taken. For example, in the peer-reviewed article on page 402, the author draws heavily on movie reviews. This is appropriate because she discusses many films and their popular reception. Movie reviews would not be used for an article on molecular science, unless, for instance, the essay focuses on how molecular science is portrayed in films.

Works Cited list. Scholarly writers include a bibliography at the end of their articles. They list sources in the format dictated by the journal they're publishing in, or according to the format favored in their discipline's professional organization, such as the Modern Language Association (MLA style) and the American Psychological Association (APA style).

Sika Dagbovie-Mullins

Mixed-Race Superstars

Sika Dagbovie-Mullins is an assistant professor of English at Florida Atlantic University, where she teaches literature and researches the representation of mixed-race identity in literature and culture. Her article, originally titled "Star-Light, Star-Bright, Star Damn Near White: Mixed-Race Superstars," first appeared in 2007 in *The Journal of Popular Culture*, a scholarly, peer-reviewed journal. The journal, based at Michigan State University and published by the Popular Culture Association, presents the works of scholars in the field as well as in the related areas of literature, film studies, and African American studies. Dagbovie-Mullins's book *Crossing Black: Mixed-Race Identity in Modern American Fiction and Culture* was published in 2013.

(*Article: Copyright © 2007 John Wiley and Sons.*

Top banner: Courtesy of The Journal of Popular Culture.)

ONLINE JOURNAL ▲
The Journal of Popular Culture
Where Sika Dagbovie-Mullins published her article. *Courtesy of* The Journal of Popular Culture.

THE JOURNAL OF POPULAR CULTURE

Submissions | Recent Articles | Editorial Board | FAQs | Subscribe | Advertise | Awards

Star-Light, Star-Bright, Star Damn Near White: Mixed-Race Superstars

SIKA DAGBOVIE-MULLINS

In an episode of *The Chris Rock Show*, comedian Chris Rock searches the streets of Harlem to find out what people think of Tiger Woods.[1] When he asks three Asian storekeepers if they consider Woods Asian, one replies, "Not even this much," pressing two of his fingers together to show no space. This comic scene and the jokes that surround Woods's self-proclaimed identity reveal a cultural contradiction that I explore in this essay, namely the simultaneous acceptance and rejection of blackness within a biracial discourse in American popular culture. Though Woods's self-identification may not fit neatly into the black/white mixed-race identity explored in this project, he still falls into a black/white dichotomy prevalent in the United States. The Asian storekeepers agree with Rock's tongue-in-cheek suggestion that Tiger Woods is as black as James Brown, opposing sentiments like "The dude's more Asian than he is anything else" on an Asian American college Internet magazine ("Wang and Woods"). Woods cannot escape blackness (a stereotypical fried-chicken-and-collard-green-eating blackness according to Fuzzy Zoeller), and yet he also represents a multicultural poster boy, one whose blackness pales next to his much-celebrated multi-otherness.[2]

Through advertising, interviews, and publicity, biracial celebrities encode a distinct connection to blackness despite their projected (and sometimes preferred) self-identification. Drawing from Richard Dyer's *Stars*, I read biracial celebrities Halle Berry, Vin

Continues next page

What is the composer, **Sika Dagbovie-Mullins**, doing?

THE RHETORICAL SITUATION

Purpose
Audience
Rhetorical appeals
Modes & media

see page 404

How do I know this is a **peer-reviewed journal** article?

THE GENRE'S CONVENTIONS

Elements of the genre
Style
Design
Sources

see page 404

THE RHETORICAL SITUATION

Purpose

As the author of a peer-reviewed journal article, Dagbovie-Mullins aims to inform her readers of how biracial celebrities present their "blackness." She also makes an argument about how American popular culture both accepts and rejects "blackness."

THE GENRE'S CONVENTIONS

Elements of the genre

Based on original research and research by other scholars. Dagbovie-Mullins examines the publicity and representations of three celebrities. She acknowledges that she uses some of the ideas from another scholar, Richard Dyer, as models for her ideas.

(Continued on p. 406.)

THE JOURNAL OF POPULAR CULTURE

Diesel, and Mariah Carey by analyzing autobiographical representations, celebrity statuses, public reception, and the publicity surrounding each of the representations.[3] Dyer writes, "Stars are, like characters in stories, representations of people. Thus they relate to ideas about what people are (or are supposed to be) like" (*Stars* 22). Recognizing that we can never know how much agency stars have in their image, I acknowledge that biographies or interviews are not necessarily "truths." However, the interviews, career moves (e.g., movie roles or music), public reception, and publicity that I examine all play a part in creating a star's image. I argue that the reception of mixed-race celebrities in popular culture reflects a national inclination to define blackness. While laws have historically defined who is black, social laws also attempted to regulate blackness, ensuring that blacks "kept their place." Similarly, in contemporary popular culture, advertisers and media attempt to define blackness. For mixed-race celebrities, this means blackness is deemed acceptable only when it upholds stereotypical white preconceptions and desires.

During and after slavery, many whites thought that mulattos were intellectually superior to "pure" blacks, a notion that confirmed white supremacy. At the same time, some whites believed mulattos were psychologically unstable, suggesting that even one drop of black blood could lead to mental and other deficiencies. Though mixed-race men were often labeled rapists and murderers, mixed-race women were seen as lascivious seductresses. Some of these same stereotypes reappeared in nineteenth and twentieth century American literature. Sterling Brown was the first to name the literary stereotype the "tragic mulatto." In "Negro Character as Seen by White Authors" he describes the archetype as "a victim of divided inheritance and therefore miserable" (162). The persistence of this stereotype has continued in contemporary popular culture, revealing America's obsession with race mixing and mixed-race bodies. Like census statisticians, America does not know what to do with "mulattos." Historically and today, mixed-race individuals are used to explore, praise, or condemn the "racial unknown."

THE JOURNAL OF POPULAR CULTURE

Though multiracial identity has become a modish identity that white Americans seek, desire, and fetishize, Americans still fear and loathe blackness, marginalizing and criminalizing black bodies. The fascination with mixed-race bodies is metaphorically synonymous to racial slumming in the late 1920s. Kevin Mumford explains, "the influx of white mainstream urbanites . . . temporarily participated in the interzones [black/white sex districts], usually for pleasure, and then returned to their homes and lives apart from the black/white vice districts" (133). Similarly, whites' obsession with black/white mixed-race bodies permits "consumption" of a more palatable form of blackness while allowing whites to return "home" or stay distanced from the supposedly less "attractive" aspects of black identity.

Some mixed-race celebrities are read as black, even when they distance themselves from blackness. Conversely, mixed-race celebrities who claim a black heritage often get labeled as multiracial, not black. In short, the contradictory desires of the American public and media, manifested in a simultaneous disavowal and celebration of mixed race, show both our discomfort and fascination with mixed-race people and their bodies in particular. In the entertainment industry, a star's biracial identity may fade, be tucked away, or even disappear according to audience perceptions and star construction. On the other hand, a mixed-race identity never satisfies. Berry may self-identify as black, yet the media often holds onto her multiracial background. Diesel's desire not to talk about his racial background unsurprisingly fuels more interest. Carey proudly asserts a biracial identity while alternately encoding blackness and "otherness" in the media. Although Berry is distinct from the two other celebrities in her constant embracing of and identification with blackness, the reception of all these celebrities groups them together. The hype surrounding Berry, Diesel, and Carey shows the inconsistencies of America's racial desires over whether to control blackness on the one hand or encourage racial harmony on the other, or perhaps to abandon race altogether.

Continues next page

THE RHETORICAL SITUATION

Audience

Readers are most likely to be educators, scholars, and/or researchers interested in race, identity, and celebrity. As readers of *The Journal of Popular Culture*, they are already interested in the topics that title suggests—such as film, television, and other areas of pop culture.

Rhetorical appeals

One way the author establishes her **ethos** is by providing a careful cultural analysis of the anecdote from *The Chris Rock Show*.

Dagbovie-Mullins appeals to readers' **logos** by reviewing historical aspects of her topic and using the quotations and source summaries she chooses to logically build toward her conclusion.

(Continued on p. 407.)

THE GENRE'S
CONVENTIONS

Reviewed by peers.
*The Journal of
Popular Culture,*
where the article
was published, is
a scholarly, peer-
reviewed journal
based at Michigan
State University.

Is thesis-driven.
Dagbovie-Mullins
begins by stating
the central issue she
will address. Her
thesis (spread over
several sentences)
provides her main
argument and its
consequences.

**Identifies and
synthesizes
sources.** The
author goes beyond
summarizing,
paraphrasing,
and quoting from
sources; she
synthesizes them to
make a point. E.g.,
when discussing
Halle Berry's role in
Monster's Ball, she
pulls together several
sources to make her
point.

(Continued on p. 408.)

THE JOURNAL OF POPULAR CULTURE

Claiming Halle Berry: Biracial or Black?

When Halle Berry won the Oscar for Best Actress in 2002, she became more widely recognized as an accomplished black actress. Berry's acceptance speech confirms her racial allegiance: "The moment is so much bigger than me. . . . It's [the Oscar] for every nameless, faceless woman of color that now has a chance because this door tonight has been opened." Despite Berry's claim, competing discourses on her ethnicity consume popular cultural discussions of her. In a 1994 interview with Lisa Jones, Berry makes clear, "I never once announced that I am interracial. I was never the one to bring it up. . . . Yet reporters constantly ask what childhood was like to an interracial person" (Jones "Blacker," 60). Berry consistently identifies as African American, evoking an identity grounded in a black politics. Jones asks Berry if mixed-race children should choose a race. Berry replies, "You've got to identify with one group or the other. It is a political choice" (60). Berry learned this, she claims, from her white mother who advised her to "accept being black, embrace it" (Kennedy 28). Berry's biracial background follows her in her movie roles and public persona, evidenced perhaps in the approval she seems to give to stereotypes of mulatta women. The media's investment in reading Halle Berry within a biracial narrative assures a biracial script both within the movies and in pseudo-liberal discussions of race. She is more easily accepted in a "role," both cinematic and stereotypic, that is familiar to Americans—that of the exotic mixed-race woman.[4]

Donald Bogle's discussion of Dorothy Dandridge is particularly helpful in thinking about Halle Berry. Bogle describes Dandridge as having "the rich golden skin tone that had always fascinated movie audiences, black and white." He continues, "she was a destructive personality, schizophrenic, maddening, euphoric, and self-destructive," all characteristics that define what the tragic mulatta has become: a beautiful, licentious, yet confused and unhappy woman (166). Dandridge's roles in films like *Carmen Jones* (1954), *Island in the Sun* (1957), and *Tamango* (1957)

THE JOURNAL OF POPULAR CULTURE

perpetuated the tragic mulatto stereotype around which her career became centered. Bogle asserts that Dandridge "epitomized the confused, unsatisfied movie star dominated by the publicity and lifestyle that informed her screen image" (174–75). Similarly, *Ego Trip's Big Book of Racism!*, a biting collection of satiric essays and lists, places Berry as number five in its "Top Ten Tragic Mulattos." The media unnecessarily emphasize her biraciality in any description of her misfortunes, including an abusive father and ex-boyfriend, two divorces, and a suicide attempt. The authors of *Ego Trip's* cite Berry's "emotionally wrenching turn as her troubled role model, Dorothy Dandridge" as partial evidence of her "tragic mulatto" status (Jenkins 81).

In an interview with Entertainment Television, Warren Beatty says, "She's a beautiful woman and she's the essence of that biracial thing in America that is so beautiful" ("Halle Berry"). Beatty, who acted with Berry in *Bulworth* (1998), romanticizes mixed-race identity as an American ideal, reducing Berry to the essence of a biracial "thing," no longer an individual but a notion or concept. Praising Berry as a national ideal inadvertently summons the history of black/white mixing in America, namely the sexual abuse of black women by white men during slavery. However, Beatty's comment also suggests a desire to interpret Berry within a "melting pot" framework, one that depoliticizes identity. This rhetoric abounds in multiracial literary interpretations, such as in Maria P. P. Root's assertion that "the accomplishment of complex identities by racially mixed persons gives us the hope that if individuals have been able to resolve conflicting values, claim identities, synthesize multiple heritages, and retain respect for individual heritages . . . perhaps it is possible for us eventually to do this as a nation" (347). Multiracial activists see a mixed-race Berry in the same way they view Tiger Woods, as an indication of racial harmony or what David L. Andrews and C. L. Cole describe as "racially coded celebrations which deny social problems and promote the idea that America has achieved

Continues next page

Modes & media

Mode = written The author's scholarly article is text based (it appears in print and as a PDF online) and includes no images or graphics. Some journals encourage authors to use images and graphics; this is especially true for business and economics journals that publish articles that analyze relationships among factors, and as you might expect, art journals make heavy use of images of the art being discussed. (See "Charts/infographics" on p. 357.)

(Continued on p. 409.)

THE GENRE'S
CONVENTIONS

Documents sources.
The author provides
in-text citations
when drawing on
outside sources.

**Uses formal
language.** The
author's choice
of terms such as
self-proclaimed and
discourse adds to
the serious feel of the
writing.

**Uses precise
language.** For
example, Dagbovie-
Mullins specifies
that *Monster's Ball*
"recycles nineteenth-
century" images,
clarifying that she
sees the film in a
particular historical
context.

Style

Descriptive title.
The author uses the
title to grab attention
and present the gist
of her argument.

**Strong author's
voice.** Dagbovie-
Mullins refers to
many sources but
her voice stays in
control; her voice
doesn't get lost
in the midst of
quotations.

(Continued on p. 410.)

THE JOURNAL OF POPULAR CULTURE

its multicultural ideal" (70).[5] Reading Berry in a biracial framework falls in line with historical and cinematic representations of mixed-race women and allows a white patriarchal system to prevail under the guise of politically correct rhetoric. In other words, other people define Berry and place her in a category that best satisfies white perceptions of race and mixed race.

The titles of articles on Berry reveal a tendency to read her as a modern day tragic mulatto. "Halle Berry, Bruised and Beautiful, Is on a Mission," "The Beautiful and Damned," "Am I Going to Be Happy or Not?" and even an unauthorized biography entitled *Halle Berry: A Stormy Life* all highlight Berry's troubled personal life, recalling mixed race literary characters whose beauty was rivaled only by their ugly misfortunes. Though the media extol Berry's beauty, their accolades always urge references to her tragic life. Films including *The Flintstones* (1994), *Introducing Dorothy Dandridge* (1999), *X-Men* (2000), *Die Another Day* (2002), and *Monster's Ball* (2002) also subtly accentuate Berry's image as tragic or exotic. In the miniseries *Queen* (1993), Berry plays Alex Haley's grandmother, daughter of a white master and a black slave. The producers stayed "true" to Queen's racial background by choosing Berry for the part and remained loyal to the "tragic mulatress text: Not only does *Queen* drag out mulatto clichés from every B movie and paperback, it luxuriates in them with eerie aplomb" (Jones, *Bulletproof Diva* 50). Yet even Berry's decidedly "monoracial" characters, like the role of Nina (a pro-black "fly girl") in *Bulworth*, repeat a tragic motif. Patricia Williams writes that Berry's role "never rises above the most ancient of clichés" by bordering "black and white," "hope and despair, good and bad, sane and insane; the positive and negative divided by two, multiplied by sex" (11). In the sci-fi comic-book-turned-movie *X-Men*, Berry's character again occupies an "in-between" space. Lynne D. Johnson asserts that Berry's role as Storm in *X-Men* did not surprise, given her mixed racial background: "Though not a tragic mulatto in the classic sense of the myth, being mixed in both the racial and genetic mutation sense

THE JOURNAL OF POPULAR CULTURE

THE RHETORICAL
SITUATION

of the word, Storm is representative of this idea." In 2004, Berry played another mutant woman, *Catwoman*, first made famous by biracial actress Eartha Kitt in a 1960s television show. Like Berry's other films, *Catwoman* capitalizes on Berry's reputation as exotic, liminal, and hypersexual.[6]

Berry's casting as Leticia Musgrove in *Monster's Ball* prompted diverse reviews from moviegoers and critics. The reaction from the black community was mixed, mostly due to Berry's casting as a stereotypical black woman in a film that "unfolds like something that was written by Simon Legree, the slave owner in *Uncle Tom's Cabin*. Just hours after they meet, the black woman lustfully seduces the startled white man" (Wickham 15A).[7] While many reviews mention the clichés in *Monster's Ball*, most fail to mention the stereotypical image of black women.[8] Actress Angela Bassett declined the role, she claims, because "I wasn't going to be a prostitute on film. . . . I couldn't do that because it's such a stereotype about black women and sexuality" (Samuels 54). Bassett does not mention the stereotypes of mixed-race women implicit in Berry's portrayal of Leticia, a woman who wants Hank to "heal" her through sex. Here the movie recycles nineteenth-century images of black and mixed-race women as oversexual.[9] More specifically, the movie encourages the myth of mixed-race women "as lewd and lascivious as the men are idle, sensual, and dishonest" (Mencke 102). Though the film does not specifically label Leticia mixed race, her characterization urges such readings. Symbolically, the movie recalls the history of miscegenation yet, more specifically, the movie reinforces general perceptions of Halle Berry as biracial. One reviewer sarcastically claims that the film suggests blacks and whites will get along only when "black women are already half white, already measure up to the white beauty standard," like Halle Berry ("Monster Balls"). Berry's role in *Monster's Ball* speaks to Berry's own tragic mulatto image, and her image never strays far from the "biracial" characters she plays.

Medium = print and digital This piece originally appeared in both the print and digital versions of *The Journal of Popular Culture*. Subscribers to the print journal automatically get online access to the digital version of the journal, enabling readers to choose which medium they'd prefer to read an article in (the two versions have no content differences). Some journals have developed apps for iPads and other mobile devices that allow readers to access the online version of an article on the go.

Continues next page

THE GENRE'S
CONVENTIONS

Authoritative and declarative tone. The author states her case with confidence. She sometimes uses first person to present her ideas as a researcher and scholar.

Use of detail. The author follows her generalizations with specific examples to back up her claims. E.g., she states that "The titles of articles on Berry reveal a tendency to read her as a modern day tragic mulatto" and then provides evidence: 'Halle Berry, Bruised and Beautiful, Is on a Mission,' 'The Beautiful and Damned,' 'Am I Going to Be Happy or Not?' and even an unauthorized biography entitled *Halle Berry: A Stormy Life* all highlight Berry's troubled personal life, recalling mixed race literary characters whose beauty was rivaled only by their ugly misfortunes."

(Continued on p. 412.)

THE JOURNAL OF POPULAR CULTURE

As so many viewers and audiences have lamented, Hollywood representations of blackness have been limited and narrow. Movies have historically slighted actors who are "too black" and, simultaneously, shunned those who are "not black enough." Like Dorothy Dandridge and Lena Horne, Berry has been hindered by her lighter complexion, and sometimes deprived of movie auditions and offers for "black" roles. Berry's manager, Vincent Cirrincione, claims that when Berry auditioned for *Strictly Business* (1991), they told her to "get a tan" (Kennedy 28). Conversely, Cirrincione says other executives have told him "milk is milk until you add a little Hershey. It doesn't matter if you add a little Hershey or a lot" (Kennedy 28). More often than not, Berry does not signify real "blackness." Philip Kerr remarks that in *Monster's Ball*:

> I didn't see a black woman who looked, well, black. Am I the only one to have noticed? Halle Berry—who let's face it, is half-white—made a lachrymose, Oscar-winning thing about being a woman of colour, and yet the reality is that she looks no more like a person of colour than I do. Is it just me, or do most of the black women cast in Hollywood films, with their straight hair, thin lips and cappuccino-coloured skins, look just a little bit white? (Kerr 44)

Kerr's offensive statement uses biology to classify Berry, relying on crude physical descriptions like "straight hair" and "thin lips" to declare Berry "not black." Though Kerr's criticism rightly addresses the prejudice against darker actresses, his critique also suggests a restrictive and monolithic view of blackness. Such physical stereotypes of African Americans neglect the wide array of physical characteristics and skin color within black communities. Berry cannot pass and does not "look" white as Kerr suggests; her physical markings represent those commonly associated with a person of color. That Berry self-identifies as black makes Kerr's statement particularly insulting in terms of his desire to read her as "half-white." The media criminalizes dark skin, associating darkness with poverty, ignorance, and physical ugliness. Cannot Leticia be poor, desperate, downtrodden, and still light skinned? Aside

THE JOURNAL OF POPULAR CULTURE

from presenting narrow-minded views on race, Kerr's description shows that the public and critics invest in Berry's "whiteness."

Public discourses about Berry belabor her looks when referring to her celebrity allure. Charlie Kanganis, who directed Berry in *Race the Sun* (1996), compares Berry with "a double espresso machiatto, a dollop of shapely foam, a shower of cinnamon and cocoa." No other actress in "Cinema and the Female Star," a collection of reflections and tributes to actresses, is so objectified. Warren Beatty claims that people laugh when they first see Berry because "they don't know how else to react. They're not used to someone that beautiful." Literary descriptions of mixed-race women in early American fiction suggest a similar exceptional, almost unreal beauty. In Charles Chesnutt's *The House Behind the Cedars* (1900), John, not yet recognizing Rena as his sister, describes her as "strikingly handsome, with a stately beauty seldom encountered" (7). These characterizations imply a uniqueness associated with mixed race that persists in popular culture. Lynn Hirschberg claims that Berry's beauty is "actually distracting; the perfection of her face would not seem to allow anything less than a perfect life" (26). Would people review Berry's beauty in the same way if she were "just black" (and not "biracial")? She represents the supposed mystique of mixed-race people, alluring because they symbolize a social taboo. Her image represents "black" and "not black," which unsettles and entices. A *Time* article begins, "Is it a curse to be beautiful?" continuing a familiar rhetoric about Berry's looks, one that intensified after *Monster's Ball*. Descriptions of Berry's beauty intimate what has become a common boasting on numerous multiracial Web sites—that mixed-race people are "prettier." This notion gets directly and indirectly repeated in advertisements and magazines that use models who physically represent racial mixture. The point here is not to judge or critique Berry's beauty, but rather to examine why it attracts so much attention. Berry cannot be taken out of a historical context of mixed-race beauty images. Her image reflects back the fantasy that makes Americans both anxious and envious.

Continues next page

THE JOURNAL OF POPULAR CULTURE

Multiracial to the Rescue: Vin Diesel

When Tiger Woods gained notoriety, he was proclaimed the new
multiracial face of America. Andrews and Cole maintain that
Woods represents the "latest in America's imagined realization
of its ideals (agency, equality, responsibility, and freedom) and its
imagined transformed sense of national self (America has become
the world that came to it)" (73). Yet Vin Diesel's recent explosion in Hollywood has introduced an even "better" Tiger Woods,
because unlike Woods, Diesel refuses to name himself racially.
Diesel, a self-described "mystery man," represents an amalgama-
tion of all races, literally in his racial ambiguity and symbolically
in his equally racially vague movie roles. In short, he is "everyman." His image enacts America's desired "other": multiracial,
de-politicized, and lacking any serious racial allegiance.

When asked about his background, Diesel firmly describes himself
as "multicultural." Diesel's name change from Mark Vincent
to Vin Diesel seems to corroborate his racial ambiguity or at
least encourage a multiracial reading of this ethnicity as "Vin"
is a stereotypical Italian American name. ("Diesel" refers to the
slang term, "cock diesel," describing a man's muscular physique.)
Diesel explains that this nickname emerged when he worked as
a bouncer: "We all had nicknames. It was wonderful to detach
a little bit" (Tesoriero 61). As an actor, Diesel appears to detach
from any racial group. Rumors abound about his Italian mother
and African American father, but he maintains, "I want to keep
my mystery" (Kirkland). Diesel denies "hiding anything": "It's not
that I don't want people to know anything. It's just that I would
rather spend more time talking about more productive things
that relate to the film [XXX]" (Kirkland). Diesel's silence seems a
strategic response not just to advertisers but also to the broader
cultural pattern that advertisers respond to, namely multiculturalism. One advertising executive asserts, "Both in the mainstream
and at the high end of the marketplace, what is perceived as good,
desirable, successful is often a face whose heritage is hard to pin

THE JOURNAL OF POPULAR CULTURE

down" (La Ferla). Diesel confirms what Danzy Senna jokingly calls "mulatto fever," telling one reporter that his "ambiguous, chameleon-like ethnicity" is "cool" (Thrupkaew). His production company, One Race, enforces his raceless image, reminiscent of Jean Toomer's early twentieth century proclamation, "I am at once no one of the races, and I am all of them." Diesel's explanation of his racial background captures how his image reflects America's desire for ethnic homogeneity. He presents no controversy and gives no reminders of black/white miscegenation.

Diesel's relationship with the black community seems dubious considering his reticence to claim any identity. Samuel Jackson, who stars with Diesel in *XXX*, tells *People Weekly*, "There's an air of mystery and danger about Vin, but he also has a little bit of the just-like-us quality" ("XXX Appeal" 87). Perhaps "just-like-us" speaks to the African American colloquial belief, "we know our own." Jackson's comments imply Diesel's blackness ("just-like-us") but also suggest his multiracial background ("air of mystery"). Despite claiming a nebulous "multicultural" description, Diesel has been somewhat accepted by the black community, at least superficially in terms of his appearances as a presenter at the 2002 NAACP Image Awards and his inclusion in *Ebony*'s 2003 top Black moneymakers list. This acceptance is, however, limited. A forum on bet.com (Black Entertainment Television) which posed the following question, "If Vin Diesel has any Black heritage, should he claim it publicly?" and articles such as "Outing Diesel" repeat a familiar resentment with celebrities who do not outwardly claim the black community (Hill). Still, that Diesel's refusal to acknowledge (or disclaim) blackness (or any race) has incited less anger and uproar than Tiger Woods's self-termed "Cablinasian" perhaps speaks to America's desire to forget about racial divisions. Similarly, publicity surrounding Vin Diesel exposes America's desires to be like Diesel, "of no particular place, and at the same time, able to be anywhere and be anything" (Iverem).

Continues next page

THE JOURNAL OF POPULAR CULTURE

Diesel's recent movies, with their over-the-top action and "heroes" of superhuman strength, seem geared toward teenagers. Diesel says he claims a "multicultural" identity because of his young audience: "I support the idea of being multicultural primarily for all the invisible kids, the ones who don't fit into one ethnic category and then find themselves lost in some limbo" (Iverem). Homi Bhabha contends that "the multicultural has itself become a 'floating signifier' whose enigma lies less in itself than in the discursive uses of it to mark social processes where differentiation and condensation seem to happen almost synchronically" (31). Diesel represents Bhabha's explication of the multicultural. The celebration over his fame both depends upon his difference as "Hollywood's new superhero: a self-made man unconfined by racial categories" (Thrupkaew) and his ability to relate to Americans as "multiethnic Everyman, a movie star virtually every demographic can claim as its own" (Svetkey). Diesel is a floating signifier, and, as *Boiler Room* director Ben Younger claims, "People seem to make him into whatever they want him to be" (Svetkey). Unlike Berry who cannot "pass," Diesel's racially uncertain physical characteristics allow him to pass as various ethnicities in his movies. For example, he plays an Italian in *Saving Private Ryan* (1998) and in *The Fast and the Furious* (2001), and a racially ambiguous person in *Boiler Room* (2000), *Pitch Black* (2000), and *The Chronicles of Riddick* (2004). While critics have charged Diesel with passing, others applaud his savvy marketing skills. Diesel admits, "Being multicultural has gone from the Achilles' heel of my career to my strength." He describes the world as a "big melting pot," deducing that "people are ready for a hero who is more ambiguous" (Thrupkaew).

XXX's advertising refers to its main character, Xander Cage, as "a new breed of secret agent," a seemingly intentional though oblique reference to Diesel's mixed-race background and his emergence in a genre once dominated by now outdated white action stars like Arnold Schwarzenegger, Sylvester Stallone, and Bruce Willis (White). Similar descriptions follow Diesel, naming him a new

THE JOURNAL OF POPULAR CULTURE

"multicultural hero" (Mora) and the "first truly All-American action hero" (White). Director Rob Cohen (*XXX* and *The Fast and the Furious*) maintains, "It has taken America a long time to acknowledge the new face of America . . . and to some degree, Vinny is that new face" (Kirkland). Such descriptions recall *Time*'s 1993 special issue cover, "The New Face of America," featuring a future mixed race, computer-made American woman. Suzanne Bost argues that *Time*'s female creation "charms . . . and yet she is taboo, bloodless, impure" (1). Lauren Berlant suggests that "new faces" like the *Time* cover respond to "problems of immigration, multiculturalism, sexuality, gender, and trans(national) identity that haunt the U.S." (398). What does it mean that this new representative (noncomputerized) face is a man, a "He-man" no less? Diesel's image, in part created through his movie roles, represents America's assimilation and capitalist impulses. In other words, his image encourages the idea that race is a commodity that people can trade, buy, or sell, virtually "e-racing" national histories of racialization. Henry Giroux writes, "National identity in the service of a common culture recognizes cultural differences only to flatten them out in the conservative discourse of assimilation and the liberal appeal to tolerance" (182). The suggestion that Diesel stands for "everyman" attempts to create a national identity that eliminates difference. Santiago Pozo, CEO of Arenas Entertainment, tells *Time*, "In the past, John Wayne and Jimmy Stewart were the face of America. . . . Today it's The Rock or Vin Diesel" (Tesoriero 61). Such a comparison suggests that biracial celebrities like The Rock or Diesel evoke a "multiracial sameness," a sugar pill oxymoron that ends up surreptitiously recentering white normative American identity.

Mariah Carey as Biracial Fantasy

If Halle Berry is America's prized mulatta, then Mariah Carey is her lascivious tragic sister. Carey's image depends on her exploitation of the mulatta stereotype.[10] On the one hand, she represents

Continues next page

THE JOURNAL OF POPULAR CULTURE

the alienated racial outsider in songs such as "Outside" (from the *Butterfly* album) where she bemoans the difficulties of not belonging. On the other hand, she exploits the notion of the racially ambiguous seductress, wearing next to nothing in music videos and publicity photos. Since Carey's self-titled debut album in 1990, she has publicly performed various "roles" including white ingenue, biracial outsider, black hiphopper, and erotic/exotic "other." Kate Lanier, a script-writer for Carey's film, *Glitter* (2002), asserts that "a lot of mixed-race girls and young women . . . hold Mariah up as a hero." Lanier claims this makes Carey "proud" because "for a long time she was encouraged to play up her white side. Since she has been allowed creative freedom, she has related more to black culture" (Beller 13). Carey's image both deflects and confirms blackness, creating an "in-between" status she teases in terms of her racialized sexuality. She wears biracial stereotypes like a blackface "costume," allowing audiences to explore racial and sexual fantasies while maintaining racial stereotypes.

Music reviews and articles have paid close attention to Carey's overt sexuality and racial shifts in a popular culture context. Vincent Stephens observes: "Along with genre changes, Carey has taken on a more sexualized visual persona and has become more outspoken about her multiracial heritage and struggles for artistic freedom" (234). Caroline Streeter sees Carey "transform[ing] from white to black before our very eyes" (311). Indeed, Carey's album covers trace her shifting racial movements from what Lisa Jones calls "a rainbow body of African descent, skin toasted almond and hair light brown" to her current whitewashed blond pin-up look (*Bulletproof Diva* 200). While other ethnic stars such as Jennifer Lopez or Beyoncé sport blond hair, Carey's hair transformation seems particularly racially motivated considering the initial marketing of Carey that concealed her blackness. In 1990, music critics labeled Carey a "white Whitney Houston" until outside pressures prompted her record company to make a statement. Carey cleared up misconceptions at a press confer-

THE JOURNAL OF POPULAR CULTURE

ence where she declared, "My father is black and Venezuelan. My mother is Irish and an opera singer. I am me" (Jones *Bulletproof Diva* 197). Following Carey's public disclosure, black publications ran articles such as "Mariah Carey Tells Why She Looks White but Sings Black" and "Mariah Carey: Not Another White Girl Trying to Sing Black," seemingly attempting to assure black audiences that Carey was not trying to pass or disregard her black ancestry. However, Carey's later physical transformation suggests an effort to depart visually from "black" and to reflect white standards of beauty.

Despite publicly claiming a multiracial heritage, Carey admits that her physical hints of blackness made her self-conscious. Recalling her *Butterfly* (1997) album cover, Carey shares that she felt pressured to cover up her face "because I had been told I looked horrible and too ethnic with my face showing" (Grigoriadis 194). As Carey's hair turns straighter and blonder, she increasingly signifies "whiteness" while contradictorily maintaining a position as ethnic "other" vis-a-vis her public assertions of biracialism. Richard Dyer suggests that "blondeness is racially unambiguous" and "the ultimate sign of whiteness" (*Heavenly Bodies* 44, 43). Carey represents a racial anomaly because her image simultaneously projects different racial tropes. These competing discourses establish Carey in a biracial narrative that depends upon her liminality.

Musically, Carey has moved from pop to hip-hop, in some ways a symbolic shift from white to black. After Carey divorced then Sony Music president Tommy Mottola, her music and image changed drastically. Carey claims that her *Butterfly* album symbolizes her feelings of personal and professional freedom impelled by her divorce. As she explained it in 1997, "I feel more free to put more of myself into my music" (Thigpen 113). With *Butterfly*, Carey has worked with more hip-hop artists and producers to tap into her "broad demographic." As she observes, "I have an audience that's urban and one that's Middle America." She continues, "So I have to really be a little bit conscious of the fact that

Continues next page

THE JOURNAL OF POPULAR CULTURE

it's broad, and also it's diverse in terms of the racial thing. I am anyway, being a mixed person racially" (Carey, Interview with Dimitri Ehrlich 338). On *Rainbow* (1999), Carey collaborated with hip-hop artists and rappers including Jay-Z, Usher, Da Brat, Missy Elliott, and Snoop Dogg. Carey's earlier albums *Mariah Carey* (1990), *Emotions* (1991), and *Daydream* (1995) demonstrated her penchant for love ballads and cross-over pop songs, save for Carey's "Dreamlover" remix with Ol' Dirty Bastard on *Daydream*. Earlier albums also feature Carey in her pre-blonde days, suggesting that Carey's physical transformation heightened after she professionally embraced black culture. In a 2002 MTV interview Carey revealed, "Most of my friends and most of the music I listen to and most of my influences are R&B and hip-hop" ("Mariah Carey: Shining Through the Rain"). Still, Carey's most hip-hop albums visually emphasize her whiteness, such as *Charmbracelet* which shows her with platinum streaks.

Carey constructs a stereotypical mulatta trope in public discussions of her biraciality. Inside the *Rainbow* CD liner Carey's message to fans expresses her desire for people of all races and hues to live with one another happily and without conflict. Her words both reveal her vision of racial unity and explain why multiracial organizations herald her as an ideal biracial "spokesperson." In "My Saving Grace" Carey positions herself as tragic, discussing how during her childhood she felt confused and suffered from low self esteem due to her mixedness. In general, she laments over the media's and public's obsession with her racial identity yet openly discusses her feelings of racial alienation and isolation. She shares always feeling "so separate from everybody, even if I never talked about it" (Udovitch 34). She attributes this alienation to various reasons: "Because my father's black and my mother's white. Because I'm very ambiguous-looking." Carey has claimed multiple descriptors including "person of color" and the glib, "I view myself as a human being" (Farley 75). Yet despite Carey's supposed desires to put the issue of her racial

THE JOURNAL OF POPULAR CULTURE

background to rest, she often brings it up in interviews and has appeared on national shows like *Oprah* to discuss such issues. In an *Oprah* show entitled "Mariah Carey Talks to Biracial Teens," Carey announces herself as somewhat of a multiracial nationalist, claiming, "I bond with mixed people" (7). Yet, Carey frequently exploits biracial stereotypes, betraying her role model status.

Carey's hypersexuality intensifies as she encodes "whiteness" via her album covers and "blackness" via her music, symbolically evoking the "warring" racial divisions and libidinous nature of the mulatta stereotype. Magazine photos play up her sexuality so that her overall image combines multiple representations: mulatta sex kitten, black performer, and white pin-up. However, Carey and her music are not considered "black" in the same way, for example, that Mary J. Blige represents "blackness." And physically, Carey is too ethnic to be a white sex symbol. The result places Carey in an in-between, mixed-race seductress narrative. For example, the *Rainbow* CD liner opens up to reveal a photo which exploits Carey as a heterosexual male fantasy: she suggestively lies on a bed in white cotton underclothes, wearing stiletto heels and licking a heart-shaped lollipop. A nearby phone lying off the hook may suggest Carey's possible roles as phone sex operator or prostitute. Magazine photos of Carey (as in *Vibe* March 2003) (Ogunnaike) are not just revealing, but border on soft porn. In one photo she wears a trench coat, partly opened to reveal her naked body. Another frames Carey lying on a couch, one hand on her breast, the other suggestively positioned below her stomach. Still another shows Carey in an unzipped miniskirt and unzipped midriff top, suggestively looking downwards at her skirt. While many pop stars like Christina Aguilera and Britney Spears also wear skimpy and sexy clothing, Carey's provocative style of dress is coupled with a publicized troubled multiracial identity, making her sexuality fetishized and tragic. Tellingly, Carey cites Marilyn Monroe, a star whose name virtually equaled sex in the 1950s and who began her career as a pin-up, as the

Continues next page

THE JOURNAL OF POPULAR CULTURE

person she most admires.[11] Not surprisingly, Barbara Walters symbolically likens the two, calling Carey "a soldier's pin-up girl come to life" while describing her Kosovo trip to visit U.S. troops (Carey, "Surviving the Glare").

Carey's semi-autobiographical box office failure, *Glitter*, confirms her racialized sexuality despite its attempts to critique biracial clichés. In one scene the music video director explains his idea for the main character's video: "She is not black, she is not white, she is exotic, OK?" This same theme follows representations of Carey's public and private life. In July 2001, Carey appeared on MTV's *Total Request Live* (*TRL*) pushing an ice-cream cart in a "Loverboy" (the name of *Glitter*'s first single) T-shirt and heels. She proceeded to perform a pseudo striptease, taking off her T-shirt to reveal a hidden skimpy outfit. Entertainment reporters and tabloids ridiculed Carey for her bizarre behavior and incoherent ramblings to *TRL* host, Carson Daly. Accordingly, *Ego Trip's Big Book of Racism!* comically named Carey their number one "Tragic Mulatto" for, among other things, "a propensity for 'whorelike attire,' a nervous breakdown, a mocked and derided cinematic debut, and a failed soundtrack" (Jenkins 81). Such descriptions urge the question, what role does Carey have in sexualizing her image? Carey reports feeling "constantly amazed" regarding her portrayal as "very loose morally and sexually," an ironic statement considering that Carey invites such readings in nearly all recent publicity photos and public outings ("Mariah Carey Discusses" 58). Though we can never know how much agency stars exert over their image, Carey seems to perpetuate wittingly an oversexual public persona. She represents a historically comfortable vision of mixed race women. Carey poses little threat to racial hierarchy because she fits a mold that showcases just enough "blackness" to intrigue but not enough to appear definitive or political.

THE JOURNAL OF POPULAR CULTURE

New Faces, Old Masks

The media commodifies biracialism by using "new" celebrity faces: Diesel's movie posters that target a younger, more multicultural and multiracial generation and Carey's seemingly produced and packaged embodiment of the mulatta seductress in videos, albums, and magazines. Despite Berry publicly announcing a black identity, her image still "sells" biracialism through media representations of her life and less obviously via her stereotyped movie roles. In this sense, all three stars symbolically represent the "multiracial neutral" in that their images "sell" the idea of racial pluralism and freedom, and yet their images remain "Other," available for audiences and consumers of all racial backgrounds to "claim" or "own." The popularity of these stars does not reflect a more racially tolerant or progressive America. Like the cliché "some of my best friends are black," which attempts to prove a supposed lack of racism, the multiracial craze only superficially embraces the dark "Other." Liberals and conservatives alike have repeatedly placed idealistic expectations on mixed-race individuals in discussions of racism and multiculturalism. Though expectations differ, this pattern gets repeated in a popular culture context with mixed-race stars. Thus, Tiger Woods is not just a superb athlete of color, but an emblem of racial harmony, the Great Multiracial Hope. When stars' images do not fit our vision, we force them into familiar stereotypes that satisfy other expectations. Halle Berry's image may not represent racial unity, but at least it does not depart from what we have learned to expect from mixed-race women. In a popular culture context, biraciality "works" for people who do not really want to confront racial issues when it exploits difference under the guise of celebrating diversity. The "new" faces of America have no racial responsibilities, loyalties, or obligations. People admire them for their beauty, celebrate them as America's future, and envy their "cool" multiracial status. However, old masks lurk alongside interpretations of what new faces represent, namely racial stereotypes. Until power relations equalize, any celebration of mixed race needs to recognize those who are not celebrating or benefiting from

Continues next page

THE JOURNAL OF POPULAR CULTURE

America's longtime fascination. Questioning what it means to be black or part-black allows one to be critical of traditional assumptions about racial identification and realize the urgency of racial responsibility in a society built upon racial inequality.

NOTES

1. See *Best of the Chris Rock Show*.

2. In 1997, golfer Fuzzy Zoeller made a racist joke during the 62nd Masters golf tournament in Augusta, Georgia. He reportedly joked that he hoped fried chicken and collard greens would not be served at the next year's tournament should Tiger win and choose the menu.

3. My essay focused on these particular celebrities because they have represented multiple racial tropes in popular culture and in their work. Their immense popularity, I argue, is also connected to their "otherness." These stars differ from other biracial stars, such as Alicia Keys, whose blackness often foregrounds their public image. This essay was written after Mariah Carey's 2002 album and after Vin Diesel's and Halle Berry's 2004 films.

4. In his classic book, *Toms, Coons, Mulattoes, Mammies, and Bucks*, Donald Bogle examines the persistence of these five common stereotypes of African Americans on film. Bogle cites *The Debt* (1912) as one of the earliest film representations of the tragic mulatto. Like the literary stereotype, the mulatta on film was often near white, exceedingly beautiful, exotic, and doomed as a result of her mixed race.

5. Such perceptions abound in Web sites and often show up in online discussions, particularly following Berry's Oscar speech, which angered many people who self identify as multiracial. For example, responding to a post in a "Moms of Biracial Children" forum, one woman writes, "I didn't watch the awards but it's pretty sad that she had to put a label on the [Black] community she was thanking. . . . It's comments like that continues the separatism of races." Another respondent writes, "My daughter a beautiful little girl loves Halle Berry and couldn't understand why she only said she was black. I think it was a very confusing statement." See "Did Halle Berry Forget Her Mom Is White?" for other postings.

6. Continuing her portrayal of "liminal" characters, Berry says she is preparing for a movie entitled *The Guide*, playing "a spiritual woman—half Native American, half African-American—who guides people through times of crisis" (Ritz 128). Most recently, she portrayed Zora Neale Hurston's mixed-race character, Janie, in Oprah Winfrey's television rendition of *Their Eyes Were Watching God*.

7. See, for example, the online discussion, "Bassett: 'Monster' Role Was Demeaning."

8. For a sample of reviews on *Monster's Ball*, see Roger Ebert, Leslie Felperin, Lisa Schwarzbaum, and Stephanie Zacharek.

THE JOURNAL OF POPULAR CULTURE

9. In *Ar'n't I a Woman?: Female Slaves in the Plantation South*, Deborah Gray White argues that the jezebel stereotype that emerged during slavery was used to justify the sexual exploitation of black women. The stereotype suggested that black women were promiscuous and invited rape and sexual abuse.

10. Ironically, an April 2005 *Essence* article on Mariah Carey begins, "This 'mulatto' is hardly tragic" (121). See Joan Morgan.

11. See "All Mariah" on Carey's homepage (http://www.mariahcarey.com).

Works Cited

"All Mariah." *Mariah*. Web. 19 Mar. 2004. <http://www.monarc.com/mariahcarey/allm/index.asp>.

Andrews, David L., and C. L. Cole. "America's New Son: Tiger Woods and America's Multiculturalism." *Sport Stars: The Cultural Politics of Sporting Celebrity*. Ed. David L. Andrews and Steven J. Jackson. New York: Routledge, 2001. 70–86. Print.

"Bassett: 'Monster' Role Was Demeaning." Online discussion forum. The Black Web Portal Forum. Web. 28 Mar. 2004. <http://www.blackwebportal.com/forums/viewmessages.cfm?Forum=5&Topic= 1872>.

Beller, Thomas. "The New M.C." *Elle* July 2001: 109+. Print.

Berlant, Lauren. "The Face of America and the State of Emergency." *Disciplinarity and Dissent in Cultural Studies*. Ed. Carey Nelson and Dilip Parameshwar Gaonkar. New York: Routledge, 1996. 397–439. Print.

Berry, Halle, as told to David A. Keeps. "Halle Berry Dishes the Dirt." *Marie Claire* Feb. 2002: 52–59. Print.

Best of the Chris Rock Show. HBO, 1999. DVD.

Bhabha, Homi K. "Culture's in Between." *Multicultural States: Rethinking Difference and Identity*. Ed. David Bennett. London: Routledge, 1998. 29–36. Print.

Bogle, Donald. *Toms, Coons, Mulattoes, Mammies, and Bucks*. New York: Continuum, 2003. Print.

Bost, Suzanne. *Mulattas and Mestizas: Representing Mixed Identities in the Americas, 1850–2000*. Athens, GA: University of Georgia Press, 2005. 1. Print.

Continues next page

THE JOURNAL OF POPULAR CULTURE

Brown, Sterling B. "Negro Character as Seen by White Authors." *Journal of Negro Education* 2 Apr. 1933: 201. Print.

Carey, Mariah. "Outside." *Butterfly*. Columbia, 1997.

———. *Rainbow*. Columbia, 1999. CD.

———. Interview with Dimitri Ehrlich. *Interview*. Oct. 1999. 338–39. Print.

———. "My Saving Grace." *Charmbracelet*. Island Def Jam, 2002. CD.

———. "Surviving the Glare: Celebrities Who Prevailed After Scandal." Interview with Barbara Walters. *20/20*. ABC. 9 May 2002. Television.

Chambers, Veronica. "Mariah on Fire." *Newsweek* 15 Nov. 1999: 80–81. Print.

Chesnutt, Charles W. *The House Behind the Cedars*. New York: Modern Library, 2003. 7. Print.

Corliss, Richard. "Halle Berry: Monster's Ball." *Time* 21 Jan. 2002: 124–25. Print.

"Did Halle Berry Forget Her Mom Is White?" Online posting. 11 Sept. 2000. "Moms of Biracial Children." Commitment.com. Web. 23 Feb. 2004. <http://www.commitment.com/boards/boardMB/MBbrmsgs/142.html>.

Dyer, Richard. *Stars*. London: British Film Institute, 1979. Print.

———. *Heavenly Bodies: Film Stars and Society*. New York: St. Martin's Press, 1986. Print.

Ebert, Roger. Rev. of *Monster's Ball*. Dir. Marc Forster. *Chicago Sun-Times* 1 Feb. 2002. Web. 1 Mar. 2004. <http://www.suntimes.com/ebert/ebert_reviews/2002/02/020101/html>.

Farley, Christopher John. "Pop's Princess Grows Up." *Time* 25 Sept. 1995: 75. Print.

Felperin, Leslie. Rev. of *Monster's Ball*. Dir. Marc Forster. *Sight and Sound* June 2002 sec. 12.6: 46. Print.

Giroux, Henry A. "The Politics of National Identity and the Pedagogy of Multiculturalism in the USA." *Multicultural States: Rethinking Difference and Identity*. Ed. David Bennett. London: Routledge, 1998. 178–94. Print.

THE JOURNAL OF POPULAR CULTURE

Glitter. Dir. Vondie Curtis-Hall. Twentieth Century Fox, 2001. Film.

Grigoriadis, Veronica. "The Money Honey." *Allure* Sept. 2001: 190+. Print.

"Halle Berry." *Road to the Red Carpet*. Entertainment Television. 3 May 2003. Television.

Haynes, Esther. "Am I Going to Be Happy or Not?" *Jane* Dec. 2003: 126–28. Print.

Hill, James. "'Outing' Diesel." Bet.com. 2 Aug. 2002. Web. 4 Mar. 2004. <http://www.bet.com.articles/o,,c3gb3453-4121,00.html>.

Hirschberg, Lynn. "The Beautiful and Damned." *New York Times Magazine* 23 Dec. 2001: 26. Print.

Iverem, Esther. "A Monster Love." Rev. of *Monster's Ball*. Dir. Marc Forster. 21 Feb. 2002. *Seeing Black*. Web. 26 Feb. 2004. <http://www.seeingblack.com/x022102/monstersball.shtml>.

Jenkins, Sacha, Elliott Wilson, Chairman Jefferson Mao, Gabriel Alvarez, and Brent Rollins. *Ego Trip's Big Book of Racism!* New York: Regan Books, 2002. Print.

Johnson, Lynne D. "Bearing the Black Female Body as Witness in Sci-Fi." 1 Dec. 2003. *Pop Matters*. Web. 1 Mar. 2004. <http://www.popmatters.com/columnsjohnson/031218.shtml>.

Jones, Lisa. "The Blacker the Berry." *Essence* June 1994: 60+. Print.

———. *Bulletproof Diva: Tales of Race, Sex, and Hair*. New York: Doubleday, 1994. Print.

Kanganis, Charlie. "Halle Berry." *Senses of Cinema*. 23 Nov./Dec. 2002. Web. 1 Mar. 2004. <http://www.sensesofcinema.com/contents/02/23/symposium1.html#berry>.

Kennedy, Dana. "Halle Berry, Bruised and Beautiful, Is on a Mission." *New York Times* 10 Mar. 2002: 2A+. Print.

Kerr, Philip. "A Shocking Cheek." *New Statesman* 17 June 2002: 44. Print.

Kirkland, Bruce. "Word's Out: Vin's In." *Toronto Sun*. 4 Aug. 2004. Web. 4 Mar. 2004. <http://www.canoe.ca/JamMoviesArtistsD/diesel_vin.html>.

La Ferla, Ruth. "Generation E.A.: Ethnically Ambiguous." *New York Times* 28 Dec. 2003, sec. 9: 1+. Print.

Continues next page

THE JOURNAL OF POPULAR CULTURE

"Mariah Carey Discusses Her Sex Life, Race, Career." *Jet* 31 May 2000: 56–60. Print.

"Mariah Carey: Shining Through the Rain." Interview with John Norris. MTV. 3 Dec. 2002.

"Mariah Carey Talks to Biracial Teens." *Oprah*. ABC. 27 Dec. 1999. Transcript.

"Mariah Carey Tells Why She Looks White but Sings Black." *Jet* 3 Apr. 1991: 56–57. Print.

Mencke, John G. *Mulattoes and Race Mixture: American Attitudes and Images, 1865–1918*. Ann Arbor: Umi Research Press, 1979. Print.

"Monster Balls." Rev. of *Monster's Ball*, dir. Marc Forster. Metaphilm. Web. 29 Feb. 2004 <http://www.metaphilm.com/philms/monstersball.html>.

Mora, Renee Scolaro. Rev. of *XXX*, dir. Rob Cohen. *Pop Matters* 9 Aug. 2002. Web. 16 Feb. 2004 <http://www.popmatters.com/film/reviews/x/xxx.shtml>.

Morgan, Joan. "Free at Last." *Essence* Apr. 2005: 118–24. Print.

Mumford, Kevin J. *Interzones: Black/White Sex Districts in Chicago and New York in the Early Twentieth Century*. New York: Columbia University Press, 1997. Print.

Norment, Lynn. "Mariah Carey: Not Another White Girl Trying to Sing Black." *Ebony* Mar. 1991: 54–58. Print.

Ogunnaike, Lola. "Through the Fire." *Vibe* Mar. 2003: 113–20. Print.

Pappademas, Alex. "Over the 'Rainbow': A Tale of Two Mariahs." *Boston Phoenix*. 22 Nov. 1999. Web. 24 Mar. 2004 <http://weeklywire.com/ww/11-22-99/boston_music_2.html>.

Prince. "Controversy." *Controversy*. Warner Bros., 1981. CD.

Ritz, David. "Heart to Heart." *Essence* Dec. 2002: 128+. Print.

Root, Maria P. P. "From Shortcuts to Solutions." *Racially Mixed People in America*. Ed. Maria P. P. Root. Newbury Park: Sage, 1992. 342–47. Print.

Samuels, Allison. "Angela's Fire." *Newsweek* 1 July 2002: 54. Print.

Sanello, Frank. *Halle Berry: A Stormy Life*. London: Virgin Books, 2003. Print.

THE JOURNAL OF POPULAR CULTURE

Schwarzbaum, Lisa. Rev. of *Monster's Ball*. *Entertainment Weekly* 25 Jan. 2002. 2 Mar. 2004. EBSCO.

Stephens, Vincent. Rev. of *Rainbow*. *Popular Music & Society* Summer 2003, sec. 26.2: 234–35. Print.

Streeter, Caroline A. "The Hazards of Visibility: 'Biracial Women,' Media Images, and Narratives of Identity." *New Faces in a Changing America: Multiracial Identity in the 21st Century*. Ed. Loretta I. Winters and Herman L. DeBose. Thousand Oaks: Sage, 2003. 301–22. Print.

Svetkey, Benjamin. "Vin at All Costs." *Entertainment Weekly* 2 Aug. 2002: 5. Print.

Tesoriero, Heather Won. "The Next Action Hero." *Time* 5 Aug. 2002: 61–62. Print.

Thigpen, David E. Rev. of *Butterfly*. *Time* 15 Sept. 1997: 113. Print.

Thrupkaew, Noy. "The Multicultural Mysteries of Vin Diesel." Alternet.org. 16 Aug. 2002. Web. 4 Mar. 2004 <http://www.alternet.org/story.html?StoryID=13863>.

Udovitch, Mim. "An Unmarried Woman." *Rolling Stone* 5 Feb. 1998: 30–32. Print.

"Wang and Woods." Asian American E-Zine at Stony Brook University. 11 Dec. 2002. Web. 1 Apr. 2004 <http://www.aa2sbu.org/aaezine/articles/sports/12-WangAndWoods.shtml>.

White, Armond. Rev. of *XXX*, dir. Rob Cohen. *New York Press* Web. 4 Mar. 2004 <http://www.nypress.com/15/33/film/film2.cfm>.

White, Deborah Gray. *Ar'n't I a Woman?: Female Slaves in the Plantation South*. New York: Norton, 1984. Print.

Wickham, DeWayne. "Bassett Criticism Has Its Merit." *USA Today* Section: News, 15A. Print.

Williams, Patricia. "Bulworth Agonistes." *The Nation* 7 June 1998: 11. Print.

"XXX Appeal." *People Weekly* 19 Aug. 2002: 87–88. Print.

Zacharek, Stephanie. Rev. of *Monster's Ball*. Dir. Marc Forster. Salon.com. Web. 28 Mar. 2004. <http://archive.salon.com/ent/movies/review/2002/01/04/monsters_ball/>.

Questions: Analyzing Dagbovie-Mullins's peer-reviewed journal article

1. Purpose. Dagbovie-Mullins discusses Halle Berry, Vin Diesel, and Mariah Carey, but how does she make it clear from the beginning that she's not writing about these actors as entertainers? What seems to be her main purpose? Does she seem to have secondary purposes?

2. Audience. What are some features of this paper that make it clear that she's writing for other scholars, rather than, say, general readers of *People* magazine, who might also be interested in reading about Halle Berry, Vin Diesel, and Mariah Carey? How would the author need to revise for a *People* magazine audience?

3. Rhetorical appeals. How does Dagbovie-Mullins establish her authority on the topic she writes about?

4. Rhetorical appeals. How does the author appeal to your sense of logic in presenting examples and details to support her points? What are some specific details she uses that appeal to your sense of logos?

5. Modes & media. This particular article does not include any images, although thousands of images of Halle Berry, Vin Diesel, and Mariah Carey are available. Why do you think the author opted not to integrate images into her article?

6. Elements of the genre. What is Dagbovie-Mullins's thesis? How easy was it for you to locate her thesis? What cues does she use in her introduction to indicate that the thesis is coming?

7. Elements of the genre. Do you have to be familiar with the author's sources to understand her point? Explain.

8. Style. Celebrities are typically considered more appropriate subjects for gossip magazines than scholarly journals. How does the author present celebrities as appropriate subjects for a researched article?

9. Design. Dagbovie-Mullins uses subheadings to break the article up into chunks. Did you find these helpful? Did you want fewer or more of them? Why or why not? Also note that some subheadings are questions, while others could be considered thought-provoking statements ("Multiracial to the Rescue: Vin Diesel"). How did these subheadings work on you as a reader? Did they make you want to keep reading? Explain.

10. Sources. Note the extensive Works Cited list. Glance through the list of sources and note how many seem to be scholarly sources and how many seem to be other types of sources. How does the use of nonscholarly sources seem appropriate or inappropriate for this article?

Drafting a Peer-Reviewed Journal Article

CHECKLIST: Drafting a Peer-Reviewed Journal Article Thinking of drafting a peer-reviewed journal article? Ask yourself the following questions.

WHAT'S MY RHETORICAL SITUATION?

☐ **Purpose.** What topic have I researched that I could inform other experts about? Have I discovered something about the topic that others like me might find interesting or conducive to their own research? Do I want to persuade readers of something? To effectively persuade readers, what will I need to inform them about?

☐ **Audience.** My readers will be experts on my general topic, but they won't know as much as I do about the aspect I'm writing about. How much background information will they need? What kind of terminology will they expect? How will my readers use the information I present?

☐ **Rhetorical appeals.** How will I establish my authority as a writer? How will I build a case for my conclusions using logic? Will I need to cite sources to establish myself as an expert? What kinds of sources will help me build my case?

☐ **Modes & media.** Can some of the information I present be shown with a chart or graphic? Do I want readers to access my article in print or digitally? Or do I want to make both options available?

WHAT GENRE CONVENTIONS MATTER?

☐ **Elements of the genre.** How can I make sure my thesis is clear and declarative? How will I refer to my sources? How can I synthesize my sources to show readers how they are in conversation with each other?

☐ **Style.** How can I project an authoritative voice? How much detail will I need to provide so that readers will understand the complexity and validity of my research?

☐ **Design.** How will I use subheadings to present my information in chunks? Will I use images to illustrate points?

☐ **Sources.** Will my readers expect sources to be cited in MLA style, APA style, or another format? Will my readers respect the types of sources I've referred to?

PRACTICE Want to experiment? Draft your own peer-reviewed journal article.

Think about a topic you are researching for this class or another class. What are some of the issues surrounding your topic? Draft an opening paragraph that establishes you as an authority and also makes it clear that you are writing for fellow students rather than a general audience.

DOCUMENTARY FILMS

As the name suggests, documentary films document something: a real-life event, person, or phenomenon. Documentary filmmakers use techniques such as investigative reporting, research of archival footage, and primary research, including interviews with people who are connected to the subject of the film. Documentaries are usually feature-length films.

A popular type of documentary is one that combines reporting and social or political critique. Michael Moore's documentaries *Bowling for Columbine*, which studied the high rate of gun violence in the United States and won the 2002 Academy Award for Documentary Feature, and *Sicko*, which focused on the American healthcare system, both got lots of attention from the public.

Another popular type of documentary is the science or nature documentary; these films are often shown in IMAX theaters in nature and science museums. The IMAX film *Everest* documents the challenges and disasters encountered by a group of climbers in the face of Mount Everest. The documentary film *Grizzly Man* traces Timothy Treadwell's summers living and ultimately dying with wild bears in Alaska.

Biographical documentaries often focus on the life of a famous person, for example, *Imagine: John Lennon*. This type of documentary often mixes present-day interviews with archival footage and audio: *Imagine* uses television and film footage from Lennon's time with the Beatles and his solo career, as well as audio voiceover clips from recorded interviews.

Documentary films are often released for theater viewing. Science and nature documentaries are often shown at museums, aquariums, and planetariums. Documentary films can also be found online at sites such as Top Documentary Films.

Have you watched a documentary lately? If so, what was your viewing experience like? What did the film require of you as a viewer? How did the experience compare to watching an action film or a drama? #Understand

Analyzing Documentary Films: What to Look For

THE RHETORICAL SITUATION

Purpose   The main purpose of a documentary film is to inform viewers about a real-life subject or event. Documentary filmmakers always present information from a particular point of view; for example, the documentary film *Scratch* by Doug Pray focuses on the perspective of hip-hop DJs themselves rather than that of their audiences. In addition to informing viewers, documentary filmmakers often seek to persuade viewers to see their subject in a particular way. Michael Moore's documentaries, mentioned above, are often politically charged; one of his implied purposes is to cast suspicion on political views he does not hold. Finally, documentaries tell a kind of story about their subjects, as the nature documentary *March of the Penguins* does. The filmmaker informs audiences about penguin migration, presenting mother penguins—who must travel to a distant sea to find food to bring back for their young—as heroes battling brutal weather.

Audience   Filmmakers create documentaries for people who are curious about a subject or who want to better understand a difficult or complex event. For example, filmmaker Alex Gibney, creator of *Enron: The Smartest Guys in the Room*, kept in mind that his film would appeal to an audience interested in corporate corruption. Films about musicians appeal to music lovers, such as the documentary *No Direction Home: Bob Dylan*. Other filmmakers document international subjects. For example, the creators of *Control Room*—which documents Al Jazeera, an Arabic news outlet—draws an audience interested in Al Jazeera and the news coverage of the Iraq war.

What types of documentary subjects are most appealing to you? Do you have to be interested in the subject to be the audience for a documentary? Why or why not? #Analyze

Rhetorical appeals   Documentary filmmakers achieve their purposes by presenting carefully selected and edited interviews and shots. Documentary filmmakers *mediate* reality, meaning that they present a version of it. For example, filmmakers choose interviewees because they are compelling speakers and/or because they're experts in the subject. Filmmakers choose images that are striking and memorable, and organize and present information coherently. Everything in the film must contribute to a sense of a story being told. Documentary filmmakers must appeal to their audience's sense of ethos, since all aspects of the film are seen as a version of truth. Additionally, documentary filmmakers might also appeal to their audience based on logos if they are building an argument and/or pathos if they want to engage their audience emotionally.

Modes & media   Documentary filmmakers use visuals and audio to convey information. Visuals can be live footage, such as shots of people or places, or historical/archival footage that they can integrate with the present. For example, in *No Direction Home: Bob Dylan*, filmmakers mixed concert footage with interviews. Audio for a documentary can include music, dialogue, sound effects, or voice-over narration. You can watch a documentary in a theater, on TV, and on your computer screen.

Elements of the genre

Based on a real-life person or event. The subjects of documentary films are typically based on actual people (*Marley*) or on events (*March of the Penguins*). This nonfiction element separates documentary films from other film genres. Even though documentaries reside in the world of nonfiction, the films usually tell a story. In the case of *March of the Penguins*, the film tells the story of penguins during one breeding cycle in Antarctica. When choosing a compelling subject for a documentary, some filmmakers decide to highlight specific social issues. For example, in the documentary film *Born into Brothels*, the filmmakers chose to highlight their experiences with children in the red-light district of Calcutta.

Based on primary research, including interviews. Documentary filmmakers interview people directly connected to the film's subject. Some are experts, such as Robert McNamara in *The Fog of War*, who was the secretary of defense during the Vietnam War and was heavily involved in its planning. Other times, filmmakers choose interviewees who have less-quantifiable expertise, as in the case of the "man on the street" interviews that Michael Moore uses in his documentaries, where random people are questioned about their opinions on a subject, such as gun violence. Interview subjects are often identified with a byline listing their name and qualification to be interviewed on the subject.

Not staged; shows people in the context of their environment. Documentary films are not usually scripted. Instead filmmakers shoot footage of actual events. For example, *Grey Gardens*, a documentary about two eccentric socialites (mother and daughter) related to the Kennedy family, shows the women in their dirty house, surrounded by cats, old food, and growing piles of newspapers. It also shows the women entertaining guests, singing, and arguing. When documentary filmmakers anticipate an event, they might set up for a particular shot. For example, a filmmaker might be shooting a documentary about the running of the bulls in Pamplona, Spain, and know that at a particular moment, bulls will charge through the street; the filmmaker might stage the shot in that case, making sure to use the proper lighting and lenses to capture the desired effect.

May include archival footage. Filmmakers working with historical subjects often rely on archival footage, including clips from older films, such as newsreels or other documentaries. This footage has been filmed by someone else, not the documentary filmmaker. For instance, in the documentary *The Agony and the Ecstasy of Phil Spector*, the filmmaker uses archival footage of Spector's 2007 murder trial, integrating it into the film to provide information and context for Spector's life story.

Uses voice-over narration. Documentary filmmakers often use voice-over narration while visuals are shown. A voice-over often provides background information or facts that provide context for what the viewer sees. A popular voice-over narrator is David Riley, who is the voice behind many National Geographic documentaries.

Style

Is carefully edited after shooting. Documentary filmmakers shoot lots of footage—but often it's in the editing room, after the filming is done, that they identify their main focus. Filmmakers and editors go through a process of reviewing all footage to decide what to highlight, what the story arc is, where to begin, how to move the film to a heightened level of tension, and how to end. During the editing process, the filmmaker might take one hour of footage and edit it down to one minute.

Provides detail. Details are crucial to bringing subjects to life in a documentary film. For example, in *March of the Penguins*, filmmakers show every aspect of the birds' yearly mating ritual. In a scene where the female moves the egg to the male, the filmmakers carefully focus on the female pushing the egg onto the male's feet. By emphasizing every bit of detail in this process, viewers can appreciate the fragility of the moment and the ultimate fragility of life in the Antarctic.

Conveys an author (or narrator's) tone and voice. Tone in a documentary film is established by its narrator, who may be the filmmaker himself or herself or an actor hired for the part. The voice typically needs to have a quality of authority in order to establish ethos—especially if the purpose of the film is not just to inform but to persuade viewers into taking action. Such was the case with Al Gore's *An Inconvenient Truth*, for example.

Includes secondary images, called B-roll, to add interest and texture. B-roll film refers to any extra footage shot; filmmakers use it during the editing process to supplement interviews, illustrate and provide context, or smooth transitions between shots that are not consecutive. B-roll footage can also establish background for an issue in the film. For example, in Al Gore's *An Inconvenient Truth*, footage from Hurricane Katrina illustrates issues of global warming.

Design

Use of shots and framing. A film shot is a continuously filmed scene. How material will appear depends on the camera angle and distance between the camera and the subject, among other elements. Filmmakers often use close-up shots to create a sense of intimacy between the subject and audience, and long shots to show a large expanse of space. For instance, the creators of *March of the Penguins* use long shots showing thousands of penguins lined up on an Antarctic ice shelf to emphasize the sheer numbers of penguins, while Errol Morris, creator of *The Fog of War*, uses many close-ups of Robert McNamara to reinforce that the documentary is told from his perspective.

Use of lighting. Filmmakers use lighting to emphasize the subject of their documentaries; they film in natural light when possible, but usually need artificial light

> Making a documentary is all about the post-shoot editing and shaping of a story. Have you ever watched a documentary that you thought could have been better edited? What would you have done differently? #Evaluate

---

👉 **Attention, documentary filmmakers!**

Editing is crucial. If you are shooting video with a cell phone or camera, check out the manual and tutorial that accompanies the device for assistance editing. The same goes for using video-editing software. Tutorials are extremely valuable.

---

to avoid glare and shadows (unless they want shadows, to create a particular effect or mood).

Use of music. Documentary makers edit music into their films to convey emotion, to draw out particular viewer responses to specific scenes, and to smooth transitions between clips. They can also use music to connect a scene to a specific historical moment. For example, if a documentary is focused on the counterculture movement of the 1960s, then the sound editor might decide to include music from the Grateful Dead to orient the viewer to that time.

Use of sound. Filmmakers use sound to emphasize mood, reinforce location, and provide a dynamic experience for viewers, among other things. For example, if filmmakers want viewers to feel a sense of intrusion, they might interrupt a quiet scene with a loud doorbell. If they want to give viewers a sense of a setting, such as a chaotic foreign city, they might use a cacophony of voices from a marketplace. They might also play with volume, varying quietness and loudness, and balancing sound between speakers.

Sources Documentary filmmakers attribute their sources in the ending credits and throughout the film by naming people being interviewed or identifying scenes being shot. Because documentary filmmakers aim to inform, scrupulous citing of sources is very important, and viewers watching a documentary usually know exactly where information in the film came from. In his 2006 documentary *An Inconvenient Truth*, for instance, Al Gore frequently cites specific scientists who provided data for the film.

> Do you have a favorite documentary? If so, how does the filmmaker use sound in that work? What would the film be like without background sound and narration?

☞ **Attention, documentary filmmakers!**

For more information on documentary films, see:

- eHow, "How to Make a Documentary"
- Kenneth Lindenmuth, "How to Make a Documentary Film"

Guided Reading: Documentary Film ▼

Doug Pray

From *Scratch*

Top Documentary Films
Watch Free Documentaries Online. Browse TDF.

Home | Browse Documentaries | Documentary List | Talks / Lectures | The

Scratch

Performing Arts   8 Comments

Scratch is a feature-length film/ DVD that explores the world of the hip-hop DJ. From the birth of hip-hop, when pioneering DJ's began extending breaks on their party records (which helped inspire break dancing and rap), to the invention of scratching and "beat-juggling" vinyl, to its recent explosion as a musical movement called "turntablism", it's a story of unknown underdogs and serious virtuosos who are radically changing the way we hear, play and create music.

The film features some of the world's best DJ's, whether they're famous for solo scratching, competing in international DJ battles, playing for rap artists, or just rocking parties with the most insane records ever dug up.

Check out dynamic performances and interviews with DJ's Q-bert, Mix Master Mike (of the Beastie Boys) Rob Swift and the X-ecutioners, Cut Chemist & NuMark (of Jurassic 5), DJ Craze, The Bullet Proof Space Travelers, Babu (of Dilated Peoples), DJ Krush, DJ Premier (Gang Starr), and others, along with "old-school" innovators like Afrika Bambaataa and GrandWizard Theodore (who is widely acknowledged as having invented the idea of scratching vinyl in the first place).

The film features some of the world's best DJ's, whether they're famous for solo scratching, competing in international DJ battles, playing for rap artists, or just rocking parties with the most insane records ever dug up.

Check out dynamic performances and interviews with DJ's Q-bert, Mix Master Mike (of the Beastie Boys) Rob Swift and the X-ecutioners, Cut Chemist & NuMark (of Jurassic 5), DJ Craze, The Bullet Proof Space Travelers, Babu (of Dilated Peoples), DJ Krush, DJ Premier (Gang Starr), and others, along with "old-school" innovators like Afrika Bambaataa and GrandWizard Theodore (who is widely acknowledged as having invented the idea of scratching vinyl in the first place).

Watch the full documentary now

GRAND WIZARD THEODORE

Filmmaker Doug Pray is the creator of *Scratch*, a 2001 documentary that examines the world of hip-hop music through the lens of the hip-hop DJ. In the film, Pray shows how various turntablists got into the world of scratching (the manipulation of a record on a turntable) and how they improvise and create their art. Pray's documentaries focus on elements of subcultures, including surfing, graffiti, and truck driving. When he chooses a subject for a documentary, he is not usually a participant in that subculture. Instead, he comes at the subject as an outsider. According to Pray, "I like filming people who are dedicated to a unique way of expressing themselves, and I celebrate their art or ideas in film." The following stills from *Scratch* (which can be viewed in its entirety here) have been annotated by the authors. (All images from *Scratch* courtesy of Ernest Meza and Brad Blondheim, Producers.)

What is the director, **Doug Pray**, doing?

THE RHETORICAL SITUATION

Purpose
Audience
Rhetorical appeal
Modes & media

Purpose

Pray's purpose is to inform viewers about different aspects of hip-hop DJing; he does this through the stories and perspectives of influential DJs who created and developed the scratch technique.

Audience

Pray's main viewers are DJs and people interested in hip-hop music and culture. However, given Pray's editorial choices, the film could also appeal to a broader audience, one that doesn't know much about hip-hop or music history.

Rhetorical appeals

Pray establishes **ethos** through the experts he's chosen as subjects; he gains authority by showing

(Continued on p. 438.)

Doug Pray, From *Scratch,* *Continued*

This opening image is accompanied by music, which is not identified by title or artist. The lyrics are "Here's a little story that must be told," a line from a song by the X-ecutioners. The introduction continues with images of driving into New York City at night.

Doug Pray, From *Scratch*, *Continued*

Grand Wizard Theodore, on how he developed the scratch technique. "This one particular day when I came home from school, you know I usually go home and practice, and I was playing music a little bit too loud. And my moms came and banged on the door, 'boom, boom, boom, boom, boom.' 'If you don't cut that music down, you're gonna have to cut it off.' So while she's in the doorway, you know, screaming at me, I was still holding the record, and rubbing the record back and forth. When she left, I was like, hm, that's a pretty good idea. So when she left, I experimented with it. A couple of months. A couple of weeks. Different records. And then, when I was ready, we gave a party, and that's when I first introduced the scratch."

Afrika Bambaataa, on the origins of hip-hop. "This is the famous Bronx River Houses, the home of hip-hop. We also used to say 'the home of God.' And also 'Little Vietnam.' It was crazy at one time, when even police wouldn't even come in. We had a lot of gang violence happening at the time. Also a lot of social awareness that was also happening at the time. So that's why we started the Universe of the Zulu Nation. Trying to take a lot of gang affiliations and turn that into something positive. . . . We started organizing a lot of different people in the street. You know, who had different dance groups. You know, B-boys, B-girls, as well as rappers and graffiti artists, all together to make the whole culture."

THE GENRE'S CONVENTIONS

Elements of the genre
Style
Design
Sources

Elements of the genre

Informs about a topic from a particular perspective. Pray gives an insider's view of scratching, through the point of view of hip-hop DJs.

Based on interviews with experts (primary research). Pray interviews people connected with the hip-hop and turntablism movement, such as Afrika Bambaataa (early hip-hop pioneer and DJ from the South Bronx).

Identifies interviewees. Pray identifies interviewees by name and location, for example, "Grand Wizard Theodore" of "New York City." The labeling also makes clear that interviewees are influential hip-hop DJs.

(Continued on p. 438.)

THE RHETORICAL SITUATION

exactly how DJs create music in a hands-on way.

Pray appeals to viewers' **pathos** (emotions) through the music he chooses, the lighting and setting he chooses, and the general "cool" atmosphere of his film. He furthers this appeal by having influential DJs, such as turntable master Mix Master Mike, discuss their careers and techniques themselves.

Modes & media

Mode = visual, audio, and written Because Pray's documentary is film, the primary mode is visual: He shows viewers what scratch artists do. Specific visuals include the faces of the people he interviewed, close-ups of the turntables, and street scenes giving the viewer a sense of location. Pray also emphasizes the audio component of his film, especially because it's about music. Pray presents the music of his interviewees and also edits in early hip-hop recordings. He uses text-based captions to make clear who is being interviewed and how that artist fits into hip-hop.

Medium = film and digital You can rent *Scratch* as a DVD or stream it for free from the Top Documentary Films site. The film might also be shown at an independent film festival or a hip-hop event.

THE GENRE'S CONVENTIONS

Not staged. Pray films interviewees in their environments. And what they say seems conversational, not scripted or rehearsed.

Use of voice-over. Pray includes narration over some of the scenes; for example, in the frames that show people break-dancing, a narrator explains some of the history of the dance style.

Style

Careful and deliberate editorial choices. For example, Pray sometimes presents a visual image without dialogue, but still conveys meaning.

Level of detail. To capture the skill that goes into turntablism, Pray often focuses the frame on the DJs fingers/hands, showing exactly what it takes to spin.

Tone of interviewees, narrator, and film. The film has a friendly, conversational tone. For example, the DJs speak directly to the camera, and viewers follow them as they shop for records.

Use of B-roll. The opening frames show B-roll footage of driving into New York City at night, which provides context, mood, and location.

Design

Range of shots / atmosphere. Pray uses close-ups and midrange shots. His framing of interviewees creates intimacy. Sometimes he shows only the DJ's hands working the record.

Use of music and sound. Because the film focuses on the art of scratching, the majority of the music and sound comes from actual compositions by the artists. Pray emphasizes the sounds of the scratching.

Sources

Because Pray is an outsider to the world of scratching and hip-hop, he relies on the expertise and experience of hip-hop and scratch artists.

Questions: Analyzing Pray's documentary film

1. Purpose. Watch the entire documentary. How does Pray put the story together? What choices does he make in telling the story?

2. Purpose. Although Pray's main purpose is to inform viewers about the world of scratching and DJing, he also makes some arguments about the DJ subculture. What are his claims regarding DJ culture? Point to specific moments in the documentary to support your answer.

3. Audience. To what extent does Pray's documentary reach beyond an audience already familiar with hip-hop music? Explain.

4. Audience. How does Pray show viewers the differences between hip-hop and rap, and how are these differences developed throughout the documentary?

5. Rhetorical appeals. How does the mix of DJs Pray interviews contribute to the film's ethos and credibility?

6. Modes & media. As you watched the film, which captured your attention more—the audio or the video? Why?

7. Elements of the genre. How does Pray organize the material in his documentary? What is the effect of this organization? How does the order of scenes contribute to his purposes?

8. Elements of the genre. Why does Pray highlight the musicians' locations? What point does he make about scratching in relationship to place?

9. Style. Comment on Pray's emphasis on hands and quick shots between subjects. How do these choices affect his presentation of scratching?

10. Style. How does Pray create smooth transitions between the different people he features? Consider his use of visuals, music, background sound, and B-roll. Look at one specific transition and discuss why you think he made the choices he did.

11. Design. Why do you think the film ends with a piece of nineteenth-century classical music, Edvard Grieg's "In the Hall of the Mountain King," performed and interpreted by the British instrumental group Apollo 100? Fast-forward the *Scratch* video to 1:21:09 (the entire film is 1:27:48); the DJ mixes in "In the Hall of the Mountain King" from that point through the film's wrap-up.

Drafting / Sketching Out a Documentary Film

CHECKLIST: Drafting/Sketching Out a Documentary Film Thinking of drafting a documentary film? Ask yourself the following questions.

WHAT'S MY RHETORICAL SITUATION?

☐ **Purpose.** Which people in my life might make good documentary subjects? Why? What questions do I have about these people? Is there a subculture that I belong to or that I'm interested in that would make an interesting subject for a documentary? Why?

☐ **Audience.** Who are my viewers? What do they care about? Why should/will subject matter to them? What do I want them to learn about my subject? Do I want my audience to be motivated to action? That is, do I want to inform them? Do I want to persuade them? Or a little of both?

☐ **Rhetorical appeals.** How will I present the narrative aspects of my documentary? And how will I establish my authority as a filmmaker? Will I use a narrator, and if so, how reliable will that voice be? To what extent will I appeal to my viewers' emotions? To what extent will I rely on logic to support my interpretations?

☐ **Modes & media.** Do I want viewers to experience my film primarily through visuals? How might I use audio in relation to visuals? Will I use text in the film? What about sound effects and B-roll?

WHAT GENRE CONVENTIONS MATTER?

☐ **Elements of the genre.** Will I use only footage that I shoot or will I integrate archival/historical footage? Should I use voice-over narration? If so, what will be the role of that narration?

☐ **Style.** How will I organize my documentary? How will I inform my viewers and tell the story I want to tell? How will I make the transition between the different parts of my documentary?

☐ **Design.** What types of shots will I want to use? Do I want to focus on close-ups, long-range shots, or midrange shots? How will I frame my subject? For what purpose?

☐ **Sources.** How many people will I interview for my documentary? Will they all be people I know? Will I need to do additional research for the film? Will I need to consult experts in a particular field?

PRACTICE Want to experiment? Sketch out a plan for your own documentary film.

Draft a paragraph or two describing a documentary film you could make about a subject you're interested in (perhaps a hobby, creative outlet, etc.) and that you could treat in an in-depth manner, the way Doug Pray treats hip-hop DJs in *Scratch*. Think about the point of view of your documentary, people you could interview, and potential audiences for your film, and what they might already know about your topic. What do you want your audience to learn from your film? To what extent do you want to persuade them about your topic? How will you organize your information? Will you frame your documentary as a story or use some other type of structure? Remember, all choices you make should contribute to your overall purpose(s) and help you reach your audience(s).

Podcasts and Videos GT

You probably know the definition of *video* and may already have experimented with shooting video on a camera, smartphone, or other device. The term *podcast* may not be as familiar, but the concept is probably more familiar to you than you realize. *Wikipedia* identifies a **podcast** as a "type of digital media consisting of an episodic series of audio files subscribed to and downloaded through Web syndication or streamed online to a computer or mobile device." As podcasts have become more popular, producers have developed video podcasts (or vodcasts) as well as enhanced podcasts that include a variety of still media, graphics, and hyperlinks embedded in the program.

Planning

Video and podcast production is usually exciting, and the resulting project can be an entertaining and powerful expression of your creativity as well as a refreshing approach to presenting your arguments. Audiovisual production is challenging and time-consuming, however, and you may find yourself with a lofty vision for a project that cannot be produced in the time allotted. Therefore, you must plan your project carefully (considering all the relevant rhetorical elements) and manage your expectations about what you can produce and what you hope to achieve (see the "Managing Expectations for Digital and Team Projects" section in Chapter 9). A good rule of thumb is to keep your final video or podcast under five minutes.

Whether you are creating this project on your own or as part of a group, you must plan carefully. Think about where you want to record (in the library, around campus, in your residence), what time of day or night, and who to feature (fellow classmates, friends, people on the street). You'll want to adhere to a well-thought-out schedule and be sure that you do not leave the bulk of your production and postproduction process until just before the project is due.

An extremely valuable tool in planning this type of project is the **storyboard**, which helps you to map out your production frame by frame or section by section. Often you create the storyboard for yourself and any other classmates with whom you are collaborating, but your instructor may also ask you to submit the storyboard as confirmation of your project development, to help ensure your success. (For more on storyboarding, see Chapter 18.)

Writing a Script

Improvisation can be fun, but it can sometimes lead to an unorganized final product. Instead, you need to create a script (which might include occasional improvisation). Not only does a script provide the content (e.g., speaking lines, guidelines about pacing, notes about visual shots, notes about pauses and transitions), it also helps when you are editing the piece: you can consult your script to ensure you have incorporated all necessary elements or to determine which pieces you can edit out while still maintaining the integrity of your project.

Checking Your Equipment

How are you going to record audio and video? Do you have a camera, a smartphone, or an e-device with a microphone and camera? Does your computer come equipped with editing software? If you need to rely on equipment and software available through the Georgia Tech Library or some other campus resource, you'll want to reserve it far in advance and have a backup plan if it is not available. Many of these projects are assigned toward the end of a semester as part of a final project, so many students want to take advantage of this equipment at the same time.

Drafting

Recording and postproduction comprise the drafting process of an A/V project. In this phase, you shoot video, choose still images and music, record interviews and voice-overs, and identify where you want to include onscreen graphics. The postproduction process includes putting all of these pieces together: editing audio and video, adding the graphics, and mixing the audio. You should approach postproduction in two phases: you first produce a "rough cut" of your project to ensure that you have the pieces you need in the proper order, and then you refine that version through a series of further edits and revisions to make it polished and professional.

Reviewing, Revising, and Editing

Video and podcasting software such as iMovie, GarageBand, and Audacity provide editing and testing modes to allow you to add, delete, and adjust any component of your project. Take full advantage of this opportunity to ensure that the graphics you have chosen show cleanly on the screen and that the soundtrack you have added fades in and out smoothly at the beginning and ending of your piece; if you use more than one piece of music in your soundtrack, check that the transitions are seamless. Also make sure that the sound levels are equalized and that a voice-over is clearly audible over the soundtrack or any other ambient noise. To ensure this professional result, you should record any voice-overs in a quiet room without distracting background noise and listen to your project through headphones to confirm that sound levels are properly balanced. You can ask your instructor how to reserve the recording booth in the Stephen C. Hall Building, a room designed just for that purpose.

Publishing and Submitting

Before you submit your video or podcast project, confirm with your instructor the format in which you should submit it. One factor in deciding how to submit your project is determining which file format your instructor is able to view. If you choose a .wmv (Windows Media Viewer) file format, for example, and your instructor uses a Mac, your instructor will not be able to open that file. Currently, three relatively easy ways exist to deliver an audio, video, or mixed media project:

1. Copy the media file to a DVD and deliver it to your instructor in person.

2. Send the file electronically (via email, T-Square, or a cloud delivery service such as Dropbox or Google Drive). If you choose this option, be aware that video files can be very large, and Wi-Fi delivery may take a significant amount of time. Your upload session may even close unexpectedly.

3. Upload the file to a media-sharing service such as YouTube. In many ways, this option may be the most efficient, since it provides a streaming browser-based experience that your instructor can access from any type of Internet-connected device. Two words of caution, however. First, choose the "not visible" setting when you upload your media file, so that only people to whom you give access may view your project. Second, keep in mind that this project may be included in your final portfolio, and you will, therefore, need to ensure that the link you submit is active until the time of your graduation from Georgia Tech.

15 PERSUASIVE GENRES

CONTENTS

TRY TO SEE THINGS FROM MY POINT OF VIEW.

◀ POLITICAL CARTOON
Rex F. May
Reprinted by permission of Rex May.

e For e-Pages content, visit **bedfordstmartins.com /bookofgenres.**

Open your Web browser, page through any magazine, or take a walk to the coffee shop, and you will be barraged by texts and media created to persuade you—to think something, do something, like something, or buy something. Depending on the source you look at, city-dwelling Americans see between three thousand and five thousand ads per day.*

For an Index of Sources & Contexts for material referenced in this chapter, see the e-Pages at **bedfordstmartins.com /bookofgenres.**

Online, advertisers individualize their messages to you. For example, when you log on to Amazon.com you are greeted with a list of recommendations based on your previous purchases. On Facebook, the ads on your page are generated according to your likes and dislikes, and other information you provide in your profile and posts.

While advertising is probably the most pervasive of persuasive genres, we create lots of other kinds of texts at home, work, and school in order to convince others to see things our way. In fact, you could argue that almost every communication—a text message to a friend about what movie to see, an online posting of a cute kitten or puppy, a Match.com profile, an editorial on CNN about the economy, a joke made on *The Simpsons* about the editorial on Fox News, or even a chapter in a textbook—has persuasive elements built into it.

The Rhetorical Situation

Purpose: Why write to persuade?

When we write to persuade, we do so because we want to convince our readers of something—usually to agree with us about a topic, issue, or idea, or to take a specific action. As a student, when you write a paper in which you take a stance on an issue or you give a speech in which you ask your audience to do something, you are writing to persuade. As a professional, when you apply for a job, you craft a resume and cover letter and make a convincing case for yourself during your

▲ AD
Match.com
Have ads like this popped up in your browser window? According to Match.com, "1 in 5 relationships start online." *Courtesy of Match.com.*

*According to a study done by the journal *Pediatrics*, "The average young person views more than 3,000 ads per day on television (TV), on the Internet, on billboards, and in magazines" (see "Children, Adolescents, and Advertising," December 1, 2006). According to an article by Walter Kirn, published in *The New York Times Magazine*, "[R]esearchers estimate that the average city dweller is exposed to 5,000 ads per day, up from 2,000 per day three decades ago" (see "Here, There, and Everywhere," February 11, 2007).

▲ BUMPER STICKER
Imagina Productions.

interview in order to persuade the person hiring that you are the best candidate. A persuasive text can be as simple as a six-word slogan.

Audience: How do we persuade others?

As citizens of a democracy, we may read persuasive texts, such as editorials, to help us figure out our own positions on specific issues. For instance, during election season, you might pay close attention to the opinion pages of local and national newspapers. The editorial boards of these newspapers publish editorials in which they try to convince you who to vote for, how to think of specific issues, and why.

Like the editorial board of *The New York Times*, any time you want to persuade your audience, you need to lay out your ideas, anticipate possible objections, and support your argument with relevant information. As with reporting information (see Chapter 14), accuracy is important when it comes to persuading others. Backing up your ideas and claims with correct information, gathered from reliable sources, will make your argument stronger.

The *Times* editorial board was well aware of their audience—which tends to be liberal, Democratic, and educated—when they wrote the piece on page 447 during the 2008 presidential election. The editors wrote: "We believe [Barack Obama] has the will and ability to forge the broad political consensus that is essential to finding solutions to this nation's problems." They supported their argument by contrasting Obama with his opponent, John McCain, and by providing carefully chosen details of Obama's platform and the choices he made as a senator.

Rhetorical Appeals: How do we use ethos, logos, and pathos to persuade?

Whether you want to convince others to agree with you on an important issue, to date you, to vote for your candidate, or to buy your product, you will be most persuasive if you relate to

What texts in your immediate surroundings (billboards, ads, etc.) are meant to persuade you of something? What persuasive techniques are evident? Which texts are most convincing? Why? #Apply #Evaluate

ONLINE EDITORIAL ▶
***The New York Times* Editorial Board**
"Barack Obama for President." *From The New York Times,*
October 23, 2013 © 2013 The New York Times. All rights reserved.

The New York Times

Opinion

EDITORIAL

Barack Obama for President

Published: October 23, 2008

Hyperbole is the currency of presidential campaigns, but this year the nation's future truly hangs in the balance.

Multimedia

K   Interactive Feature
New York Times Endorsements
Through the Ages

Related

Times Topics: Barack Obama

The United States is battered and drifting after eight years of President Bush's failed leadership. He is saddling his successor with two wars, a scarred global image and a government systematically stripped of its ability to protect and help its citizens — whether they are fleeing a hurricane's floodwaters, searching for affordable health care or struggling to hold on to their homes, jobs, savings and pensions in the midst of a financial crisis that was foretold and preventable.

As tough as the times are, the selection of a new president is easy. After nearly two years of a grueling and ugly campaign, Senator Barack Obama of Illinois has proved that he is the right choice to be the 44th president of the United States.

Mr. Obama has met challenge after challenge, growing as a leader and putting real flesh on his early promises of hope and change. He has shown a cool head and sound judgment. We believe he has the will and the ability to forge the broad political consensus that is essential to finding solutions to this nation's problems.

In the same time, Senator John McCain of Arizona has retreated farther and farther to the fringe of American politics, running a campaign on partisan division, class warfare and even hints of racism. His policies and worldview are mired in the past. His choice of a running mate was so evidently unfit for the office was a final act of opportunism and bad judgment that eclipsed the accomplishments of 26 years in Congress.

Given the particularly ugly nature of Mr. McCain's campaign, the urge to choose on the basis of raw emotion is strong. But there is a greater value in looking closely at the facts of life in America today and at the prescriptions the candidates offer. The differences are profound.

Mr. McCain offers more of the Republican every-man-for-himself ideology, now lying in shards on Wall Street and in Americans' bank accounts. Mr. Obama has another vision of government's role and responsibilities.

In his convention speech in Denver, Mr. Obama said, "Government cannot solve all our problems, but what it should do is that which we cannot do for ourselves: protect us from harm and provide every child a decent education; keep our water clean and our toys safe; invest in new schools and new roads and new science and technology."

Since the financial crisis, he has correctly identified the abject failure of government regulation that has brought the markets to the brink of collapse.

The Economy

The American financial system is the victim of decades of Republican deregulatory and anti-tax policies. Those ideas have been proved wrong at an unfathomable price, but Mr. McCain — a self-proclaimed "foot soldier in the Reagan revolution" — is still a believer.

Mr. Obama sees that far-reaching reforms will be needed to protect Americans and American business.

Mr. McCain talks about reform a lot, but his vision is pinched. His answer to any economic question is to eliminate pork-barrel spending — about $18 billion in a $3 trillion budget — cut taxes and wait for unfettered markets to solve the problem.

Mr. Obama is clear that the nation's tax structure must be changed to make it fairer. That means the well-off Americans who have benefited disproportionately from Mr. Bush's tax cuts will have to pay some more. Working Americans, who have seen their standard of living fall and their children's options narrow, will benefit. Mr. Obama wants to raise the minimum wage and tie it to inflation, restore a climate in which workers are able to organize unions if they wish and expand educational opportunities.

Mr. McCain, who once opposed President Bush's tax cuts for the wealthy as fiscally irresponsible, now wants to make them permanent. And while he talks about keeping taxes low for everyone, his proposed cuts would overwhelmingly benefit the top 1 percent of Americans while digging the country into a deeper fiscal hole.

National Security

The American military — its people and equipment — is dangerously overstretched. Mr. Bush has neglected the necessary war in Afghanistan, which now threatens to spiral into defeat. The unnecessary and staggeringly costly war in Iraq must be ended as quickly and responsibly as possible.

While Iraq's leaders insist on a swift drawdown of American troops and a deadline for the end of the occupation, Mr. McCain is still talking about some ill-defined "victory." As a result, he has offered no real plan for extracting American troops and limiting any further damage to Iraq and its neighbors.

Mr. Obama was an early and thoughtful opponent of the war in Iraq, and he has presented a military and diplomatic plan for withdrawing American forces. Mr. Obama also has correctly warned that until the Pentagon starts pulling troops out of Iraq, there will not be enough troops to defeat the Taliban and Al Qaeda in Afghanistan.

Mr. McCain, like Mr. Bush, has only belatedly focused on Afghanistan's dangerous unraveling and the threat that neighboring Pakistan may quickly follow.

Mr. Obama would have a learning curve on foreign affairs, but he has already showed sounder judgment than his opponent on these critical issues. His choice of Senator Joseph Biden — who has deep foreign-policy expertise — as his running mate is another sign of that sound judgment. Mr. McCain's long interest in foreign policy and the many dangers this country now faces make his choice of Gov. Sarah Palin of Alaska more irresponsible.

Both presidential candidates talk about strengthening alliances in Europe and Asia, including NATO, and strongly support Israel. Both candidates talk about repairing America's image in the world. But is seems clear to us that Mr. Obama is far more likely to do that — and not just because the first black president would present a new American face to the world.

Mr. Obama wants to reform the United Nations, while Mr. McCain wants to create a new entity, the League of Democracies — a move that would incite even fiercer anti-American furies around the world.

Unfortunately, Mr. McCain, like Mr. Bush, sees the world as divided into friends (like Georgia) and adversaries (like Russia). He proposed kicking Russia out of the Group of 8 industrialized nations even before the invasion of Georgia. We have no sympathy for Moscow's bullying, but we also have no desire to replay the cold war. The United States must find a way to constrain the Russians' worst impulses, while preserving the ability to work with them on arms control and other vital initiatives.

Both candidates talk tough on terrorism, and neither has ruled out military action to end Iran's nuclear weapons program. But Mr. Obama has called for a serious effort to try to wean Tehran from its nuclear ambitions with more credible diplomatic overtures and tougher sanctions. Mr. McCain's willingness to joke about bombing Iran was frightening.

The Constitution and the Rule of Law

Under Mr. Bush and Vice President Dick Cheney, the Constitution, the Bill of Rights, the justice system and the separation of powers have come under relentless attack. Mr. Bush chose to exploit the tragedy of Sept. 11, 2001, the moment in which he looked like the president of a unified nation, to try to place himself above the law.

Mr. Bush has arrogated the power to imprison men without charges and browbeat Congress into granting an unfettered authority to spy on Americans. He has created untold number of "black" programs, including secret prisons and outsourced torture.

The president has issued hundreds, if not thousands, of secret orders. We fear it will take years of forensic research to discover how many basic rights have been violated.

Both candidates have renounced torture and are committed to closing the prison camp in Guantánamo Bay, Cuba.

But Mr. Obama has gone beyond that, promising to identify and correct Mr. Bush's attacks on the democratic system. Mr. McCain has been silent on the subject.

Mr. McCain improved protections for detainees. But then he helped the White House push through the appalling Military Commissions Act of 2006, which denied detainees the right to a hearing in a real court and put Washington in conflict with the Geneva Conventions, greatly increasing the risk to American troops.

The next president will have the chance to appoint one or more justices to a Supreme Court that is on the brink of being dominated by a radical right wing. Mr. Obama may appoint less liberal judges than some of his followers might like, but Mr. McCain is certain to pick rigid ideologues. He has said he would never appoint a judge who believes in women's reproductive rights.

The Candidates

It will be an enormous challenge just to get the nation back to where it was before Mr. Bush, to begin to mend its image in the world and to restore its self-confidence and its self-respect. Doing all of that, and leading America forward, will require strength of will, character and intellect, sober judgment and a cool, steady hand.

Mr. Obama has those qualities in abundance. Watching him being tested in the campaign has long since erased the reservations that led us to endorse Senator Hillary Rodham Clinton in the Democratic primaries. He has drawn in legions of new voters with powerful messages of hope and possibility and calls for shared sacrifice and social responsibility.

Mr. McCain, whom we chose as the best Republican nominee in the primaries, has spent the last coins of his reputation for principle and sound judgment to placate the limitless demands and narrow vision of the far-right wing. His righteous fury at being driven out of the 2000 primaries on a racist tide aimed at his adopted daughter has been replaced by a zealous embrace of those same win-at-all-costs tactics and tacticians.

He surrendered his standing as an independent thinker in his rush to embrace Mr. Bush's misbegotten tax policies and to abandon his leadership position on climate change and immigration reform.

Mr. McCain could have seized the high ground on energy and the environment. Earlier in his career, he offered the first plausible bill to control America's emissions of greenhouse gases. Now his positions are a caricature of that record: think Ms. Palin leading chants of "drill, baby, drill."

Mr. Obama has endorsed some offshore drilling, but as part of a comprehensive strategy including big investments in new, clean technologies.

Mr. Obama has withstood some of the toughest campaign attacks ever mounted against a candidate. He's been called un-American and accused of hiding a secret Islamic faith. The Republicans have linked him to domestic terrorists and questioned his wife's love of her country. Ms. Palin has also questioned millions of Americans' patriotism, calling Republican-leaning states "pro-America."

This politics of fear, division and character assassination helped Mr. Bush drive Mr. McCain from the 2000 Republican primaries and defeat Senator John Kerry in 2004. It has been the dominant theme of his failed presidency.

The nation's problems are simply too grave to be reduced to slashing "robo-calls" and negative ads. This country needs sensible leadership, compassionate leadership, honest leadership and strong leadership. Barack Obama has shown that he has all of those qualities.

your audience through the rhetorical appeals—ethos, logos, and pathos.

Ethos, the authority and trustworthiness that you establish as a writer, composer, or speaker, is crucial when you want to persuade others. For example, if your boss asks you to review several possible locations for an important fund-raising event and recommend one, you will want to establish yourself as dedicated to getting a high-quality venue for a reasonable price. To do this, you'll need to demonstrate that you've taken the assignment seriously, studied the options objectively, and weighed your company's needs and priorities carefully.

Here's another example. Way back in 1981, horror writer Stephen King wrote an essay about why horror films are popular. Because he was already established as a best-selling horror author with titles like *Carrie* (1974) and *The Shining* (1977), both of which had already been made into successful horror movies, he had instant credibility, with which he developed an ethos as an expert on his subject. He went further than that, however, citing many examples throughout the essay to establish that he knows more than just his own experience. Here is an excerpt from the essay:

> We also go to re-establish our feelings of essential normality; the horror movie is innately conservative, even reactionary. Freda Jackson as the horrible melting woman in *Die, Monster, Die!* confirms for us that no matter how far we may be removed from the beauty of a Robert Redford or a Diana Ross, we are still light-years from true ugliness.
> —**Stephen King,** from "Why We Crave Horror Movies"

Are there particular types of persuasive texts you automatically trust? Distrust? Why? #Apply

King furthers his ethos by taking his subject seriously and speaking specifically about it.

Logos, the logical chain of reasoning that you provide for readers, is extremely important when you are making any kind of argument. Imagine you are taking a car for a test drive to decide whether you will buy it. You might mention to the salesperson that you are interested in a car that won't be too bad for the environment. The salesperson might then present you with some facts about the mileage the car gets, the measures the manufacturer has taken at the factory to protect the environment, and the paper-free policy the dealership has initiated by conducting as much business as possible electronically. By talking to you about these factors, the salesperson is creating a chain of reasoning that—she hopes—will lead you to conclude that the car you are driving is an environmentally responsible choice.

Let's look at an example of a verbal argument made by media scholar Johanna Blakley. She gave a presentation about social media that was videotaped and published online by TED, a nonprofit open-source site devoted to "ideas worth spreading." In her TED talk, Blakley makes a case for how people connect. She says:

> [People] don't aggregate around age, gender, income. They aggregate around the things they love, the things that they like. And if you think about it, shared interests and values are a far more powerful aggregator of human beings than demographic categories. I'd much rather know whether you like *Buffy the Vampire Slayer* rather than how old you are. That would tell me something more substantial about you.
> —**Johanna Blakley,** from "Social Media and the End of Gender"

Notice how—after making her claim that people aggregate around their interests—she gives a specific example about interest in *Buffy the Vampire Slayer* being a better indicator than age of how much people have in common with each other.

Pathos is the appeal that you use when you want to evoke your readers' emotions. This comes in handy when you are trying to persuade someone to do something. An appeal to pathos connects you with your audience, and vice versa. For example, when a salesperson asks you about yourself and then tells you a bit about himself and you find some commonalities, that salesperson is appealing to your pathos. When he later tells you that he loves the stereo you are looking at, you're more likely to buy it because you've already identified with him.

Advertisers often appeal to pathos. For example, a commercial for Tide Free & Gentle detergent begins with a little girl trying on pairs of tights as a motherly woman's voice says:

> "Picking the right tights isn't always easy. Picking a free detergent is."

As the commercial continues, the girl frolics around her room, posing in front of her mirror in different pairs of tights, as the motherly voice continues talking about how Tide Free & Gentle detergent will ensure that whichever tights the girl picks, they will be clean and free of anything that can irritate her skin.

By focusing on the cuteness and innocence of the little girl, the ad equates a mother's desire to keep her daughter safe with choosing Tide Free & Gentle detergent. The advertisers associate protectiveness and love with the detergent itself.

Modes & Media: How can they help you persuade?

Following is a breakdown of the modes and media of some of the compositions presented in this chapter:

PERSUASIVE GENRES	Mode	Medium
AD Match.com (p. 445)	VISUAL AND WRITTEN	DIGITAL
BUMPER STICKER Imagina Productions, "Don't Text & Drive" (p. 446)	WRITTEN	PRINT
ONLINE EDITORIAL *The New York Times* Editorial Board, "Barack Obama for President" (p. 447)	VISUAL AND WRITTEN	DIGITAL

ONLINE & TV AD	VISUAL AND AUDIO	DIGITAL
Tide Free & Gentle detergent commercial (p. 450)		(ONLINE AND ON TELEVISION)

The Genre's Conventions

Elements of the Genre: What does all persuasive writing have in common?

Persuasive writers aim to change the reader's or viewer's mind in some way. Different authors and artists may use different strategies for achieving this, but most effective persuasive communication has two elements in common:

1. *Makes an explicit argument/position statement.* When writers state exactly what they'd like readers or viewers to do or think, then there is no guesswork involved. Many persuasive writers present an explicit position statement, such as "Voters should support Proposition 2 because it will reduce taxes in the long run." Others may strongly imply, but not explicitly state, the case they're making. The text of an ad won't always say, "Buy this product," but you get that idea from the use of persuasive images and text; ad writers make clear what they're trying to persuade you of, often without using direct language.

2. *Taps into audiences' values and emotions.* Most persuasive writers appeal to their readers' or viewers' sensibilities in some way. While this is true of most writers, it's particularly true of writers who want to persuade; it's essential to tap into ethos, pathos, and/or logos. Ethos is especially important because most readers will not be convinced by an unreliable author.

Style: How does it help you persuade?

When you want to persuade others, present your ideas in a way that will hold your readers' (or listeners' or viewers') attention. You will need their attention before you can make your specific arguments. You can do this with certain stylistic techniques—as well as through the voice and tone you use.

Let's look at an example. On January 8, 2011, Congresswoman Gabrielle Giffords and eighteen others were shot in a supermarket parking lot in Tucson, Arizona. Six people died. A few days later, President Obama gave a speech in Tucson that paid tribute to the injured and killed; the speech was also designed to persuade Americans not to blame each other or a particular political party for the tragedy (though the gunman was later described as mentally ill by the judge at his sentencing, early reports had circulated that his politics had inspired his actions). He began with a greeting to those present, noted the occasion for the speech, and said something about each person killed in the shooting. Then Obama moved on:

> [A]t a time when our discourse has become so sharply polarized—at a time when we are far too eager to lay the blame for all that ails the world at the feet of those who happen to think differently than we do—it's important for us to pause for a moment and make sure that we're talking with each other in a way that heals, not in a way that wounds. . . .
>
> Yes, we have to examine all the facts behind this tragedy. We cannot and will not be passive in the face of such violence. We should be willing to challenge old assumptions in order to lessen the prospects of such violence in the future. But what we cannot do is use this tragedy as one more occasion to turn on each other. That we cannot do. That we cannot do.
>
> As we discuss these issues, let each of us do so with a good dose of humility. Rather than pointing fingers or assigning blame, let's use this occasion to expand our moral imaginations, to listen to each other more carefully, to sharpen our instincts for empathy and remind ourselves of all the ways that our hopes and dreams are bound together.
>
> —**Barack Obama,** from his speech "Together We Thrive: Tucson and America," University of Arizona, January 12, 2011

Notice the structure of the excerpt above. Obama moves from providing context to actively presenting an argument to his listeners. One of his techniques is to use repetition to reinforce what he says. For example, he uses the phrase "at a time when" twice in the first sentence to keep listeners engaged; he uses the line "we cannot do" three times in order to emphasize his case that we cannot "turn on each other" during a divisive moment. Notice, too, the mix of long and very short sentences that create variety for listeners.

In this speech, Obama's tone is friendly but also serious and presidential.

Design: What is the best format for persuading?

Consider the Nike logo. Ever wonder who designed it? As it happens, in 1971 a graphic arts student at Portland State University named Carolyn Davidson created the Nike swoosh symbol, which became one of the most successful logos of all time. Years later, the ad firm Wieden + Kennedy penned the slogan "Just Do It." The campaign is noted by *Advertising Age* as one of the Top 100 Advertising Campaigns of the twentieth century. Why? Because the swoosh design and the slogan are clear, simple, and memorable. These are the qualities that make the campaign persuasive.

The design of a piece can contribute to its persuasiveness or work against it. Consider someone trying to convince you that he is a calm and patient person. Imagine that he is wearing a bright red T-shirt with the slogan "Don't think! Just *act!*" Chances are that the design of this person's wardrobe would work against persuading you that he is calm and patient.

Sources: What research should you draw on to persuade others?

To be persuasive, use sources to develop your credibility, to draw on for facts, and to support your claims and objectives. For example, if Liz wants to persuade her dean to send her to a conference, she'll need to do some research about the conference and then make a case for how the conference and the dean's goals are related.

In the composition on page 454, artist Dominic Episcopo aims to persuade viewers that, figuratively, America is "made of meat." In creating this piece, which is part of his "Meat America" series, he may have had in mind any or all of the following factors: high U.S. obesity rates, high levels of cholesterol and heart disease, or the country's dependence on a system of raising cattle that is hard on the environment and animals.

To support the argument he makes in his sculpture, Episcopo could draw on sources of information on meat consumption in the United States and its effects. For example, he could draw on the data in the chart on page 455 that shows the rise of Americans' beef consumption—from 63 pounds per person per year in 1950 to 85.56 pounds per person in 2010 (with the greatest consumption in 1975). Published by the Humane Society, this chart uses government census and USDA data, which makes it a particularly solid source.

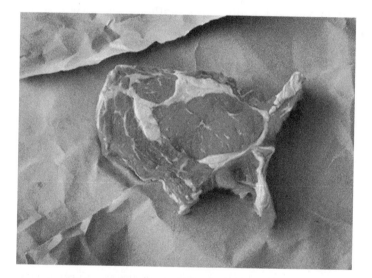

◀ PHOTO
▶ SCULPTURE &
▼ WEB SITE
Dominic Episcopo
"United Steaks of America" (right), a work included at meatamerica.com (bottom). *Three images: Dominic Episcopo.*

MEAT AMERICA | By Dominic Episcopo

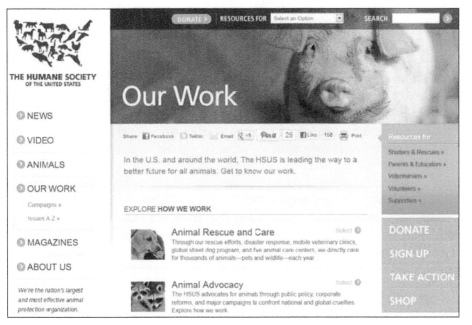

When you write to persuade, how do you use sources to support your argument? What types of sources are most persuasive? Why? #Understand

▲ WEB SITE & ▼ CHART

The Humane Society of the United States

"U.S. Per Capita Meat Consumption" and humanesociety.org. *The Humane Society of the United States homepage.*

ADVERTISEMENTS

An advertisement is any text created to persuade consumers to purchase a product or service. Print advertising is as old as the first newspapers, which appeared in England in the 1600s. Today, ads are everywhere and are presented in a variety of print and digital media. Advertisers spend large amounts of money to research potential customers and then tailor and distribute sales messages that will appeal to those consumers and translate into sales. The money they spend on Web advertising, in particular, is on the rise, especially display ads (banners and video ads). The Interactive Advertising Bureau (IAB), in its 2012 report, indicates record online ad revenues, with a 15 percent and more than $1 billion increase over 2011. The *Los Angeles Times* and eMarketer.com report that while advertisers still spend on print ads, they're spending more of their budgets on digital ads; by 2016 online ad spending is likely to nearly double ($62 billion), leaving print far behind ($32 billion).

How do you know when you are (or aren't) the target audience for an ad? Have you ever been offended or alienated by an ad? If so, why?
#Understand
#Evaluate

CHART ▶
eMarketer.com/
Los Angeles Times
"U.S. Print vs. Online Ad Spending, 2011–2016." *eMarketer, Inc.*

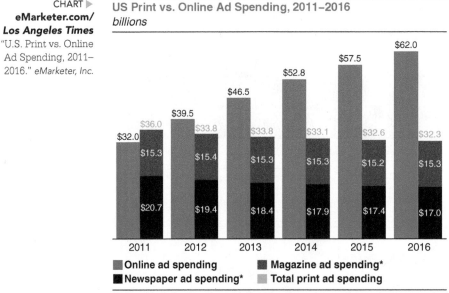

US Print vs. Online Ad Spending, 2011–2016
billions

$62.0
$57.5
$52.8
$46.5
$39.5
$36.0 $33.8 $33.8 $33.1 $32.6 $32.3
$32.0
$15.3 $15.4 $15.3 $15.3 $15.2 $15.3
$20.7 $19.4 $18.4 $17.9 $17.4 $17.0

2011   2012   2013   2014   2015   2016

■ Online ad spending   ■ Magazine ad spending*
■ Newspaper ad spending*   ■ Total print ad spending

Note: eMarketer benchmarks its US online ad spending projections against the IAB/PWC data, for which the last full year measured was 2010; eMarketer benchmarks its US newspaper ad spending projections against the NAA data, for which the last full year measured was 2010; *print only
Source: eMarketer, Jan 2012
136019   www.eMarketer.com

Analyzing Advertisements: What to Look For

Purpose   To sell their products and services, companies need to publicize information about what they're offering. They also need to win business from competitors. For example, the well-known Progressive auto insurance commercials advertise the company's "comparison shopping" feature, as shown below, to inform shoppers of their rates versus those of other carriers and support their claim that with Progressive, "You could save over $475 on car insurance."

◀ONLINE AD
Progressive
"Compare Rates."
Courtesy of Progressive.

Audience   When major advertising firms such as the Ad Agency, Arnold Worldwide, and Wieden + Kennedy create ads, they have a very clear picture of their target market, and they aim their branding, visuals, messages, and other persuasive tools squarely at that market. For example, the Old Spice commercials of 2010, featuring the actor Isaiah Mustafa, clearly target a young, tech-savvy, heterosexual female demographic. The creators of these quirky ads (Wieden + Kennedy) dusted off an old brand of men's cologne and made it more appealing to a new audience by using humor, personality, and a supersuave ladies' man. Originally released on YouTube and then as a Super Bowl commercial, the "Old Spice Guy" ad went viral within a few days, getting more than thirty-four million views in less than a week.

In the ad, Mustafa says: "Hello, ladies, look at your man, now back to me, now back at your man, now back to me. Sadly, he isn't me, but if he stopped using ladies' scented body wash and switched to Old Spice, he could smell like he's me. Look down, back up, where are you? You're on a boat with the man your man could smell like. What's in your hand, back at me. I have it, it's an oyster with two tickets to that thing you love. Look again, the tickets are now diamonds. Anything is possible when your man smells like Old Spice and not a lady. I'm on a horse." Then comes the voiceover: *Smell like a man, man. Old Spice.*"

Rhetorical appeals   Advertisers use appeals to ethos (authority), logos (logic), and pathos (emotion). Many ads that feature expert testimonials or celebrity endorsements, for example, make use of ethos; if you trust the expert giving the testimonial, you are more likely to trust the product. A product that has been long established, such as Old Spice, which has been around for more than seventy years, has its own built-in ethos. The advertisers of Old Spice further establish its ethos by emphasizing the macho quality of the product and choosing a super-fit actor with a deep voice to star in the commercial. The advertisers also appeal to viewers' sense of pathos—tapping into their desire to buy the product, even though it is a nonessential item.

Modes & media   As more reading and viewing happen online, more advertising will happen there too. A digital ad, such as the Old Spice commercial mentioned above, has the potential to spread through social media and YouTube, giving advertisers more "bang for the buck." In terms of the medium, some online ads are static (e.g., display ads that don't move) while others are videos or animations that incorporate sound. There are even reports of a new medium called "smell-vertising": a product's scent is broadcast in an area with potential consumers of the product.

Think of an ad that features a visual image that doesn't directly relate to the product being promoted. What is the product? The visual? Why might the ad creators have made this choice? #Analyze

Elements of the genre

Headlines. Advertisers use headlines to immediately attract the reader's attention. The headline often conveys the product's benefits through concise language. Additionally, advertisers pay special attention to the placement of the headline, ensuring that it is not obscured or overwhelmed by a visual element. In the case of some electronic ads, a headline may be read aloud by a narrator.

Visuals. Graphics work together with the headline to attract the reader. They also illustrate the point or provide visual evidence that supports the product's claim. In television commercials, advertisers edit the visuals to hold viewers' attention, maintaining a quick pace and not lingering for too long on one image.

Ad copy. Advertisers use the words of an advertisement, or ad copy, for specific purposes. They use a headline to get a consumer's attention and then draw the reader in further with an intriguing subheading. Copy that is not a headline or heading is called body text, and it tells about the benefits of the product or service and either implicitly or explicitly tells the consumer to make a purchase. Digital and TV ads also feature ad copy—it can be spoken and/or animated on the screen.

Advertising slogans. Advertisers often associate sayings or phrases with a product. For example, Nike's slogan is "Just Do It."

Signature. Usually found toward the bottom of a print ad, the signature includes the advertiser name and contact information. In digital and TV ads, contact information is not normally provided, but the brand and product name is made clear.

Style

Technique. The writing tends to be brief and directive. For example, in the original Smokey the Bear advertisements, Smokey addresses the reader: "Only YOU can prevent forest fires!" Words are usually secondary to visuals. Visuals are carefully selected as persuasive tools (see "Design" below). Because digital and TV ads are very short (usually thirty seconds or less), words are limited.

Details. Advertisers usually keep details (and words, in general) to a minimum.

Voice and tone. In a commercial, voice and tone can give the viewer an impression of the product's benefits. For example, if a company is promoting its product's ability to relieve stress, then the tone of the ad is usually soothing. If a financial company is advertising its services, then the tone is usually reassuring. Written ad copy conveys its tone through word choice and phrasing, while digital and TV ads convey tone through vocal intonation, pacing, and the qualities of the voice itself (male or female, deep or high, etc.).

Design

Visual of the product. Advertisers need to provide an image of what they're selling so consumers can identify and purchase it. If the product is less tangible (or not an object), such as an auto insurance policy, then some kind of visual emphasizes the message. For example, in some Geico ads, a caveman is the main visual, emphasizing how easy it is to purchase auto insurance.

Additional pathos-building images. Advertisers use visuals to convey ideas and tap into viewers' emotions. For example, in a commercial for Abilify (a drug used mainly to treat depression), the advertiser presents "before" and "after" images. The commercial begins with a series of people looking stressed, sad, and unable to do anything. The drug is introduced, followed by a series of visuals showing the same people engaged with life and smiling.

Color. Advertisers can further appeal to pathos by using images and colors associated with particular emotions.

Product logos. Advertisers carefully design product logos to convey particular ideas and values about a product. For example, the Nike swoosh indicates speed and movement. All Nike products and advertisements feature the swoosh, which is instantly identifiable and long established.

Layout. In a print-based ad (or a static Web ad), the layout orients the reader and establishes the most important pieces of information. The main visual and headline are the most prominent in the advertisement; contact info and fine print are usually somewhere toward the bottom of the piece. Advertisers use similar principles in digital and TV commercials to make the featured product and message clear and conspicuous.

Sources   Advertising agencies conduct market research before creating ad campaigns so they can most efficiently identify and target their main audience and tailor their overall message accordingly. Once they've identified some possible directions for the content and design, they may ask a test audience to determine which ad will be most successful. Sources noted within an ad can include a company Web site where consumers can find more information about the product.

Danone/Evian and Havas Worldwide

Detox with Evian

The Evian brand of spring water is promoted as a natural product "from the heart of the French Alps." The Danone company introduced Evian to the United States in the 1970s, mostly in luxury hotels and expensive restaurants. Since then, they have associated the brand with luxury and have often used celebrities and people from the fashion industry to build its appeal.

Among the many ads for Evian is the notable "Detox" campaign of 2006. This campaign stressed the health benefits of drinking Evian, arguing that the water helps people maintain youthfulness and purity. Youthfulness is a theme that recurs in Evian's campaigns, including their current "Live Young" campaign that invites customers to post photos and participate in a video campaign.

To create the "Detox" campaign, Danone/Evian worked with the ad firm Havas Worldwide (formerly known as Euro RSCG). The firm also created Evian's popular "Live Young" campaign. Havas Worldwide creates ads and marketing plans for many major companies and is one of the largest advertising and marketing agencies in the world.

Danone/Evian also hired a firm called Codegent to create the digital marketing pieces for the "Detox" campaign. Copy on Codegent's site reads: "We've worked on Evian campaigns for a couple of years, now: the Detox with Evian campaign that was in conjunction with the on-pack promotion and the Evian Live Young campaign which also featured TV advertising. Bringing brands to life online, it's a great job."

Annotations in the margins of the Evian ad on page 462 point out the choices that Evian made in terms of their purpose, sense of audience, and use of rhetorical appeals. You'll also see notes on how this work reflects the conventions of the advertising genre—in terms of its persuasive appeal and specific techniques. *(Source for image on p. 462: various publications.)*

▲ WEB SITE
Danone
Owner of Evian spring water.

The ad copy reads: "Return to purity with water from the French Alps that's been naturally filtered for over 15 years."

THE RHETORICAL SITUATION

Purpose

Havas Worldwide, the creators of this ad (hired by Danone/Evian), hope to persuade consumers to buy Evian water.

Audience

The ad creators are aiming at people looking for health benefits and/or people who want to "detoxify." (Note that this ad appeared right after New Year's Eve 2006, and the idea of detoxifying had been very popular that year.) The audience reads magazines (where the print ad appeared) and spends time online (notice the Evian URL in the ad copy).

Rhetorical appeals

The ad appeals mainly to readers' **pathos** (emotion)—by displaying a beautiful landscape and model and by equating both with Evian. The model's nudity implies snow-angel-grade purity. It also—in combination with the giant falling drop—suggests sex. The idea of "detoxing" also plays on readers' worries about health and an "impure" lifestyle.

The ad also conveys Evian's **ethos** through the presentation of the bottle and the emphasis on branding.

Modes & media

Mode = written and visual The advertisers use visuals and a small amount of text to persuade viewers to purchase Evian water. Evian's "Detox" campaign stresses the purity and health benefits of the water, so both the visuals and text convey this point. The text emphasizes this through the headline ("Detox with Evian") and also the body copy ("Return to purity"). The visuals make the claim with pictures of snow-covered alps and a beautiful woman.

Medium = print and digital While this ad appeared in print magazines, it can also be found digitally. Evian's campaigns are designed not only for print, but also for TV and the Internet.

THE GENRE'S CONVENTIONS

Elements of the genre

Presents an argument (visual and textual) for purchasing a product.

The headline, "Detox with Evian," is brief, direct, and directive. The ad copy, "Return to purity with water from the French Alps that's been naturally filtered for over 15 years," suggests the benefits of the water and the process used to filter it; the writers also used directive language (i.e., "Return").

Style

Brief text, with an emphasis on visuals. A central image—a naked woman making a snow angel in the Alps—is used to sell the Evian water.

Design

Color is used to create drama and focus attention. The writers and designers chose cool tones—blue and white—for the snow and water to suggest purity, and chose bright colors—red and pink—for the product name and product shot to highlight the brand.

The layout focuses on the woman's body; the composition suggests purity but also sexuality to entice consumers.

The spatial arrangement emphasizes the Alps, where the water originates. The placement of the woman below the mountain suggests that drinking water that comes from the mountain can make you young and beautiful.

The use of a sans serif typeface and lowercase letters suggests freshness and a contemporary quality. The clean lines of the font reinforce the pure/natural message.

Sources

Havas Worldwide most likely researched a variety of images before choosing the final one. The source of the water itself (the Alps) also plays into the choice of setting/backdrop for the ad.

Questions: Analyzing Danone/Evian and Havas Worldwide's advertisement

1. Purpose. What information did the creators of the ad provide (textually and visually) about Evian water? How interesting is the information? How persuasive is it? Explain.

2. Audience. How do the various images in the ad speak to its audience? Who is the primary target audience for this ad? Is only one audience being addressed by the ad or several? Why do you think so?

3. Rhetorical appeals. How many different ways is the concept of "purity" conveyed in the ad? How is this used to persuade the audience?

4. Rhetorical appeals. Why do the ad's creators focus on Evian water's "detoxifying" properties? And what does this suggest about Evian's target audience?

5. Rhetorical appeals. Look up the word *detox* in a dictionary. Which of the definitions listed seems most appropriate in the case of the ad? Why?

6. Modes & media. The ad copy mentions the French Alps but does not mention the woman, although both are central visuals in the ad. Why do you think the creators chose not to include the woman in the ad copy?

7. Elements of the genre. The ad headline is very brief and directive. Does it have the same catchiness as the Nike slogan "Just Do It"? Why or why not?

8. Elements of the genre. What is the relationship between the visual images and the text? If the bottom portion of the ad with the text were eliminated, what would your reaction to the image be? How does your reaction change when you see the text?

9. Style. How would you characterize the tone of the ad copy? Does the tone fit the advertisement's purpose? Why or why not?

10. Design. Describe the visuals in the ad. What do the visuals suggest about what the advertisers want consumers to think/ believe/feel about Evian?

11. Design. Water drops are used twice in the ad. What purpose do they serve?

12. Sources. Is it effective to use an image of the mountains where Evian water comes from as a backdrop in the ad? Why or why not?

Drafting an Advertisement

CHECKLIST: Drafting an Advertisement Thinking of creating an ad? Ask yourself the following questions.

WHAT'S MY RHETORICAL SITUATION?

☐ **Purpose.** What product do I use that I want to convince others to use? What are the reasons to use that product? Why would someone besides me want to use the product?

☐ **Audience.** Who are the people in my target audience? Who will use the product? When will they use the product? Where will they use the product? How will they use the product?

☐ **Rhetorical appeals.** How will I establish my credibility in my advertisement? How will I illustrate the product's reliability and ethos? How will I use emotions to persuade my reader to use the product? To what extent will I use logic to support my claim about the product?

☐ **Modes & media.** Will my ad be print-based or digital or made for TV? How will I use visual images to persuade? Will I use one primary image or others that are secondary? How will my text work with my images? Will text explain visuals? Complement them? Will I use animation?

WHAT GENRE CONVENTIONS MATTER?

☐ **Elements of the genre.** Will my visuals be literal or symbolic? What type of catchy slogan can I create to make my product memorable? Will I use the slogan as my headline or within the ad copy?

☐ **Style.** What tone will work best for selling my product? How will my intended audience respond to my tone?

☐ **Design.** What typeface should I use? What size type will work best with my visuals? How can I use layout in order to feature the most important elements and leave the least important for final viewing? How can I use color and other design elements to guide my viewers' experience?

☐ **Sources.** What kind of market research will I conduct? Will I test out my headline/slogan on a potential audience? Will I show them a series of visuals to see which is most persuasive?

PRACTICE Want to experiment? Draft your own advertisement.

Think of a product you consume or use, such as an energy drink, candy bar, computer, or article of clothing. Create a draft of a print advertisement that highlights a specific property/aspect of that product, such as the detoxifying properties of Evian. Use symbolic visuals to sell your product. Alternatively, create a digital or TV ad in which you use images, sound, and text.

EDITORIALS & OPINION PIECES

Editorials are related to **news articles**. Both types of writing are presented by news organizations (such as *The New York Times*, CNN, and your campus paper); however, editorials present opinions (which are subjective) and articles present facts (which are objective).

Editorials and opinion pieces are texts that convey a writer's opinion on a particular topic, sometimes a controversial topic. This type of writing can be called by different names, such as *opinions*, *perspectives*, *commentaries*, and *viewpoints*, and can take the form of a letter to the editor or an online comment in response to an issue or other piece of writing.

Editorials appear in newspapers and magazines, on TV and radio, and in blogs and other online publications. Editorials also include editorial cartoons. An editorial represents the opinion of a news agency's editorial board and, therefore, represents the opinion of the publisher. An opinion piece, on the other hand, could take the form of opinion columns by regular featured writers, and letters from readers in which they share their views. Many newspapers, such as the *Denver Post*, feature editorials and opinion pieces side by side; the *Denver Post* calls the page simply the Opinion Page. If your school publishes a newspaper, it probably also includes a section dedicated to editorials or opinions.

EDITORIAL PAGE ▶
**The *Denver Post*
Opinion Page**
Printed with permission from The Denver Post.

Analyzing Editorials & Opinion Pieces: What to Look For

THE RHETORICAL SITUATION

Do you read editorials? What issues or events are most important to you? To what extent do we benefit from the opinions of others? #Evaluate

Purpose

Individual writers. An average citizen or student who writes an editorial or letter to the editor does so to convey his or her view on a specific issue, with the intent of persuading other readers. For example, in one issue of the *Oregon Daily Emerald*, a University of Oregon student wrote a column titled "Students Should Have Wider

denverpost.com Opinion

Editorial: Trim feds' role in policing pot

As more and more states legalize medical marijuana, it's time for Congress to end the conflict between federal and state law.

PRINT   EMAIL
23 COMMENTS

POSTED: 06/25/2011 01:00:00 AM MDT

By The Denver Post

The nation's marijuana laws are an overlapping mess. Possession is illegal under federal law while an impressive list of states, including Colorado, brazenly defy Washington's edict by allowing marijuana for medical use. Congress should have resolved this conflict years ago but now at last it has its chance.

A bill, whose sponsors include Rep. Jared Polis, D–Boulder, would not legalize marijuana, but rather remove it from the federal government's list of controlled substances. That would enable states that have legalized medical marijuana — which include such major population centers as California, New Jersey and Michigan — to craft and enforce their own laws without conflict with the feds.

Those states may be operating outside of federal law, but it's with their citizens' consent. State and local officials, as well as dispensaries and their clients, deserve a reprieve from this twilight zone in which federal authorities could change their mind at any moment and charge them with crimes.

Earlier this year, the clash between state and federal law came into sharp focus when federal prosecutors essentially fired warning shots at proposals in several states despite previous assurances they would not target those who followed state laws.

John Walsh, U.S. attorney for Colorado, took issue with a proposed law that would have created a license for large-scale marijuana-infused manufacturing facilities. Similarly, other U.S. attorneys threatened enforcement of federal law against big operations.

The result was trepidation among medical marijuana business owners who had operated in line with what they thought was a relaxation of federal enforcement.

We haven't and won't defend the ambition of medical marijuana businesses that seem determined to interpret the 2009 Justice Department pronouncement in the most expansive light.

We also have said on several occasions that we do not think voters were approving back-door legalization when they supported a 2000 state constitutional amendment allowing medical marijuana. Indeed, straight-up legalization failed overwhelmingly in Colorado in 2006 and would probably fail again if voters are given another shot at the issue in 2012.

If voters were to approve legalization, of course, the conflict with federal law would only sharpen.

That's why we think this congressional measure makes sense.

To be sure, the bill still would allow for some federal enforcement — in cases, for instance, of trafficking between states. But mostly it would take the feds out of the enforcement equation.

Such a change would all but eliminate the confusion between state and federal law and allow for clear enforcement of established rules.

Gun Liberties," in response to an article discussing how the university campus prepares for a campus shooting. The student's purpose is clear—as is his opinion.

The same is true for an individual columnist—a staff or syndicated writer for a specific newspaper, magazine, or other news organization; that is, the columnist conveys his or her own opinion in the editorial and not the opinion of a publisher, though there is some gray area here because the writers are usually employed by the publisher.

Editorial board writers. Texts that are written by the editorial board of a newspaper or magazine convey the opinion of the publisher. These editorials are intended to educate and persuade readers to agree with a specific idea and/or to take a specific action. For example, in the *Denver Post* editorial "Trim Feds' Role in Policing Pot," the *Post* argues in support of a congressional measure that would eliminate marijuana from the federal government's list of controlled substances. The editorial boards of most newspapers reflect a conservative or liberal point of view through their editorials; for example, the editorial board of *The New York Times* has a reputation for being fairly liberal, while the editorial board of the *News-Gazette* of Champaign-Urbana, Illinois, has a reputation for being conservative.

Audience   Anyone with access to newspapers, magazines, television, radio, or the Internet can access editorials and opinion pieces. As a reader, you might scan the

E-mail | Print | RSS

When teachers cut class

Remember those days when your teacher unexpectedly called in sick? Some hapless substitute walked in, briefly struggled to teach a lesson and then surrendered class time to "study hall."

Despite anecdotal and academic evidence that students don't learn as much from substitutes, many school districts appear to have a problem with truant teachers, especially on sunny Fridays. An *Orlando Sentinel* reporter recently found that one district had 35% more teachers sick on Fridays than Wednesdays. A Minneapolis reporter found similar absentee problems there.

Besides hurting kids' education, these suspicious absences deplete school funds that could be spent on other education priorities. Substitutes generally cost districts $60 to $100 a day.

Academic and financial costs incurred when teachers skip class argue for tougher attendance measures. But a recent *Education Week* survey of superintendents found little taste for confronting teachers' unions. One Florida superintendent threw up her hands in helplessness. She had no choice but to accept the word of teachers that they were sick, she said, and challenging teachers on skipping school wasn't something she was going to make into an "issue."

That's not good enough, especially considering recent evidence from researchers at Duke and Harvard universities confirming what common sense already suggests: Teacher absences affect student performance. The Harvard study found that 10 days of teacher absence is equivalent to a student drawing a rookie teacher rather than a second-year teacher. The Duke University study of North Carolina schools found similar results.

A few superintendents have launched programs to reward teachers who take fewer sick days than the contract allows. Other programs pay bonuses to schools that reduce their overall absence rates.

None of this should be necessary. Most teachers work hard in demanding jobs for modest pay, but they get home for dinner, have plenty of school holidays and breaks, and get summers off. It's grossly unprofessional for those who aren't really ill to take long weekends during the school year.

Perhaps supervisors need to start treating truant teachers like children and demanding notes from their parents and doctors.

opinion pages of newspapers regularly, or mainly during an election or controversy, in order to read the opinions, analysis, and interpretations of others on these issues.

Writers of editorials keep their readers—primary and secondary audiences—in mind as they compose. For example, the editorial board of *USA Today* published an editorial titled "When Teachers Cut Class" (May 1, 2008), aimed primarily at a conservative audience of parents, taxpayers, and citizens opposed to teachers' unions; it is also aimed at the teachers they critiqued in the editorial. Among the responses

Time to show respect to America's educators

I take exception to USA TODAY's characterization of teachers in its editorial about high sick-leave rates in school districts on Fridays ("When teachers cut class," May 1).

After the terrorist attacks on Sept. 11, 2001, I pondered what I would do if my job situation changed. I went back to school and earned a master's degree in education.

Having spent nearly 30 years in business, where responsibilities are well-defined and employees are compensated for their work, I sometimes look at the options in teaching and wonder why such an important job is so poorly compensated yet receives more criticism than respect from the American public.

No one seems to consider that many teachers are the breadwinners in their families. Summers are often spent taking courses to keep up with licensure renewal or mandates.

Teachers don't exit school on the day students are released for the summer or return on the same day in the fall when students arrive. There are reports to complete, rooms to organize and lesson plans to write. Teachers spend hours writing lesson plans and aligning them to standards. I have done this, and it requires much effort.

Every teacher I know works hard to achieve success for his or her students. In business, we are expected to suffer failures in the pursuit of success. Teachers are held to a standard of 100%, and I cannot think of another profession, even medicine, that mandates 100% success, pays little and then harps when a person takes a day off — personal, sick or otherwise.

Myra Warne

Zanesville, Ohio

Opinion
Opinion Home
Editorials and Debates
Columnists' Opinions
Readers' Opinions

E-mail | Print | RSS

Do you listen to editorials read on the radio? What is your experience as a listener? As a writer, how would you decide on the best mode and medium for your editorial message? #Apply

to the editorial was a letter to the editor from Myra Warne, an Ohio teacher who took exception to *USA Today*'s opinion.

Rhetorical appeals   Editorial and opinion piece writers rely most on ethos and logos to persuade readers of the validity of their positions. As shown on page 468, the editorial board at *USA Today*, for example, uses evidence to appeal to readers' sense of logic. If the reader accepts the results of the university studies about the ill effects of teacher absences on student learning, then the reader should make the logical leap that teacher absences need to be dealt with seriously. Myra Warne responds to the editorial using a variety of appeals, including pathos. She establishes her ethos by discussing all her years in business, establishing her expertise in the work world. Additionally, she appeals to readers' emotions by illustrating the amount of work teachers do during the summer when they are not working, hoping that her readers sympathize with the dedication of teachers.

Modes & media   Newspaper editorials and opinion pieces are usually presented as written texts; sometimes they're accompanied by a small photo of the writer to establish the writer's credibility. Some editorials include charts or other infographics. Some editorials are presented as audio texts, such as the commentaries offered by National Public Radio. Editorials and opinion pieces can be found both in print, such as in newspapers and magazines, and digitally, such as on the sites for *The New York Times* and NPR.

THE GENRE'S CONVENTIONS

Elements of the genre   Editorial and opinion piece writers do the following:

Clearly present their work as opinion writing. The distinction between an editorial or opinion piece and a news article is important: Editorials or opinion pieces are opinions based on research and analysis whereas news articles are objective reporting based on research. That is, editorials reflect a personal view while news articles are supposed to be totally free of opinion. Editorials or opinion pieces are usually clearly labeled as *editorials* (or with another name such as *opinion*, *viewpoint*, *perspective*, or *commentary*).

Write concisely. An editorial or opinion piece is typically about five or so paragraphs long, which means the author needs to make his or her point quickly.

Begin with an introduction that gets readers' attention. For example, the authors of the *USA Today* piece on teachers' cutting class opens with a rhetorical question asking readers, "Remember those days when your teacher unexpectedly called in sick?" followed by a remark about the useless substitute. Immediately, readers are reminded of their own experiences and identify with the writers.

Identify and address counterarguments. Editorial and opinion piece writers make their strongest cases when they anticipate objections and opposition to their views. In the *Denver Post* editorial arguing for state control of marijuana (p. 467), the writers anticipate that readers might bring up the fact that state marijuana laws operate in conflict with federal laws. In response to this, the writers argue, "Those states may be operating outside of federal law, but it's with their citizens' consent."

Offer potential solutions. Often after explaining a problem, writers will examine potential solutions and suggest one over another. In the *USA Today* editorial, the writers mention some solutions but then conclude that the best one would be for teachers to simply stop taking sick days unless they are sick.

Close with a simple but memorable statement. For example, the final paragraph of the *USA Today* editorial is particularly memorable because of the writers' tone—and the sarcastic suggestion that, like absent children, absent teachers should provide a sick note from their parents.

Invite readers to respond. Many online editorials, such as the *USA Today* editorial, become discussion starters in which hundreds or even thousands of readers post replies to the original editorial and to other posts.

Style   Editorial and opinion piece writers do the following:

Include concise detail. Editorial and opinion piece writers use specific facts throughout their texts to support their position. Because they are making a case, they need to use enough evidence to convince readers, but they still need to keep the entire piece fairly brief.

Use a variety of techniques. To engage and persuade readers, editorial and opinion piece writers:

» Include quotations from experts to support their claims.

» Avoid errors in reasoning; such errors are known as logical fallacies. Here are some of the most common types:

  » *Red herring*: Distracting the reader from the real issue being argued; for example, "Global warming needs to be addressed, but people are struggling with gas prices."

  » *Ad hominem*: Attacking the person making an argument instead of addressing the argument; for example, "She says women should have equal rights, but look at how ugly she is."

  » *Hasty generalization*: Extrapolating unrealistically from one example; for example, "He lied; therefore all men are liars."

  » *Slippery slope*: Assuming that if one step is taken, then all sorts of catastrophic results will inevitably follow; for example, "If we increase taxes by 1 percent today, tomorrow our children will be paying more in taxes than they take home."

» *Circular reasoning*: Defining a word by using the word, where the start is the same as the ending; for example, "The reason we should outlaw guns is that guns should be made illegal."

» *Post hoc*: Confusing chronology with causality; for example, "The cat peed on the bedspread because I just washed it."

» Use analogies and refer to cultural and historical events so that readers will identify with the issue.

» Avoid jargon and instead use language that will appeal to readers who may not be familiar with the issue.

» Use rhetorical questions to spark readers' attention.

Convey a clear, personable voice and tone. Writers use clear, persuasive language as they present their opinions and support them with facts. Editorial writers often write in the first person (*I*) and in a friendly and inviting tone to reach a wide readership.

Design   Editorial and opinion piece writers—and the designers they work with—do the following:

Write clear, interesting headlines. Whether they're published in print or online, editorials, like news articles, are presented with a headline designed to get readers' attention and to make it clear what the editorialist is writing about. Editorials and opinion pieces are also clearly labeled as such, or with other terms, such as *opinions* or *commentaries*, that denote subjective writing.

Repeat design features on the page. Whether you're reading an editorial or opinion piece in print or online, you'll see certain design elements on every page; these elements include the name of the newspaper, perhaps presented as a logo or otherwise branded, at the top and bottom of the page. This helps the writers and designers establish the news organization's identity. You might also find a heading indicating what part of the paper or site you've navigated to ("Editorial," "Opinion," etc.). The date also appears in these spots for easy reference.

How do editorial writers use sources to support their arguments? What sources are most persuasive? Can anecdotal evidence be as convincing as statistical data? #Analyze #Evaluate

Note: Design features of editorials and opinion pieces are generally similar to those of newspaper articles. See Chapter 14, page 385, for more on news article design.

Sources Editorial and opinion piece writers do the following:

Refer to specific examples. The editorial board of *USA Today* offers several specific pieces of evidence to make its point (p. 468), such as the actual cost of substitutes, the results of the *Education Week* survey, and the results of the Harvard and Duke studies. The writers make the case by offering a variety of support from credible sources.

Use attribution phrases. Editorialists present evidence to support their points, often using attribution phrases to let readers know where the data came from. For instance, in the *USA Today* editorial, "An *Orlando Sentinel* reporter recently found" cues readers that the source of the information on the most common sick days is an *Orlando Sentinel* article.

Guided Reading: Opinion Piece ▼

Katha Pollitt

Adam and Steve—Together at Last

Katha Pollitt is a regular columnist for *The Nation* magazine, where she writes an opinion column called "Subject to Debate," which has won the National Magazine Award for Columns and Commentary. *The Nation*, like Pollitt's column, tackles political and social issues, usually from a left-wing political perspective. Pollitt's work has appeared in other magazines including *Harper's* and *The New Yorker*. Her persuasive essay "Adam and Steve—Together at Last" first appeared in the December 15, 2003, issue of *The Nation*. The essay disputes the legitimacy of arguments against same-sex marriage. Although same-sex marriage is legal in many countries, such as Canada and South Africa, it has been a controversial issue in the United States, with supporters claiming that allowing same-sex unions extends basic rights to homosexuals, and opponents maintaining that legalizing same-sex unions would jeopardize all marriages. *(Pages 474–76: Text © Katha Pollitt. Art Courtesy of The Nation.)*

▲ AUTHOR PHOTO
Katha Pollitt
Christina Pabst.

What is the composer, Katha Pollitt, doing?

THE RHETORICAL SITUATION

Purpose
Audience
Rhetorical appeals
Modes & media

see page 475

Adam and Steve--Together at Last

Will someone please explain to me how permitting gays and lesbians to marry threatens the institution of marriage?

Katha Pollitt

Will someone please explain to me how permitting gays and lesbians to marry threatens the institution of marriage? Now that the Massachusetts Supreme Court has declared gay marriage a constitutional right, opponents really have to get their arguments in line. The most popular theory, advanced by David Blankenhorn, Jean Bethke Elshtain, and other social conservatives is that under the tulle and orange blossom, *marriage* is all about procreation. There's some truth to this as a practical matter— couples often live together and tie the knot only when baby's on the way. But whether or not marriage is the best framework for child-rearing, having children isn't a marital requirement. As many have pointed out, the law permits marriage to the infertile, the elderly, the impotent, and those with no wish to procreate; it allows married couples to use birth control, to get sterilized, to be celibate. There's something creepily authoritarian and insulting about reducing marriage to procreation, as if intimacy mattered less than biological fitness. It's not a view that anyone outside a right-wing think tank, a Catholic marriage tribunal, or an ultra-Orthodox rabbi's court is likely to find persuasive.

So scratch procreation. How about: Marriage is the way women domesticate men. This theory, a favorite of right-wing writer George Gilder, has some statistical support—married men are much less likely than singles to kill people, crash the car, take drugs, commit suicide—although it overlooks such husbandly failings as domestic violence, child abuse, infidelity, and abandonment. If a man rapes his wife instead of his date, it probably won't show up on a police blotter, but has civilization moved forward? Of course, this view

How do I know this is an opinion piece?

THE GENRE'S CONVENTIONS

Elements of the genre
Style
Design
Sources

see page 475

HOME | BLOGS | COLUMNISTS | CURRENT ISSUE | MAGAZINE ARCHIVE | MULTIMEDIA   COMMUNITY | NATION BUILDERS | STUDENTS
POLITICS   WORLD   BOOKS & ARTS   ECONOMY   ENVIRONMENT   ACTIVISM   SOCIETY   LIVED HISTORY   NEW YORK: THE GILDED CITY

of marriage as a barbarian-adoption program doesn't explain why women should undertake it—as is obvious from the state of the world, they haven't been too successful at it, anyway. (Maybe men should civilize men—bring on the Fab Five!) Nor does it explain why marriage should be restricted to heterosexual couples. The gay men and lesbians who want to marry don't impinge on the male-improvement project one way or the other. Surely not even Gilder believes that a heterosexual pothead with plans for murder and suicide would be reformed by marrying a lesbian?

What about the argument from history? According to this, marriage has been around forever and has stood the test of time. Actually, though, marriage as we understand it—voluntary, monogamous, legally egalitarian, based on love, involving adults only—is a pretty recent phenomenon. For much of human history, polygyny was the rule—read your Old Testament—and in much of Africa and the Muslim world, it still is. Arranged marriages, forced marriages, child marriages, marriages predicated on the subjugation of women—gay marriage is like a fairy tale romance compared with most chapters of the history of wedlock.

The trouble with these and other arguments against gay marriage is that they overlook how loose, flexible, individualized, and easily dissolved the bonds of marriage already are. Virtually any man and woman can marry, no matter how ill assorted or little acquainted. An eighty-year-old can marry an eighteen-year-old; a john can marry a prostitute; two terminally ill patients can marry each other from their hospital beds. You can get married by proxy, like medieval royalty, and not see each other in the flesh for years. Whatever may have been the case in the past, what undergirds marriage in most people's minds today is not some sociobiological theory about reproduction or male socialization. Nor is it the enormous bundle of privileges society awards to married people. It's love, commitment, stability. Speaking just for myself, I don't like marriage. I prefer the old-fashioned ideal of monogamous free love, not that it worked out particularly well in my case. As a social mechanism, moreover, marriage seems to me a deeply

Continues next page

THE RHETORICAL
SITUATION

Purpose
Pollitt wants to convince readers that gay marriage should be accepted as a "constitutional right."

Audience
Pollitt's readers are interested in the gay marriage debate. They may be socially liberal or conservative; if they are regular readers of *The Nation*, they're probably socially liberal.
(Continued on p. 476.)

THE GENRE'S
CONVENTIONS

Elements of the genre
Pollitt makes it clear that this is an opinion piece, beginning with the tone of her title, a play on Adam and Eve, and her first sentence: "Will someone please explain to me. . . ." She goes on to **relate her opinions** on gay marriage.

Pollitt **grabs attention** by starting with a question and a reference to a court decision.
(Continued on p. 476.)

Katha Pollitt, *Adam and Steve—Together at Last*

Nation.

HOME | BLOGS | COLUMNISTS | CURRENT ISSUE | MAGAZINE ARCHIVE | MULTIMEDIA   COMMUNITY | NATION BUILDERS | STUDENTS

POLITICS   WORLD   BOOKS & ARTS   ECONOMY   ENVIRONMENT   ACTIVISM   SOCIETY   LIVED HISTORY   NEW YORK: THE GILDED CITY

unfair way of distributing social goods like health insurance and retirement checks, things everyone needs. Why should one's marital status determine how much you pay the doctor, or whether you eat cat food in old age, or whether a child gets a government check if a parent dies? It's outrageous that, for example, a working wife who pays Social Security all her life gets no more back from the system than if she had married a male worker earning the same amount and stayed home. Still, as long as marriage is here, how can it be right to deny it to those who want it? In fact, you would think that, given how many heterosexuals are happy to live in sin, social conservatives would welcome maritally minded gays with open arms. Gays already have the baby—they can adopt in many states, and lesbians can give birth in all of them—so why deprive them of the marital bathwater?

At bottom, the objections to gay marriage are based on religious prejudice: The marriage of man and woman is "sacred" and opening it to same-sexers violates its sacral nature. That is why so many people can live with civil unions but draw the line at marriage—spiritual union. In fact, polls show a striking correlation of religiosity, especially evangelical Protestantism, with opposition to gay marriage and with belief in homosexuality as a choice, the famous "gay lifestyle." For these people gay marriage is wrong because it lets gays and lesbians avoid turning themselves into the straights God wants them to be. As a matter of law, however, marriage is not about Adam and Eve versus Adam and Steve. It's not about what God blesses, it's about what the government permits. People may think *marriage* is a word wholly owned by religion, but actually it's wholly owned by the state. No matter how big your church wedding, you still have to get a marriage license from City Hall. And just as divorced people can marry even if the Catholic Church considers it bigamy, and Muslim and Mormon men can only marry one woman even if their holy books tell them they can wed all the girls in Apartment 3G, two men or two women should be able to marry, even if religions oppose it and it makes some heterosexuals, raised in those religions, uncomfortable.

Gay marriage—it's not about sex, it's about separation of church and state.

THE RHETORICAL SITUATION

Pollitt establishes her **ethos** by writing with authority and showing her familiarity with historical facts and theories (such as those put forth by Blankenhorn and Elshtain).

Modes & media

Mode = written The digital version also includes a visual, a small headshot of Pollitt. Most editorials and opinion pieces are written or audio. Words are vital to an editorialist making his or her point because the specificity and clarity of the editorialist's position is so important.

Medium = print and digital The content is the same in both versions, but the design and context are different. In the print version, the essay gets one complete page of the magazine. In the digital version, the column shares space with a menu bar at the top and several items that occupy the left-hand side of the screen, including a small headshot of Pollitt and links to related articles on *The Nation*'s Web site. These differences result from the varying needs and desires of print and digital editorial audiences.

THE GENRE'S CONVENTIONS

Style

Pollitt **uses specific facts** to back up her views; e.g., she provides details of aspects of George Gilder's theories and refers to other source texts, including the Bible.

She **uses rhetorical questions** effectively; for example, to hold the reader's interest, she asks, "Why should one's marital status determine how much you pay the doctor?"

Her tone is personal and informal. For example, she writes, "Speaking just for myself, I don't like marriage."

Design

The "Subject to Debate" **headline and its visual design draw readers in.** For easy reference, *The Nation*'s title appears at the top of the page. In the online version of this article, there are "About the Author," "Also by the Author," and "Related Topics" headings to orient readers within the site and expand their reading.

Sources

Pollitt **refers to several specific sources** (the voices of opposition), such as David Blankenhorn, the founder and president of the socially conservative Institute for American Values, and ethics professor Jean Bethke Elshtain, as well as the Old Testament. While sources are linked in some online editorials and opinion pieces, that's not the case here.

Questions: Analyzing Pollitt's opinion piece

1. Purpose. Does Pollitt convince you that gay marriage is "not about sex, it's about separation of church and state"? Why or why not?

2. Audience. How do you think a person opposed to gay marriage might respond to Pollitt's essay?

3. Rhetorical appeals. List the counterarguments Pollitt addresses. Do you think she's left out any? If so, why do you think she chose to focus on the ones she did?

4. Rhetorical appeals. How does Pollitt build her case? How does she appeal to her audience using logos?

5. Rhetorical appeals. To what extent does Pollitt come across as authoritative and knowledgeable? What does she do to convince you she is (1) authoritative and knowledgeable or (2) lacking in authority and knowledge? Explain.

6. Modes & media. Imagine that Pollitt had included a large black-and-white photo of two men kissing at the top of the essay. How would the addition of this image add to or detract from the effectiveness of the editorial?

7. Elements of the genre. Although Pollitt's essay doesn't feature a clearly stated position or thesis statement at the beginning, how does she make her position clear from the beginning? Where does Pollitt state her position most clearly?

8. Elements of the genre. How do the organization and paragraph structure help you pick out the specific counterarguments Pollitt addresses in her column?

9. Style. How would you characterize the tone of Pollitt's essay? How does it affect you as a reader? Do you think anyone would consider her language inflammatory? How does this work for or against her position?

10. Style. What does the title allude to? Why is that allusion appropriate for this essay?

11. Design. The final sentence is set off in its own paragraph. How does this add to the impact of Pollitt's conclusion?

12. Sources. Pollitt does not cite sources in every paragraph. How does she convince you that she is familiar with source material about, say, the history of marriage, without directly citing sources?

Drafting an Editorial or Opinion Piece

CHECKLIST: Drafting an Editorial or Opinion Piece Thinking of writing an editorial? Ask yourself the following questions.

WHAT'S MY RHETORICAL SITUATION?

☐ **Purpose.** What is my purpose? And what do I want to persuade others to think or do? Do I want readers to see things from a different perspective? To take action? Do I want them to completely change their minds on an issue? How feasible is it to try to change a person's mind?

☐ **Audience.** Who am I trying to persuade? What are my audience's concerns about the issue I'm writing about? What do they fear? What is their stake in the issue (what do they personally have to risk losing if they do what I want)?

☐ **Rhetorical appeals.** How will I establish myself as reasonable and authoritative on this issue? How can I use organization to appeal to my audience's sense of logos? Will my audience respond to emotional appeals or will I seem manipulative if I appeal to pathos?

☐ **Modes & media.** Will I use written words or audio or video to convey my point? Based on the audience I have in mind—are they more likely to read or listen to an editorial in print, on the radio, or on the Internet?

WHAT GENRE CONVENTIONS MATTER?

☐ **Elements of the genre.** How can I make it clear that I'm writing an opinion piece? How can I get my audience's attention immediately and show them how important and relevant this issue is to their lives? Which potential objections and counterarguments should I address? How can I make the closing of my editorial memorable?

☐ **Style.** Would my case be strengthened by bringing in quotations from experts? Are there analogies that I could use that would appeal to my readers? What types of rhetorical questions would be most compelling for my editorial? How will I keep my language persuasive yet friendly?

☐ **Design.** Do I want to design a heading or logo for my column to identify myself as the author? How can I use a heading, logo, or other design element to develop my ethos?

☐ **Sources.** What kinds of sources will be most useful and most interesting and persuasive to my audience? How might I bring in sources to address potential objections and opposing arguments?

PRACTICE Want to experiment? Draft your own editorial or opinion piece.

Think about an issue you care deeply about. Think about what your position is on the issue. Then brainstorm a list of reasons/evidence that supports your position. What are some of the counterarguments? Do research so that you can provide some support, as Pollitt does with different theorists and their positions. Then combine your research and ideas into an editorial or opinion piece that convinces your audience that your position is a valid one.

RESEARCHED ARGUMENTS

A researched argument is any work in which a writer presents an argument and backs it up with solid sources. Most academic research papers are researched arguments (see also the peer-reviewed journal article discussed in Chapter 14, p. 402). Writers of researched arguments do the following:

» Investigate a topic and work with sources

» Make a specific and persuasive case about that topic

» Incorporate in their writing voices of their sources through summary, paraphrase, and quotation

» Cite those sources in the body of the composition

» List the sources at the end

When you read an argument text, are you more swayed by personal opinion and anecdote or research as support? Does it depend on the subject matter? Your expertise on the subject? The genre itself? Explain. #Understand

The main purpose of writing a researched argument is to persuade your readers of the merits of your argument. Drawing on and citing your sources builds a case for your argument.

Researched arguments appear in the same places that research papers do: in the classroom, in peer-reviewed journals, in magazines, and on the Internet in the form of blog entries and other argumentative pieces. Depending on what level of research they've conducted and where they publish their work, authors of this genre may be scholars, recognized by other scholars as experts on the subject they are writing about, or they may be reporters, bloggers, or other types of experts on their subject. For example, an experienced snowboarder who researches different snowboarding designs and blogs in favor of one would be considered an expert on the subject she's writing about.

At work, researched arguments often take the form of reports or memos. When an employee wants to persuade an organization to change a policy or procedure, he may write a memo or report in which he refers to specific research or to policies at similar organizations.

Analyzing Researched Arguments: What to Look For

Purpose   We write researched arguments because we want to persuade others to share our point of view on a topic. We may be looking for readers to simply agree or maybe to take a specific action. When you write a researched argument, you begin by conducting research in hopes that the quality and quantity of the data you present will convince readers. For example, Liz had the following experience: her department at Metro State recently considered whether or not to change the amount of credit students will receive for certain AP scores. Liz and a colleague argued their position about how much credit Metro State should give students in a memo to the department that cited the AP credit policies of several other similar universities and colleges. Their purpose was to get their colleagues to agree with them and to take action.

Henry Fong, host of the blog *FitBomb*, writes to persuade readers to adopt or at least consider the exercise and eating plans he favors. In the post on page 482, he argues for the Paleo Diet, citing research to back up his views on the benefits of "eating like a caveman." As you can see, he uses hyperlinks to cite his sources, furthering his ethos and logos. This is an example of a researched argument presented as a blog post.

Audience   Authors of researched arguments usually write for others who are interested in the topic being discussed. Readers may or may not agree with the argument the writer proposes, but they're generally curious enough to read about the perspectives of others. If you're an expert writing a researched argument for a peer-reviewed journal, then your audience is other experts. If you're writing a memo or report at work, then your audience is your colleagues. If you're writing a blog, such as Henry Fong does at *FitBomb*, you're writing for others who most likely share your enthusiasm for fitness—but who may or may not agree with everything you propose.

In the case of the *FitBomb* post on the Paleo Diet, the author is clearly aware of his readers' potential skepticism. The Q&A format he adopts for the argument takes into account potential objections, and he addresses the reader directly: "What? Not good enough? I hear you. Frankly, I resisted going Paleo for quite a while."

Do any of the blogs you read feature researched arguments? How persuasive do you find them? Have you ever changed your view on a topic because of a researched argument you read on a blog? #Understand

👉 **Attention, researchers & writers!**

Poorly integrated and cited research casts doubt on you as an author and seriously compromises your ethos—while a smart use of sources does a lot to build it. See Chapter 20 for more on integrating and citing sources.

BLOG POST ▶
Henry Fong
"What Is the Paleo
Diet?," a researched
argument at *FitBomb*.
*All images on pages
482–89: Henry Fong/
Fitbomb.com.*

START HERE   ABOUT   CROSSFIT   WHAT IS THE PALEO DIET?   MOST POPULAR   SHIRTS   NOM NOM PALEO APP

What Is The Paleo Diet?

INTRODUCTION

Even after eating this way for years, we still manage to catch
some of our dining companions off-guard. Their eyebrows
shoot up when we order our food sans bread, pasta, rice,
polenta or beans. The questions are always the same:

"Are you on Atkins or something?"

"Trying to lose weight?"

"You don't even eat *whole* grains?"

"What the hell is the matter with you?"

Well, here exactly is the matter with me: I EAT PALEO. As in
the Paleolithic (or "Paleo") Diet. You may have heard of it as
the Caveman Diet.

If you're feeling bookish, Loren Cordain's "The Paleo Diet" and Mark
Sisson's "The Primal Blueprint" introduced the concept of ancestral
eating approaches to tons of people. (Sisson, in particular, is an
excellent resource for tips and information on implementing this type of
nutritional template. Check out his massively popular site, Mark's Daily
Apple, for more.)

If you'd rather gaze into a computer screen, start with Cordain's Paleo
Diet FAQ, Sisson's how-to on living "Primally," and J. Stanton's "Eat
Like a Predator, Not Like Prey." This page on Melissa McEwen's site
also contains lots of useful resources for newbies. Hivelogic's Paleo
link primer is a great starting point, too. (And I'm not just saying that
'cause my wife's blog is listed as a Paleo cooking resource.)

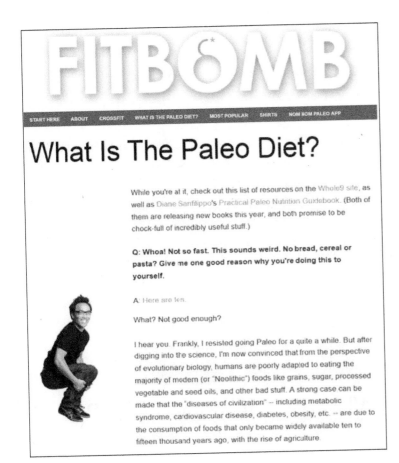

FITB☉MB

START HERE ABOUT CROSSFIT WHAT IS THE PALEO DIET? MOST POPULAR SHIRTS NOM NOM PALEO APP

What Is The Paleo Diet?

While you're at it, check out this list of resources on the Whole9 site, as well as Diane Sanfilippo's Practical Paleo Nutrition Guidebook. (Both of them are releasing new books this year, and both promise to be chock-full of incredibly useful stuff.)

Q: Whoa! Not so fast. This sounds weird. No bread, cereal or pasta? Give me one good reason why you're doing this to yourself.

A: Here are ten.

What? Not good enough?

I hear you. Frankly, I resisted going Paleo for a quite a while. But after digging into the science, I'm now convinced that from the perspective of evolutionary biology, humans are poorly adapted to eating the majority of modern (or "Neolithic") foods like grains, sugar, processed vegetable and seed oils, and other bad stuff. A strong case can be made that the "diseases of civilization" -- including metabolic syndrome, cardiovascular disease, diabetes, obesity, etc. -- are due to the consumption of foods that only became widely available ten to fifteen thousand years ago, with the rise of agriculture.

Rhetorical appeals   When writing a researched argument, authors can establish ethos in the following ways:

» Describing their research methods

» Explaining the data they collected and how they analyzed it

» Discussing their findings and conclusions in detail

» Citing their sources appropriately

» Writing as directly and persuasively as possible

Writers can establish logos in the following ways:

» Stating their position clearly

» Stating each aspect of their argument clearly—and in an order that makes sense

» Anticipating and addressing objections

» Supporting their claims with evidence—including the views of others (drawn from their sources)

Do you prefer an author to sound like a know-it-all or would you rather an author admit that he or she doesn't know everything about the topic? #Evaluate

The author of the *FitBomb* post outlines his information and argument clearly. He explains what the diet is and also makes a case for adopting the diet.

As this book goes to press, Henry Fong of *Fitbomb* presents his information on the Paleo Diet in the following parts, which are in turn broken out into a Q&A format:

Introduction

1. What to Eat and Why

FITBOMB

START HERE   ABOUT   CROSSFIT   WHAT IS THE PALEO DIET?   MOST POPULAR   SHIRTS   NOM NOM PALEO APP

What Is The Paleo Diet?

PART 1: WHAT TO EAT AND WHY

Let's start with the basics:

Q: What foods can you eat on a Paleo diet? And what can't you eat?

A: I do my best to stick to whole, unprocessed foods: meat, eggs, seafood, non-starchy vegetables -- and some (but not a ton of) fruit, nuts and seeds. I try to avoid eating things with sugar, grains (yes, whole grains, too), legumes (and not just because of their fart-inducing properties), and polyunsaturated fats. In short, I eat anything that can be hunted or gathered, and try to avoid stuff that's processed, cultivated, or sealed in colorful plastic packaging.

2. What's Wrong with What We Eat?

3. You Aren't What You Eat (So Eat Some Fat)

4. Why I Eat Paleo

5. Mythbusting

6. Foods to Avoid and Why

7. Transitioning to Paleo

What voice and tone are appropriate for a researched argument? How might this vary, depending on context and medium? #Understand

Whether or not you agree with his take on "eating like a caveman," the author of the *FitBomb* post appeals to readers by doing much of what is described in the above section on ethos and logos. Further, he appeals to pathos through his use of humor, as in the excerpt that follows.

Modes & media   Researched arguments published as articles in peer-reviewed journals, as memos, and as reports are text based and may include visuals such as charts, graphs, and images to support and illustrate points. These types of pieces can be available in print or online. For example, the memo about AP scores that Liz wrote was circulated by e-mail. Blog entries, of course, are digital.

THE GENRE'S CONVENTIONS

Elements of the genre

Author states a thesis or makes a clear claim. To make a position clear, a writer can (1) indicate the topic at hand and his or her position on it right in the title, (2) provide a clear thesis, doing so right at the beginning, or (3) combine both. In the *FitBomb* post on the Paleo Diet, the author uses clear subheadings for the various sections. In the section titled "What Really Causes Obesity?," he answers the question in a clear thesis in paragraph 1:

> The short answer: Excess carbohydrates. Especially sugar.

This clearly shows that the writer will argue against the commonly held belief that consuming too much fat leads to obesity; instead, he will argue that sugar causes us to be overweight.

Authors present an argument. For example, the *FitBomb* blogger writes to explain the Paleo Diet—but mainly to persuade readers to adopt it. He supports his main argument with seven sections—moving from what the diet is, to what research shows about the diet, to why he likes it—and ends with advice on how readers can transition to it themselves. In each part of his argument, the writer supports himself with evidence.

Authors base their arguments on solid research. All researched writing relies on research of some kind. Most writers support their ideas by drawing on the research of others—of experts and leaders in the field. As a student, unless you do primary research (such as conducting interviews), you most likely draw on the research of others in your researched writing.

Some authors—mainly academics writing for peer-reviewed journals—draw on their own research, particularly if they've conducted a study or survey of some kind that brings in data. Arguments for peer-reviewed journals are usually written in a formal style using precise language. They are also reviewed by others in the field for accuracy and reliability. (For more on peer-reviewed journal articles, see Chapter 14.)

When Liz and Amy present papers at conferences, they draw on and cite specific research done by academic experts and colleagues to support their arguments. The *FitBomb* blogger cites more than two hundred sources, including research by established experts, such as the Weston A. Price Foundation, which focuses on nutrition education.

Authors address counterarguments. To build logos, writers need to acknowledge contrasting or opposing arguments and either (1) refute them by exposing their holes or presenting evidence that outweighs them or (2) concede that they are legitimate and then explain why, despite this legitimacy, the audience should take the author's position. In Liz's AP score memo, she conceded to the opposing argument that some students with AP scores of 3 in English might no longer apply to Metro State if they wouldn't receive credit for a composition class. However, she explained that in the long run, these students would actually be more successful if they were required to take a composition class at Metro State.

Authors synthesize and attribute the work of others. As noted above, citing sources—and specific examples—builds ethos. It's also a good idea to pull information from multiple sources and to synthesize it by showing readers how these sources align and differ. When a writer relies on only one source, it makes the argument look weak to readers and, therefore, much less persuasive.

Style

Authors title their work to make their position clear. Authors of researched arguments title their work to make clear what topic they're writing about and what their position is. For example, for her memo subject line, which serves as the memo's title, Liz wrote: "Why we should raise AP scores for composition credit."

Authors write with authority. Writers use a strong voice and tone to convey expertise on a topic, support their ethos, and persuade their readers.

Authors get readers' attention with simple but memorable introductions and closing statements. For example, the *FitBomb* blogger starts with an anecdote.

Toward the end of his argument, the blogger concedes that the Paleo Diet isn't for everyone, but he does so with humor—subtly critiquing the "low-fat approach" and presenting a mental image of grass-fed beef, a central part of the Paleo Diet.

Authors use detail. The more specific writers are—in terms of both the main point and the research they're drawing on—the better and more persuasive the argument.

Design

Authors use subheadings. Many writers divide their arguments into sections with subheadings that make a long, complex piece easier to navigate. (See p. 484.) Subheadings also signal readers that an author is shifting his or her focus.

Authors support their arguments with images. Photos, charts, and illustrations convey complex information visually—and can serve as sources. For example, the *FitBomb* blogger uses images to back up his argument about the Paleo Diet, such as the infographic on page 490, taken from a like-minded site, PaleolithicDiet.com.

Sources

Authors curate sources carefully. Authors of researched arguments use sources that their readers will respect. When Liz wrote the AP credit memo, she knew her audience—colleagues in the English department—would be swayed by what other English departments do. In the case of the *FitBomb* post, the author draws on sources by writers he identifies as experts on the Paleo Diet.

Authors cite sources—according to genre conventions. An author of a peer-reviewed journal article would include a bibliographic list at the end of the article and use parenthetical citations throughout. A blogger simply embeds links to his or her sources, as the *FitBomb* blogger does.

INFOGRAPHIC ▶
PaleolithicDiet.com
"The Paleolithic Diet
Explained," from the
FitBomb post.

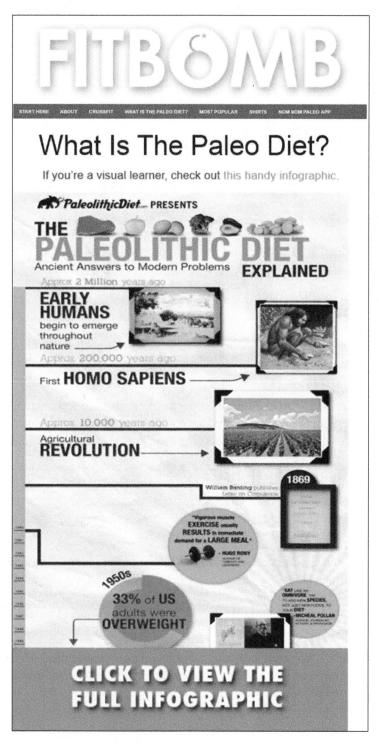

Chase Dickinson (Student)

Are Kids on a One-Way Path to Violence?

Chase Dickinson, a student from Herriman, Utah, wrote the following researched argument when he was a freshman at Weber State University, where he studied geoscience. As he mentions in the following essay, Dickinson worked for a video game vendor called Play N Trade, which factors into the argument he makes about video games in "Are Kids on a One-Way Path to Violence?" The essay, which he wrote for his English composition course, was also published in Weber State's journal of student work, called *Weber Writes*, edited in 2010 by Scott Rogers and Sylvia Newman.

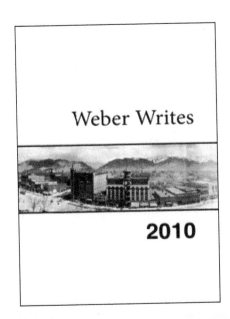

▼ STUDENT PHOTO, JOURNAL COVER, ▶ & UNIVERSITY WEB SITE ▼
Chase Dickinson; Weber Writes, the student journal that published Dickinson's researched essay; and **Weber State University's site**.
Author photo: Chase Dickinson. Journal cover: Weber State. Weber State homepage: Weber State.

What is the composer, **Chase Dickinson**, doing?

THE RHETORICAL SITUATION

Purpose
Audience
Rhetorical appeals
Modes & media

see page 493

How do I know this is a **researched argument**?

THE GENRE'S CONVENTIONS

Elements of the genre
Style
Design
Sources

see page 494

Chase Dickinson
Are Kids on a One-Way Path to Violence?

In the popular video game *Grand Theft Auto* (GTA), players are thrust into a world without laws, free to do just about anything they want. Stealing cars, killing civilians, and causing general mayhem are common occurrences in the fictitious world of Liberty City. In fact, GTA is about as lawless as games get. But can a game such as *Grand Theft Auto* actually fuel real-world violence? There are many who believe so, and violent video games have therefore become a hotly debated topic in today's headlines.

If you were to listen to politicians and critics, the relationship between video games and crime is blatantly clear: children who play video games will either become more aggressive or actually commit real-world acts of violence. According to the lawyers of Lee Malvo, the young "DC Sniper," Malvo learned to shoot by playing "very realistic and gory" video games. These games were also said to have "desensitized (him) . . . to train him to shoot human forms over and over" (qtd. in Provan). Another popular argument against violent video games comes in the form of the infamous Columbine shootings in which Dylan Klebold and Eric Harris killed thirteen students and injured twenty-three more before killing themselves. During the investigation that followed, it was discovered that both teenagers enjoyed playing the bloody first-person shooter *Doom*, and that they went on the rampage shortly after their parents took the game away from them. It has also been speculated that the pair created a level in *Doom* with the same layout as their school in order to plan out their attack (Mikkelson). Yet another argument finds Jack Thompson, a leader in the fight against violent video games, blaming the Virginia Tech shooting on the first-person shooter *Counter-Strike*, saying that once again the shooter trained for his crime by playing the popular first-person shooter (qtd. in Benedetti).

Dickinson, *One-Way Path to Violence?* *Continued*

THE RHETORICAL
SITUATION

With video games rapidly gaining popularity, we have to ask ourselves if these crimes are actually caused by the increasing violence in games. While there are many who tend to think so, I believe that it is not the fault of the games themselves, but the lack of parental supervision and interaction with today's youth. Also, preexisting mental disorders have been found to play a huge role in how different people will react to video games.

Take, for example, the DC sniper shootings. *Halo*, the game that Malvo supposedly used to prepare for his crimes, employs the use of unrealistic guns to shoot giant alien bugs. Such actions are hardly effective ways to learn how to shoot a sniper rifle at human beings. Malvo even admitted that he trained by shooting a real gun at makeshift targets with paper plates for heads (Provan). Similarly, the claims that the Columbine shooters created a level with their school's layout were never found to be true. In fact, all of the levels they made were later found on their Web site, and all of them were based on fictitious locations on alien planets (Mikkelson). Lastly, no one was ever reported to have seen Seung-Hui Cho, the Virginia Tech shooter, playing any video games. His roommate told the New York Times that he would sometimes enter Cho's room and find Cho sitting at his desk, staring into nothingness (Biggs). He wasn't staring at a computer and playing *Counter-Strike*, but was rather staring at nothing at all.

In addition, Seung-Hui Cho had been diagnosed with selective mutism, a severe anxiety disorder, as well as major depressive disorder (Adams). The DC shooter had a long history of anti-social and criminal behavior, including the torturing of small animals (Kutner 8). Similarly, FBI investigations were able to conclude that Klebold was significantly depressed and suicidal, and Harris was a sociopath (Kutner 8).

Ultimately, it falls upon the parents to filter what gets to their kids, and, when a known mental problem exists, parents should

Continues next page

Purpose

Dickinson wants to persuade readers that video games do not cause violent behavior in mentally healthy children.

Audience

His readers are his instructor, his classmates, and the students at Weber State University who read the journal *Weber Writes*.

Rhetorical appeals

Dickinson develops his **ethos** by stating that he is a gamer himself and that he's even worked in the industry.

By noting that the DC Sniper trained at a shooting range, Dickinson appeals to readers' sense of **logos** to question the connection between the DC Sniper and his video game experience.

(Continued on p. 495.)

Dickinson, *One-Way Path to Violence?* *Continued*

THE GENRE'S
CONVENTIONS

Elements of the genre

States a thesis or makes a clear claim.
Dickinson's is "I believe that [violent behavior in people who play video games] is not the fault of the games themselves, but the lack of parental supervision and interaction with today's youth."

Presents an argument based on research.
He presents his argument in paragraph 3 and develops it in subsequent paragraphs—reasoning that the DC Sniper, Columbine shooters, and Virginia Tech shooter had histories of mental illness and that is what the crimes should be attributed to. He argues that parents should monitor children's use of games and take mental health into account when deciding what their children can handle.

(Continued on p. 496.)

be that much more strict on what their kids play. As an avid gamer myself, and as someone who has worked in the industry, I understand the sense of accomplishment received from a well placed shot in *Modern Warfare* just as much as I understand that video games are not real. I was personally raised buying and playing games under the supervision of my parents, and am a strong supporter of such supervision. Even so, according to Jack Thompson and others with his mindset, I should be a ball of boiling hatred ready to explode at the slightest provocation.

Contrary to the claims of many naysayers, it is becoming easier to filter what a child does and does not play. A rating system implemented by the Entertainment Software Rating Board (ESRB) provides a fantastic way for parents to monitor what their kids are playing. This rating system issues an age range for each game, disclosing the full contents of the game. The most common ratings include E (Everyone, suitable for everyone age six and older), T (Teen, suitable for ages thirteen and older), and M (Mature, suitable for ages seventeen and older). The AO rating (Adult Only) is the only one higher than the M rating, and is actually considered to be a death sentence for games because brick-and-mortar stores will not sell them. AO- and M-rated games are the ones that come under the most fire from the media because they contain the most violent and bloody content. However, many people don't realize that in order to purchase an M-rated game from any major retailer, the customer must be at least seventeen years of age. Because of this age restriction, it is harder for young children to get their hands on violent content without parental approval.

There is no denying that video games have matured since their introduction in the '70s. Back then, games meant playing *Pong* or *Space Invaders* with friends and family. Today, games are becoming more and more complex, with violence playing a large role in almost all modern titles. Still, with parents staying involved in their kids' lives, it is possible to filter violent

Dickinson, *One-Way Path to Violence?* Continued

content and keep it to a minimum, which can prevent any type of aggressive behavior from developing. And with the ESRB and Web sites like *What They Play*, it is becoming easier and easier to keep children from playing games that are not age appropriate. Rather than focusing on trying to ban video games for their so-called influence on violent crime, an emphasis on parental supervision should be implemented in the fight against modern-day crime.

Works Cited

Adams, Duncan. "The Alienation and Anger of Seung-Hui Cho." *Roanoke.com*. The Roanoke Times, 31 Aug. 2007. Web. 27 Jan. 2010. <http://www.roanoke.com/vtinvestigation/wb/130177>.

Benedetti, Winda. "Were Video Games to Blame for Massacre?" *MSNBC.com*. MSNBC, 20 Apr. 2007. Web. 27 Jan. 2010. <http://www.roanoke.com/vtinvestigation/wb/130177>.

Biggs, John. "Why Video Games Don't Cause Violence." *CrunchGear.com*. CrunchGear, 18 Apr. 2007. Web. 27 Jan. 2010. <http://techcrunch.com/2007/04/18/why-video-games-dont-cause-violence/>.

Kutner, Lawrence, and Cheryl Olson. *Grand Theft Childhood: The Surprising Truth About Violent Video Games and What Parents Can Do*. New York: Simon & Schuster, 2008. Print.

Mikkelson, Barbara. "Columbine Doom Levels." *Snopes.com*. Snopes, 1 Jan. 2005. Web. 27 Jan. 2010. <http://www.snopes.com/horrors/madmen/doom.asp>.

Provan, Alexander. "The Education of Lee Boyd Malvo." Bidouan.org, 13 Jan. 2009. Web. 27 Jan. 2010. <http://www.bidoun.org/magazine/16-kids/the-education-of-lee-boyd-malvo-by-alexander-provan/>.

THE RHETORICAL SITUATION

Modes & media

Mode = written
Dickinson's assignment specified that he write an essay; however, sometimes assignments allow students the latitude to choose another mode, such as video or audio essay. Dickinson could have included visuals with his essay, perhaps screen shots of the video games mentioned in the essay or mug shots of the DC Sniper.

Medium = print
Again, Dickinson was required by his assignment to produce an essay in print form, but researched arguments often appear digitally, on blogs, for example.

Dickinson, *One-Way Path to Violence?* Continued

THE GENRE'S CONVENTIONS

Acknowledges counterarguments. For example, in paragraph 2, the author mentions that lawyers claimed there were connections between their clients' violence and use of video games.

Refutes or concedes counterarguments. For example, in paragraphs 4 and 5, the author discredits the links others have made between specific criminals and video game habits.

Cites specific examples, synthesizing them into his main argument. Rather than being general, the author specifies shooters (DC Sniper, Columbine, and Virginia Tech) and particular games (*Grand Theft Auto*, *Doom*, *Halo*, and *Counter-Strike*).

Style

Descriptive title. Dickinson's title makes clear that his essay deals with kids and violence.

Gets readers' attention in the introduction. Dickinson accomplishes this by stating that players are "free to do just about anything they want" in the game *Grand Theft Auto*.

Closes with a simple, memorable statement. His final sentence reads: "Rather than focusing on trying to ban video games for their so-called influence on violent crime, an emphasis on parental supervision should be implemented in the fight against modern-day crime."

Strong authoritative voice and tone. The author chooses to avoid phrases such as "I think" and "in my opinion" but is still present in the essay.

Uses detail. For example, he names the names of violent criminals and identifies the games they're associated with.

Design

For this brief essay, the author decided that subheadings and explanatory notes would be inappropriate. When he submitted it for class, it was double-spaced. For use in *Weber Writes*, it was single-spaced to conform to that journal's design.

Sources

The author cites sources in the body of the text and at the end in a Works Cited list. His sources are varied and include Snopes.com, a respected Web site.

Questions: Analyzing Dickinson's researched argument

1. Purpose. Has Dickinson persuaded you that video games cannot be conclusively linked to violent behavior in players? Why or why not?

2. Audience. Besides Dickinson's professor and classmates, who else do you think might be an appropriate audience for this essay? Would Dickinson need to revise his essay to make it accessible for other audiences?

3. Rhetorical appeals. What are two techniques Dickinson uses to develop his ethos?

4. Rhetorical appeals. Dickinson's appeals to ethos and logos are discussed in the annotations. Can you find any appeals to pathos in the essay?

5. Modes & media. How would the inclusion of screen shots of the video games mentioned add to or detract from the essay?

6. Elements of the genre. How effective do you think Dickinson's refutation of the counterarguments is? Can you think of other refutations he could have used?

7. Style. Dickinson begins his essay by stating that players are "free to do just about anything they want" in *Grand Theft Auto*. What are some other ways Dickinson could have gotten readers' attention at the very beginning? For example, how could a reference to one of the criminals mentioned in the essay be used in the introduction?

8. Style. Dickinson writes in a strong, declarative voice rather than in a tentative "I'm just a student" voice. Find two or three sentences that are particularly strong and analyze the techniques Dickinson uses to come across as authoritative in these sentences.

9. Design. Because this is a short essay, Dickinson opted against using subheadings. If the essay were developed into a longer one, say fifteen pages, what are some subheadings he might use?

10. Sources. Look over Dickinson's Works Cited list. Are there some sources that appear to be more reliable than others?

Drafting a Researched Argument

CHECKLIST: Drafting a Researched Argument
Thinking of writing a researched argument? Ask yourself the following questions.

WHAT'S MY RHETORICAL SITUATION?

☐ **Purpose.** What topic am I researching that might lend itself to an argument? What are some potential persuasive claims I could make about that topic? Have I discovered something about the topic that would contribute to other scholarly research?

☐ **Audience.** Assuming my readers are my classmates and professor—I need to think about how much they already know about my topic. How much background information will they need? What kind of terminology will they expect? How will they use the information I present?

☐ **Rhetorical appeals.** How will I establish my authority as a writer? How will I build a case for my conclusions using logic? What kinds of sources establish me as an expert and work to build my case?

☐ **Modes & media.** Can some of the information I present be shown visually with a chart or graphic? Do I want readers to access my article in print or digitally? Or do I want to make both options available?

WHAT GENRE CONVENTIONS MATTER?

☐ **Elements of the genre.** How will I make my thesis clear and declarative? How will I refer to my sources? How can I synthesize my sources to show readers that my sources are in conversation with each other?

☐ **Style.** How can I project an authoritative voice? How much detail will I need to provide so that readers understand the complexity and validity of my research?

☐ **Design.** How will I use design elements to my advantage? Will I use subheadings to organize and chunk information? Will I use images to illustrate points?

☐ **Sources.** Will my readers expect me to cite my sources in MLA, APA, or another format? Will my readers respect the types of sources I've referred to?

PRACTICE Want to experiment? Draft your own researched argument.

Think of a controversial topic you are curious about, perhaps even a bit uninformed about. Maybe campaign finance reform, the safety of bottled water, or the future of AIDS research. Ask your instructor or a librarian to help you find three reliable sources on the subject. Read the sources and then draft an argumentative thesis statement in which you take a position on the topic. Sketch out at least two counterarguments and your refutations of them.

Creating Blogs 🔲

Blogs began as "Weblogs"—logs that people kept on the newly emerging web of computers connected to what is now called the Internet. Evolving from the notes and correspondence of early Internet pioneers, blogs now provide a space online for people of any technical ability to post writing, pictures, links, and videos to share publicly or privately. Blogs can be used beyond personal applications as accessible platforms for carefully researched arguments, which you just read about. The discussion below provides more information about setting up a blog and maintaining it for a course assignment at Georgia Tech.

Setting Up a Blog

Signing up for a free blog is easy and simply requires creating a username, password, and a personalized URL. At the end of this section, you will learn about options for creating a free blog through Georgia Tech. Most blogging platforms (like WordPress, Blogger, and Tumblr) also allow a user to create a free account and run a blog from the blog domain (so you don't need your own server space); in this case, your blog address will contain the name of the blog host (i.e., www .GeorgeBurdell.wordpress.com). If you do have access to server space, you can run a blog through a service like WordPress or Blogger, but the address will not contain the blog domain (i.e., www.GeorgeBurdell.com).

▼ SCREENSHOT
WordPress Dashboard
The dashboard allows you access to administrative features of a WordPress site.

Once you have created your blog account, you can choose the name of your blog and design the appearance. Users can choose from a selection of predesigned "themes" and then add a variety of tools (sometimes called "widgets") such as a links menu, a calendar, or an RSS feed button. Most blogs provide the option to download plug-in tools that add extra functionality (such as sending out a tweet when you post or parsing out spam from your comment stream).

Privacy   When you are setting up your blog, you need to choose your privacy settings. You can make your blog completely open to the public or limit it to only those people to whom you have given access. Some blogs give you the option of leaving your blog open but selecting not to allow search engines to index the blog (so people can't find your blog using an Internet search). You can also decide about other issues at this stage: you can select if you want to allow any visitor to your site to leave a comment on your blog or if you will require commenters to be registered users. Your best choice is to select "comment moderation," which means that no comments will appear on your site until you have approved them. This way, no inappropriate content or spam will show up on your site without your knowledge. Maintaining control over your content and personal information helps you make the best impression when you apply for future internships or job opportunities.

Blogging for a Course Assignment

Blogs are a useful venue for completing different types of assignments for a course. For your class, you may be asked to keep an individual blog in which you write carefully researched posts about the reading for the course or reflect on what you are learning and experiencing. Alternatively, you might be allowed to use the blog for brainstorming, drafting, or linking to related content on the Web. Sometimes you will be given access to a centralized class blog and asked to regularly post content there viewable by everyone in the course.

Design considerations play a significant role in blogging for a course assignment. You can customize blogs by choosing a theme; changing the default banner image, font color, and menu options; and selecting other design and functionality features. While you will probably have a blog assignment that requires you to post a certain number of times per week or respond to specific prompts, you can use the blog for other types of writing such as brainstorming, drafting, and reflecting. Your blog is also a great space for thinking about multimodal communication, as you can post images, videos, audio, and links to external content. Regardless of whether you have an individual blog or are contributing to a centralized class blog, be sure to check with your instructor about the requirements for voice, style, and grammar: your instructor might be interested in just letting you write casually about your ideas or might be focusing on the quality of your writing—or both.

Georgia Tech Blogs

At Georgia Tech, you might work with blogs in different capacities and with different levels of participation and ownership. The following list outlines some common roles you might have in a blog and considerations for each.

Class Blog   The most common type of blog you'll participate in is a class blog—often hosted on a WordPress blog server. In this case your professor establishes and administers the blog, and you participate as an author who contributes content. If your English 1101/1102 instructor is using the GT Ivan Allen College of Liberal Arts (IAC) blogging platform, the server is set to automatically allow you access through your GT account. However, you should pay close attention to your privacy and permission settings, whether you are using the IAC WordPress blogs or a blogging platform of your own choosing. Before you change your settings for the IAC blogs, carefully consider the following issues:

» By default, IAC blogs require login with a GT account, though your instructor may choose instead to make blog content public if it suits the purposes of the class.

» For public IAC blogs, student names are anonymized when viewed from outside of the campus network; the purpose of this is to protect your private information such as course enrollment.

» By default, posts to an IAC blog will allow others to comment on them. However, to comment, the user must be logged into the blog with their GT account.

With class blogs, your instructor takes responsibility for the overall presentation of the blog, including design and navigation elements, as well as any additional themes or plug-ins. Your primary contributions to a class blog are content, participation in the comments, and addition of effective terms for tagging and sorting posts.

Individual GT IAC Blog   In some cases, you may create and manage your own blog—that is, instead of being one of many participants within a class blog, you or a small group may have a site containing your own content, which you control. In this case, one option is to establish a blog on the same IAC WordPress blog server that often hosts class blogs. In this situation, you would assume more responsibility for the blog but would still benefit from default security settings and GT account authentication.

If you want to use the GT IAC blogging platform for your English 1101 and English 1102 classes, you can go to http://blogs.iac.gatech.edu/ to get started. As a blog administrator, you take responsibility for the design and appearance of the blog as well as for all blog content. If you want others to participate in your blog as commenters or authors, you need to ensure that the blog is set to allow them the access permissions they need.

Personal Third-Party Blog   If you need to run your own blog, you can use a third-party blog hosting service such as WordPress or Blogger, or you can install your own version of WordPress or other blogging software, either in server space provided by GT or off-campus third-party providers. You might do this if you need maximum control over the design of the blog (selecting or designing your own themes) or need extended blog functionality (installing your own or third-party plug-ins). In this case, GT account integration is not built in; you must assume greater responsibility for managing access to the blog, user accounts, and passwords, as well as for determining who is allowed to comment on blog posts and what kind of authentication is required. Blogs with inadequate security often fall victim to "blog spam," where human or automated agents create irrelevant posts or comments containing advertisements and links to scams.

Selecting a blog for your medium requires you to carefully balance access to information with privacy and security. Make sure you weigh your options before choosing the type of blog and hosting service you want to use.

AUTHOR'S/ARTIST'S STATEMENTS

Composers of all sorts often write a statement for their audience that explains their inspirations, intentions, and choices in their creative and critical processes. The liner notes that come with a CD, the program you receive at the theater or symphony, the Director's Commentary on a DVD, the Artist's Statement pinned to the wall at an art gallery—these are all forms of Authors' or Artists' Statements.

The magazine *Cook's Illustrated* is in the business of providing recipes, often with accompanying critical discussions. The point of the discussion—or what you could call a Cook's Statement—is to explain and discuss what went into the creation of the recipe, what went well, and what could have gone better, for example, and to discuss process. In the following discussion of the recipe for Thai Grilled-Beef Salad, recipe writer Andrew Janjigian explains what his goals were and the thought processes behind the decisions he made as he tinkered with the recipe. Janjigian is an associate editor for *Cook's Illustrated* and also works for America's Test Kitchen.

An Author's or Artist's—or Cook's—Statement assists the reader in understanding the process that led to the product. If you've watched a DVD recently, you may have found a Director's Commentary included along with the feature film or documentary. In Director's Commentaries (or Statements), the director—or an actor, choreographer, or other person associated with the film—talks about the considerations that went into making the film, such as casting, lighting, music, and blocking. The Director's Commentary, like an Author's Statement, makes visible, to some extent, the behind-the-scenes work that is invisible in the final product.

When our students create assignments—whatever genre or media they create in—we ask them to write an accompanying Author's or Artist's Statement that can give us insight into what they set out to do, how they did it, and what they might do to further improve the piece.

What are some examples of Authors' or Artists' Statements that you've seen lately? How does understanding a composer's perspective and intent contribute to how you relate to their work? #Understand #Analyze

AUTHOR PHOTO ▶
Andrew Janjigian
America's Test Kitchen.

Thai Grilled-Beef Salad

Our goal was to look no further than the supermarket to replicate this salad's complex range of flavors and textures. Along the way, we learned a neat trick for grilling meat.

≋ BY ANDREW JANJIGIAN ≋

A scoop of rice turns this steak salad into a meal.

High-Steaks Decisions

Five Tastes of Thai Grilled-Beef Salad—and One More

One of the keys to this salad is balancing the signature flavor elements of Thai cuisine. In addition to achieving this, we added one more complementary flavor: the earthiness of toasted cayenne and sweet paprika.

HOT	SOUR	SALTY	SWEET	BITTER	EARTHY

Falling Water

Well Dressed

THAI GRILLED-BEEF SALAD

SERVES 4 TO 6

Unbeadable Thai Trick: Knowing When to Flip

TIME TO FLIP

Look: The Moisture Beads

Video available FREE for 4 months at www.CooksIllustrated.com/aug11

Analyzing Author's/Artist's Statements: What to Look For

THE RHETORICAL SITUATION

Purpose   The purpose of an Author's Statement is for an author (or artist or other composer) to discuss the decisions and choices he or she made in composing a specific text or other work. Let's say you've created an ad or a documentary film for your course. By writing an accompanying Author's or Artist's Statement, you can persuade your readers to see your finished piece in a particular way. A successful Author's Statement reflects your understanding of your chosen genre (and the elements, style, design, and use of sources that characterize it)—and of your specific rhetorical situation (your reasons for composing, your audience, how you use rhetorical appeals, and your choice of mode and medium).

Following is an example of a Director's Statement. It relates to the film *The Social Network*, directed by David Fincher. In the Director's Commentary for the film (included on the DVD), Fincher aims to persuade viewers that his choice in how to cast the main character was motivated by his desire to be realistic:

> I was looking for somebody who could just come out of the gates and be relentlessly who he is, and um, this QuickTime of an audition ended up on my computer and I turned it on and I watched Jesse Eisenberg. I think he did two takes of this scene, and I just thought, "Wow, like, that's pretty undeniable," and I remember dragging Aaron [Sorkin, the screenwriter on the film] into my office and saying, "Just watch this," and he looked at it and he said, "Well, our job's done."
>
> —**David Fincher**, from Director's Commentary for *The Social Network*

If you're writing an Author's Statement in an academic setting, your main purpose is to inform and persuade readers—your peers, your instructor, your audience—of the critical and creative thought you put into your composition.

Audience   The audience for an Author's Statement is usually a particularly engaged and interested reader or viewer. Not everyone who saw the film *The Social Network* listened to David Fincher's Director's Commentary. Only the most interested viewers did; the ones who wanted to better understand the behind-the-scenes process. In an academic setting, your audience is made up of invested and critical readers and viewers, such as your professor and peers, who want to confirm that you've made deliberate choices throughout your composing process.

Rhetorical appeals   In an Author's Statement, writers persuade readers by appealing mainly to logos and ethos. The author's credibility (ethos) is particularly important because, as with most persuasive pieces, the writer needs to come across as honest and thoughtful. Authors can establish ethos through the reasoning (logos) they present in their Authors' Statements. When writers logically present evidence to readers about the choices they made in organizing and presenting their work, readers are more likely to accept the claims the author makes.

To persuade, composers may sometimes appeal to their audience's emotions. For example, if a composer wrote a piece of music as a memorial and wanted it performed a certain way, that message would appear in the program.

Modes & media   Authors choose modes and media for their Statements that are appropriate for those of the work they're discussing. An artist showing work online would probably create a digital Artist's Statement, whereas an artist showing work in a brick-and-mortar gallery would probably print out a text-based statement to hang next to his or her masterpieces.

Elements of the genre   In their Authors' and Artists' Statements, writers do the following:

Discuss a specific composition—and make an argument. In an Author's or Artist's Statement, writers discuss a particular composition—such as an essay, painting, photo, documentary, ad, or other work. They refer directly to that work and provide specific details as they explain the "what, why, and how" of their creation. For example, in the Cook's Statement example from *Cook's Illustrated*, Andrew Janjigian explains that he set out to create a dressing that would successfully blend "the four Thai flavor elements: hot, sour, salty, and sweet." He then explains how he did that.

Writers also make a case for their compositions in order to persuade readers to see their work in a particular way. For example, David Fincher (p. 505) wants us to believe his casting was motivated by a desire for realism. Andrew Janjigian wants us to see that his beef salad recipe succeeds in blending desired flavors.

Address readers directly. Writers use the *I* construction, which allows them to speak plainly to readers about their choices. They also refer to the works they're discussing in the Statement as "my essay" (or "my painting," "my photograph," etc.), indicating their ownership of the composition and the choices they made.

Explain their choice of genre—and how they worked with its conventions. The Author's or Artist's Statement is a place for a composer to explain why he or she chose to work in a particular genre. For example, let's say that for your composition course, you chose to write an opinion piece on gun control. In a separate statement, submitted with your opinion piece, you might explain to your instructor and classmates why you chose this genre. Pointing out your specific choices builds your ethos and persuasiveness. You might note, for example, that the opinion piece was the best choice of genre, because it allowed you to:

» Clearly present your opinion on the topic of gun control (and write in the first person)

» Be brief (just a few paragraphs) and lively

» Deal with potential objections and offer potential solutions

» Invite readers to respond

What are some arguments a musician might make about a song or album? What are some claims a fashion designer might make about a new line of clothing? #Understand

Alternatively, maybe you created a photo essay, for your class or a wider audience. An accompanying statement—in which you explain why you found the photo essay to be the best way to communicate your ideas about gun control—would go a long way toward helping your viewers get the most out of your work.

Discuss their specific rhetorical situation—and related choices. The Author's or Artist's Statement gives you, as a composer, an opportunity to explain to audiences:

» Your purpose: why you composed the work—on that specific topic, in that specific way

» Your audience and use of rhetorical appeals: what you understand about your readers and how you connected with them through choices regarding ethos, pathos, and logos

» Your mode and medium: why you chose them and how they benefit your work overall

For example, if you created a collage—perhaps on the topic of body art and identity—in your Artist's Statement, you could explain to viewers:

» Your purpose or main point in creating a collage on the relationship between body art and identity—and what the relationship is

» Why you chose specific central images, how they contribute to your message, and how you hope your viewers will read them and relate to the collage overall

» How you wanted to connect with your viewers through pathos, logos, and ethos (for example, your arrangement of images might appeal to their logic or emotions)

» Why you decided to create the collage, say, in a digital format

Reflect on their compositions—and discuss successes and limitations. Writers use Authors' Statements as an opportunity to look back at a composition and to evaluate the extent of their achievement; they might also note what they would have done differently or better. For example, say you created an advertisement showing how marines achieve strength without steroids. You might note in an accompanying Author's Statement that you felt you'd succeeded in providing a captivating visual, an original slogan, and an emotional appeal. On the other hand, don't hesitate to mention in your Statement places where you could improve your work editorially or technically. The point here is to do your best and reflect on what you did well and talk about what you'd like to improve. This all adds to your ethos as a composer and to the persuasiveness of your work.

Provide context. In the Author's or Artist's Statement, it's useful for writers to give some background on their composition (their editorial or collage, etc.), such as how they became interested in the topic, what their inspirations were, or, if they've created a series of related works, how the piece fits in with other pieces. Andrew Janjigian explains in his Cook's Statement that he decided to create his own beef salad recipe because he hadn't found one that came close to achieving the quality of beef salads he'd eaten in Thai restaurants.

Style Statement authors do the following:

Use detail. The persuasive and critical nature of the Statement depends on the use of specific detail. Janjigian, for example, names particular ingredients that he tried and describes the exact result he got, such as in his discussion of what happened when he used cayenne pepper instead of powdered Thai bird chiles: "Just ½ teaspoon of cayenne, in fact, overpowered the meat's smoky char."

Write in a tone that builds ethos. In their Statements, authors use critical, analytical language to make their points. They choose words related to their subject of inquiry to establish themselves as experts. When you write such a Statement, even though you're writing in the first person (*I*), use a serious, straightforward tone to emphasize that you have made deliberate, thoughtful choices.

Design Authors' Statements can often look very much like an academic essay, with indented paragraphs and little or no decoration except for subheadings that offer structure and organization. However, a writer might choose to design an Author's Statement to reflect the genre of the composition. For example, an Author's Statement might take the form of a letter written to a professor, a Director's Commentary, or a one-page Artist's Statement.

Sources The most persuasive authors discuss the sources that informed their composing process. For example, in his Statement, student Michael Kipp mentions specific sources by title or author's name, including page numbers. Depending on the audience, sources may be cited according to MLA or APA or other academic formats, as in Michael Kipp's Statement on page 510. An artist who is inspired by another artist usually names his or her inspiration and cites specific works by that artist.

Besides the essay format, what other forms might you use for an Author's or Artist's Statement? When might writing a song for this purpose be appropriate? Are there forms that would never work as a Statement? What forms? Why? #Understand #Analyze

Michael Kipp (Student)

Artist's Statement: Why and How I Created My Collage: "Thank You"

Michael Kipp, a student at Red Rocks Community College, became interested in the concept of gratitude and happiness when he took a psychology course and studied positive psychology. As part of a second-semester research-based composition class, Kipp decided to focus his semester-long multigenre project on the idea of gratitude, looking at research in the field and reflecting on his own experience with feeling gratitude. One of the pieces Kipp created for the project was a collage illustrating gratitude, which includes a quote. Accompanying the collage is his Artist's Statement, analyzing the choices he made in creating the collage, such as design and organization, and illustrating how his collage achieves his purpose and uses rhetorical appeals to persuade his audience. *("Artist's Statement: Why and How I Created My Collage: 'Thank You.'" Reprinted Courtesy of Michael Kipp.)*

▲ STUDENT AUTHOR PHOTO & ◀ COLLAGE
Michael Kipp and his composition, *Thank You*, the subject of his Artist's Statement on page 510. *Michael Kipp.*

What is the composer, Michael Kipp, doing?

THE RHETORICAL SITUATION

Purpose
Audience
Rhetorical appeals
Modes & media

see page 511

How do I know this is an Artist's Statement?

THE GENRE'S CONVENTIONS

Elements of the genre
Style
Design
Sources

see page 511

Michael Kipp
Artist's Statement: Why and How I Created My Collage: "Thank You"

"Psychologists have repeatedly shown that perceptions are more important than objective reality" ("Positive Thinking"). This quote embodies the message behind my collage. It ties in with messages from other research I've done on the science of happiness, including my reading of the article "Psychological Research: Gratitude," by Jerry Lopper. In that piece, Lopper quotes psychologist and researcher Dr. Alex Wood as saying: "Gratitude is a life orientation towards noticing and appreciating the positive in the world." These quotes suggest that feeling grateful requires mental work (Emmons, *Thanks!* 6). Gratitude is a part of our perception, a "life orientation," and without effort that perception will not arise or be maintained. Thus, to have an attitude of gratefulness, we must change our outlook on life. My purpose in creating this collage is to promote the idea that we make choices about how we perceive experience, and that practicing gratitude can make us happier.

My intended audience is made up of people who like art, psychology, and philosophy, who appreciate the abstract expression of concepts, and who may be persuaded to think about how a grateful attitude could be more important than one's objective reality—and how they may practice that in their own life to be happier.

In my collage I used *pathos* to convey these ideas—I wanted to sway my viewers emotionally, to cause them to feel curious and inspired when looking at the collage. I did this through my choices of composition, colors, and subjects, which are discussed in depth below. I used striking contrast and positioned the objects in ways the viewer would not expect, thus drawing attention to them. I also used *logos* by putting the piece together in a logical manner, and by grounding my concept in positive psychology research. Furthermore, by including the quote about perception and reality, I ask viewers to think about how the collage illustrates that concept. My goal is that my audience will ponder what each part of the collage represents and come to logical conclusions about the collage's representation of gratitude.

During my research, the following passage stood out for me: "A grateful outlook does not require a life full of material comforts but rather an interior attitude of thankfulness regardless of life circumstances" (Emmons and Shelton, "Gratitude" 465). I wanted to convey this idea visually by emphasizing contrasting experiences; a negative or challenging objective reality is represented by the black background, which is supposed to have a feel of encompassing and surrounding the sitting figure, which is asymmetrically placed within the piece. The figure herself is creating a positive perception of her reality, the potential of which is represented by the landscape and the rainbow, which arches upward and out—drawing the eye forward and to a higher point. A Spanish study confirmed that positive affect rises in persons who practice gratitude, which was found in a previous study (Martinez-Marti, Avia, and Hernandez-Lloreda 893).

Also, the landscape refers to the fact that grateful people experience a positive memory bias—they are more likely to recall positive memories, similar to the negative memory bias experienced in depression (Watkins 63). The idea of creation is also suggested by the plant, whose roots surround the woman's head. Her efforts to be thankful and practice gratitude are nourishing the plant, which grows upward, changing her reality, subjective and objective, for the better. The figure's pose is reminiscent of *The Thinker*, a nineteenth-century sculpture by Rodin, which suggests that changing one's attitude takes intentional, active thought. "People adapt quickly to positive changes in their lives and thus derive diminishing happiness returns" ("Positive Thinking"), so it may be that practicing gratitude helps counteract that adaptation.

Continues next page

THE RHETORICAL SITUATION

Purpose

Kipp's purpose is to persuade readers that "practicing gratitude can make us happier" and that his collage furthers that goal. He wants readers to know that he made thoughtful decisions when composing the collage.

(Continued on p. 512.)

THE GENRE'S CONVENTIONS

Elements of the genre

Kipp **discusses a specific composition** (his collage)—and makes an argument about it. He supports claims with evidence; for example, Kipp discusses how he used color and composition in the context of Emmons and Shelton's concept of an "interior attitude of thankfulness."

Kipp **addresses readers directly** (e.g., "I considered adding words") and uses *my* throughout (e.g., "my collage" and "my research").

(Continued on p. 000.)

Kipp, *Artist's Statement,* *Continued*

THE RHETORICAL
SITUATION

Audience

His readers are his
instructor and fellow
students. They want
to know why he
created a collage
and what research
informed it.

THE GENRE'S
CONVENTIONS

Kipp **explains why
he created a collage**
and how he worked
with established
conventions. For
example, he writes
that choosing this
genre meant he
could use a variety
of images—and
also use a black
background as part
of the composition.

He **talks about
his rhetorical
situation**—and
specific related
choices. For
example, he appeals
to his audience
through pathos,
hoping they "feel
curious and inspired"
when viewing the
collage.

The embracing arms in the collage represent several things: first, they represent the tendency for people who practice gratitude to be more prosocial, more likely to help others or return a favor, than less grateful people (Tsang 139). They also represent the positive social benefits we receive when we regularly practice gratitude (Watkins, Grimm, and Kolts 65). Finally, they represent that gratitude is an acknowledgment that one is dependent on others (Emmons and Shelton, "Gratitude" 463). The angle of the arms to the rainbow creates a triangle, which leads the eye to the point where they get close together and hit the frame. The frames represent precisely that—that gratefulness is a frame of mind. What is outside that frame is objective reality. The parallel lines created by the frames again pull the eye upward; their top ends create a diagonal line with the part of the plant where the last leaf connects to the stem, as well as the top of the mountain, which pulls the eye back to the left center of the piece, and finally back to the central figure. The shelf the books rest on and the bench the woman sits on repeat the parallel lines created in the frames, but are perpendicular to them. The red "Thank You" at the bottom of the piece pulls in the warm colors in the arms at the opposite side and serves as a sort of name tag—indicating that the collage is based on thankfulness, as is the woman's perception of her life.

All of these pieces contribute to the composition of my collage—even the use of a canvas was intentional, enhancing the idea of active creation. I used a collage because even though I am unfamiliar with the genre, I am familiar with painting and drawing, so I have some, although limited, background in composition and got to try something new. I also wanted to create in a medium other than text or a computer-based visual. Collages often have more cut out pieces pasted together, but the more I added, the less I felt like the collage conveyed the intended message. Covering too much of the black background defeated the purpose of that background—the

Kipp, *Artist's Statement,* *Continued*

negative space is as important as the positive space. I considered adding words, but found that I liked the collage better when no words were used, that it was more powerful without text—this is also why I moved "Thank You" off the canvas; it complements the idea behind the picture, but is not included within the composition itself. I added the perception and reality quote last—I think it gives the viewer more to think about, particularly because it is the quote that inspired the entire piece. It also extends the ideas I've presented, asking viewers not only to feel and practice gratitude, but to affect their own experiences of reality by doing so.

Works Cited

Emmons, Robert A. *Thanks! How the New Science of Gratitude Can Make You Happier.* New York: Houghton Mifflin Harcourt, 2007. Web. 10 Oct. 2012. <http://books.google.com/books?id=tGCcH2l4jUUC>.

Emmons, Robert A., and Charles M. Shelton. "Gratitude and the Science of Positive Psychology." *Handbook of Positive Psychology.* Eds. C. R. Snyder and Shane J. Lopez. New York: Oxford University Press, 2002. 459-471. Print.

Lopper, Jerry. "Psychological Research: Gratitude." *Suite101.* Suite101, 19 May 2008. Web. 10 Oct. 2012. <http://www.suite101.com/content/psychological-research-gratitude-a54399>.

Martinez-Marti, Maria Luisa, Maria Dolores Avia, and Maria Jose Hernandez-Lloreda. "The Effects of Counting Blessings on Subjective Well-Being: A Gratitude Intervention in a Spanish Sample." *Spanish Journal of Psychology* 13.2 (2010): 886-896. Web. 25 Nov. 2012. <http://www.ucm.es/info/psi/docs/journal/v13_n2_2010/art886.pdf>.

Continues next page

THE RHETORICAL SITUATION

Rhetorical appeals
Kipp establishes his credibility, or **ethos,** in paragraph 1 by showing he's done research on positive psychology, including quotes from experts.

(Continued on p. 514.)

THE GENRE'S CONVENTIONS

Kipp **reflects on his successes and limitations.** For example, he mentions that though he has a "limited" background in design and visual composition, he was pleased by achieving a "striking contrast" for viewers through his positioning of images.

Kipp **provides context** by discussing his interest in the concept of gratitude and his goal to show readers "that practicing gratitude can make us happier."

(Continued on p. 514.)

Kipp, *Artist's Statement***,** *Continued*

Pursuit of Happiness.org / Teaching Happiness, Inc. "Positive Thinking: Optimism and Gratitude." *The Pursuit of Happiness*. Pursuit-of-Happiness.org (Teaching Happiness, Inc.), n.d. Web. 26 Nov. 2012. <http://www.pursuit-of-happiness.org/science-of-happiness/positive-thinking/>.

Rodin, Auguste. *The Thinker*. 1880-81. Bronze sculpture. Cleveland Museum of Art, Cleveland.

Tsang, Jo-Ann. "Gratitude and Prosocial Behaviour: An Experimental Test of Gratitude." *Cognition & Emotion* 20.1 (2006): 138-148. *Academic Search Premier*. Web. 25 Nov. 2012.

Watkins, Philip C., Dean L. Grimm, and Russell Kolts. "Counting Your Blessings: Positive Memories among Grateful People." *Current Psychology* 23.1 (2004): 52-67. *Academic Search Premier*. Web. 25 Nov. 2012.

THE RHETORICAL SITUATION

Kipp appeals to **logos** by explaining his choices logically and using evidence from his collage to support his claims. For example, when he discusses his use of **pathos**, he shows how he used contrast and layout to make readers curious.

Modes & media

Mode = written
Kipp uses only words to make his case for his collage. He uses both his own analysis and outside research to deliver his reflections and analysis.

Medium = print
Because Kipp composed his statement as a researched academic essay, he chose to print it out and submit it to his instructor that way. Of course, he could also have submitted the statement digitally. In digital format, readers could easily click on the sources in his Works Cited page, for example.

THE GENRE'S CONVENTIONS

Style

Kipp **uses specific detail.** For example, he talks about the image of embracing arms, and what they represent in terms of gratitude, how their angle orients the reader toward a certain point, and how the arms relate to the frame.

His **word choice reflects his critical thought** (e.g., intentional, sway, ponder, grounding, bias).

Design

Kipp structures and designs his statement as a traditional researched essay with an introduction, body paragraphs, conclusion, parenthetical citations, and Works Cited list.

Sources

Kipp's sources for the Artist's Statement are the collage itself and the research he conducted on gratitude. He refers to source material, such as a study by Martinez-Marti, Avia, and Hernandez-Lloreda, and relates that back to his collage.

He cites his sources per MLA style and connects them to the decisions he made in composing his collage.

Questions: Analyzing Kipp's Artist's Statement

1. Purpose. How does Kipp convince you that his collage illustrates that "practicing gratitude can make us happier"?

2. Audience. Although the primary audience for the piece is Kipp's instructor, are there other audiences that might be interested in reading the piece? If so, who? Why?

3. Rhetorical appeals. One of the ways Kipp establishes his ethos is by including research. How else does he establish his ethos?

4. Rhetorical appeals. Why would it be inappropriate for Kipp to use pathos in an Artist's Statement? Are there any circumstances where pathos might be appropriate for an Artist's Statement? What circumstances? Why?

5. Modes & media. How would including visuals enhance Kipp's Artist's Statement? Where might he incorporate visuals?

6. Elements of the genre. What types of evidence does Kipp use to support his claims? How effective is the evidence? Are there places where he might have included different evidence? If so, where and what?

7. Elements of the genre. Throughout the statement, Kipp shows how research influences his choices and motivations. Do you learn anything about Kipp's own personal motivation for exploring this subject? If so, how? If not, what would this add to the Artist's Statement?

8. Style. How does Kipp use language to establish his credibility?

9. Design. Kipp chose to submit his Artist's Statement in a traditional academic essay form. Would the piece be strengthened if he had used subheads and divided the Artist's Statement into sections? If so, what would be the different sections?

10. Sources. What are the different purposes the research serves in Kipp's Artist's Statement?

Drafting an Author's/Artist's Statement

CHECKLIST: Drafting a Statement Thinking of drafting an Author's/Artist's Statement? Ask yourself the following questions.

WHAT'S MY RHETORICAL SITUATION?

☐ **Purpose.** What is the central claim I want to make about my piece? What particular elements do I need to justify? What choices did I make as I created the piece? What motivated me to create the piece?

☐ **Audience.** Am I writing this Statement for my instructor? For fellow students? Will my Statement be read by people outside the academic setting? If so, how will this affect what I write?

☐ **Rhetorical appeals.** What makes me a credible writer on this subject? How will I show readers my credibility? How will I organize my information to support my claims?

☐ **Modes & media.** Will I present my Statement only in written form? Is it appropriate to incorporate visuals? If so, what types of visuals? How would the inclusion of audio enhance my Statement? Would it be appropriate to just use audio? Do I want to present my work in print or digital form?

WHAT GENRE CONVENTIONS MATTER?

☐ **Elements of the genre.** What persuasive point do I want to make about my piece? How can I support that point with specific examples and details from my composition and process? Are there aspects of the context that readers should know to fully understand and appreciate my work?

☐ **Style.** How can I use my tone to convey the seriousness with which I view my work? What details can I use to support the generalizations I make?

☐ **Design.** How will I organize my Statement? What visuals should I include? Should I use subheadings, or is my Statement short enough that subheadings aren't necessary?

☐ **Sources.** Is the piece I composed informed by source material? What inspired me? Where did I get the facts and information that I used? Will my audience expect formal citations?

PRACTICE Want to experiment? Draft your own Author's/Artist's Statement.

Look at a piece you wrote earlier in the semester or for another class. Reflect on the choices you made as you thought through and created the piece. Where did you put most of your energy and why? Where did you get your ideas? What did you tinker with? Then draft a brief statement in which you discuss your process and thoughts.

COLLAGES/VISUAL ARGUMENTS

Collage is an art form that involves gluing pieces of paper, ribbon, newspaper, photos, gems, buttons, and other small items to a paper, poster board, wood, or canvas background. Artists use a combination of everyday or "found" materials, assembling them to create a piece of art. Collage techniques have been used since tenth-century Japanese calligraphers glued colored pieces of paper to their poems; today, scrapbookers and other DIY artists use collage techniques.

Have you ever made a collage? If so, why? And for what audience? What was the overall message of your collage? #Understand #Apply

Iconic artists, including Pablo Picasso (1881–1973), have used collage to express ideas—and to make arguments. One of Picasso's well-known collages is *Guitar, Sheet Music, and Glass*, completed in 1912, in which the artist glued pieces of sheet music and newspaper to a background.

◀ COLLAGE
Pablo Picasso
Guitar, Sheet Music, and Glass (1912).
© McNay Art Museum/ Art Resource, NY.

Let's look at Picasso's collage as a visual argument. What is Picasso arguing? And what choices make his argument(s) clear? Let's look at two of the choices he made.

1. Picasso chose to represent the objects in the collage in an abstract, rather than a realistic, way. Possible argument: Picasso is making a case for a break from traditional forms of art such as lifelike or still-life painting.

2. Picasso chose to use everyday materials drawn from everyday life (wallpaper, a cast-off piece of sheet music, etc.). Possible argument: Picasso is making the case for the value of the everyday in fine art. (This was a revolutionary idea back in 1912.)

What are some other examples of visual arguments? This book is filled with them—ads, comics, bumper stickers, photos, and other images. While the focus of this section is on the collage as a visual argument, much of the advice here also pertains to any type of visual argument.

POLITICAL CARTOON ▶
**Rex F. May
(a.k.a. Baloo)**
*"My Point of View."
Reprinted by permission
of Rex May.*

Analyzing Collages/Visual Arguments: What to Look For

Purpose   We (artists, nonartists, students) create visual artwork, including collages, in order to convey ideas or aesthetic concepts—and often to make a visual argument or commentary on a controversial issue, a moment in time, or a cultural theme. Some collage artists, for example, choose a particular shape for their composition to emphasize their point.

Audience   Visual artists often appeal to a particular audience through their choice of subject. For example, the artist Kara Walker, who works with issues of race and gender, knows that her art appeals to people who are interested in slavery, racism, and feminism. In the piece on page 520, taken from an exhibit entitled "Kara Walker: Annotating History," Walker superimposes a figure over an original illustration from *Harper's Pictorial History of the Civil War* of 1866/1868.

◀ ARTIST PHOTO
Kara Walker
With her work at her 2007–08 installation at the Whitney Museum of American Art. *Librado Romero/NY Times.*

▲ COLLAGE
Kara Walker

*A Warm Summer
Evening in 1863.*
Walker uses a silk-
screening process to
create layers in this
mixed-media print.
*Untitled collage on
paper, Artwork G Kara
Walker/Image courtesy
of Sikkema Jenkins &
Co., New York.*

Rhetorical appeals   Visual composers use image, line, color, and other visual elements to express concepts and arguments. Depending on an artist's main point—
and how he or she chooses to reach viewers—the artist will emphasize ethos,
pathos, or logos. For example, the composer of the *Business Collage* on page 523
appeals to viewers' sense of logos by creating a chain of reasoning for the reader.
The "$" and "Only" on the glasses in the collage tell the reader that the consumer
organizes the world according to money and perceived bargains. Additionally, the
composer appeals to viewers' sense of pathos by presenting a relationship between
the pressure of consumerism (as symbolized by the coupons) and addictive
behavior (as symbolized by the cigarette and the beckoning finger). The piece is

persuasive because of the textual messages, the visual representation of a consumer, and the juxtaposition of all the elements.

The *Coffee Break* collage below was created in response to a contest called the NASA Remix Challenge. The composer combined real NASA photos and a picture of a café on Route 66. The artist establishes ethos by using real photos to remix ideas about the moon landing, and also appeals to viewers' pathos through humor. The original caption reads: "After 109 hours, 39 minutes in the lunar module, Neil Armstrong and Buzz Aldrin enjoy a double cafe mocha." The collagist persuades the viewer that Starbucks has no boundaries—they will even take their product to the moon.

Modes & media   Visual composers use a variety of visual elements to create their work. Collagists, specifically, cut images out of magazines, incorporate found objects and fabrics, and work with photos to create their assemblages. When text is a part of a collage, it is usually "found text" taken from something else rather than written specifically for the collage. Collages are delivered in a variety of media—in galleries, print magazines, and digital collections.

Visual composers arrange images in certain ways to create connections. Have you ever seen two images side by side and been struck by the combination? How does seeing an image on its own—or paired with another—alter how you experience it? #Understand

◀ COLLAGE
Jerry Taylor
Coffee Break. "Coffee Break" NASA remix, Jerry Taylor (jrtcel).

Elements of the genre   Visual composers do the following:

Convey a theme. If you think of a visual work as an argument, then the visual artist, like an editorial writer or film reviewer, for example, creates works that convey a central idea or commentary. In collages, artists juxtapose different images or use shape and form to convey a theme. For example, among the images the *Business Collage* artist chooses are a dollar sign and a price tag, which contribute to the overall commentary on greed, consumption, and "business."

Connect with culture and history. Visual artists—especially those making an argument—often create or incorporate images that allude to a cultural or historical phenomenon. For example, in one of her collages, Kara Walker features an image of Ulysses S. Grant, the eighteenth U.S. president and commander of the Union army in the Civil War, and pastes onto it an image of an African American woman. Walker's collage makes clear the differences between her perspective and that of the nineteenth-century creators of the Grant image and puts her work in the context of the Civil War.

Use layers and juxtapose images and materials. By definition, collages are composed of a variety of objects. Collagists use a variety of objects to bring texture and dimensionality to their work. All visual artists, especially those presenting an argument, consider how presentation and positioning of different items affect how viewers see the work.

Use color to direct the attention of the viewer. In Kara Walker's collage, the superimposed silhouette stands out against the pale background image. Collage artists use the same principles as composers of advertisements, who might contrast the color of the text with the background of the page or screen so that the text is more prominent for the viewer.

Assemble parts. When artists assemble a collage, they use a variety of materials, such as scissors, glue, newspapers, magazines, books, and paint. Because you can make a collage out of anything, you can use materials you find in the kitchen or at a bus stop. For example, the Romanian-born Swiss artist Daniel Spoerri uses familiar objects in his pieces, such as kitchen plates and leftover food. Although collagists have the broadest range of materials, all visual artists use a variety of materials to assemble their pieces.

Style   Visual composers do the following:

Present varying degrees of detail. The amount of detail in a visual argument varies. In Picasso's collage (p. 517), he uses just a few elements to create his piece. In the *Coffee Break* collage (p. 521), the artist uses detail to emphasize the Starbucks brand.

Convey a tone. Artists convey their attitudes toward the subjects of their work. Some artists use parody to persuade viewers, for example, the creator of the *Coffee Break* collage.

Design   Visual composers do the following:

Vary the size and shape of their compositions. Collage artists, like other visual artists, are not limited by a particular size or form for their creations. Some pieces might be the size of a sheet of paper, while others might occupy an entire wall. In collage, in particular, by using shape in a deliberate way the artist conveys a point.

Embrace (or reject or remix) traditional artistic conventions. Collagists generally follow the con-

▲ COLLAGE **Stock Artist,** *Business Collage*
CSA Images/Printstock Collection/Getty Images.

ventions of visual art, in terms of balance, contrast, and perspective. These conventions allow the artist to make sure that nothing in the piece gets more attention than he or she wants it to. Artists generally divide their canvases into sections. For example, the collagist who created *Coffee Break* divides his work into thirds, with each astronaut on the outer third of the piece. This keeps the artist from putting an image right smack in the middle, where it would dominate the piece. As with other art forms, when artists violate the rules of perspective and other conventions, they do it with a purpose, to call attention to the violation.

Present patterns/repeat certain elements. All visual artists must give their work a sense of order or coherence. This is true of collagists, whose works are made of seemingly random pieces, but which can be given order through the repetition of elements such as color or shape. The *Business Collage*, for instance, is held together visually by the predominant use of black and white, and by the curved shapes of the ears, chin, and glasses. Other artists use similar strategies, repeating shapes and colors to give a piece an overall sense of unity.

Use lines (or not). Collagists use the lines created by the edges of the images they've assembled to direct the audience's attention to particular elements, just as an arrow would. Notice, for example, how the flagpole in *Coffee Break* directs your attention to both the café flag and the astronaut's arm. Visual artists working in other media use lines similarly. Click through a museum Web site and find a painting and notice how the lines in the painting direct your attention.

Look around you and find three visual pieces in any medium—posters, ads, billboards, and so on. Which pieces are divided into thirds? What is the effect? #Understand

Sources   To create collages, artists do the following:

Incorporate found objects. The cutouts and items that a collagist uses are considered "found objects" because they are not created for artistic purposes; rather, they are items that have been repurposed by an artist. Source material is often paper based, such as photos and cutouts from magazines and newspapers, but can be any item an artist chooses. Collage artists have used small objects like buttons and ribbons, parts of items like tree branches, and larger items, too. Visual artists working in other media get ideas and inspiration from many sources; for example, an artist might paint a portrait based on a photograph of a person or place.

Incorporate cultural materials. Artists may include cultural and historical materials such as documents and images.

Richard Hamilton

Just What Is It That Makes Today's Homes So Different, So Appealing?

On page 526 is a collage created in 1956 by artist Richard Hamilton (1922–2011), entitled *Just What Is It That Makes Today's Homes So Different, So Appealing?* The dimensions of the original are 10¼ × 9¾ inches. When the collage was first displayed as part of an exhibit titled *This Is Tomorrow*, the image of the tape player in the collage had a sound source behind it, making the piece not just a collage but a multimodal composition. The *This Is Tomorrow* exhibit kick-started the pop art movement, and *Just What Is It That Makes Today's Homes So Different, So Appealing?* became one of the most recognized pieces of pop art ever produced. Pop art raised everyday materials and techniques to art status, featuring more ingenuity and cleverness than high art sensibility. The background of this collage is a flooring ad torn from a 1950s *Ladies' Home Journal*. *(Image on page 526: © R. Hamilton. All Rights Reserved, DACS 2013.)*

What do you think of pop art? Is everyday or "lowbrow" life worth looking at? How do the sensibilities of Hamilton, "the father of pop art," compare with your own? Learn more in his obituaries in digital editions of the *Guardian* and *The New York Times*. #Understand

◀ ARTIST PHOTO
Richard Hamilton
Chris Morphet/Getty Images.

Hamilton, *Today's Homes,* Continued

What is the composer, **Richard Hamilton**, doing?

THE RHETORICAL SITUATION

Purpose
Audience
Rhetorical appeals
Modes & media

see page 527

THE GENRE'S CONVENTIONS

Elements of the genre
Style
Design
Sources

see page 527

How do I know this is a **collage/visual argument**?

Hamilton, *Today's Homes, Continued*

THE RHETORICAL SITUATION

Purpose

Hamilton makes an argument about 1950s domesticity, sexuality, and consumerism. He wants to persuade us that having all the new consumer culture wouldn't lead to a perfect life—it would merely lead to a perfect-*looking* life. He also comments on 1950s body ideals.

Audience

His viewers appreciate visual art, pop culture, and humor. When the piece was originally displayed in 1956, many audience members were probably curiosity seekers attracted by the hoopla around the exhibit.

Rhetorical appeals

The artist appeals to **pathos** by presenting erotic images—a bodybuilder and a nude woman on a couch—in a domestic situation. He establishes his **ethos** by including items that might be found in a home in the late 1950s.

Modes & media

Mode = visual and audio The visual aspect is most obvious. When the piece was exhibited in 1956 in *This Is Tomorrow*, it also had an audio element because of the sound source behind the radio.

Medium = paper In the original exhibition, the piece was viewed face-to-face. Reproductions can be conveyed in print, as in this book, or digitally, as in images of the piece on the Internet. Artwork typically makes a more profound impression when viewed face-to-face, in part because a small reproduction in a book simply can't make the same impact as a large piece can in person. Textures that are evident in a face-to-face viewing are usually lost in print or digital renderings.

THE GENRE'S CONVENTIONS

Elements of the genre

Presents a theme. Hamilton's collage connects 1950s home life with romance (e.g., the framed comic book page), convenience (e.g., the canned ham), and tradition (e.g., the formal portrait on the wall).

Connects with history and culture. The images from 1950s pop culture invite viewers to make associations. For example, the canned ham connects with World War II, when fresh meat was scarce and convenience foods like Spam hit the market.

Layers images. The artist cut images from ads and magazines, then arranged them into a layered composition.

Works with color. Hamilton chooses mainly black and white, but uses color very deliberately. For example, the Tootsie Pop and the framed comic stand out.

Assembles the pieces. Hamilton used a transparent material to attach the pieces, so that it would not interfere with the visual impact.

Style

Brings in specific detail. For example, the artist makes sure the brands of the canned ham and the lollipop are visible.

Conveys a tone and attitude. Most living rooms don't feature a naked bodybuilder holding a giant lollipop, yet Hamilton uses images such as these to create an ironic and satirical tone.

Design

Consciously uses size and shape. Hamilton works with scale to create emphasis—note the different sizes of the women in the image.

Works with traditional art conventions. While this collage looks very modern, Hamilton conforms to established principles of balance, contrast, and perspective.

Repeats elements. For example, the rectangular shapes (the couches) highlight the idea that people are constrained by consumerism rather than liberated by it.

Uses lines. Hamilton creates strong horizontal and vertical lines with the edges of the cutouts, such as the couch, window, portrait, and framed comic.

Sources

The collage is made up of clippings from magazines (e.g., *Ladies' Home Journal*) and advertisements of the time.

Questions: Analyzing Hamilton's collage

1. Purpose. Hamilton is considered a creator of pop art. In an interview, he said that he considered pop art to be "popular (designed for a mass audience); transient (short-term solution); expendable (easily forgotten); low cost; mass produced; young (aimed at youth); witty; sexy; gimmicky; glamorous; and last but not least, Big Business." In what ways does Hamilton's collage seem consistent with his thoughts on pop culture? Explain.

2. Purpose. Hamilton's collage is titled *Just What Is It That Makes Today's Homes So Different, So Appealing?* How does the title direct your thinking about the artist's point in making the collage? How effective is the title? Why?

3. Audience. The collage uses images current for audiences in 1956. View some of the modern adaptations created by students at Joliet Junior College at www .redmagazine.com/web2012/feature_what_ the.html. How do you think the audiences for Hamilton's collage and the students' collages are similar and/or different?

4. Rhetorical appeals. How does Hamilton appeal to your emotions? What emotions is he appealing to and how?

5. Rhetorical appeals. What other rhetorical methods does Hamilton use to try to persuade us, his viewers, of his take on 1950s domestic culture?

6. Modes & media. You are viewing this piece at a smaller size than the original. Check out a bigger version of this collage from the Tate museum site, in London. What details do you notice in it that you didn't notice when you looked at the small printed reproduction in the book?

7. Elements of the genre. What ideas or themes do you notice in the collage?

8. Style. How would the collage be different if the canned ham and lollipop weren't associated with particular brands?

9. Style. Do certain parts of the collage seem to attract more of your attention? For example, do your eyes more readily go to the romance comic book page on the wall or to the Tootsie Pop acting as a loincloth? Why?

10. Design. How many different materials can you identify in the collage? How does the use of different materials affect you as a viewer?

11. Design. How do the lines and use of color in the collage direct your attention toward particular elements?

12. Sources. The collage is made up of "found objects" rather than created from scratch. How does the fact that the collage is constructed of rather mundane scraps from magazines and advertisements, rather than painted or drawn, lend meaning to it? Keep in mind that the purposes and audiences for the scraps are probably different from the purposes and audiences of the collage. For example, the Tootsie Pop cutout in the collage was probably originally intended for an advertisement, not an artistic collage.

Drafting/Sketching a Collage/Visual Argument

CHECKLIST: Planning a Collage
Thinking of sketching out a collage or other visual argument? Ask yourself the following questions.

WHAT'S MY RHETORICAL SITUATION?

☐ **Purpose.** What idea do I want to represent in a collage or other visual argument? Do I want to persuade others about a political issue? Do I want my viewers to take some type of action? What themes might I use to advance my ideas or arguments?

☐ **Audience.** Will my collage or other visual argument be viewed in a public space? Private space? What type of viewer is interested in my subject? Who do I want to influence?

☐ **Rhetorical appeals.** How will I establish my credibility? How will I persuade my viewer? Do I want to appeal to viewers' emotions through humor? Do I want to shock viewers? How will I organize my material to appeal to viewers' sense of logos?

☐ **Modes & media.** To create a visual argument, will I use only visuals, such as photographs? Will I incorporate text? Will the text be something I create or something I take from existing material? Do I want viewers to see the piece face-to-face, such as hanging on a wall? Or do I want to digitize the piece so that anyone can view it?

WHAT GENRE CONVENTIONS MATTER?

☐ **Elements of the genre.** What theme do I want to convey? How can I use shape, color, image, and other elements to convey this theme? What connotations and cultural associations do I want my audience to catch?

☐ **Style.** How can I layer and juxtapose materials to add dimensionality? What colors will convey my point? What materials will I use to put everything together? How much detail will I need to persuade my audience? Do I want to convey a satirical tone? A serious tone? Some other tone?

☐ **Design.** What size and shape will my visual argument be? Is there a particular shape I can use to convey my point? How will I use balance, contrast, perspective, and line to focus my audience's attention on particular elements? What elements can I repeat to give the piece a sense of order?

☐ **Sources.** What sources will I use? Should I consider cutting photos or pictures out of magazines, or printing images from the Internet (or embedding them if I'm creating a digital file)? What about objects, such as buttons, jewelry, or scraps? How about found objects such as a grocery list, a cocktail napkin, or a restaurant's bar coaster? Do I know particular cultural or historical associations that I'd like to emphasize for my audience? If so, I need to consider working with (or from) these types of materials.

PRACTICE Want to experiment? Sketch your own collage.

Think of a point you'd like to argue about modern life, such as "social networking is making us lose our ability to communicate in person," and create a collage to make your argument. Begin by going through some magazines and cutting out images that you think will assist in making your point. Play with different ways of arranging the images together, overlapping them in different ways. Then think about other items you might want to add, such as buttons and pins, scraps of fabrics or other materials, printouts of images from the Internet, photos, or jewelry (for example, to make the argument mentioned about social networking, you might want to find and print out from the Internet an image of an old-fashioned calling card).

Alternatively, create a digital collage. Instead of cutting out images from magazines, find images online and incorporate them or take your own digital photos. Instead of buttons, pins, and fabric scraps, you can use a photo-editing application to create different effects, such as blurred photo edges or the addition of a particular pattern, similar to a pattern added with a rubber stamp in a traditional collage.

Creating Electronic Posters GT

Creating a poster used to be a matter of buying some craft paper and either handwriting or cutting and pasting documents and images onto a trifold poster board. Not anymore. Today, with the availability of software and online tools, creating a professional poster is much easier, but you need to learn how to use these tools. For traditional posters that you can print and display, PowerPoint is an easy-to-use platform that allows you to design a poster to a specified size and format. For more dynamic, interactive posters that can be viewed online, Prezi allows you to create an electronic poster that can be viewed as a zooming slide show or printed as a poster.

Try advanced software such as Adobe InDesign to design your poster. These programs offer many more features for customizing your poster, but they also require significantly more effort to learn. Learn InDesign to create sophisticated designs with the extra tools available. #Create

PowerPoint

Essentially, in PowerPoint you design a poster as one slide, but you change the dimensions of the slide to the size of the poster you wish to create (for example 20" × 30"). Ask your instructor about the required size for the assignment and whether to submit a print poster (some instructors only need the electronic version, while some ask you to print and mount the poster). If you will be printing your poster, you need to identify the dimensions *before* you design it to make sure that the scale is correct.

◀ SCREENSHOT
**Page Setup in
PowerPoint**
Setting the custom
dimensions allows
you a larger canvas to
design your poster.

On campus, you have three main options for printing: You can go to Paper & Clay in the Student Center or the library's Multimedia Studio, both of which charge a nominal fee. Check the library Web site or the Paper & Clay Web site to find out what size paper is available and how much each size costs to print. You can also use the plot printer in the Communication Center if you have participated in one or more official tutoring sessions about your poster project.

Once you know what dimensions you need, you can begin creating your poster. In PowerPoint, select a new slide and then go to Design > Page Setup and select "Custom," which enables you to choose the dimensions you need. You can also choose the orientation of your poster.

Now you can begin designing your poster. You can use the "Insert" tab to add pictures, text, shapes, charts, and other custom features. Remember to follow guidelines for effective visual design and go to the print preview to check how your poster looks before you print it. PowerPoint is only one option (and not the most refined one) to create posters, but it is serviceable. You might also use a program dedicated to image manipulation to increase the elements and conventions that you can control. The MultiMedia Studio has computers with software such as the Adobe Creative Suite. Use the studio and the free classes the librarians offer to help you make effective posters and data visualizations.

POSTER ▶
Exploring the Designing in Designing Things.
This student project for an English 1102 course uses design characteristics such as contrast, repetition, alignment, and proximity to help viewers further understand the poster's argument about design. Depicted here are both the full poster and a close-up of one specific section. The student elected to use Adobe InDesign to have more design capabilities. *Courtesy of Miyeon Bae.*

A CLOSER LOOK
What is the design actually like, and what is it doing?

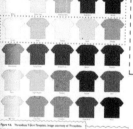

Visual Aesthetics in Designing Things

Contrast

The contents (heading, body, and captions) are distinguished by the use of different fonts and font sizes. This is so that the reader will clearly know what part is what. Different shades of gray are used to set off emphasis and to show differences in colors.

Repetition

The same styles of font, font size, and spacing are maintained throughout, constituting a repetition.

Alignment

The layout utilizes the "grid system," with the contents arranged in balanced proportions. The top edge of Figure 4.5 on the left side matches with the top edge of Figure 4.6; in another words, each diagram is measured to fit the column structure. This exact alignment gives the whole page a sense of sharpness and adds more balance to the overall picture. Paragraphs are single-spaced and the beginnings of new paragraphs are all indented. The single-spacing allows the reader to read without making drastic eye movements.

Proximity

Captions are placed directly under the diagrams, so that the reader can easily make visual connections with the written words. In addition, Figure 4.6 is placed on the same page as the paragraph that's on "flexible/agile manufacturing." In this way, the reader will know that the figure is related to that topic.

Prezi

Like PowerPoint, Prezi allows you to create presentation slide shows, but it can also be used to create a more innovative and multimodal form of a poster. If you are considering using Prezi for an interactive poster assignment, be sure to confirm with your instructor that it is an acceptable format.

Prezi is an online tool that allows you to create slide shows that "zoom" along a path from one image or text element to the next. They can be viewed online or offline and can be viewed as a slide show or as a presentation the user can interact with, zooming in and out of interesting content. Like PowerPoint, Prezi allows you to embed images and text, but it also supports video and audio files, making it multimodal. For a full demonstration of how Prezi works, visit the Prezi Web site.

If you plan to use Prezi to make a poster, consider these factors:

» Unlike a Prezi slide show, which guides the viewer logically through a preprogrammed sequence, a poster contains elements that can be viewed in any order. Accordingly, as the designer, you need to make the logical sequence of the poster clear by carefully applying visual design principles.

» Because of Prezi's zooming feature, you may find that when you zoom all the way out to print a poster, some of the text features become too small to read. When you are designing the poster, double-check that you are not creating content that will be too small to view in poster format. Make sure you consult Prezi's online help for information about how to print your Prezi.

Video and audio content can print as an image, but choosing a clear screenshot to represent dynamic content is more difficult than representing static content.

To use Prezi, you need to make sure the software is on your computer or that you have Internet access.

A film review—or a review of any product, restaurant, or performance, for that matter—is at its heart a persuasive genre. Reviewers evaluate with the purpose of influencing readers to accept their judgment on the item or work they've reviewed.

Most film reviews, such as the ones you read in The New York Times, for example, are written by journalists with knowledge of film; these reviews are aimed at a popular audience. The purpose of this type of film review is to persuade readers to see (or not see) a movie that's out in the theaters. Popular film reviewers include critics such as Roger Ebert, Joel Siegel, Lisa Kennedy, Kurt Loder, and David Edelstein. Their reviews appear on TV, in popular newspapers and magazines, and online. Audiences expect these reviews to be of films that are either just out in theaters or just out in DVD form, so they have the kind of currency associated with journalism. Just as a newspaper editorial covers current events, reviews that appear in newspapers cover current films.

Other film reviews are written by scholars for academic audiences and are known as "film criticism." Scholarly film critics write to persuade their readers—not so much to see or not see a film—but to accept their interpretations of it. As authors, film critics are similar to writers of peer-reviewed journal articles in terms of purposes and audiences. In their reviews, film critics draw on established theory developed by scholars who have studied film in depth. They include Pauline Kael, Andrew Sarris, and Phillip Lopate; their reviews appeared in publications including the *Journal of Film and Video* (published by the University Film and Video Association) and Film Comment. Because a film critic doesn't seek to persuade audiences to attend specific films, the currency of the film discussed is not as important as it is in a journalistic review aimed at a popular audience. While a journalistic film reviewer might review the rerelease of the 1994 film *Pulp Fiction*, a film critic would take a different angle, examining the career of Quentin Tarantino, for example.

In this section, we focus on the journalistic film review geared toward popular audiences.

Analyzing Film Reviews: What to Look For

THE RHETORICAL SITUATION

Purpose   Film reviewers write partly to inform readers about a particular movie; they discuss the film's story and the way it's conveyed, and contextualize the film in terms of its director and actors, for example. However, the reviewer's main

Do you read film reviews? If so, do you read them before or after you see a particular movie? How much do reviews influence whether you go to see a film? What sources—for example, *Rolling Stone* or the *Los Angeles Times*— do you like best for film reviews? #Understand

purpose is to persuade readers about the movie's overall quality and whether (from the reviewer's perspective) it's worth seeing. When a reviewer pans a film, some readers may decide not to spend money to see it in a theater; they might skip the movie altogether or wait for it to come out on DVD or through Netflix.

Reviewers make an argument about a film by analyzing certain aspects of it. For example, they may discuss the success with which the writer and director used narrative techniques such as flashbacks; they might consider the use of film techniques such as special effects, as well as cinematography and the use of close-up shots, for example. They may weigh in on the quality of the performances and comment on the overall cohesion of the work.

Audience   Film reviewers write for popular audiences: general readers who get their entertainment news on TV, in local papers, and online at news and other sites. They may visit film-focused sites such as *Rotten Tomatoes* and the *Internet Movie Database*. Film reviewers know that their readers want (1) to decide whether to see a particular movie or (2) to get a reviewer's perspective on a film they've already seen. For example, Liz often likes to read reviews after seeing a film so she can process her thoughts about it. Reviewers' work might also be read by movie insiders,

◀ WEB PAGE
The Internet Movie Database (IMDb)
Page for *The Hobbit*.
IMDB (http://imdb
.com/title/tt 1170358)

including directors and actors who want to know how their work is being received. Reviewers may keep this audience in mind as well when they critique a film.

Rhetorical appeals Film reviewers persuade readers by appealing to their sense of ethos, pathos, and logos. Reviewers need to develop their ethos as experts so readers will trust their judgment about a film. For example, in his review of the film *Bridesmaids*, Roger Ebert writes:

> Three of my good female friends, who I could usually find overcoming hangovers at their Saturday morning "Recovery Drunches" at Oxford's Pub, once made pinpricks in their thumbs and performed a ceremony becoming blood sisters. They were the only people I have actually known who could inspire a Judd Apatow buddy movie, and all three could do what not all women do well, and that is perfectly tell a dirty joke.
>
> Maybe I liked *Bridesmaids* in their honor.

By mentioning that he knows women who "could inspire a Judd Apatow buddy movie," Ebert builds his ethos. He establishes that he's qualified to speak about the realism of the movie and the experience of women like his friends, women such as those the *Bridesmaids* characters were modeled on.

Film reviewers also tap into emotion as they seek to convince readers to agree with their critiques of specific movies. For example, reviewer David Edelstein appeals to pathos when, in his assessment of the final *Harry Potter* movie, he writes:

> Seeing Daniel Radcliffe, Rupert Grint, and Emma Watson together for presumably the last time brought a tear to my eye.

The most persuasive film reviewer will also rely on logos, systematically building a case with evidence from the movie to support his or her main argument. For example, in a review of the film *Cowboys & Aliens*, Tom Long makes the claim in his title that the film is "big dumb summer fun." He then gives specific examples to back this up. He discusses the film's special effects, which constitute the "big" part of the argument, and also the silliness of the film, which constitutes the "fun" part of the argument. He writes:

> [L]aser beams are blowing buildings up and metallic lassos are coming down from assorted flying machines and scooping people up.

Modes & media Film reviewers publish their work in written form (as discussed above), on paper and digitally online. They present their reviews as part of TV broadcasts, such as the reviews shown on E! Entertainment, as part of radio broadcasts, such as the audio reviews aired by National Public Radio, and on the Internet at ComingSoon.net, for example.

Think of something—films, restaurants, or products and services—that you regularly read reviews of. Have you ever doubted a reviewer's credibility? Why? #Evaluate

THE GENRE'S CONVENTIONS

Elements of the genre   Film reviewers do the following:

Create titles that identify the film and hint at their critique. For example, reviewer Karina Longworth titled her review of *Crazy, Stupid, Love* as follows: "*Crazy, Stupid, Love* Isn't Crazy Enough."

◀ FILM REVIEW
Katrina Longworth
First published in *Miami New Times*, a Miami News Times, LLC publication.

Crazy, Stupid, Love isn't crazy enough

By **Karina Longworth** *Thursday, Jul 28 2011*

Comments (0)

In the first scene of *Crazy, Stupid, Love*, Emily (Julianne Moore) tells Cal (Steve Carell), her high school sweetheart and husband of 20-plus years, she wants a divorce. She goes on to mention she had an affair with a co-worker named Dave Lindhagen (Kevin Bacon), at which point Cal tells her that he has heard enough. (He's not kidding: By the time Cal makes it to the bar that night, the name "Dave Lindhagen" will have become a kind of negative mantra for him.) But Emily can't stop talking. "I think I'm having a midlife crisis," she confesses a few scenes later, when the now-estranged couple meet again. "Can women even have midlife crises? In the movies, it's always men."

And in this movie too. Would that an actress of Julianne Moore's age and talent get a chance to explore an identity crisis in a real way in a venue other than Showtime, but whatever Emily might be going through, it's swiftly pushed to the background. Following *Friends With Benefits* as the second romantic comedy in as many weeks to ostentatiously point up its awareness of romantic comedy cliché several times over the course of a narrative that ultimately validates far more of those clichés than it deflates, here *Crazy, Stupid, Love* makes the mistake of suggesting a path untrodden by films of its genre, only to deliver a

Steve Carell and Julianne Moore in *Crazy, Stupid, Love.*

Details

Starring Steve Carell, Ryan Gosling, Julianne Moore, Emma Stone, and Kevin Bacon. Directed by Glenn Ficarra and John Requa. Written by Dan Fogelman. 117 minutes. Rated PG-13.

scramble of the romantic-comedic familiar. Directors Glenn Ficarra and John Requa were last seen as the auteurs of *I Love You Phillip Morris*, one of the smartest comedies of recent years and quite possibly the best gay relationship film ever made featuring Hollywood stars. *Crazy, Stupid, Love* isn't nearly as groundbreaking, but its love-positive dramedy is notably big-hearted, and enlivened by the work of a few good actors.

So Moore recedes, popping up mostly as a foil to Cal's effort to Regain His Manhood via new clothes and anonymous sex. He takes tutoring in both fields from Jacob (Ryan Gosling), a hard-bodied, harder-hearted player who is moved to Change His Ways when he falls for Hannah (Emma Stone), a stunning lady/neurotic law student whose Focus On Career has left her in lack of a satisfying romantic life. In a less successfully integrated story thread, Cal's 13-year-old son nurses an obsessive crush on his 17-year-old babysitter, who in turn only has eyes for 40-something Cal — a roundelay whose bawdy sentimentality feels airlifted from a John Hughes movie.

Carell and Gosling, each willing to take their characters to the point of caricature in order to find

the truth in them, have a nicely barbed chemistry together, never more convincing than in the scene, indicative of *Crazy*'s treatment of cinematic tropes, in which they establish their pupil-mentor relationship. Strangers negotiating in a bar, they use gangster film lingo ("Maybe you remind me of somebody," "You in or you out?") to cement a bond whose first destination is necessarily a shopping montage.

Carell's film choices as far back as *The 40-Year-Old Virgin* suggest a tendency toward middle-aged, every-nerd romantic leads — the unlikely love interest who spends an entire film proving his charms — but here he's given a realistically complicated person to play. As Gosling's character puts it, he has "kind eyes and a good head of hair," both of which go a long way toward boosting the credibility of a character who bounces between oblivious dad, hopeless romantic, and calculating Lothario. In contrast to Carell's contrived "transformation" into romantic hero, Gosling is treated like an ingenue, with the directors building an entire scene around the awesome spectacle of his rock-hard midsection, giving his ass and hulking muscles their own key light in a sex scene in which his partner is mostly in shadow.

Dan Fogelman's script is snappy, if too proudly referential (it's difficult to say if a motif involving the use of *Dirty Dancing* as a seduction tool was outright stolen from last year's French rom-com *Heartbreaker* or if the similarity is mere coincidence). The film is more interesting at its least cute; in its second half, the dialogue seems looser, less bound to punch line. Characters who previously talked over one another, too deep in their own heads to actually have an exchange, slow down and begin to listen. Shooting on grainy, high-speed film stock with an often hand-held camera, working with a suite of actors who are game to both play light and silly and dig deep, Ficarra and Requa lend a naturalism to highly contrived, patently absurd situations.

Spoiler alert: There are two plot twists, neither of which seems particularly necessary, but I admit

---

Write juicy lead paragraphs. Film reviewers want to grab readers' attention right away, which is why their opening paragraphs tend to be provocative. A writer might begin by naming the film, identifying its genre, hinting at her evaluation and the argument she will present, and provide a hook to keep you reading. For example, Manohla Dargis writes in paragraph 1 of her review of *Elizabeth: The Golden Age*.

> A kitsch extravaganza aquiver with trembling bosoms, booming guns and wild energy, *Elizabeth: The Golden Age* tells, if more often shouts, the story of the bastard monarch who ruled England with an iron grip and two tightly closed legs.

Discuss the film's genre. As noted above, reviewers usually say what type of film they're writing about, whether it's an action, horror, or science fiction movie, or a comedy or drama. For example, in her review of *Crazy, Stupid, Love*, Karina Longworth comments on the film's genre by pointing out its "romantic comedy clichés."

Summarize the film's narrative. Reviewers provide a brief outline of the film's plot, characters, and setting, but they do not give away specific details such as endings and plot twists. (Doing so is called "spoiling" and it is frowned upon.)

Evaluate the filmmakers and actors. Reviewers name the key contributors to the film and mention a few of their other works in order to provide context. They also critique the success of each participant, for example, rating the writer's and director's editorial choices and the performances of the lead actors, while drawing on examples from specific moments from the movie to support the analysis.

Analyzing Film Reviews: What to Look For

Make a clear argument, critiquing the film overall. Reviewers make arguments about the overall success (or failure) of filmmakers—to achieve their purpose and reach their audience through specific films—in several ways. For example, a reviewer might begin by assigning a film they deem successful with four out of five stars, then build this case throughout the body of the review. Longworth, for example, states her main argument:

> *Crazy, Stupid, Love* isn't nearly as groundbreaking [as *I Love You Phillip Morris*], but its love-positive dramedy is notably big-hearted, and enlivened by the work of a few good actors.

She then praises the performances of the film's stars, Julianne Moore, Steve Carell, Ryan Gosling, and Emma Stone, while opining that Moore deserved more screen time. So while her overall critique is that the film is not worth seeing, Longworth does point out some of the positives.

When a reviewer gives a film a thumbs-down, readers expect the writer to build an argument about how the film fails to entertain—in terms of the plot's weaknesses or the actors' poor performances, for example. Similarly, when a reviewer loves a film and recommends it, readers expect the writer to offer insights on how and why the film succeeds—in terms of the writing, filmmaking, directing, drama, excitement, acting, and special effects, for example.

Style   Film reviewers do the following:

Use specific writing techniques, such as quoting from the film. Reviewers often quote from memorable or crucial-to-the-plot dialogue from the film in order to discuss the plot and characters in the work. They also quote from the dialogue to support their specific arguments and opinions about the movie.

Incorporate specific details. Reviewers persuade their readers that their generalizations about a film are legitimate by illustrating their points with specific details. Notice how Karina Longworth begins with a fairly general comment, then describes the details of a particular scene:

> Carell and Gosling, each willing to take their characters to the point of caricature in order to find the truth in them, have a nicely barbed chemistry together, never more convincing than in the scene, indicative of *Crazy's* treatment of cinematic tropes, in which they establish their pupil-mentor relationship. Strangers negotiating in a bar, they use gangster-film lingo ("Maybe you remind me of somebody." "You in or you out?") to cement a bond whose first destination is necessarily a shopping montage.

Use voice, tone, and word choice to convey ethos. To be persuasive, reviewers need to come across as knowledgeable film buffs. For example, Karina Longworth establishes that she's knowledgeable about romantic comedies when she compares the one she's reviewing (*Crazy, Stupid, Love*) to another film of the same genre (*I Love You Phillip Morris*). She also writes as an authority on performance, as evidenced in the excerpt from her review, above, about the chemistry between actors Carell and Gosling.

Design Film reviews:

Are formatted like news articles and editorials. Like other journalistic works that appear in print and online, a film review includes a headline, a title, and a byline identifying the reviewer (often with a photograph). Reviews are formatted in columns if printed or in single-spaced paragraphs if digital, and include masthead information, such as the name of the newspaper or Web site and the date.

Present a star rating system. Most reviewers work with a system in which they can assign up to five stars (or other symbols) to rate the success of a film. The star rating is often provided at the top or bottom of the review.

Include production credits. In some cases, reviewers include a list of the film's credits, usually at the end of the review.

Feature a still photo from the film (or video if online). Many reviews include an image from a crucial moment in the film. For example, Longworth includes a photo of Carell and Moore.

Sources Film reviewers, like other journalists, do not include a Works Cited list or references list; they simply name their sources within their reviews as they refer to them. For example, many reviewers refer to other films to provide context for the one they're writing about and to establish their own credibility as experts, as Karina Longworth does when she compares *Crazy, Stupid, Love* to another romantic comedy, *I Love You Phillip Morris*.

And in this movie too. Would that an actress of Julianne Moore's age and talent get a chance to explore an identity crisis in a real way in a venue other than Showtime, but whatever Emily might be going through, it's swiftly pushed to the background. Following *Friends With Benefits* as the second romantic comedy in as many weeks to ostentatiously point up its awareness of romantic comedy cliché several times over the course of a

◀ FILM REVIEW
Katrina Longworth
First published in
Miami New Times, a
Miami News Times,
LLC publication.

Steve Carell and Julianne Moore in *Crazy, Stupid, Love.*

Roger Ebert

Ratatouille: Waiter, There's a Rat in My Soup

Roger Ebert is a famous film critic who has written film reviews for the Chicago Sun-Times since the mid-1960s. From 1986 to 1999, Ebert cohosted the television show *At the Movies* with Gene Siskel, another Chicago film reviewer. Known for their lively banter, the two critics often disagreed with each other, providing their audience with sometimes-clashing views about a film. Ebert's reviews are syndicated in numerous newspapers, and he was the first film reviewer to win a Pulitzer Prize. Below is his review of *Ratatouille*, an Oscar-winning animated feature film. The review appeared in the *Chicago Sun-Times*, a respected paper that was awarded the Pulitzer Prize for Journalism in 2011. (Text of review: From *Chicago Sun Times* 8/30/2007 © 2007 Sun-Times Media. All rights reserved. Used by permission and protected by the Copyright Laws of the United States. The printing, copying, redistribution, or retransmission of this Content without express written permission is prohibited.)

WEB PAGE ▶
Roger Ebert
Page at the *Chicago Sun-Times*. Everett Collection.

What is the composer, **Roger Ebert**, doing?

Roger Ebert, *Ratatouille*, *Continued*

▲ Gently persuasive, Remy (left) finds a way to communicate with Linguini, and together they electrify Paris with their cooking in *Ratatouille*. *Everett Collection.*

Release Date: 2007
Ebert Rating: ★★★★
August 31, 2007

A lot of animated movies have inspired sequels, notably *Shrek*, but Brad Bird's *Ratatouille* is the first one that made me positively desire one. Remy, the earnest little rat who is its hero, is such a lovable, determined, gifted rodent that I want to know what happens to him next, now that he has conquered the summit of

cast & credits

With the voices of:
Remy: **Patton Oswalt**
Skinner: **Ian Holm**
Linguini: **Lou Romano**
Anton Ego: **Peter O'Toole**
Gusteau: **Brad Garrett**
Colette: **Janeane Garofalo**
Emile: **Peter Sohn**
Django: **Brian Dennehy**
Horst: **Will Arnett**

Walt Disney Pictures presents a film by Pixar Animation. Directed and written by Brad Bird. Running time: 110 minutes. Rated G.

THE RHETORICAL SITUATION

Purpose
Audience
Rhetorical appeal
Modes & media

Purpose

Ebert's purpose is to persuade readers to accept his view and argument about *Ratatouille*.

Audience

Ebert's readers include movie fans who may be thinking of seeing *Ratatouille*, and fans who have already seen it and want Ebert's opinion as a film buff.

Rhetorical appeals

Ebert builds **ethos** by showing he's an expert on animated films and the achievements of *Ratatouille*'s director, Brad Bird.

Ebert appeals to **pathos** by using humor to persuade his audience. For example, he remarks that "there's something de Gaullean about [Remy's] snout."

(Continued on p. 545.)

Continues next page

How do I know this is a **film review?**

THE GENRE'S CONVENTIONS

Elements of the genre
Style
Design
Sources

Elements of the genre

Strong title. Ebert identifies the film and grabs attention with the headline "Waiter, there's a Rat in my Soup."

Juicy lead paragraph. Ebert piques interest with an introduction to the protagonist, Remy, who is a "gifted rodent" who "has conquered the summit of French cuisine."

Discussion of genre. Ebert identifies *Ratatouille* as an animated film and connects it with related films, such as *The Incredibles.*

Summary of narrative. In the body of the review, Ebert relates the basics of the plot and Remy's escapades—without spoiling the ending.

French cuisine. I think running for office might not be beyond his reach, and there's certainly something de Gaullean about his snout.

Remy is a member of a large family of rats (a horde, I think, is the word) who ply the trash cans and sewers of a Parisian suburb, just like good rats should. "Eat your garbage!" commands Remy's father, Django, obviously a loving parent. The rats are evicted from their cozy home in a cottage-kitchen ceiling in a scene that will have rat-haters in the audience cringing (and who among us will claim they don't hate rats more than a little?), and they are swept through the sewers in a torrential flood. Students of Victor Hugo will know that the hero Jean Valjean of *Les Miserables* found the Seine because he knew that every sewer must necessarily run downhill toward it, and indeed Remy washes up near the river, in view of the most famous restaurant in *tout le* France. This is the establishment of Auguste Gusteau, author of the best-seller *Anyone Can Cook,* a title that might not go over very well in France, which is why the book appears to be in English, and might well be titled, *Anyone Can Cook Better Than the English.* (Famous British recipe: "Cook until gray.")

Remy (voice of Patton Oswalt) has always been blessed, or cursed, with a refined palate and a sensitive nose, and now he starts skulking around the kitchen of Gusteau, his culinary hero (voice of Brad Garrett). Alas, when the monstrous food

THE GENRE'S CONVENTIONS

Evaluation of filmmakers and actors. Ebert names the director and producer and gives his opinion of their work on the film: "[T]hey have taken over the leadership in the animation field right now."

Overall critique of the film. In the opening, body, and closing of his review, Ebert gives a clear thumbs-up. In his final paragraph, he states, "This is clearly one of the best of the year's films."

Style

Quotes. Ebert supports his argument with quotes from the film's dialogue, such as "I would do anything for you, *monsieur. . . .*" and "Eat your garbage!"

Detail. Ebert supports his case with specifics. For

Roger Ebert, *Ratatouille*, *Continued*

critic Anton Ego (Peter O'Toole) issues a scathing indictment of Gusteau's recent cooking, the chef dies in a paroxysm of grief or perhaps it is not a paroxysm, but I like the word, and the kitchen is taken over by the sniveling little snipe Skinner (Ian Holm). Lowest of the low is Gusteau's "nephew" Linguini (Lou Romano), who must be hired, but is assigned to the wretched job of *plongeur*—literally, one who washes the dishes by plunging them into soapy water.

Linguini and Remy meet, somehow establish trust and communication, and when Linguini gets credit for a soup that the rat has saved with strategic seasonings, they team up. Remy burrows into Linguini's hair, is concealed by his toque, can see through its transparent sides, and controls Linguini by pulling on his hair as if each tuft were a joystick. Together, they astonish Paris with their genius.

All of this begins as a dubious premise and ends as a triumph of animation, comedy, imagination, and, yes, humanity. What is most lovable about Remy is his modesty and shyness, even for a rat. He has body language so expressive that many humans would trade for it. Many animated characters seem to communicate with semaphores, but Remy has a repertory of tiny French hand gestures, shrugs, and physical expressiveness. Does any other nationality have more ways of moving a finger and an

---

THE RHETORICAL SITUATION

Ebert states his argument and presents it logically, appealing to logos. For instance, he says he's already looking forward to the film's sequel and then goes on to build a case for Remy (1) as a character (a determined hero) and (2) as an unforgettable animated creature (Ebert notes his "repertory of tiny French hand gestures").

Modes & media

Mode = written and visual Ebert's review is word/text based. And, because films are visual, he also includes a still image from the film to illustrate for readers the central characters, Remy and Linguini.

Medium = print and digital Ebert's review appeared in the print and digital versions of the *Chicago Sun-Times.*

THE GENRE'S CONVENTIONS

example, he argues for the film's "triumph of animation" by describing Remy's "so expressive" body language.

Voice, tone, and word choice. Ebert writes with authority and a pleasant, humorous tone. For an example, see his description of Remy in paragraph 5. The words he chooses—including *triumph*, *astonish*, and *lovable*—reflect his positive opinion of the film.

Design

The review looks like any other journalistic work and includes an author byline. It features a star rating system (Ebert gives the movie four out of four stars) and includes a still from the movie. It ends with a cast and credit list, and info about the film.

(Continued on p. 546.)

Roger Ebert, *Ratatouille*, *Continued*

THE GENRE'S
CONVENTIONS

Sources

Ebert's main source
for this review
of *Ratatouille* is
the film itself. He
also draws on his
existing knowledge
of animated films,
the director, and
France (he refers to
de Gaulle, the Seine,
and Victor Hugo).

eyebrow less than an inch while signaling something as complex as, "I would do anything for you, *monsieur,* but as you see, I have only two hands, and these times we live in do not permit me the luxury of fulfilling such requests."

Brad Bird and his executive producer, John Lasseter, clearly have taken over the leadership in the animation field right now. Yes, Bird made *The Incredibles,* but the one that got away was his wonderful *The Iron Giant,* in which a towering robot was as subtle, gentle, and touching as Remy. His eye for detail is remarkable. Every prop and utensil and spice and ingredient in the kitchen is almost tangible, and I for one would never turn off the Food Channel if Remy hosted a program named *Any Rat Can Cook.*

This is clearly one of the best of the year's films. Every time an animated film is successful, you have to read all over again about how animation isn't "just for children" but "for the whole family," and "even for adults going on their own." No kidding!

Questions: Analyzing Ebert's film review

1. Purpose. What evidence does Ebert use to convince the reader to see *Ratatouille*? How convincing is his argument?

2. Audience. Who is the primary audience that Ebert addresses in his review? Use specifics from the review to support your answer.

3. Rhetorical appeals. What are some ways Ebert establishes his ethos? What makes evident Ebert's experience as a film reviewer?

4. Rhetorical appeals. Ebert uses some humor to make his case. Is this an effective strategy to use in his film review? Why or why not?

5. Modes & media. Ebert's review includes a still from the movie. How does that contribute to your reading of the review? After reading the review, can you think of other visuals that you wish Ebert had chosen to accompany the text? Explain.

6. Elements of the genre. Ebert does not overtly state his evaluation until the end. Are there places prior to the end that give you a sense of the writer's judgment of the film?

7. Elements of the genre. What is the impact of Ebert's references to previous films of the director?

8. Style. How does Ebert's inclusion of specific quotes of dialogue make his case for going to see the film? Do the quotes give you a better sense of character or plot? Or do they give you an equal sense of both?

9. Design. Before you read the review, you know that Ebert has given the film four stars. How does this affect your reading of the review? Does he show you why he has given the film four stars? Why or why not?

10. Sources. Ebert uses references from France in his review. Were you familiar with these references? How do these references give you a sense of the film?

Drafting a Film Review

CHECKLIST: Drafting a Film Review
Thinking of drafting a film review? Ask yourself the following questions.

WHAT'S MY RHETORICAL SITUATION?

☐ **Purpose.** What is my opinion of the film? Do I think others should rush out and see it? Or do I feel like I've just wasted two hours of my life? What are some of the key things in the film that helped me form my opinion?

☐ **Audience.** The people most likely to want to see the film I'm reviewing: What are the things this audience values? How can I appeal to those values?

☐ **Rhetorical appeals.** How will I establish my credibility? What specifics will I include in my review to gain readers' trust in my opinion? To what extent will I appeal to their emotions? Should I try to shock my readers? Make them laugh?

☐ **Modes & media.** Do I want my audience to read my review in print format (on paper) or online? If online, how will I take advantage of a digital environment? Will I embed links, for example? Stream video? What visuals will I include? What visuals will be most persuasive?

WHAT GENRE CONVENTIONS MATTER?

☐ **Elements of the genre.** What might be a catchy title for my review? What is the film's genre? What do I need to know about that particular genre to include in the review? Who is the film's director? Do I want to incorporate other films by this director into the review? Who are the main actors? What's important to share about their previous films? How do I feel about the actors' performances in the film? How will I support my views?

☐ **Style.** What bits of dialogue convey why the film is worth viewing or not? What examples from the film are the most convincing for my purpose? What tone do I want to use? How will I use diction to show my point of view?

☐ **Design.** Do I want my reader to know my rating before reading the review or after? Did I include my byline? Do I have all the information needed for the production credits? How much of the production credits do I want to include with the review?

☐ **Sources.** What do I know about the film's director? The key performers? Do I know enough or do I need to do research to get more information? What do I know about the film's genre?

PRACTICE
Want to experiment? Draft your own film review.

Think of a film you've seen recently. Do you want to convince others to see the film or to avoid it altogether? How many stars would you give it? Draft a review that includes a brief plot summary (without giving away any of the ending), refers to other works by the director, and gives a clear evaluation of and argument about the film. Be sure to work in details that support your overall argument about whether readers should rush out to see the film—or forget they ever heard about it. Be persuasive by choosing your words, tone, and voice effectively.

PRESENTATIONS

Most presentations are brief talks about a particular topic delivered by a knowledgeable speaker to a specific audience. Often they are persuasive—aimed at getting audience members to agree with the speaker about something, and/or to take action. For example, a salesperson might give a presentation to try to convince a potential client to adopt a particular product. Or you might give a presentation to persuade your classmates to agree with you about a specific topic or issue.

With software available on the Web, you can reach more viewers and listeners, and make your presentation more visual and multimodal. For example, in the workplace, you might use online meeting products such as WebEx, Microsoft Live Meeting, or Elluminate to reach people at remote locations. You can also record a presentation and then post it online for future viewing, such as in Matthew Inman's Ignite talk featured in the guided reading.

To put a presentation together, you can use software to organize your ideas. For years, PowerPoint, part of Microsoft Office, was the standard in many workplaces and classrooms. However, some presenters are now turning to more visually engaging tools, such as Prezi.

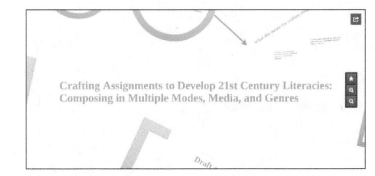

Crafting Assignments to Develop 21st Century Literacies: Composing in Multiple Modes, Media, and Genres

◀ SLIDE
Liz and Amy's Prezi
The opening of Liz and Amy's Prezi from a presentation they gave at an academic conference. *Courtesy of Elizabeth Kleinfeld and Amy Braziller.*

Analyzing Presentations: What to Look For

THE RHETORICAL SITUATION

Purpose   Presenters always have a goal for their presentations. In a speech class, you might give a presentation about a problem, persuading your audience that your solutions are the best route to take. For a research composition class, you might present your research strategies in order to persuade your audience that the strategies you chose were the most appropriate for your topic and approach. At work, you might give a presentation to persuade others of an idea. Over the last several years, a presentation series called Ignite talks have sprung up in cities around the world. The tagline for Ignite is "Enlighten us, but make it quick." Presenters persuade others about their ideas and passions within a very small time frame. Ignite presenters can use only twenty slides, which in turn automatically advance every fifteen seconds. A similar phenomenon is the PechaKucha, a slideshow of twenty slides that show for twenty seconds each.

Audience Presenters tailor their talks to their audiences. By knowing their audiences, they know what kind of background information they'll need to present, what terminology is useful, and what cultural references their listeners will connect

WEB PAGE ▶
Ignite
"How to Produce
an Ignite Event."
*igniteshow.com
/howto.*

with. For example, writer and professional speaker Scott Berkun gave a talk "How and Why to Give an Ignite Talk." When he drafted his talk, he knew that his audience would be potential Ignite performers, so he geared his talk to persuade them that they all have a story to tell, something worth sharing on the Ignite stage.

Rhetorical appeals Any time you want to persuade, you need to establish your ethos in order to get your audience to embrace your ideas. If you are giving a persuasive talk, some ways to build ethos are to state your argument clearly, support it with accurate data and appropriate evidence, and, if you're working with slides, to provide slides that are free of spelling and grammatical errors and that are well designed. When presenting, you can boost your ethos through good posture and eye contact. To be persuasive, you'll also need to appeal to your audience's sense of logic. If you want to convince a client to purchase a product, then you need to provide the reasons and benefits in a logical order. You might also appeal to pathos by being funny or surprising. The humorous and unexpected can work well, depending on your audience. Berkun establishes his ethos by showing he knows how to present within the constraints of Ignite—he uses twenty self-advancing slides within five minutes.

Modes & media   Presenters use a combination of audio, visual, and text. If slides are involved, they may include text, visuals, and even hyperlinks to multimedia, such as Web pages, animated visuals, movie clips, music, and audio clips. Some speakers use physical props (for example, in the guided reading/viewing in this chapter, the speaker holds up a doll). Some provide their listeners with printouts of their slides. Some deliver their presentations face-to-face or in a digital environment (such as WebEx) where the talk can be replayed anytime, anywhere. Scott Berkun gave his presentation live at a conference; it was recorded and is now available on YouTube.

Do your professors use PowerPoint or Prezi or other presentation software during class? If so, what is your experience as a viewer? How might you improve it? #Evaluate

THE GENRE'S CONVENTIONS

Elements of the genre   Effective presenters do the following:

Give a bold introduction to capture their audience's attention. For example, Scott Berkun opens with "I think storytelling is everything," which prepares his audience for the persuasive claims he will make later in the presentation. Presenters also:

» Introduce themselves

» Establish credibility and their relationship to the topic

» Preview what they will cover during their talk

An introduction is where speakers make a first impression on their audience—and also where they need to persuade the audience that the presentation is worth a listen.

Provide enough background so that the audience can understand the content of the presentation. Presenters must clarify acronyms and define unfamiliar terminology.

Present their information and arguments in the body of their talks. This is where speakers make claims and back them up with facts, data, personal stories, and quotes from experts.

Address objections and counterarguments to make the best case possible.

Conclude with a summary and solid message. This ensures that the audiences have understood the argument presented, have gotten a clear message, and know what the speaker is asking of them in terms of agreeing and/or taking action (for example, against a particular injustice). Many speakers end by inviting the audience to ask questions.

Use visuals, video, audio, and other media to support their arguments. Most presenters use slides as a way to present key points, infographics, photos, and links to various multimedia—and to provide context and support for their arguments. For example, if a presenter wants to persuade listeners of the need for a program to reduce childhood obesity, he might include an image of obese children, or a chart that shows the relationship between childhood weight and diabetes. To take another example, when Berkun mentions famous people who were "lousy speakers," he backs this up with a visual of Abraham Lincoln. Visuals and other media should not distract the audience. And it's a good idea to bring handouts of slides so audiences have something to refer back to.

Make transitions to move the audience from one point to the next. Presenters can do this by advancing slides or by cuing listeners through speech (for example, "This brings me to my second point . . .").

Style   Effective presenters do the following:

Organize their material so that it's clear and persuasive. Presenters must make it enable audiences to follow what they're saying—and to accept their claims and arguments. Some speakers may arrange their talks into three or so main parts, for example, built around separate but related concepts. Others might use a chronological organization, which is especially useful for laying out the history of an idea or movement. For example, a speaker arguing about the factors that led to the AIDS crisis might organize his talk chronologically, while a speaker arguing about possible ways to curb the spread of the disease might organize his talk by first focusing on the problem, and then focusing on potential solutions and actions.

Tailor their level of detail. Presenters consider their subjects and audiences when deciding on the level of information to share. For an introduction to a topic, a speaker doesn't need to provide as much complex detail as he or she would for a more advanced approach to a subject. Similarly, for an audience of experts, a presenter would provide more depth and detail—such as a speaker talking about climate change and changing geologic formations to a group of geologists.

What makes a presentation memorable? What should the balance be between the spoken word and visuals and other media?

Make eye contact with the whole room and stand tall. These nonverbal cues connect speakers with audiences and convey their confidence, knowledge, and persuasiveness.

Vary their delivery and show emotion. Speakers vary the volume of their voices, speaking softer at some points and louder at others to stress certain aspects of what they have to say. For example, a speaker may raise his voice to show anger at a situation or excitement about a future possibility. Speakers also vary their pacing between speaking slowly and more quickly, depending on their content and what they want to stress. However, it's important to not speak too quickly, as Scott Berkun demonstrates, and to pause so that audiences digest information. Many speakers work in a couple of funny stories or anecdotes: Humor can connect them with the audiences they want to persuade.

Design   For presenters creating slides, a smart, clean, nondistracting design will persuade audiences by allowing them to focus on content. Most successful slides reflect the following design features:

» Fonts are usually sans serif—at 20 points or larger for easy reading.

» There is contrast between backgrounds and text. Light-colored text on dark backgrounds or dark-colored text on light backgrounds works best. It's best to avoid clashing colors such as pink text on an orange background. For example, Scott Berkun presents white text on a black background.

» Slides are not crowded with lots of points and images. Each slide should have only one main point with a few supporting points.

Sources   To persuade their listeners, presenters, like anyone building an argument, may do the following:

» Draw on their own expertise of a subject

» Confer with others who are knowledgeable in the field or subject

» Read articles, reports, books, or other reference material

» Provide a Works Cited list on a slide at the end of the presentation (and/or provide brief citations throughout the slides)

» Credit charts, photos, or any other graphics, usually on the slide where the visual appears, underneath the visual

Sunni Brown

From *The Doodle Revolution*

Sunni Brown is a visual thinker, researcher, and self-described "large-scale Infodoodler and Leader of the Doodle Revolution" who believes in the power of doodling. She argues that focused doodling, in any scenario, gets our minds and memories working better. Brown's academic background is in journalism and linguistics and she holds a master's degree in public affairs. She lives in Austin, Texas, owns a design company, works as a consultant and creative director, and is the coauthor of *Gamestorming*, a book on innovation and visual thinking.

Brown gave a talk at an Ignite event in which she makes her case for the Doodle Revolution. Ignite hosts events around the country where speakers talk about things (in their lives, in their work, etc.) that they care about most. An Ignite talk can be no longer than five minutes and is supported by twenty slides that advance every fifteen seconds. In her presentation, Brown uses images and statistics to support her points on the value of doodling. The Doodle Revolution *is presented here by permission of Sunni Brown, Infodoodler-in-Chief, Author and Leader of the Doodle Revolution, http://igniteshow.com/videos /doodle-revolution.*

Courtesy of igniteshow.com/howto.

Sunni Brown, *From The Doodle Revolution*, Continued

[Transcript]

"I am what I refer to as a large-scale strategic doodler. So people pay me to track auditory content and display it to them in a visual language format. And I have a series of "whoa" moments when I do this."

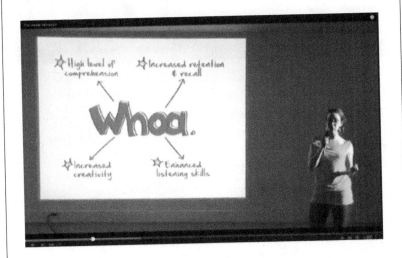

What is the composer/ presenter, Sunni Brown, doing?

THE RHETORICAL SITUATION

Purpose
Audience
Rhetorical appeals
Modes & media

see page 556

How do I know this is a presentation?

THE GENRE'S CONVENTIONS

Elements of the genre
Style
Design
Sources

see page 556

Sunni Brown, *From The Doodle Revolution,* Continued

Purpose

Sunni Brown wants
to persuade her
audience that
doodling, though
considered socially
unacceptable in
many settings,
is actually a very
effective tool for
recording, absorbing,
and retaining
information. As she
seeks to persuade,
she also seeks
to entertain her
audience and hold
their interest with
visuals, humor,

THE GENRE'S
CONVENTIONS

**Elements of the
genre**

**Ethos-building
introduction to her
argument.** Brown
establishes her
ethos by explaining
that people pay her
to doodle, makes
clear that she will
argue for a "Doodle
Revolution," and lays
out the reasons that
focused doodling
should be taken
seriously. Brown sets
a tone that indicates
she's knowledgeable;
at the same time

[Transcript]

"I have a significantly high level of comprehension of the information that I doodle. I also have increased attention and recall of that content, weeks and months later, and I can easily immerse myself back into it. Additionally, I've noticed that when I do strategic doodling, I have increased creativity and I can make solutions to problems that are even surprising to me. And finally, my listening skills are like, ninja-like. I can discern immediately what's relevant and what's not relevant."

[Transcript]

"So I have this series of 'whoa' moments, and simultaneously I notice that our society frowns on doodling in learning environments. In the board room, in the situation room, and in the classroom. So, I find that problematic. . . ."

Sunni Brown, *From The Doodle Revolution,* *Continued*

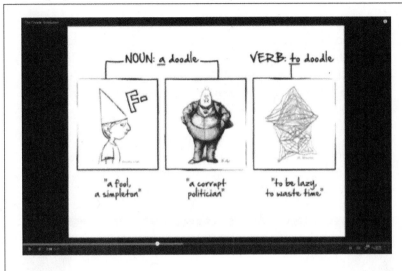

[Transcript]

"I discovered five interesting things. One of them is that there is no flattering definition of a doodle. In the seventeenth century, a 'doodle' was a fool; in the eighteenth century, a 'doodle' was a corrupt politician; and in the modern-day society, in the 1930s we see the emergence of our verb 'to doodle,' and it means to be

THE RHETORICAL SITUATION

focused statements, and brisk pacing.

Audience
Brown's audience is made up of information geeks, designers, writers, and doodle enthusiasts who appreciate irony, comedy, comics, and pop culture.

Rhetorical appeals
Brown builds **ethos** as a creator of doodles and expert on visual thinking. As a professional, scholar,
(Continued on p. 558.)

THE GENRE'S CONVENTIONS

she uses humor, even before the presentation officially begins, that has her audience listening and laughing.
Thoughtful conclusion. Her ending sums up the essence of her presentation—and the humor of her delivery, her slides, and the statistics she shares—with
(Continued on p. 558.)

Sunni Brown, *From The Doodle Revolution*, *Continued*

lazy or waste time. . . . [Later] there was a period in time when
the ballpoint pen came into play, and people had access to mass-
produced pulp paper. So they actually were kind of like flipping
around, just like, 'wee, look at these tools we have!' But [doo-
dling] wasn't necessarily meaningful at that point in time."

[Transcript]

"In the 1930s, Freudianism was at its height, and people believed
that you could actually psychoanalyze someone based on their
doodles, and dig into the recesses of their freaky psyches. And
naturally, people have an aversion to that. [laughter]

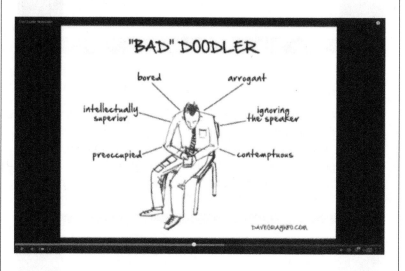

[Transcript]

"And finally . . . the physical gesture of doodling gives people the
impression that you're not present, right? So, whenever there's a
speaker, um, not me, but if there were another speaker [up here]
they would think that it was rude and that you're not paying
attention."

Sunni Brown, *From The Doodle Revolution,* Continued

[Transcript]

". . . Also, in our society, we don't think that national leaders doodle. We don't think it's appropriate. But that's patently false. These are Ronald Reagan's doodles. . . . Every president, ever, in our history has been a doodler. Republicans are actually more prolific doodlers than Democrats, which I find interesting."

THE RHETORICAL SITUATION

Modes & media:
Mode = audio and visual Brown uses a combination of audio and visuals throughout her presentation. The audio is her voice presenting ideas, along with laughter from the audience. Her visuals are the images on her slides, which include doodles, comics, and hand-drawn infographics.
(Continued on p. 560.)

THE GENRE'S CONVENTIONS

for persuasive and humorous impact.

Clear transitions. Brown uses the slides themselves to advance the points of her talk (the Ignite format is five minutes, twenty slides, each slide advances after fifteen seconds). She also uses verbal cues to lay out the structure of her ideas and to transition from one
(Continued on p. 560.)

THE RHETORICAL SITUATION

Medium = face-to-face and video This talk was originally delivered before a live audience. In the example given, the presentation is digital, since it is a recording of the original talk that can be found on the Ignite Web site.

THE GENRE'S CONVENTIONS

idea to the next ("I discovered five interesting things. One of them . . ." and "finally").

Use of supporting examples. Throughout the presentation, Brown shows an example to support her pro-doodle argument. In fact, she uses twenty examples (each slide is one idea).

Style

Smart use of detail. Brown offers just enough detail to

"Here's a better definition of 'doodle,' which is: scribblings to help a person think. And that definition came out of a 1936 movie called Mr. Deeds Goes to Town. . . . So what do we know about the doodle? We know that doodlers retain 30% more information than non-doodlers."

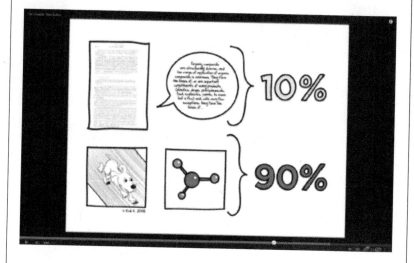

[Transcript]

"We also know that there's a phenomenon called the "picture superiority effect," which means that after this event is over, you're only going to remember 10% of what I say, but you're going to remember 90% of what I showed you. And so when you're doodling and you're creating pictures that you get to reflect back on, it actually is a way of processing and retaining information. . . . So the doodle's not a joke, okay? Ya get it?" [laughter]

Sunni Brown, *From The Doodle Revolution,* Continued

[Transcript]

"We also know that almost every genius inventor and innovator and scientist and screenwriter and poet, they all use sketches and doodles in order to get to a solution they wouldn't otherwise have gotten to. This is Alexander Graham Bell's sketches of the telephone."

THE GENRE'S CONVENTIONS

illustrate her ideas. She chooses very specific images, each for a reason. For example, to support her claim that scientists use doodles to work out solutions to complex problems, she shows a doodle by Alexander Graham Bell and moves on. **Delivery technique.** Throughout her talk, Brown faces the audience comfortably (she does not fidget). Her facial expression and hand gestures are not distracting but rather make the audience feel as though she is just having a casual (and funny) chat with them.

Persuasive, friendly voice and tone. Brown speaks with an even pace throughout, never rushing through any parts of the talk. Her pacing works with her humor; for example, after she's laid out considerable evidence supporting her claims that

(Continued on p. 562.)

Sunni Brown, From *The Doodle Revolution*

doodling should be taken seriously, she says, "So doodling isn't a joke. Okay?" The audience laughs as she reinforces her point.

Design

The speaker does not use traditional slides with text; rather, she uses specific visuals to support the points she's making.

Sources

Brown's sources for her presentation are her own experience and background, and information that she's gathered as a researcher on doodling, visual thinking, and memory. If this were a research paper and not a presentation, she would have a References list or Works Cited page that would include, for example, a source for her information about the phenomenon of "picture superiority effect," and the film *Mr. Deeds Goes to Town*, which she mentions in her talk.

Sunni Brown, *From The Doodle Revolution*, Continued

[Transcript]

"There are three learning pathways, primarily, that we all have. . . . In order to lock in information, you have to engage at least two. . . . Or, you have to have an emotional experience coupled with one of those things."

[Transcript]

". . . These are the three things that you have to do in order to engage the pathways. And I think the reason why the doodle is so powerful for so many people around the world and throughout time is that it actually employs all three of your learning pathways simultaneously."

Sunni Brown, *From The Doodle Revolution,* Continued

"... I think that the doodle is actually most appropriate in those situations where society actually believes it to be the least appropriate, which is where you have an informationally dense situation, and people are accountable for learning that information. So I say bring on the freaking doodle revolution." [laughter, applause]

Questions: Analyzing Brown's presentation

1. Purpose. How does Brown use examples to support her central argument and purpose? Why does she choose to incorporate these specific examples in her talk "Doodle Revolution"?

2. Audience. What assumptions do you think Brown holds about her audience at Ignite? Why do you think that?

3. Rhetorical appeals. One way Brown establishes her ethos is through her demeanor. How else does she establish ethos throughout the presentation?

4. Rhetorical appeals. What does Brown's appeal to pathos and use of humor add to the presentation? To what extent do pathos and humor make her presentation more (or less) persuasive?

5. Modes & media. What effect would it have had on the presentation if, rather than using illustrations, doodles, and infographics, Brown had used traditional slides with headings and explanatory text? Also, how is the experience of watching the talk digitally different from experiencing it as a live audience?

6. Elements of the genre. At the start of the presentation, Brown mentions that as a professional strategic doodler she has lots of "whoa moments," and that, thanks to strategic doodling, she has "ninja-like" listening skills. What effects do you think these statements have on her audience? Is this a good strategy for beginning her talk? Why or why not?

7. Elements of the genre. What are some of the choices that Brown makes to present her argument? Why does she make those choices, and which parts of her talk are most convincing? To what extent does she persuade you that a "Doodle Revolution" would be a good idea?

8. Style. How does Brown create a sense of a personal conversation throughout the talk? How do her delivery, tone, and pacing foster this?

9. Design. Brown says that most people remember 10% of what they hear and 90% of what they see / are shown in a presentation. Does this seem right to you? How does this apply to your experience of her talk?

10. Sources. Why do you think Brown chose the specific evidence (and visuals) that she uses in her talk (aside from Ignite's parameters of twenty slides)? Do the slides work? Why or why not?

Drafting a presentation

CHECKLIST: Drafting a Presentation Thinking of drafting a presentation? Ask yourself the following questions.

WHAT'S MY RHETORICAL SITUATION?

☐ **Purpose.** What subjects am I passionate about? What current issues are most important to me? Do I want to motivate my audience to action? Do I want to persuade them to think differently about an idea? Do I want them to see things from a different perspective?

☐ **Audience.** When I deliver my presentation, will I be speaking to experts in the field? Or, will I want to persuade a more general audience? What do I expect is my audience's attitude toward my topic? How will I inspire and persuade my audience? Will I post my presentation online to attract a wider audience?

☐ **Rhetorical appeals.** How will I establish my ethos? Do I want to use emotion to appeal to my audience? If so, how will I make sure my audience continues to see my approach to the subject as reasonable? Will I use logic in my appeal? How can I use logic to persuade my audience to accept my claim?

☐ **Modes & media.** Will I prepare slides with text to accompany my presentation? What visuals might I add to the slides? Should I embed video clips from YouTube? Should I provide handouts? Would audio enhance my presentation? Do I want my presentation to be viewed live (face-to-face)? Do I want it available for future viewing online?

WHAT GENRE CONVENTIONS MATTER?

☐ **Elements of the genre.** How will I grab my audience's attention at the start of my presentation? What background information or terminology do I need to cover first in my presentation? How will I anticipate and address my audience's opposition to any of my persuasive claims? How could slides and visuals enhance my presentation? Will they clarify concepts? Expand ideas? Persuade?

☐ **Style.** What organization is best for my presentation? Do I want to examine a problem and persuade my audience to adopt a solution? To what extent do I need to examine causes and effects? How much time have I allotted to practicing my delivery? What strategies can I use to make sure I stay composed while presenting? Do I want to incorporate humor? Shock?

☐ **Design.** Are my slides simple, uncluttered, and readable? Is my font size large enough for the room and screen? Do I have enough contrast between my font and the background? Is each slide focused around one main point?

Sunni Brown, From *The Doodle Revolution*

PRACTICE Want to experiment? Draft your own presentation.

In the presentation featured in this unit, Sunni Brown argues that visualizing ideas—in a variety of contexts, including the workplace—boosts creativity and memory. What ideas do you have about boosting creativity and memory? Or for improving a process or learning environment? Plan out your argument and gather supporting evidence, then put together an **Ignite-style talk** that:

- is no longer than 5 minutes
- is supported by 20 slides (that will advance every 15 seconds)

As you plan your presentation, review the annotations provided in the Guided Reading of Sunni Brown's talk and keep the following in mind.

- Think about your rhetorical situation—your purpose, audience, and how you will use rhetorical appeals and media. For example, will you be most persuasive if you are also funny?
- Think about the genre's conventions—the elements of a presentation such as a strong introduction and conclusion, interesting visuals, and clear transitions, as well as appropriate style, design, and use of sources. For a 5 minute talk, you'll want to streamline your major points, perhaps sticking to only three or so, and being sure to support each one.
- Ask yourself: What do I most want my audience to remember about my presentation?

TED Talks GT

TED Talks have become ubiquitous in many parts of the academy, community, and workplace. TED is a nonprofit organization, describing itself as a "global community . . . [that believes] passionately in the power of ideas to change attitudes, lives and, ultimately, the world." The ideas are shared in short, powerful talks (usually fewer than 18 minutes); they are well-crafted and well-rehearsed. Originally, the talks were about technology, entertainment, and design (thus, TED), but now the presentations address "almost all topics—from science to business to global issues."[1]

Some critics berate TED Talks for being expensive, rehearsed, and slick, for using audience-engaging camera angles and dramatic visuals. TED Talks are criticized for not including Q&A, not providing citations, and not using a conventional rating system. They're criticized for taking many "capable-but-ordinary speakers, doing old talks they've performed many times elsewhere, and [dressing] them up in a production that makes you feel like you're watching Kennedy announce the race to the moon." All of these criticisms appear to be well-founded.[2]

And yet, TED Talks are frequently engaging and compelling. Further, the staging, timing, visuals, and presentation style all provide models from which you can learn to be a more effective designer and presenter. Carmine Gallo analyzed 500 TED Talks and identified the following characteristics that he believes are valuable for any presenter to use.

» **Engagement.** Gallo states that you should "express an enthusiastic, passionate, and meaningful connection to your topic." If you're engaged and interested, the audience is more likely to be as well.

» **Storytelling.** Tell stories that resonate. They'll strike a chord, and you'll have a connection with the audience.

» **Practice.** Gallo's findings show you should "practice relentlessly and internalize your content so that you can deliver the presentation as comfortably as having a conversation with a close friend." Practice. Practice. Practice. Is 10 time enough? No. Is 50 times? No.

Some TED Talks are winners and some aren't. Try evaluating two TED Talks, using criteria Gallo identifies as characteristics of effective presentations. Begin with these two short talks: Adam Grosser's "A Mobile Fridge for Vaccines" and Joe Landolina's "This Gel Can Make You Stop Bleeding Instantly." #Evaluate

[1]SOURCE: TED. Our Organization. http://www.ted.com/about/our-organization
[2]SOURCE: Robbins, Martin. The Trouble with TED Talks. *New Statesman.* 2012.

» **Novelty.** Give the audience something new. Gallo quotes explorer Robert Ballard who said "your mission in any presentation is to inform, educate, and inspire. You can only inspire when you give people a new way of looking at the world in which they live."

» **Emotion.** Incorporate emotionally provocative content. Gallo advocates adding what "scientists call . . . an 'emotionally competent stimulus'—. . . anything in a presentation that elicits a strong emotional response such as joy, fear, shock, or surprise."

» **Humor.** Use gentle humor (and avoid outright jokes).

» **Brevity.** Keep it short . . . if possible, just a bit briefer than the time limits.

» **Visualized Support.** Design for the medium. Use very little text. Use more images than text. Use minimal bulleted lists.

» **Be yourself.** Gallo found that the best speakers were "open, authentic, and, at times, vulnerable."[3]

This textbook asks you to view a number of TED Talks as examples. Why, especially given the criticism that they are sometimes received as glossy and superficial? In spite of the criticism, the best TED Talks can be excellent models for creating coherent and informative presentations. If you can be as confident and engaging as the best TED Talk presenters, you'll have a distinct advantage in both academic and workplace presentations.

---

[3]SOURCE: Gallo, Carmine. "9 Public-Speaking Lessons From The World's Greatest TED Talks." *Forbes*. 2014.

16 CONSIDERING COMMUNICATION: PERFORMANCE, DIFFERENCE, LANGUAGE, AND CULTURE GT

CONTENTS

To learn more about the nonverbal mode and the ways our bodies influence our communication, view Amy Cuddy's TED talk "Your Body Language Shapes Who You Are."

Being an effective communicator means more than not making mistakes. It often means engaging your entire body. It means knowing when to follow and when to flout rules. It means being aware of and responsive to the culture in which communication is created and interpreted. It means knowing how to be perceived as part of a community because of the dialect or variation of English you select. This section of the book asks you to try new ideas that will help you become a more effective communicator.

Theatrical Training and Multimodal Composition GT

You've probably taken several years' worth of high school English classes that taught you the basics of writing. But have you ever studied oral and nonverbal communication? Most students arrive at Georgia Tech with little training in these modes: a public speaking course here, a dance class there, a few performances in school plays, or maybe nothing. As a WOVEN teacher, I think that's a problem, but also an opportunity. You might never have thought about how to use your voice

---

"Theatrical Training and Multimodal Composition" was contributed by Dr. Jonathan Kotchian, a Marion L. Brittain Postdoctoral Fellow alumnus at Georgia Tech.

and body more effectively. If you're a relative beginner, you can make a lot of progress very quickly. But if you are a beginner, you might also be asking, "How do I get better at nonverbal communication and public performance?" Your English 1101 and English 1102 courses can help you develop your awareness of these elements and maybe even gain some practice performing.

I trained for years as an actor at Yale University, and I draw on that training to teach my English class as a performance workshop several times each semester. If you were to visit these special workshops in my class, here are some of the things you might see:

» Physical and vocal warm-ups

» Movement and dance experiments

» Improvisation games

» Observation exercises

» Imagination training

» Scene study

» Discussion of literary characters' motivations and actions

All of this work, in addition to being fun, is designed to change the ways students think about the oral and nonverbal modes. You should think about your work in these modes as performances—think like an actor does when preparing and enacting a role. To do this effectively, you need to distinguish between this **performance** model and a more traditional **presentation** model. Learning how to give a good business presentation or an academic research talk is a valuable skill; in fact, strategies for these kinds of presentations are covered in Chapters 10 through 12 of this textbook. However, oral and nonverbal communication involves more than just this approach to presentations. Too much focus on the presentation model might limit you because it often prescribes a narrow range for your voice and body: think of the stereotypically serious, polished, commanding "good" public speaker standing behind a podium and microphone. Following that stereotype can lead you to think too much about errors, about fixing what you're doing wrong. Worrying too much about making mistakes can get in the way of your natural creativity.

My teaching of composition and my teaching of acting share a goal: *making natural a role and circumstances that at first seem difficult and artificial.* Weak essays, weak speeches, or weak performances might seem empty because the authors/speakers/actors are only going through the motions, trying to sound "right" without really making the role their own. By contrast, the audience doesn't perceive strong actors/speakers/authors as trying at all; the performances seem natural, as though they were not pretense but real. This kind of natural performance can be learned through actor training using the tradition of the Stanislavski system. This method of acting aims at truthful performances in which you actually feel and express vocally and physically the emotions of your character rather than merely indicating them. To achieve this goal, you must imagine yourself in the character's shoes, picturing what the character sees, hearing what the character hears; you must clearly identify the character's motivation or objective to be able to act and react as your character would. When you've successfully imagined and internalized this life, you don't have to laboriously ponder the ways you ought to walk, talk, or create your facial expressions. These elements of the performance emerge intuitively and organically, just as they do in real life.

Extending this system to nontheatrical contexts is a matter of "getting into the part," even when you're writing essays, creating Web sites, or making professional speeches. Sometimes, the role you play isn't that different from your own: "academic writer," "business professional," "architect," "engineer," or "scientist." Sometimes, though, you need to think of ways to expand your range as a speaker and presenter by trying *sharply* different roles. For example, I might tell a writer in English 1101 or English 1102 to try writing as George Orwell for a while, assign a student reading *King Lear* to attempt the part of Goneril, or even ask a shy speaker to try being a dragon. Regardless of the role, students go through the same imaginative steps, getting into the part as naturally as possible. As a result, their multimodal projects look and sound more natural and better motivated. I'll show you what I mean. What would happen if I suddenly threw a ball at your head?

> Creativity and expression are easier when you're not too worried about getting it wrong. If you're self-consciously trying to conform to preconceived rules of being a good speaker, your performance may become unnatural. However, since we don't have any rules for being a dragon, you may naturally find yourself speaking loudly and clearly with a confident command of the space.

Would you consciously calculate exactly how to move your body to catch (or dodge) the ball? No. You'd just react in the moment. Your movements would emerge naturally and organically from the circumstances. In fact, you'd do a much better job of catching/dodging than you would have if you'd stopped to analyze your movements and the possible mistakes you might make. Most American actors are trained to access this kind of organic "composition," to

PHOTO ▶
Throw, Catch, or Dodge?
Georgia Tech student Shane Connelly tries to anticipate how to catch two balls being tossed to him.
Photo © R. E. Burnett.

stay involved in the present moment. Once they immerse themselves in a role, they can act and react naturally, without thinking, letting the subconscious take over. They give more creative and more effective performances as a result. Your goal is to find ways to learn to act naturally, even in roles and circumstances that might at first seem difficult and artificial.

Acting Naturally

Acting naturally may be easier said than done. In fact, when you have to move and speak in front of others, you sometimes feel tense, unnatural, and very self-conscious, especially in situations where the stakes are high and the fear of failure is strong. You can call this "stage fright" if you want to, and I think everyone knows what it's like—when you walk into a party alone and you don't know anyone, maybe? Or when you try to start a conversation with someone you're interested in romantically? The awkwardness can hurt your performance; you might end up stuttering, mumbling, or even tripping over yourself. The great Russian teacher Constantin Stanislavski (the inventor of the Stanislavski method mentioned earlier) tells a story in his book *An Actor Prepares* that helps us understand the oppressive effects of intense, awkward self-consciousness and also helps us see how we can move past them. His narrative persona (the novice actor, Kostya) is terrified by the idea of everyone in a large theater watching him:

> I went out to the front of the stage and stared into the awful hole beyond the footlights, trying to become accustomed to it and to free myself from its pull, but the more I tried not to notice the place the more I thought about it. Just then a workman who was going by me dropped a package of nails. I started to help pick them up. As I did this, I had the very pleasant sensation of feeling quite at home on the big stage. But the nails were soon picked up, and again I became oppressed by the size of the place. (7)

▲ PHOTO
Portrait of Stanislavski
Constantin Stanislavski (or Konstantin Stanislavsky), director of the Moscow Art Theatre. *Library of Congress LC-82-5898-7.*

The trick, as Kostya discovers, is that if you can genuinely focus on something (or someone) else, you'll forget about yourself. You won't be thinking about your voice and body anymore, and you can get out of your own way. I usually call that someone/something else a *source*, to emphasize that an actor can react to it and draw energy from it, instead of focusing on herself or himself. A source is usually another person, but it can also be a physical object or even an *image*, something you picture in your mind's eye. What should you do when you feel self-conscious or paralyzed? Re-*invest* in your source; attend to those dropped nails, to your partner, or to your visualized image. If you can do this, you'll feel quite at home in any role, whether playing a Shakespearean role, confidently walking into a party, or giving an engaging product pitch to potential investors.

Relieving Tension

Any exercise you can do to relieve tension helps because tension can imprison your voice and body in a tiny jail cell. That's the most important lesson of my physical and vocal warm-ups. Rather than teaching my students to put in more effort to "project" their voices or muscle up their bodies, I instead try to get them to relax. This is particularly important to Georgia Tech students, 90 percent of whom described themselves in 2011 as "very stressed," compared to a 53 percent national average for all students. (Read the full text of the "Mental Health Task Force's Report and Recommendations" from October 2013 to discover what Georgia Tech proposes to do to create a healthier environment on campus. Search for it by name on the Institute's main Web site.)

▲ PHOTO
Warming Up
Georgia Tech students Shane Connelly and Lindsey Hollenbeck demonstrate a tension-relieving warm-up. *Photo © R. E. Burnett.*

You can try the following warm-up (or something similar) on your own: I usually start with a vigorous shaking-out of the limbs, asking my students to flail about generally, then, before they have a chance to worry about how they look, we do a "spine-fold": a standing collapse, bending from the hips, letting the head and arms dangle freely; then we build the spine back up, veerrry slowly, vertebra by vertebra, until the head floats up and the shoulders roll back; then a giant sigh. Almost everyone feels a little better, more awake, more observant, less worried.

I give extra focus to two major trouble spots: the jaw and the belly. Most of us have been taught since childhood to hold these areas in an artificial tension: we hold our mouths closed to avoid tongue-lolling and drooling, and we suck in our guts so as not to look fat. We're more presentable that way, but these actions clamp down on vital resonating areas. Bouncing and shaking these areas—at first with unvoiced sighs, then with voiced sighs—helps to expand the voice's range. Most people are accustomed to living their entire lives using only a very narrow range of both voice and body, but we're capable of much more once freed from some of our tension. Instead of replacing our existing narrow range with a "correct" one that's just as narrow—a risk of using the stereotypical presentation model—our goal should be to develop the maximum possible range of our physical instruments. "Try softer," I tell my students if they become frustrated.

Borrowing from Kristin Linklater's widely used manual for actors, *Freeing the Natural Voice*, you can think about this work as "freeing," reminding yourself that you don't need to force anything because your bigger range already exists in potential. Recall a time when relaxing led to more effective communication with your audience. #Remember

Sending Action

Probably the most important performance concept I teach is called "sending action." This vocabulary comes from my practical theater work, especially from my studies with James DePaul, Bill Walters, James Luse, Michael Tracy, and Alison Chase. If the *action* is *X*, *sending* or *releasing X* is making your source feel *X*. For example, you might make the source feel excited, scared, weird, or beautiful.

▲ PHOTO
Sending Actions
Georgia Tech student Lindsey Hollenbeck sends the action "disgust" to another student. *Photo © R. E. Burnett.*

Rather than *indicating* how she herself is supposedly feeling—trying to contort her face, body, and voice into an artificial imitation of, say, pain—the actor instead invests in her source, trying to make the other person feel *X*, where *X* is "mean" for inflicting the pain, or "powerful" enough to cause the pain, or "merciful" as the other person comes to her aid. Sending "mean" is a way for her to play "I'm angry or aggressive or in pain" more organically, with her attention on her source, not herself. Conscious indication is unnecessary; the face, body, and voice naturally express the emotion without the actor thinking about it. You've probably realized by now that action isn't something only actors use; we can all think of ourselves as sending actions all the time, as we live our lives. Whenever you've made a connection to a source, you're sending action, no matter the circumstances—academic, professional, personal. That's vital to acting naturally.

Here's how I teach sending action: my class gathers in a circle, and each student tries to send action to another, one at a time. Each student picks a source across the circle and sends that person action *X* (I start off with easy ones, like "ugly" or "amazing") while saying some nonsense text. To keep students' attention off the way they look and sound, I have them throw an inflatable ball around the circle as they send each action. They know how to throw a ball, just as Kostya knows how to pick up nails. I ask them to increase their actions' specificity and urgency by using Stanislavski's *magic if*. Try imagining something extreme: how would you send the action "scared," *if* you had only seconds to save your source's life by frightening that person away from an electrified fence? I follow this work with a partner exercise designed to open students up to truthful emotional connection: you might find a trusted friend and try speaking the text "I could really be hurt by you" while sending chosen actions such as "loved" or "hated." After a while—as the photos in "Performance and Nonverbal Modes" on pp. 576–577 show—you'll gain confidence in identifying the actions sent by others and in responding to them naturally.

Consider your own facial expressions, body language, and vocal expressiveness. Using what you've learned in this chapter, decide what your greatest strengths are. #Evaluate

Creating a Role

When creating a role, whether it is Goneril or "savvy business person," ask yourself these five questions:

1. Who am I?

2. Where am I?

3. What do I want?

4. How do I go about getting what I want?

5. What do I do after I do/don't get what I want?

The third question is the most important because it makes you define your *objective*, or motivation. The objective, in turn, leads you to choose certain actions (the answer to question 4). For example, as King Lear's daughter Goneril, I might want Lear to get out of my house; this would be my objective. As my scene progressed and my circumstances (developed through questions 1 and 2) changed, I would try different actions to achieve the objective. I might send to Lear the action "powerful," then "presumptuous," then "stupid," then "frightened," and finally "annihilated," matching these with my spoken lines. When working with a dramatic scene, I ask my students to identify only one objective per scene, but choose several actions that might help them get what they want; this helps to create a natural variety in performance. We also examine the ways different performance choices might lead to different literary interpretations.

You can treat as a role—even something less obviously theatrical, like a business presentation—and prepare the role by answering the questions above. If you don't feel confident or authoritative enough in making a sales pitch, for example, you might place yourself into the role of *Star Trek*'s Captain Picard (minus the accent), or you might instead imagine a businessman, "Joey Pitcheroo," much more experienced and slicker than yourself. You could then choose the objective and actions that Joey might use to make his sale. This technique might help you discover a counterintuitive, but effective, action. Instead of sucking up to them, you might decide to make your audience feel "not even cool enough to buy my product!" and moreover imagine them as overeager schoolchildren instead of corporate executives. Exercises like these allow us to range far beyond the stereotypical presentation personae. Imagining 30 of your character's likes and dislikes is one way to ensure specificity in preparing a role; it's essential not to skimp on the imaginative work, as it's what creates the broad range of possibilities for performance.

When we use the above techniques to perform a role, are we really acting genuinely and truthfully? After all, the role is still a role. Doesn't that suggest at least

Performance in Oral and Nonverbal Modes

Responding in the Moment
Rather than trying to plan every word and gesture in advance, learn to let your subconscious respond naturally, as it does when you're catching a ball.

Sending Action
Sending action—trying to make your source feel an emotion, such as joy or annoyance—wards off self-consciousness and ensures a more organic performance.

Warming Up

Use vocal and physical exercises to stretch out your voice and body, expanding your range of possible characters and actions.

All photos © R. E. Burnett.

Theatrical Training and Multimodal Composition

How will you make your own academic performances genuine and truthful? #Apply

some artificiality? Perhaps, but consider that metaphor we sometimes use for the work of an actor expertly playing a part: we say that he has "made the role his own." Those words suggest that a role can become, in a way, part of the performer. Consider the role of "academic writer," one with which you're familiar. Most professional scholars have successfully made this role their own. I think of my "academic writer" persona as an aspect of myself because I actually think and feel the things I write, even if I write them in a style different from the one I use in ordinary conversation. Yes, I frequently alter my writing to fit various circumstances, but I'm not being fake. The role is second nature to me now. I'm being genuine in a different way, one I've had to figure out as I go along.

Once you understand that a valid part of your job is figuring out the gritty details of getting into the part—how to stop faking it, how to more naturally perform your thinking, reading, writing, speaking, and moving—you might feel liberated. Attending to your own processes of self-transformation, rather than attempting to conceal, rush, or deny them, removes the burden of pretense, as you no longer feel compelled to construct a false front to please your teacher. Rather, you can reflect on how you wish to fit into your new roles, how to inhabit them organically, and how to use them as the means to explore projects of your own. Your life as a student, professional, and human being may be more fully and truthfully lived as a result.

I'd like to leave you with another passage from Stanislavski. The story that follows, from Stanislavski's autobiography, *My Life In Art*, explains the difference between fake work and truthful work—not only in the theater, but in composition, literature, and beyond. Understanding those differences and creating presentations that are themselves truthful will make a difference in your life.

Excerpt from Stanislavski's Autobiography, *My Life In Art*

This took place on our estate, about thirty versts from Moscow, in one of the wings of our house. A small children's stage was erected there, with a plaid cloth instead of a curtain. As custom has it, the entertainment was composed of tableaux, in this case the four seasons of the year. I was about two or three years old at that time, and impersonated Winter. The stage was covered with cotton; in the centre there was a small evergreen, also covered with cotton, and on the floor, wrapped in a fur coat, with a fur hat on my head, and a long beard that would insist on crawling up my forehead, sat I, without knowing where to look and what to do. This impression of aimlessness, bashfulness and the absurdity of my presence on the stage, was felt by me subconsciously at that time, and even now it is alive in me and frightens me when I am on the stage. After the applause, which I remember was very much to my liking, I was placed on the stage again, but in a different pose. A candle was lit and placed in a small bundle of branches to make the effect of a fire, and I was given a small piece of wood, which I was to make believe I put into the fire.

"Remember, it is only make-believe. It is not in earnest," the others explained to me.

And I was strictly forbidden to bring the piece of wood close to the candlelight. All this seemed nonsensical to me. Why should I only make believe when I could really put the wood into the fire? And perhaps that was what I had to do, just because I was forbidden to do it?

In a word, as soon as the curtain rose, I put out the hand with the piece of wood towards the fire with great interest and curiosity. It was easy and pleasant to do this, for there was meaning in the motion; it was a completely natural and logical action. Even more natural and logical was the fact that the cotton caught fire. There was a great deal of excitement and noise. I was unceremoniously lifted from the stage and carried into the big house, where I was severely scolded. In short I had failed cruelly, and the failure was not to my taste. These four impressions, of the pleasure of success, of the bitterness of failure, of the discomfort of unreasonable presence on the stage, and *the inner truth of reasoned presence and action on it, control me on the stage even at the present day.* (23–24)

Works Cited

Linklater, Kristin. *Freeing the Natural Voice*. Hollywood: Drama Publishers, 2006. Print.

Stanislavski, Constantin. *An Actor Prepares*. Trans. Elizabeth Reynolds Hapgood. New York: Routledge, 1989. Print.

———. *My Life in Art*. Trans J. J. Robbins. Cleveland: Meridian, 1963. Print.

Assumptions, Audience, and Access **GT**

Although we rarely give assumptions conscious thought, we almost constantly make them. Assumptions are rooted in inductive reasoning: when something seems obvious or proves to be true often enough, people begin to treat it as fact. Doing so provides a foundation of knowledge: without assuming that scientific laws are true and that mathematical theorems are valid, for example, our culture would make little technological progress. Similarly, people would have trouble functioning in our daily lives if we had to verify each of our beliefs or perceptions before acting on it.

Not questioning every assumption is convenient and reasonable. For instance, we can rationally assume that a sturdy-looking chair will not collapse when someone sits on it. However, if one of the legs falls off the chair and sends a person sprawling on the ground, the fact that the initial assumption was incorrect in one particular instance does not mean it is necessary to question the sturdiness of every chair. We can reasonably continue to assume that sturdy-looking chairs are generally sturdy (and that exceptions are rare).

Inductive reasoning: movement from general conclusion to individual instances; conclusion probably follows from the premises.

Deductive reasoning: movement from individual instances to general conclusion; conclusion necessarily follows from the premises.

"Assumptions, Audience, and Access" was contributed by Dr. Britta Spann, a Marion L. Brittain Postdoctoral Fellow alumna at Georgia Tech.

The same holds true for the assumptions made in communication: all communication includes assumptions about audience. You usually don't give conscious thought to these assumptions, and you don't need to examine every assumption. However, when one of your assumptions, no matter how reasonable, proves incorrect, the result can be somewhat like sitting in a chair that breaks—something that you relied on falls apart, you look a bit silly, and ultimately you fail to accomplish your purpose.

Assumptions are inherent in each rhetorical appeal (ethos, pathos, logos). For instance, let's say that I am making dinner plans with a friend and want to convince her to go to a particular pizza restaurant. If I appeal to ethos by telling her that a local food critic gave it five stars, I am taking it for granted that she will consider the critic a credible authority. This could be a fair assumption, depending on the critic's reputation, but my friend's acceptance of the argument depends on her personal opinion. If I appeal to logos by pointing out that the restaurant is selling large pepperoni pizzas for half price, I am assuming that she likes pepperoni pizza and will consider the low price a compelling reason to visit the restaurant. This is a reasonable assumption given the food's popularity and the fact that most people value a good deal. However, my argument will fail if my friend is a gluten-intolerant vegan. If I burst into tears and say not eating at the restaurant will ruin my day, I am assuming that my friend will feel pity and be persuaded by my appeal to pathos. Such an assumption is generally unreasonable—most people would probably not sympathize with an adult who claims that her happiness depends on pizza—but the assumption could be correct, depending on my friend's personality. If my friend finds my behavior obnoxious, my faulty assumption invalidates my argument and, moreover, damages my credibility.

Assumptions and Inclusivity

When you have close relationships with people, you tend to know their personalities, values, likes and dislikes, life experiences, and subject positions. These elements contribute to a nuanced understanding of the rhetorical situations in which you communicate. When you do not know your audience well (or at all), you are likely to draw from your own perceptions and experiences to fill in the information. Because your perceptions and experiences are limited, you might overlook crucial details. The less you know about audience members, the more likely you are to make incorrect assumptions about them. The extent to which a faulty assumption damages your communication depends on how well your audience knows you: if I ask a friend who practices Judaism what he received for Christmas (mistakenly assuming that he observes a holiday originating in the Christian tradition), he might focus more on my good intentions than my oversight and gently correct me. A casual acquaintance or stranger, on the other hand, could perceive me as ignorant and even find my question offensive.

Here, *subject position* refers to the combination of qualities such as race, gender, sexual identity, age, and socioeconomic status that contributes to your identity.

English 1101 and English 1102 help you develop your ability to evaluate rhetorical situations and your ability to choose effective communication strategies, but you need to pay careful attention to assumptions about your audience, your classmates, and your instructor. The following practices can help you avoid making false assumptions by making your communication more inclusive of the many types of diversity that might exist among your audience members.

Consider Your Assumptions

Watch the 20-minute video, "Georgia Tech It Gets Better," on YouTube. The video was conceived, created, directed, shot, edited, and produced by former Marion L. Brittain Postdoctoral Fellow Jesse Stommel (now a professor at the University of Wisconsin–Madison) and his student Julie Champion, then a biomedical engineering major and president of Pride Alliance at Georgia Tech.

Be mindful. The more you pay attention to your own performance of assumptions, the more likely you are to avoid mistakes and to improve your strategies. Simply putting conscious effort into recognizing your assumptions can help you adjust those that might be invalid. Over time, you'll likely find that your ability to make accurate assumptions improves as you become familiar with more rhetorical situations.

Leave room for exceptions. Be wary of using all-encompassing language: Could "anyone" really perform a given action? Is "everyone" truly familiar with a concept? Do "students" (which implies *all* students) really face a particular challenge? Qualifiers such as "generally," "often," and "tend to" make diction broad and *inclusive*. On the other hand, language that is *exclusive* fails to take certain groups of people into account, thus implying that they do not exist or that their experiences do not matter. A speaker who makes faulty assumptions about inclusion or exclusion might appear insensitive or even alienate audience members. A strategy for avoiding exclusive assumptions during planning and revising is to ask yourself questions such as "What type of person might not have experienced this situation?" or "Who might have trouble relating to this example?"

Be especially cautious when using the second-person perspective. Directly addressing the reader with "you" or asking the audience to do something, such as imagine a scenario, can make one's communication more engaging. To engage students using this textbook, the authors frequently use "you" because the word directly addresses students using the book as part of their work in English 1101 and English 1102. However, directly addressing the reader with "you" can also be a risk. If the earlier analogy had said, "we can rationally assume that a sturdy-looking chair will not collapse when you sit on it," the sentence would exclude people who are not physically able to do so. Even seemingly innocent phrases such as "as you can see" or "you will be able" can exclude audience members unable to see or do what you claim. Words and phrases that allow room for exceptions are helpful.

Seek information about your audience. Knowledge is power. If you are communicating with live audience members, their body language and even the sounds they make can provide valuable information. Hypothetically, you might reasonably assume that some touches of humor could engage the audience's interest at the beginning of a speech only to find yourself facing an audience full of stern, serious faces and impatiently tapping feet. In that case, you might rethink your assumption and skip your opening joke, getting straight to your main point instead. You can conduct research in advance to identify useful information. Reading about the culture of a country that you are planning to visit could help you avoid behaviors that you assume to be polite or friendly but that are traditionally considered rude or offensive, such as showing up on time for a dinner invitation in Argentina, smiling at strangers in Russia, or giving someone a thumbs-up in Iran.

Ask questions. While you will not always be able to ask your audience questions, doing so is often an effective strategy for gaining information. Sometimes you may have difficulty determining whether an assumption is valid. A student giving an oral presentation about the Battle of Gettysburg might, in looking over her audience before she begins, realize that she cannot assume that her peers, many of whom are international students, will have already learned about the U.S. Civil War. Starting her presentation by asking the audience how many are familiar with the battle could help her determine how much background information to include.

Consider the size of the audience. The larger an audience, the more diverse it is likely to be. Your audience members might seem to have many things in common, but even if you are writing a blog accessible only to blond-haired female electrical engineers from Atlanta who are allergic to cats and drive white Honda Accords, they will have different opinions and experiences. If only three people who fit this description visit your blog, you might safely assume that all of them enjoy their jobs, but if you were to have 3 million visitors, your assumption is likely to be incorrect. The greater the diversity of the audience, the less information you can assume to be universal among the members, so when you plan and create a multimodal artifact, consider the amount and types of diversity that might be present in your audience.

Making Communication Accessible

Each mode of communication assumes that the audience can access it: a written text, for example, takes for granted that the audience is literate. However, access is sometimes more complicated. Many people experience temporary or permanent conditions that impair their ability to access a given mode of communication. For example, people who have visual impairments may struggle to read standard-size fonts. People who have auditory impairments may have difficulty understanding a speaker if even a slight amount of background noise in the room exists. You almost certainly have communicated with such audiences. To make your texts as widely accessible as possible, you can make a conscious effort to apply universal design principles to your work.

Universal design is the concept of making objects and environments that enable access by all people, regardless of ability or disability. Elevators and wheelchair ramps are examples of universal design features. If a building were constructed without these features, some people with movement disorders would be unable to travel between floors or even to enter the building on their own. Universal design features are potentially beneficial to all users: taking an elevator rather than navigating stairs can help a person who has a sore ankle, is pushing a stroller, or is carrying a heavy load. Similarly, applying universal design principles to an artifact can benefit all members of an audience: a set of instructions that includes diagrams in addition to written text provides users who cannot read a way to access the information, but diagrams could also clarify the directions for those who prefer visual learning.

◀ VISUALIZATION
Universal Design
Universal design is not only used by architects, contractors, and city planners but also by graphic designers, computer programmers, and technical writers. This image describes how the USDA, a federal agency, plans to meet employees' expectations for universal design throughout their careers. *"Discover What to Expect from Universal Design," Target Center, U.S. Department of Agriculture, Office of Operations, 2014.*

The communication strategies covered in this text embody universal design principles. The guidance you receive about such elements of visual design as font size and the use of color, for example, can help you make a PowerPoint, poster, or Prezi more readable and appealing to your general audience. However, making effective choices could also determine whether your work is legible to someone who is visually impaired or color-blind. Moreover, multimodality can be a universal design feature. Presenting information in several modes provides multiple means of access. Below are some specific examples that illustrate the ways multimodality can facilitate access for audience members who have conditions that may impair their ability to interpret and use texts:

» **Attention Deficit Hyperactivity Disorder (ADHD).** ADHD is a disorder that affects people's ability to focus. People with ADHD tend to be easily distracted and often take longer on average to process information. They have an "attention battery" that does not hold its charge well. Primarily oral or written modes of communication tend to require sustained focus, quickly draining that battery; people with ADHD become distracted as their attention is pulled in new directions. Communicating information in several modes provides people with ADHD an opportunity to shift their attention without being distracted from an artifact. Visual elements are especially productive for conveying information to people with ADHD. Pictures or graphs in an essay, video clips embedded in a Prezi, or the hand gestures of a speaker provide a break from processing purely written or oral information, allowing audience members with ADHD to recharge their attention battery.

▲ PHOTO
Tools of Scholarship
Sometimes disabilities are minor and visible. Other times, disabilities are major and not necessarily visible. Universal design helps everyone access your information. *Amanda Mills/Centers for Disease Control and Prevention.*

» **Aural and Visual Impairments**. An artifact that communicates information through both visual and auditory elements is accessible to people who experience an impairment of one of those senses. Electronic communication is one of the most efficient ways to produce and disseminate such texts. Unlike a printed hard copy of an essay, an electronic document can be read aloud by a universal reader application. Similarly, whereas a simple oral explanation of a process might not clearly convey the information to someone with a hearing impairment, playing a video that animates the process while one describes it could.

» **Dyslexia.** Dyslexia is a language processing disorder that affects one's ability to read and write. The brain of a person with dyslexia has difficulty recognizing and deciphering letters, numbers, and words. Characters might appear upside down or backward, the spacing between words and letters might be disrupted, text might appear distorted or move about the screen, and orientations might change, causing a writer to begin writing upside down or backward. Often, multiple symptoms are present at once. To a person with dyslexia, the first sentence of this paragraph could look something like this: *Dy slxeia isalau gnage dro cessingbisor der taht af fe cst oue'sadil ity to rbae or rwtei.* Presenting ideas in more than one form facilitates access. Dyslexia specifically affects written information, so oral and nonverbal visual communication are beneficial; as with ADHD, dyslexia can cause the brain to tire quickly, so images and audio clips often provide welcome breaks. Electronic media can be readily adapted to incorporate both visual and auditory elements. Further, they can allow viewers to make changes; many people with dyslexia find reading easier if the background behind the text has a slight tint or if certain fonts are used.

When Ability Is Impaired

If you have been diagnosed with a condition that affects your ability to communicate or to understand communication in one or more modes, then you have probably devised strategies for coping with the challenges you face and might even have requested official accommodations from your previous school, from Georgia Tech, or from an employer. However, no system of accommodation can be perfect. Further, impairments (temporary or permanent) can happen unexpectedly — you might find yourself losing your voice on the day of a presentation or simply unable to focus your attention due to stress or insufficient sleep. The information and strategies that follow offer ideas that can help you communicate more effectively when you face such limitations. (If you have any kind of disability, contact ADAPTS, the Office of Disability Services at Georgia Tech, discussed below.)

Apply universal design principles. If you have difficulty communicating fluently in a given mode, devise ways to supplement your communication with other modalities. If you have a speech disorder or will be perceived by your audience as having a strong accent, you can use visual and nonverbal communication to facilitate the audience's comprehension during an oral presentation. For example, you could include a short video clip to explain a concept that you might struggle to articulate out loud. Similarly, if you struggle with written communication, you can use pictures or graphs to supplement written descriptions and explanations.

Try Visual Note Taking

If you don't find traditional written notes helpful, consider creating sketches—visual notes—that capture the main points of what you are researching, listening to, or watching. Using a visual form might improve your understanding and increase your ability to recall material. To get started with visual note taking, check out Claudine Delfin's YouTube video, "Sketcho Frenzy: The Basics of Visual Note-taking" or Craighton Berman's three-part series, "Sketchnotes 101: Visual Thinking."

Make the planning process multimodal. You have likely been advised, if not trained, to use prewriting strategies such as brainstorming, visual note taking, freewriting on a topic, and outlining to help you devise, refine, and organize ideas before you begin drafting a written assignment. For some people with ADHD, dyslexia, and verbal processing disorders, these activities seem like obstacles. If writing is already a challenge, how can *more* writing make it easier? If this question resonates with you or if you don't find prewriting activities helpful, experiment with shifting the modality. Rather than writing a list of potential topics for an essay or freewriting about a topic to refine a thesis, turn on a recorder and start talking. Recording gives you access to your ideas later, so you do not have to worry about forgetting anything you talk about. Instead of writing an outline, record yourself talking through your ideas or, even better, record a conversation with a willing friend or colleague. The flow of ideas in the conversation could provide clues about an effective organizational strategy.

Customize your composition and revision processes. Obviously, you would not want to turn in a lab report written in 20-point boldfaced font and printed on pink paper. But you can certainly draft it that way. Compose and revise your work in a format that you find easy to access. You could, for example, highlight your entire text in light blue before revising if the stark contrast between black font and white background causes you visual strain. If, like some people with dyslexia, you find the infamous **Comic Sans** font easier to read than Times New Roman, go ahead and use it (Dyslexia Style Guide). Once you have finished making your revisions, you can adjust the document's formatting to ensure that your work has a professionally appropriate appearance.

Advocate for yourself. According to the U.S. government's ADA Web site, "the Americans with Disabilities Act of 1990 (ADA) prohibits discrimination and ensures equal opportunity for persons with disabilities in employment, state and local government services, public accommodations, commercial facilities, and transportation." If you are granted accommodations by your employer or school in compliance with the ADA, those accommodations are not suggestions or tips: they are your civil right. You also have a right to request reasonable accommodations if you have a documented disability. Unfortunately, some ill-informed people talk about some accommodations as though they were "special treatment"; these people do not understand that giving extra time on quizzes to someone with ADHD is like providing a ramp to someone in a wheelchair. If you encounter a boss or professor with such an attitude, do not take it personally, and prepare yourself for the possibility of having to politely, but firmly, insist on your accommodations. If you are refused, notify

Use Collaborative Planning

Professionals mentally rehearse the ways they'll respond to various rhetorical elements (e.g., content, context, purpose, audience, argument, organization, support, visuals, design, conventions). They ask themselves questions about the ways they'll address and manage these elements. You can do the same thing with a partner who asks you questions about your plans for an artifact, creating questions for each rhetorical element. If you engage in **collaborative planning** enough, the process eventually becomes internalized.

the appropriate party (Human Resources at your job or ADAPTS at Georgia Tech) as soon as possible.

Remember that accommodations can change. Typically, accommodations are decided based on what is standard and on what a specific person has been granted in the past, so they may not account for your particular circumstances. If you know that a certain accommodation could help you, such as being allowed to take notes with a laptop in class, ask for it—explain to your professor or to an ADAPTS official

Understand Multiple Intelligences and Preferences for Different Approaches to Learning

People have different strengths as learners. Perform Internet searches for <multiple intelligences>. The multiple intelligences theory developed by Howard Gardner defines seven kinds of intelligence: visual-spatial, bodily-kinesthetic, musical-rhythmic, interpersonal, intrapersonal, linguistic, and logical-mathematical. As a communicator, incorporating as many of these intelligences as possible in your artifacts promotes universal access and helps you reach everyone in your audience. Visit Gardner's Web site (http://multipleintelligencesoasis.org/) for more information.

Moreover, identifying which of these intelligences you prefer can improve your learning experience. Do some research on the intelligences that most resonate with you, and identify how you can apply that self-knowledge to selecting your approach to your learning. Educators have identified a number of learning preferences, which are often grouped into three categories of preference: **visual** (you prefer to learn by seeing and visualizing), **auditory** (you prefer to learn by listening), and **kinesthetic** (you prefer to learn by touching or doing hands-on activities). Search for and complete a few free online learning preference inventories—knowing your preferred approaches to learning can help you develop techniques to increase the efficiency and variety of your study and preparation practices.

» If you prefer visual learning, visual note taking might be more effective or efficient for you than traditional written notes. You will likely find that you more readily understand concepts if you draw yourself diagrams or pictures to illustrate your learning.

» If you prefer auditory learning, consider recording your lectures or listening to podcasts. Listening to your material may be more effective than handwritten notes. You might also consider setting your notes to a certain rhythm or tune to aid your recall.

» If you prefer kinesthetic learning, try setting up practice experiments or physical models you can interact with. You might also find that performing small, simple actions like handling note cards or playing with a small object (pen, ball, etc.) while you study helps your recall.

Don't assume you should study exactly like your friends or classmates! Rereading lecture notes and reviewing slides work for some students, but for others the practice feels difficult and therefore becomes more time-consuming. If you find yourself frustrated when preparing for an exam or recalling your reading for English 1101 or English 1102, try a different approach to learning. Draw character relationships; create a song expressing the main points an author makes; sketch a visual concept map to express the relationships among ideas; make a flip book of your notes and impressions. Understanding more about approaches and preferences to learning can certainly improve your quality of life as a student, but it also increases your audience awareness when communicating with others.

how the accommodation could improve your experience and why you think it would be reasonable. Even if you don't get exactly what you have requested, you might still be able to improve your situation. If nothing else, you are helping your professor, school, or employer better understand your needs.

Finally, encourage yourself not to settle. Many people never seek accommodations that would benefit them because they can make do without them. You'll experience a world of difference, however, between getting by and excelling. You might easily be able to pass a test or perform a job function without accommodations, but what if having them allowed you to earn an A or achieve a promotion? You might even discover that you have a natural aptitude you never expected. Impaired ability or disability is not the same as inability.

Resources and Tools

ADAPTS is the Office of Disability Services at Georgia Tech. If you have a documented disability, ADAPTS professionals will help determine and coordinate your accommodations. They can also assist you with questions about acquiring accommodations and testing for disabilities.

Dyslexia-friendly fonts exist and are continually being improved. Dyslexia Reading Well provides a thorough list of the fonts that people with dyslexia find easiest to read as well as links to downloadable fonts designed especially for people with dyslexia.

Storyboard That is a free online program for creating storyboards, a multimodal alternative to the traditional outline that you might find especially useful for planning comics, graphic novels, videos, or even written narratives.

Universal reader software programs such as Universal Reader Plus and Jaws convert text to speech. Some are only compatible with certain types of files while others will read any text on the screen, which can be beneficial for revising work. Programs vary tremendously in quality, price, and the number of functions available, so do research before downloading and, especially, before purchasing any program.

Voice-recognition software such as Dragon Naturally Speaking transcribes spoken words to written text and can thus be of great use to people whose ability to write is impaired by a physical or neurological condition. As with universal readers, research is necessary to find the program best-suited to your individual needs.

Works Cited

2010 ADA Regulations. N.p., n.d. Web. 28 Nov. 2014.

"Dyslexia Font and Styles." *Dyslexia Reading Well.* N.p., n.d. Web. 28 Nov. 2014.

"Dyslexia Style Guide." *British Dyslexia Association.* N.p., n.d. Web. 28 Nov. 2014.

Voice, Culture, Language, and Dialect GT

Considering your communication style includes more than thinking about your performance and role or acknowledging and adapting to linguistic difference and bias. As an effective communicator, you need to thoughtfully use language to help you craft your artifacts. The next three subsections discuss important questions you need to answer and practical techniques for using language as part of your communication process, including establishing your voice, addressing cultural factors, and considering dialects and languages. For further help with writing and communication, you should consult an online handbook such as the *Purdue Online Writing Lab* or *Writing Commons*, make an appointment in the Communication Center (in Clough), and use class-related resources such as your instructor's office hours and the course's T-Square site or Web site.

Linguistic culture involves more than oral and written language. Let's consider two dramatically different kinds of language that are an important part of the world in which you live, study, and work. These examples are drawn together with poetry. The first example involves what is called **interlanguage**, a system that allows speakers to use the familiar *sounds* of their native language to be combined in new ways that enable them to speak an entirely unfamiliar language. The second example involves American Sign Language (ASL), which is a distinct language used by many people. As you watch these two examples online, reflect on the ideas about voice, culture, dialects, and languages, thinking as well about how interlanguage and ASL broaden your understanding of WOVEN communication.

Language of Poetry

1. Search for and view Jonathan Stalling's TEDxOU talk, "How Chinese Characters Can Change English Language Education," which is about how interlanguage can help writers and speakers better understand poetry.

2. Search for and view the ASL performance at the 2009 Nationals of Poetry Out Loud; the performance includes a reading of Archibald MacLeish's poem "Ars Poetica," first aloud and then translated/interpreted in ASL.

Voice

As Chapters 13, 14, and 15 discuss, each genre, whether narrative, informative, or persuasive, permits certain voices but considers others atypical, ignorant, or offensive. **Voice** in this section refers to the way you address your audience using

---

"Voice, Culture, Language, and Dialect" was contributed by Dr. Malavika Shetty, a Marion L. Brittain Postdoctoral Fellow alumna at Georgia Tech. She received her PhD in Linguistics from the University of Texas at Austin.

diction, tone, grammar, and other verbal and nonverbal factors. In many ways, voice and audience are critically connected: your choice of voice is determined by the intended audience for your communication. As a writer and communicator, you must learn how to adjust your voice to reach your audience. Simply put, all communication efforts fail if your audience is not persuaded to participate.

In your academic writing, you can usually assume that your primary audience is your instructor; however, your instructor also represents your intended audience, so you still have to adjust your voice accordingly. For a formal essay or report, you generally assume that your audience is composed of informed, scholarly readers who have some background knowledge about your topic. Therefore, your voice is formal and the grammar is conventional; your tone might be persuasive. However, your instructor might give you an assignment that requests you to address a different audience—a publisher or editorial board, a committee of venture capitalists, a group of teenagers, or a prospective employer—which would require you to modify your voice to best reach that person or demographic.

You should **modulate** your voice in academic writing, which is easier in a formal context than when you are using social media. Emails, blogs, text messages, and Facebook posts all have an informal feeling to them, and you might be tempted to use an informal voice when communicating online. However, remember that your voice is determined by the audience, not just by the conventions of the genre, mode, or medium. Use the conventions to help you approach your audience in the way its members expect, but carefully consider the kind of relationship you want to create with those members. If you want to build credibility as a source of important information, you might choose a more formal voice.

> Modulating your *speaking voice* means both varying your vocal intensity (literally, high and low) and adjusting your diction and grammar to the context, purpose, and audience. Modulating your *writing voice* also means varying your intensity—for example, adjusting diction, grammar, and other factors (e.g., punctuation, graphic elements such as bullets and boxes, and page layout).

Since online forms of communication (e.g., Twitter, Facebook, LinkedIn, email, and blogs) offer an immediate availability to the audience that formal writing (e.g., journal articles, books, and essays) does not, don't let the speed of sending trick you into forgetting to carefully select your approach, voice, tone, and language. Email, for example, can be an informal "what's up" for friends or a formal request made in the workplace or the classroom. When sending an email, remember to whom you are writing (a friend? an instructor? a social club? a prospective employer?) and adjust your word choice, grammar, and tone accordingly. Even in informal electronic communication, you should follow a process similar to the one in all of the genre sections of Part 5 of this textbook. Make yourself a checklist and think about the two main questions posed in each genre section: "What's my rhetorical situation for these modes and media" (purpose, audience, and rhetorical appeals) and "What genre conventions matter?" (elements of the media, style, design, and sources).

Your communication is shaped as much by design, images, and nonverbal cues as by words. Your nonverbal behaviors influence your voice as well. For example, a short, two-word email might seem encouraging when you write it, but the message might feel abrupt to readers when they see it on the screen. Similarly, long sentences without punctuation to break up the cadence may visually reinforce to the audience that you are rambling. In electronic communication, we often use visual elements to stand in for oral or nonverbal cues. These elements help indicate the formality of your voice. A medium's conventions help you establish meaning without written exposition. For example, ALL CAPS in an email or text usually signals shouting, which is useful occasionally but can offend an audience if used unintentionally or frequently.

You might also communicate nonverbally in your electronic communication through *emoticons* or *emoji*, which convey emotions that are hard to capture outside of a face-to-face setting (e.g., a winking face to indicate sarcasm). However, they are inappropriate in formal situations, so pay attention to your diction and perceived tone when you need to respond without these indicators. To ensure that your style or brevity is not misinterpreted, consider how others will perceive your text if they don't have your particular background knowledge.

Emoticons and emoji are related; however, *emoticons* are represented with keyboard characters whereas *emoji* are small digital pictures. Both are popular ways of indicating tone and voice in electronic communication. Compare the Wikipedia definitions for *emoticons* and *emoji*. #Analyze

Social media posts and text messages are examples of media that often require an informal voice. However, when writing informally on social networking sites (e.g., Facebook, Twitter, blogs), you should still be mindful of your voice. Texts and tweets, for example, are inherently quick and use limited characters but should still be thoughtfully composed, or you might confuse your recipient. In "short" messaging systems such as text messaging, chat programs, or Twitter, the conventions allow you to use abbreviations, unconventional grammar, and emoticons or emoji to more effectively convey your message within the character limits. To use these conventions successfully, you need to select them with your audience in mind. Would you use the same text message abbreviations with your grandparents, your parents, and your friends? If your recipient does not know what your abbreviations mean, can't interpret your random characters as an identifiable emoticon, or considers your raised fist emoji as a sign of violence rather than a congratulatory fist bump, your communication is unsuccessful. While appropriate within social media, these tactics for conveying emotion would make readers question your ethos and professionalism in an academic venue.

Be careful not to transfer your "text speak" over into other venues (e.g., academic papers, scientific studies, business proposals, or résumés) where it might be inappropriate. If you are blogging, text messaging, or tweeting for a class assignment, check with your instructor about whether you are required to write in formal English or if less formal writing is acceptable. One important reminder about informal communication using electronic media: these messages can easily be taken out

Digital Privacy

Even though Snapchat is designed specifically to give you control over how long a viewer sees a picture or video you send before erasing it, many third-party apps and other methods enable viewers to capture your images. The best rule of thumb to protect your privacy is to avoid digitally capturing and sending anything you would not want to see as front-page news.

of context and become public on a global scale. As with all electronic communication, text messages (or Twitter posts, Facebook messages, and even Snapchats) you send are likely to be forwarded or copied without your permission. Do not send messages that you do not want everyone to see.

Cultural Factors and Writing Style

Language is a product of society and culture. The languages we speak and the cultures we grow up in influence not only the way we speak but also the way we write and communicate with each other. The view that the language we speak determines how we think is often called **linguistic determinism**, and the view that speakers of different languages think about the world in quite different ways is known as **linguistic relativity**.

The linguist Benjamin Lee Whorf, in 1940, proposed a controversial theory that the language we speak influences the way we look at the world and process information. For example, he claimed that if a language does not have a future tense, the speakers of that language might not have any concept of future time. His theory, which later came to be known as the Sapir-Whorf hypothesis (named after Whorf and his teacher Edward Sapir) has been criticized as being too simplistic. For example, if a language has no equivalent word for *tomorrow*, speakers of that language may still grasp the concept that another day follows the present one.

In recent years, however, the Sapir-Whorf theory has been revisited, and researchers have discovered that certain aspects of our thinking are influenced by the languages we speak. For example, some languages (like Spanish, French, and German) assign a gender to objects, unlike English, which is a gender-neutral language. An article from the *New York Times* describes how French and Spanish speakers were asked to assign human voices to a fork in a cartoon. French speakers, for whom "fork" (*la fourchette*) is feminine, gave it a woman's voice, but Spanish speakers, for whom "fork" (*el tenedor*) is masculine, gave the fork a male voice. The languages we speak and the cultures we grow up in do influence our ways of thinking and communicating. In written artifacts, you can see this connection between culture and language through assumptions about who is responsible for understanding the communication and through the tone considered appropriate for communication.

Referring to a discussion as an "inside joke" indicates the influence of culture, situation, and context on the language being used. Do you have any special words, phrases, or inside jokes that make sense only within your family? What cultural clues from your family group give this communication special meaning for you but not others? #Understand #Analyze

Writer-Responsible and Reader-Responsible Cultures Japanese discourse linguistics scholar John Hinds, in an influential 1987 article titled "Reader Responsibility versus Writer Responsibility: A New Typology," put forth the argument that readers who belong to certain cultures have a greater responsibility to successfully comprehend a written communication. The article introduced the notion of **reader responsibility**, in contrast to **writer responsibility**.

According to Hinds, differences in rhetorical styles depend on culture and language background. In the United States, whether in the academy, community, or workplace, the communicator is responsible for effective written, oral, and visual communication. For example, the writer—not the reader—is responsible for establishing the intention, purpose, and coherence of a written document. More specifically, academic essays are expected to have a clear thesis or focus. The thesis indicates the purpose and direction of the essay and is usually stated in the first few paragraphs. The writer is expected to use topic sentences that focus the paragraphs, and the paragraphs are expected to support the thesis. A well-written essay is clear, focused, and makes strong points. No room exists for ambiguity. Connections between and among ideas are clearly drawn out, and readers are not expected to connect the dots. Remember the researched argument by student Chase Dickinson in Chapter 15 (on p. 491) "Are Kids on a One-Way Path to Violence?" It presents a clear thesis in paragraph 3, which indicates the purpose and stance of the essay. Dickinson writes

> For a verbal and visual discussion of cultural factors influencing language, search YouTube for <How they talk in KY, OH and TX (from AMERICAN TONGUES)>. This clip from the documentary American Tongues by Louis Alvarez and Andrew Kolker explains how culture and speech are interrelated, using many examples from linguistically diverse speakers.

> While there are many who tend to think so [video games increasing crime], I believe that it is not the fault of the games themselves, but the lack of parental supervision and interaction with today's youth. Also, preexisting mental disorders have been found to play a huge role in how different people will react to video games.

He makes his purpose and claims explicit for the reader from the beginning, and we expect he will follow through in the order he has established.

In some other cultures, however, readers are responsible for figuring out the purpose and focus of the written communication. For example, the following essay, written by a student from South Korea, has no clear thesis indicating the purpose of the essay. Readers will realize the main idea behind the essay only after reading the conclusion. The essay is compelling because of its indirect structure, but it would not be considered conventional in a U.S. academic context, even though it would be effective in the student's home country. A U.S. reader expecting an academic essay might be confused by the indirect structure.

This I Believe
Joowon Jun

> I grew up in a wealthy family. My parents were both doctors and I could get anything I wanted. I always thanked my parents for the precious life I had, but that was not enough.

My father was a very home-oriented guy who tried to spend his time with family. He grew up in a very wealthy family. However, somehow his family became poor, and he had to study using his own means. He worked himself through college when he was young. He went to medical school, paying all his tuition himself. He tried to not make any appointments or meetings with his friends on the weekends or weeknights. Since my mother was not good at cooking, my father tried to make food for my family. He did everything to make his family's life more comfortable and full of love. Then, my father had a neck surgery when I was around 11. I did not know he had surgery at the time. When my father was in the hospital, I never wondered why my father did not come home. When I discovered a few years later that my father had had surgery, I realized how ignorant and indifferent to my family I was. It opened my eyes to my love for my family, and I tried harder and harder to show my love to my family. Even on Christmas, I decided to stay with my family even though I had girlfriend. Since then, I never went out on the weekends because that was the only time that my family could stay and spend time together.

My mother had been sick since I was 15, due to problems with two of her spinal cord discs. She had suffered since then, but I only noticed it 2 years ago. I did not know how much she had to suffer to pay for my sister and my tuition studying abroad. It costs a lot even though my parents are doctors. They had to spend their savings to pay for us. I thought that was what all parents in the world should do. I thought that was guaranteed and took it for granted, but I was so wrong. I had to thank my parents. Even if I had realized my ignorance since my father's surgery, I wasn't really grown up. My mother still suffers from her back pain. It takes an hour for her to just get out of bed on the morning. She cried every morning and night because of her pain, and I had nothing to do for her. I felt so weak. Then I realized that the only thing I could do is to spend more time with her, study harder, and express my love more.

Since then, I always say "I love you" to my parents. Even though I am far away from my home, I try to call my parents as much as possible. Because that is the best thing I can do for them. I always live with a thankful mind, and my parents are the best and the most important people, valuable to my life now. I believe in and love my beloved family.

To make smart communication decisions, you need to be aware of the context of the communication. The genre sections in Chapters 13 through 15 provide practice establishing your rhetorical situation and genre conventions related to your selections. Remember to ask, "Who is the intended audience for the communication?" In the United States, which is a writer-responsible culture rather than a reader-responsible culture, you need to make sure that you clearly lay out the purpose and direction of the essay for readers. U.S. readers do not expect they will have to guess the author's intention or purpose, so indirect approaches are often interpreted as ineffective writing.

Tone in Academic Language   The rhetorical situation of communication helps you answer the question, "Is the tone I selected appropriate to the context, purpose, audience, and genre?" For example, your instructor might ask you to write a research essay about a certain topic. In this situation, your tone needs to be formal, with established claims, supporting evidence, and careful attention to writing in academic English (such as writing in full sentences, establishing topic sentences and paragraph transitions, and using collegiate-level vocabulary). In contrast, your instructor might ask you to write a blog post responding to a reading or an event. A blog post, according to convention, is less formal than a research essay and includes your opinion about the event or reading. See, for example, the blog post below in response to a prompt about whether dying languages that are threatened with extinction should be saved.

Blog assignment prompt. The *NY Times* article "Listening to and Saving the World's Languages" speaks about efforts to identify speakers of endangered languages and to preserve some of these languages. The questions prompted by the blog are as much philosophical as practical: Should endangered languages be saved? Why should we try to save a language that its speakers no longer find useful? Should languages be left to die a natural death, or should we do our utmost to save these languages? Should endangered languages be given the same attention that is given to the protection of endangered species of animals?

Blog Response to "Listening to and Saving the World's Languages" by Student Writer Rebecca Lally

Before reading this article, I was stuck in the mind-set that languages that are endangered should just die out, and no effort should be made to save them. I think things die out when they're supposed to; the effort to keep them alive isn't worth it.

After actually reading the article, however, my opinion changed. A language can really define people and their background, and knowing and enjoying your background is accompanied by a sense of comfort and a better understanding of who you are. A lot of effort is required to keep these languages alive, and they are bound to die out eventually, but the people are happier if they can use a language in their lifetime and if they feel as if they prolonged its life just a little bit longer. A big difference exists in trying to preserve your mother tongue in your native country and trying to preserve it here in America. Kids of my generation have to know English to grow up in America and survive. They probably don't see the point in learning their parents' mother tongue, and if they do learn it, they do not use it outside of the home. I think languages like that are bound to die here in America. Even with more popular ones like Spanish, if the Spanish-speaking children marry English-speaking Americans, they will spend the majority of their lives speaking English when outside of the home. English is used across the US, so preserving languages like Garifuna or Neo-Aramaic is difficult.

I think no matter how large of an effort is given, these languages will soon enough serve little to no purpose. They will only be spoken in the small communities that use them, but outside of the home and small communities, they will not be effective. I think the approach that Mr. Lovell was taking is a good approach. It teaches the children their heritage and what the words mean, but he doesn't expect them to speak it all day every day. That is a good balance. Language should be preserved in order to teach people their heritage and culture, but they shouldn't have to be fluent in it.

Lally's response contains her personal opinion about endangered languages and the efforts made to save them. Her tone is less formal in this blog post than her tone would be in a formal essay, but she is still following writing conventions because of her audience and purpose.

Languages and Dialects

What is the difference between a language and a dialect? Unfortunately, the response to this question is not as clear as one might expect. Very often, political and social rather than linguistic criteria determine whether or not a language is a dialect.

How can we distinguish a situation of several separate languages from a situation with several dialects of the same language? One of the linguistic tests to determine whether two people are speaking separate languages or whether those two people are using dialects of each other's language is mutual intelligibility. Two languages or dialects are mutually intelligible if one can be understood by speakers of the other and vice versa. For example, speakers of Scandinavian languages like Danish, Norwegian, and Swedish can understand each other because they speak similar languages:

Danish: *Hun sidder i vinduet og ser ud over gaden.*
Norwegian: *Hun sitter i vinduet og ser ut over gatan.*
Swedish: *Hon sitter i fönstret och ser ut över gatan.*
English: She is sitting at the window and is looking out over the street.

In the case of Danish, Swedish, and Norwegian, the three languages are mutually intelligible, so linguistically speaking, these languages could be considered dialects of each other, rather than separate languages. However, these languages are spoken by people who live in different countries who want to have separate linguistic identities. Hence, Danish, Norwegian, and Swedish are politically and socially identified as separate languages that are spoken by people in Denmark, Norway, and Sweden.

On the other hand, in China, Mandarin and Cantonese are looked upon as Chinese dialects, even though these two languages are not mutually intelligible. Mandarin and Cantonese are, in reality, two separate languages rather than dialects of each other. Thus, in practice, a language can be called a dialect, and a dialect can be called a language for social and political reasons.

Three elements distinguish languages from one another:

1 **Lexicon:** The thing a chicken lays is "egg" in English, *oeuf* in French, and *huevo* in Spanish.

2 **Syntax:** English has subject-verb-object word order. For example: *Jill kicked the ball*. Japanese has subject-object-verb word order. For example: *Jiru wa, bōru o ketta* (Jill ball kicked).

3 **Morphology:** English has a plural morpheme *s*, which is added to transform a word from singular to plural. For example, one *ball* becomes several *balls*. Chinese, however, does not have such a way of marking plurals.

Four elements distinguish dialects from other dialects:

1 **Lexicon:** *Knock up* means "wake up" in British English but "make pregnant" in American English.

2 **Syntax:** Some southern American dialects have the construction "I *might could come* for the movie tonight" where two auxiliaries *might* and *could* are combined within the same sentence. Similarly, in many Midwestern American dialects, speakers perfectly normally say, "The crops *need watered*," a phrase that may be frowned upon in certain academic settings.

3 **Morphology:** The reflexive pronouns *hisself* and *theirselves* are used in some American and British dialects of English, while the more standard forms, *himself* and *themselves*, are used in others.

4 **Phonetics:** The *r* sound is trilled in some British and Scottish dialects of English, but not in most American dialects.

> ### Important Definitions for Linguistic Terms
>
> *Lexicon:* vocabulary
>
> *Syntax:* arranging words and phrases to construct sentences
>
> *Morphology:* identifying, analyzing, and describing parts of a language, including words and parts of speech
>
> *Phonetics:* study and classification of speech sounds

Visual Language and Dialects

> Nations and regions all over the world have their own sign languages with gestures developed by their specific deaf communities. American Sign Language (ASL), the most common language used by deaf people in North America, is not based on English but rather is derived from French sign language. Signs in ASL do not have a one-to-one translation with spoken English. In ASL, nonverbal posturing, facial expressions, and even the position of the eyebrows change the grammatical function of the gestures in a sentence. For example, if you ask a yes or no question, ASL signers expect to see your eyebrows arch up. Furthermore, consider how often you use a form of "to be" in your sentences. ASL has no form of "to be" — instead of saying, "The dog is brown," one might sign DOG BROWN.
>
> Not only is ASL a distinct language, it also has many dialects. According to the National Institute on Deafness and Other Communication Disorders, "Just as certain English words are spoken differently in different parts of the country, ASL has regional variations in the rhythm of signing, form, and pronunciation. Ethnicity and age are a few more factors that affect ASL usage and contribute to its variety."
>
> For more information about sign languages, visit the sign language library guide on Gallaudet University Library's Web site. NB: Gallaudet is the only university in the world designed specifically to accommodate the deaf and hard-of-hearing although they do admit a very small percentage of hearing students as well.
>
> Work Cited: "American Sign Language," National Institute on Deafness and Other Communication Disorders.

The *Dictionary of American Regional English (DARE)* is an online resource that documents varieties of American English. Visit its Web site if you speak American English and want to discover what variety you speak. You can also visit the Cambridge Online Survey of World Englishes and participate in their initiative to document the language's variety. To hear some accents in action, visit the Speech Accent Archive to listen to dialects of English from around the world. You might also refer to the companion Web site for the PBS film *Do You Speak American?* to discover the social and geographical reasons dialects of English developed.

What Are Dialects of English and Why Do They Exist? Is the sweet fizzy drink called *soda*, *pop*, or *coke*? Well, the answer depends on where in the United States you ask this question. Various dialects of English are spoken all over the world. British English is spoken in the United Kingdom, Indian English is spoken in India, and American English is spoken in the United States. The dialect you see and hear on television and radio in North America is largely Standard American English (SAE). However, many different dialects of American English are spoken across the country. If you move from one region of the United States to another, you might find you comprehend the individual words people say, but the accent, dialect, emphasis, and idiomatic expressions may be hard for you to follow. The southern dialect of English spoken in the United States, for example, is distinctive. For a humorous look at southern English in comparison to Standard American English, watch Lemonette's YouTube video "On Being Bilingual." Do you recognize any of the markers of southern English from living in Georgia?

Dialects are created by differences in geographical location, differences in customs and traditions, and other factors such as age, gender, and context. Young people tend to speak differently than older people. The word *like*, for example, is used far more frequently by young people in various grammatical contexts than by older people.

Similarly, gender plays a role in determining the dialect of a language one speaks. In some languages, like Japanese, for example, women may choose to speak a distinct female dialect. Japanese has many honorific words (words that convey politeness and signal social status); women tend to use polite forms more often than men. Women also use formal speech (formal verbal inflections) more often than men.

Learn more about Baugh's study from Patricia Rice's article "Linguistic Profiling: The Sound of Your Voice May Determine If You Get That Apartment or Not" on the Washington University in St. Louis Web site. Find out more about Labov's study in his book *The Social Stratification of English in New York City* (2006).

Dialects and Prejudice Linguistically speaking, no one dialect or language is better than another. All languages and dialects are rule-governed, rational, human creations. However, over time, certain dialects have assumed greater or lesser social prestige than others. Unfortunately, dialects are very often used as a basis of discrimination. People who speak a socially nonprestigious dialect could find themselves discriminated against in certain contexts. For example, John Baugh, the linguist who coined the term **linguistic profiling**, found that people who

spoke certain dialects of English were discriminated against when they were looking for places to live. Equally interesting, William Labov's influential 1972 study of
class-based dialects in New York revealed that people react differently to different
dialects and that certain dialects are associated with higher prestige than others.

Some dialects are often made fun of on television, and the speakers of those dialects are perceived as being lazy and stupid. One dialect that is frequently the
subject of jokes is the southern dialect of American English. For example, *The Daily
Show*'s former host, Jon Stewart, made fun of Texas governor Rick Perry's southern dialect. You can view this clip by searching for "Indecision 2012—The Great
Right Hope." Whether these dialects are labeled nonprestigious or prestigious is
not clear-cut. For example, African American English (AAE), a dialect of American
English spoken, with several variations, by some African Americans in the United
States, is in certain contexts a nonprestigious dialect and in certain other contexts
a preferred dialect.

Translating between Languages   Translation (or lack of translation) can be a
serious issue that influences access to medical care and education, among other
important services. Imagine seeking medical care for yourself or a family member
in a country where you have only a basic understanding of the language. How
would you be able to understand the ramifications of particular procedures?

When you translate written language, you must be careful to capture not just the literal meaning of the words but also the context, connotations, and intent associated
with them. One particularly dramatic example deals with the challenges of translating an experimental novel written as a lipogram, a type of writing that purposefully
and systematically omits a particular letter. In Georges Perec's French novel *La Disparition*, the letter *e*—the most frequent letter in both French and English—never
appears (except in the author's name). The novel was translated by Gilbert Adair
into English as *A Void*. To maintain fidelity with the experimental constraints of
the original, Adair had to translate the text carefully to not reintroduce the letter *e*.
Thus translation becomes far more challenging than just selecting the right word to
convey the intention; the translation must also attend to the constraint the author
imposed on himself. A literal translation of Perec's novel might be readable, but it
would be devoid of its artistic inspiration and of the original intention and meaning.

More and more multilingual writers now use online translators such as the popular
Google Translate to translate between English and other languages, as least as a
place to start. However, you can see that an online translator would be inadequate
in a task such as translating *La Disparition*. While online translators can sometimes be useful tools in translating between languages, keep in mind that different
languages assign different meanings to the same concept. Online translators are
good at providing a literal translation of text from one language to another. How-

Which dialects are preferred in the academic environ-ment? #Apply

Watch the YouTube video "ASL—Your Right to an Inter-preter (with Cap-tions)" about the rights of hearing impaired people. Construct a position statement about what qualities must be considered for fair and equitable communication. #Create

Read Miguel Helft's 2010 *New York Times* article "Google's Comput-ing Power Refines Translation Tool" to see how Brin is pushing to improve Google Translate because the task is so challenge. #Understand

ever, a literal translation might give results such as the one Google founder Sergey Brin obtained in 2004 using Google Translate for a message in Korean saying that Google was a favorite search engine. The result read: "The sliced raw fish shoes it wishes. Google green onion thing!" The capabilities have since improved, but they're still not as good as using an expert, bilingual human.

Relying on an online program to translate your writing is not a very good choice for multilingual writers. The best translator, even as online translators get more sophisticated, is still a human. A good strategy would be to write in English by looking up words using an online translator; then make sure a friend who is a native speaker reviews your text before you submit it.

Assumptions about Gender   English is one of the few Western languages that do not assign gender to nouns and pronouns. For example, in French using the pronoun *he* is correct when referring to the indefinite pronoun *someone*.

> French: *Si quelqu'un veut de la pizza, il doit chercher une assiette.*
> English translation: *If someone wants pizza, he should get a plate.*

In this example, the word *quelqu'un* translates into English as *someone* and the word *il* translates as *he*. In French, this pronoun use would be appropriate in all contexts even if the *someone* were female. In Standard American English, a person might more appropriately say, "If someone wants pizza, he or she should get a plate" or "If someone wants pizza, a plate is required" or "Eating pizza usually requires a plate." Follow this simple guideline: avoid using *he* in English when the gender of a person is unknown or if you're making a generalization about people rather than a generalization about males.

The pronoun one. How can you use the gender-neutral pronoun *one*? While the use of *one* is commonplace in British English, some in the United States believe the usage is stilted. Using *one* can also distance speakers or writers from the audience, which may reduce the effectiveness of the communication. If you are speaking or writing informally, you can replace *one* with *you*. For example, in an email, a blog post, a TED talk, or a podcast, you could say, "You really have to be careful when walking alone at night on campus" instead of "One really has to be careful when walking alone at night on campus."

He or she. You can use *he or she* to refer to a gender-neutral noun such as *lawyer*: "A lawyer must pass the bar exam before he or she can begin to practice." Reserve such use for formal writing, such as in an academic paper; in informal writing or oral presentations, the usage can appear awkward. If possible without altering the sentence's meaning, revise it to make the pronoun plural and increase concision: "Lawyers must pass the bar exam before they can begin to practice."

He, she, or they? After reading the preceding sections, you may be surprised when you read a news article in which the author refers to *he* or *she* when talking about someone of unknown gender. For example, you may read something like "When a child grows older, she needs more guidance from her parents" or "When a student fails a test, ask him to retake it." Another confusing example might be "When a patient needs more medicine, they should get it." Why do these examples appear? No authoritative consensus yet exists on which pronoun should replace a singular, gender-neutral noun like *child*. Using *they* for the unknown *he* or *she* as in *the child* or *the student* is becoming common, but violates the conventions of Standard American English. The word *they* is a third-person plural pronoun and cannot replace a singular noun like *child* if you are following formal grammatical rules. You should avoid using *he*, *she*, or *they* to replace a singular gender-neutral noun. You could sometimes repeat the noun: "When a student fails a test, ask the student to retake it."

Watch "What if? Georgia Tech" on YouTube. Assess the creators' choice to speak out against sexual violence using only male speakers, especially given Georgia Tech's demographics. Also, how does the video suggest our language is part of the problem that must be addressed? #Understand #Evaluate

Political Correctness **Political correctness** is a common concept in the United States. The term's usage and definition have been widely debated by political, ethnic, social, and intellectual groups. Political correctness is influenced by a range of factors. What counts? Demographic factors such as gender, age, race, ethnicity, and sexual orientation matter. Geography and culture matter. Personal choice matters, including occupation as well as religious and political beliefs. And physical characteristics matter, including body type and disabilities. One goal of political correctness is to avoid insulting or offending people. Another goal is to identify yourself as a person who is aware that careless use of language can hurt or insult. Some people believe that political correctness denotes language, ideas, policies, and behavior that seek to minimize the use of terms to describe people who might cause offense. Others argue that political correctness provides inclusive language to talk about the diversity of people who live in the United States. For example, the term *African American* is the preferred term of many people who, decades ago, used to be called *Negro* or *colored*. Many consider *African American* or *black* to be a politically correct terms while considering *Negro* and *colored* politically incorrect. Patricia Aufderheide's *Beyond PC: Toward a Politics of Understanding* (1992) gives an interesting account of this phenomenon in the chapter entitled "A Short History of the Term 'Politically Correct.'"

Despite the ongoing debate about political correctness, many international students find that, on a daily basis, people in the United States use more terms for the nation's diverse population than in their home countries, where political correctness may be reserved for government officials. Richard Yam, international student adviser at the University of Massachusetts, Amherst, in his editorial "Cultural Adjustment and Transitioning," writes that Americans' "openness and political correctness can be overwhelming" to international students.

Voice, Culture, Language, and Dialect

According to Georgia Tech's Office of Diversity Programs, the Institute has a non-white population of 49 percent, which makes it one of the most diverse universities in the world. The Institute has a mission to support diversity:

> We realize that, in order to achieve our vision for Georgia Tech as a leader in influencing the major technological, social, and policy decisions in the 21st century, we must recruit and retain faculty, staff, and students from a wide array of backgrounds, perspectives, interests, and talents. In doing so, we will create a community that exemplifies the best in all of us—our intellectual pursuits, our diversity of thought, and our personal integrity. Our mission to achieve inclusive excellence means unleashing the full potential of Tech's human capacity to create a better, sustainable future for us all.

Georgia Tech's Office of Diversity Programs provides guidelines about approaching diversity when trying to become an effective writer or communicator in the United States. Consider the following tips about ways to address a diverse audience (adapted from those provided by our Office of Diversity Programs):

Adapt to your audience

» Know your audience (age, race, ethnicity, ability/disability). Consider questions such as these: Do you need an interpreter? Are there people in your audience with visual impairment? Does hand and finger dexterity of the audience permit the use of a personal recording system (PRS)? Do you have people who are color-blind?

» Consider your audience's prior and common knowledge.

Adjust your dialect and diction

» Avoid slang, jargon, and acronyms.

» Avoid using or referring to culturally specific language, examples, customs, and so on.

» Rectify any language patterns or case examples that exclude or demean any group.

» Do your best to be sensitive to terminology that refers to specific ethnic or cultural groups.

» Use inclusive language.

» Try to express your own displeasure without spicing up your language with exaggerations or inflammatory words.

Respect your audience's values

» Be culturally sensitive and culturally appropriate.

» Recognize that your worldview is typical of that of your country (or even state) of origin. People from different countries may not share the same worldview.

Do an Internet search for <Beloit mindset list> and select the year you entered college. Compare and contrast your class with a much earlier one. How do they differ? What difference might those discrepancies make when communicating with that group? #Apply

For example, people in the United States often value youth over age, but this attitude may not be the same in Asian countries.

» Examine and recognize your own attitudes, beliefs, biases, and stereotypes.

» Seek information about the history and culture of groups other than your own.

» Do not assume the audience will recognize cultural, literary, or historical references familiar to you.

Use appropriate oral language and actions

» Make sure the rate of your speech is not too fast.

» Speak clearly and use proper enunciation.

» Make sure the audience seems engaged and they are following you with appropriate nonverbal feedback.

» Demonstrate sincere interest through tone and body language.

» Know that listening is not agreement.

Use humor appropriately

» Use humor with caution. Humor is relative.

Use visuals thoughtfully

» Use visual aids for clarity.

» Be aware of cultural differences in the meaning of images, design, and color.

The Office of Diversity Programs also provides the following list of ways students may differ from one another. Consider these factors carefully before you create artifacts for your classmates:

» Race

» Ethnicity

» Gender, gender identity, or gender expression

» Socioeconomic group

» Family situation (e.g., two-parent household, marital status, children)

» Disability/ability

» Learning style

» Political affiliation

» Age

» Sex

» Sexual orientation

» Geographic location

» Major

» Country of origin

» Travel experiences

Think about your own culture of origin (whether from another part of the United States or another country entirely). What are stereotypes some people believe about this culture? #Understand #Apply

Further information

Georgia Tech's Office of Diversity Programs: http://www.diversityprograms.gatech.edu/

Office of the Vice President of Institute Diversity (VPID), which provides institute leadership to establish priorities, policies, and programs that support our mission as a leading technological university in the 21st century: http://www.diversity.gatech.edu/

International Student Guide to the United States for information about foreign students and cultural transitions to the United States: http://www.internationalstudentguidetotheusa.com/articles/cultureadjust.php

PART 6
HOW DO I USE PROCESSES FOR STRATEGIC COMMUNICATION?

Read This First! GT

The most effective communicators understand that developing artifacts is a process and that process changes based on your rhetorical situation, your access to resources, and the time you have to research, develop, and revise. The chapters in this section will help you focus on the various stages of creating projects and point you to resources such as the Georgia Tech Library that can help you build a strong and credible foundation for your projects.

Screenwriter Dustin Lance Black talks about his process—the invention, the pain, the excitement, the drudgery that is involved in creating a script for a film. Go to YouTube and search <Creative Spark Dustin Lance Black> to find his video interview. Take seven minutes to listen to (and watch) Dustin as he explains his process, showing you his research closet, note cards, and file folders. Developing your own thoughtful process will help you produce projects that readers, viewers, and listeners will find compelling and believable. Pay attention—from the beginning of your process—to being responsible and ethical. Notice that Dustin thinks about his projects a lot; he doesn't just sit down to write a draft and hope things will somehow turn out all right. Instead, he carefully plans each stage of his process and knows how to move through that process, from research and interviews to note cards and outlines to a "shitty first draft" and more refined drafts. He's thoughtful and careful in his research, keeping his sources organized so he can retrieve them from a particular file or box. You can't retrofit responsible and ethical behaviors, which affect everything from brainstorming ideas to documenting sources.

Which of Dustin's practices might you adopt for yourself? #Understand #Apply

If you analyze, evaluate, and document sources as you go along, rather than wait until the final draft, your process will very likely be more accurate, thorough, and easy. For example, if you start the research early, you have an opportunity to identify and use more sophisticated materials and thus create a more mature argument; however, if you procrastinate, you'll find yourself grabbing the first source from a hurried Internet search and only having time to create a shallow argument. Or, if you wait until the end to question the credibility of a source, you may find you have built an argument on a shaky foundation.

While your particular process will change based on the modes and media you use, the following chapters outline basic stages that are essential to projects: begin by exploring topics and proposing a plan; develop the project through mock-ups, storyboards, or outlines; build the project by evaluating, documenting, and integrating source material; and, finally, shape the project to best accomplish your goals through revising and envisioning the project's future life. These stages apply to all projects, regardless of the emphasis on written, oral, or visual modalities, and regardless of whether the project is presented in print or electronic media.

In Chapter 2, "Critical Concepts of Communication," you read about strategic and tactical decisions. Remember that **strategic decisions** typically address big-picture concerns, and **tactical decisions** address immediate concerns. Thinking about your overall process focuses your attention on the big picture, the strategies you'll use. Your specific tactics usually involve immediate, short-term decisions. Effective communicators often shift back and forth between these two kinds of decisions. Dustin talks about the big picture, his overall concept for a film, as well as the specific (and sometimes difficult) decisions he needs to make to get to the work done. Remember that he laid out all the note cards on his table and said that if they didn't all fit in the space, he knew he needed to cut something. His process allowed him to evaluate his material both tactically and strategically.

Your audience's perception of your reliability and trustworthiness is a key element of using your work to solve problems and to become an engaged member of your communities. The material in the following chapters will help you tackle topics that can inform and change your answers to the following metacognitive questions and to improve your knowledge of credibility and ethical considerations in communication.

Mentally reviewing your ethical considerations is essential, not only to streamline your project process but also so that you know the values that underpin your decision making; when you select certain videos, images, or words to present to an audience, you are shaping the way that audience understands its world. If you've never asked yourself how credibility is formed or why correct citation matters beyond an assignment requirement, you won't be prepared to tackle communication tasks in your future workplace.

Metacognitive Questions to Leverage Your Knowledge: Credibility and Ethics

You can start to answer these metacognitive questions now, but you'll have much more detailed and credible responses when you finish reading all the chapters in Part 6.

» **REMEMBER:** Recall a time when you questioned the credibility of a source. What made you suspect its accuracy or authenticity? **#Remember**

» **UNDERSTAND:** Compare the credibility of the *New York Times* (tagline: "All the news that's fit to print") and the tabloid newspaper the *Weekly World News* (tagline: "The world's only reliable news"). Visit and compare their homepages. **#Understand**

» **APPLY:** What can you do to establish your credibility in an academic paper? **#Apply**

» **ANALYZE:** Do an Internet search for Matt Cutt's TED talk "Try Something New for 30 Days," and watch his three-minute presentation. How does he establish his credibility? He uses lots of different strategies. See if you can classify them. **#Analyze**

» **EVALUATE:** Matt Cutt's TED talk "Try Something New for 30 Days" is rated as highly persuasive. Explain why you agree or disagree. **#Evaluate**

» **CREATE:** Create a tagline describing yourself on a social media site such as Twitter. Limit yourself to 160 characters—Twitter's maximum length for your personal bio. **#Create**

17 PROCESS: EXPLORING TOPICS AND CREATING A RESEARCH PROPOSAL

CONTENTS

▲ STUDENT AUTHOR
Jasmine Huerta
iStockphoto.
RESEARCH PROPOSAL ▶
Jasmine Huerta
Diabetes Project.

ENG 101, Professor Braziller

Research Proposal Assignment: What Is Your Focus?

Jasmine Huerta
Professor Amy Braziller
English 101
October 6, 20—

Research Proposal

1. Your research question

   How can diet—specifically, monitoring the intake of sugar, calories, and sodium—help someone with diabetes manage the disease and avoid taking insulin?

2. A working title for your project

   The working title for my project is "Living with Diabetes: Diet Is the Answer." I chose this topic because although some people are predisposed to diabetes because of genetics, they do have some control over the situation. For example, through their choices related to food and diet they can manage or perhaps even prevent the disease.

CHOOSING A TOPIC THROUGH INITIAL RESEARCH

What issues do you care most about? What have you blogged or posted about lately? What topics from the news or your studies keep you up at night? What would you like to learn more about?
#Remember
#Understand

The Internet offers an unlimited source of topics, and beginning your reading can be exciting but overwhelming: You can easily locate millions of resources on any topic simply by doing a quick online search. That's why it's important to go about the process in an orderly fashion. This chapter will show you the steps you need to take.

Whenever you write—as a student in a composition classroom or a professional in a workplace—you focus on a specific topic. Sometimes you may be provided with a general theme or a specific topic or issue. For example, your instructor might ask you to respond to an essay you've read for class, or your manager at work might ask you to share your plans to improve business or increase sales in the next quarter. Other times, most often in the course of college work, you get to start from scratch and choose a topic purely out of your own interest and curiosity.

So how do you choose a topic? Where should you start?

1. Brainstorm Topic Ideas: Read, Talk, Sketch, Enjoy.

For an Index of Sources & Contexts for material referenced in this chapter, see the e-Pages at **bedfordstmartins .com/bookofgenres.**

The best way to get started on identifying a topic that is meaningful to you is to get your ideas flowing. Here are some ways to do that.

Begin by reading for ideas and discussing those ideas with others.

Do some preliminary reading online, but be disciplined about it   Googling your topic is a way to explore your initial ideas, but at this stage, limit yourself to a few major sources in order to get a flavor for the topic. Some general sources might be *Salon, Slate, The New York Times,* or CNN. If you want to skim scholarly sources, try Google Scholar (scholar.google.com). If you go to *Wikipedia,* be sure to look at the source links for the entries you read. That's where you'll find the best leads. And don't be all day about it: Remember, you're generating ideas, not surfing mindlessly. For example, let's say you are interested in the topic of road rage: the problem of aggressive driving. While the *Wikipedia* "Road Rage" entry (see p. 611) may not be exceptionally informative (or particularly trustworthy), the "Sources," "Further reading," and "External links" sections can connect you to better sources, such as the National Highway Traffic Safety Administration's campaign to stop aggressive driving (see p. 612), and AAA's (the Automobile Association of America's) study on controlling road rage.

Talk to people   Discuss your topic ideas and questions with classmates, friends, family, and coworkers to find out what others have to say about the topic you're considering. Often, explaining why you're interested in a topic can help you focus. When others ask you to clarify your ideas, you will often discover what you really want to say.

Continue to generate ideas through brainstorming and sketching techniques.

Make a list   What do you care most about? Begin by making a list of things you are passionate about, your pet peeves, things you are curious about, things you don't understand, or things you'd like to change about the world. From your initial

WEB SITE ▶
National Highway Traffic Safety Administration "Stop Aggressive Driving." The "Sources" and "External Links" sections of *Wikipedia*'s "Road Rage" entry point readers to this authoritative government source (nhtsa.gov/ Aggressive). *Courtesy of the National Highway Traffic Administration.*

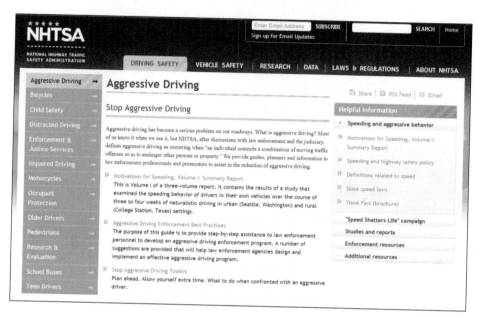

Ideas come out of conversations. What comes up in your talks with friends? What was the topic of your last discussion or disagreement? What are some of your unresolved questions about the topic? #Remember #Understand

list, force yourself to double or triple the size of the list. Often the best topic ideas are the less obvious ones—ideas that will come to you when you push yourself to keep listing.

Freewrite   If you've identified a general topic area, or some of the ideas you've generated in your lists interest you, try freewriting. The goal here is to get your ideas written down, without judging what you're writing, or editing yourself, or trying to write beautifully. Experiment by making yourself write nonstop for ten to thirty minutes. As you keep your fingers moving, don't worry about making sense, or about readers being confused or impressed. No one is going to read this document but you. When you take away the pressure of producing smooth prose, you may be surprised to see the ideas you generate.

Mind map   Like list making and freewriting, mind mapping gives you a creative format for sketching out your early ideas about a topic. To begin, write the topic or idea you are exploring in the middle of a blank piece of paper (alternatively, you can use mind-mapping software such as MatchWare OpenMind or a free Web-based mind-mapping application such as Bubbl.us). As you think of details and related ideas, write them around the central topic, connecting them with lines that indicate their relationships.

Guided Process: How to Choose a Topic

Sharon Freeman (Student)

From Coffee to Germs

Below are three lists made by student Sharon Freeman. In the first list, she simply wrote down everything on her mind. For the second list, she wrote a question or two about each topic. By the third, she focused on germs and specific questions related to that topic.

▲ STUDENT AUTHOR
Sharon Freeman
Here we look at this student's early brainstorming on a possible research topic (germs). *Shutterstock.*

TOPIC BRAINSTORM 1

Coffee

Chocolate

Democracy

Taxes

Germs

TOPIC BRAINSTORM 2

Coffee—is it worth it to pay more for organic or sustainably grown coffee?

Chocolate—is dark chocolate really good for you?

Democracy—how much say do citizens have compared with corporations these days? How much difference do huge campaign contributions make in how politicians vote and make laws?

Taxes—how much do I really pay in taxes (income taxes, sales taxes, property taxes, etc.), and how does it all get spent?

Germs—is antibacterial soap really necessary?

TOPIC BRAINSTORM 3

Germs

Do I need to use antibacterial soap, or does it make things worse?

Do you need both antibacterial soap and hand sanitizer, or just one?

How much money do people spend these days on antibacterial products and is it all just a hoax?

Aren't some germs actually good for you?

Has anyone actually gotten sick from someone at the gym not wiping down a machine? Seriously, what can you catch from someone else's sweat?

Why do some people get colds and other people don't?

How contagious are you when you have a cold? Should you really skip class and work?

How can you build your immunity against colds?

After brainstorming, Sharon did some freewriting about germs:

TOPIC FREEWRITE: "GERMS"

It seems like everyone I know is obsessed with germs. My roommate has little bottles of hand sanitizer stashed everywhere and she's constantly using the stuff and offering it to me. I feel weird when I say no, but honestly, I'm suspicious of the stuff. I wash my hands before cooking or eating and of course, after using the bathroom, and I almost never get sick, so it seems to me that I'm doing everything I need to do. What would spending money on hand sanitizer and obsessing over germs do for me? I think it's a moneymaking scheme. The companies that make soap now want to sell us soap AND hand sanitizer. And now we have to pay extra to get antibacterial soap, too. My parents don't use that and they're perfectly healthy. My dad hasn't had a cold in twenty years.

Sharon also sketched out a mind map in order to explore different views and aspects of her topic. In the map below, she broke out "Germs" into two aspects or subtopics:

TOPIC MIND MAP: "GERMS"

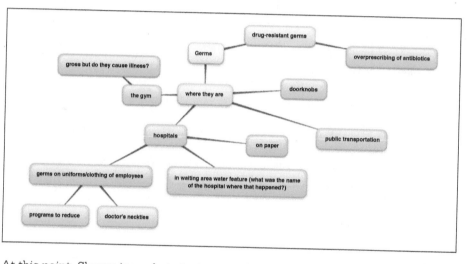

At this point, Sharon is ready to test some of her questions with some preliminary research, with a focus on:

1. Where germs are

2. How germs become drug resistant

From there, she focuses on the first subtopic—where germs are—and further breaks it down into aspects she could explore (in darker green):

» The gym

» Public transportation

» Hospitals

» Doorknobs

When you research a topic, how do you know what is fact and what is opinion (an argument supported with facts)? If you wanted just plain facts about how germs are spread—and not, say, an argument for or against hand sanitizers—what sources would you turn to? Medical reports? Editorials? #Understand

Next, Sharon focuses on hospitals—and programs that hospitals could adopt for reducing the spread of germs among staff and patients. For example, "asking doctors not to wear germ-transporting neckties" could branch off the "programs to reduce" bubble.

Plenty of unexplored topic areas are still represented in this map. For example, Sharon could go back to her "Germs" bubble and add other aspects, such as the views of scientists, parents, and schools. Or she could focus on the relationship between drug-resistant germs and the use of hand sanitizer.

2. Explore Topic Ideas through Preliminary Research: Ask Yourself, Who's Saying What?

Once you've identified a topic area (road rage, germs, or something else), you're ready to dig a little deeper to better understand it. Keep a few possibilities in mind and conduct preliminary research on several related topics (or subtopics) so you can make an informed decision about which one to commit to; the viability of each topic will depend on what you find out at this point. As with the preliminary reading you did during brainstorming, you'll continue to draw on sources written for nonexperts. Later in your process, you'll move on to more specialized sources. As you conduct preliminary research, focus on the following:

Words and facts: Ask yourself some questions. Are there terms you need to define? And what are the facts?   For example, if you are exploring road rage, you might ask yourself: How do law enforcement agencies define "road rage"? When is this term used, and why? What are the degrees of road rage that police recognize? And how does the court system define and prosecute road rage? For example, the Automobile Association of America (AAA), in a report it commissioned (see p. 616), makes a distinction between "road rage" and "aggressive driving."

As you gather facts, ask yourself: How many incidents of road rage have been recorded nationally? How many in your state, city, or neighborhood? What were the circumstances? What were the repercussions?

Opinions: Find out what others have to say on the subject, and notice what evidence they use to support their opinions   In addition to facts, what opinions surround your topic? Who writes about the topic, and why are they concerned? On what sources do they base their statements or arguments? What sources do they draw on? And what sources might you want to use, too? In relation to the road rage topic, you might find out that some psychologists consider road rage a mental health issue or that law enforcement in different places defines road rage as a crime, depending on whether someone is injured or killed. Source material for road rage might include legal statutes and news reports of incidents.

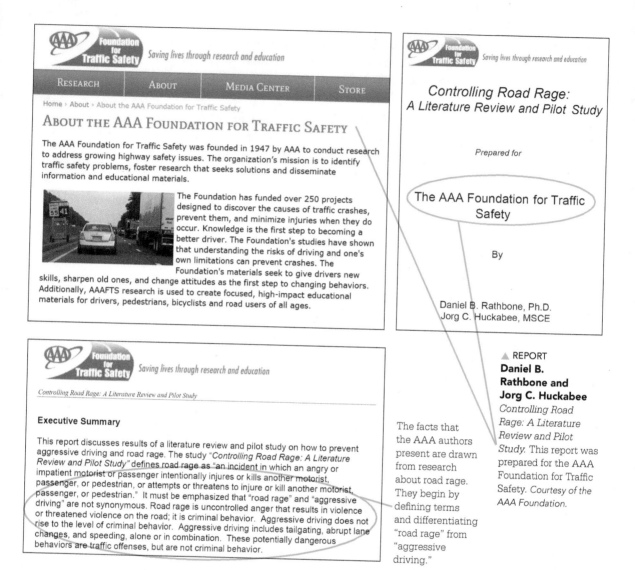

REPORT
Daniel B. Rathbone and Jorg C. Huckabee *Controlling Road Rage: A Literature Review and Pilot Study.* This report was prepared for the AAA Foundation for Traffic Safety. *Courtesy of the AAA Foundation.*

The facts that the AAA authors present are drawn from research about road rage. They begin by defining terms and differentiating "road rage" from "aggressive driving."

As you gather opinions on your topic, ask yourself: What are the advantages of—and motivations behind—each argument? For example, an organization that wants to stop road rage might define it as a mental health issue; this might make it easier for the organization to get funding for a safe driving program.

Your perspective: Form your own arguments in response to others As you research, you will begin to form your own ideas and opinions about your topic. For example, learning how others define road rage might lead you to form your own definition. Or learning how psychologists understand and treat road rage could lead you to put forth an argument about how it should be handled by law enforcement. In other words, you will naturally begin responding to the ideas of others and kicking around possible arguments.

Conflicting views: Notice who disagrees about your topic   When you begin reading sources related to your topic, you might begin to notice that there are viewpoints that stand opposed to each other. Furthermore, as you dig into these disagreements, you might realize that the differing viewpoints are well-researched and should not be immediately dismissed. In the case of road rage, you might find one article by a psychologist arguing that road rage is a result of a mental disorder and another article written by a sociologist claiming that road rage is not a mental condition but rather a cultural condition based on societal behavior. Discovering well-researched, well-reasoned opposing stances related to your topic forces you to accept that one "correct" viewpoint does not necessarily exist; reasonable people can disagree.

The irrational: Avoid arguments that are just too "out there"   In the course of your research, you may stumble upon the ideas of people who are unreasonable, ill informed, or both. For example, say you are researching *Apollo 11*, the first manned landing on the moon, in 1969, and the cultural impact of this event. You may encounter arguments by those who believe the landing was a hoax, despite factual evidence to the contrary. Moon landing deniers are considered by most people to be out of touch with reality; in this case, pursuing this strand of research is not worthwhile. Keep a critical eye as you read sources.

Comfort zone: Use sources that are right for you   While plenty of source material exists about the topics of road rage and *Apollo 11*, other topics, especially those that are very narrow or specialized, can be problematic. In certain cases, the information you need might be held in archives or scientific labs that you don't have access to; another problem is that the information you find might be so complex that you can't understand it. For example, a scholarly journal article on advanced economic theory is probably not an appropriate source for your purposes (unless you happen to be an expert in this area).

Detective work: Keep an eye out for subtopics   In your preliminary research you'll uncover subtopics you hadn't thought of before. For example, you may not have known that the phenomenon of road rage is discussed and researched by doctors and psychologists; a subtopic of road rage might be personality predictors for road rage.

The search: Pay attention to key terms   As you conduct preliminary research, you'll notice that certain terms pop up. For example, if you research road rage, you'll see that *defensive driving*, *aggressive driving*, *reckless driving*, and *intermittent explosive disorder* are terms that appear frequently in source materials. Follow up on these key terms by using them in your searches of the Internet and library databases.

What works: Test the viability of your topic by asking yourself a few questions   Following is an assignment we give our students during their preliminary research phase. It includes the responses of a student, Jasmine Huerta, whose research topic is diabetes. (Note: We will see more of her work on this project later in the chapter.)

Through answering the assigned questions, Jasmine realizes that she has several interesting potential research questions to pursue. The list of key terms helped her continue and refine her research. She realized that the glycemic index is not 100 percent accepted, which surprised and intrigued her. By using the Internet to find key terms, exploring some of these potential subtopics, previewing and reading sources, and then reflecting on her process and discoveries, Jasmine narrows her topic from diabetes to the role of nutrition in the diabetic patient.

▲ STUDENT AUTHOR
Jasmine Huerta
In this chapter, we follow this student as she chooses and investigates a topic (diabetes). Jasmine appears next on page 626.
iStockphoto.

TOPIC ASSIGNMENT ▶
Jasmine Huerta
Shown here are Jasmine's very early ideas about her diabetes project and some information on what she's discovered during preliminary research.

ENG 101, Professor Braziller

Topic Assignment: What Is Your Topic? How Viable Is It?

Jasmine Huerta
Professor Amy Braziller
English 101
September 26, 20—
Topic Idea: Diabetes

You've begun your preliminary research. Now, respond to the following questions to see how workable your topic may be.

1. What is the general topic area you are considering?

   I am interested in researching and writing about diabetes.

2. Why? Are you truly fascinated/curious/passionate about the topic? How did you become interested in this topic? (If your answer is no, explain why and then move on to the next topic without answering any more questions.)

   Diabetes runs in my family, so it's something I want to understand more about in case I am faced with it at some point. My six-year-old cousin has type 1 diabetes. My mother had gestational diabetes when she was pregnant with me. Most recently, my grandfather, who is a bit overweight (as is my cousin), was diagnosed with diabetes. I'm wondering if I am just destined to develop it at some point because of my family history. I also wonder if perhaps there are things I can do to prevent the disease, since I presently don't have diabetes. I worry about both my cousin and grandfather, so I'd like to see if there are some things they could do to keep their diabetes under control, rather than just relying on traditional medicine.

3. What surprising facts have you gathered so far about your topic? What further questions do you have that you need answered with data? And what sources are you thinking of using?

Huerta, *Topic Assignment, Continued*

Surprising facts/data:

- According to *Wikipedia*'s entry "Diabetes" (accessed on 9/20/13): "Diabetic patients with neuropathic symptoms such as numbness or tingling in feet or hands are twice as likely to be unemployed as those without the symptoms."

- A link found on the American Diabetes Association to an article on SmartBrief .com stated that those who are exposed to secondhand smoke have a greater risk of contracting diabetes.

- According to an article about lifestyle and home remedies, found on the Mayo Clinic's page, diabetes can contribute to gum infections.

Potential sources:

- *Wikipedia*

- American Diabetes Association

- Mayo Clinic

4. Do reasonable people disagree about the topic? If so, what aspects of the topic do they disagree about? Who disagrees with whom? Name names. Articulate at least three positions you have found. (If your answer is no, explain why and then move on to the next topic without answering any more questions.)

There seems to be a bit of a debate about what makes the best approach for a diabetic diet. While surfing around on the Internet, one of the big debates I found discussed the glycemic index and how it relates to managing diabetes. It seems that people used to think you just had to avoid high-sugar foods, but after reading a few articles, I realized that many researchers want to look more closely at using the glycemic index (taking into account carbohydrates) in working with diabetic diets.

In an article titled "Low–Glycemic Index Diets in the Management of Diabetes," Miller et al. argue that this is a positive approach. I found an editorial written by Marion Franz in the publication *Diabetes Care* that argues with this approach: "The Glycemic Index: Not the most effective nutrition therapy intervention." In the Mayo Clinic's advice column, "Ask a Diabetes Specialist," someone wrote to Dr. Maria Collazo-Clavel, asking, "Is the glycemic-index diet useful for people with diabetes?" She responds that it's very complicated to use this as a measure, cautioning that it might not be the best approach for everybody.

5. Is the topic researchable in the time you have? Will you be able to conduct primary research? (If your answer is no, explain why and then move on to the next topic without answering any more questions.)

I don't see any issues with researching the topic this semester. In a short amount of time I was able to find many sources and potential ideas. Primary research also should be easy. As I mentioned in my answer above, I have a number of family members who deal with diabetes. I can easily interview them. I also would like to contact a doctor who treats people with diabetes and arrange an interview, perhaps by phone or e-mail. Another possibility for primary research is to find some blogs written by diabetics, so I could draw on some of their firsthand experiences.

Continues next page

Choosing a Topic through Initial Research

Huerta, *Topic Assignment,* Continued

6. What are some subtopics that have emerged in your research?

- Nutrition to manage diabetes
- Medication to manage diabetes
- Alternative treatments for diabetes
- Prevention of diabetes
- Social issues connected to diabetes

7. What questions might you pursue in further research, based on what you've discovered during preliminary research?

- What types of diets are best for people with diabetes?
- How can diet prevent someone from getting diabetes if he or she has a family history of diabetes?
- How can following certain nutritional guidelines make diabetes go away?
- How can alternative treatments or natural medications be used instead of insulin?
- What countries have the highest rate of diabetes? What contributes to the high rate?

8. What are some key terms that keep coming up in relation to this topic?

- glycemic index
- metabolism
- blood sugar
- hypertension
- obesity
- glucose monitoring
- insulin

3. Commit to a Single Viable Topic: What Are You Most Curious About?

Once you've identified a general topic area, you need to commit to one specific topic within it. The "What Is Your Topic? How Viable Is It?" assignment (p. 618) can assist you with this choice, as can the following questions:

Is your topic compatible with your assignment? And can you make a strong argument about it? If your instructor has given you an assignment, read it carefully and consider the degree to which your topic will work. If you've been asked to make an argument, you might find yourself gravitating toward controversial issues—such as gun control, abortion, and censorship. However, we urge you to consider other, less obvious topics. For example, if you are interested in the subject of gun control, rather than choosing the topic of concealed weapons and constitutional rights, you might take the topic of gun control and examine the power that gun control groups, such as the NRA, hold in the political arena.

Do you like your topic enough to stick with it? If you are not truly curious about your topic, you probably won't remain interested in your research beyond the first week or so. Choose something you really want to learn about, that has some connection to you and your life.

What is your deadline, and how will it affect your plans for research? If your completed project is due in two weeks, choose a topic for which you have plenty of information that you can access easily. If you have more time, say an entire fifteen-week semester, you have the luxury of using a range of sources and conducting interviews or surveys, for example, so you can select your topic accordingly. On the other hand, if your topic is so obscure that your only sources need to be ordered through interlibrary loan (which can take several weeks), it is not a good topic for either a two-week or fifteen-week deadline.

Will you find appropriate sources for your topic? Some topics are so current that little or no published research is available. For example, a friend who works in the field of bioengineering might tell you that scientists are developing crops with deeper roots to reduce the amount of carbon dioxide in the atmosphere, but because the research has just begun, no published articles about it are available. In this case, you might want to shift your topic toward an aspect of bioengineering that is more researchable in the present.

4. Form a Working Research Question—and Refine as You Go.

What's your general topic? What questions will move you from a basic, broad idea to more specific ideas? Creating research questions focuses your attention from a general topic to a specific aspect of the topic, as follows:

GENERAL TOPIC	Race
WORKING RESEARCH QUESTIONS	Is the criminal justice system in the United States racist?
	Is racial profiling a form of racism?
	What is it like to be an immigrant in America?

☞ **Attention, researchers! Looking for something to argue about?**

Almost any topic offers argumentative angles: The key is to find the angles.

For example, while "reading" may not seem like the most provocative topic, a quick Google search reveals that it's the subject of much debate. Some questions around this debate include: Do college students read more or less than in the past? Is online reading cognitively different from reading books? What is the relationship between how much we read and our development of critical thinking skills?

The point is to keep an open mind to topics that seem vanilla. You may find some spice under the surface.

While you'll ask (and answer) lots of questions in your research, your "research question" is the big question, the one that you are ultimately interested in answering. Once you've done some preliminary searching—and have a sense of what people are saying about your topic and what some of the subtopics are—you can formulate a working research question. As you continue your research, you will refine your question. For instance, you might decide to begin as follows:

WORKING RESEARCH QUESTION   Is racial profiling a form of racism?

But as you discover more about your topic, you might revise your question to reflect what you're learning, as follows:

REVISED RESEARCH QUESTION   How does racial profiling help or hinder law enforcement policies?

WEB SITE ▶
The American Civil Liberties Union. The ACLU is an excellent resource for racial profiling data and perspectives. *American Civil Liberties Union.*

The ACLU argues that the practice of racial profiling hinders law enforcement and alienates communities.

ACLU
AMERICAN CIVIL LIBERTIES UNION

BECAUSE FREEDOM CAN'T PROTECT ITSELF.

KEY ISSUES   TAKE ACTION   VIDEOS+   ABOUT US   DONATE˅

Racial Profiling

The ACLU's Campaign Against Racial Profiling fights law enforcement and private security practices that disproportionately target people of color for investigation and enforcement. We represent individuals who have been victims of racial profiling by airlines, police, and government agencies. Our work also encompasses major initiatives in public education and advocacy, including the creation of essential resources, lobbying for the passage of data collection and anti-profiling legislation, and litigation of airline and highway profiling cases.

HOME › DEFENDING TARGETS OF DISCRIMINATION › RACIAL PROFILING

Share

> Blog Series - The Three Faces of Racial Profiling

Racial profiling is a practice that presents a great danger to the fundamental principles of our Constitution. Racial profiling disproportionately targets people of color for investigation and enforcement, alienating communities from law enforcement, hindering community policing efforts, and causing law enforcement to lose credibility and trust among the people they are sworn to protect and serve. We rely on the police to protect us from harm and to promote fairness and justice in our communities. The despicable practice of racial profiling, however, has led countless people to live in fear and created a system of law enforcement that casts entire communities as suspect.

BLOG OF RIGHTS

RELATED POSTS

The Legacy of Trayvon Martin

The U.S.-Mexico Border: Safer than Ever

Worried About Police Accountability in New York City? There's an App for That

See All »

TRENDING TOPICS

What questions—focused on finding facts and defining terms—can move you toward a final research question? As you begin your research, many of your questions will be focused on gathering facts and defining terms. If, as in the example above, you're researching the general topic of race, you will ask questions at the outset such as the following:

QUESTIONS TO HELP YOU UNCOVER FACTS & TERMS	What is the definition of *race*?
	What is the difference between *race* and *ethnicity*?
	Has the definition of *race* changed over time?
	What statistical data is there concerning race in the United States?

Your research question, however, should focus on more complex *analysis*. Following are some examples of revised, more final research questions:

RESEARCH QUESTIONS	How is race portrayed in the news media?
	What are the real-life effects of the news media's portrayal of race?
	What can news media outlets do to ensure that race is portrayed responsibly?
	What would happen if the portrayal of race in the news media were regulated by a governing body?

Notice how these questions require extensive research and even speculation, especially the last question. These would make solid research questions, while the first set of questions would not, although they would be useful questions to ask in the course of researching one of the questions in the second list.

Let's look at another example. Imagine you are researching graphic novel heroes. As you begin to familiarize yourself with your topic, you might ask:

QUESTIONS TO HELP YOU UNCOVER FACTS & TERMS	When did graphic novels become popular?
	What are some popular themes in graphic novels?
	What are the most commercially successful graphic novels?
	Who is the audience for the most commercially successful graphic novels?

With the answers to these questions, you can then focus on answering more critical, complex research questions, like these:

RESEARCH QUESTIONS   How do graphic novels subvert female stereotypes?

How does the portrayal of females in graphic novels differ from the portrayal of females in comic books?

How do graphic novels extend and build upon the archetypes of comic books?

How does the subversion of female stereotypes in graphic novels affect female readers?

WEB SITE ▶
**Graphic Novel
Reporter**
A good source for
facts and opinions on
graphic works, and
for investigating the
themes, assumptions,
and stereotypes built
into graphic novels.
*Copyright 2008–2010,
GraphicNovelReporter
.com. All rights reserved.*

What is the general topic of your
research? What
are your questions
about it so far?
Which questions
have to do with
finding facts? Which
ones are more about
analysis? What, in
your early research,
has surprised you
most? #Understand
#Analyze

As with the research questions about race, the final questions about graphic novels are much more focused on analysis than on simple fact-finding.

The chart below shows some working research questions as they move from general concepts drawing on facts to more complex ideas involving speculation. As you read from left to right, you can see beginning/working research questions evolving into more final research questions. Notice also that as the questions get more speculative, they also become more debatable and argumentative.

	QUESTIONS TO HELP YOU UNCOVER FACTS & TERMS			RESEARCH QUESTIONS	
	Broad/general ──────────────────►			Specific, analytical, complex	
TOPIC: Race	What is the definition of *race*? What is the difference between *race* and *ethnicity*?	▶ Has the definition of *race* changed over time?	▶ How is race portrayed in the news media? What are the effects of the news media's portrayal of race?	▶ What can news media outlets do to ensure that race is portrayed responsibly?	▶ What would happen if the portrayal of race in the news media were regulated by a governing body?
	Broad/general ──────────────────►			Specific, analytical, complex	
TOPIC: Graphic novels	When did graphic novels become popular? What are the most commercially successful graphic novels? Who is the audience for the most commercially successful graphic novels?	▶ What are some popular themes in graphic novels?	▶ How do graphic novels subvert female stereotypes? How does the portrayal of females in graphic novels differ from the portrayal of females in comic books?	▶ How do graphic novels extend and build upon the archetypes of comic books?	▶ How does the subversion of female stereotypes in graphic novels affect female readers?

▲ CHARTS
Refining a research question.
This chart shows the movement from broad topic questions to more specific research questions. Notice the movement from "What is race?" to "What if the government had a say in the portrayal of race in the media?"

CHECKLIST Refining Your Research Question

What are the qualities of a really good research question?

☐ **It is open-ended,** meaning it cannot be answered with a simple yes, no, or maybe, or a single number.

☐ **It uses specific, rather than general, terms.**

☐ **It can be answered in the time you have—and with the resources you have access to.** You might have a fascinating and specific research question, but if you can't feasibly research it in the time you have, it just won't work.

☐ **It is one you really want to find answers to.** The best research grows out of curiosity. No matter how good your research question is, if it isn't backed up by your genuine interest, it won't lead you to rich, interesting research.

MOVING FROM A RESEARCH QUESTION TO A PROPOSAL

Now that you've got an understanding of how to explore a topic and form working research questions, let's look at some next steps. In the following Guided Process, we circle back to Jasmine Huerta (remember her from the assignment on p. 618?) to see how she proceeds in her research on diabetes.

Guided Process: How to Research a Topic

Jasmine Huerta (Student)

Diabetes Project

While you may not follow every step that Jasmine takes as you work on your own research topic, tracing her process (through p. 645) may give you ideas for how to proceed.

Exploring a Topic: Diabetes

When Jasmine got started on her project, she knew she wanted to write about diabetes, but she wasn't sure how to focus. So she began with a few broad questions:

▲ STUDENT AUTHOR
Jasmine Huerta
Moves from her working research question to a final proposal in this Guided Process section. *iStockphoto.*

QUESTIONS TO HELP YOU UNCOVER FACTS & TERMS	What causes diabetes? Who is affected by it, and why?
	What are the statistics of diabetes in the United States and around the world?
	What is the latest medical research on diabetes?
	What alternative treatments are there (as opposed to insulin)?
	How can people avoid getting diabetes?
	What is the relationship between nutrition and diabetes?
	What is the relationship between metabolism and diabetes?
	What is the role of glucose and the glycemic index?

From these fact-finding questions, which she investigated through research (we'll outline this process in a moment), Jasmine began to narrow the scope of her topic from the list of questions above to:

| WORKING RESEARCH QUESTION | What is the relationship between nutrition and diabetes? |

After still more research and analysis, she pursued this question:

REVISED RESEARCH QUESTION   How can diet—specifically, monitoring the intake of sugar, calories, and sodium—help someone with diabetes manage the disease and avoid taking insulin?

Ultimately, Jasmine moved from a research question to the argument she made in her final paper, which also became her title:

FINAL RESEARCHED ARGUMENT   Getting off insulin: A case for a nutritional approach for managing diabetes

Finding Facts about Diabetes

What was Jasmine's process? First, through her early reading, and as a person with a family history of the disease, Jasmine realizes that what interests her most are the dietary concerns of diabetics. With this in mind, she begins to explore a few more sources.

Wikipedia is her starting point. Even though her instructor has cautioned the class against using *Wikipedia* as a source, Jasmine sees it as a good starting point for general information and perhaps some leads related to dietary concerns. She begins with the "Diabetes mellitus" page (when she typed in "Diabetes," she was redirected there). ▼

▼ WIKIPEDIA ENTRY
"Diabetes mellitus"
Jasmine reads through this entry with special attention to the "References" and "External links" sections for further resources—as well as the "Management" and "Lifestyle" portions for information on diet, which are shown on page 628. *Courtesy of Wikimedia Foundation, Inc. All rights reserved.*

WIKIPEDIA
The Free Encyclopedia

Article   Talk

Read   View source   View history   Search

Diabetes mellitus

From Wikipedia, the free encyclopedia

"Diabetes" redirects here. For other uses, see Diabetes (disambiguation).

Diabetes mellitus, or simply **diabetes**, is a group of metabolic diseases in which a person has high blood sugar, either because the pancreas does not produce enough insulin, or because cells do not respond to the insulin that is produced.[2] This high blood sugar produces the classical symptoms of polyuria (frequent urination), polydipsia (increased thirst) and polyphagia (increased hunger).

There are three main types of diabetes mellitus (DM).

- Type 1 DM results from the body's failure to produce insulin, and currently requires the person to inject insulin or wear an insulin pump. This form was previously referred to as "insulin-dependent diabetes mellitus" (IDDM) or "juvenile diabetes".
- Type 2 DM results from insulin resistance, a condition in which cells fail to use insulin properly, sometimes combined with an absolute insulin deficiency. This form was previously referred to as non insulin-dependent diabetes mellitus (NIDDM) or "adult-onset diabetes".
- The third main form, gestational diabetes occurs when pregnant women without a previous diagnosis of diabetes develop a high blood glucose level. It may precede development of type 2 DM.

Other forms of diabetes mellitus include congenital diabetes, which is due to genetic defects of insulin secretion, cystic fibrosis-related diabetes, steroid diabetes induced by high doses of glucocorticoids, and several forms of monogenic diabetes.

Untreated, diabetes can cause many complications. Acute complications include diabetic ketoacidosis and nonketotic hyperosmolar coma. Serious long-term complications include cardiovascular disease, chronic renal failure, and diabetic retinopathy (retinal damage). Adequate treatment of diabetes is thus important, as well as blood pressure control and lifestyle factors such as stopping smoking and maintaining a healthy body weight.

Main page
Contents
Featured content
Current events
Random article
Donate to Wikipedia
Wikimedia Shop

▼ Interaction
Help
About Wikipedia
Community portal
Recent changes
Contact Wikipedia

▶ Toolbox

▶ Print/export

▼ Languages
Afrikaans
አማርኛ
العربية
Aragonés

Diabetes mellitus
Classification and external resources

Universal blue circle symbol for diabetes.[1]

ICD-10	E10🔗–E14🔗
ICD-9	250🔗
MedlinePlus	001214🔗
eMedicine	med/546🔗 emerg/134🔗
MeSH	C18.452.394.750🔗

After reading through the overview, Jasmine realizes that she needs information about the differences between type 1 diabetes and type 2 diabetes (which the entry explains is the more common form, and the one that can be treated through diet). She discovers she'll also need to explore diabetes in terms of blood glucose levels, metabolism, body weight, and insulin.

Of particular interest are the "References" and "External links" sections of the "Diabetes mellitus" page, which offer Jasmine a head start on exploring other sources.

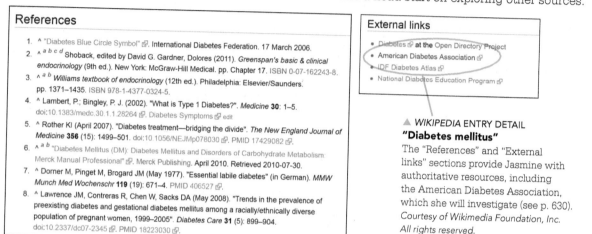

References

1. ^ "Diabetes Blue Circle Symbol" ⟲. International Diabetes Federation. 17 March 2006.
2. ^ a b c d Shoback, edited by David G. Gardner, Dolores (2011). *Greenspan's basic & clinical endocrinology* (9th ed.). New York: McGraw-Hill Medical. pp. Chapter 17. ISBN 0-07-162243-8.
3. ^ a b *Williams textbook of endocrinology* (12th ed.). Philadelphia: Elsevier/Saunders. pp. 1371–1435. ISBN 978-1-4377-0324-5.
4. ^ Lambert, P.; Bingley, P. J. (2002). "What is Type 1 Diabetes?". *Medicine* **30**: 1–5. doi:10.1383/medc.30.1.1.28264 ⟲. Diabetes Symptoms ⟲ edit
5. ^ Rother KI (April 2007). "Diabetes treatment—bridging the divide". *The New England Journal of Medicine* **356** (15): 1499–501. doi:10.1056/NEJMp078030 ⟲. PMID 17429082 ⟲.
6. ^ a b "Diabetes Mellitus (DM): Diabetes Mellitus and Disorders of Carbohydrate Metabolism: Merck Manual Professional" ⟲. Merck Publishing. April 2010. Retrieved 2010-07-30.
7. ^ Dorner M, Pinget M, Brogard JM (May 1977). "Essential labile diabetes" (in German). *MMW Munch Med Wochenschr* **119** (19): 671–4. PMID 406527 ⟲.
8. ^ Lawrence JM, Contreras R, Chen W, Sacks DA (May 2008). "Trends in the prevalence of preexisting diabetes and gestational diabetes mellitus among a racially/ethnically diverse population of pregnant women, 1999–2005". *Diabetes Care* **31** (5): 899–904. doi:10.2337/dc07-2345 ⟲. PMID 18223030 ⟲.

External links

- Diabetes ⟲ at the Open Directory Project
- American Diabetes Association ⟲
- IDF Diabetes Atlas ⟲
- National Diabetes Education Program ⟲

▲ **WIKIPEDIA** ENTRY DETAIL
"Diabetes mellitus"
The "References" and "External links" sections provide Jasmine with authoritative resources, including the American Diabetes Association, which she will investigate (see p. 630). *Courtesy of Wikimedia Foundation, Inc. All rights reserved.*

In addition, the "Lifestyle" section of the page links her to another entry titled "Diabetic diet."

WIKIPEDIA ▶
ENTRY DETAIL
"Diabetes mellitus"
The "Management," "Lifestyle," and "Medications" sections refer Jasmine to related entries. She notices that the "Lifestyle" section links to an entry for "Diabetic diet," which she decides to check out (see p. 629). *Courtesy of Wikimedia Foundation, Inc. All rights reserved.*

Management

Main article: Diabetes management

Diabetes mellitus is a chronic disease which cannot be cured except in very specific situations. Management concentrates on keeping blood sugar levels as close to normal ("euglycemia") as possible, without causing hypoglycemia. This can usually be accomplished with diet, exercise, and use appropriate medications (insulin in the case of type 1 diabetes, oral medications, as well as possibly insulin, in type 2 diabetes).

Patient education, understanding, and participation is vital, since the complications of diabetes are far less common and less severe in people who have well-managed blood sugar levels.[24][25] The goal of treatment is an HbA1C level of 6.5%, but should not be lower than that, and may be set higher.[26] Attention is also paid to other health problems that may accelerate the deleterious effects of diabetes. These include smoking, elevated cholesterol levels, obesity, high blood pressure, and lack of regular exercise.[26] Specialised footwear is widely used to reduce the risk of ulceration, re-ulceration, in at-risk diabetic feet. Evidence for the efficacy of this remains equivocal, however.[27]

Lifestyle

See also: Diabetic diet

There are roles for patient education, dietetic support, sensible exercise, with the goal of keeping both short-term and long-term blood glucose levels within acceptable bounds. In addition, given the associated higher risks of cardiovascular disease, lifestyle modifications are recommended to contr blood pressure.[28]

Medications

Oral medications

Main article: Anti-diabetic medication

Metformin is generally recommended as a first line treatment for type 2 diabetes, as there is good evidence that it decreases mortality.[29] Routine u of aspirin, however, has not been found to improve outcomes in uncomplicated diabetes.[30]

Insulin

Main article: Insulin therapy

Article   Talk

Read   Edit   View history   Search   🔍

Diabetic diet

From Wikipedia, the free encyclopedia

There is much controversy regarding what diet to recommend to sufferers of diabetes mellitus. The **'diet'** most often recommended is high in dietary fiber, especially soluble fiber, but low in fat (especially saturated fat). Recommendations of the fraction of total calories to be obtained from carbohydrate intake range from 1/6 to 75% – a 2006 review found recommendations varying from 40 to 65%.[1] Diabetics may be encouraged to reduce their intake of carbohydrates that have a high glycemic index (GI), although this is also controversial.[2] (In cases of hypoglycemia, they are advised to have food or drink that can raise blood glucose quickly, such as lucozade, followed by a long-acting carbohydrate (such as rye bread) to prevent risk of further hypoglycemia.) However, others question the usefulness of the glycemic index and recommend high-GI foods like potatoes and rice.

Display showing low fat and/or high fiber foods

Display showing refined, high fat/carbohydrate foods

Contents [hide]

1 History
2 Exchange scheme
3 Later developments
4 Carbohydrates
5 Low-carbohydrate alternatives
6 Vegan/vegetarian
7 Timing of meals
8 Special diabetes products
9 Alcohol and drugs
10 Specific diets
11 See also
12 Further reading
13 References
14 External links

History   [edit]

There has been long history of dietary treatment of diabetes mellitus – dietary treatment of diabetes mellitus was used in Egypt as long ago as 3,500 B.C., and was used in India by Sushruta and Charaka more than 2000 years ago. In the eighteenth century, these authors note, John Rollo argued that calorie restriction in the diabetic diet could reduce glycosuria in diabetes. However, more modern history of the diabetic diet may begin with Frederick Madison Allen, who, in the days before insulin was discovered, recommended that people with diabetes ate only a low-calorie diet to prevent ketoacidosis from killing them. This was an approach which did not actually cure diabetes, it merely extended life by a limited period. The first use of insulin by Frederick Banting in 1922 changed things, and at last allowed patients more flexibility in their eating.

Jasmine looks closely at the "External links" section of the *Wikipedia* page (p. 628) and decides to investigate the American Diabetes Association. She finds out that the ADA is a nonprofit group whose purpose is to control diabetes, especially through improving healthcare access and funding research and prevention.

◀ *WIKIPEDIA* ENTRY **"Diabetic diet"** Jasmine reaches this page through the "Lifestyle" section of the "Diabetes mellitus" entry (see p. 629). *Courtesy of Wikimedia Foundation, Inc. All rights reserved.*

▲ WEB SITE
American Diabetes Association

Jasmine investigates the ADA site, where she focuses on the following content categories: "Diabetes Basics," "Prediabetes," "Living with Diabetes," "Recently Diagnosed," "Food & Fitness," and "MyFoodAdvisor," as shown below and through page 635. *Copyright 2013 American Diabetes Association. From http://www.diabetes.org. Reprinted with permission from The American Diabetes Association.*

The ADA site is organized into topics, including "Diabetes Basics," which in turn is broken down into related subtopics. In this section, Jasmine uncovers some interesting data, including:

» Prediabetes is a condition that develops prior to type 2 diabetes.

» Seven million people in the United States have undiagnosed diabetes.

» It is a myth that people get diabetes just because they eat too much sugar.

◄ WEB SITE DETAIL
American Diabetes Association.

Jasmine is especially interested in the "Diabetes Basics" category and wonders what the ADA has to say about prediabetes, type 1, and type 2. *Copyright 2013 American Diabetes Association. From http://www.diabetes.org. Reprinted with permission from The American Diabetes Association.*

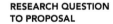

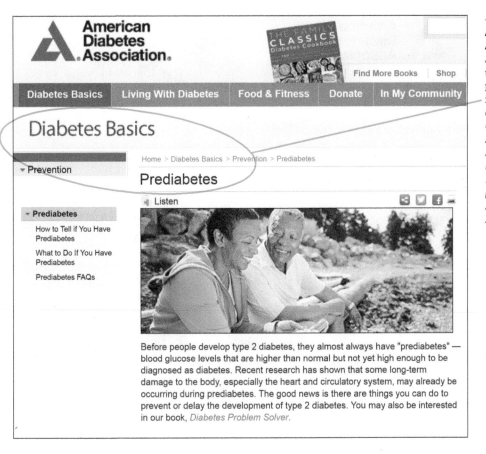

Jasmine is also interested in "Living With Diabetes," which is broken down into smaller topic areas.

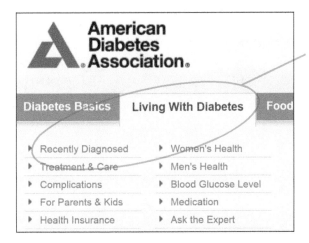

WEB SITE DETAIL ▶
**American Diabetes
Association**
On the "Recently
Diagnosed" page,
Jasmine reads some
concrete advice on
type 1 and type 2
diabetes, including
how to manage
both. Copyright 2013
American Diabetes
Association. From http://
www.diabetes.org.
Reprinted with permission
from The American
Diabetes Association.

She's especially drawn to the "Food & Fitness" section, because of her interest in nutrition.

WEB SITE DETAIL ▶
**American Diabetes
Association**
The "Food & Fitness"
page is a great find
for Jasmine, because
she wants to learn
more about the
connections among
eating, exercise, and
managing diabetes.
Copyright 2013
American Diabetes
Association. From http://
www.diabetes.org.
Reprinted with permission
from The American
Diabetes Association.

In the "Food & Fitness" section, Jasmine is surprised by the emphasis on recipes and meal planning as ways to control the disease. She finds the following information especially interesting:

» Beans, berries, and tomatoes are diabetes "superfoods."

» We shouldn't just look at the sugar content on food labels. It's more useful to examine the total carbohydrate number.

» Recipes for diabetics are not dull. The site includes recipes for Texas Tuna Burger, Asian Roast Pork Sliders, and Whole-Wheat Pancakes.

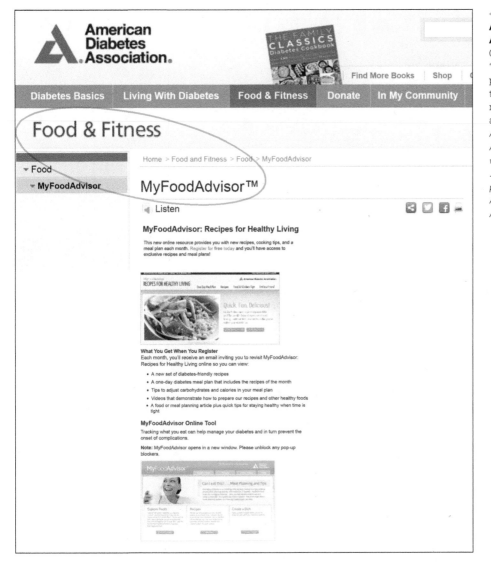

◀ WEB SITE DETAIL
American Diabetes Association
On the "MyFoodAdvisor" page, Jasmine is thrilled to find specific recipes and nutritional advice. *Copyright 2013 American Diabetes Association. From http://www.diabetes.org. Reprinted with permission from The American Diabetes Association.*

As Jasmine continues to read through the ADA site, she gets more absorbed in the idea that eating specific kinds of foods can assist in managing diabetes. She decides her next step is to find more information on nutrition, maybe even some more recipes designed for diabetics. A hospital or research facility might be another good source, she thinks, and she decides to check out the Mayo Clinic site.

WEB SITE ▶
Mayo Clinic
On their "Diabetes" page, the Mayo Clinic provides a definition of the disease. Jasmine is interested to see how this information compares to that of the ADA. *Mayo Foundation for Medical Education and Research.*

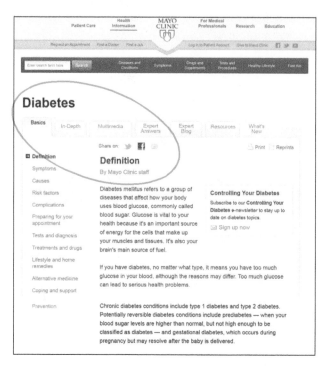

There she finds information on diabetes, along with meal plans and recipes. She gets even more interested in the relationship between diet and diabetes management.

WEB SITE DETAIL ▶
Mayo Clinic
On the "Diabetes meal plan recipes" page, Jasmine is pleasantly surprised by the range of foods that the Mayo Clinic recommends. *Mayo Foundation for Medical Education and Research.*

The following recipe, among many others, catches her eye.

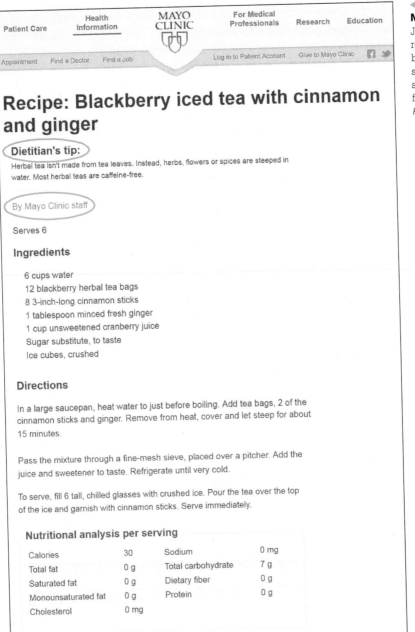

◀ WEB SITE DETAIL
Mayo Clinic
Jasmine finds that the recipes are created by Mayo Clinic staff and include specific pointers from a dietitian. *Mayo Foundation for Medical*

The recipe itself, and the surrounding information, presents Jasmine with a few things to think about. First, the "Dietitian's tip" mentions that most herbal teas are caffeine-free, which makes her wonder about the connection between caffeine and the health of a diabetic. She also notices the use of cinnamon and ginger and wonders how these natural ingredients might benefit a diabetic. In the nutritional analysis of the recipe, Jasmine sees that the drink is low in calories and does not contain any sodium. She wonders if these are important concerns; before she started browsing recipes at the ADA and the Mayo Clinic, Jasmine knew that diabetics should avoid sugar, but she hadn't been taking sodium and calorie content into consideration.

At this point, Jasmine's working research question has evolved from:

WORKING RESEARCH QUESTION What is the relationship between nutrition and diabetes?

to:

**REVISED, MORE SPECIFIC,
WORKING RESEARCH QUESTION** How can diet—specifically, monitoring the intake of sugar, calories, and sodium—help someone with diabetes manage the disease?

Now that Jasmine has done some exploratory, informational reading, she's ready to see what others have to say about managing diabetes through diet. She moves on to look for sources that will offer viewpoints and arguments about diabetes and nutrition.

Gathering Opinions about Diabetes

Jasmine looks for other sources—including a journal article, a Web site, and a YouTube video—to provide current viewpoints on nutrition as prevention/treatment for diabetes.

American Diabetes Association.

At the ADA site, Jasmine finds an article (in their journal, *Diabetes Care*) that provides the organization's position on diabetes and nutrition. The ADA argues:

> There is not sufficient, consistent information to conclude that low–glycemic load diets reduce the risk for diabetes.
>
> —**ADA,** from "Nutrition Recommendations and Interventions for Diabetes"

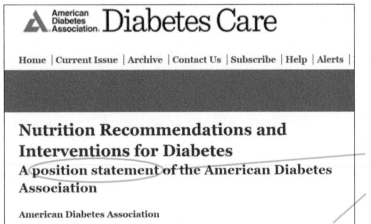

◀ JOURNAL ARTICLE/
POSITION STATEMENT
**American Diabetes
Association**
Jasmine goes back to the ADA to see if that organization offers any opinions or recommendations about diabetes and nutrition. She finds this position statement. (Shown here: the introductory paragraph and recommendations.) *Copyright 2013 American Diabetes Association. From http:// www/diabetes.org. Reprinted with permission from The American Diabetes Association.*

Diabetes Care

Home | Current Issue | Archive | Contact Us | Subscribe | Help | Alerts |

Nutrition Recommendations and Interventions for Diabetes

A position statement of the American Diabetes Association

American Diabetes Association

Medical nutrition therapy (MNT) is important in preventing diabetes, managing existing diabetes, and preventing, or at least slowing, the rate of development of diabetes complications. It is, therefore, important at all levels of diabetes prevention (see Table 1). MNT is also an integral component of diabetes self-management education (or training). This position statement provides evidence-based recommendations and interventions for diabetes MNT. The previous position statement with accompanying technical review was published in 2002 (1) and modified slightly in 2004 (2). This statement updates previous position statements, focuses on key references published since the year 2000, and uses grading according to the level of evidence available based on the American Diabetes Association evidence-grading system. Since overweight and obesity are closely linked to diabetes, particular attention is paid to this area of MNT.

Recommendations

- Among individuals at high risk for developing type 2 diabetes, structured programs that emphasize lifestyle changes that include moderate weight loss (7% body weight) and regular physical activity (150 min/week), with dietary strategies including reduced calories and reduced intake of dietary fat, can reduce the risk for developing diabetes and are therefore recommended. (A)

- Individuals at high risk for type 2 diabetes should be encouraged to achieve the U.S. Department of Agriculture (USDA) recommendation for dietary fiber (14 g fiber/1,000 kcal) and foods containing whole grains (one-half of grain intake). (B)

- There is not sufficient, consistent information to conclude that low–glycemic load diets reduce the risk for diabetes. Nevertheless, low–glycemic index foods that are rich in fiber and other important nutrients are to be encouraged. (E)

- Observational studies report that moderate alcohol intake may reduce the risk for diabetes, but the data do not support recommending alcohol consumption to individuals at risk of diabetes. (B)

2. The Joslin Diabetes Center.

At this site, Jasmine read the views of Amy Campbell, a Joslin nutritionist and the coauthor of a book titled *16 Myths of a Diabetic Diet*. Campbell states that there is no such thing as a "diabetic diet." Jasmine finds the following quote from Campbell on a Joslin page titled "The Truth about the So-Called 'Diabetes Diet'":

A person with diabetes can eat anything a person without diabetes eats.

—**Amy Campbell,** from "The Truth about the So-Called 'Diabetes Diet'"

RESEARCHED ▶
ARGUMENT
Joslin Diabetes Center and Amy Campbell

At the Joslin Diabetes Center page, Jasmine is surprised to see an argument against "the so-called 'diabetes diet.'" It seems to contrast with what she's read elsewhere at the American Diabetes Association Web site. *Copyright © 2012 by Joslin Diabetes Center (www.Joslin.org). All rights reserved. Reprinted with permission.*

Joslin Diabetes Center

Affiliated with Harvard Medical School

| Diabetes Information | Adult Clinic | Pediatrics | Healthcare Professionals | Research |

Diabetes Information | Diabetes Resource » Diabetes & Nutrition » The Truth About the So-Called "Diabetes Diet"

The Truth About the So-Called "Diabetes Diet"

Despite all the publicity surrounding new research and new nutrition guidelines, some people with diabetes still believe that there is something called a "diabetic diet." For some, this so-called diet consists of avoiding sugar, while others believe it to be a strict way of eating that controls glucose. Unfortunately, neither are quite right.

The "diabetes diet" is not something that people with type 1 or type 2 diabetes should be following. "That just simply isn't how meal planning works today for patients with diabetes," says Amy Campbell, MS, RD, LDN, CDE, a nutritionist at Joslin and co-author of *16 Myths of a Diabetic Diet*.

"The important message is that with proper education and within the context of healthy eating, a person with diabetes can eat anything a person without diabetes eats," Campbell states.

What's the truth about diabetes and diet?

We know now that it is okay for people with diabetes to substitute sugar-containing food for other carbohydrates as part of a balanced meal plan. Prevailing beliefs up to the mid-1990s were that people with diabetes should avoid foods that contain so-called "simple" sugars and replace them with "complex" carbohydrates, such as those found in potatoes and cereals. A review of the research at that time revealed that there was relatively little scientific evidence to support the theory that simple sugars are more rapidly digested and absorbed than starches, and therefore more apt to produce high blood glucose levels.

3. Nature's Factory Products.

On YouTube, Jasmine finds a video produced by a business called Nature's Factory Products, which makes aloe vera–based products and markets them for various ailments. Jasmine was surprised by the company's claim that aloe helps treat diabetes. In their video, "How Aloe Vera can help Diabetics," the manufacturer claims that:

> Aloe vera can help regulate blood sugar levels and control inflammation caused by diabetes.
>
> **—Nature's Factory Products**

While she is skeptical about Nature's Factory Products' claims, Jasmine doesn't dismiss their argument altogether. She decides to keep this source in mind and to fact-check the claims made in the video by researching medical studies.

Now that she's gathered some facts and arguments about diabetes, Jasmine decides to meet with her instructor to talk about a final research question and plan her research proposal.

What is Aloe Vera?

Member of Lily family
Known as "Miracle Plant"
Full of natural Antioxidants!
   Polysaccharides
   75 vitamins & minerals
   Enzymes
   Anti-microbial agents

◀ VIDEO AD
Nature's Factory Products, From "How Aloe Vera Can Help Diabetics"
Jasmine discovered a video on YouTube by a company that makes nutritional supplements. In the video advertisement, Nature's Factory Products addresses the question: "What is Aloe Vera?" and argues that among its many benefits, the plant helps reduce blood sugar. Jasmine is intrigued by this and by the claims that aloe vera may improve the circulation, immune systems, and overall internal health of diabetics. She decides to keep this source in the mix—and to verify some of the claims made by Nature's Factory Products. She'll do this by reading medical studies on the relationship between aloe vera—and potential health benefits to diabetic patients.

CHECKLIST Choosing a Topic

As you start your research, consider following these steps:

☐ **Brainstorm topic ideas.**

   ☐ Read what others have said.

   ☐ Google your topic (but stay focused).

   ☐ Discuss what you find with others.

☐ **Start writing informally.**

   ☐ Make a list of topics that interest you, then double it, then double it again.

   ☐ Freewrite about your topic.

   ☐ Sketch out a mind map.

☐ **Do preliminary research.**

   ☐ Ask questions of fact and definition so that you will understand the more complex research you do later.

   ☐ What arguments have others made about your topic? How do they support their views?

   ☐ Note key terms to aid in later research.

☐ **Commit to a topic. Consider these factors:**

   ☐ Is the topic compatible with the assignment?

   ☐ Have you found an argumentative angle?

   ☐ Will you stay interested in this topic?

   ☐ Are there enough appropriate sources available for you to research in the time you have?

   ☐ Overall, how viable is the topic? (See Jasmine Huerta's assignment, "What Is Your Topic? How Viable Is It?" on p. 618.)

☐ **Form a research question. Consider these factors:**

   ☐ Does your question focus more on stating facts and defining terms? Or are you making an argument? Providing an analysis?

   ☐ Is your question open-ended?

   ☐ Is your question specific enough? If not, how will you move from a general question to a more specific one?

   ☐ Are you truly interested in finding answers to this question?

   ☐ What are some challenges you may come up against as you research this question, and how can you deal with these challenges?

Creating a Research Proposal

A research proposal sets forth a writer's rationale for choosing a particular research question. For Jasmine, the proposal gives her an opportunity to fine-tune her research question and her focus. Your instructor may ask you to turn in a proposal or a working bibliography that outlines your sources (pp. 646–49). Or your instructor might simply ask you to think about your research before looking more carefully at sources.

Even if your instructor does not assign a formal research proposal, it can be a great tool for use in planning your project. Following is a research proposal assignment that we give our students.

ENG 101, Professor Braziller

Research Proposal Assignment: What Is Your Focus?

This proposal will help you solidify your ideas for your semester's research. Your proposal should be approximately two double-spaced pages in MLA manuscript format. Your proposal should include the following:

1. Your research question

2. A working title for your project

3. A summary of your project. Identify your topic and describe what you will be looking at in terms of the topic. Include some key terms and additional questions that will guide your research.

4. A description of your purpose for working on this project. Why did you choose this topic? What do you hope to learn from this project?

5. A discussion of the key challenges you will face or you imagine you will face. What concerns do you have regarding the research/project?

Following is Jasmine's research proposal, in response to the above assignment.

ENG 101, Professor Braziller

Research Proposal Assignment: What Is Your Focus?

Jasmine Huerta
Professor Amy Braziller
English 101
October 6, 20—

Research Proposal

1. Your research question

   How can diet—specifically, monitoring the intake of sugar, calories, and sodium—help someone with diabetes manage the disease and avoid taking insulin?

2. A working title for your project

   The working title for my project is "Living with Diabetes: Diet Is the Answer." I chose this topic because although some people are predisposed to diabetes because of genetics, they do have some control over the situation. For example, through their choices related to food and diet they can manage or perhaps even prevent the disease.

3. A summary of your project. Identify your topic and describe what you will be looking at in terms of the topic. Include some key terms and additional questions that will guide your research.

   I plan to research and write about different ways you can control diabetes through nutritional choices. While there are medications used to control the disease, such as

▲ STUDENT AUTHOR
Jasmine Huerta

insulin, I'm more curious about natural approaches, such as diet. I want my readers to understand that diabetes doesn't have to be a death sentence and that even if you are predisposed to it, there are some simple things you can do to keep it from taking over your life or causing other health issues.

I also think, based on my research, that diet and nutrition might be just as powerful as insulin for some people. I wonder if doctors are too quick to prescribe insulin.

Much of the debate around diabetes has to do with the connection between diabetes and obesity. I wonder to what extent diabetes can be prevented by a healthy diet, one that helps people avoid obesity. Also, are there specific foods that children need to avoid? Are these different from what older people should avoid?

Besides researching different diabetes-related diets, I want to find out how people learn about these diets. Are there specific programs, initiatives, or educational tools used to get this information out to the public? How might schools and doctors share this information?

Following are some **key terms** I've discovered during my preliminary research: *glycemic index, metabolism, blood sugar, hypertension, obesity, glucose monitoring,* and *insulin.*

Following are some of the **questions that will guide my research:**

- What diets are best for diabetics?
- What foods do diabetics need to avoid?
- Can diet cure diabetes? If so, how?
- Can diet prevent someone from getting diabetes, even if he or she has a family history of the disease? If so, how?
- Can diet prevent someone's diabetes from getting worse? If so, how?
- Can dietary changes prevent or reduce a diabetic's dependence on insulin?

4. A description of your purpose for working on this project. Why did you choose this topic? What do you hope to learn from this project?

Diabetes runs in my family, so it's something that is very close to me. My cousin, who is only six years old, has type 1 diabetes. Just last month, my grandfather, who is somewhat overweight, but definitely not obese, was diagnosed with diabetes. When my mother was pregnant with me, she had gestational diabetes.

I believe I may be predisposed toward the disease, and I want to find out what I can do to avoid it. I also want to help my family by sharing what I learn—especially in terms of natural alternatives rather than traditional medicine.

5. A discussion of the key challenges you will face or you imagine you will face. What concerns do you have regarding the research/project?

My biggest challenge so far has been making sense of some terms I've encountered in my research. Some articles go into a lot of detail about the relationship of the glycemic index to insulin levels. Authors of these pieces also use technical terms such as *pancreatic islet cells, resistant starches,* and *macronutrients.*

Another challenge I might face is that my topic may be too narrow. Based on my research so far, it seems that many sources say yes, diet does contribute to diabetes prevention and management. But how might I expand on that? Will I end up just listing foods to eat and not to eat?

I think that trying to figure out if nutritional changes can actually replace insulin as treatment gives my project a good argumentative angle, but I am a little worried that I may end up arguing more strongly against insulin than I really want to.

I am also afraid of getting sidetracked and focusing too much on the obesity problem, especially in regard to children, and losing my focus on diabetes. While obesity is related, I really want to focus on preventing and managing the disease—and not so much on the causes of diabetes. While it's important to understand some of the causes, especially as they relate to nutrition, I'm more interested in prevention and treatment.

Now that Jasmine has written her proposal and submitted it to her instructor, she is ready to begin the next stage of her research.

CHECKLIST Creating a Research Proposal

What does a good research proposal do?

☐ **It assists you in organizing your project,** and includes five major components:
- Research question (the main thrust of your research)
- Working title
- Summary of the project (a sketch of the research you've done, the questions you've raised, and the possible direction you will take, including the potential argument you may make)
- Overall purpose (why you want to pursue this topic and project)
- Potential challenges

☐ **It shows that you have a clear focus for your research.** Your research question and working title are specific, showing your reader the angle you are researching. Throughout the proposal, you include details rather than vague generalities. For example, Jasmine doesn't just write, "I want to learn how people find out about these diets." She adds these details: "Are there specific programs, initiatives, or educational tools. . . ."

☐ **It illustrates that you have done some preliminary research.** Your summary includes key terms that you discovered while doing research. While Jasmine might have previously thought of the key terms *obesity* and *insulin*, she probably had not considered such terms as *glycemic index* and *glucose monitoring*.

☐ **It gives reasons why you have selected your area of research.** By communicating why you chose your topic, your reader understands your choice, and you see why this research matters to you. By articulating these reasons, you stay more engaged.

☐ **It shows that you have considered potential challenges.** Anticipating challenges prepares you for the bumps you might hit during research. Additionally, a good research proposal tells your reader about those challenges so that you might be given assistance. For example, when Jasmine writes that she has encountered technical terms such as *pancreatic islet cells*, her reader might point her to resources where she can get help deciphering these terms.

Moving from a Research Question to a Proposal

ORGANIZING YOUR SOURCES

Once you have a research question and a rough plan (as Jasmine does), you'll begin to gather and read more sources. In Chapter 19, we're going to take you deeper into the research process. But before that, here's some advice on staying organized.

Be sure to keep track of every source you look at so that you can:

» Easily retrieve sources to verify facts

» Check that you aren't plagiarizing

» Make connections among sources

» Document your sources in your final paper

Use Simple Strategies: E-mail, Bookmark, Copy/Paste, Screen Capture

Following are some strategies for keeping track of your sources:

E-mail sources you find online to yourself. Store the e-mails in a folder on your computer.

Bookmark sources on your computer. Create folders for your bookmarks.

BOOKMARK TOOLS ▶
Featured on most PCs.

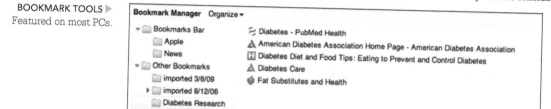

Use social bookmarking tools. Sites such as Diigo have bookmarking/information storage functions.

BOOKMARK TOOL ▶
Diigo

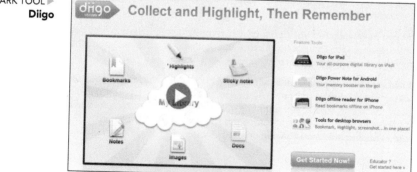

Copy and paste content from Web sites into a Word document. Below is a Word document into which we've pasted a section of the text of a commencement speech by the late novelist, David Foster Wallace, published by Kenyon College.

◀ WORD DOCUMENT
David Foster Wallace
2005 commencement speech at Kenyon College, "This is Water," copied/pasted from *Kenyon College Alumni Bulletin*.

👉 **Attention, researchers! A note on cutting and pasting.**

If you copy and paste from a source, do so very carefully. Make sure you have a way of reminding yourself which words belong to others—and which ones belong to you. If you decide you want to capture something exactly from a Web site, then copy and paste as above, highlighting the source information.

Create screen captures of online content. For this option, you would capture screens of your sources and paste them into a Word document (or save the screens as image files). We highly recommend this method of recording source material. Why? Because it prevents any potential confusion about what content came from where—and prevents you from inadvertently mixing up your own words with those from your source. A screen capture of the David Foster Wallace commencement speech as it appears online is on page 646.

WEB PAGE ▶
**David Foster
Wallace**
"This is Water," his
2005 commencement
speech at Kenyon
College, from *Kenyon
College Alumni
Bulletin* (bulletin
.kenyon.edu).

Create a List of Sources: Keep a Working Bibliography

We also highly recommend that you create a working bibliography—or, even better, an annotated working bibliography, which includes more detail. A working bibliography is simply a list of the sources you've gathered and plan to refer to. Keeping a list will provide you with the information required by all documentation styles, including MLA and APA.

Your working bibliography, which you add to and revise as you research, will be the basis for your final Works Cited list and in-text citations. It will also help you evaluate your sources as a group, so you can make sure they represent a good range and so you can make any useful connections among your sources. (For information on evaluating, integrating, and documenting sources, see Chapters 19 and 20.)

Better Yet, Keep an Annotated Working Bibliography

An annotated bibliography is a working bibliography (a list of your sources) that includes your own brief notes about each source. In your annotations, you summarize each source, capturing its essence in a few sentences. If the source is argumentative, you also note the main points of the writer's argument. In addition, note the potential reliability of the source: Is it from a reliable site, news organization, or publication? Was it created by a source you can trust? How well do the source and its author fit with your research? What might the source add? What might be its drawbacks? (For details on evaluating sources, see Chapter 19.)

Guided Process: How to Create a Bibliography

Jasmine Huerta (Student)

Diabetes Project: Bibliography

▲ STUDENT AUTHOR
Jasmine Huerta
iStockphoto.

Jasmine's Working Bibliography

Below is Jasmine's working bibliography for her project on nutrition and diabetes. In this case, Jasmine uses the MLA style of documentation.

Jasmine writes of her working bibliography:

> I pulled together a good range of dependable sources—including, for example, a peer-reviewed journal called *Diabetes Care*, the American Diabetes Association, and the Harvard School of Public Health. My sources are connected: Three focus on diabetes and the glycemic index and two focus specifically on low-glycemic foods. I made sure to include the detailed source information my instructor expects, and in MLA format.

Huerta 1

Working Bibliography
(for diabetes project-in-progress)

Brand-Miller, Jennie, et al. "Low–Glycemic Index Diets in the Management of Diabetes." *Diabetes Care* 26.8 (2003): 2261-2267. Web. 15 Sept. 2013. <http://
care.diabetesjournals.org/content/26/8/2261.long>.

"Diabetes Mellitus." *Wikipedia.* Wikimedia Foundation, 7 Sept. 2013. Web. 15
Sept. 2013. <http://en.wikipedia.org/wiki/Diabetes_mellitus>.

"Glycemic Index and Diabetes." *American Diabetes Association.* American Diabetes Association, n.d. Web. 15 Sept. 2013. <http://www.diabetes.org/
food-and-fitness/food/planning-meals/glycemic-index-and-diabetes.html>.

"Glycemic Index and Diabetes: Low-Glycemic-Index Foods." *WebMD Diabetes
Health Center.* WebMD, n.d. Web. 15 Sept. 2013. <http://
diabetes.webmd.com/glycemic-index-good-versus-bad-carbs>.

"Simple Steps to Preventing Diabetes." *The Nutrition Source.* Harvard School of
Public Health, n.d. Web. 15 Aug. 2013. <http://www.hsph.harvard.edu/
nutritionsource/diabetes-prevention/preventing-diabetes-full-story/
index.html>.

Continues next page

Attention, bibliographers!

Although the latest MLA guidelines say it's okay to omit source URLs, we recommend that you include them in your papers, as shown in Jasmine's bibliographies. Including URLs (or embedding hyperlinks in your paper) leaves no room for confusion about where you obtained information, and makes it easier and faster for your readers to check your sources.

Jasmine's Annotated Bibliography

Here is how Jasmine describes her process:

I began each entry with a basic summary. In my summaries, I note specific examples, such as unfamiliar terms or important evidence. I've also indicated my evaluation of how dependable each source is. When I quoted exact language from a source, I used quotation marks. I also made connections among my sources.

Huerta 1

Annotated Working Bibliography

Brand-Miller, Jennie, et al. "Low–Glycemic Index Diets in the Management of Diabetes." *Diabetes Care* 26.8 (2003): 2261-2267. Web. 15 Sept. 2013. <http://care.diabetesjournals.org/content/26/8/2261.long>.

The authors explore the controversy about whether a low-glycemic diet actually helps someone manage his or her diabetes. The article presents the research methods used, along with the results. Ultimately, the results of their study show that a low-glycemic diet did help patients manage their diabetes—in contrast to patients whose diets consisted of high-glycemic foods. The article is filled with unfamiliar terms such as "acarbose therapy." At the end is a list of footnotes and references that will be useful as I continue my research. This is a very reliable source because *Diabetes Care* is a peer-reviewed journal; also, the use of documentation reinforces the authors' ethos.

"Diabetes Mellitus." *Wikipedia*. Wikimedia Foundation, 7 Sept. 2013. Web. 15 Sept. 2013. <http://en.wikipedia.org/wiki/Diabetes_mellitus>.

This article gives a very comprehensive overview of diabetes. It begins by briefly explaining the different types of diabetes, such as types 1 and 2. It also includes a discussion of symptoms, causes, and ways to control the disease. Throughout the article, there are numerous hyperlinks to other Wikipedia pages that explain concepts further. Since I'm focusing on nutrition, I found the hyperlink to the "Diabetic Diet" page most useful, since this page included information on various diets and potential research sources. *Wikipedia* gears its information to someone beginning research, looking for possible angles to explore related to the topic. Additionally, it establishes its reliability by providing many source references at the end of the article. Many of the references were from medical journals.

"Glycemic Index and Diabetes." *American Diabetes Association*. American Diabetes Association, n.d. Web. 15 Sept. 2013. <http://www.diabetes.org/food-and-fitness/food/planning-meals/glycemic-index-and-diabetes.html>.

The ADA's page on the glycemic index and its relationship to diabetes is an informative summary on the topic. It has three subheads, so readers can immediately find information: "What is the glycemic index?" "What affects the GI of a food?" And, "Is the GI a better tool than carbohydrate counting?" The article discusses how the glycemic index is affected by many things and is not simply determined by a food's type. For example, factors such as length of ripening and cooking time affect a food's glycemic index. The article is written for a general reader, so I found that I could understand all its terms and get a beginning grasp of the glycemic index. This article, too, is very reliable since the American Diabetes Association is a respected and noted organization related to the field.

"Glycemic Index and Diabetes: Low-Glycemic-Index Foods." *WebMD Diabetes Health Center*. WebMD, n.d. Web. 15 Sept. 2013. <http:// diabetes.webmd.com/glycemic-index-good-versus-bad-carbs>.

WebMD's article provides a good overview of the glycemic index. The article briefly discusses how a diet of high-glycemic-index foods (pasta, rice) can contribute to weight gain and health issues. The article encourages readers to choose low-glycemic-index foods (vegetables, fruits) for a healthier diet. While the article tends to be fairly general, it does bring up some useful points; for example, it explains that several factors might alter the glycemic index, such as the combination of foods eaten. I trust the information presented here since WebMD is a trusted Web source for medical information, especially in terms of providing basic ideas to readers.

"Simple Steps to Preventing Diabetes." *The Nutrition Source*. Harvard School of Public Health, n.d. Web. 15 Aug. 2013. <http://www.hsph.harvard.edu/ nutritionsource/diabetes-prevention/preventing-diabetes-full-story/ index.html>.

This article focuses on ways to prevent type 2 diabetes. It gives statistics on the number of people affected by the disease and lists illnesses that the disease may cause, such as blindness. Prevention strategies are offered, such as diet and exercise. The writers sum up these strategies by saying, "Stay lean and stay active." This article, like the Brand-Miller piece, also includes a list of references, so I will add that to my potential project sources. Since this piece was published by a Harvard University site, I trust the information presented.

Drafting a Research Question, Proposal, & Bibliography

CHECKLIST: Beginning Your Research As you begin drawing on sources, forming your research questions, drafting your research proposal, and creating a bibliography, ask yourself the following questions.

WHAT'S MY RHETORICAL SITUATION?

☐ **Purpose.** What am I learning as I research? And how can I develop what I'm learning into a solid research question? Once I identify a research question, I'll need to refine it. Does it simply focus on facts (if so, it's not refined enough)? Or is it geared toward analysis and argument (if so, I'm heading in the right direction)? Once I come up with a research plan, I need to clearly articulate my approach, purpose, and potential challenges in my research proposal.

☐ **Audience.** What expectations will my readers (my instructor, classmates, and any audience beyond) have regarding the quality of my sources? (See Chapter 19 for more on evaluating source quality.) As I gather sources into an annotated bibliography, how can I make certain that my notes on each source show readers its potential usefulness?

☐ **Rhetorical appeals.** As I begin research, how will I know whether to trust an author and source? What about a given author and source gives me confidence, or doubts? What techniques and appeals do authors use that I can adopt for my own purposes? To what degree do they use logos (logic) and pathos (emotion) to reach readers? As I draft my research question, proposal, and bibliography, I need to make a solid case for my readers. Do I convey the reliability of my sources in my proposal and bibliography?

☐ **Modes & media.** How do modes and media come into play as I'm reading and choosing sources? My sources should represent a range of modes and media.

HOW DOES GENRE MATTER?

☐ **Elements of genres.** As I look at potential sources, I need to ask: Does the author of this source draw on other sources? Does the author document the work of others? For example, I'd expect a journalist to attribute quotations to specific people in a news article, but bloggers may not be meticulous about naming people quoted. How many different genres should I include among my sources—and in my bibliography?

☐ **Style.** When I look at a potential source, how much attention should I pay to the author's style? Are informal first-person pieces the right fit for my topic? Do I need to gather sources written in a variety of styles? To what extent do tone and level of detail contribute to a source's reliability? I should note each author's style and tone in my annotated bibliography.

☐ **Design.** When I look at a potential source, how important are design considerations? Some sources are very visual and graphically designed, but I should find a good mix.

☐ **Sources.** What makes a source particularly trustworthy? For example, if an author draws on documented sources, I may want to pay more attention to that text. If a source is drawn on by more than one author, I should check out that source and consider adding it to my working bibliography and commenting on it in my research proposal.

PRACTICE Want to experiment? Draft a research proposal. Create a working bibliography and annotate it.

Find a topic that interests you and work through the points in the above checklist until you develop a research question you are interested in. Then do the following:

1. Draft a research proposal for your professor that includes:

   - A working title for your project (you can always change the title later, when you have a better idea of what your finished project will actually cover).
   - A summary of the project, including which aspects of the topic you will research.
   - A list of the keywords you've identified in the research you've done so far.
   - A discussion of your purpose in working on the project. This is where you'll discuss why you are interested in answering the research question.
   - A discussion of the challenges you anticipate facing in your project and strategies you can use to deal with them.

2. Keep a working bibliography of all the sources you use, even ones you think you won't refer to in your final written report. You never know.

3. Annotate three sources you find particularly interesting or thought provoking. In your annotation, discuss:

   - What the summary is about
   - The argument the source makes
   - How reliable you judge this source to be and why
   - How this source might be used in your project

RESEARCH AND LIBRARY RESOURCES AT GEORGIA TECH 🗨️GT

The Georgia Tech Library is essential to your success as a student. Whether you are looking for a place to study, access to particular software or hardware, or help with a research project, the library can help you meet your research and technology needs, especially for English 1101, English 1102, and LMC 3403. The following section describes some of the resources and services the library provides for conducting successful research and creating multimodal projects.

The Georgia Tech Library is now open 24/7 for all Georgia Tech students, faculty, staff, and researchers. Check the library's Web site for variations in the schedule.

Research Support

The Georgia Tech Library offers several forms of research assistance. **Research Guides** for selected disciplines direct you to subject-specific resources, and links to contact information such as email addresses, chat, and a list of subject librarians are available on the library's Contact Us! page. For English 1101, English 1102, and LMC 3403 research assistance, contact Sherri Brown, first-year English instruction librarian and subject librarian for the School of Literature, Media, and Communication.

Identify a research guide that you anticipate will be useful to you. Explain why you think it's credible and why it will be useful. #Apply #Create

The library holds walk-in workshops on a variety of topics—many of them helpful for learning ways to create multimodal projects using multimedia software. For a list of upcoming classes, choose the **Library Classes** link on the library's homepage. These are some of the classes you may find useful:

» Communication Ethics: Avoiding Plagiarism

» EndNote X7 Training Session: Citation Management

» Tips & Tricks in Photoshop CS5

» Crash Course: Web Design

Technology Resources

The library has many important technology resources, including expert assistance from trained professionals and peers, spaces for individual and collaborative work, software applications to support your work, and equipment you can borrow.

Library West Commons (LWC). The *LWC Productivity Cluster* is located on the first floor west of the Main Library. The cluster's 85 general-use workstations provide access to a variety of software. The cluster houses scanners and both black-and-white and color printers. See the LWC Web site for a list of current resources.

The LWC is also where you will find the **Library Services Desk**, which is staffed whenever the library is open. In addition to being the starting place for circulation, research, or technology troubleshooting, the Library Services Desk has a variety of gadgets available, including laptops and peripherals, digital cameras and camcorders, audiovisual accessories, and more. Loan times vary by item.

Library East Commons (LEC). The LEC is a flexible, mixed-use space designed for long-term collaborative work and academic socializing. It is located on the first floor east of the Main Library. The LEC offers computers, a black-and-white and a color printer, comfortable furniture, and a café. The LEC also houses the Innovation & Design Collaborative (IDC), with technology to support creative design and development.

The Multimedia Studio, located on the ground floor of the Main Library, is equipped with high-end Mac workstations with multimedia applications and video-editing software and hardware. The Multimedia Studio also contains a large-format plotter printer (good for posters and other large-print artifacts), a large-format scanner, and the Beck Multipurpose Room, which can be used for high-end audio creation and editing, for Web conferencing, or for small classes. You will find a list of current Multimedia Studio software and information about the space on the Multimedia Studio Web site.

Lynda.com is another terrific resource you can use for software assistance. Go to lynda.gatech.edu to log on to this excellent online tutorial service. The Web site provides in-depth video support for many applications you might use to complete class projects. Georgia Tech has an Institute-wide subscription, so you can access it for free.

Printing.   All students are allocated $2.20 each week on their Buzzcards for printing at any Pharos Station on campus, including in the Library East and West Commons, the Multimedia Studio, and the Clough Commons. Students can also add funds to their Buzzcard to purchase additional prints after their allocation is spent. Additional printing costs are listed as follows, but make sure to double check your printing allowance and printing costs as they can change:

» Black-and-White (with or without finishing) = $.04/page

» Color = $.19/page

» CentralPS = no charge; double-sided, black-and-white only, 1,200 page quota per semester

Technology Support Center.   Supported by the Office of Information Technology (OIT), the Technology Support Center is located on the second floor of the Clough Undergraduate Learning Commons. The Technology Support Center provides assistance with hardware, software, and computer networking.

Research Basics

The library's homepage is the place to start when conducting academic research. From there, you can locate, reserve, and request the material you need.

Locating Course Material on Reserve.   Professors often place materials on reserve for their courses. You can search for these items by course name, department, or instructor through the Course Reserves link on the library's homepage. Reserve materials include printable PDF files and print or multimedia items located at the Library Services Desk. Loan periods for print and multimedia items are generally for two hours of in-library use only.

Finding Books at Georgia Tech.   You can find books owned by the library using the GT Catalog. You can search the catalog either by using the **GT Catalog** link or the search box at the top of the library's homepage (see below):

Once you enter search terms and find a book that you want, you need to write down the call number of the book in order to locate it in the stacks (see below):

Courtesy of the Georgia Tech Library.

Book Catalog Record.   Note the location and call number of the item. In this example, the item is located in the stacks on the fourth floor west of the Main Library, under the call number PN1995.3 .B48 2012.

Each record indicates where the item is located. The following list explains a few of the most common locations:

» *Main Library*: use the call number to locate the book in the stacks on floors 2 through 6.

» *Library Services Desk*: items that list this location may be on reserve for a class (either your class or another). Please ask at the Library Services Desk in the Main Library to see if the item can be checked out and for how long.

» *Reference*: Reference books are located either on the second floor east or on the Ready Reference Shelves behind the Library Services Desk. These items are for in-library use only.

» *Archives*: items that list this location must be used in the Archives, located behind the Main Library building. These items may not be checked out. The Archives are regularly open Monday–Friday, 9:00 AM–5:00 PM.

» *Architecture Library*: Located on the first floor of the Architecture West Building (247 Fourth Street), the Architecture Library houses items on art, architecture, and design.

Once you have located an item that can be checked out, you can take it to the Library Services Desk, located on the first floor east of the Main Library.

If the item is an electronic book, you should see a link in the GT Catalog record that takes you to the e-book online (see below):

Courtesy of the Georgia Tech Library.

Requesting Books from Other Libraries. If Georgia Tech does not own a book that you need or if the book is unavailable, you may be able to request it through the Universal Catalog/GIL Express, assessed through the Main Library's homepage. The Universal Catalog searches the holdings of all of the libraries in the University System of Georgia. If you find a book available at another University System of Georgia library, you can place a GIL Express Request to have it delivered to Georgia Tech for free.

If you need a book, journal article, or other item that is not available at Georgia Tech or through GIL Express, you can request the item through **Interlibrary Loan (ILLiad)**. Once you log in, you can request a photocopy of a journal article or book chapter or request a loan of a book or other item. From the Interlibrary Loan Web site, you can view articles sent to you electronically, request renewals for Interlibrary Loan books, and more. The service is free to students as long as it costs less than $25 for the library to obtain the item.

Finding Articles. From the library's homepage, use the **Articles (Databases)** link to find articles indexed in general and subject-specific databases. For literary research, for example, you may want to search in databases such as these:

> » MLA International Bibliography
>
> » Literature Resource Center
>
> » Project Muse
>
> » JSTOR

You can use the Research Guides or Ask for Assistance links to locate databases in a particular subject area.

Finding Articles from a Citation. The Library's **eJournals** page allows you to find articles based on citation information (what journal, newspaper, or magazine published the article, and in what volume, issue, year, and page it appeared). Search eJournals using the journal/newspaper/magazine title, *not* the article title. If the periodical is not listed in the eJournals section, you can check the **GT Catalog**.

Evaluating Sources.[1] Chapter 19 introduces you to evaluating and choosing sources in detail, which is an essential part of the research process. You can use

---

[1] Adapted from: Terry Taylor, "Evaluating Information," *100% Information Literacy Success* (New York: Thomson, 2007), 101–39; and *Evaluating Information: Applying the CRAAP Test*, Meriam Library, California State University, Chico, 1 Oct 2008.

the short list of evaluation criteria included here as a quick reference when conducting research. Consider the following when using books, articles, or Web sites:

» **Credibility:** Who wrote or created the work? Is the author an expert in the field of study? Is the piece from a peer-reviewed journal or a popular magazine? Who published the work—a university press, trade press, vanity press, or an individual? Who sponsored a particular Web site?

» **Relevancy:** How relevant is the information to your research needs? Would something else better fit your needs?

» **Currency:** How up-to-date is the information? If it is a Web site, when was it created? How often is it updated? If it is a book or an article, is it current enough to meet your needs?

» **Reliability:** Consider the possible agenda of the person writing the piece. How biased is the information? Are references provided for the information used? Does the information in this work match what you have read in other sources? Do you trust the source?

Reliability. The text to the left uses the word *reliability* to describe whether a source is "reliable"—that is, trustworthy. However, in your business, math, engineering, and science classes, you'll hear the word *reliable* used as a statistical term to refer to the overall consistency of a psychometric measure. Both uses of the word are correct and common in academic and workplace communication.

18 PROCESS: COMPOSING IN GENRES AND DESIGNING YOUR PROJECT

CONTENTS

FILM STILL ▶
**Hugh Jackman
as Wolverine**
From *X-Men*: a source
for student Gwen
Ganow's superhero
project. *Everett
Collection.*

By now you are familiar with a variety of genres (introduced in Chapter 4 and Chapters 13–15) and the choices writers and designers make. You've experienced a range of rhetorical situations and seen how composers work with genres. You've experienced a range of rhetorical situations and seen how composers work with genres. You've learned to think about your preliminary processes by performing initial research, creating proposals, using the library as a resource, and organizing your sources (Chapter 17). This material has built your foundation; now you must further develop your process by making strategic and tactical choices to select your genre and make your own composition. To help you with this process, we've provided a model. In this chapter, we'll follow Gwen Ganow, one of Amy's former students, as she drafts, chooses her genre, revises, finishes, and polishes a film review and an accompanying Author's Statement.

As you'll see, choosing a genre and drafting are related activities that sometimes overlap. Sometimes you need to start drafting before you can decide on a genre, or vice versa.

In this chapter, we'll guide you through the following processes, along with Gwen, as she moves from exploratory draft to finished genre composition and accompanying Author's Statement. *(Gwen Ganow's superhero project presented in this chapter appears by permission of Gwen Dalynn Ganow.)*

▲ STUDENT AUTHOR PHOTO
Gwen Ganow
Amy's student at Red Rocks Community College. *This image appears throughout chapter by permission of Gwen Dalynn Ganow.*

ROUGH DRAFTING

At this stage, you know your topic. You've formed a research question and gathered sources, and have a general idea of what you want to say. (For help with topics and research questions, see Chapter 17.) You may have decided on your genre, but don't worry if you haven't. Perhaps you know you want to persuade your audience about the importance of spaying and neutering pets, but aren't sure whether you'll create an editorial, a collage, or an ad, for example. Regardless, you'll want to get your ideas out of your head and down on paper (or up on your computer screen).

Advice for Rough Drafting

As you begin your rough/exploratory draft, remember that it is just for you. No one else ever needs to see it. Think of your first draft not as an organized, perfect piece of writing with a clear purpose, but as a messy opportunity for creativity and experimentation.

Don't worry about a thesis, or about being logical or eloquent. Instead, focus on quantity rather than quality. That's right: quantity not quality. Think of words in the first draft as raw materials. You want as much raw material to work with as possible. Imagine an artist beginning a painting. Would she have only the exact

☞ **Attention, composers! Wondering how to begin?**

As you think about what form your composition will take, ask yourself the following:

• What do I want to accomplish? Who is my primary audience, and how will I connect with my audience?

• What genre will work best for my rhetorical situation and be most persuasive?

• What genre(s) am I already an expert in? Which are the most challenging? Which work best with my schedule?

For an Index of Sources & Contexts for material referenced in this chapter; see the e-Pages at **bedfordstmartins.com /bookofgenres.**

amount of paint she needs to create her piece? What if she changes her mind midway through the painting and wants to use more yellow than red? Wouldn't it make sense for her to begin with extra paint in each color to allow her the flexibility to modify her ideas? Writing and other kinds of composing are similar. Beginning with more words than you need gives you more options. Here are some pointers for getting your first draft written:

1. Set a timer for thirty minutes and force yourself to write for the entire time, not stopping for anything. That means no stopping to reread and correct or to refer to sources or models, and definitely no stopping to check Facebook.

2. Don't stop to correct or edit what is on the page.

3. Write until you have five thousand words or you run out of time.

Don't worry about grammar, punctuation, spelling, transitions, topic sentences, organization, titles, and so on. Don't even worry about genre or what the finished piece will look or sound like. Once you have your thoughts down, you can think logically about your purpose, audience, and the points you want to convey.

At this stage, if you're putting pressure on yourself to write flawless, beautiful prose, remind yourself of the term *rough draft*—with *rough* being defined as coarse, rugged, crude, unrefined, graceless, unfinished, tentative, imperfect, or approximate. Take a little more pressure off by thinking of Anne Lamott's phrase "shitty first draft." Everybody, including published authors, writes them.

Let's take a look at one student's drafting process. When Gwen Ganow took a composition class with Amy at Red Rocks Community College, she composed an argument about superheroes and social attitudes, starting with this question:

RESEARCH QUESTION
To what extent do superheroes reflect real-world values and attitudes?

She then moved from that question to an exploratory rough draft.

▲ STUDENT AUTHOR PHOTO
Gwen Ganow

Guided Reading: A Rough Draft ▼

Gwen Ganow (Student)

Superhero Project: Rough Draft

Gwen began with some exploratory drafting to solidify what she wanted to say about superhero comics and social attitudes.

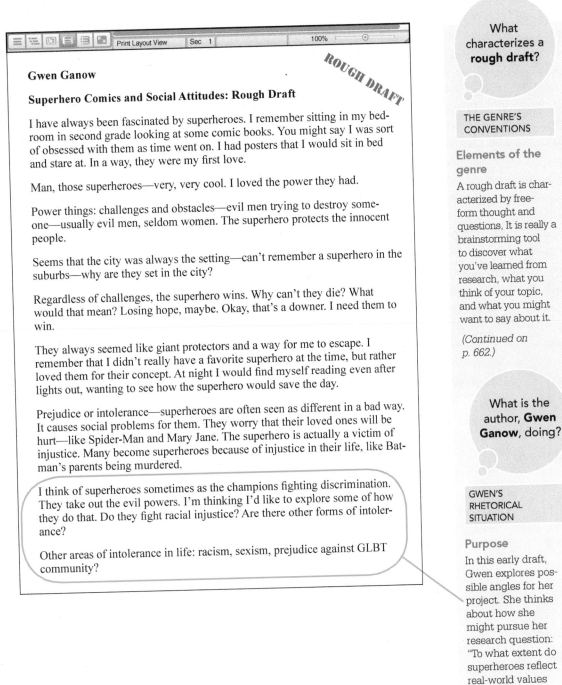

Print Layout View   Sec 1   100%

Gwen Ganow

Superhero Comics and Social Attitudes: Rough Draft

ROUGH DRAFT

I have always been fascinated by superheroes. I remember sitting in my bedroom in second grade looking at some comic books. You might say I was sort of obsessed with them as time went on. I had posters that I would sit in bed and stare at. In a way, they were my first love.

Man, those superheroes—very, very cool. I loved the power they had.

Power things: challenges and obstacles—evil men trying to destroy someone—usually evil men, seldom women. The superhero protects the innocent people.

Seems that the city was always the setting—can't remember a superhero in the suburbs—why are they set in the city?

Regardless of challenges, the superhero wins. Why can't they die? What would that mean? Losing hope, maybe. Okay, that's a downer. I need them to win.

They always seemed like giant protectors and a way for me to escape. I remember that I didn't really have a favorite superhero at the time, but rather loved them for their concept. At night I would find myself reading even after lights out, wanting to see how the superhero would save the day.

Prejudice or intolerance—superheroes are often seen as different in a bad way. It causes social problems for them. They worry that their loved ones will be hurt—like Spider-Man and Mary Jane. The superhero is actually a victim of injustice. Many become superheroes because of injustice in their life, like Batman's parents being murdered.

I think of superheroes sometimes as the champions fighting discrimination. They take out the evil powers. I'm thinking I'd like to explore some of how they do that. Do they fight racial injustice? Are there other forms of intolerance?

Other areas of intolerance in life: racism, sexism, prejudice against GLBT community?

What characterizes a rough draft?

THE GENRE'S CONVENTIONS

Elements of the genre

A rough draft is characterized by free-form thought and questions, It is really a brainstorming tool to discover what you've learned from research, what you think of your topic, and what you might want to say about it.

(Continued on p. 662.)

What is the author, Gwen Ganow, doing?

GWEN'S RHETORICAL SITUATION

Purpose

In this early draft, Gwen explores possible angles for her project. She thinks about how she might pursue her research question: "To what extent do superheroes reflect real-world values and attitudes?"

(Continued on p. 662.)

THE GENRE'S CONVENTIONS

Style

Gwen is not worried about style, grammar, or how the draft reads. It's not meant to be perfect. Her writing is very casual, as if she's writing in a journal to herself.

Sources

Gwen does not discuss sources in this draft, but she could have, depending on how far along she was in her research process.

Design

A rough draft is not designed. It's typically a Microsoft Word document.

GWEN'S RHETORICAL SITUATION

She allows herself to be unfocused as she starts with her fascination with superheroes. After doing this low-stakes drafting she realizes that she wants to cover how superheroes fight intolerance.

Audience

At this point, Gwen is writing for herself and her instructor, Amy. They'll go over this draft together to try to pin down a direction. Gwen will later identify a specific outside-of-the-classroom audience.

Rhetorical appeals

Gwen is not concerned right now about ethos, logos, and pathos. She's in exploration mode.

Modes & media

Gwen e-mailed this Word document to her instructor.

After writing her first draft, Gwen talked with Amy about directions she might take with her topic. Together they decided that Gwen should look back at her initial research, specifically the sources dealing with the history of comics.

CHECKLIST Getting Started on a Rough Draft? Keep the following questions in mind.

Exploration

☐ **What do I already know about my topic?** What intrigues me about this topic? What questions do I still have about it?

☐ **Based on my research so far, what arguments am I familiar with about this topic?** Are there some that resonate for me more than others? Do I have an opinion on this topic?

☐ **Is there a way to narrow my topic** by time, place, demographics, or something else? For example, if I write about gun control, do I focus on guns on college campuses (narrow by place) or the growth of shooting ranges geared toward women (narrow by demographics)?

Rhetorical Situation

☐ **What is my purpose?** What do I want to say—and how do I want to say it? Do I want to tell a story? Inform? Persuade? Some combination?

☐ **Who am I composing for?** Is my primary audience mainly the other students in this course? My instructor? Anyone with access to the course space or blog? Or to the campus newspaper or Web site? Who makes up my secondary audience? Am I writing for a broader, more public audience too? For others on campus? For anyone with an Internet connection?

☐ **How will I connect with my audience?** How will I establish my authority as a composer (ethos) so that my readers will trust me? What is the most logical way for me to present what I have to say? To what extent will I want to appeal to my audience's emotions? For example, if I want to persuade people to take a certain action, how will I cultivate their enthusiasm?

REREADING & ANNOTATING SOURCES

We believe that critical reading is a crucial part of the composing process. By critical reading, we mean more than simply moving your eyes across a page of text. When you read critically, you read with an eye for detail, noticing not just *what* another author or artist says but *how* she says it. For example, imagine you are reading an article in *The Onion* that you think is hilarious. As you read, you relate to the content and subject, but you might also zoom in on what the author does to make the piece so funny: maybe using a lot of exaggeration and sarcasm, as well as clever details. You might then try using exaggeration and sarcasm in a piece you are writing, to heighten the humor.

Earlier in this book, we focused on reading a variety of genres (Chapters 4 and 13–15), on reading to explore topics and creating a research plan (Chapter 5), and on previewing, evaluating, and choosing sources (Chapter 19). When you read as part of your composing process, we recommend the following steps.

Steps for Rereading & Annotating Sources

Step 1. Preview each source.   If you've already done this earlier in your process, do it again to refresh your memory. (For a more thorough explanation, see "How Do I Preview a Source Critically?" on pp. 724–31.) Ask yourself the following:

» Who is the author of this text (remember, a text can be written words, video, an audio podcast, or something else)? What, if anything, do I know about him or her? Are any details or credentials provided?

» What can I figure out from the title? A title will usually hint at an author's topic and purpose. Consider two titles: "How to Conserve Water at Home" and "Political Factors Affecting Nationwide Water Conservation Efforts." Both pieces are obviously about saving water, but the titles make clear that the authors wrote for different purposes and audiences. The first piece is most likely aimed at homeowners and is probably very straightforward; the second piece sounds more technical and may have been written for scientists, a government agency, or some other specialized audience.

» What can I determine about this piece based on where it was published or appeared?

Step 2. Mark up each source.   This means writing notes on the piece you are reading (or if the piece is not text-based—say you're working with video—using the annotating tools at your disposal). Annotating is different from highlighting. Highlighting allows you to remind yourself of what you found interesting or important as you read, but it doesn't allow you to record why you found things interesting or important. Annotating is more active; it gives you the chance to record your critical thoughts as you read more closely. It also keeps you engaged with the text, as it allows you to "talk back" to it.

We advise that you follow steps 3–7 as you annotate, incorporating these points into your notes.

Step 3. Identify each author's purpose and main points. What is the author's purpose? How clear is it? Can you put it in your own words? This is a good way to check your own understanding of what you're reading. If you can summarize what you've read in your own words—that is, without quoting the piece you've read—then you probably understand it. By the same token, if you can't summarize it in your own words, chances are you don't fully grasp what you've read and you should reread more carefully.

Step 4. Identify each author's audience. Who do you think is the composer's primary audience? What makes you think so? Can you tell who the author's secondary audiences might be? How does the author address his or her audience? What kind of relationship does the author try to create with the audience? For example, if the author writes in the first person and addresses the audience as "you," that creates a sense of intimacy. How do you feel toward the author and why?

Step 5. Analyze each author's use of sources, evidence, and rhetorical appeals. Notice whether the piece presents statistics, anecdotes, personal experiences, or other types of evidence to support its points. Also note whether the piece is using ethos, pathos, or logos. As you notice these things, keep in mind that if you are positively affected by the use of evidence and rhetorical appeals in the piece, you might want to try the same techniques in your own writing.

Step 6. Pay some attention to the genre and the conventions that are evident. Keep your eyes open for how genre conventions help you identify the genre. Begin thinking about how you could incorporate the conventions into your own genre piece. Which features and conventions get your attention and guide you through the piece? For example, do images give you a clearer picture of statistics that would otherwise confuse you?

Step 7. Notice each author's style and techniques. Be aware of how the writing affects you, and notice techniques you might want to try yourself. Whenever you see an author doing something particularly effective or interesting—say, integrating dialogue or introducing an image or presenting an argument—note how the author does it so that you can try it yourself.

CHECKLIST **Analyzing Sources & Genres as You Draft?** Keep the following questions in mind.

The Rhetorical Situation

☐ **Purpose.** What seems to be the author's purpose? How is that purpose made clear? How is that purpose achieved? How could I use similar techniques to establish my purpose in the piece I'm drafting?

☐ **Audience.** Who seems to be the targeted audience for the piece? How is that made clear? How are vocabulary, examples and details, organization, and other elements geared toward the targeted reader? How could I use similar techniques to engage my audience?

☐ **Rhetorical appeals.** How does the author use rhetorical appeals to connect with the audience? How could I use similar appeals in my own piece?

☐ **Modes & media.** How does the author's choice of mode and medium affect my level of engagement with the piece? For example, if the piece is a video, does the background music keep me interested or distract me? Can I use the author's choices about mode and medium as models for my own choices? Or as cautionary tales?

The Genre's Conventions

☐ **Elements of the genre.** How does the author use the elements of the genre to guide me through the piece? If I am composing in the same genre, how can I use the elements of the genre to guide readers through the piece?

☐ **Style.** How do the word choices, sentence structures, use of literary devices (like metaphor), and other stylistic techniques used by the author get me engaged in the piece? How can I use similar stylistic techniques to keep my readers engaged?

☐ **Design.** How has the author used design elements, such as color, images, and font, to emphasize the purpose and main point? How could I use similar design elements to convey my purpose and main point?

☐ **Sources.** What kinds of sources does the author refer to? How are these sources cited? How does the author make it clear when source material has been consulted? How can I use the author's strategies with sources as a model (or anti-model) for what I want to do?

Guided Process: How to Reread & Annotate a Source

Gwen Ganow (Student)

Superhero Project: An Annotated Source

▲ STUDENT AUTHOR
PHOTO
Gwen Ganow

Gwen decided to return to her sources, which included Dwight Decker's essay "Fredric Wertham: Anti-Comics Crusader Who Turned Advocate" (see p. 667), Brandford Wright's book *Comic Book Nation*, and various comic books by Alex Ross. She focused on the Dwight Decker essay, which she had found through a simple Google search on the history of comics. She especially liked how the author of the piece approached comics as a subject worthy of serious study. She also liked the author's tone and thought she might want to use a similar tone in her own writing. In this way, Gwen read this piece as both a source of information and a source of inspiration for *how* to write about her topic.

Gwen found Dwight Decker's article at *The Art Bin*, a magazine published by Karl-Erik Tallmo of Slowfox Press and archived at the press's blog. Decker notes at the end of his article: "This is a re-written version of an article that appeared in the magazine *Amazing Heroes* in 1987. Also available in Swedish. © Dwight Decker, 1987, 1997." *Amazing Heroes* (1981–1992, published by Fantagraphics Books) was a magazine about comics for comic book fans.

Also included with Decker's article is the following biography:

"Born 1952, Dwight R. Decker has been an active comics fan since 1967. By day he is a technical writer in the electronics industry, and by night he works as a freelance comics translator for publishers in the United States and Europe. [Decker] publishes his own fanzine, *Torch*, [and is] presently living in Phoenix, Arizona."

("Fredric Wertham—Anti-Comics Crusader Who Turned Advocate" by Dwight Decker is reprinted here by permission of the author, © Dwight Decker.)

Fredric Wertham - Anti-Comics Crusader Who Turned Advocate

by Dwight Decker

Illustration:
Asa Harvard

In the late 1940s and early 1950s, a distinguished psychiatrist named Dr. Fredric Wertham made a name for himself in the United States by leading a crusade against violent comic books. His 1954 book exposing the comic-book industry, *Seduction of the Innocent*, is still remembered in American comics fandom as a wildly exaggerated and overwrought polemic and has gone on to become a collector's item in its own right. Even the comic books mentioned in the text or used as source illustrations have also become collector's items because of their association with him and the book. Facing a public relations nightmare and hearings by the U.S. Senate subcommittee on juvenile delinquency, fearful publishers either went out of business or banded together to form a Comics Code Authority that would censor comic books before some outside body did it for them.

American comics fans have no cause to love Dr. Wertham. They remember him as the man who attacked comics with his hysterical book, helped kill EC Comics (the one publisher doing anything like adult-level material), and brought on the Comics Code that reduced American comics to a childish mentality. Many fans have associated Dr. Wertham with Senator Joseph McCarthy, well-known for his anti-Communist crusade at about the same time, and legends circulate of Dr. Wertham accusing comic books of being a Communist plot or some such.

"*Seduction of the Innocent*—the influence of comic books on today's youth." On the book's inner flap you could read: "90,000,000 comic books are read each month. You think they are mostly about floppy-eared bunnies, attractive little mice and chipmunks? Go take a look."

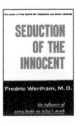

The actual story is somewhat different, and much more complicated. As an indicator of the general trend of Dr. Wertham's thinking, consider these three quotes from his various books:

> I have known many adults who have treasured throughout their lives some of the books they read as children. I have never come across any adult or adolescent who had outgrown comic-book reading who would ever dream of keeping any of these "books" for any sentimental or other reason. —*Seduction of the Innocent* (1954)

> When *Seduction of the Innocent* appeared in the middle fifties, it started a grass-roots social reaction. . . . A change occurred. Murder in comic books decreased, and so did the number of crime-comic-book publishers. Within a few years after the publication of *Seduction of the Innocent*, twenty-four out of twenty-nine crime-comic-book publishers went out of business. But it was only a partial victory. We now meet some of the child

Continues next page

Gwen's notes on Decker's article

I see from his bio that the author, Dwight Decker, is a freelance comic translator.

The title suggests a focus on one man, with the purpose of showing how Wertham changed his stance on the value of comics.

Decker's purpose seems to be to inform readers about the complex life of a man who rejected and then embraced comics. The article also seems to be a commentary on the value of comics, to some extent.

At the end of the piece, Decker notes that the article originally appeared in *Amazing Heroes*. I Googled "Amazing Heroes" and found out it's a defunct magazine for comic book fans. So Decker was writing to an audience who knew something about comics. It doesn't seem to be an analytical journal, per se, but this piece seems rather scholarly to me.

Gwen Ganow, *An Annotated Source*

**Gwen's notes on
Decker's article**

Decker draws on a
bunch of sources,
including passages
from Wertham's
books, articles, and,
later, his fanzine, as
well as a *New York
Times* obituary.

Decker builds
ethos through his
authoritative tone,
and logos by back-
ing up his points
with specific evi-
dence, organized
chronologically.

Decker informs and
draws on sour-
ces—but presents
his opinions about
Wertham's crusade
against comics and
the contradictions
when Wertham
reinvents himself.
So I'd character-
ize the piece as a
researched argu-
ment.

Researched argu-
ments are charac-
terized by, well,
research and are
typically docu-
mented according
to a scholarly style,
unless they are
created for a popu-
lar, nonacademic
audience (as is the
case here).

comic-book readers as parents of the "battered child" or in similar roles. Moreover, very many of the old comic books are still around at reduced prices. —*A Sign for Cain* (1966)

Comic-book collecting which started as a nice nostalgic hobby is in some danger of becoming an overpriced, overcommercialized transaction. —*The World of Fanzines* (1974)

A man probably has a right to change his mind over the course of twenty years, but did Dr. Wertham really change his? How did a prominent psychiatrist and author get mixed up with comic books in the first place?

Fredric Wertham, 1895–1981.

According to his obituary in the *New York Times* (December 1, 1981), Fredric Wertham was born in Munich, Germany, in 1895. He studied at Kings College in London and at the Universities of Munich and Erlangen, and received his MD from the University of Würzburg in 1921. He did post-graduate study in London, Vienna, and Paris, and correspondence with Sigmund Freud led him to take up psychiatry as his life's work. He settled in the United States in 1922, becoming a citizen in 1927.

Wertham's subsequent career was impressive. He held the posts of senior psychiatrist for the New York City Department of Hospitals and director of the mental hygiene clinics at Bellevue Hospital and later Queens General Hospital. He was also director of the Lafargue Clinic in Harlem, a mental hygiene clinic for the poor in a mostly black section of New York City. His article for the *American Journal of Psychotherapy*, "Psychological Effects of School Segregation," was submitted to the United States Supreme Court as an important piece of evidence in the legal case that led to the 1954 ruling that declared racial segregation in schools to be unconstitutional.

Where Dr. Wertham made his name was as a consulting psychiatrist for the court system. The psychiatric clinic he directed for the New York City court was probably the first clinic in the United States in which all convicted felons received a psychiatric examination. His recommendations led to the modernization of facilities and methodology at many mental and criminal holding institutions.

Dr. Wertham was also an author. His first book was *The Brain as an Organ* (1934), a straightforward scientific work. *Dark Legend,* however, was a psychological case history of a seventeen-year-old boy who murdered his mother, written for a more general audience and with literary allusions. The reviews were mostly favorable, though an MD referred to "slips and inconsistencies which definitely mar the book as a scientific study." Criticisms of sloppy writing would dog every book Wertham wrote. His 1949 book, *Show of Violence,* is a general study of murder in which he discusses some of the major murder cases he was involved with as either a court witness or a consultant.

Parents and educators had been complaining about comic books for years. As early as December, 1940, when comic books were still in their infancy, the *National Education Association Journal* ran an article discussing "An Antidote to the Comic Magazine Poison." Dr. Wertham ran into comic books in the course of his work with juvenile offenders, and noting that many of the delinquents read them avidly, concluded that they were important environmental factors leading the kids to crime and violence. He presented his case in an article published in the May 29, 1947, issue of the *Saturday Review of Literature,* and after that he was off and running in his crusade against violent comic books. Over the next seven years, he would give lectures, write articles, and testify as an expert witness before legislative committees investigating the comic-book menace, culminating in the publication of his book *Seduction of the Innocent* in 1954.

Latterday American comics fans, who look back at the anti-comics crusade with fear and loathing, and fret nervously over whether it might happen again, tend to ignore the point that comics publishers of the early '50s virtually cut their own throats. While Dr. Wertham overstated his case to a sometimes ludicrous degree, he didn't have to: comics really were as crude, violent, and tasteless as he claimed, as any parent or legislator could easily confirm. With the postwar eclipse of costume heroes, comic books moved into increasingly violent and graphic crime and horror. Parents and legislators were worried enough about children seeing pictures of endless murders and mutilations and severed body parts in comics that were anything but fuzzy bunny books; then a distinguished psychiatrist came along and told them exactly what they had suspected all along—yes, children who read crime comic books became hardened to violence, and even accepted it as a useful problem-solving device. Comic books taught children to be cruel, sexually warped, dishonest, and contemptuous of soft virtues like pity or love. Comic books were still relatively mild in 1947 when Dr. Wertham began his crusade, but some publishers lost all restraint into the 1950s, running increasingly violent and gory stories that only confirmed everything he said.

Outside the forbidden pages of de Sade, you find draining a girl's blood only in children's comics.

One of Dr. Wertham's samples from the book, with his own caption.

Seduction of the Innocent is a remarkable book. Like most of Dr. Wertham's publications, it is short on proof of its assertions and long on polemics, anecdotes related without any sources cited, and literary quotations or allusions crowbarred into the text. Several generations of comics fans have had a chance to discover the book and react to it now, and everything you've heard about it is probably true. Dr. Wertham does accuse Superman of being a fascist, Batman and Robin of being a homosexual fantasy of a man and a boy living together, and Wonder Woman of being just plain kinky (judging from the early years of that strip, with all the downright astonishing emphasis on bondage and submission, I'd have to say he called that one pretty well). He does make the claim that comic-book drawings contain "pictures within pictures" for "those who know how to look," his Exhibit A being the shading of a man's shoulder muscles that supposedly evoke a woman's naked torso when squinted at right. Dr. Wertham does badly misinterpret a few stories, notably an EC one in which some overly patriotic citizens beat a man to death for not saluting the flag, only to discover at the end that he was blind and couldn't see it; Wertham claimed that the story *favored* rough treatment of insufficiently patriotic individuals, somehow missing the point of a fairly heavyhanded story.

Mr. Decker's own fanzine *Torch*.
By permission of Douglas Jones.

NOTE: Several paragraphs are intentionally omitted. Decker's final paragraphs appear below. —*Eds.*

Continues next page

Gwen's notes on Decker's article

This researched argument originally appeared in *The Art Bin*, an early online magazine, now archived by its publisher, Karl-Erik Tallmo.

This researched argument, in effect, is posted on a blog, but does not reflect the typical conventions such as hyperlinks and comments, for example. This may be because it was published in the early days of the Internet, before blog conventions were what they are now.

I like the use of text and images—and also Decker's personable but authoritative style. He isn't simply an excited comics fan; he seems like a scholar and takes comics seriously. He persuades me that comics are a worthy topic of study and that I could write about them seriously myself.

Dr. Wertham's account in the introductory chapter [of his book *The World of Fanzines*] of how he got involved with fanzines is interesting, as he doesn't mention *Seduction of the Innocent* or his anti-comic book work in the '50s. The unknowing reader is left with the impression that Wertham is simply a public figure known for his "writings or talks on such subjects as mass media, youth problems, or violence," and fanzine editors sent him their publications just to communicate pleasantly with the nice gentleman in response. Wertham gives no hint of his personal position in the world of fanzines as a near-legendary bogeyman, regarded by many of their editors and contributors as incarnate evil walking the earth.

He seemed to only reluctantly acknowledge comic books and science fiction as the source of fanzines and fandom, and gave a couple of the most skewed capsule histories of the genres I've ever seen, concentrating on their anti-war and non-violent aspects. In discussing the comics fanzines' emphasis on superheroes, he offered the remark that "the creative imagination of fanzine writers and artists, especially the younger ones, tends in the direction of heroes, maybe in that lies a message for our unheroic age." This is more than a little remarkable coming from the man who in *Seduction* classified superheroes as a bizarre variant of "crime comics" and thought Superman in particular was a fascist avatar. Mostly, he glosses over the comic-book connection of comics fandom, treating it puzzledly or condescendingly when he can't avoid it, and seems to proceed on the premise that fandom just spontaneously organized itself as a communications vehicle for teenagers, with comic books only an incidental, even accidental aspect of it all. As usual, Dr. Wertham concentrates on violence and is delighted to report that there isn't any in the world of fanzines.

The World of Fanzines is a masterpiece of scholarship gone off the track. It's the only book you'll find about its subject in most libraries even though the author never quite understood what he was writing about. He never said as much—he couldn't admit it for the sake of professional pride, perhaps—but *The World of Fanzines* contradicts everything Dr. Wertham wrote about comic books and their readers in his previous books.

In the end, he decided, we'd turned out pretty much all right.

CHOOSING A GENRE TO COMPOSE IN

After reviewing your sources and creating a rough, exploratory draft, you should have a better sense of what you want to say about your topic. Your next decision is to choose a genre. You may find the checklist on page 672 helpful.

Steps for Choosing a Genre to Compose In

Step 1. Revisit your topic & research question. Remember that rough draft? Since you've done more reading and analyzed a variety of genres, what's changed for you? How might that affect your focus?

Step 2. Focus on your purpose. Look over your initial draft and highlight some of the main ideas you want to explore. Make a list of four or five of them. Next, choose the idea that energizes you the most, the one that you will be most excited to write about. Then, decide on the primary purpose of the piece you are composing.

Step 3. Really think about your audience.   Consider your audience. Keep in mind that aspects of your topic that are obvious to you may not be obvious to your audience.

Step 4. Strategize on how you'll use rhetorical appeals.   Start thinking about how to appeal to your audience's senses of ethos, logos, and pathos. Many composers begin with only a general sense of how they will use rhetorical appeals, but while drafting realize which appeals will be most effective.

Step 5. Consider your mode & medium.   Once you have narrowed the scope of your purpose and audience, think about whether you want to work with text, visuals, video, audio, or some combination. Consider the advantages of each, as well as your skills and the tools available to you. If you have access to a multimodal composing lab on campus, you may be more interested in experimenting with sound and images than if you have to teach yourself how to use sound- and image-editing software.

Step 6. Narrow your choices down to three possible genres.   Now that you have your purpose and audience, and are developing a sense of how you'll work with text and other media, put together a short list of potential genres you want to consider composing in. At this point, it can be helpful to look at the particular conventions of the genres you are considering.

Step 7. Look at examples of the three genres you're interested in.   There are many features to consider when looking at genre:

» **Is point of view important for your purpose and audience?**   Determining the point of view for your genre piece helps you narrow your genre selection. If you need your piece to be first person so that it includes your perspective, then make sure you choose a genre that accommodates this point of view.

» **What type of connection do you want to establish with your audience?**   If you want to remain at a critical distance from your audience in order to establish a more authoritative voice, you might choose a genre that emphasizes ethos in its rhetorical appeal. If you want to make a closer connection with your audience, perhaps appealing to their emotions regarding the topic, then you might choose a genre that emphasizes pathos.

» **What tone do you want to use in order to achieve your purpose?**   Some writers, especially those composing a scientific report, for example, adopt a formal tone, one that perhaps incorporates jargon from the field that will be familiar to his or her readers. If you want your piece to have that level of formality, make sure to choose a genre that utilizes formality. On the other hand, if you desire to convey your message using a more informal tone, look for genres whose style is marked by a less formal tone.

Step 8. Zero in on how you'll use your sources. Finally, you'll need to think about how you will use sources in your piece—and how the genre you're considering typically deals with sources. You may realize that you need to do more research or simply reread the sources you've gathered more carefully. You'll also want to look at samples of the genre you're thinking of working in. Keep this in mind: Genre decisions at this point are still tentative; as you draft, you may stumble upon a completely different genre idea that fits your purpose, audience, and other aspects of your rhetorical situation. Keep an open mind as you draft. Remember that the drafting process is a process of discovery.

CHECKLIST **Choosing a Genre?** Keep the following questions in mind.

The Rhetorical Situation

- ☐ **Purpose.** What is my purpose? Which genres are best for what I want to do? If I want to persuade, should I consider creating an advertisement? An editorial? Something else?

- ☐ **Audience.** How familiar is my audience with my topic? What assumptions might my audience make about my topic? What expectations will my audience have about my piece?

- ☐ **Rhetorical appeals.** How will I connect with my audience? For example, if I create an ad or an editorial, how will I work within that genre to be as compelling and convincing as possible?

- ☐ **Modes & media.** What is the best mode for saying what I want to say? If I rely on text only, will anything be lost? And what medium would be best?

The Genre's Conventions

- ☐ **Elements of the genres.** What are my favorite genres? Which ones do I know the most about? Which ones do I want to try out? Which ones can I get help with? Among the sources I've drawn on in my research, which ones stood out? What are their genres? What features make a particular genre what it is? How would I use (or not use) those features?

- ☐ **Style.** What are my strengths as a writer/composer? What tone will be most appropriate for my composition, considering the genre I choose to use? For example, if I create an ad, can I be funny? What kind of vocabulary would I use? How much detail would be appropriate?

- ☐ **Design.** Once I choose the genre for my composition, how will it look (or sound)? Will I use a conventional design, or perhaps tailor a standard layout or structure to my own purposes?

- ☐ **Sources.** What do I already know about my topic? What sources have I gathered? Which ones will work best as sources for my composition, and why? To what extent will I need to draw on my sources? Will I need to quote from them? Document them?

Guided Process: How to Choose a Genre to Compose In ▼

Gwen Ganow (Student)

Superhero Project: Brainstorm to Refine Topic & Purpose

▲ STUDENT AUTHOR
PHOTO
Gwen Ganow

In the following pages, Gwen Ganow decides which genre she'd like to compose in. She does so by:

1. Brainstorming about her topic and rhetorical situation
2. Looking at three examples of persuasive genres: an ad, a researched argument, and a film review
3. Deciding how she wants to use sources—and which genre will work best overall. In this section, Gwen moves from brainstorming about a possible genre to compose in—to making a final choice about which genre will be best for her project. (Spoiler alert: It's a film review.)

| ☰ ☷ ▣ ☰ ▤ ▦ | Print Layout View | Sec 1 | 100% ─○─ |

Gwen Ganow

Superhero Project: Brainstorm

BRAINSTORM

WHERE AM I WITH MY TOPIC AND RESEARCH QUESTION?

Okay, I've sketched out a rough draft and looked at an argument about superheroes. But I need to think through my topic a little more. Here are some ideas and questions I'm tossing around:

- Now that I've read some more, I may focus totally on superheroes, rather than comics as a whole. Good idea?
- Most comics have superheroes. Why? Also, they are kind of underdogs with power. What does that have to do with the real world?
- Superheroes are sort of in the real world—but also in a kind of magical world where they always persevere. Why this duality?
- Superheroes use their power to protect others. Why do they care so much? And why do fans seem to need superheroes to win?
- Superheroes mainly fight injustice. Superheroes are themselves almost always victims of injustice.
  - I like the injustice angle, which gets back to my idea of writing about a social issue. Not sure what I'll say, but I may present an argument about superheroes, power, and social inequality.

WHAT IS MY PURPOSE?

I need to decide what I want to say. Also, how and why. What do I want to present to my audience about superheroes? Do I want to:

Continues next page

Gwen's notes on her project

My early research question about comics and social attitude—"To what extent do superheroes reflect real-world values and attitudes?"—is too broad.

Will revise to something like: How/why are superheroes victims of injustice? What does that have to do with their fight against injustice?

Ganow, Superhero Project: Brainstorm, Continued

**Gwen's notes on
her project**

What I really want
to do is present
some type of per-
suasive argument
about superheroes.

Tell a story?

I could tell a story about a superhero fighting some evil. The story would show some societal intolerance, maybe racism, and it would show how the superhero struggles but ultimately wins. But that's not really a fresh concept. Also, what would be the advantage of telling a story? Would I create a work of fiction with a moral or lesson—or a narrative essay? I'm not sure that's right for my topic.

Report information?

I might present information about how a superhero fights injustice. Instead of telling a story, I would give concrete information so that my reader sees how the superhero ultimately promotes tolerance. How do superheroes promote tolerance? If I took on that question, I'd need to provide information. I'd also offer analysis through my perspective. More like arguing a case. Hmm.

Persuade?

I could try to convince people that we need superheroes in the world to fight intolerance. I might use my idea of how we need hope and how superheroes give us that hope. Also, what are superheroes—and why do we need them? So I'd be defining superheroes, but also creating a persuasive argument. The question now is, how? Would an advertisement be a good idea, or some other persuasive genre?

WHO IS MY AUDIENCE?

Okay, who do I want my target readers/viewers to be?

Mainly, people who enjoy comics. Probably they read them as children and teens because they loved the stories and heroes. Also, my classmates and in-structor. Beyond the people in my course, I'd like to aim at a primary audience of people who are really into comics—who know something about them and their history. A kind of expert audience.

I know I want to
make a case about
superheroes. I see
my primary audi-
ence as comic and
superhero fans like
me. I see my sec-
ondary audience
as people who may
have less interest
in superheroes.

So I have a mix of potential readers—my primary, expert audience of comics fans—and people in my classroom who may have varying levels of knowledge and interest in the topic.

What do they know about superheroes?

My primary audience already knows something about superheroes. They aren't necessarily as obsessed as I am, but they have a certain passion about the topic. They do have some level of specialized knowledge, which means I'll have to craft my argument in ways to hook in uninterested people—but also speak to my core readers (appreciative fans).

What expectations will they have?

As comic book lovers/experts, my target audience will expect me to be well-informed about superheroes. If I'm going to persuade them of something, I'll need to draw on evidence and details from comics to support my points. Whatever genre I choose for my composition, something visual and narrative will appeal to this audience.

Ganow, *Superhero Project: Brainstorm,* *Continued*

≡ ≣ ▣ ▤ ▥ ▣ | Print Layout View | Sec 1 | 100% |○

What assumptions might they already hold about superheroes?
For most comic readers, superheroes save the day. They represent good battling evil (or vice versa) and usually do a lot of rescuing (or sabotage). At least
these are my own assumptions as a comics expert.

HOW WILL I USE RHETORICAL APPEALS?
Ethos
I think of ethos as having to do with authority. As an author, if I want to
persuade my audience, it's going to be crucial to convince them that my information and argument are credible—and that I am qualified (or authorized)
to make the argument. I've grown up with comics and have a good base of
knowledge; I'll establish that in my composition. That will help me with my
ethos.

Logos
I associate logos with logic. I'll need to build a logical case for my audience.
How to do this will become clearer once I choose a genre, I think. But I'll
need to be methodical and organized. Depending on the form my composition takes, I'll have to find ways to present and support my argument clearly.
Thinking back to some of my sources, I like how Dwight Decker does that in
his researched essay. Maybe reread?

Pathos
Emotions. Hmm. I'm not totally sure how I'll work with pathos. But part of
what makes me care about superheroes is my emotional connection to them as
people who care—who put themselves "in harm's way," as they say, to help
and rescue others. I hadn't thought of tapping into emotions in my piece, but
it might come in handy, especially if I emphasize superheroes as righters of
wrongs and fighters of injustice. I also may want to use humor as a persuasive
strategy.

WHAT MODES AND MEDIA WILL I WORK WITH?
Even though I don't know what genre I'll compose in, I should probably think
of the media I'm most comfortable with. That might impact my choice of
genre. Okay, so will my composition be:

Visual? Textual?
My composition will probably have more text than visuals. My comics-fan
audience may expect visuals, but I'm more comfortable working in text—and
presenting arguments that way. Also, I'll be drawing on sources. How would
I do that in a nontextual medium? Though it might be fun to branch out into
working with images.

I'm a good writer, but I feel less comfortable as an artist. Maybe I can use
existing images from comics in my work to support my points. (Many of my
sources are visual.) Or maybe it doesn't matter that creating visuals isn't my
strong suit. Should I experiment?

Continues next page

Gwen's notes on her project

I'll be making an
argument, so it
makes sense to
emphasize ethos
(my own authority
as a comics fan)
and logos (logic) to
reach my audience.
Also pathos—my
primary audience
has an emotional
relationship with
comics.

I think I'll use both
words and im-
ages—but mainly
words. I'd like my
sources to be ap-
parent, especially
to online readers.
I'd also like to be
able to integrate/
embed media such
as video.

Ganow, *Superhero Project: Brainstorm,* *Continued*

Print Layout View   Sec   1   100%

**Gwen's notes on
her project**

I want to be
persuasive—what
genres will help
me convince my
audience of comics
lovers of my views
on superheroes?
Given my skills
and timeframe,
I'd consider three
possibilities: an
ad, a researched
argument (which I
could morph into a
presentation), or a
film review.

Sound? Motion (video or animation)? Other digital delivery?
I probably won't use sound, but I would consider using video clips from
superhero films or animated works. I'd need to use existing content because I
don't have expertise in creating this stuff myself. Also, I have a limited time
frame. In a future iteration of this project, I might use other media. I might
even collaborate with someone who knows how to work with video.

If I create a written text for a digital environment, I can embed links. That
might be an easy way to bring in my sources. I'd like to build into my work
some existing clips from films and animations.

WHAT ARE SOME PERSUASIVE GENRES? WHICH ONE SHOULD I CHOOSE?
Here are the genres I'm familiar with that are associated with persuading.
Which option do I like best?

Ad?
I like that I could mix visuals with text if I made an ad. Where would I publish
this ad? It would need to be somewhere that comic book fans would see it. Not
sure where that would be. I also like the idea of making a commercial. Sounds
fun. An ad is very obviously persuasive. This could work for me, though it
wouldn't showcase my sources. But I could include them in an Artist's Statement. If my ad is image centered, then I will be creating a type of visual argument. That may be a good way to reach comic book lovers.

Editorial?
I could easily write an editorial, and maybe include some images. But I've
done a lot of research, and I'd really like to show off my sources. How might
this work? Most editorials are pretty short, and I'm not sure how much space
I'll need to make my case. Yeah, I don't think a traditional newspaper-type
editorial will work, given that I want to use images. But maybe a researched
argument?

Researched argument?
This may be a better option than an editorial. I've done research and want to
draw on that. If I choose this genre, I won't have to worry about length problems and could easily include visuals to make my case. I'm now thinking I
could present this online in a magazine, journal, or blog. I see researched arguments and presentations as related genres. Could work. This genre would give
me a framework for arguing about superheroes, and I could include related/
supporting images and clips.

Collage or other visual argument—such as a comic?
It would be cool to create a persuasive comic, but I'd want help with the images and don't have a lot of time. While I love the idea of creating some kind
of visual argument—I think my best bet is to work existing visuals into my
composition in a meaningful way.

Presentation?
I can see myself translating a researched argument into a presentation at some
point.

Ganow, *Superhero Project: Brainstorm, Continued*

For more on **rhetorical appeals**, see Chapter 4, page 89.

☰	⁝	▢	▤	▤	▣	Print Layout View	Sec 1	100% ━━━━◉━━━

Personal statement? Resume & cover letter?
These genres don't apply to my topic, purpose, or audience. Onward!

Film review?
Hmm, this is a possibility. I love superhero / comics movies, and there are a lot of them out there. And as an avid film-viewer I do read a lot of film reviews. I could review a film that focuses on a superhero. Interesting thought. A film review is kind of like an editorial or researched argument in that I'd make a case mainly through writing.

For more on **argument and persuasion**, see Chapter 15, "Persuasive Genres."

Gwen Ganow (Student)

Superhero Project: 3 Annotated Persuasive Genres

Now that Gwen has narrowed her choice of genre down to three types—an ad, a researched argument, and a film review—she looks at an example of each:

» AD: **Douglas & Gordon,** "He Was No Ordinary Estate Agent," from the Douglas & Gordon Web site

» RESEARCHED ARGUMENT: **Shannon Cochran,** "The Cold Shoulder: Saving Superheroines from Comic-book Violence," from *Bitch* magazine online

» FILM REVIEW: **A. O. Scott,** "*Iron Man*: Heavy Suit, Light Touches," from *The New York Times* online

She annotates these sources, reading them not only for information about her topic, but also to find out more about the genres and their conventions. For example, how did the composers of these works incorporate sources?

As she reads these sources closely, she asks herself: Which of these persuasive genres—an ad, researched argument, or film review—should I ultimately choose for my composition?

Gwen analyzes and annotates each piece according to the author's/artist's rhetorical situation and use of genre conventions.

How do I know
this is **an ad**?
And do I want
to create
one?

THE GENRE'S
CONVENTIONS

**Gwen's notes
on Douglas &
Gordon ad**

**Elements of the
genre**
I like this ad's
simplicity. The
real estate agent
superhero is vivid
and colorful. The
name of the agency
is easy to find; the
brand is reinforced
by the logo on the
hero's chest and
beside the company
name.

Style
Not much text—
mainly the head-
line—and what's
there is conversa-
tional. Effective.

Design
The image plays
on pop culture.
The ad creators
mimic comic books
with the speech
bubble and text
boxes.

Sources
The ad makers
draw on the image
of Superman. But
they don't have to
cite this source.
That's handy.

What are the
ad's composers,
**Douglas &
Gordon**,
doing?

THE RHETORICAL
SITUATION

**Gwen's notes
on Douglas &
Gordon ad**

Purpose
Douglas & Gordon
want to persuade
viewers that their
agents can save the
day. If I created an
ad, what would my
argument be?

Audience
This ad is aimed at
people buying or
selling real estate.
I've identified my
main audience as
comic book lovers.
But where would
I place an ad so it
reaches my audi-
ence?

Rhetorical appeals
The ad creators
appeal to pathos/
emotion through
the message that
their agents can
rescue you. They
appeal to ethos
through the com-
pany branding.

Modes & media
This ad is online,
but could easily
translate to a print
magazine, for ex-
ample. I like that.

Text of ad:
He was no ordinary estate agent.
With over 45 years experience in property and a team of more
than 150 well trained, enthusiastic everyday superheroes, D&G is
dedicated to providing you with an extraordinary service. We're
here to fight for truth, justice and the best deal on your property.
Ad reprinted here by courtesy of Douglas & Gordon.

Next, Gwen looks at an example of a researched argument, asking herself: Would I want to compose in this genre? *(Shannon Cochran's article is reprinted here courtesy of Bitch Magazine.)*

The Cold Shoulder — Shannon Cochran

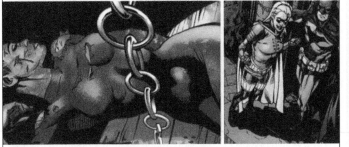

Saving Superheroines from Comic-book Violence

There's a new Bat in Gotham City. Like Bruce Wayne, she's a rich socialite by day and a black-clad vigilante at night. And, also like Bruce Wayne, in both incarnations she's apt to sweep the ladies off their feet. Kate Kane, the new, revamped Batwoman, isn't the first lesbian character to debut in the DC Comics universe, but she might have the highest profile. Last June, DC Executive Director Dan DiDio issued a press release saying the move was intended "to get a better cross-section of our readership and the world."

But the new Caped Crusader may find Gotham City a hostile work environment. Many of the series' previous female characters met with unfortunate fates. An earlier Batwoman was murdered, a female Robin was tortured to death with a power drill, one Batgirl was shot by the Joker, and another one was turned to villainy. In fact, it's so common for female superheroes to be killed in gruesome ways, comic-book fans have a term for it: "women in refrigerators." The phrase was coined in 1999 by comic-book writer Gail Simone, whose many credits include a stint on the Superman title *Action Comics* as well as current authorship of the *Birds of Prey* series.

The women-in-refrigerators syndrome got its name from a 1994 *Green Lantern* story arc, in which the titular hero's girlfriend is strangled and later discovered in a fridge. In an e-mail interview, Simone explains: "I and some male friends started making a list of the characters that had been killed, mutilated, or depowered (also a telling trend, as the more powerful a female character was, the more likely it was that she would lose those powers). It was shockingly long, and almost no one in the already small pool of valid superheroines escaped the wave of gynocentric violence."

Continues next page

---

bitchmedia

But so what? Don't superheroes die all the time in comic books, regardless of their biology? Sure, but as Simone says: "First, there's [always been] a larger selection of male characters, so a handful killed made barely a ripple. Second, they didn't seem to be killed in the same way—they tended to die heroically, to go down fight-ing. Whereas in many cases, the superLADIES were simply found on the kitchen table already carved up." Furthermore, she points out, most of the men recovered with lightning speed. Take Batman and Batgirl: "Both had their backs broken [Batman broke his in a dramatic Batcave confrontation with the villain Bane; Batgirl broke hers when she was ambushed in her home and shot in the spine by the Joker, never given a chance to fight]. Less than a year later, Batman was fine. Batgirl—now named Oracle—was in a wheelchair and remained so for many years."

Alan Moore, the writer responsible for the story arc that led to Batgirl's shattered spine, provides some insight into the editorial perspective behind the decision. As he told the industry magazine *Wizard*: "I asked DC if they had any problem with me crippling Barbara Gordon—who was Batgirl at the time—and if I remember, I spoke to Len Wein, who was our editor on the project, and he said, 'Hold on to the phone, I'm just going to walk down the hall and I'm going to ask [former DC Executive Editorial Director] Dick Giordano if it's alright,' and there was a brief period where I was put on hold and then, as I remember it, Len got back onto the phone and said, 'Yeah, okay, cripple the bitch.'"

Moore later regretted the story arc that retired Batgirl, stating in several interviews that he felt the decision was shallow and ill-conceived. However, Barbara Gordon was far from the only victim of the women-in-refrigerators syndrome. The list Simone created in 1999 included more than 90 female characters, among them Aquagirl, Hawkwoman, Elasti-Girl, Nova, Lady Flash, and at least two different Supergirls. In the eight years since, few of the list's characters have returned to life or regained their powers.

Simone also contacted other comic creators, both male and female, asking for their reactions to the list. Her letters were cir-culated on message boards and fan sites, provoking widespread debate and discussion in the comic-book world. Simone and her compatriots decided to create a Web site detailing the women-in-refrigerators phenomenon (now archived at http://unheardtaunts .com/wir/). The site includes Simone's original list, along with a number of the responses it sparked.

For female fans like myself, Simone had pinpointed a problem we felt keenly but had not been able to articulate. "WiR syndrome" was the terminology we needed to make our discontent with the indus-try's sexism coherent, and Simone's list was the ammunition behind

bitch media

our arguments. And it seemed that her observations impacted the industry. "For whatever reason," Simone notes, "the next generation of writers paid a great deal more attention to making fun, entertaining, kick-ass superheroines." Notable examples include characters like Mark Andreyko's Manhunter at DC, or over at Marvel, Brian Michael Bendis's Jessica Jones, Tamora Pierce's White Tiger, and Dan Slott and Juan Bobillo's She-Hulk (thankfully reinvented as much more than a green slice of cheesecake). According to Simone, these characters have generated more female fans.

But many female fans are still angry over treatment of past characters. Although Stephanie Brown might not be well known to casual fans of the Batman mythos, readers of DC's Batman titles knew her for 12 years as Spoiler, a young and impulsive vigilante with a sunny optimism that made her an endearing foil to Batman's endlessly brooding ways. Robin's girlfriend for many years, Stephanie eventually filled out Robin's tights herself when the former Boy Wonder resigned his post. Shortly after, in 2004, Stephanie met her grisly end by the aforementioned power-drill torture by the supervillain Black Mask. The sequence spanned multiple issues and featured graphic artwork that blatantly sexualized the teenage heroine during her bondage and torture. An action figure of Black Mask, complete with power drill, was subsequently issued. No action figure of the Girl Wonder was ever made.

It felt like comics were backsliding badly. Before Stephanie Brown took over for Robin, I'd gone years without reading a *Batman* comic. It was a cover picture of Stephanie in action under the brassy logo "Robin: Girl Wonder" that had reinvigorated my interest. Soon I was buying four *Batman*-related titles every month and splurging for the occasional *Teen Titans* crossover. Stephanie's brutal death felt like a kick in the gut. I'd been a rube to fall for a promise that DC never intended to keep.

And I wasn't the only one angry about it. Mary Borsellino, a graduate student in cultural studies at Melbourne University, posted a rant on her blog that articulated her "rage and disgust" at Stephanie's treatment. Within two hours, her post had gathered about a hundred comments from like-minded fans.

"I felt like this was a sign," Borsellino wrote in an e-mail exchange, "that this was something that needed to be sustained. So I registered Girl-Wonder.org that evening."

Project Girl Wonder was initially dedicated to protesting the treatment of Stephanie Brown, but quickly took on a life of its own. While Stephanie remains the site's official symbol, Girl-Wonder.org's mission has expanded into a campaign demanding better treatment for *all* women in comics. As the site proclaims: "Batman and other

Continues next page

superhero stories are the modern age's fables, and if we don't stop the spread of this rot now they will be irrevocably corrupted by it. Stephanie Brown is a symbol of the need for change. And we're going to see that the change begins." The site attracted more than 100,000 visitors in its first couple months, with hundreds of registered users filling the message boards. In the years since, Girl-Wonder.org has organized a letter-writing campaign, distributed literature about the WiR problem to conventions and local comic stores, and sparked a new wave of debate within the industry.

For Borsellino, the Girl Wonder campaign is fueled not only by depictions in the comics, but also by the apparent disdain shown by industry editors toward their female audience. In an e-mail interview, Borsellino wrote: "Less than a week [after Stephanie's death], [DiDio] started shooting his mouth off in an interview, and described Stephanie's death-by-torture as having a 'major impact' on the lives of heroes." This statement bothered Borsellino because it was untrue (Stephanie's death didn't seem to impact male superheroes) and because of what it implied. "It completely failed to acknowledge that anybody could possibly have the girl as their hero. No, the girls are the ones who die and thereby make the boys, the real heroes, sad. It's pathetic." DiDio provoked another wave of outrage when, in response to a question from a fan at a comics convention, he allegedly intimated that Stephanie Brown deserved her torture and death because she had failed to obey Batman's orders to stay out of the fight with Black Mask.

Simone believes the anger against DiDio may be misdirected: "I'm not against shock and repulsion as story elements at all, in fact. I think comics that are slightly lurid are wonderfully compelling, and my own work regularly contains things that are simply inappropriate for anyone, thank God. And thankfully, Dan is dead serious about more diversity in both the characters and creators. It's not just more good female characters we need—it's more good gay characters, more good Asian characters, more good African-American characters, and on and on."

But the reality isn't so rosy. A former industry employee who maintains a blog at occasionalsuperheroine.blogspot.com recently removed all of her previous posts and replaced them with a twelve-part "Goodbye to Comics," in which she referenced the sexual harassment that had been a daily part of her job until she was driven to resign.

DiDio and other industry honchos might make the right noises about increasing diversity and female audiences, but even in death, Stephanie Brown has been treated unfairly. While another fallen Robin (Jason Todd, now resurrected as Red Hood) was honored with a permanent memorial in the Batcave, no sign of Stephanie's service has been installed. According to Coordinating Editor Jann

Jones, no plans for a memorial are in the works. For the boys: glorious deaths and dramatic returns. For the girls: punishment, torture, and forgotten fates.

Meanwhile, Girl-Wonder.org has expanded to include three regular columnists who keep tabs on the ongoing portrayals of female superheroes in the mainstream and alternative comics; they also recommend comics featuring strong female characters. Academic papers with titles like "The Secret Origins of Jessica Jones: Multiplicity, Irony and a Feminist Perspective on Brian Michael Bendis's *Alias*" or "Wonder Woman: Lesbian or Dyke? Paradise Island as a Woman's Community" are archived on the site. Two independent Web comics are hosted by Girl-Wonder.org, and Borsellino says she'd like to see the support for creators expand: "Someday I'd love to generate the funds to get more female creators to conventions, so their work can be seen by editors, and to perhaps have a Girl-Wonder.org publishing imprint to get titles into stores, even if only in small numbers."

The future will belong to those creators. "We are making strides at DC," Simone affirms. "I write a book with an Asian lead [*The All-New Atom*], another with a nearly all-female cast [*Birds of Prey*], another with a cast of senior citizens [*(Welcome to) Tranquility*], and another with an openly lesbian couple, among others. That would have been almost unimaginable a few years back. We've got a lot to do, but I'm very optimistic and excited to be part of it."

Borsellino is also looking forward to a brighter future for female characters and fans, but she thinks that groups like hers will be necessary to keep the industry in line. "I want Girl-Wonder.org to stand like a watchdog. We're working on forging contacts with media groups, so that the next time DC or Marvel try to do something as sickening as [the arc in which Stephanie Brown was murdered], they'll have to consider that there's this group of very noisy, very angry feminists watching their every move and hitting their speed-dial as they do it."

Both Simone and Borsellino are optimistic about DC's new Batwoman. "I think it could be an amazing book," Simone says. But Borsellino notes that her presence has come with a price. "To get Kate Kane, we lost Cass Cain, Stephanie Brown, and Leslie Thompkins entirely [the latter, though not killed, was exiled to Africa]. Barbara Gordon and Helena Bertinelli were permanently relocated to Metropolis. Onyx has vanished without any follow-up. So that's six female characters—one Asian, one poor, one elderly, one disabled, one Italian, and one black—traded off the team in order to get one rich, white, young, pretty, gay woman."

Hopefully, Batwoman will be strong and capable enough to navigate the streets of Gotham City on her own. But it can't hurt that there's a legion of real-life Girl Wonders to watch her back. We've lost enough of our heroines already.

Gwen then looks at an example of a film review. *(A. O. Scott's review reprinted here from* The New York Times, *May 2, 2008. © 2008 The New York Times. All rights reserved.)*

How do I know this is a **film review**? Do I want to write one?

THE GENRE'S CONVENTIONS

Gwen's notes on Scott's review

Elements of the genre
In a film review, a writer presents an argument about a movie and backs that up by drawing on moments from the film, and even from film history. Here, Scott's lead paragraph gets readers' attention and identifies the genre of the film. In his review Scott makes clear what he thinks of the film.

Style
Scott writes in the third person. His tone is mostly formal but is sometimes informal, e.g., his use of exclamation points and phrases including: "Yeah, that guy." He even addresses the reader as "you." I like that informality a lot.

The New York Times

Movies
Heavy Suit, Light Touches
By A. O. SCOTT

MOVIE REVIEW | 'IRON MAN'
Iron Man (2008)

Zade Rosenthal/Paramount Pictures

Iron Man, based on the Marvel comic and with Robert Downey Jr. as the title character, opens on Friday nationwide. Jon Favreau directed.

The world at the moment does not suffer from a shortage of superheroes. And yet in some ways the glut of anti-evil crusaders with cool costumes and troubled souls takes the pressure off of *Iron Man*, which clanks into theaters today ahead of Hellboy, Batman, and the Incredible Hulk. This summer those guys are all in sequels or redos, so *Iron Man* (a Marvel property not to be confused with the Man of Steel, who belongs to DC and who's taking a break this year) has the advantage of novelty in addition to a seasonal head start.

And *Iron Man*, directed by Jon Favreau (*Elf*, *Zathura*), has the advantage of being an unusually good superhero picture. Or at least—since it certainly has its problems—a superhero movie that's good in unusual ways. The film benefits from a script (credited to Mark Fergus, Hawk Ostby, Art Marcum, and Matt Holloway) that generally chooses clever dialogue over manufactured catchphrases and lumbering exposition, and also from a crackerjack cast that accepts the filmmakers' invitation to do some real acting rather than just flex and glower and shriek for a paycheck.

There's some of that too, of course. The hero must flex and furrow his brow; the bad guy must glower and scheme; the girl must

What is the composer, **A. O. Scott**, doing?

THE RHETORICAL SITUATION

Gwen's notes on Scott's review

Purpose
Scott wants to persuade readers that *Iron Man* is a film to see. He shows readers that it's a "superhero movie that's good in unusual ways." I like that his purpose is extremely clear and that he draws on moments in the film to support his claims.

Audience
As a film critic for *The New York Times*, Scott writes for anyone generally interested in movies. In this case, his audience also consists of people familiar with the Marvel comic, people who like Robert Downey Jr., and people who like imagined worlds. My audience is similar: They are fans of comics and people who like superheroes.

The New York Times

shriek and fret. There should also be a skeptical but supportive friend. Those are the rules of the genre, as unbreakable as the pseudoscientific principles that explain everything (An arc reactor! Of course!) and the Law of the Bald Villain. In *Iron Man* it all plays out more or less as expected, from the trial-and-error building of the costume to the climactic showdown, with lots of flying, chasing and noisemaking in between. (I note that there is one sharp, subversive surprise right at the very end.)

What is less expected is that Mr. Favreau, somewhat in the manner of those sly studio-era craftsmen who kept their artistry close to the vest so the bosses wouldn't confiscate it, wears the genre paradigm as a light cloak rather than a suit of iron. Instead of the tedious, moralizing, pop-Freudian origin story we often get in the first installments of comic-book-franchise movies—childhood trauma; identity crisis; longing for justice versus thirst for revenge; wake me up when the explosions start—*Iron Man* plunges us immediately into a world that crackles with character and incident.

It is not quite the real world, but it's a bit closer than Gotham or Metropolis. We catch up with Tony Stark in dusty Afghanistan, where he is enjoying a Scotch on the rocks in the back of an armored American military vehicle. Tony is a media celebrity, a former M.I.T. whiz kid and the scion of a family whose company makes and sells high-tech weaponry. He's also a bon vivant and an incorrigible playboy. On paper the character is completely preposterous, but since Tony is played by Robert Downey Jr., he's almost immediately as authentic and familiar—as much fun, as much trouble—as your ex-boyfriend or your old college roommate. Yeah, that guy.

Tony's skeptical friend (see above) is Rhodey, an Air Force officer played with good-humored sidekick weariness by Terrence Howard. The girl is one Pepper Potts (Gwyneth Paltrow, also in evident good humor), Tony's smitten, ultracompetent assistant. His partner and sort-of mentor in Stark Enterprises is Obadiah Stane, played by Jeff Bridges with wit and exuberance and—spoiler alert!—a shaved head.

These are all first-rate actors, and Mr. Downey's antic energy and emotional unpredictability bring out their agility and resourcefulness. Within the big, crowded movements of this pop symphony is a series of brilliant duets that sometimes seem to have the swing and spontaneity of jazz improvisation: Mr. Downey and Ms. Paltrow on the dance floor; Mr. Downey and Mr. Howard drinking sake on an airplane; Mr. Downey and Shaun Toub working on blueprints in a cave; Mr. Downey and Mr. Bridges sparring over a box of pizza.

Those moments are what you are likely to remember. The plot is serviceable, which is to say that it's placed at the service of the

Continues next page

The New York Times

actors (and the special-effects artists), who deftly toss it around and sometimes forget it's there. One important twist seems glaringly arbitrary and unmotivated, but this lapse may represent an act of carefree sabotage rather than carelessness. You know this ostensibly shocking revelation is coming, and the writers know you know it's coming, so why worry too much about whether it makes sense? Similarly, the patina of geopolitical relevance is worn thin and eventually discarded, and Tony's crisis of conscience when he discovers what his weapons are being used for is more of a narrative convenience than a real moral theme.

All of which is to say that *Iron Man*, in spite of the heavy encumbrances Tony must wear when he turns into the title character, is distinguished by light touches and grace notes. The hardware is impressive, don't get me wrong, but at these prices it had better be. If you're throwing around a hundred million dollars and you have Batman and the Hulk on your tail, you had better be sure that the arc reactors are in good working order and that the gold-titanium alloy suit gleams like new and flies like a bird.

And everything works pretty well. But even dazzling, computer-aided visual effects, these days, are not so special. And who doesn't have superpowers? Actually, Iron Man doesn't; his heroism is all handicraft, elbow grease and applied intelligence. Those things account for the best parts of *Iron Man* as well.

Iron Man is rated PG-13 (Parents strongly cautioned). It has a lot of action violence, none of it especially graphic or gruesome. Also, Iron Man has sex, and not with the suit on. But not completely naked either.

Opens on Friday nationwide.

Directed by Jon Favreau; written by Mark Fergus, Hawk Ostby, Art Marcum and Matt Holloway based on the character created by Stan Lee, Larry Lieber, Don Heck and Jack Kirby; director of photography, Matthew Libatique; edited by Dan Lebental; music by Ramin Djawadi; production designer, J. Michael Riva; visual effects by John Nelson; produced by Avi Arad and Kevin Feige; released by Paramount Pictures and Marvel Entertainment. Running time: 2 hours 6 minutes.

With: Robert Downey Jr. (Tony Stark), Terrence Howard (Rhodey), Jeff Bridges (Obadiah Stane), Shaun Toub (Yinsen) and Gwyneth Paltrow (Pepper Potts).

Gwen Ganow (Student)

Notes on Final Genre Choice

Now that Gwen has decided she wants to write a film review, she needs to think about that genre in terms of how she'll pull in sources and work with evidence. She does some more brainstorming to think this through.

She wants to figure out how she might work in the research she's done, and what kind of evidence she'll need to draw on to convince readers to agree with her evaluation of whatever film she will review.

 Print Layout View   Sec 1   100%

Gwen Ganow

Genre Choice: Film Review

I like the idea of composing an ad or a researched argument, but
I think that a film review is a genre that my target audience can connect with. Why? Because superheroes are a big part of pop culture and tons of films feature them. I assume that, like me, my comic- and superhero-loving audience sees these films and reads reviews of them.

How will I draw on sources in my genre composition?

Okay, I'm going to write a film review. Now what?

- **What film will I review?** It has to be one about superheroes. Should I choose something contemporary? Or a classic? And once I choose, should I read others' reviews of that film or will those sources just distract me?
- **How will I work with research I've done? What more do I need to find out about?** Once I know what film I'll review, I will need to learn about other works the director, writer, and producer have been involved in. Maybe the actors too. Also, how can I draw on research I've already done? I'm thinking that one of my sources in particular—a book I've read titled *Who Needs a Superhero?* by H. Michael Brewer—could come in handy, in addition to the film itself, which is my main source.
- **What do I know about film reviews?** I may need to do more reading on the film review as a genre. What makes a film review successful? Maybe I should look at more examples. I'll reread the section in Chapter 15 on film reviews and take a closer look at the Roger Ebert example. He's a known and respected reviewer.
- **Do I need to know more about how comics fans think of superhero movies?** Especially when a story is moved from the page to the screen? I might need to do some primary research on this. Maybe I should interview some comics fans.

Gwen's notes on her genre choice

The film review is a genre I know, and a great venue for presenting an argument about superheroes.

I need to choose a superhero film to review. But which one?

I need to read more film reviews—especially those by Roger Ebert.

I need to look back at my other sources—and maybe interview people from my potential audience.

COMPOSING YOUR GENRE PIECE

Remember that "shitty first draft" we mentioned at the beginning of this chapter? Let's circle back to that. It might not look much like an editorial or an investigative journalism piece or whatever genre you've chosen. That's okay. But now that you've followed Gwen to this point, you may have more ideas about what you want to do—and why and how. Hopefully you have a more solid sense of your own rhetorical situation and have focused in on a genre that you want to compose in.

When you do return to your draft, try this: Review the conventions of the genre you've chosen, and start nudging your rough draft into the shape of your chosen genre. For example, if you're writing an editorial, you'll want a pithy first paragraph that makes the issue you're discussing and your position on it clear. If you're composing an ad, step back and think about how visuals could work with your text.

Steps for Composing

You have your topic, your basic ideas, and the genre figured out. Now it's time to start composing in the genre.

Step 1. Write a solid draft.   Review the exploratory rough draft you created earlier in this process and begin fleshing it out so it has a beginning, middle, and end, or whatever elements are appropriate for your chosen genre. It should include, at least in rough form, the main points you want to make, and include some examples or evidence you'll use to support your points.

Working from this draft, follow the steps below to evaluate and revise it.

☞ **Attention, composers! Wondering about media?**

What medium will best suit your genre and rhetorical situation? Will you reach your audiences best through a print or physical medium—or in a digital environment? If you're composing online, will you use audio? How about video or animation? What medium will your primary audience respond to best?

Step 2. Evaluate your use of sources and evidence.   Look at a really good example of the genre you're working in—and compare it to yours. How does that author support claims with evidence? Draw on sources? What kind of evidence will your audience expect and respond to? Will anecdotes and personal stories be convincing to your audience, or will they be more convinced by statistics and references to peer-reviewed studies?

Note: Refer to the sample of your genre as you complete steps 3–7.

Step 3. Confirm the scope of information to provide.   How much coverage of the topic is appropriate for the genre you've selected? Examine the sample of the genre you're comparing your draft to. Does it present an overview of the subject? What is the level of detail?

Step 4. Consider your use of style.   Think about voice, tone, language, and point of view. Is the genre you're composing in characterized by the use of first or third person? How explicit and present will your voice and experience be in the piece? Look at the example you're comparing your piece to. Does that composer use an objective, authoritative tone, or a personal, subjective tone, or something else?

Step 5. Look at how you use rhetorical appeals. Look at your draft and the sample genre piece you're consulting. To what extent does the other author use ethos, pathos, and/or logos? How effective is his/her approach, and what might you want to adapt for your own work?

Step 6. Look at your organization. How have you organized your content? Is this the best way, considering who your audience is and what you're trying to achieve? Is it logical? Persuasive? Does the sample you're consulting have anything to offer you in terms of a model for improving your work?

Step 7. Consider your mix of words and images. This is also a moment to think about design and medium. Are you being as effective as you could be? Again, consult your example.

Step 8. Make a list of what you want to work on when you revise. Base your list on what you've determined in steps 2–7.

Step 9. Revise your draft based on your revision list. After you've revised, reread your work and make notes to address things you want to improve for the next draft.

Step 10. Revise a little more. Get your work in the best shape you can in the time you have.

☞ **Attention, composers! A word on design.**

What are the design features of the genre you're composing in? How will you use design? Consider:

Layout. In your genre, how are elements typically arranged spatially? How are visuals presented? How will your layout help readers/viewers quickly orient themselves?

Color. How can you use color to guide your audience's attention? What colors are often associated with your genre? For example, many ads are designed with bright colors.

Chunking and fonts (if you're working with text). Will it be best to present information in short paragraphs organized under headings? Or are you going to do something else? How can a font help you achieve your purpose and reach your audience? What fonts are associated with your genre? For example, Times New Roman works in newspapers; sans serif fonts work well in a digital environment.

Context. Is the design you have in mind appropriate, considering when and where and how your audience will encounter the piece?

Guided Process:
How to Compose a Genre Piece ▼

▲ STUDENT AUTHOR
PHOTO
Gwen Ganow

Gwen Ganow (Student)

Superhero Project: Film Review Draft 1

Gwen has a clear sense of her genre—as well as her rhetorical situation. She now gets down to writing. In the following section, she writes a first draft of her film review. She then spends time evaluating it—reading it against a published film review—to see how she might improve her own. In this process, she reviews her work for how well she deals with purpose, audience, and other rhetorical concerns, as well as how well she works in the genre of the film review itself. After this process, she revises her work, creating a second and third draft.

**Gwen's notes on
her film review**

I decided to review
the film *X-Men*—
it's a significant
film in the super-
hero genre that my
audience will be
familiar with. This
is my first attempt
at a draft.

≡ ≔ ▣ ▤ ▥ ▣   Print Layout View   Sec 1   100% ──○──

Gwen Ganow

Film Review Draft 1

DRAFT 1

X-Men

The punctuated equilibrium concept of Niles Eldredge and Stephen Jay Gould states that evolution and speciation occur at a rapid rate followed by long periods of stasis. The film *X-Men* explores how a modern American society would react to its own punctuated equilibrium in which a new, superhuman species rises and suddenly integrates with "normal" humans. Through the events and emotions of the movie *X-Men*, our past and current social issues of prejudice and intolerance as an American society become exposed.

X-Men opens with a powerful image of prejudice and intolerance, a Nazi concentration camp. While unloading a new trainload of Jews, Nazi soldiers rip a young boy from the arms of his parents. He sits in the rain crying and watches helplessly as his parents are herded off to other buildings. His yellow Star of David, his label of difference, is the only color against the dismal backdrop of rain, mud, and hate. The young boy survives his Nazi captors and grows up to be a mutant with the power to move and control metal.

The movie leaves the scene of war and enters the chambers of Congress where a Senate committee hearing is taking place. Magneto attends this committee hearing of the Senate because he is curious about what the American government is doing about the so-called "mutant problem" in the United States. Senator Kelly, a staunch supporter of the Mutant Registration Act, is debated by Dr. Jean Grey (a mutant herself). Jean Grey argues against the Mutant Registration Act and says, "Mutants who have revealed themselves publicly have been met with fear, hostility, and violence." To this, Senator Kelly responds with the questions, "Are they dangerous? Do you want your children in school with mutants? Do you want your children to be taught by mutant teachers?"

Ganow, *Film Review Draft 1,* *Continued*

To shield the younger generation from the violence created by the words of intolerance spoken by Senator Kelly, Charles Xavier (a mutant with powerful psychic abilities) creates Xavier's School for Gifted Youngsters and makes it a place for young mutants who have recently discovered that they are very different from their peers and have run away from home. Here he offers these young men and women a place of refuge and sense of inclusiveness. This is a safe environment where they can be taught how to control their developing minds and powers by some of Xavier's finest past students like Storm, Cyclops, and Jean Grey, who become mentors to a new generation of young mutants, afraid of the world around them. Charles Xavier never gives up hope that humanity will come to realize the error of their judgment. He teaches his students that intolerance should not be returned with even more intolerance.

Magneto's view of humanity is radically different from the views of Charles Xavier. Magneto sees nothing wrong with trying to solve the plight of mutants by using violence and fear against humans. He devises a plan using his own powers combined with a radiation-generating machine to change non-mutants into mutants. By doing this, he feels that vengeance will be carried out by putting would-be persecutors into the lives of the people they sought to persecute and chooses Senator Kelly as his first test subject. Magneto tells the senator, "Humankind has always feared what it doesn't understand. You have nothing to fear from God and nothing to fear from me. Not anymore."

The fear, intolerance, and violence toward mutants that is conveyed in *X-Men* closely ties in with the fear, intolerance, and violence endured by the GLBT community today. Sometimes, the reality of the comic book universe resembles our own reality more than we would like to admit. The movie *X-Men* questions whether we as Americans really believe in freedom for all or whether we really mean freedom for some.

Gwen Ganow

Superhero Project: Evaluation of Film Review Draft 1

Next, Gwen evaluates her film review by comparing it to an excellent example of the genre: A. O. Scott's review *"Iron Man*: Heavy Suit, Light Touches," which she looked at earlier. She evaluates Scott's use of evidence and sources, his scope and use of rhetorical appeals, and his organization and use of visuals. Then she applies this lens to her own review. *(A. O. Scott's review reprinted here from* The New York Times, *May 2, 2008.* © 2008 The New York Times. *All rights reserved.)*

Gwen's notes on Scott's review

Scott's use of evidence & sources

Scott contextualizes *Iron Man* with other movies of the same genre. He also refers to the director, his other films, and the scriptwriters.

He gives lots of plot details but never gives the story away. He supports each claim with brief snippets from the plot. E.g., when he talks about the "brilliant duets" (paragraph 7), he backs that up with evidence from specific scenes.

Scott's scope

Scott's scope is in line with his purpose: to evaluate the film overall—to make an argument in favor of it. He chooses key details about characters and from specific scenes to support his claims and overall case.

He summarizes quite a bit: He offers just a snapshot of the plot by providing setting, character descriptions, and parts of the story.

The New York Times

Movies

Heavy Suit, Light Touches

By A. O. SCOTT

MOVIE REVIEW | 'IRON MAN'
Iron Man (2008)

Iron Man, based on the Marvel comic and with Robert Downey Jr. as the title character, opens on Friday nationwide. Jon Favreau directed.

The world at the moment does not suffer from a shortage of superheroes. And yet in some ways the glut of anti-evil crusaders with cool costumes and troubled souls takes the pressure off of *Iron Man*, which clanks into theaters today ahead of Hellboy, Batman, and the Incredible Hulk. This summer those guys are all in sequels or redos, so *Iron Man* (a Marvel property not to be confused with the Man of Steel, who belongs to DC and who's taking a break this year) has the advantage of novelty in addition to a seasonal head start.

Print Layout View   Sec 1   100%

Gwen Ganow

Film Review Draft 1

DRAFT 1

X-Men

The punctuated equilibrium concept of Niles Eldredge and Stephen Jay Gould states that evolution and speciation occur at a rapid rate followed by long periods of stasis. The film *X-Men* explores how a modern American society would react to its own punctuated equilibrium in which a new, superhuman species rises and suddenly integrates with "normal" humans. Through the events and emotions of the movie *X-Men*, our past and current social issues of prejudice and intolerance as an American society become exposed.

Gwen's notes on her own review

My use of evidence & sources

In my own review, I contextualize *X-Men* in terms of the theory of "punctuated equilibrium" (and cite Eldredge and Gould as my source).

I support my claims about the "powerful image of prejudice and intolerance" (paragraph 2) with plot details and specifics from a scene.

Like Scott, the evidence I use to support my argument includes details from the plot and other aspects of the film and its creators.

My scope

I go into way more detail than Scott does, maybe because I am retelling the plot chronologically. Is this a problem? Do I need to pull back from some of my details to give more summary? Should I choose my details more carefully?

Ganow, *Film Review Draft 1,* Continued

Gwen's notes on Scott's review

Gwen's notes on Scott's review

Scott makes broad statements when he delivers snappy and fun one-liners. E.g., in his line "The hero must flex and furrow his brow," Scott makes a generalization about action movies.

Scott's style

I like Scott's writing style. It's almost as if I can hear him speaking, especially in lines such as: "The hero must flex and furrow his brow; the bad guy must glower and scheme; the girl must shriek and fret."

He chooses each word carefully and keeps his language varied and interesting. E.g., he uses a variety of terms (*film*, *picture*) to refer to the movie.

Scott writes in the third person, but I like how he sometimes invites the reader in by using the word *we*.

X-Men opens with a powerful image of prejudice and intolerance, a Nazi concentration camp. While unloading a new trainload of Jews, Nazi soldiers rip a young boy from the arms of his parents. He sits in the rain crying and watches helplessly as his parents are herded off to other buildings. His yellow Star of David, his label of difference, is the only color against the dismal backdrop of rain, mud, and hate. The young boy survives his Nazi captors and grows up to be a mutant with the power to move and control metal.

The movie leaves the scene of war and enters the chambers of Congress where a Senate committee hearing is taking place. Magneto attends this committee hearing of the Senate because he is curious about what the American government is doing about the so-called "mutant problem" in the United States. Senator Kelly, a staunch supporter of the Mutant Registration Act, is debated by Dr. Jean Grey (a mutant herself). Jean Grey argues against the Mutant Registration Act and says, "Mutants who have revealed themselves publicly have been met with fear, hostility, and violence." To this, Senator Kelly responds with the questions, "Are they dangerous? Do you want your children in school with mutants? Do you want your children to be taught by mutant teachers?"

To shield the younger generation from the violence created by the words of intolerance spoken by Senator Kelly, Charles Xavier (a mutant with powerful psychic abilities) creates Xavier's School for Gifted Youngsters and makes it a place for young mutants who have recently discovered that they are very different from their peers and have run away from home. Here he offers these young men and women a place of refuge and sense of inclusiveness. This is a safe environment where they can be taught how to control their developing minds and powers by some of Xavier's finest past students like Storm, Cyclops, and Jean Grey, who become mentors to a new generation of young mutants, afraid of the world around them. Charles Xavier never gives up hope that humanity will come to realize the error of their judgment. He teaches his students that intolerance should not be returned with even more intolerance.

Gwen's notes on her own review

My style

I'm not sure my voice comes through enough in my review. I think I sound knowledgeable, but I'm not so sure how present I am in the writing in terms of voice, personality, or humor.

My review does not seem as personal or subjective as Scott's. I think my perspective is more objective. Is that a strong point? Or a problem?

My use of rhetorical appeals

I want to establish myself as a kind of expert on superheroes and film. I like how Dwight Decker established his ethos in his researched essay. I'm modeling my language on his. Is it right for a film review? I'm not sure how well I've conveyed my ethos. I also need to persuade my audience, so I need to appeal to pathos.

Gwen's notes on Scott's review

Scott's use of rhetorical appeals

Scott builds his ethos by drawing on evidence and by crediting the film's creators. He also makes it clear that he is very qualified to write about superhero action flicks.

He also appeals to readers through pathos. He entices readers to go see *Iron Man* through his language and tone.

Scott's organization

Scott begins with general comments about superheroes and the popularity of superhero movies before he moves onto *Iron Man*.

Next, he situates the film within its genre, hinting at his opinion of the movie. He outlines some of his expectations.

He makes claims that he supports with details of the plot and characters; he closes with a final evaluation of the film.

Scott's use of visuals

He includes a few visuals. The large still featuring Robert Downey Jr., who plays the lead, is pretty striking. There is also a small picture further into the review.

Gwen's notes on her own review

My organization

I move through the plot, giving readers a general sense of the story.

I don't discuss the film in terms of a broader context. Should I? I'm also not sure I present my argument clearly enough. I think I need to be more direct.

My use of visuals

I haven't yet incorporated any images/film stills into my review, but I need to. Which characters/key scenes do I want to show? Why?

What to focus on when I revise

Revise/reorganize the review so it isn't just a chronological plot summary. Will be challenging. Maybe I should think about the main points I want to make, and then choose supporting details from the plot as needed, much as Scott does.

Establish a clearer sense of voice. Also, should I worry about the shift from third to first person? How much personality can I inject into my review?

Make sure I'm giving a clear evaluation of the film. I need my argument about the film to be stronger. Is it worth seeing? Why or why not? Also, I want readers to see the dilemma of the hero as related to that of the GLBT community.

Do more to establish ethos and appeal to readers' emotions.

Pay more attention to language. For example, don't just use the word *movie* throughout.

Incorporate visuals—also maybe embed video.

Gwen Ganow (Student)

Superhero Project: Film Review Draft 2

Gwen returns now to her draft and begins to rework it, based on her evaluation of it, her comparison of it to the A. O. Scott review, and her list of what to focus on when she revises.

Gwen Ganow

Film Review Draft 2

X-Men: Mutants R Us

As a "hard-core" comic book fan, I always considered the 2000 *X-Men* film the epitome of a true comic book movie. What sets the *X-Men* apart from other comic book films is that the story behind the X-Men is not overshadowed by special effects. In *X-Men*, equilibrium is punctured; humans face a sudden and dramatic evolutionary change, one that results in the existence of "mutants." The mutants are humans with superhuman powers, who look human enough to integrate invisibly into society. The movie explores how American society might react to the existence of these mutants, exposing our past and current social issues of prejudice and intolerance. Bryan Singer, best known for 1995's *The Usual Suspects*, directs from the screenplay written by David Hayter.

Created by Stan Lee and Jack Kirby in 1963, X-Men are children of parents who were exposed to atmospheric radiation and became genetically altered. The mutant kids are outsiders in the world, and are envied and feared by "normal" humans. The alienation of the X-Men is similar to that of other groups of people who have experienced prejudice, like African Americans, Jews, Japanese, and homosexuals. Singer makes this parallel explicit with the opening scene.

X-Men opens with a powerful image of prejudice and intolerance, a Nazi concentration camp. While unloading a new trainload of Jews, Nazi soldiers rip a young boy from the arms of his parents. He sits in the rain crying and watches helplessly as his parents are herded off to other buildings. His yellow Star of David is the only color against the dismal backdrop of rain, mud, and hate. The young boy survives his Nazi captors and grows up to be a mutant known as Magneto with the power to move and control metal.

The movie leaves the scene of war and enters the chambers of Congress where a Senate committee hearing is taking place on the Mutant Registration Act, which would require mutants to register with the government and list their special abilities, making it impossible for them to blend in unnoticed with the rest of society. Magneto, played by Ian McKellen, attends this committee hearing because he is curious about what the American government is doing about the so-called "mutant problem." Senator Kelly, played by Bruce Davison, a staunch supporter of the Mutant Registration Act, is debated by Dr. Jean Grey, a mutant herself, played by Famke Janssen. Kelly supports the Mutant

Continues next page

Gwen's comments on her film review

Overall, I've done a better job evaluating the film and making an argument about it. It's clear what I think of the movie and why.

This draft is more interesting and readable. I've done more to appeal to my audience of superhero/comic lovers. For example, my first sentence and paragraph are aimed at drawing them in.

My writing still seems stiff in places. I want to make the style and tone a little more casual; also, I want to tighten up the wording and do more to make this flow.

Ganow, *Film Review Draft 2*, Continued

Gwen's comments on her film review

This doesn't look like a film review yet. I'll need to apply design principles and add at least one image. Maybe some links, too. If this is going to be delivered digitally, I should take advantage of hyperlinking.

| ☰ | ⋮ | ▤ | ▤ | ▤ | ▣ | Print Layout View | | Sec 1 | | | 100% | ⊙ |

Registration Act, believing that mutants are a danger to "normal" humans and should be locked away, while Grey argues that forcing mutants to register would create the potential for them to be treated as freaks.

The performers share good chemistry, with Hugh Jackman's Wolverine's and James Marsden's Cyclops's one-upmanship bringing humor to their scenes. Patrick Stewart's Charles Xavier seems both fatherly and professorial, and Anna Paquin as Rogue does a fine job conveying fear about her future as a mutant and lovesickness over Wolverine. Rebecca Romijn makes an impression in a role that relies more on physical presence than lines.

In *X-Men*, responses to prejudice by the victims of prejudice are explored through the actions of two important mutants, both leaders of mutant groups. Charles Xavier, a mutant with powerful psychic abilities, creates a school for the gifted for young runaway mutants. Here he offers these young men and women a place of refuge and a sense of inclusiveness. This is a safe environment where they can be taught how to control their developing minds and powers by some of Xavier's finest past students like Storm, Cyclops, and Jean Grey, who become mentors to a new generation of young mutants, afraid of the world around them. Xavier's "turn the other cheek" philosophy links him to the Jesus Christ of the Christian culture. The fact that Charles Xavier provides a safe house for people rejected by humanity also links him to our real-life organizations like NAACP, GLBT (gay, lesbian, bisexual, and transgender) resource centers, and some of our churches.

The other leader is Magneto, who fronts the Brotherhood of Mutants. Magneto's perspective on humanity stems from his experiences as a young boy at a WWII concentration camp, which was captured in the film's opening scene. This experience left Magneto distrustful of humanity and convinced that mutants are bound to suffer the same fate met by the inmates of the Nazi death camps. To preserve the survival of his mutant species, Magneto declares war on humankind. Magneto's view of humanity is radically different from the views of Charles Xavier. Magneto sees nothing wrong with trying to solve the plight of mutants by using violence and fear against humans.

Although the film is worth seeing for the performances and direction alone, the special effects, while relatively low-key for a superhero movie, are stunning. Magneto's spinning contraption, the fight scenes, and Storm's weather conjuring add to the fun. Finally, while there is seldom a clear right and wrong in real life, Singer's film makes it easy for us to take the right side. The heroes of the film are clearly Professor Xavier's X-Men. In this way, Singer allows us to imagine the consequences of violence and anger, as shown by Magneto's band of mutants, and ultimately root for Xavier's more tolerant gang.

Gwen Ganow (Student)

Superhero Project: Film Review Final

Gwen revises some more: this time with plenty of attention to design, images, and embedded links. She also polishes her writing, and continues to evaluate her choice of mode and medium, with thoughts of future iterations of her project. Below is an excerpt from her final review.

| ≡ ≡ ◫ ≡ ≡ ◲ | Print Layout View | Sec 1 | 100% | ⊙ |

Gwen Ganow

Film Review Final

FINAL

X-Men: Mutants R Us

As a "hard-core" comic book fan, I always considered the 2000 *X-Men* film the epitome of a true comic book movie. What sets the *X-Men* apart from other comic book films is that the story behind the X-Men is not overshadowed by special effects. In *X-Men*, it's the story that matters. In the world of this film, the equilibrium of existence has been punctured; humans face a sudden and dramatic evolutionary change, one that results in the existence of "mutants." The mutants are humans with superhuman powers, who look human enough to integrate invisibly into society. The movie explores how American society might react to the existence of these mutants, exposing our past and current social issues of prejudice and intolerance.

Bryan Singer, best known for 1995's *The Usual Suspects*, directs from the screenplay written by David Hayter. . . .

The performers share good chemistry, with Hugh Jackman's Wolverine's and James Marsden's Cyclops's one-upmanship bringing humor to their scenes. Patrick Stewart's Charles Xavier seems both fatherly and professorial, and Anna Paquin as Rogue does a fine job.

Hugh ▶
Jackman as
Wolverine,
from *X-Men*
(2000).
*Everett
Collection.*

Gwen's notes on her film review

My writing is a little smoother now and flows better.

I've decided that I want to deliver my film review digitally. I'm taking advantage of digital tools, including embedded links. E.g., I've added a link to the film trailer at Amazon, which illustrates the points I make in paragraph 1, and included another link to the director's bio at IMDb. I like the digital format, too, because I can give readers the option to comment on my work and to share it on social media.

As for future versions of this material, I'd consider an audio podcast. Podcasts give a clear sense of the writer's voice, views, and personality, something I'm striving for.

COMPOSING AN ACCOMPANYING AUTHOR'S OR ARTIST'S STATEMENT

What is an Author's or Artist's Statement? It's a piece of reflective and persuasive writing in which you explain the choices you made in a separate composition. Artists, filmmakers, novelists, and other composers commonly write statements of the intentions, processes, and inspirations behind a particular work or body of work. In this case, we're talking specifically about the Statement that you can write to accompany the genre piece you've created.

Advice for Composing Your Statement

Your Statement is a critical analysis of what you did and why, how successful you think you were, what you might have done differently, and any plans you may have for further revision—or even of repurposing the project for something else. If your genre piece is not ultimately as successful as you'd hoped, consider the Statement a chance to explore what didn't work and what you might do differently next time. The Statement is an opportunity to explain to your audience (particularly your peer and instructor audience) such specifics as why you chose your genre, what your rhetorical purposes were, how you wanted to affect your audience, and how your research informed your composition.

If your instructor asks you to write such an accompanying Statement, approach the drafting of it just as you would for any persuasive writing that brings in sources. Refer to the pieces you worked with along the way when composing your genre piece: Draw on any brainstorm lists, notes, and revisions of drafts. This will help you reconstruct your process and remember the choices you've made. Just as with any other composition, you'll want to get reader feedback and revise. (For more on Author's and Artist's Statements, see pp. 503–16.)

Following are instructions that we give our students for creating their Statements. Note: This is the assignment that Gwen will respond to on pages 698–99.

> **ENG 101, Professor Braziller**
>
> **Assignment: Compose an Author's or Artist's Statement**
>
> For this course, every genre piece you create must be accompanied by an Artist's or Author's Statement. In that document, please explain:
>
> - **The rhetorical choices you made as you composed your genre piece.**
>   Define your purpose, audience, and how you wished to affect your audience.

Please also cover your use of rhetorical appeals, and the mode and medium you chose to work in.

- **How you worked within (or broke out of) genre conventions.**
  Discuss the elements that define the genre most typically, and how you responded to those in your composition. Discuss your style (written and other), your use of design, and how you drew on sources. In fact, as you write, please draw on sources and cite them in the text of your paper and in a list at the end.

Note: Your Statement should be documented in MLA or APA style. Within the text of your Statement, please draw on specific sources that informed your composition. Include *both* in-text citations and a list of Works Cited or References at the end of your Statement. Remember, you're reflecting on your process—and persuading your readers that you made thoughtful choices. Maybe your choices weren't all perfect, but that's okay. This is your chance to explain your intentions.

Use these questions to guide your Statement.

Rhetorical choices

- What was your purpose? For example, did you set out to tell a story, report information, or present a persuasive argument? Or some combination? How well do you think you achieved your purpose? What, if anything, might you have done differently?

- Who was your intended primary audience? Secondary audience? Why? Characterize the people in each group. What are their assumptions and expectations about your topic? How did you speak to these audiences? What message did you want them to take away from your composition? For example, did you want them to take a specific action?

- Did you use one or more of the rhetorical appeals (ethos, logos, pathos), and how effective were you in reaching your audience through the appeals?

- How and why did you choose the mode and medium you decided on? What are the advantages to these choices? How might you alter your choices in future iterations of the project?

Genre conventions

- Why did you choose the genre you did? What elements of the genre interested you most? How did you use or subvert the conventions of the genre?

- What choices did you make in terms of style (including organization, language, voice, and tone)? What did you consider in making these choices?

- Evaluate your design. Why did you choose to work with text, images, video, and audio (and any other elements) as you did? How effective do you think you were? What might you have done differently if you had had more time?

- What sources did you draw on for this piece? How did you decide which sources were right for you? How did you integrate them into your composition? Did you cite them according to the conventions of your genre?

Guided Process: How to Compose an Author's Statement ▼

Gwen Ganow (Student)

Superhero Project: Author's Statement Draft 1

Following is Gwen's first draft of her Statement to accompany her film review.

**Gwen's notes
on her Author's
Statement**

My purpose
Do I convey clearly
and persuasively
enough why I
chose to write a
film review? Not
sure. Also, should I
comment more on
process? And what
might I have done
differently or better?

My audience
Have I succeeded
in explaining my
choices to readers?

**My use of rhetorical
appeals**
I focused on using
pathos and logos.
Have I emphasized
one over the other?
Is that a good idea?

**My choice of and
use of modes &
media**
I should talk more
directly about
modes and media.
I'll ask my instruc-
tor about this.

≡ ≣ 🗔 ≡ ≣ 🗔	Print Layout View	Sec 1		100% ◁ ─○─ ▷

Gwen Ganow

DRAFT 1

Author's Statement Draft 1

Why I Wrote a Film Review of *X-Men*

There are two reasons I chose to write a film review. As a "hard-core" comic book fan, I always considered *X-Men* as a good example of what a true comic book movie should be. What sets the movie apart from other comic book mov-ies is that the story behind *X-Men* is not overshadowed by special effects. The second reason I chose to do a film review was to show another perspective on how comic books are interrelated with our modern culture. Superheroes, heroes, antiheroes, and villains don't just come to us through the pop culture pages of a comic book. They have also expanded their influence to include the American silver screen. The stories of these comic book characters are now told by our Hollywood actors and actresses.

Created by Stan Lee and Jack Kirby in 1963, the X-Men are the children of humans who were exposed to atmospheric radiation and became genetically altered. These children are born with "differences" and become outsiders in a world that considers them mutants. Even though they do not show any outward signs of difference, their extrahuman powers evoke the envy and fear of ordinary people (Brewer 134). We can link the alienation of the X-Men to groups of people who have gone through their own form of prejudice in real life. African Americans, Jews, Japanese, and homosexuals have all endured the pain of living in an American society that is quick to respond in fear to someone who may be different from the norm.

In *X-Men*, solutions to the problems of prejudice are explored through the actions of two important mutants. Both of these men are leaders, one being the leader of the X-Men, the other the leader of the Brotherhood of Mutants. Charles Xavier creates a school for the gifted for young ostracized mutants. He teaches his mutant students to use their powers to benefit humanity, even if that same humanity hated and distrusted them (Brewer 142). Xavier's "turn the other cheek" philosophy links him to the Jesus Christ of Christian culture. The fact that Xavier provides a safe house for people rejected by humanity also links him to our real life organizations like NAACP, GLBT resource cen-ters, and some of our churches.

Magneto's perspective on humanity stems from his experiences as a young boy at a WWII concentration camp. This experience left Magneto distrustful of humanity, and he is convinced that mutants are bound to suffer the same

---

Ganow, *Author's Statement Draft 1*, *Continued*

fate met by the inmates of the Nazi death camps (Brewer 143). To preserve the survival of his mutant species, Magneto declares war on humankind. We can link the thoughts and actions of Magneto to our own real-world thoughts and actions. We, as humans, have always wanted to put our persecutors into the shoes and lives of the persecuted. If we were given the technology to right the wrongs against us, would we create a machine similar to Magneto's? As humans, why are we quick to return violence with more violence?

Overall, I wanted my readers to see my passion for the subject. I wanted to persuade them, using pathos, to understand that you could read the film as a larger statement on the intolerance GLBT people often face. One of the ways I achieved this was by relying on logos, helping my readers follow the film logically, using strategies employed in other film reviews, such as giving snippets of the plot and using some of the plot summary to highlight the film's strength.

I studied several film reviews to help me figure out how to best create my review. One of the things that was missing from my initial draft was placing the film in a broader context. Thus, in my revision I began the review by discussing my relationship to comics (even if briefly) and then moved on to the film itself. I also incorporated the theory of punctuated equilibrium to help establish my ethos; I know about the theory because of my zoology/biology major. Another thing I wanted to make sure to achieve in the film review was a clear evaluation of the film. My earlier draft did not really make this clear; it primarily consisted of a retelling of some of the plot. In the revision I made sure to include this, not only in the close of the review but with some word choices in the review, such as "powerful image," "good chemistry," and "fine job."

When comic book fans or superhero film fans finish reading my review, I hope that they will see that *X-Men* is definitely an appealing film. More importantly, though, I want my audience to realize that lessons about ourselves can be learned through the story of the X-Men. By witnessing and learning from the actions of a misguided mutant like Magneto, humankind can learn how to be more understanding and tolerant—like Charles Xavier.

Works Cited

Brewer, H. Michael. *Who Needs a Superhero? Finding Virtue, Vice, and What's Holy in the Comics.* Grand Rapids: Baker Books, 2004. Print.
X-Men. Dir. Bryan Singer. Perf. Hugh Jackman, Ian McKellen, and Patrick Stewart. Marvel Studios, 2000. Film.

From this point, Gwen will discuss the draft with her classmates and instructor, and revise her Statement.

Gwen's notes on her Author's Statement

My use of sources
My instructor has asked me to use MLA-style citation in this Statement. I've supported my claims with evidence, but need to double-check my in-text citations in the next draft.

Should I include images in my Statement, too? Would that help me make my case?

After reading Gwen's Statement and considering her purposes, do you think she made a good choice of genre? Why or why not? Has she observed all the conventions of film reviews? Has she ignored any? What are the effects of her choices? #Analyze #Evaluate

If you were Gwen, what would be your main goals in revising this draft Statement? #Evaluate

DESIGNING YOUR PROJECT

As you saw with Gwen's project, composing a multimodal artifact involves complex processes of development. Drafting, seeking feedback, and revising are crucial to creating a project that responds to your rhetorical situation and best fits your audience. But how do you create drafts for a multimodal project that you can evaluate with others? This section describes two different strategies that will work with a variety of projects: mock-ups and storyboards. Consider how these two strategies might be added to your existing drafting processes to help you plan an effective multimodal project.

A **mock-up** is a rough layout of a screen or page. It is most commonly used for drafting Web sites, but it can also be used for drafting any type of still composition that is primarily visual, such as a poster, an album cover, a brochure, or an instruction set.

A **storyboard** is a sequence of drawings, much like a comic book or visual outline, that represents the movement, spatial arrangement, and soundtracks of objects or characters in shots, screens, or scenes. Storyboards work best for projects that include a timeline, such as videos, audio pieces, or animations.

Mock-Ups

Essentially, a mock-up is an outline of a visual project. A good mock-up should include the proposed layout, colors, images, fonts, and recurring elements such as headers. Though mock-ups may include the actual textual content, often they do not. The idea is to create a kind of road map that shows where everything will eventually go, not to actually create the finished product. Web authors often compose mock-ups by hand, on paper, or in some type of screen-based software such as Photoshop. You can also create mock-ups using word processors, spreadsheets, or slideshow software. It's not so much how you create the mock-up that's important as it is *what* the mock-up illustrates.

Figure 18.1 shows a professional Web design mock-up for The Kitchen Sync, a boutique kitchen supply store located in Wenatchee, Washington. The clients (the owners of the store) wanted a Web site that would help advertise their store by providing a professional boutique feel while also showcasing the different products the store had to offer. The main goal was to get people to visit the store itself. While the clients had some ideas about what they wanted the site to look like, the Web designer wanted to show them a rough layout with a few different color and image options. Notice that on the left-hand side of this mock-up you see possible colors, textures, and images. On the right-hand side you see possible headings and buttons.

◀ FIGURE 18.1
**A Mock-Up Design for
The Kitchen Sync**
This Web site mock-up
shows how the basic
features of the proposed
site will look and offers
different color options.

Mock-ups will also let you know where you might need to make adjustments *before* you put lots of time and effort into building your project. As writer/designers, we often find that our first ideas about how to arrange elements need tweaking, and they sometimes don't work at all. By first sketching out really rough layouts and then revising and making changes, we ultimately save ourselves time and create more successful designs.

The mock-up of a veterinary hospital Web site in Figure 18.2 shows where the main content on each page of this site will be (where the picture and caption are now) as well as how the navigation will work within the drop-down menus at top and along the left-hand side.

Mock-Up Guidelines   Here are some questions to consider as you design a mock-up:

» Is the proposed layout evident? Is it consistent across all possible iterations (pages) of the text? If the layout needs to change to indicate different sections or areas of a text, are those variations indicated in separate or supplementary mock-ups?

» Is the color scheme clearly indicated? Is it appropriate for the rhetorical situation and for readability?

FIGURE 18.2 ▶
**Tapiola Veterinary
Hospital Web Site
Mock-Up**

Tapiola Veterinary Hospital

About Us	Forms	Services	Contact Us	Pet Care Info
Veterinarians *Philosophy* *History* *Staff* *Map to Clinic*	*New Client* *Boarding* *Dental* *Sedation* *Pain Meds*	*Vaccinations* *Surgery*	*Address* *Email* *Phone* *Hours*	*AKC* *Annual Exam* *Puppy* *Kitten* *Senior Cat* *Senior Dog* *Winter* *Summer*

Routine Prevention

Surgical Care

Microchip

Flea, Tick,

Heartworm

Pet Pharmacy

Laboratory

Client Education

Practice Philosophy

Service

Forms

Contact Us

We at Tapiola Veterinary Hospital are
committed to providing you and your pet with
the best possible care.

Taking into consideration the rhetorical situation for The Kitchen Sync mock-up in Figure 18.1, use the Mock-Up Guidelines to determine whether that mock-up is effective. Then compare it to the actual Kitchen Sync Web site at http://thekitchen-sync.com. Did the stakeholders make the same choices you would have made? #Understand #Evaluate

» If images are used, is their relative placement on the page or screen mock-up purposeful and consistent across all versions?

» Are example fonts provided, and if so, do they adequately reflect the rhetorical needs of the text (e.g., did you use display type for headlines and body type for larger amounts of written content)?

» Are the navigational elements shown or indicated? Are they clear for users? Are they consistent across all iterations?

Storyboards

Unlike a mock-up, which represents a static text, a storyboard represents a text that moves through time, such as a video or an animation. Like mock-ups, storyboards may include rough visuals, but they use visuals to show the sequence of the text, as well as written descriptions of the actions or sound effects that need to take place at each moment. Storyboards can be incredibly complex but a simple storyboard consisting only of stick figures and a few arrows to show directionality can also be surprisingly effective. As with mock-ups, the important thing is not how artistic the storyboards are but that they indicate what elements (im-

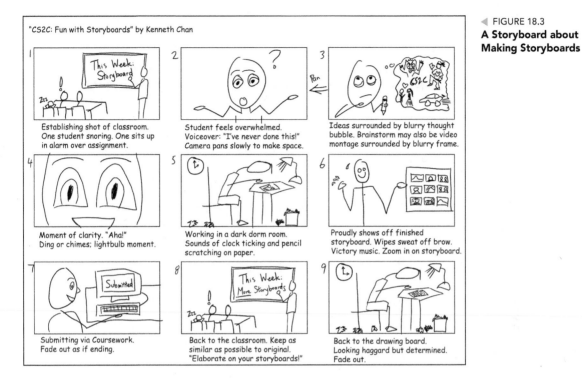

ages, audio) and actions (movement, lighting, camera angle, etc.) need to occur at which point.

The goal of an effective storyboard, no matter its level of complexity, is to capture as much information as possible and help you decide what shots you'll need to film, what audio you'll need to record, or what images you'll need to capture *before* the filming, recording, or animating begins. Similar to a mock-up, a storyboard can also help you get feedback on your basic design so that you can adjust it if it isn't working for your audience.

When creating your storyboard, you'll want to think about including notes on the following elements:

» Setting

» Movement by characters or objects

» Script/dialogue

» Soundtrack or sound effects

» Shooting angle

Of course, depending on the genre of your project, you may want to make notes on other elements as well.

For instance, Courteney was creating a three-minute video-based analysis on effective action films and had 64 panels in her storyboard. Figure 18.4 is a small segment of Courteney's entire storyboard. You can see that you don't need to be an amazing artist to compose an effective storyboard; you just need to include enough detail so that your audience or instructor can figure out what you intend to do and give you feedback on it, and so that you have an outline to work with once you do start capturing your content.

FIGURE 18.4 ▶
**The First Six Panels
of Courteney's
Storyboard**
These panels show
her introduction of
the topic (Panel 1),
the beginning of her
narrative-based analy-
sis (Panels 2–3, in
Courteney's bedroom),
and the main char-
acters in the analysis
(Panels 4–6, Courteney
and her "muse").

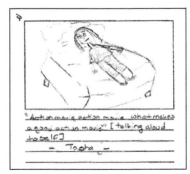

▲ FIGURE 18.5
**Courteney's Drawing of Herself in
Bed (Panel 2 of 64)**

▲ FIGURE 18.6
Courteney's Video of That Scene

▲ FIGURE 18.7
**Courteney's Drawn Introduction of
Her "Muse" (Panel 6 of 64)**

▲ FIGURE 18.8
Courteney's Muse as She Appears in the Video

Storyboard Guidelines   Here are some questions to consider as you design a
storyboard:

» Is the initial setting or context clearly evident? How is each setting or segment
change represented auditorially, visually, spatially, or linguistically — via intertitles, transitions, or other means?

» Is each character/interview/subject matter differentiated in some way (if it's
necessary to do so)?

» Are important character or object movements indicated? (For example, if it's
important that a character is seen rolling his or her eyes, have you used arrows
around the eyeballs or something else to indicate that movement? Or if a car is
supposed to exit the right side of the frame, how have you shown that?)

» Are snippets of major dialogue included underneath the story-board visuals? If
not, what are the key ideas that need to be expressed in each scene or segment?

Designing Your Project

Drafting Your Mock-Up or Storyboard

Are you creating a static, visually based project that would need a mock-up? Or are you creating a temporally based project such as a video, an audio project, or an animation that would be better served by a storyboard? Decide which method will work best for your text and begin drafting! Refer back to your genre conventions checklist and your conceptualizing documents/drawings from Chapter 6 to make sure you have included all major design features (or have purposefully not included them). Also keep in mind the guidelines for mock-ups and storyboards from earlier in this chapter, and make sure you've included everything you need for planning your project and for helping others understand what you are going to compose.

» Are sound effects or musical scores noted (usually under the dialogue or scene)? Do you indicate what these audio elements will be and how long or loud they will be?

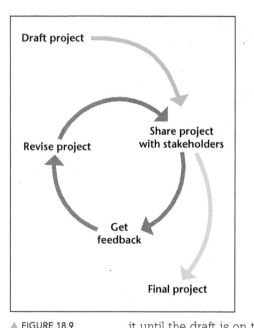

▲ FIGURE 18.9
The Feedback Loop

The Feedback Loop

After you've completed your mock-up or storyboard, you'll want to use it to get feedback on your project. Feedback can happen throughout the process and often results in multiple revisions. This process is rarely linear and is often referred to as a loop. That is, you share your project, receive feedback, make revisions and move forward, and then receive more feedback, continuing on until you and/or the stakeholders (ideally both!) are satisfied. You can also participate in others' feedback loops: your fellow students or colleagues may ask you to give feedback on their early work.

Finding out what your audience sees at this stage will forecast whether your design draft will successfully match what they want, need, and expect from the finished project. If your current plan isn't working, the feedback you receive should help you make changes to the draft and re-present it until the draft is on the right track for its rhetorical situation. You don't want to start composing the project itself if you're not sure it will suit the rhetorical situation. It's much easier to change a mock-up or storyboard than to change a finished multimodal project, so take advantage of your feedback loop.

When you give feedback on someone else's design concept, you will want to consider a range of questions, such as those we listed in the Mock-Ups and Storyboards sections of this chapter, so as to ensure that the writer/designer's design choices are suitable for the rhetorical situation.

Case Study Using the Feedback Loop

A graduate student in fine arts digital media was asked to design a cover for *Pank Magazine*, a literary magazine that describes itself as "fostering access to emerging and experimental poetry and prose, publishing the brightest and most promising writers for the most adventurous reader." The designer contemplated his rhetorical situation. The **purpose** of this text was to serve as an eye-catching cover for an edgy literary magazine, so that the magazine would stand out among the other literary journals (**genre**) displayed on a bookfair table or store bookshelf (**context**). *Pank* also uses the cover image as a digital advertisement for the issue itself, which is another **context** the designer had to consider. For example, the editors of *Pank* change the magazine's Facebook icon to the issue cover for the run of that issue, and they promote the issue by posting the cover image in their Facebook followers' feeds. The cover needed to be simple so that it would stand out at a range of sizes and in a variety of media, yet it also needed to meet the needs of the intended **audience**: those who enjoy literary magazines and think of themselves as being on the cutting edge of literary arts.

The editor of the journal provided the designer with two possible photographs, both taken by artist Elena Duff, along with some information about the journal itself. The designer carefully considered this information and then designed four mock-ups (see Figs. 18.10–18.13).

After sharing the mock-ups with the editorial board (the stakeholders), the editor sent this email to the designer:

▲ FIGURE 18.10
Pank **Mock-Up #1**

▲ FIGURE 18.11
Pank **Mock-Up #2**

▲ FIGURE 18.12
Pank **Mock-Up #3**

▲ FIGURE 18.13
Pank **Mock-Up #4**

Word back from all the editors is overwhelmingly positive, but with a strong preference for the second of the two girl/hair designs. While we like the playfulness of the other two designs, they feel a bit too disorganized/graffiti-like for our intended aesthetic. The hair designs feel a bit more serious while still keeping an edgy sensibility. The second of the two feels the most polished to us, and we like that it helps to emphasize the journal name itself. I'm wondering if I can see 2 or 3 variations on the theme, leaving the image(s) as is, but playing with the typography a bit? We'll choose a final design from this next round.

FIGURE 18.14 ▶
Final *Pank* Cover

While most of the designs didn't make the cut, the designer was now able to focus on mock-up #2 (Fig. 18.11) and offered the editor a range of different typefaces for that design. The stakeholders eventually decided on the cover shown in Figure 18.14. As this example illustrates, designing a mock-up usually involves creating several options and playing around with design combinations to get a sense of what might work best for your text's rhetorical situation. Your first design choice is most often not the best or only way to get your multimodal point across.

write/design assignment

Getting Feedback

Present your mock-up or storyboard to your instructor or other stakeholders for feedback. Your presentation may be formal (presenting to a client) or informal (conferencing with a teacher or workshopping with classmates), depending on your writing situation. Research the genre requirements for your presentation situation and prepare accordingly. (This may be similar to your pitch in Chapter 6.)

Be able to say why you've made the design choices you have — for example, you might explain that you chose the color scheme and navigation system for your Web site mock-up to match the interests of the site's intended audience, or that the nontraditional sequence of your storyboard's scenes is crucial to your text's purpose.

Refer to the checklists in the Mock-Ups and Storyboards sections to determine the areas that you might want your reviewers to focus on, and provide reviewers with your genre checklist (if appropriate) as they review your documents. If your stakeholders or colleagues offer feedback, assess that feedback for its usefulness in relation to your project's rhetorical situation, and revise your mock-up or storyboard accordingly.

Making Sure You Have What You Need

After you create your final storyboard or mock-up, you'll want to go back to your list of assets and sources and make sure it contains everything you'll need.

Assets The following questions can help you plan for gathering and editing your assets, which you will do as part of the final Write/Design assignment for this chapter.

» Which assets do you need to spend time creating or editing in order to prepare them for your project? For example, you may need to capture video clips, crop sound files, or visually manipulate images.

» What hardware (cameras, sound recording equipment, markers, paper) and software (sound editing software, photo manipulation software, etc.) do you need access to in order to turn your mock-up or storyboard into a reality?

» How much time will it take to get these assets ready for your project? As with any project, especially ones utilizing digital technology, remember that you will almost certainly need some extra time to troubleshoot.

For instance, Courteney went back to her assets list and created the chart below to make sure she'd covered everything. In the "Needs" column she listed all the assets and other materials she needed for her project; in the "Solutions" column she figured out how to get them. Working from this chart, she made sure her room was clean, asked her actor friends for help in advance, and made sure the camera's battery was charged well before she set out to film anything.

Courteney's Assets Chart

Needs	Solutions
Bedroom setting	Use my bedroom when roommate is in class
Narrator (actress)	Me
Muse (actress)	Sarah, my friend in the theater department
Release form for actress	Get a sample copy from instructor; print out before filming with Sarah
Additional research on genre features of action movies, including: • which movies I want to use • how I will find/get them • credible sources to cite (either linguistic or multimodal) to support my analysis	• I own *The Dark Knight*, *Inception*, *Star Wars*, and *The Matrix* • I want to get copies (Netflix?) of *The Lord of the Rings* trilogy and *Terminator 2* • I will create an annotated bibliography of five print and multimodal sources (per my teacher's assignment requirements)
Video camera	Check this out from the school library (what are its hours?)
Video editing program for PC	I can't use the Mac lab at school because I work during open hours, so I'll use my laptop, which has Movie Maker on it

Timeline   Collecting assets sometimes takes longer than an author has planned for in his or her proposal timeline, whether because equipment or actors become unavailable or because deadlines for other projects and meetings interrupt the author's work. It's not unusual to have to repeatedly revisit a project timeline to make adjustments for different obstacles and constraints. Before collecting assets, authors should ask themselves these questions:

» Is this timeline still manageable? Think backwards from the project's due date and include any major milestones (internal, personally imposed deadlines or external, instructor- or client-based deadlines) that you need to meet.

» Are there any logistics you need to keep in mind as you proceed, such as computer lab hours or instructional technology check-out limits?

FIGURE 18.15 ▶
Timelines for Complex Collaborations
Professionals collaborated for more than a year to make the *New York Times'* "Snow Fall" multi-media project happen. Read their process reflection at bedfordstmartins .com/writerdesigner.

HOW WE MADE SNOW FALL

A Q&A with the New York Times team

The New York Times' astonishing Snow Fall: The Avalanche at Tunnel Creek, launched in the final days of 2012, capped a year of extraordinary work in interactive journalism, both at the Times and in newsrooms around the world. In the six days after Snow Fall's launch on December 20th, 2012, it had received more than 3.5 million page views and 2.9 million visitors, nearly a third of whom were new visitors to the Times website.

January 1, 2013

By Steve Duenes, Erin Kissane, Andrew Kueneman, Jacky Myint, Graham Roberts, Catherine Spangler

💬 25 Comments

---

write/design assignment

Gathering Your Assets

Revisit your source list from Chapter 20 and your proposal (with your timeline) from Chapter 9 to make a list of everything you'll need to compose your project: assets, tools, people to help you, etc. Use Courteney's two-columned approach, listing what you need in one column and where and how you'll get it in the other. Remember to follow the categorizing and file-naming guidelines from Chapter 9.

PROCESS: EVALUATING AND CHOOSING SOURCES

CONTENTS

WIKIPEDIA
The Free Encyclopedia

◀ WIKI ENCYCLOPEDIA
Wikipedia
Courtesy of Wikimedia Foundation, Inc. All rights reserved.

In Chapter 13, we discussed how to begin your research to explore topics—and ultimately to come up with a research question and proposal. We assume in this chapter that you've done your preliminary research, you have a topic, and you are ready to focus in on an important aspect of that topic. In the following pages, we will discuss research in greater depth, covering how to identify a source that is appropriate, reliable, and useful to you.

GETTING STARTED WITH SOURCES

What Are Sources?

For an Index of Sources & Contexts for material referenced in this chapter, go to **bedfordstmartins .com/bookofgenres**.

The word *source* comes from the Anglo-French word *surse*, which means "to rise or to begin." Think of a source as a starting point. To cook something you've never made before, you might first refer to a cookbook, an online recipe database, or the Food Channel for inspiration. To plan a trip, you might begin with sources including maps, photos, and brochures. To begin a research paper, you might refer to Google and online databases such as *EBSCOhost* and *ProQuest*, and consult research librarians and professors to shape and define your ideas and narrow your topic.

LIBRARY HOMEPAGE ▶
Auraria Library Homepage
This library serves the Metropolitan State University of Denver and other institutions in the Denver area. Like most libraries, this one offers access to a range of databases, organized by title and subject area. *Auraria Library.*

What research have you done for other courses? Where did you seek advice? What sources worked especially well? What do you wish you'd done differently or better? #Remember #Evaluate

In the context of this book, we see everything you read (or view, or listen to, or experience in any way), every text you encounter, every conversation you have, as a potential source for your writing. When you compose—whether in college or on the job—you draw on sources for information and opinions. These sources do more than get you started; they are also the texts that you'll converse with throughout your composing process, from your earliest topic ideas to your final project. (For more on early topic ideas, see Chapter 17. For information on integrating and documenting sources, see Chapter 20.)

The Crème Brûlée Truck
also known as the Crème Brûlée Cart, is based in San Francisco. Researching food? A food truck or other eatery can be a valuable source of firsthand information. *The Crème Brûlée Cart.*

Can a food truck be a source? Sure. Especially if you're researching the trend of food trucks, or the growing number of people who identify themselves as "foodies." Maybe you're interested in comparing the old-time ice cream truck to the phenomenon of the food truck. Depending on your argument, you might use the truck as a starting point for your research, talking with its chef or operator to learn more about the business: its operation, clientele, and profitability. Or maybe about the food itself: the source of its ingredients and its nutritional value. (See Cremebruleecart .com: Better Living through Dessert.)

Where Do I Find Sources?

Sources are everywhere. Imagine that a friend tells you about an upcoming debate about the presence of the ROTC on campus; because she has provided you with information, your friend is a source. Let's say you become interested in the ROTC debate and decide to search your online campus newspaper for articles and editorials on the topic. Your campus paper and the materials it contains are sources.

From there, you could learn more by talking to a member of the ROTC or a military recruiter, or a local activist organization opposed to military recruiting. The people you talk with and the discussions you have with them are sources.

What Can Sources Do for Me?

For one thing, they help you make decisions. You use sources all the time—not only to inform your school and work projects, but to aid you in making informed choices. For example, you want to choose a movie to see this weekend. You'd probably consult a variety of sources: Maybe you'd read film reviews, watch current movie trailers, or talk with a film-buff friend. Or imagine you're shopping for a car. You would probably do some research; you would probably visit some manufacturers' sites, talk to your mechanic and other car owners, or visit dealerships for test drives. You might check out the advice at Cars.com.

Quick Start Guide

Cars.com's editors help find the right vehicle for you.
Click on a Step below for detailed guidance, or select directly from the resources below.

Step 1 Determine what you can afford
Learn How ▸

Step 2 Decide which vehicles you should consider
Learn How ▸

Step 3 Prepare to deal with sellers
Learn How ▸

Step 4 Find the right car for you
Learn How ▸

Resources

Financing Advice Read about financing options and strategies.

Buying Guides Research current and previous year models.

Used-Car Listings See asking prices for cars in your area.

Payment Calculator Determine how much you'll pay each month.

Resources

Research See photos, prices and specs for any car.

Buying Guides Sort new and used cars by class or price.

Certified Pre-Owned Cars Understand and compare programs.

Used-Car Listings See what's available in your price range.

Build a New Car Select and price styles and options.

▪ **Read Car Reviews**

Resources

Kelley Blue Book Values Look up fair sale or trade-in prices for used cars.

Rebates and Incentives Check for deals on the car you want.

Negotiating With Dealers Learn how it works and how to do it.

How to Buy a Used Car Read tips to avoid getting burned.

▪ **How to Read a Window Sticker**

Resources

Used-Car Listings Find the exact car you want and contact the seller.

Build a New Car Get price quotes from local dealers.

Dealer Locator Find dealers near you and see their inventory.

Sell It Yourself Get more cash for your car.

Now that you have a sense of what sources are, the rest of this chapter will show you how to:

» Locate and preview sources

» Identify sources in terms of general versus specialized academic; and of primary versus secondary

» Read sources critically, with attention to author, purpose, audience, and other rhetorical concerns

» Evaluate what sources will be best for your own research and writing

What's a General Source?
What's a Specialized Academic Source?

When you look at a source, think about who created that text, and for what purpose and for what audience. That will guide you as to when and how to use that source.

General Sources

General sources are aimed at a general audience; that is, they're written by knowledgeable authors and are meant to be understood by nonexperts. For example, a

Did you ever start reading a source and realize that you were in over your head? What were the indicators? Have you ever had the opposite experience—you started reading a source and realized it was much too simple? What were the indicators? #Evaluate

journalist who regularly covers local politics for your newspaper might write a piece to inform readers about a scandal at city hall. To get the gist of the story, you don't have to know anything about local politics or politicians. General sources help you:

» Begin to understand the overall topic

» Begin to see what the subtopics are

» Discover keywords

» Find the different conversations that are related to the topic

» Begin to explore your research questions

ARTICLE: ▶
GENERAL SOURCE
Psychology Today
Amy Alkon's article,
"The Truth about
Beauty," is aimed at
a general audience.
Courtesy of Psychology Today. *Photo by Art Steiber/August Images.*

An example of a general source is "The Truth about Beauty," an article written by Amy Alkon, a journalist and writer for the magazine *Psychology Today*. Alkon's purpose is to persuade her audience, primarily middle-aged women, about how men define beauty. Her ultimate goal in the article is to empower women so that they can understand their choices and the effects of their choices when it comes to beauty and landing a man. This is an example of a general source.

Specialized Academic Sources

These sources are aimed at (you guessed it!) specialized academic readers. They are usually written by scholars and other experts—professors, scientists, doctors, and researchers—who have studied the subject extensively. An example of a specialized academic source is an article from *JAMA* (*The Journal of the American Medical Association*) on a new clinical trial and its success. Readers of such an article would include doctors interested in new treatments that they can incorporate in their own practice. Although academic articles are aimed at people with expertise on a given subject, that doesn't mean you should avoid these sources. They may include information that you can use—and may become easier to understand as you deepen your research and gain an understanding of your topic (and associated terms and vocabulary). You might turn to these sources once you've built a foundation of understanding with your general sources. Specialized academic sources help you:

» Delve into a topic in depth

» See how experts view the subject

» Access the latest research in the field

» Access critiques of research in the field

» Find other academic sources through Works Cited lists and bibliographies

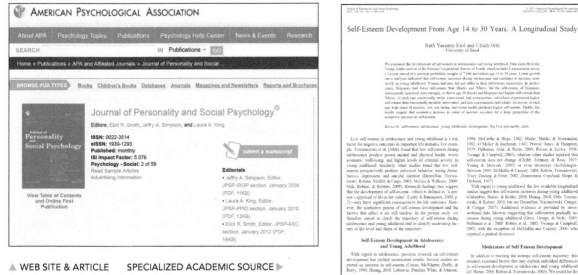

▲ WEB SITE & ARTICLE   SPECIALIZED ACADEMIC SOURCE ▶
American Psychological Association

This article from the *Journal of Personality and Social Psychology* is aimed at an audience of experts. *The APA Web site screenshots are reproduced with permission. Copyright © 2013 by the American Psychological Association, all rights reserved. No further reproduction or distribution is permitted without written permission from the American Psychological Association.*

An example of a specialized academic article is a piece on self-esteem development by Ruth Yasemin Erol and Ulrich Orth (see p. 719), which appeared in the American Psychological Association's publication, the *Journal of Personality and Social Psychology*. In the article, the authors examine the ways that early self-esteem affects health and happiness in later life. The primary audience for this piece consists of psychology and sociology scholars interested in social behavior.

☞ **Attention, researchers! A word about specialized sources.**

In addition to specialized academic sources, depending on your topic, you might also deal with specialized technical sources, such as technical manuals or drawings. For example, if you are researching ecotourism, you might use as a source a schematic drawing of a water treatment plant, one that an engineer might refer to on the job.

What Are Primary and Secondary Sources? Tertiary Sources?

What kinds of sources do you use every day that would be considered primary sources? What about secondary sources and tertiary sources? When you have a choice between different types of sources, say between asking your friend what time a concert starts and looking it up on the Internet, which do you usually choose and why? #Understand

Sources can be categorized as primary, secondary, or tertiary, based on the type of information an author uses—and the distance between the author and that information. A primary source is a record of information encountered firsthand, such as original photographs, interviews, correspondence, or historical documents. For example, if you read a letter written by a slave, that letter would be considered a primary source. However, if you read the letter in an anthology that also includes historical interpretations about the letters, then that book would be considered a secondary source. The categories of primary, secondary, and tertiary are not always clear-cut. Sometimes, something that would be a primary source in one circumstance would be a secondary source in another. For example, if Liz interviews Amy, the interview is a primary source for the researcher Liz; however, if Liz publishes this interview, and our editor Ellen reads the interview, it is a secondary source for Ellen.

We advise you to keep these distinctions in mind, but not to get too caught up in categorizing sources precisely in these terms. That said, here are a few rules of thumb to keep in mind:

1. A **primary source** is an original artifact, like a journal entry or photograph. If you were conducting research on the author Virginia Woolf, you might use one of her journal entries to get a sense of how her personal experiences shaped the novels she wrote.

2. A **secondary source** is written about an original artifact and often includes interpretation or analysis. If you were conducting research on Virginia Woolf, you might read a biography of her to get a sense of how her life intersected with historical events and to get a sense of the overall themes of her life.

3. A **tertiary source** is based on multiple secondary sources and presents uncontested information about a topic. In your hypothetical Virginia Woolf project, you might consult an encyclopedia of famous women to get a quick sense of the achievements Woolf is most famous for.

Primary Sources

In a primary text, a writer reports directly what he or she has witnessed, experienced, or created. For example, a piece of original music can be considered a primary source. Composers of primary sources rarely create their compositions to analyze, interpret, or evaluate data. If you are doing scientific research and encounter a rare plant specimen in the field, that plant specimen would be considered a primary source. If you are doing research on the Civil War and you find a map of a battlefield, that map would be considered a primary source. A place where you can find such a primary source is at the Library of Congress site, particularly in the American Memory collection, where the map of Gettysburg shown on page 722 and other Civil War maps are housed.

◄ WEB SITE FOR
PRIMARY SOURCES
The Library of Congress
An authoritative public archive of primary sources. The map on page 722 is from the LOC American Memory collection. *Library of Congress.*

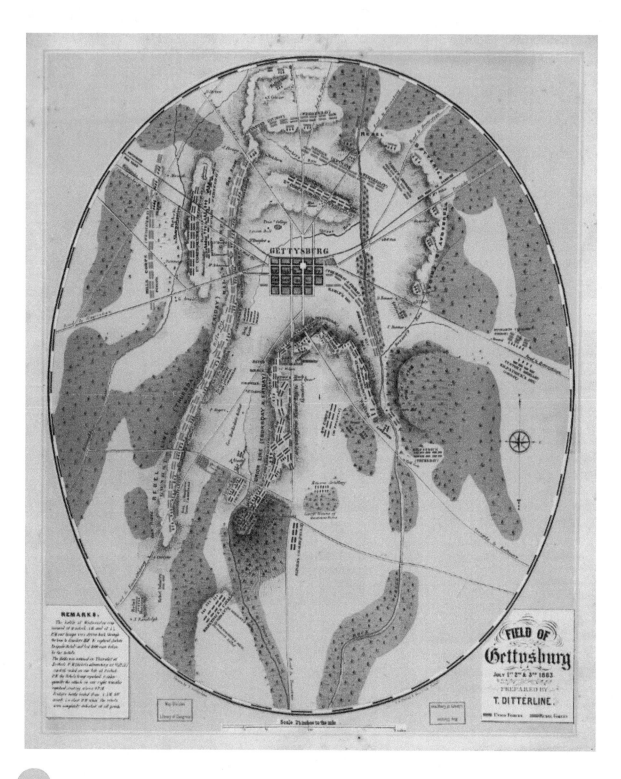

Secondary Sources

In a secondary source, a writer looks at a primary source—and offers an analysis, interpretation, or evaluation of that source. For example, a critique of a song (a primary source) is a secondary source. A critique of Lady Gaga's album *Born This Way* found in *Rolling Stone* magazine would be considered a secondary source; a YouTube video of Lady Gaga performing a song from *Born This Way* would be considered a primary source. If you were researching George Washington and found the biography *His Excellency: George Washington* by Joseph J. Ellis, that book would be considered a secondary source, while the George Washington Papers, original documents collected by the Library of Congress, are a primary source. (For more original documents, see the Manuscript Division at the Library of Congress.)

Tertiary Sources

Authors of tertiary texts synthesize, critique, and/or analyze secondary sources without adding new information. Essentially, authors of tertiary (or thirdhand) sources compile primary and/or secondary sources. They tend to present a generalized view of a given subject. For example, a music encyclopedia that mentions the critique (secondary source) of a piece of music (primary source) would be considered a tertiary source. *Wikipedia* is considered a tertiary source because it essentially summarizes information found in secondary sources.

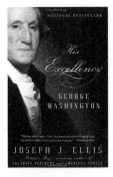

▲ SECONDARY SOURCE: BOOK
Joseph J. Ellis
His Excellency: George Washington. Copyright © 2004 by Alfred A. Knopf, a division of Random House, Inc. from His Excellency: George Washington by Joseph J. Ellis. Used by permission of Alfred A. Knopf a division of Random House, Inc. Any third party use of this material, outside of this publication, is prohibited. Interested parties must apply directly to Random House, Inc. for permission.

The Library of Congress

George Washington Papers of the Library of Congress 1741-1799

Manuscript Division, Library of Congress

Search by Keyword | Browse the Collection

The complete George Washington Papers collection from the Manuscript Division at the Library of Congress consists of approximately 65,000 documents. This is the largest collection of original Washington documents in the world. Document types in the collection as a whole include correspondence, letterbooks, commonplace books, diaries, journals, financial account books, military records, reports, and notes accumulated by Washington from 1741 through 1799. The collection is organized into nine Series or groupings. Commonplace books, correspondence, and travel journals, document his youth and early adulthood as a Virginia county surveyor and as colonel of the militia during the French and Indian War. Washington's election as delegate to the First and Second Continental Congresses and his command of the American army during the Revolutionary war are well documented as well as his two presidential administrations from 1789 through 1797. Because of the wide range of Washington's interests, activities, and correspondents, which include ordinary citizens as well as celebrated figures, his papers are a rich source for almost every aspect of colonial and early American history. In its online presentation, the George Washington Papers consists of approximately 152,000 images. This project is funded by Reuters America, Inc. and the Reuters Foundation.

◀ PRIMARY SOURCE: DOCUMENTS
The Library of Congress
The George Washington Papers. *Library of Congress.*

▼ TERTIARY SOURCE: WIKI ENCYCLOPEDIA
Wikipedia
Courtesy of Wikimedia Foundation, Inc. All rights reserved.

◀ PRIMARY SOURCE: MAP
The Library of Congress
"Field of Gettysburg." American Memory collection. *The Library of Congress.*

WIKIPEDIA
The Free Encyclopedia

When Should I Draw on a Primary Source? When Might a Secondary or Tertiary Source Be Best?

The kind of source you turn to depends on your purposes as a researcher and writer:

» When you want to get an overall sense of a topic or find uncontested factual information, look for a **tertiary source**.

» When you want original artifacts without the interpretation or analysis of others, look for a **primary source**.

» In most other cases, when you want to know how others have made sense of or interpreted primary sources, you should look for **secondary sources**.

Imagine you are conducting research about graphic novels and their presentation of female characters. Following are some sources you might turn to. They are organized into general and specialized academic categories. They are further divided by whether a given source is primary, secondary, or tertiary.

CHART ▶
Types of Sources
Primary, secondary, and tertiary, for a project on graphic novels and female characters. As you begin your research of any topic, keep in mind the variety of sources out there, aimed at different audiences, and composed for different purposes. Which are right for you?

	General sources	Specialized academic sources
PRIMARY SOURCES	• An interview with a graphic novelist that appears in the entertainment section of the newspaper • A graphic novel • A blog entry written by a graphic novelist about the creation of graphic novel characters • A movie poster for a film adaptation of a graphic novel	• An interview with a graphic novelist that appears in a peer-reviewed journal (an academic journal containing research by scholars in the field, reviewed by an editorial board of peers, such as other academic experts) • A professor's lecture about graphic novels in a literature course
SECONDARY SOURCES	• A book about the history of graphic novels geared toward a general audience • A blog entry by a fan of graphic novels that summarizes and comments on several different graphic novels	• A scholarly article about a graphic novel • A scholarly article that offers a feminist critique of graphic novels
TERTIARY SOURCES	• An encyclopedia entry about graphic novels • A review of a film adaptation of a graphic novel • A specialized encyclopedia of comic books and graphic novels	• A review of literature in a scholarly book on graphic novels • An annotated bibliography of articles about graphic novels

How Do I Preview a Source Critically?

Previewing your sources before committing to them is worth the effort. Ask yourself the following questions to identify what you might expect from a particular source, and whether you will want to use it in your research.

1. What Is the Overall Rhetorical Situation?

That is, what is the context of the source? Who wrote this piece, why, for whom, and how? And how does this impact the value of this text as a potential source?

Following is an example that we'll refer to throughout this section. It's an editorial published at Bloomberg.com.

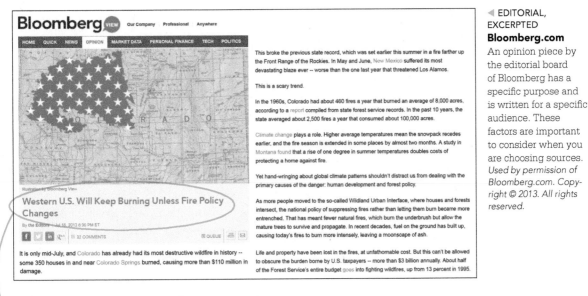

What's the Rhetorical Situation?

Bloomberg Editors, "Western U.S. Will Keep Burning Unless Fire Policy Changes"

To get a sense of the rhetorical situation of this Bloomberg editorial—or any potential source—ask and answer some basic questions:

▶ **Who wrote this piece?** The editorial board at Bloomberg, an influential news organization focused on business and finance and with clout in both of these areas.

▶ **Why?** The Bloomberg editors wanted to address the disastrous Colorado fires of the summer of 2012. Their purpose was to persuade readers that the government could adopt a course of action that could prevent future fires—and also save taxpayers money.

▶ **For whom?** Bloomberg's audience includes general readers with Internet access interested in business news and a "business take" on issues—both in Colorado and across the country—as well as business and government leaders who could do something about the problem.

▶ **How?** The editors collaborated to come up with their collective view on government policies regarding fires in the Rockies. They published their editorial in the opinion section of their Web site. The editorial includes hyperlinks to related materials, and there are options for commenting and linking out to social networking.

As you look at sources, think about the rhetorical context of each by paying attention to the authors and their purposes, their target audiences and how they appeal to them, and the modes and media that they use for delivering their messages.

Purpose   First, ask yourself: Who is the author of this piece? What are his or her reasons for writing? What assumptions does the author make? How does all of this fit in with what I'm looking for? Keep in mind:

» *What is the author's background?* This information will give you a sense of the author's credibility (ethos) and his or her perspective on the topic at hand. Begin by reading any biographical information provided and see if there are links to any other writing the author has done on this topic. For example, an article from a collection published by the surgeon general about the causes of heart disease is very likely to be more dependable than an article written by someone who is not a doctor. The authors of the editorial about fire policy (p. 725) are the members of Bloomberg's editorial board. Bloomberg is a well-respected news group focused on money and the marketplace, part of what makes this source a trustworthy one.

» *Is the author seeking to persuade?* Report information? Tell a story? All of the above? How does this fit with the type of information you're looking for? Begin by examining the title and then skim the piece with a critical eye.

Have you ever discovered something about a writer that made you question his or her reliability? Have you ever been unsure about a writer's trustworthiness and then made a discovery that changed your mind? #Understand

» *What are the author's biases?* While you're skimming, keep an eye out for assumptions built into the text. For example, an article by Facebook founder Mark Zuckerberg on the value of social networking will be biased in favor of social networking, while an article written by a more neutral, objective author not employed in the social networking business may be less biased. While both sources may have value, you need to keep in mind the authors' viewpoints and how they fit with what you want to say. The Bloomberg editorial (p. 725) represents the viewpoints of editors whose priorities are business growth and other financial concerns rather than the environment and other aspects of fire policy.

Audience   Ask yourself: Where did I find this text? Was it published in a popular magazine? A specialized academic journal? At a particular Web site? If so, who is the main audience for that magazine, journal, or Web site?

» *Am I part of the author's primary audience?* Based on the text's origin and a quick read of its contents, is the author aiming at a general readership or a narrower, more specialized audience? Evaluate the piece in terms of whether you find it readable, challenging, or perhaps oversimplified or condescending. Ask yourself: How much subject knowledge does the author assume readers have? For example, an engineer writing for a technical journal will assume readers are also engineers or specialists in related fields. That engineer is not writing to a general reader. As for the editors at Bloomberg (p. 725), they write for business-people, not environmentalists, so their take on fire policy is likely going to mesh better with the concerns of the business community than those of tree huggers.

» *Am I* not *part of the author's primary audience?* Don't dismiss a source just because you're not part of the author's primary audience. There may be something to learn from the piece. Let's say you're researching mining safety violations and settlements, and you locate a brochure created by a mining company. The target audience for the brochure is the local community—including relatives of people killed in a recent disaster at the mine. Perhaps the brochure oversimplifies the situation and denies responsibility, or perhaps it offers an apology and reparations. In either case, understanding an author's rhetorical situation (in this case, a company trying to appeal to employees and families) is valuable to you as a researcher.

Rhetorical appeals   In general, what strategies does the author use to build his or her case and connect with readers?

» *Does the author use humor?* Again, examine the title and skim the composition. If the author uses humor, does it work to strengthen the piece? How well does a humorous piece fit in with your topic and research?

» *Does the author use ethos, logos, and pathos to connect with readers?* How much authority does the author convey in the writing? Is the writing logical? To what extent does it appeal to your emotions? For example, you might realize as you analyze an author's appeal to pathos that his or her argument is not logical. At that point (unless you want a piece that is not logical, perhaps so you can critique it), you might decide not to use the source. It's a good sign when authors of a source incorporate statistical data, as the Bloomberg editors do (see p. 725), for example, to build a logical case that current fire policy must change. In the case of the Bloomberg editorial, the numerical data particularly appeals to their business and government audience.

Modes & media

» *Modes* In what mode was the source produced—written, audio, video, or something else? How does the composer's choice of mode contribute to the composition? What assumptions do you have about the mode? For example, it's fair to assume that hearing an audio essay, which features the composer's voice, is a more intimate experience than reading an article online. By considering mode you're more aware of how the author appeals to his or her audience. For example, a documentary film can have more of a dramatic impact on viewers than a researched article on readers because viewers use multiple senses to experience a film.

Do you think that some modes are more reliable than others? For example, do you assume that printed sources are more authoritative than stories you hear on the radio? Why or why not?
#Understand
#Evaluate

» *Media* In what medium is the source delivered—print, digital, or something else? What does the composer's choice of medium tell you about his or her assumptions about the audience? For example, digital sources are used primarily by audiences with access to computers or smartphones. Think, too, about the relationship between medium and the currency of information. A composer who publishes online can make revisions to the piece, adding links to newer articles on the topic at hand. For example, the Bloomberg editorial (p. 725) is digital, with written and visual components. The digital nature allows for the composers to update hyperlinks throughout the editorial, connecting readers with the latest writing on the topic.

2. What Is the Genre of the Piece?

What are you looking at? What kind of composition is it? What qualities is this genre known for? What makes this text a potentially workable source, or not?

Following is an example that we'll refer to throughout this section. It's a photo essay published at *Time* magazine's Web site. The photos are by Danny Wilcox Frazier of Redux photography, and the text was written by editors at *Time*.

PHOTO ESSAY ▶
Time. This photo essay, "In Boise, Housing Struggles to Emerge From Its Malaise," includes photos by Danny Wilcox Frazier of Redux, and captions by *Time* editors. As you consider sources, think about the genre of those sources (see the box on p. 729). *Photo essay: Danny Wilcox Frazier / Redux. Time branding: © 2009. Time Inc. Reprinted/ Translated from TIME. COM and published with permission of Time Inc. Reproduction in any manner in any language in whole or in part without written permission is prohibited. TIME and the TIME logo are trademarks of Time Inc. Used under license.*

What's the Genre?

Time and Danny Wilcox Frazier/Redux, "In Boise, Housing Struggles to Emerge From Its Malaise"

When you look at a potential source, you want to understand its rhetorical situation (see the Bloomberg editorial on p. 725)—its authorship, purpose, audience, etc.

You also want a sense of the genre that the composer chose—will it work for you?—as well as the style, design, and other sources drawn on. Ask and answer the following questions:

▶ **What am I looking at?** The image on page 728 is from a photo essay published online, created by *Time* editors and a photographer.

▶ **What qualities is this genre known for?** Photo essayists combine images and words to tell a story and/or to make an argument. Here, the editors at *Time* show the impact of an economic crisis—and hoped-for recovery—on a community. The title, "In Boise, Housing Struggles to Emerge From Its Malaise," suggests the argument being made.

▶ **What makes this text a potentially workable source, or not?** The authorship of this photo essay and its publication in a respected magazine make it a promising source. Also promising is that the journalists who composed the piece also conducted interviews with residents. The genre makes it useful to a researcher looking for a persuasive visual/textual argument based in primary research.

Elements of the genre   Ask yourself: What do I know about the genre? What can I expect or assume about it? Keep in mind:

» *What is the scope of the information?* Different genres present different amounts and degrees of information: An encyclopedia entry provides an overview of information, while a peer-reviewed journal article provides in-depth treatment.

» *How reliable is the information?* Some genres are known for their reliability and objectivity, others less so. For example, in terms of factual accuracy, a peer-reviewed journal article is probably more reliable than a political ad. (See also Chapter 4, "Understanding Genres.")

» *What is the connection between genre and purpose?* There is a relationship between an author's purpose and his or her choice of genre. For example, an author writing a blog probably wants to inform and/or persuade others. On the other hand, the author of an encyclopedia entry seeks to provide uncontested knowledge, while the creator of a TV ad is definitely out to convince viewers to buy something. Previewing a source in terms of its genre gives you a set of expectations to consider before you decide whether to read the source more closely. (See also Chapter 4, "Understanding Genres.") For example, the authors of the photo essay (see p. 728) chose that genre for a reason. The *Time* editors and photographer Danny Wilcox Frazier, who collaborated on the photo essay, chose to focus on the human side of the housing crisis in Boise. Consider how differently the business-oriented Bloomberg editorial board might have dealt with the same issue, perhaps writing an opinion piece on the financial aspects of the crisis rather than on how people deal with losing their homes.

Style   When evaluating a source, pay attention to the style of the author. Ask yourself:

» *How does the author use language?* As you skim, pay attention to the writer's word choice and vocabulary level. To what extent do they contribute to (or undermine) the author's ethos? How formal or informal is the language? Does the writer use slang? If so, keep in mind that slang is not an indicator of unreliability, just as formal language is not an indicator of reliability.

» *What is the author's tone? How does he or she use voice?* Describe the author's presence in the text. How does he or she use stylistic techniques to create a memorable voice and tone? For example, if you want to learn about the day-to-day impact of Asperger's syndrome, you may be drawn to a first-person text (or video, etc.) created by someone who is being treated for Asperger's and who can explain it from an intimate point of view. For any source, pay attention to tone—some authors may be off-putting, while an author with an engaging voice and tone might get you to read a piece that you weren't initially sure about.

» *How well does the author's style work with the chosen genre?* Think of the author's style in the context of the genre the author composed in. For example, if the author has written an editorial, ask yourself: Is the style generally in keeping with other editorials? For example, is it direct and persuasive?

» *What special techniques does the author use? How much detail does he or she provide?* Does the author use literary techniques, such as dialogue, setting, and metaphor? How do these techniques work to get and keep your attention? And how specific does the author get in terms of detail? Paying attention to these factors will assist you in deciding whether to commit to the source; in the best cases, other authors provide examples of techniques that you can adapt in your own writing. Consider the *Time*/Frazier photo essay as a source (p. 728). The editors don't go into much detail in the textual part of the essay, but the photos they chose highlight the personal connections people have with their homes.

Design   All compositions—from the lowliest e-mail to the biggest-budget film—are designed. Ask yourself: Is the source I'm looking at presented in a way that draws me in?

» *How are text and images laid out?* How does the author use spatial arrangement to guide your reading? How does formatting, such as use of capital letters, bold, or special fonts, direct your attention or shape your understanding of the source's organization? Is color used to highlight information? As with style, you might notice how an author uses design elements to communicate with a reader and decide to try some of the same techniques yourself. Designs that you find annoying or gimmicky may turn you off to a source, and the opposite may happen too: Clever design that resonates with you can draw you in.

» *How are sound and other nontext/nonimage elements arranged?* How does the composer use sound to guide your listening? How does the composer use sound to evoke emotion? How do these elements direct your attention toward or away from aspects of the piece? Note, for example, how in the *Time*/Frazier photo essay (p. 728), the photos stand out against the black background.

Sources When you preview a text, learn what you can about its author's research methods, and therefore the text's validity. Ask yourself:

» *How did the author gather and analyze data?* For example, if you're looking at an article that draws its data from surveys of large groups, you expect to encounter a lot of statistics and charts that compile the data. You'd also hope that the data is dependable. For example, the *Time* editors who created the photo essay on the housing situation in Idaho visited the location and conducted interviews, gathering information firsthand.

» *What types of sources did the author draw on?* Pay attention to where the author obtained the information on which the piece is based. Also, keep in mind the type of information you're looking for. For example, if you want facts on a specific topic and the source you're looking at is anecdotal or only relies on the author's experiences rather than on scientific research, you might decide the source won't be of use to you after all.

» *Did the author document sources?* Are sources listed in a bibliography or Works Cited list? Within the text, are specific details about sources given, such as page numbers and dates of publication for written sources? For example, in the *Time*/Frazier photo essay (p. 728), the writers refer to the names of the homeowners in the text of the piece.

» *Did the author not conduct research?* Not all authors conduct outside research, especially when they compose in particular genres such as the memoir. In the case of the memoir, the source that informs the piece is the author himself or herself—it's based on his or her own experiences.

What is the price of drawing on unreliable sources? Have you ever lost faith in an author because of the sources he or she used? What were the sources? What made them seem unreliable? #Evaluate

PREVIEWING A SOURCE

Emily Kahn: Women in Comic Books Project

▲ STUDENT AUTHOR
Emily Kahn
iStockphoto.

Let's follow a student, Emily Kahn, as she previews a possible source. Emily is interested in comics and graphic novels, and she plans to write an academic argument about the portrayal of women in these works. She locates a promising-looking article on the topic of women in graphic works in *Lightspeed: Science Fiction & Fantasy*, a weekly online magazine for fans of sci-fi and fantasy literature. The article, "The Objectification of Women in Comic Books," is by a writer named Jehanzeb Dar.

Before Emily reads the article in depth or adds it to her working bibliography, she will preview it. This means she'll dig around to better understand the context of the article. Keeping in mind the factors outlined above, Emily will set out to learn basic information about the publisher and author of the article—in addition to the author's purpose, audience, choice of genre, and more.

☞ **Attention, researchers! A word about previewing.**

When you find a source, do basic detective work before you commit to it. Start by getting to know its publisher and author. Ask yourself:

1. Where did the piece appear? Was it published by a scholarly journal? A well-known news outlet? An obscure but solid-looking blog? To what extent does the publisher have a specific point of view or agenda (e.g., *The Weekly Standard* states that it is a conservative publication)? How will this perspective fit in (or compare/contrast) with my project?

2. Who is the author? Someone I've heard of? Someone I don't know, but who seems to be a good writer?

---

1. What Is *Lightspeed* Magazine?

Emily first considers who publishes the magazine in which the article appears. She asks herself:

» What type of magazine is this?
» Who publishes it?
» What is the quality of the work presented there?
» Who is the main audience?
» Are the articles in the magazine peer-reviewed? Scholarly?

On the "About" page, she reads a note from the publisher:

ABOUT

Lightspeed is an online science fiction and fantasy magazine. In its pages, you will find science fiction: from near-future, sociological soft SF, to far-future, star-spanning hard SF—and fantasy: from epic fantasy, sword-and-sorcery, and contemporary urban tales, to magical realism, science-fantasy, and folktales. No subject is off-limits, and we encourage our writers to take chances with their fiction and push the envelope.

Lightspeed was a finalist for the 2011 & 2012 Hugo Awards, and stories from Lightspeed have been nominated for the Hugo Award, the Nebula Award, and the Theodore Sturgeon Award.

Edited by bestselling anthologist John Joseph Adams, every month *Lightspeed* brings you a mix of originals and reprints, and featuring a variety of authors—from the bestsellers and award-winners you already know to the best new voices you haven't heard of yet. When you read *Lightspeed*, it is our hope that you'll see where science fiction and fantasy comes from, where it is now, and where it's going.

For Emily, the fact that *Lightspeed* has been nominated for a number of awards and that the editor seems to be knowledgeable are important selling points. While at first glance *Lightspeed* might look like a fanzine, she sees when she browses the contents that the nonfiction pieces published there seem sophisticated in terms of subject matter, cultural analysis, and the use of sources and Works Cited lists. *Lightspeed* may be more scholarly than she'd originally thought, though it's very readable for a general audience. She's not sure what to assume about it, so she reads on.

2. Who Are the Editors and Staff Members at *Lightspeed* Magazine?

Emily scrolls down to the masthead to find out more about the magazine's editorial staff.

She asks herself:

»   What can I learn about who runs the magazine?

»   Who is the publisher or main editor? What are his or her credentials? Is this an independent company, or is a parent company in charge?

»   Who are the other editors and regular contributors to the magazine? What else have they written, and for what publications?

»   Are the editors and contributors scholars? Critics? Fans of the genres of science and fantasy fiction? Authors themselves?

Emily is curious about the publisher and editor-in-chief, John Joseph Adams, and sees that he has won several awards as an anthologist and also is affiliated with Wired.com. She notices that *Lightspeed*'s monthly sponsor is Orbit Books, an imprint of Hachette, which publishes books by authors she has read, so that adds to the magazine's credibility. Reading down the masthead, she sees that many editors are published authors themselves who also write critical articles for other magazines devoted to fantasy, science fiction, horror, culture, and comics. Emily is pleasantly surprised that the editors of *Lightspeed* are more than enthusiastic consumers of science fiction and fantasy: They are experts as well. From the information Emily reads on the "About," "Our Staff," and "Our Sponsor" pages, she finds that *Lightspeed* magazine may be an appropriate source for her paper.

◀ MAGAZINE
Lightspeed
Excerpt from the masthead on the "Our Staff" page. Emily browses *Lightspeed*'s staff page to learn about who puts the magazine together. *John Joseph Adams.*

Our Staff

John Joseph Adams
Publisher/Editor-in-Chief

John Joseph Adams, in addition to serving as publisher and editor of *Lightspeed* (and its sister magazine, *Nightmare*), is the bestselling editor of many anthologies, such as *The Mad Scientist's Guide to World Domination, Oz Reimagined, Epic: Legends of Fantasy, Other Worlds Than These, Armored, Under the Moons of Mars, Brave New Worlds, Wastelands, The Living Dead, The Living Dead 2, By Blood We Live, Federations, The Improbable Adventures of Sherlock Holmes,* and *The Way of the Wizard.* He has been nominated for six Hugo Awards and four World Fantasy Awards, and he has been called "the reigning king of the anthology world" by Barnes & Noble.com. John is also the co-host of Wired.com's *The Geek's Guide to the Galaxy* podcast. Find him on Twitter @johnjosephadams.

Robert Barton Bland
Assistant Publisher

Robert Barton Bland dabbles in writing, independent film, and, when struck by fancy, will even patronize the arts. He subsidized and helped found his sister's start-up dance company, Company Stefanie Batten Bland, currently a Baryshnikov Arts/Jerome Robbins New Fellow. Rob also produced the touring and creation of "Chapters an Evening of Repertory," which toured at Symphony Space in New York City, Saratoga Arts Festival, and in 2010 at Ris Orangis in France. In film, Rob is a two-time CINE Eagle Award winner for the independent shorts, "On Time" and "Writer's Block," and is currently executive producing a feature length independent film, *79 Parts,* directed by Ari Taub. Rob is also an alum of Jeanne Cavelos's Odyssey Workshop (2001), and he is currently pecking away at an urban fantasy novel, *Divinity Bind.*

Rich Horton
Reprint Editor

Rich Horton is a Software Engineer living in the St. Louis area, working for a major Aerospace corporation. His job sometimes has a science fictional side, but he'd go to jail if he told you why. He also writes a monthly column for *Locus Magazine,* and columns and reviews for *Black Gate, SF Site,* and other publications. He edits *The Year's Best Science Fiction & Fantasy* series of anthologies for Prime Books, as well as such other anthologies as *War and Space: Recent Combat* and *Superheroes.*

Jack Kincaid
Podcast Host

Jack Kincaid is best known as the creator and producer of the cyberpunk audio drama series, *Edict Zero - FIS.* He is a speculative fiction writer with a handful of short stories published and many novels waiting in the wings. One novel, *Hoad's Grim,* he released as a podcast in 2008-2009. He is also a diverse voice actor whose work can be heard in audio dramas on the web and in podcasts such as *The Geek's Guide to the Galaxy,* among other places. His background includes theatre, A/V production, music, games, sound design, and early machinima. Find him on Twitter at @jackkincaid9.

Jim Freund
Podcast Editor

Jim Freund has been involved in producing radio programs of and about literary sf/f since 1967, when he began working at New York City's WBAI-FM at age 13. Jim has been sole host of the radio program, *Hour of the Wolf,* since 1974. Over the years, he has produced many radio dramas and lost track long ago of how many interviews and readings he has conducted. His work has been twice nominated for and was once a winner of the Major Armstrong Award for Excellence in Radio Production. Jim is currently Producer and Executive Curator of The New York Review of Science Fiction

Karen Jones
Art Director

Karen Jones is a freelance User Interface Designer based in Brooklyn, New York. Her creative pursuits include photography, vector-based art, and character design for video games. When she isn't working in Photoshop or Illustrator or looking for artists on Cool Vibe and Deviant Art, she's being chased by zombies on the Xbox 360, reading about the art and architecture of the ancient world, or traveling. Follow her on Twitter at @karenjUX.

Christie Yant
Assistant Editor

Christie Yant has published fiction in the magazines *Beneath Ceaseless Skies, Crossed Genres, Daily Science Fiction, Fireside, Shimmer,* has been featured on io9 and Wired.com, and has been included in the anthologies *The Way of the Wizard, Armored,* and *The Year's Best Science Fiction & Fantasy, 2011 Edition.* In the past, she has served as a book reviewer for Audible.com, and she occasionally narrates for StarShipSofa and blogs at Inkpunks.com, a website for aspiring and newly-pro writers. She lives in a former Temperance colony on the central coast of California, where she sometimes gets to watch rocket launches with her husband and her two amazing daughters. Learn more at inkhaven.net.

Our Sponsor

Lightspeed's sponsor this month is Orbit Books:

Orbit US is the Science Fiction and Fantasy imprint at Hachette Book Group USA. Our authors include Joe Abercrombie, Iain M. Banks, Gail Carriger, Lilith Saintcrow and Brent Weeks. They publish a wide range of fiction from both established and debut authors.

Orbit also publishes digital short stories from their authors. The stories are available at all major ebook retailers —currently in the US and Canada, and further afield in the very near future. You can find their short fiction program at www.orbitshortfiction.com.

3. Who Is Jehanzeb, the Author of the Article?

Emily sees that *Lightspeed* attributes the article to a writer named Jehanzeb, for whom no last name is given. She asks herself:

» How can I discover the last name of the author, so that I can learn more about this writer?

» Is there a biography somewhere? Maybe a link to a blog or personal Web site?

» What else has this author written—whether on this topic or others? And where has his work been published?

» How much credibility does the author convey?

Emily first needs to discover Jehanzeb's full name. She notices a brief biography at the end of the article, which links to Jehanzeb's blog, where the article was first published. She also sees that *Lightspeed* has published three other articles by Jehanzeb on the topic of women in comics. To learn more, Emily follows the link to Jehanzeb's *Broken Mystic* blog, where he posts poems, personal writing, and articles. There she links to

Jehanzeb is a film student who writes about Islam, Feminism, Politics, and Media. This piece was originally published on his blog.

Tagged as: comics

Related Posts

○ A Critique of Muslim Women in Comics -- AK Comics' Jalia and Aya

○ A Critique of Muslim Women in Comics -- The 99

○ Female, Muslim, and Mutant

Muslim Reverie ~ "*With a daring brow, encounter every ill you meet; grapple boldly with each sorrow, dream not of defeat.*" - *Zeb-un-Nisa*

I am a Pakistani Muslim who advocates anti-racist, anti-colonial feminism. I often write anti-racist feminist critiques of media representations concerning Muslims, Arabs, Iranians, South Asians, and other communities of color, but also like to write poetry, short stories, and spiritual prose. I studied social psychology in undergrad and am also an independent filmmaker. I've always been inspired to implement spirituality into my efforts for social justice and believe in a politics of mutual accountability and interrelatedness.

In 2010, a chapter I wrote on the vilification of Muslims in mainstream American comic books was <u>published</u> in a textbook entitled <u>"Teaching Against Islamophobia,"</u> As described by the publishers, the book "contends that teachers must have the tools with which to combat unilateral politicization of Arabic and Muslim peoples. 'Teaching Against Islamophobia' creates a pedagogical space for educators to engage with necessary issues and knowledges regarding the alienation of Islamic culture, religion, knowledge, and peoples." I also wrote another chapter on the objectification of women in mainstream American comic books that will appear in a forthcoming publication.

♦ CATEGORIES

▪ Anti-racism
▪ Feminism
▪ History
▪ Introduction
▪ Islamophobia
▪ Media
▪ Pakistan
▪ Poetry
▪ Spirituality

◀ PHOTO & BIO
Jehanzeb Dar, blog,
Muslim Reverie
Emily discovers that Dar has an Internet presence; he's the author of a blog, and has been quoted in an Associated Press article (see below). *Jehanzeb Dar.*

a second blog, called *Muslim Reverie*, where Jehanzeb posts about "politics, current events, feminism, and media literacy." Here Emily discovers that his last name is Dar. She notices e-mail links at both blogs, so she can contact him directly. She thinks she might do that if she decides to use his article as a source in her research.

Now that Emily knows Jehanzeb's full name, she does a quick Google search to learn more about him. She wonders: Has Jehanzeb Dar published elsewhere—besides *Lightspeed* magazine and his blog? To what extent is he considered an expert on comics? A critic? She's interested to discover that Jehanzeb was interviewed by the Associated Press about the film *Prince of Persia*. In the AP article, which also appeared in media outlets including MSNBC's *Today, The Huffington Post, The Washington Times,* and *Bloomberg Businessweek,* among others, Jehanzeb argues that the role played by Jake Gyllenhaal (a white actor) should have gone to an actor of Middle Eastern descent. Dar also posted on his blog about the topic (see "This Prince Is Not Persian"). He is noted in different sources as a blogger, filmmaker, video gamer, and critic.

Critics: 'Airbender' & 'Prince' were 'whitewashed'
DEEPTI HAJELA, Associated Press
May 25th, 2010

NEW YORK (AP) — The hopes of many are resting on the shoulders of 12-year-old Aang.

Ever since he first came out of a block of ice in the Nickelodeon cartoon series "Avatar: The Last Airbender," the other tribes in his fictional, Asian-inspired world saw Aang and his power over the elements as their last chance for peace after a century of conflict.

Now Paramount Pictures and director M. Night Shyamalan also have high hopes for Aang; that he will attract audiences to see their big-screen — and big budget — version of "The Last Airbender," opening July 2.

"This part really needed to go to someone who's Persian," said Jehanzeb Dar, a blogger and independent filmmaker who is a fan of the video game but has no intention of supporting the movie.

"It's not only insulting to Persians, it's also insulting to white people. It's saying white people can't enjoy movies unless the protagonist is white," he said.

◀ ARTICLE EXCERPT
Associated Press /
Deepti Hajela
Excerpt from "Critics: 'Airbender' & 'Prince' Were 'Whitewashed,'" in which Jehanzeb Dar is quoted. *The YGS Group.*

By tracking down information through the bio that appeared with the article, through Jehanzeb's blogs, and through a Google search, Emily has turned up some rich information. As her mental picture of Jehanzeb gets clearer—as a writer, and as a thinker and critic who takes part in larger, public conversations about the presentation of race in popular culture—she becomes more interested in his article on women in comics as a source for her paper.

4. What Type of Article Is This? Will It Work for My Topic?

Now that Emily has a better sense of *Lightspeed* magazine and the writer Jehanzeb Dar, she's ready to do a closer reading of the article itself. Below is Dar's article, along with Emily's notes in the margins—you can see how she identifies her assumptions and also begins to read the piece closely and critically. At this point, she is still deciding on whether to use this source. Once she's done some annotating, she's ready to make her final call.

☞ **Attention, readers! A little history on this article.**

Jehanzeb Dar's article on women in graphic works was originally published at *Lightspeed* magazine (formerly *Fantasy* magazine). The piece included here is an updated version of the essay that Dar sent us for publication in this book. How did he revise his work? Why not read both versions of the article to find out? (Go to fantasy-magazine.com and search by author and title.)

Guided Process: How to Preview a Source ▼

Emily Kahn (Student)

Women in Comic Books Project: Previewing Jehanzeb Dar

As she reads, Emily asks herself the following questions:

▲ STUDENT AUTHOR
Emily Kahn
iStockphoto.

» What is Dar's main purpose? And how does this fit in with my research questions?

» Who is his primary audience? Am I part of it? How does he connect with readers through rhetorical appeals?

» What genre is this piece? Based on what I know about the genre, what assumptions can I make?

» What is Dar's writing style? How do his techniques, voice, and tone affect me as a reader? How much detail does he use?

» Does the design of the article support what Dar seeks to achieve?

» What sources does he draw on? Does he document them? What type of sources are they— and how reliable are they?

(The following article appears by permission of Jehanzeb Dar. The Lightspeed *branding appears by permission of John Joseph Adams.)*

The Objectification of Women in Comic Books

by JEHANZEB

During World War II, a handsome American intelligence officer, Colonel Steve Trevor, crash-lands his plane on a mysterious island inhabited by the beautiful Amazons of Greek mythology. This new world is known as "Paradise Island" (what else would an island populated by Amazonian women be called, right?) and changes the course of human destiny. A princess by the name of Diana attends Trevor's wounds and subsequently falls in love with him. When she learns about the U.S. war against the Nazis, she dons a costume of America's red, white, and blue, and departs for the "Man's World." She becomes Wonder Woman— "beautiful as Aphrodite, wise as Athena, stronger than Hercules, and swifter than Mercury." She can fly like Superman and hurl heavy objects like the Hulk, and if you refuse to tell her the truth, she'll crack out her golden lasso and tie you up (especially if you're a heterosexual man).

At first glance, she may look like an empowered, kick-butt, feminist superheroine amidst a realm dominated by white heterosexual male superheroes. But is Wonder Woman really empowered? Is she really a symbol of feminism in comic books? Is her message really all about defending sisterhood, freedom, and democracy?

A historical overview is necessary to examine the role women have played in mainstream comic books as well as how intersecting dynamics of race and gender have impacted the way women are presented.

Continues next page

Emily's notes on Dar's essay

What genre is this?
Definitely an article/essay. The title indicates the author is making an argument about sexism in comics. I know it's a researched argument because there is a references/Works Cited page at the end.

What can I assume about this genre?
I assume Dar will make claims (and maybe counterarguments) and support them with evidence from outside sources.

What is the author's style?
His style is serious and scholarly, but the tone is kind of entertaining—he uses terms such as "kick-butt." He also uses lots of detail.

How does the author use design?
I like the subheadings. They divide the article into sections on different portrayals of women in comics.

Emily's notes on Dar's essay

How does the author work with sources?

He cites sources in the text and in a References list. Looks like APA format.

Sources look to be from experts on comics and feminist and cultural critics. He also draws on comics themselves.

Who is the author?

Dar is a writer concerned with comics and critical of the portrayal of women in them. He also writes about issues related to race and popular culture.

What is the author's purpose?

The title says to me that Dar wants to persuade readers that women are objectified in comic books. As I read further, I see that he argues that even strong female characters are created to be alluring.

1. The Damsel in Distress

Originally, the only women that appeared in mainstream American comic books were white women, though they played very small roles. In the late 1930s, superpowered heroes like Superman and Captain Marvel dominated the stage while women scarcely had any presence. If women made appearances, they were depicted as dependent and "damsels in distress"—victims (typically of male violence) needing to be rescued by the male protagonist (who typically exerts more violence over the male villain). The "damsel in distress" is not only a prize that needs to be won by either the male villain or hero, but also an object that measures the masculinity of the male characters. For example, Superman's "masculinity is defined by what it is not, namely 'feminine,' and by all its associated traits—hard *not* soft, strong *not* weak, reserved *not* emotional, active *not* passive" (Brown, 2001, p. 168). The manner in which women service masculinity is apparent in the first issue of *Superman*, where news reporter and future love interest Lois Lane is kidnapped by criminals and eventually saved by Superman. A romantic relationship is not developed between the two characters and nothing is learned about who Lois is—she is only a weak "feminine" body reinforcing Superman's strong "masculinity" and "savior" role. Superman simply rescues her from villains, flies her to safety, and then flies away. Such one-dimensional portrayals were evident in other ways women were depicted: as the "girl-Friday . . . seductive vamp, or perhaps, the long-suffering girlfriend" (Lavin, 1998, p. 93). The stereotypical gender roles were quite obvious: men alone are capable of succeeding independently and being courageous, while women are dependent and weak beauties relegated to the background. These early attitudes toward women in comic books are quite suggestive of common sexist-defined role patterns where women are thought to be less intelligent than men and only have a place in the house as a caretaker and/or source of emotional support. As New York cartoonist Jules Feiffer states, "The ideal of masculine strength, whether Gary Cooper's, Lil Abner's, or Superman's, was for one to be

so virile and handsome, to be in such a position of strength, that he need never go near girls. Except to help them" (1965).

2. Women as Sex Objects

The role of women changed dramatically during World War II when patriotic characters emerged and surprisingly attracted the interest of new readers, who were both men and women. Arguably, the most noteworthy female character was Wonder Woman. As mentioned above, she possesses enormous superhuman strength, has the ability to fly, and can overcome any obstacle that comes her way. Even more interesting is how her love interest, Colonel Trevor, is constantly being rescued by her, as if he is the male version of the aforementioned Lois Lane. Rather than the male rescuing the female in every episode, it is reversed in the Wonder Woman comics. In the following years, other strong superheroine characters surfaced like Miss America—the female version of Captain America—Mary Marvel, Supergirl, She-Hulk, and many others. They carried the symbolic message that "girls could do anything boys could do, and often better, especially if they stuck together" (Robbins, 2002).

However, despite these new portrayals of strong and powerful female characters like Wonder Woman, something else was occurring: they were being depicted as sex objects. As stated by Michael Lavin: "Powerful super-heroines like DC's Wonder Woman or Marvel's She-Hulk may easily overcome the most overwhelming threats and obstacles, but they are invariably depicted as alluring objects of desire, wearing the scantiest of costumes." The images of women with large bust sizes, hourglass figures, bare legs, and half-naked appearances became enormously popular after the success of Wonder Woman. Believe it or not, comic books were filled with so many sexual images of women that they were known as "headlight comic books" (crudely referring to the female anatomy). Comic book historian Ron Goulart writes: "In the days before the advent of *Playboy* and *Penthouse*, comic books offered one way

Continues next page

Emily's notes on Dar's essay

Looks like this is a feminist critique of comics. He also includes a section on the future of comics, so he's looking forward too.

Who is the author writing for?

For the editors and readers of *Lightspeed* magazine; the audience is mainly people who are experts on comics and interested in critical commentary about comics.

How does the author use appeals?

Dar appears to make his points using logic; he establishes his ethos/intelligence/expertise and uses sources. In this article he doesn't appeal to readers' emotions as a strategy.

Emily's notes on
Dar's essay

How do the mode
& medium impact
readers?

The article appears
online, so it prob-
ably has a wider
potential audience
than a print article
would. This allows
for hyperlinks to
sources and other
pages. Also, read-
ers can add com-
ments and interact
with the author
and each other.

to girl watch" (quoted in Lavin, p. 93). A prime example of "headlight comics" was in Bill Ward's *Torchy*, a series that ran from 1946 to 1950. The comic books contained dull and uninteresting storylines where the scriptwriters were merely making an excuse to draw Torchy as a tall, bare-legged blonde, who walked around in her underwear.

The escalating amount of sex and violence in comic books eventually led to complaints, particularly by psychologist Fredric Wertham who held a symposium in 1948 on the "Psychopathology of Comic Books." He also wrote a book, *Seduction of the Innocent*, which correlated a connection between "juvenile delinquency and comic book reading" (Lavin, 1998, p. 95). As a result, the Comics Code Authority estab-lished a written code that set the guidelines for comic book publishing. During this time, the comic book industry took a remarkable new turn where the constant objectification of women was seized. The brief period where comic books were geared more toward teenage girls wouldn't last long, as superheroes reemerged in the late 1960s, along with their scantily clad superheroines and damsels in distress. Women were drawn in the same stereotypical fashion, but this time, the art-ists took it one step further on the skimpy scale. Consider the White Queen, a female villain who appeared in the *X-Men* comics during the 1980s. She was "the stuff of male sexual fantasy: a push-up bustier, panties, and high-heel boots, all in white" (Lavin, 1998, p. 94).

Today, women are becoming more and more sexualized. As described by Jones and Jacobs (1995, p. 341):

> Females, perpetually bending over, arching their backs, and heav-ing their anti-gravity breasts into readers' faces, defied all laws of physics . . . the Victoria's Secret catalogue became the Bible of every super-hero artist, an endless source of stilted poses ripe for swiping by boys who wanted their fantasies of women far removed from any human reality.

One study conducted by Jessica H. Zellers shows an examination of how women are depicted in eighteen comic books. She finds that "of the suggestively clad, partially clad, or naked individuals . . . about three times as many were women (296) than men (107)." From the comic book sample where there were 1,768 male characters and 786 female characters, only 6 percent of all males were suggestively clad, partially clad, or naked; while of all the females, 38 percent were suggestively clad, partially clad, or naked. Additionally, of all males, 2 percent were naked, while of all females, 24 percent were naked. Zellers writes: "It is incredible that almost one out of every four females was, at some point, depicted in the nude" (2005, p. 34).

3. "Women of Color" as "Exotic Others"

Often in the analysis of women in comic books, nonwhite women, or women of color, are marginalized or given no mention at all. Without discussing the way women of color are depicted in mainstream American comic books, the analysis remains centered on white women and ignores the manner in which sexism and racism intersect. It would be a mistake to assume that "all women" suffer from the same mistreatment or objectification in comic books. As feminist bell hooks explains:

> A central tenet of modern feminist thought has been the assertion that "all women are oppressed." This assertion implies that women share a common lot, that factors like class, race, religion, sexual preference, etc. do not create a diversity of experience that determines the extent to which sexism will be an oppressive force in the lives of individual women. (1984, p. 5)

During the early history of comic books, which is often referred to as the Golden Age (late 1930s to early 1950s), people of color rarely appeared as superheroes. Lothar, Prince of the Seven Sons, was the first black character to appear in a comic strip titled *Mandrake the Magician*. Lothar was an "illiterate strongman dressed in animal skins" and catered to stereotypical images of "poverty and servitude" (Hogan, 2004, para. 3). A young black male superhero was featured in the 1940s war comic *Young Allies*, but was "nothing more than a minstrel stereotype in a zoot suit, who supplied comic relief"

Continues next page

Emily Kahn, *Women in Comic Books Project*

(Lendrum, 2005, p. 365). Such demeaning caricatures of black men in comic books paralleled the blackface performances in minstrel shows and American cartoons, which featured white actors and cartoon characters, including Mickey Mouse, wearing black makeup to create stereotypical depictions of African Americans. By the civil rights movement in the 1960s, significant changes had been made and new black characters emerged. However, the changes didn't guarantee a departure from stereotypes.

While black male superheroes, such as Black Panther, Luke Cage, Black Lightning, and Black Goliath, made their debuts in the 1960s and 1970s, they were presented as hypermasculine bodies (also note that three of the four black characters mentioned have their race emphasized in their names). That is, they were drawn with larger muscles than their white counterparts, were portrayed as more violent, and reinforced racial stereotypes of black men being "overly masculine" (Lendrum, 2005, p. 365). When black superheroines were introduced in the 1970s, particularly with the appearance of Storm, a mutant who has the ability to control the weather, their bodies were subjected to both sexist and racist stereotypes. In Storm's origin story, for example, she is recruited by X-Men leader Professor X, who finds her being worshipped as a rain goddess by a tribe in Africa. Storm is depicted as mythical and topless, although her long, flowing white hair conveniently covers her breasts. Not only is Storm depicted as a sex object, but she is also exoticized as a *racialized* sex object. As Jeffrey A. Brown, author of *Dangerous Curves: Action Heroines, Gender, Fetishism, and Popular Culture* (2011, p. 170), explains:

> In particular, women of color are consistently marketed and consumed as more bodily, more sexual, and more mysterious than their Caucasian counterparts. In short, ethnically identified women are routinely overwritten by cultural stereotypes and expectations of exotic Otherness, and all the sexual fantasies that implies.

While Storm adds diversity and challenges whiteness in the comic book genre, she also perpetuates the Otherness of women of color. In other words, due to her blackness, not only must she be a character from "over there," but she must also embody popular stereotypes and expectations white writers have about the continent of Africa. One can find a similar pattern when observing the Afghan Muslim super-heroine named Sooraya Qadir, or Dust, who made her 2002 debut in *X-Men*. Although she is intended to be a "positive" representation of Muslims in comic books, her character reinforces Orientalist stereotypes, that is, inaccurate presentations of "the East," particularly the Middle East, in order to reinforce "cultural superiority" of western civilization. Her face and body are fully veiled, though that didn't stop the artists from showing off her curvy figure.

She also needs to be rescued by a white man, namely Wolverine, from misogynist Afghan men who try to take off her clothes and molest her. When Wolverine brings Dust to the X-Men headquarters, she repeatedly says "*toorab*," the Arabic word for "dust." According to Wolverine, "It's all she says."

Dust is not only an "exoticized beauty" who speaks (one word) in a "foreign language" and hides her voluptuous figure behind a black veil, but also a vehicle for a disturbing imperialist narrative. For instance, if one considers how Wolverine slaughters a pile of Afghan militants and saves Dust from sexual molestation, one can see how Wolverine represents a western military intervention to "liberate" the "oppressed Muslim woman." In other words, Wolverine's violent presence in Afghanistan is justified because Dust needs rescuing from Afghan Muslim men (because Orientalism teaches us Islam is misogy-nistic). This narrative demonstrates how the woman of color, per-ceived as being "victimized" by her own people, becomes an object of imperial heteropatriarchal possession because her body, like her land, is violable and obtainable for Western masculinist power. Similarly, in Western politics and war propaganda, the struggle of Afghan women against sexist oppression is used to justify U.S. war and occupation

Continues next page

Emily Kahn, *Women in Comic Books Project*   745

in Afghanistan, despite the fact that bombs and bullets kill Afghan women, men, and children (Smith, 2005, p. 7).

It is worth noting that more superheroines of color are appearing in contemporary comic books, specifically in those produced by the two major comic publishers, DC and Marvel. Brown (2011, p. 168) lists a significant number:

> Latina characters Arana, White Tiger, Fire, and Tarantula; the African American or African heroines Storm, Vixen, Onyx, Steel 2.0, Thunder, Lady Hawk, Misty Knight; the Asian Psylocke, Colleen Wing, Katana, and the most recent Batgirl, the Native North American Rainmaker, Dawnstar, and the most recent Shaman. . . .

These characters have undoubtedly enriched comic books with immense diversity, but only a quick glance at their names is needed to see how they're accompanied by racial stereotypes. Sexual objectification of women of color is accentuated as they are seen as "exotic" and "physically different, but in an exciting way." As Brown (2011, p. 176) states: "While white superheroines are clearly fetishized as sexual ideals as well, the inscription of hypersexuality coupled with ethnicity perpetuates specific cultural stereotypes of exotic Otherness."

4. Exploitation and Sexism

Although some comic book artists argue that drawing women voluptuously and provocatively is a symbol of their strength and power, there are other points that can be emphasized to argue that women are being exploited. Consider the creator of Wonder Woman: a psychologist named William Moulton Marston (pen name: Charles Moulton) who also invented the lie detector. Revealing Marston's intentions and goals on the character of Wonder Woman sheds light upon new attitudes toward women in the world of graphic novels. The fact that Wonder Woman comes from a woman-only "Paradise Island" is enough to suggest heterosexual male fantasy, but Marston also states, "Give [men] an alluring woman stronger than themselves to submit to, and they'll be proud to become her willing slaves." Though Wonder Woman is not subordinate to or weaker than her surrounding male characters in terms of strength and powers, she is being exoticized and idolized by her male creator. Her weapon is a golden lasso, which critics have called an erotic symbol of sexual control since she uses it to make her adversaries obey her commands. Marston has been criticized for his bondage fixations—a recurring theme of Wonder Women tying up both men and women. This theme was so prevalent that the editor of DC comics, Sheldon Mayer, was uncomfortable with it and tried to tone it down (but was unsuccessful). In one 1948 story of Wonder Woman, there are no fewer than seventy-five panels of Wonder Woman tying up men or women in ropes.

One may also find sexist undertones in how many other female characters have abilities and superpowers ranging from being skilled in mundane arts like gymnastics and mind control (Maher, 2005, para. 11). Women of color like the aforementioned Dust have powers that align with dull and unimaginative racial stereotypes. That is, since Dust is from Afghanistan, which is presented as a dusty landscape, she has the ability to manipulate, you guessed it, dust! Sarah Rainmaker, of Apache descent, has the ability to control the weather and, yep, make it rain! White female characters like Madame Mirage, White Queen, and Malice have the ability to use mind control to manipulate their opponents, mostly men! White Queen specifically uses her powers of mind control to manipulate and deceive men in order to gain wealth and power (Lavin, 1998, p. 94). The voluptuous Catwoman uses her beauty to manipulate Batman, Poison Ivy uses her seductive and deadly love potions to gain what she wants, and Malice is able to control the emotional centers of the brain. Hmm, what's next? A female character who marries a rich old man only to have him killed off just to inherit the wealth and property? Wait, they already have a character like that: White Rabbit from the Spider-Man comics!

Continues next page

Emily Kahn, *Women in Comic Books Project*

Sexist representations of women can be found in the work of Frank Miller, one of the most popular and successful comic book writers/artists, who is also notorious for his racist (see his *300* series) and sexist undertones. The misogyny in his comic books is too obvious to be missed. Elektra, for example, is a troubled female assassin and antiheroine. Miller named her after the Greek mythological character of the same name and, as in the myth, Elektra's character develops a sexual attraction to her father (which is the symptom of the Electra complex in neo-Freudian psychology). Early in her life, her Electra complex is strengthened when her father rapes her, but then she is told that it never really happened. "It was only a fantasy . . . and she wanted it to happen. Her belief in her desire for the father grows, but her father dies before she can resolve the Electra complex" (Baughman, 1990, p. 28). One can't help but ask, "What purpose does Elektra's Electra complex serve?"

Frank Miller has also subjected other female characters to subordinate positions, such as Ava Lord in his series *Sin City*. Ava Lord says to a male character: "You're right about me! I'm nothing but a selfish slut who threw away the only man she ever loved . . . I'm such a fool. Such a selfish stupid slut" (Maher, 2005, para. 13). Another character he sexualizes is Vicki Vale in his *All Star Batman and Robin the Boy Wonder* comics. She is drawn in her pink bras and panties while thinking about her upcoming date with Bruce Wayne (a.k.a. Batman). On one panel, she is sucking her finger suggestively, and on the bottom panel, there is a shameless close-up of her buttocks. Below is an excerpt from Frank Miller's script for artist Jim Lee. It speaks for itself:

> OK, Jim, I'm shameless. Let's go with an ASS SHOT. Panties detailed. Balloons from above. She's walking, restless as always. We can't take our eyes off her. Especially since she's got one fine ass.

As analyzed by a feminist comic book reader, Vicki Vale's character is there to "reassure the readership of their hetero-masculinity." She is quintessentially "watched by male watchers: the writer/director (Frank), his artist, and the presumed male audience that buys the book" (Rubinstein, para. 7).

5. The Heterosexual Male Gaze

One could argue that what is at work here is the concept of the "male gaze." This feminist theory was first introduced in the essay "Visual Pleasure and Narrative Cinema" by film theorist Laura Mulvey in 1975. Male gaze is described as "a symptom of power asymmetry" that "projects its fantasy onto the female figure." A defining characteristic of male gaze is how the heterosexual male lets the camera "linger on the curves of the female body." The male gaze "denies women agency, relegating them to the status of objects" (p. 7). When applied to comic books, what we see presented about women is through the gaze of the male. The women are presented as men would want to see them. Similarly, the same images are presented to women as something they should aspire to be if they want to be with a man. In other words, the power and control that characters like Wonder Woman have may be perceived as a woman's control or power over a man, but it is in fact fake control. The male writers can take it away at will. Consider the following "adjustments" made by male writers on the storylines of female characters: "Batwoman is killed, Batgirl is paralyzed, Mirage is raped, while Black Canary is tortured, made infertile, and de-powered!" (Maher, 2005, para. 14). In other words, femininity has no control at all, as long as male writers and artists persist with these depictions and attitudes.

However, the concept of the male gaze needs to be expanded upon in order to recognize the white heterosexual male gaze that is at work. When women of color are objectified, they are seen in the way white heterosexual men want to see them: as exotic, hypersexualized Others. A 2005 Marvel comics series titled *Daughters of the Dragon: Samurai Bullets* starred the black superheroine Misty Knight and her Asian partner Colleen Wing. Misty falls victim to "hypersexualized characterization," which begins early in the series when "her naked body is glimpsed in the shower over the course of two full pages"

Continues next page

(Brown, 2011, p. 178). After losing a half-naked fight with a white female villain, Misty has rough sex with Iron Fist to "blow off some steam." Brown elaborates:

> Though the act is not depicted (thanks primarily to comics code restrictions), the aftermath is shown and it is clear the encounter was aggressive—headboards and lamps are broken—and as Misty dresses Danny [Iron Fist] lies spent in the broken bed, declaring "I think I need an I.V. drip and some pancakes." This scene has no bearing on the story except to mark Misty's assertive and animalistic hyper-sexuality. Rarely, if ever, do white superheroines hook up for random sexual encounters just to "blow off some steam."

Dust also serves as an example of how a Muslim woman is typically perceived in mainstream western media: veiled, oppressed, shy, and mysterious. Through the lens of the heterosexual male gaze, she is veiled and oppressed, but also "sexy," as is illustrated by her skin-tight *abaya*, or outer garment.

I found countless images of female characters in extremely provocative poses: bending over, arching their heads back, tossing their hair, fighting in the rain, and so on. Even the popular characters like Wonder Woman, Storm, Supergirl, and Jean Grey were not spared.

6. What Is the Future for Women in Comic Books?

According to the article "Why Don't 'Black Books' Sell?" by Alan Donald, the comic book industry and readership is dominated by young white men (2003, para. 6). Comics writer-artist Terry Brooks observes that most attendees at comic book conventions are white men. In addition to the racial homogeny, fans are "treated to the sight of several scantily clad professional models dressed in the costumes of popular comic book babes." The models are hired by comics companies to promote upcoming publications, and "for a small fee, any fan can immortalize the fantasy by having his picture taken with one of the role-playing women" (Lavin, 1998, p. 96).

This is not to say women and people of color don't read comic books. There certainly are some who do, but one may also argue that the sexism and racism contribute to the lower number of women readers, particularly women of color. According to comic book artist Trina Robbins:

> Women just don't go into comic-book stores. . . . A woman gets as far as the door, and after the cardboard life-size cut-out of a babe with giant breasts in a little thong bikini and spike-heel boots, the next thing that hits her is the smell. It smells like unwashed teenage boys, and it has this real porn-store atmosphere.

While one may argue that Robbins is generalizing about the nonpresence of women in comic books, she raises an important point about the atmosphere comic book stores create. The images on the covers of comic books featuring Wonder Woman, Catwoman, and other scantily clad superheroines (or random women dangling from the necks of their male saviors) are comparable to the sexualized images featured on the covers of "men's magazines" like *Maxim* and *Playboy*.

The increasing popularity of comic books has influenced other entertainment industries, especially Hollywood. Comic books are being adapted into movies more than ever before. Consider films like *The Dark Knight*, *X-Men*, *Iron Man*, and the Spider-Man films. These films are not only successful, but critically acclaimed as well. Now consider the protagonists of these films: predominantly white men. Has there been a Wonder Woman film in recent years? There have been two comic book films in the past decade with a female protagonist: *Catwoman* and *Elektra*. However, these films were critical and financial failures at the box office. Catwoman is portrayed as a shy black woman who transforms into a hypersexual, animalistic vigilante, while Elektra does battle in a midriff and has an onscreen kiss with another woman (I wonder how heterosexual male fans would react if Batman kissed another man?). Not only are the films taken less seri-

Continues next page

Emily Kahn, *Women in Comic Books Project*   751

ously than the aforementioned comic book movies, but they also seem to be poor excuses to watch Halle Berry and Jennifer Garner fight crime in skintight and revealing costumes.

If there were a Wonder Woman movie, would she have the same fate as Catwoman and Elektra? Considering that Wolverine earned his own spin-off film, would we see a movie about Storm? If so, would the filmmakers depict these superheroines as complex and three-dimensional characters with dilemmas and inner struggles? The X-Men include powerful female characters who can move objects with their minds, control the weather, and run through walls, among other things, but the male characters take center stage. Also, if we look at characters like Supergirl, Batgirl, and Spider-Girl, we notice what they all have in common. That is, they would not have existed if it were not for the original male characters: Superman, Batman, and Spider-Man, respectively. Superman tells Supergirl that he will take care of her like a "big brother," but if Supergirl is the cousin of Superman, then why in the world would she need to be looked after? This is an example of how male dependency is prevalent in comic books, both implicitly and explicitly.

Sexist undertones and stereotypical images are getting worse and increasingly sleazier. Comic books have a unique blend of complex narratives and visual art, which makes them a very popular and appealing form of art, but they also reinforce stereotypes about women—stereotypes about the "ideal" feminine body image: large breasts, thin waists, toned buttocks, long legs, and so on. These "ideals" are misleading because they are setting a standard for beauty in women, and considering the growing popularity of the superhero genre in Hollywood films, more viewers are being attracted to comic books.

We need new interpretations of female comic book characters. Wardrobes have been reinterpreted in the *X-Men* films directed by Bryan Singer; instead of wearing tight leather or spandex, the characters are wearing less provocative clothing (see Anna Paquin's Rogue). However, if we focused only on clothing, we would be overlooking the way in which women are relegated to marginalized and/or stereo-typical roles. In *X-Men: First Class*, the character Angel is a woman of color with superhuman powers, but she is depicted as a stripper. I mention this not to degrade real women who work in the profession, but rather to highlight the pattern in which women of color are consistently hypersexualized in media. Furthermore, Angel decides to betray Professor Xavier's human-friendly mutants by joining the more militant and antihuman mutants led by Magneto. Instead of seeing these stereotypes about gender and race reproduced in comic books and their film adaptations, we need to see more realistic, diverse, and complex female characters—characters that we can not only relate to, but also learn from.

Some admirable efforts have been produced by comic book writer Chris Claremont, who introduced "a string of independent, strong-willed, and generally admirable heroines" in the mid '70s (Lavin, 1998, p. 97). Fourteen-year-old Kitty Pryde (or Shadowcat) of the X-Men is an excellent example of a multilayered female character. She is a teenager who suffers from anxiety, peer pressure, and loneliness, and she has a longing to be treated as an adult. In addition to being a well-developed character, she is not drawn unrealistically with large breasts like Wonder Woman. Another positive female character, Jubilee, is also from the *X-Men* series.

As more female writers and artists make contributions to the industry, male writers and artists will need to be inspired to work against sexism, the objectification of women, and the sexualization of women of color. The more sexualized images and stereotypical roles of women in comic books persist and are left unchallenged, the more sexist ideals for beauty will be reinforced and the less we will see of inspiring superheroines—of all racial backgrounds—truly taking a stand for truth, justice, and liberty.

Continues next page

Emily Kahn, *Women in Comic Books Project*

References

Baughman, L. (1990). A psychoanalytic reading of a female comic book hero: *Elektra: Assassin. Women and Language, 13,* 27–30.

Brown, J. A. (2001). *Black superheroes, Milestone comics, and their fans.* Jackson: University Press of Mississippi. 168.

Brown, J. A. (2011). *Dangerous curves: Action heroines, gender, fetishism, and popular culture.* Jackson: University Press of Mississippi. 168, 170, 176, 178.

Donald, A., et al. (2003, September 9). The panel: Why don't 'black books' sell?" *Silver Bullet Comic Books.* Retrieved from http://www.silverbulletcomicbooks.com/panel/1063121223602.htm

Feiffer, J. (1965). *The great comic book heroes.* New York: Dial Press. 21.

Gorman, M. (2003). *Getting graphic! Using graphic novels to promote literacy with preteens and teens.* Worthington, Ohio: Linworth Publishing.

Hendrix, G. (2007, December 11). Out for justice. *The New York Sun.*

Hogan, E. (2004, February 5). Afros, icons, and spandex: A brief history of the African American superhero. *Open Your Mouth.* Retrieved from http://www.comicbookresources.com/?page=article&id=14623

hooks, b. (1984). *Feminist theory: From margin to center.* Cambridge, MA: South End Press. 5.

Jones, G., & Jacobs, W. (2005). *The comic book heroes* (rev. ed.). Rocklin, CA: Prima Publishing.

Lavin, M. (1998). Women in comic books. *Serials Review, 24,* 93–100.

Lendrum, R. (2005). The super black macho, one baaad mutha: Black superhero masculinity in 1970s mainstream comic books. *Extrapolation, 46,* 360–372.

Maher, K. (2005, June 2). Comic contempt. *The London Times.* Retrieved from http://www.thetimes.co.uk/tto/arts/film/article2429806.ece

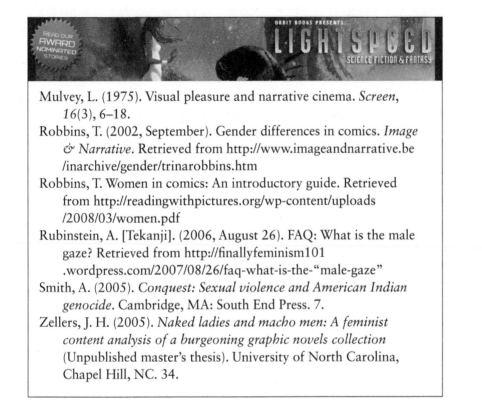

Mulvey, L. (1975). Visual pleasure and narrative cinema. *Screen*, *16*(3), 6–18.

Robbins, T. (2002, September). Gender differences in comics. *Image & Narrative*. Retrieved from http://www.imageandnarrative.be /inarchive/gender/trinarobbins.htm

Robbins, T. Women in comics: An introductory guide. Retrieved from http://readingwithpictures.org/wp-content/uploads /2008/03/women.pdf

Rubinstein, A. [Tekanji]. (2006, August 26). FAQ: What is the male gaze? Retrieved from http://finallyfeminism101 .wordpress.com/2007/08/26/faq-what-is-the-"male-gaze"

Smith, A. (2005). *Conquest: Sexual violence and American Indian genocide.* Cambridge, MA: South End Press. 7.

Zellers, J. H. (2005). *Naked ladies and macho men: A feminist content analysis of a burgeoning graphic novels collection* (Unpublished master's thesis). University of North Carolina, Chapel Hill, NC. 34.

5. Should I Add This Source to My Working Bibliography?

Emily is now satisfied that the author of the article is knowledgeable and that the article itself is interesting, readable, and potentially quite useful for her research project. She decides to add it to her working bibliography. She will return to the piece again later. Emily's next step is to create a research plan. (See pp. 774–75 for information on research plans.)

EVALUATING A SOURCE

Evaluating a source is much like previewing a source (see pp. 732–38), only with more depth and attention to specifics. Once you've decided that a source is a potential "keeper," it's time to do a closer reading of it and decide whether it fits in with your research plan. Your main questions include:

» Is this a trustworthy source—do the author and publication convey an ethos of credibility?

» Will it work for my assignment—and further my purpose?

Calvin Sweet: Hurricane Katrina Project

▲ STUDENT AUTHOR
Calvin Sweet
Shutterstock.

In the following pages, we will follow student Calvin Sweet as he looks at three different sources related to his topic, Hurricane Katrina. These sources, which appear on pages 764–73, are:

» **Madison Gray**, "The Press, Race and Katrina," an argument/editorial from *Time* magazine online.

» **Lincoln Shlensky**, "Hurricane Katrina, Race and Class: Part I," an argument/editorial from Shlensky's blog, titled *Aulula*.

» **Amardeep Singh**, "Race and Hurricane Katrina: two questions," an argument/editorial from Singh's self-titled blog, *Amardeep Singh*.

You'll read these sources along with Calvin in the next few pages. For now, here is information on each author, and the context in which his work appeared.

Madison Gray, "The Press, Race and Katrina"   Madison Gray, a journalist and the Home Page Producer for *Time*, makes choices about the content that appears daily at Time.com. On his LinkedIn page, he describes himself as a "writer, online editor, breaking news monitor, and critical thinker." Gray was educated at Central Michigan University and his experience includes work with AOL Black Voices and the Knight Digital Media Center. He writes in his biography for *Time*: "Looking at my years in this craft, you could call me jack-of-all trades, but I'm really a student. Beginning in my hometown of Detroit, first writing [for] business, then doing radio, transitioning to a major daily, and finally finding my way to the East Coast to find a place in Internet news, the surprises keep on coming." Madison Gray wrote

◀ AUTHOR PHOTO
Madison Gray
On his Twitter page, Madison Gray comments on his career to date: "Two decades, three continents, no apologies. I deliver news like Thelonius, baby: straight, no chaser." Gray's experience contributes to his ethos as a trustworthy source. *Kenneth Goldberg.*

his editorial about Hurricane Katrina in 2006, almost one year after the storm. In it, Gray calls attention to his views on how journalists handled the reporting of Katrina, especially in terms of race. Gray's editorial appears on page 764.

Lincoln Shlensky, "Hurricane Katrina, Race and Class: Part I"   Dr. Lincoln Shlensky, author of the blog *Aulula*, is an assistant professor of English at the University of Victoria. During Hurricane Katrina, Shlensky was an assistant professor of English at the University of Alabama in Mobile. As a resident of Mobile, he was directly affected by Katrina. In his blog entry titled "Hurricane Katrina, Race and Class: Part I," he discusses his perspective on Katrina in relation to how the press covered the event. An excerpt from Shlensky's blog entry appears on page 768.

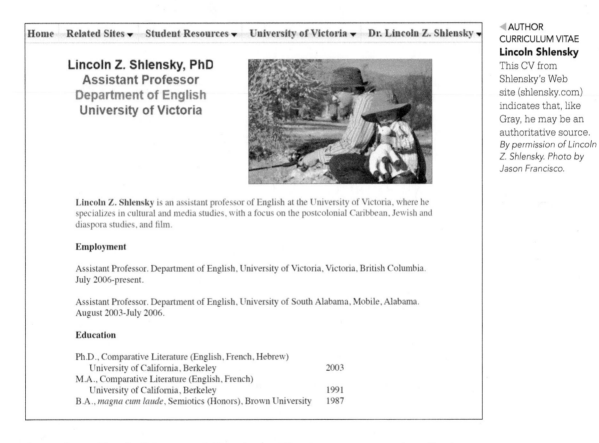

| Home | Related Sites ▾ | Student Resources ▾ | University of Victoria ▾ | Dr. Lincoln Z. Shlensky ▾ |

Lincoln Z. Shlensky, PhD
Assistant Professor
Department of English
University of Victoria

Lincoln Z. Shlensky is an assistant professor of English at the University of Victoria, where he specializes in cultural and media studies, with a focus on the postcolonial Caribbean, Jewish and diaspora studies, and film.

Employment

Assistant Professor. Department of English, University of Victoria, Victoria, British Columbia. July 2006-present.

Assistant Professor. Department of English, University of South Alabama, Mobile, Alabama. August 2003-July 2006.

Education

Ph.D., Comparative Literature (English, French, Hebrew)
University of California, Berkeley   2003
M.A., Comparative Literature (English, French)
University of California, Berkeley   1991
B.A., *magna cum laude*, Semiotics (Honors), Brown University   1987

◄ AUTHOR CURRICULUM VITAE
Lincoln Shlensky
This CV from Shlensky's Web site (shlensky.com) indicates that, like Gray, he may be an authoritative source. *By permission of Lincoln Z. Shlensky. Photo by Jason Francisco.*

Amardeep Singh, "Race and Hurricane Katrina: two questions"   Amardeep Singh is an associate professor of English at Lehigh University. His Lehigh blog includes postings on a variety of subjects: his vacation in Ireland, a book writ-

AUTHOR'S FACULTY ▶
HOMEPAGE
**Amardeep Singh and
Lehigh University**
Singh's biography on
his university's Web
site helps establish him
as a potentially reliable
source. *By permission of
Amardeep Singh.*

ten by a graduate school friend, Bollywood, and Hurricane Katrina, the topic of the posting below. In his blog posting titled "Race and Hurricane Katrina: two questions," Singh briefly explores how race played into the response to the hurricane. (Note: Singh now has a more current blog.) An excerpt from Singh's blog posting appears on page 771.

Before we read these sources on Hurricane Katrina in depth, we'll identify some guidelines for evaluating sources.

How Do I Evaluate a Source? How Is This Different from Previewing?

While some of this overlaps with advice on previewing sources, we are asking you to do a more in-depth analysis of texts than you did earlier in the chapter. To evaluate whether a source is strong enough to draw upon for your own writing, ask yourself the questions posed in the following section.

1. Is this source relevant to my project?   First, determine whether the source you're looking at is related to and useful for your project and research question(s). Ask yourself: Does the information in the source generate additional research questions related to my original question—does it get me deeper into my research? Does the source contribute to my knowledge on the topic—did I learn something new about the subject? In other words, does the author simply rehash what others have said, or does he or she say something new—or provide an alternative perspective? If the author simply duplicates knowledge, then the source is probably not a good choice for your project.

2. What is the author's level of credibility? When evaluating a source, you need to figure out how trustworthy the author is. Ask yourself:

» *What can I find out by Googling the author?* Learn about the author's education, degrees held, and any institutional, organizational, or professional affiliations. Find out whether the author is mentioned in other sources on the topic, and to what extent he or she is considered to be an "expert" on the subject by other experts in the field. Research other works by the author: One indicator of expertise is whether someone has published numerous times on the subject. However, don't discount the author's credibility just because this is the author's first piece on the subject—the author could be a rising scholar in the field.

» *What if I can't figure out who the individual author is?* If there is no obvious author, look at the reliability of the organization sponsoring the Web site. For example, if the site is the American Diabetes Association, you can assume that the information presented is researched and reliable because it is an organization that publishes researched articles on diabetes. Additionally, this organization funds research. On its Web site, the association states, "We provide objective and credible information."

No matter how much you might agree with the viewpoint conveyed in a source or how much you might like the way the author has presented information, establishing the author's credibility is absolutely necessary if you are to use this source in your research. If you cannot trust the author, then you should not use the source.

3. What is the author's purpose? To persuade? Inform? Tell a story? Some combination? Identify the author's purpose by reading the source critically and carefully. As you read, ask yourself the following questions to determine the author's objectives:

» What is the author's thesis? Does the thesis make an argument?

» Is the author trying to get me to agree with an opinion?

» Is the author presenting facts and information to teach me about the subject?

» Does the author use a narrative structure (include characters, conflict, setting)?

Once you have determined the purpose, ask yourself whether the author's purpose fits with your research question(s). A persuasive source can provide information that you can use to support or refute your argument. Informative and narrative sources may provide background for you or lend a personal perspective to your subject. For example, student Calvin Sweet's sources (see p. 756) are three

Have you ever Googled someone? If so, how did what you discovered affect your view of that person? If you've ever Googled yourself, how accurate was the information you found? What type of person did the information portray? #Understand

Evaluating a Source 759

editorials in which authors seek to persuade readers about Hurricane Katrina. One of these texts, Madison Gray's "The Press, Race and Katrina" (p. 764), presents an argument critiquing the way the press handled the reporting of Katrina in relationship to race. Calvin knows this because as he reads the article, he notes that the author discusses and provides specific examples from the media. He also circles explicit related statements such as, "many journalists who monitored the coverage felt in hindsight that African Americans caught in Katrina's wake were misrepresented in the press."

When determining an author's purpose, remember that genre might be able to give you a clue. For example, if the source is an editorial, you can assume that the author's purpose is to persuade you; however, the author might also be telling a story to support that opinion. You need to read the source carefully to fully know the author's purpose.

Ultimately, by knowing the author's purpose you can determine whether the source is a good fit for your research topic. If your goal is to persuade your reader, then a source that provides useful evidence is a good fit. If the author's purpose is to tell a story and none of the information helps you advance your own claim, then you shouldn't use that source.

4. Who is the author's target audience? How does the author use rhetorical appeals to reach that audience? When you preview a source, you determine the author's audience (see "Previewing a Source," p. 732). In order to determine the audience, ask yourself the following questions:

» Does the place of publication offer clues about audience? (For example, an editorial in *Bloomberg Businessweek* is clearly aimed at a business audience.)

» Does the author use a formal or informal tone?

» What level of detail is presented in the piece?

» Does the author include information that assumes previous knowledge?

» Does the author use jargon or vocabulary used by experts?

When Calvin reads Shlensky's blog entry about Katrina (p. 768), he notices that the author uses informal language, such as "I'm doing okay." This tells Calvin that Shlensky's primary audience is people concerned about how Hurricane Katrina affected him.

Once you've determined the audience for the text, take a look at how the author appeals to that audience. Is the author establishing a sense of credibility that speaks to particular readers? Is the author using an emotional appeal to connect with the audience? Calvin notices that Shlensky begins his blog with an emotional appeal to those who know him, discussing the long lines for gas he experiences and his concern for those who live closer to where the hurricane hit.

Besides identifying the audience and analyzing rhetorical appeals, you also need to examine the evidence the author provides and determine whether it is appropriate for his or her intended audience. Pay attention, too, to how the author keeps readers' perspectives in mind, so that they will continue to read the piece. For example, when Calvin reads Singh's piece (p. 771), he notices that the author is mindful that his audience might be put off if he makes huge generalizations about racism, so he qualifies his statements by saying "I'm not trying to imply racism is afoot."

Knowing whether a source is written for a general audience or experts in the field helps you determine how appropriate the source is for research. For example, you may want to choose more specialized sources, written for a specific audience, if you're looking for detail and research so you can dig deeper into your topic inquiry. Or, if you want to make an argument—supported by research and data—about the impact of global warming on animals, you might turn to the journal *Nature* (written for a specialized audience), rather than *USA Today* (written for a general audience).

5. What is the source's genre? Does the author make the most of its conventions? Let's say you're considering using a news and opinion blog as a source. As you evaluate it, look at a few other examples to see how other bloggers typically convey information—and the types of conventions they tend to adhere to. How does your potential source compare with other blogs? Does your blogger take advantage of the conventions of the genre? For example, does he clearly identify himself as the author? Does he embed hyperlinks to additional details or sources? Does he invite feedback? If not, you might want to consider using a different source. When an author chooses to ignore the traditional conventions of a genre, he may also ignore other things, such as using reliable evidence to support opinions.

6. How does the author use evidence—and how reliable is that evidence? As you evaluate a source, pay close attention to how the author supports his claims and arguments. Look at:

> » *Sufficient support: Does the author use enough evidence?* If not, that's a problem. A skilled persuasive writer will back up each claim with an appropriate example. Read the source and (1) make a note every time the author makes a claim, and (2) also note whether the claim is supported. Notice also whether the evidence is vague and general, or specific and detailed. For example, Madison Gray, the author of one of Calvin Sweet's sources on Hurricane Katrina, race, and the media, writes:

Do you read any blogs regularly? If so, think of two or three that you particularly enjoy. What do they have in common in terms of how the bloggers present information? Do they share design elements, such as headings and lists? Are there things that are done better on one blog than on the others? #Understand

CLAIM

"In fact, many journalists who monitored the coverage felt in hindsight that African Americans caught in Katrina's wake were misrepresented in the press."

Gray follows that claim with evidence—a quote from one person—that shows that at least one person believed there was misrepresentation. However, he doesn't sufficiently support his statement that "many journalists" felt that way. He could have made a stronger case by drawing on, say, a study of many journalists, or providing multiple quotes from journalists, for example.

INADEQUATE EVIDENCE

"I don't think African Americans were portrayed in the best light," said Camille Jackson, a staff writer for the Southern Poverty Law Center's Tolerance.org Web site. "It came out just how uncomfortable the media is when it comes to race, with the exception of a few."

☞ **Attention, researchers! A note about evidence.**

Wondering what we mean by "evidence"? Evidence is facts, examples, and source citations that authors use to illustrate and support each point they make in their compositions. Skilled authors use evidence to develop their arguments as well as their ethos. The type of evidence authors choose reflects upon them; for example, citing a celebrity gossip magazine as evidence suggests shallowness, while citing the *Wall Street Journal* suggests professionalism.

When you're evaluating a source, look at how the author uses evidence: Think of the evidence as the foundation upon which the argument is built. A shoddy foundation can cause even the most beautiful building to crumble.

» *Timeliness: Is the source and evidence current?* In most cases, you'll want to draw on sources that are as recent as possible. For example, if you are researching current trends in social media and how they affect elections, you would want the most up-to-date information. With this same topic, you might also choose to draw on perspectives from the past in order to compare how things might have changed. In either case, be sure to check the dates of your sources and when they were last updated, especially when you research online.

Timeliness mattered to Calvin Sweet when he conducted research on Hurricane Katrina. He knew he wanted a contemporary account of the hurricane, told by someone who had survived it. He wanted reporting based on actual events that occurred at the moment of the storm—so he looked for sources published on or around the storm date. He was excited to find Lincoln Z. Shlensky's blog entry, "Hurricane Katrina, Race and Class: Part I," dated September 2, 2005, just a few days after the August 29, 2005, landfall of the hurricane.

If Calvin had wanted a source focused on the longer-term aftermath of the storm—perhaps a yearlong study on the impact of the hurricane on people's lives—he'd probably have searched for sources written in 2006 or later. Such a source would likely draw on research conducted over time; the author could report the information provided in a study, or perhaps reflect on the situation, drawing on the study's data as supporting evidence for his claims. Depending on how you plan to use a source, its timeliness could make a difference. If you are looking for a contemporary account of an incident, then obviously a reflection written ten years later would not be appropriate.

7. Does the author cite sources?   As you evaluate a source, ask yourself: Does the author give credit to others? Does he mention the work of others in the text itself—perhaps with hyperlinks or a list of credits? How easily can I tell where the author obtained his or her information? If you can't tell what sources the author drew on, it's possible that the information isn't well researched or can't be supported.

Citation conventions—and by this we mean the format in which an author identifies his sources—can vary across genres. Before you can judge whether an author has cited sources properly, you need to be aware of the documentation conventions for the genre you are looking at. For example:

» Authors of newspaper articles usually cite sources in the body of the article itself, by using quotations and naming people and publications they've drawn on.

» Authors of blogs usually cite sources by providing hyperlinks to them, assuming the sources are online sources. You can see this in the two blog entries on Katrina featured in this chapter.

» Authors of peer-reviewed journal articles usually use strict source-citing conventions; for example, *The American Journal of Family Therapy*, a peer-reviewed journal on family behavioral health, requires authors to cite sources in accordance with the *Publication Manual of the American Psychological Association*. (See Chapter 7 for information on APA documentation style.) Considering that professional counselors rely on information in *The American Journal of Family Therapy* to inform their professional practice and research, it makes sense that source citation would be taken very seriously by the editors.

Once you know something about the citation conventions of a genre, ask yourself: Does the author of the source I'm evaluating cite sources the way he should? For example, a journalist who doesn't mention any sources in an article or editorial should raise eyebrows—but a blogger who uses hyperlinks (rather than an academic style such as APA) should not. In a reliable text, an author makes it clear where he or she drew from the material of others. The author provides this information in the format that is common to that genre. If the source you're looking at falls short on this score, you may want to look for a different one.

The Internet has made it possible to invent new genres quickly and easily. For example, just a short time ago, a "tweet" did not exist, but now the genre is incredibly popular. How do you think creators and users of these new genres decide how to cite their sources? What factors might contribute to their decisions? #Understand #Analyze

Guided Process: How to Evaluate Sources ▼

Calvin Sweet (Student)

Hurricane Katrina Project: Evaluating 3 Sources

▲ STUDENT AUTHOR
PHOTO
Calvin Sweet
Shutterstock.

Let's circle back to Calvin Sweet, who has identified a research question—and three sources that he's thinking of using.

RESEARCH QUESTION

How did the press treat race and class in their coverage of Hurricane Katrina and what are the consequences of that treatment?

Using the guidelines on pages 758–63, Calvin now evaluates his sources. His notes in the margins of each source show his thinking. He begins with Madison Gray's editorial for *Time*. (For biographical information on Madison Gray, see p. 756.) *(Article & Time branding: © 2009. Time Inc. Reprinted/Translated from TIME.COM and published with permission of Time Inc. Reproduction in any manner in any language in whole or in part without written permission is prohibited. TIME and the TIME logo are trademarks of Time Inc. Used under license.)*

Calvin's notes on Gray's argument

Relevant to my topic?

Yes. I want to look at media coverage of Katrina, as it relates to race and class. Madison Gray's critique of the storm coverage relates directly to my topic.

Credible author?

Yes. Gray writes for *Time*, so I trust he's a reliable journalist. He's also reported for the AP, *The New York Times*, and the *Detroit News*; he's a member of the New York Association of Black Journalists.

TIME

VIEWPOINT
The Press, Race and Katrina
Madison Gray

Home	NewsFeed	U.S.	Politics	World	Business	Tech	Health	Science	Entertainment	Style	Opinion	Photos

If you watched any television, listened to any radio, picked up a newspaper or visited a news Web site in the days that followed Hurricane Katrina last year, you probably were witness to the result of dozens of on-the-spot editorial decisions made by news managers around the country.

As much as we may have wanted to avoid the issue in those first confusing days, because New Orleans was 67% African American prior to the storm, race played a significant role in criticisms of government, both local and federal, humanitarian aid and not surprisingly, the media. Fortunately, the fourth estate has its own self-policing mechanisms and is much faster than government and other industries at evaluating and scrutinizing itself. But it is only in recent years that the media has taken a look at how it relates to the country's racial divisions, and Katrina provided an opportunity to do just that.

Keith Woods, faculty dean of the Poynter Institute, a St. Petersburg, Florida–based journalism training organization, said many

TIME

Home   NewsFeed   U.S.   Politics   World   Business   Tech   Health   Science   Entertainment   Style   Opinion   Photos

mistakes were made by the media, but in bringing attention to the crisis, the press got it right.

"The media brought a palpable sense of outrage with the coverage from the very beginning," said Woods. "If you looked at NPR, CNN, and scattered sightings of the networks and newspapers, where they did well was to recognize the size of the story and the need to stay with it."

But where race comes in is more difficult, he told me. Where journalism failed is not in any lack of emphasis on how disproportionately blacks were affected, but in how "too many people were making the surface observation that there were lots of blacks affected without spending the time parsing the facts that would make it meaningful or informative."

In fact, many journalists who monitored the coverage felt in hindsight that African Americans caught in Katrina's wake were misrepresented in the press.

"I don't think African Americans were portrayed in the best light," said Camille Jackson, a staff writer for the Southern Poverty Law Center's Tolerance.org Web site. "It came out just how uncomfortable the media is when it comes to race, with the exception of a few."

Jackson authored a series of articles for the Web site that spoke to media outlets referring to victims as "hoodlums," "animals" and "thugs." But she said it comes from cultural insensitivity in the media, which led to false news reports and eventually to a curtailing of emergency response.

She warned that the important lesson to be learned is "to be an honest journalist, to tell the whole story, and be aware of your

Continues next page

Calvin's notes on Gray's argument

I did a search for Gray on Google and found his 2008 article on Rodney King that won a journalism award. Race definitely factors into some of his articles.

Author's purpose?

Gray wants to persuade readers that "African Americans caught in Katrina's wake were misrepresented in the press." He also wants to inform about how journalists dealt with race in reporting the storm.

Audience?

Gray is writing for *Time* readers, especially African Americans who experienced Katrina and whose stories were not properly reflected in the press. His readers are also probably interested in journalism and concerned about media bias. Gray relies on ethos to appeal to readers' concerns.

Calvin's notes on Gray's argument

Identifiable genre/mode/media?

This magazine article is an editorial: Gray's column is titled "Viewpoint." Its mode is written and it is published online.

Essentially, Gray's article is an argument. He presents his case in short paragraphs and works in sources and quotes: This technique is common to editorials and other journalistic writing.

Reliable evidence?

Gray's sources include a journalism dean, a journalist, and other media experts; he also refers to a congressional report. That all seems solid.

Gray writes: "many journalists who monitored the coverage felt in hindsight that African Americans caught in Katrina's wake were misrepresented in the press."

TIME

Home   NewsFeed   U.S.   Politics   World   Business   Tech   Health   Science   Entertainment   Style   Opinion   Photos

own personal biases. I know it's scary, but we're going to have to start talking about race so that we can get at the fear."

Buttressing criticisms of the press response to Katrina was a bipartisan Congressional report released in February that outright accuses the media of making a bad situation worse. It does not specify race in its pages, but its accusations implicate press reports that it says contributed to the confusion.

The report from the bipartisan House committee investigated preparations for and responses to Katrina and found that media reports of gunshots fired at rescue helicopters, rapes and murders in the Superdome, and mass rioting in the streets were unsubstantiated at best, and many were simply false. "It's clear accurate reporting was among Katrina's many victims," the report says. "If anyone rioted, it was the media."

But Margaret Engel, managing editor of the Newseum, an Arlington, Virginia–based interactive news museum, said there are more important things to consider, like images that seemingly cast a divide between black and white survivors. Two in particular were now-infamous captions placed with Agence France-Presse and Associated Press photos. The AFP photo caption described two whites as "finding" food, while the AP caption described a black youth as "looting" a store.

"That to me is much more troubling than reporters quoting cops who didn't really know," said Engel. "I think you'll find that some of the stories on that day of looting were wildly overstated. It's not good that the press reported that, but it is a footnote to the overall coverage which riveted the nation over the lack of response." She added: "I think for Congress to cast the media response as rumor-mongering is to miss the forest for the trees."

TIME

Home   NewsFeed   U.S.   Politics   World   Business   Tech   Health   Science   Entertainment   Style   Opinion   Photos

Despite the varied points of view, two things are clear. First, mistakes were made. As Woods pointed out, there has never been a how-to book on covering a disaster that nearly wipes out a whole city. Secondly, and most importantly, if African Americans in New Orleans are to be fairly served, the story must be told. "Now that the initial event has passed, the problem is maintaining people's attention," said Richard Prince, chairman of the National Association of Black Journalists' Media Monitoring Committee. "People are desperate for media attention because they fear the country will forget them. While a lot of reporters have covered the follow-up, it has not been compelling enough."

Prince said that the way to learn from what happened is for journalists to continually go to the Gulf Coast Region and find new stories, which are abundant. "They call it one of the worst natural disasters in the history of the country. So many people have a story to tell; somehow those stories have to be told."

Calvin's notes on Gray's argument

He supports this claim by mentioning one specific journalist. Are there others he could mention to back this statement more strongly?

Sources cited?

Gray attributes his information to sources when he quotes people and names them in the body of the editorial.

He also provides hyperlinks so readers can get more information. For example, I clicked on the Keith Woods link and it took me to the Poynter Institute, where Woods was faculty dean (until 2010 when he joined NPR).

After reading through the informative and persuasive piece in *Time*, Calvin decided he wanted a more personal lens into the issues of the press and its reporting of Katrina. He found Lincoln Shlensky's blog containing writing about his views related to press coverage of Katrina. Additionally, he found that Shlensky provided the argumentative take on the situation that he was looking for. (For more biographical information on Lincoln Shlensky, see p. 757). *(The following blog post is reprinted here by permission of Lincoln Z. Shlensky.)*

Calvin's notes on Shlensky's argument

Relevant to my topic?

Yes. Shlensky focuses on issues of race and how they affected the media's response to the disaster. This will be a valuable source for my research.

Credible author?

Yes. Shlensky is a college professor, and I trust that his research and sources are valid. His area of specialty is Caribbean literature (he holds a PhD), and according to his CV, he's presented numerous times on this subject, looking at issues of race in relationship to literature.

Because he's regularly subject to the peer review of fellow academics, I'd imagine Shlensky is careful with how he states things. Also, as an educator, he may look at his loss during Katrina through a more analytical than emotional lens.

AULULA
A LYTTELL POTTE

LINCOLN Z. SHLENSKY

Hurricane Katrina, Race and Class: Part I

I have been in Pensacola, Florida, since late Tuesday because my house in Mobile still is without electricity. I'm doing okay here, but I look forward to getting back home as soon as electricity is restored. The University is supposed to reopen on September 6th, but that may change, depending on conditions. Yesterday and today the gas stations here in Pensacola were mainly without gas, and I waited in a long line at the one station that (only briefly) had gas to offer. It's scary to see people begin to panic when basic commodities are in short supply; I can only imagine to what degree such a sense of panic must be magnified nearer to the epicenter, where essential necessities such as water, food, and sanitation are in severe shortage.

From my vantage—geographically and emotionally near the disaster, but safely buffered from its worst deprivations—much of the press coverage has not adequately dealt with the most difficult social issues that mark this still unfolding catastrophe. It is difficult to avoid concluding that one important cause of the slow response to the debacle has to do with the fact that most of the people who are caught up in it are poor and black. Here in Pensacola I keep hearing blame expressed towards the victims: "they should have heeded the call to evacuate." Even the FEMA chief said as much in a news conference today. So where, I must ask, were the buses he should have provided to take them away before Katrina hit? Where were the troops to supervise evacuation? Where were the emergency shelters and health services? People who ought to know better do not seem to understand or acknowledge the enormous differential in available resources—access to transportation, money, information, social services,

AULULA

etc.—that forms the background to this human catastrophe. Terms such as "looting" are tossed about in the press and on TV with no class or race analysis at all. In recent news reports, there is an emerging discussion of the *political* background to the calamity: the Bush administration's curtailment of federal funding for levee repair in order to pay for the war in Iraq, rampant commercial housing development on environmentally protected wetlands, financial evisceration of FEMA, and so on. But there's been little or no discussion of the economic background that makes New Orleans a kind of "Third World" nation unto itself, with fearsomely deteriorated housing projects, extraordinarily high crime and murder rates, and one of the worst public education systems in the country.

Major newspaper editors and TV producers have prepared very few reports about issues of race in this disaster, and those reports that have appeared so far seem to me deeply insufficient in their analysis of endemic class and race problems. I've been communicating with a national magazine reporter friend of mine since Tuesday night about the issues of race and class in this catastrophe; here's my email comment on this topic from earlier today:

CNN addressed the race question today on TV, but only to ask softball questions of Jesse Jackson, who to his discredit didn't exhibit even a modicum of the anger of one Louisiana black political leader, who said: "While the Administration has spoken of 'shock and awe' in the war on terror, the response to this disaster has been 'shockingly awful.'"

The *Washington Post* also ran a puff piece that doesn't ask any of the relevant questions, such as whether the Administration's response would have been faster if these were white people suffering the agonies of a slow motion disaster. Here's the link to the *Post*'s piece.

Michael Moore also had this to say in a letter to President Bush circulated today:

Continues next page

Calvin's notes on Shlensky's argument

Author's purpose?

Shlensky writes his post to persuade readers that "much of the press coverage has not adequately dealt with the most difficult social issues that mark this still unfolding catastrophe . . . [because] most of the people who are caught up in it are poor and black."

Audience?

Shlensky writes to those critical of the media. He appeals to his audience with ethos (using quotes and evidence from media coverage) and pathos, hoping his audience gets angry enough to demand attention to the issues of race.

Calvin Sweet, *Hurricane Katrina Project*   769

Calvin's notes on Shlensky's argument

Identifiable genre/ mode/medium?

Shlensky mixes information and opinion. He uses blog conventions such as hyperlinks, comments, and an archive of his previous posts.

Reliable evidence?

There is a good amount of evidence and it's varied, including firsthand observations and references to a news report and Michael Moore's letter to President Bush. The entry is timely (he wrote it within days of Katrina making landfall).

Sources cited?

Shlensky attributes quotes and information throughout. He also uses hyperlinks to take you to the full source, such as when he discusses the *Washington Post* article.

AULULA

No, Mr. Bush, you just stay the course. It's not your fault that 30 percent of New Orleans lives in poverty or that tens of thousands had no transportation to get out of town. C'mon, they're black! I mean, it's not like this happened to Kennebunkport. Can you imagine leaving white people on their roofs for five days? Don't make me laugh! Race has nothing—NOTHING—to do with this!

(See Michael Moore's full letter here.)

A member of the Congressional Black Caucus had to remind reporters today to stop referring to those displaced by the flooding with the blanket term "refugees" (recalling, of course, the waves of Haitian or Central American or Southeast Asian refugees who sought shelter in the United States): these people are citizens, she said, deserving of the full protections guaranteed to all Americans.

The federal government promised on Wednesday that those receiving food stamps could get their full allotment at the beginning of September, rather than the usual piecemeal distribution throughout the month. How very generous. What these people need is relief money and access to services now—even the 50,000 or so exhausted and traumatized people whose images we've seen at the N.O. Superdome and at the Civic Center are just a few of the far larger number of those residents of the region displaced by the hurricane, many of whom live from monthly paycheck to paycheck. It will be months at the very least before these people can return home; their jobs may be gone for good. The mayor of New Orleans was actually caught off camera crying in frustration today at the slow pace of the federal response.

If there is a hopeful side to this tragedy, it is perhaps that Hurricane Katrina's damage and efforts to relieve those displaced by the storm may spark a wider national discussion about the ongoing and unaddressed issues of race and economic disparity in America. If that doesn't happen, I fear that there will be even further

AULULA

deterioration in the living conditions and economic predicament of those left destitute and homeless by Katrina—a situation in which our own government's years of neglect must be included as a crucial contributing factor. We must not let such a deterioration of conditions for those hardest hit by Katrina occur.

What happens next, when tens or hundreds of thousands of Americans require long-term recovery help, will be an important barometer of our society's ability to heal itself.

After realizing that Shlensky's blog contained a lot of evidence to support the writer's opinion, Calvin decided that another blog might give him additional anecdotes related to Katrina. Even though Amardeep Singh was not directly affected by the hurricane, his blog entry reflects his reaction to what occurred and raises questions to help Calvin dig deeper into his research. (For biographical information on Amardeep Singh, see p. 761.) *(The following blog post is reprinted here by permission of Amardeep Singh.)*

Amardeep Singh

Race and Hurricane Katrina: two questions

Though I haven't written about it this week, I've been watching and reading the coverage of Katrina in New Orleans with a mixture of awe and horror.

Two quick thoughts for discussion.

Continues next page

Calvin's notes on Singh's argument

Relevant to my topic?

While Singh touches on issues of race and raises an interesting point about how some media compared the devastation to

Calvin's notes on Singh's argument

that of third-world countries, I'm not sure that there's enough informa- tion here to be useful. The source, though, does make me think about the issues.

Credible author?

Like Shlensky, Singh is a profes- sor subject to peer review. He has published re- searched articles, so I expect this same expertise in his blog entries.

Like Shlensky, Singh takes an analytical, academic-seeming, approach, with no direct experience of Katrina.

Author's purpose?

Singh wants read- ers to consider why the media is not examining the issue of race in relationship to Katrina.

Audience?

Singh's audience is most likely his fel- low academics and those who read his blog.

Amardeep Singh

First, have you noticed that numerous articles refer to the affected region as "third world" in its devastation? (Example: CNN) I always cringe when I read that.

But it's worth thinking about. Remember how after the Bombay flood last month (37.1 inches in 24 hours), there were numerous articles in the Indian media lamenting the city's inability to keep things running smoothly? Well, it doesn't just happen in India. Natural disasters happen to everyone; it isn't something to be embarrassed about. (Still, I wish they wouldn't use poorer parts of the world as a benchmark for the scale of the disaster.)

Here the authorities had access to good predictions for the storm, and were able to execute a large-scale evacuation of *part of the population* quickly. It would be great if monsoon rains could be predicted with as much accuracy. Does anyone know the science behind this? Why did no one have any idea that 37 inches of rain were about to hit the city of Bombay last month?

[Update: The fact that they had good predictions makes it all the more unbelievable that the post-hurricane evacuation of New Orleans has been so inept.]

It is also worth considering that the area in question with Katrina is much less densely populated than Bombay (1.5 million people in the entire New Orleans metro area; compare to 20 million– plus in greater Bombay).

The second issue circles around race within the United States. If you watch the news footage of the post-Katrina rescue opera- tions, you'll notice again and again that the people being rescued seem to be overwhelmingly African American.

There could be any number of reasons for this. One is, it's quite plausible to infer that more African Americans ignored or didn't get the message about the mandatory evacuation before the storm. Some folks may not have had the physical means to get

Amardeep Singh

out (i.e., a car & a credit card), or a place to go. Another factor might be topography: it's possible that many black neighborhoods are in low-lying areas (though I admit I don't know the New Orleans area very well). And finally, one shouldn't forget that in terms of sheer demographics, these areas as a whole have large African American populations.

I'm not trying to imply racism is afoot. Only this: the fact that blacks seem to have been disproportionately affected by this tragedy reminds us of the inequities that existed before the Hurricane happened. When we see folks being airlifted to safety, it should probably be on our minds that they were the ones who lived in the most vulnerable housing to begin with, and were also in many cases unable to think of leaving it behind.

I wish the mainstream media would take notice of this issue; thus far, though, I haven't seen anyone make reference to it. (Maybe after the shock of the storm dies down.)

The mayor of Biloxi, Mississippi, called Katrina "Our Tsunami", and judging from the pictures of Biloxi and Jackson, he may be right (though, as massive as the disaster is, it is still much smaller in scale than the Tsunami, which caused huge damage in *eight countries*, and left nearly 1000 times more people dead). But as with the tsunami, there is here a story behind the tragedy—a pattern of ongoing suffering that existed before the storm—that people aren't talking about.

This Boing Boing story doesn't help matters. Apparently, in some AFP photo captions, blacks who are carrying goods retrieved from closed or damaged stores are referred to as "looting," while white people doing the same thing are described "finding" the goods they're carrying.

Calvin's notes on Singh's argument

Identifiable genre/mode/medium?

Like Shlensky, Singh blogs his argument. He uses hyperlinks, a comments section, links to previous posts, and lists contact information.

Reliable evidence?

Singh refers to CNN, *Boing Boing*, and the mayor of Biloxi's statement, but some generalizations either are not backed up or are backed with sparse evidence. For example, the statement "numerous articles refer to the affected region as 'third world' in its devastation" is followed up by only one example.

Sources cited?

Singh attributes his quotes, such as when he quotes the mayor of Biloxi, but doesn't cite common knowledge (such as the population of Bombay versus New Orleans).

Calvin Sweet (Student)

Hurricane Katrina Project: Research Plan

Following his evaluation of the works of Gray, Shlensky, and Singh, Calvin maps his research out in a little more detail.

Research Assignment: Research Plan

Calvin Sweet
Professor Elizabeth Kleinfeld
English 102
February 1, 20—
Research Plan: Hurricane Katrina Project

1. Your research question.

   My research question is twofold: How did the press treat race and class in their coverage of Katrina, and what are the consequences of that treatment?

2. Your goals.

   My starting point was to find out how the press covered Katrina. I want to be a journalist, and I remember my cousin who interned at a newspaper in 2007 saying that the writers at that paper were still talking about how "slanted" the Katrina coverage was. One of my goals is to discover what the Katrina coverage was. In the research I've done so far, it looks like some people think the coverage treated both race and class unfairly. If my research continues to support this view, I'll argue that press coverage didn't adequately take race and class into account and that there were serious consequences because of that. I believe my research would be considered inductive, because I truly haven't made up my mind and even these thoughts I have now are completely based on the three sources I've read. The next source I read could make me see things differently.

3. Types of sources.

   I will continue reading blogs about Katrina. I think reading about people who experienced it gives me an understanding of what actually happened and how race and class mattered in what happened. I also need to read the press coverage, which I have just begun with the *Time* article. In fact, analyzing the press coverage itself will be a major part of my research. I can do *EBSCOhost* searches to find articles. To make my argument that there are consequences because of the coverage, I need to follow up on things like Shlensky's idea that this could all lead to more discussion of race and class. For example, I need to find out if there have been more discussions of race and class, maybe by

---

comparing how many articles a particular newspaper published on race and class issues in the two years before and the two years after Katrina. I will also watch Spike Lee's documentary *When the Levees Broke*. My assumption is that it will be like all of Lee's other films, in which race and class are examined.

For primary sources, I will look for YouTube videos by Katrina survivors to see how they portray race and class. I will also interview Professor Hughes in the African American studies department to see if she can share any insights with me.

4. Your timeline.

- Find and read more blogs: March 20-31

- Schedule interview with Professor Kleinfeld: April 1

- Write interview questions: April 5

- Conduct interview: April 7

- Watch Spike Lee film on Netflix: April 8-10

- Find and read press coverage: April 11-25

- Draft: April 25-May 6

- Revise: May 7-14

- Edit: May 14

- Submit: May 15

20 PROCESS: INTEGRATING AND DOCUMENTING SOURCES

CONTENTS

When integrating sources—whether written, oral, visual, or electronic—into a project, authors and composers usually have two goals, both of which are necessary for the ethical use of sources:

1. Signaling sources: the clear indication of the sources from which the ideas and materials of the project originate

2. Fair representation: the accurate description and representation of the ideas and materials of sources, using a combination of quotation, paraphrase, and summary.

Working with Sources **GT**

Ethically representing other people's ideas is important for a number of reasons. Let's look at the big picture first. Your purpose in using sources, rather than creating a project that doesn't reference anyone else's ideas, is to participate in an ongoing conversation about a topic. Failing to signal your sources—that is, the other participants in the conversation—or fairly represent their ideas means your

---

This chapter on integrating and documenting sources was contributed by Dr. Patricia R. Taylor, a Marion L. Brittain Postdoctoral Fellow at Georgia Tech.

own contributions won't be taken seriously. On a more pragmatic level, if you don't integrate sources in a way that makes clear where you got your ideas or materials, you are plagiarizing, which can result in receiving a failing grade on an assignment or for a class.

Signaling Sources

The ways authors or composers signal their sources can differ from genre to genre or mode to mode. Blog posts, news articles, and editorial pieces use different types of citations than do academic papers. Films might rely on narration, captions, or even camera angles to signal a source instead of in-text citations, while Web sites might use embedded links rather than parenthetical citations. As a creator, you are responsible for investigating the particular genre you select and its citation conventions. For coursework, you need to make sure that your instructor finds your approach reasonable and appropriate. Composers who don't signal sources in a reasonable way, whether accidentally or intentionally, are guilty of plagiarism, which is a serious academic offense that can result in failure for an assignment or a class, and in extreme or repeated cases, expulsion or the revocation of a degree.

To help you reference your sources responsibly, you have three major tools at your disposal for signaling your sources. Most projects will use a combination of all three: signal phrases, in-text citations or links, and bibliographies or credits. Signaling sources in these ways allows readers to understand how composers or authors use material from various sources and evaluate the credibility and reliability of the information.

Signal Phrases

Sometimes called attributive tags, signal phrases let readers know when an idea, piece of information, or quotation comes from a source. Such tags or phrases usually identify who created the source, what type of information is being taken from the source, and what is interpreted as the author's attitude toward the material. For example, a project about the 2014 Ebola outbreak might use a signal phrase this way:

> A recent report from the CDC indicates . . .

Here, the signal phrase alerts readers that the information following in the rest of the sentence originated with the Centers for Disease Control and Prevention and that the information is timely and appropriate to the project. Using a verb such as *indicates* shows that the information is factual and verifiable. If the information had not come from a credible source or had been presented in an inflammatory way, a verb other than *indicates* would be appropriate. For example, you might make a point about the credibility of an article in the tabloid *Weekly World News* by writing: "A recent article in the *Weekly World News* disparages. . . ."

Sometimes communicators who are not proficient with signal phrases include a page number as their primary signal, writing something like, "On page 64, we see," or "In Chapters 4 and 5, we find," before moving into the quotation or paraphrase. However, this is not helpful for your audience, who may have read the text but probably will not remember the page or the chapter number. Instead, you should provide the specific context of the passage or source you are discussing by describing the elements of the argument or narrative that appear before or after the passage.

In-Text Citations

Citation practices differ from field to field, but most academic projects (and some nonacademic projects) require in-text citations—that is, indications of where readers might find the original information. Different style guides require communicators to use different information as part of the citation. In MLA format, in-text citations provide the author and page number; in APA, in-text citations provide author, year, and page number. Nonacademic electronic publications might use embedded links to source material. Other citation systems prioritize different types of information, so check your discipline's or profession's style guides to see what is necessary and appropriate.

In most cases, in-text citations appear in parentheses at the end of the sentence where the information is presented. For example, a project that paraphrases an idea from Nicholas Carr's book *The Shallows: What the Internet Is Doing to Our Brains* using MLA in-text citations might include this sentence:

> Carr argues that using the Internet can change how our minds work, due to the brain's inherent plasticity (49).

Notice that this sentence includes a signal phrase with the author's name in it. Because the name appears in the sentence, it is not needed in the parenthetical citation at the end of the sentence. In this example, only the page number from the book is needed.

If the author's name does not appear in the sentence or paragraph, it should instead appear in the parentheses with the page number:

The underlined portion of the sentence—"report from the CDC"—signals a hyperlink that, in an electronic document, links readers to the actual CDC report.

> Some writers believe that using the Internet may be changing how our minds work, due to the brain's inherent plasticity (Carr 49).

Electronic projects might include links instead of in-text citations, especially when the sources cited are also electronic. These links might not appear at the end of the sentence, but instead can be embedded in the signal phrase:

> A recent report from the CDC indicates . . .

Bibliographies or Credits

In addition to signal phrases and in-text citations, most academic projects (and many nonacademic ones) that use sources include a bibliography or works cited page, depending on the citation system being used. These bibliographies include all of the sources cited throughout the project, following whichever citation format the author used in the body of the project.

Nonacademic projects often provide the equivalent of a bibliography through "credits": films use both opening and closing credits to recognize all the people and institutions who contributed, often also citing source materials in the closing credits. Singers and songwriters recognize their sources in liner notes. Visual artists might give credit in their artists' statements.

Fair Representation of Source Materials

You might use source materials for a number of different purposes. Most students are familiar with providing evidence for or illustrating a claim. You might also use sources to establish the boundaries of a larger conversation, thus providing the context for your own argument. Your sources might provide useful counterarguments that you can use to make your project more nuanced. Using sources can also help you build ethos: this documentation demonstrates that you've done the research necessary for the particular project, which in turn can add to the credibility of your own specific position, even if you're representing ideas with which you disagree.

Three standard tools are useful for integrating sources into your writing: summary, paraphrase, and quotation. These three tools are appropriate at different moments and sometimes all at the same time: a summary might include small bits of paraphrase and quotation within it; a paraphrase might include small pieces of quotation; and a paraphrase or summary might serve as the introduction for a quotation.

As you are choosing whether to summarize, paraphrase, or quote, remember that your sources should buttress your own position and language, not replace the work of communicating the idea yourself. You should always have substantially more of your own language on a page than a source's language.

The most important (and difficult) element of integrating sources can be making sure that your representation of a source is *accurate* and *fair*. Whenever you are using ideas or materials, such as quotations or images from sources, you must fairly and accurately represent the ideas of others. Representing a text fairly does not mean you have to agree with it; however, it does mean you need to provide sufficient context (to avoid misrepresenting a statement by taking it out of context) and accurate summaries. You may need to represent not only the literal content of the source but also its tone or goal. A satirical source may actually say that to solve an economic crisis, poor people should sell their children as food (as Jonathan Swift argues in *A Modest Proposal*), but if a summary only lables this as Jonathan Swift's argument, it will fail miserably as an accurate or fair summary of the source; in addition, it also needs to accurately represent his satirical tone or his goal of critiquing the British government's attitude toward the Irish poor. Using sources accurately and fairly helps your audience use your information to make informed decisions in their own lives.

Quotations

Quotations are used to provide readers with specific bits of information when the source's original wording is essential or memorable; sometimes, you will quote because no way exists to convey the author's ideas without a verbatim repetition. Quotations must be identical to the original source, must use a small part of the source text, and must be attributed to the original author. They should always be introduced, so that readers know both the source of the quotation and its importance. Quotations are usually integrated into the text of a sentence that starts with a signal phrase:

> While Carr acknowledges that "language itself is not a technology," he goes on to argue that reading and writing are different from speaking in this regard: "reading and writing are unnatural acts, made possible by the purposeful development of the alphabet and many other technologies" (51).

Quotations that aren't integrated into a sentence in this way are sometimes called "dropped quotes" or "quote bombs." Dropped quotes are problematic because they allow the source text to temporarily overpower your own voice and argument. For the same reason, be especially careful not to overuse quotations; they are more likely than paraphrase or summary to overshadow your own work, destroying the ethos you would otherwise create by using sources.

Quoting Literary Sources Quoting a literary text (e.g., a novel, a short story, a poem) requires special care. While in many cases you can assume your readers know the literary text you are discussing, they may not remember many details. To help your readers, your signal phrase should indicate the context of the quotation (which might include items such as the speakers, the plot situation, the other characters involved). Your goal is to provide information to help your readers recognize the part you are quoting so that you can move along and make your point. Ideally, you present your evidence and quotation in such a way that readers never have to pick up the original text unless they want to double-check your point.

Generally speaking, the integration of long quotations into a paper follows a standard paradigm:

1. Provide the context for the quotation, including a signal phrase that introduces it.

2. Insert the quotation (embedding an in-text citation at the end of the quotation).

3. Follow the quotation with analysis, drawing readers' attention to the elements that support your argument.

This sequence is a guideline, not a rule; in some cases, your analysis might precede the quotation as part of the context for the quotation, or the context might be expanded as part of the concluding analysis.

Example Quotation The following paragraph from a student's paper about Jane Austen's *Pride and Prejudice* argues that characters in her novel often treat social class in a hypocritical manner. The context in the student's paper appears in boldface and the analysis in italics to show how the writer employs both to advance her argument:

> **When Elizabeth's sister Jane becomes ill while visiting Mr. Bingley's sisters at Netherfield,** *Miss Bingley and Mrs. Hurst make comments that imply that the Bennets' connections in society are far below their own.* **For example,** Miss Bingley states, "I have an excessive regard for Jane Bennet, she really is a very sweet girl, and I wish with all my heart she were well settled. But with such a father and mother, and such low connections, I am afraid there is no chance of it" (25). *According to the two women, based strictly on these family relations, regardless of the good qualities that Jane possesses, Jane's chances of achieving a good marriage are slim. If Mr. Bingley's sisters represent society's thoughts on the role of extended family, then it may be believed that Jane, Elizabeth, and the rest of the Bennet girls are undesirable mates. The irony in this situation, of course, is that* **the Bingley fortune was originally gained in trade,** *and thus they possess the same "low" relations (11).* Thus, even from the very beginning of the novel, Austen creates a situation where judgments concerning social class are often hypocritical or at least somewhat myopic.

This paragraph starts with general contextualization or summary, including the major characters involved in the scene, and then moves to a general statement about the purpose of the quotation. After giving the quotation and citation, it analyzes and expands the quotation, connecting it with earlier material and information and eventually moving back to the thesis.

Summaries and Paraphrases

Summarizing and paraphrasing are similar activities; their primary differences are scope and level of detail. **Summarizing** puts the big idea of a source into your own words, including only the main point(s). Summaries are substantively shorter than the original and take a broad overview of the source material. **Paraphrasing** puts a shorter passage from your source into your own words, often including much more detail from the original source. Unlike quotations, paraphrases are used to represent ideas where the original wording is less important.

When you are summarizing or paraphrasing, the first thing you need to do is decide which information from the source is necessary to your project. Not all of the material from any given source will be crucial to supporting your argument to your audience. You'll want to decide if particular phrases or words from the source are irreplaceable; you can integrate these quotations into your paraphrase or summary.

Once you have made these initial decisions, you'll need to work on putting the ideas into your own words. Remember that in the case of both paraphrase and summary, changing the words of the source is not enough to avoid plagiarism; you also need to avoid replicating the syntax or structure of the sentences that you are paraphrasing. Some textbooks recommend that students close the book and set it aside so they don't accidentally plagiarize; however, some students find that their memories are good enough that they still accidentally replicate language or syntax, even with the book closed. If this is true for you, you may choose to keep the book open to check to see that your paraphrases and summaries are distinctly different in vocabulary and structure.

Finally, just as quotations should be followed by your own analysis, summary and paraphrase should be integrated with or followed by your own analysis.

Example Summary and Paraphrase   Imagine you are writing a paper in which you include a definition of *science fiction*, using the ideas of an award-winning science fiction writer. Here's the original text written by Robert Heinlein:

> Science Fiction is speculative fiction in which the author takes as his first postulate the real world as we know it, including all established facts and natural laws. The result can be extremely fantastic in content, but it is not fantasy; it is legitimate—and often very tightly reasoned—speculation about the possibilities of the real world. This category excludes rocket ships that make U-turns, serpent men of Neptune that lust after human maidens, and stories by authors who flunked their Boy Scout merit badge tests in descriptive astronomy.
>
> —Robert Heinlein, *Expanded Universe*

Your **summary** of this source could identify a single central idea that can be extracted and put into other words. Your summary would not use the vivid elements of the passage; instead, it would provide a succinct account of Heinlein's definition. You would use a clear and direct signal phrase:

> Robert Heinlein defines science fiction as a genre in which genuine scientific principles serve as the foundation for an author's conjectures about the future and technology (374).

By contrast, your **paraphrase** below could draw attention to the most memorable language from the passage:

> According to Robert Heinlein, science fiction is "fantastic . . . but not fantasy," dealing with the "real world"; it is rational and incorporates scientific ideas, without ignoring the rules governing how things work (374). Ultimately, science fiction examines the extreme

possibilities of the world as we know it, and simply writing about aliens, advanced weapons, and spaceships is not enough. As Heinlein put it, science fiction "excludes rocket ships that make U-turns, serpent men of Neptune that lust after human maidens, and stories by authors who flunked their Boy Scout merit badge tests in descriptive astronomy" (374). Heinlein's examples highlight the necessity that science fiction express an intrinsic knowledge of the rules by which our universe works and the willingness to work within those boundaries.

Here, the final sentence of your paraphrase provides some analysis. One of the most common uses of paraphrasing is to "unpack," or explain, a piece of text that you have already quoted. Here, the paraphrase is combined with analysis to get at the larger meaning of the passage that goes beyond the explicit statements that Heinlein made.

The sources cited section of the paper would include one of these citations, depending on the citation style—either MLA or APA:

Heinlein, Robert. "Ray Guns and Spaceships." *Expanded Universe*. New York: Ace, 1981. Print. [MLA]

Heinlein, Robert. (1981). Ray guns and spaceships. *Expanded universe*. New York, NY: Ace. [APA]

Citing Summaries and Paraphrases   Sometimes communicators forget that summarizing and paraphrasing require the same level of citation as quoting. They neglect to cite summaries or paraphrases because they work from memory rather than look at specific pieces of a text. However, they still need to attribute summarized and paraphrased ideas to the original source. A signal phrase ("According to Jon Stewart" or "The Centers for Disease Control and Prevention Web site reports") might be sufficient citation for a summary if no quotations exist within the summary. Paraphrases require signal phrases and parenthetical citations if the material is from a paginated source. In all cases, the goal is to give readers enough information about the source to find the specific place that you obtained your information.

Integrating Media

Tables and figures (including photos, diagrams, maps, drawings, screen shots, and videos) need to be treated as the equivalent of a quotation in your project—but with some added requirements. Each embedded figure should be labeled, often using the notation "Figure" (or "Table" if it's a table) with a number, a title, and caption for the image: "Figure 1: Neurons firing in the brain." You should also indicate your source at the end of the label or caption (check the documentation system you are using for conventions).

Refer to the figure or table in the text, using the label you gave the image:

As Figure 1 demonstrates, neurons in the brain fire in response to stimuli . . .

You may want to combine the reference with a signal phrase, just as you would with a quotation:

As a recent CDC report indicates (see Figure 2), . . .

Figures and tables require analysis and explanation just as quotations do. Readers are unlikely to interpret figures and tables the way you want them to without some guidance. Instead, comment on or explain the figures and tables and the ways they are relevant to your argument.

Make sure to position a visual as close as possible *following* the first reference to the visual, to help your readers connect the text and the visual. How you position the figure within a page (aligned left, right, or centered, with or without text wrap) may depend on the style of the project or the significance of the visual in your argument.

If you are posting your project on a Web site, media from other sources may require special permission. Make sure the visual is not under copyright or that you have the right (either through fair use or permission from the rights holder) to include the material.

Working with Multimodal Sources

Working with multimodal sources and assets often requires strategies for collecting, citing, and sharing that are different from the research processes you may be familiar with. This section covers how to collect multimodal assets, what ethical issues to consider when collecting assets, and how best to cite multimodal texts. By the end of the section, you will have a list of the sources and assets you plan to use, an understanding of the ethics of this use, and citation information for your assets.

Sources and Assets

You probably know the term *sources* already, but what are *assets*? Sources are texts, such as books, articles, Web sites, etc., that you can use to gather information about a topic or genre. Assets are the pieces of content that you'll actually use in your project. An asset might be a quotation, an image, a video clip, or a screenshot. For instance, let's say that for your project you need a twenty-second clip from a two-minute YouTube video. The source is the two-minute video (akin to a book or an article you pull from a shelf or the Web). The twenty-second clip that you pull from the video is your asset. You'll gather assets from your sources—and depending on your project, you may create your own assets (for example, by filming an interview with a friend).

Web sites and other digital media are updated frequently, so when you first find an asset, you should save a copy if you think you may want to use it. Things on

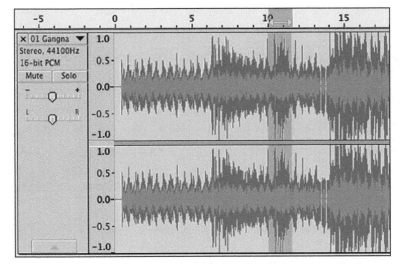

◀ FIGURE 20.1
A Source and an Asset
In this waveform illustration of an audio clip, the entire song is the **source**, while the grayed-out selection between the ten-second mark and the eleven-and-a-half-second mark is the **asset** that will be used in the project.

the Web disappear. Jenny was giving a presentation about online adoption profiles and had planned to show a couple's Web site while she talked. She did not take a screenshot or save any of the images. Sure enough, the Web site was taken down the day before her presentation, and she had to scramble to find and analyze a new example. You can save screenshots of Web sites in an online bibliography program like Zotero or in your own filing system (see Chapter 9 for file storage and sharing tips).

write/design assignment

A Multimodal Annotated Source List, Part 1

Gather the texts you used in Chapter 6 to research your project idea. Use the questions in the credibility section on pages 00–00 to make sure that your sources are appropriate and that they will build your ethos as an author. If you need to find more credible sources, talk to your instructor, classmates, stakeholders, and librarian, and use the different text, image, video, audio, and other options your Web search engine provides.

Create a list in which you annotate each source, including the following elements where possible:

» the source's author, title, publication venue, and Web address (if relevant). Later in this chapter, you'll be asked to turn this information into a citation, but for now just document enough information so that you, your collaborators, or your instructor can go back and find the source.
» the asset(s) you're planning to use from this source
» a summary of the source, including the medium it's in; a description of how the content relates to your project pitch, including any important/major issues it discusses that you can use to support your project idea; and any important/major issues the source leaves out that your project will cover

Ethics of Collecting Sources and Assets

As you search for credible sources for your project, you should be aware of some ethical issues associated with collecting lots of assets that don't belong to you. The majority of the ethical issues we'll address in this section relate to copyright law; those issues include the fair-use principle, obtaining permissions, and the use of copyrighted material that authors have purposely given others more freedom to use under certain Creative Commons designations.

Copyright   Copyright is a legal device that gives the creator of a text—that is, a work that conveys ideas or information—the right to control how that text can be used. For a work to be copyrighted, the United States Copyright Office demands that it meet the following criteria:

1. **Originality.** The work must be an original creation—though it's not really as simple as that because a work that is an adaptation or a transformation of a previous work can be copyrighted.

2. **Fixity.** The work must be capable of being stored in some way. An unrecorded speech cannot be copyrighted; once the speech is written down or videotaped, however, it can be copyrighted.

3. **Minimal creativity.** The work needs to be at least somewhat creative. This category is subjective, but for the most part anything that includes some original work will be eligible for copyright protection. Very short works such as names, phone numbers, and recipes can't be copyrighted, however, because the amount of creativity required to formulate any of those types of texts is considered to be too minimal. In other words, under copyright law "creativity" is considered to take some effort. How *much* effort is often a matter for lawyers and judges to decide.

The point of copyright is to give an author control over how his or her text is used. Authors are the only ones who can legally distribute and/or sell their work—in short, they are the only ones who should be able to profit from it. The moment an author "fixes" an original idea into a text, he or she immediately has copyright over that text, unless the author signs the rights over to another person or to a group such as a publishing company.

When you're composing a multimodal project, copyright needs to be a prime consideration. As you'll learn in the next section, some of your assets may fall under the guidelines for fair use, but if you plan to ever share your project, you need to make sure that you observe general copyright principles. Sometimes it's easy to forget about copyright because of how easy it is to find images or songs through a quick Web search. But just because you find a source online doesn't mean that it is copyright-free. When planning your asset list, make sure you note who the copyright holders of your sources are.

Fair Use Having to consider copyright law for your multimodal project may make you feel as though your creativity is being limited, but you need to remember that copyright exists in large part to protect an author's original work—and you may be very protective of your own work. However, while copyright does exist to protect original authors, the fair-use doctrine limits an author's total control.

The principle of fair use was established to allow authors to use portions of other authors' texts without permission for educational, non-profit, reportorial, or critical purposes. Anyone working on a multimodal project should pay attention to the rules of the fair-use game. Unfortunately, those rules aren't always clear-cut. But keep the following four criteria in mind, and remember that your usage of the copyrighted work should meet these criteria as stringently as is possible in order to qualify as fair use:

1. **The purpose of use.** Is the work being used for nonprofit or educational purposes? Is it being used for criticism, commentary, news reporting, teaching, scholarship, or research? Fair use looks more favorably on texts that meet these criteria.

2. **The nature of the copyrighted work.** Is it factual? Has it been published? Fair use favors factual published works over unpublished works or forms of artistic expression.

3. **The amount of the work used.** The smaller the portion of the original text you use, the more likely this use is to be protected as fair use.

4. **The market effect of the use.** Will the new use of the text be available to a small group of people for a limited time? The broader the distribution, the less likely fair use will come into effect.

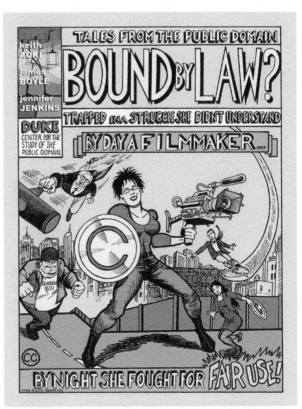

▲ FIGURE 20.2
Tales from the Public Domain
Some works—usually those that are very old—aren't covered by copyright. These fall into what's known as the public domain. For more information on the public domain, read the comic *Bound by Law?* at bedford stmartins.com /writerdesigner.

Search the Web for "fair use cases" and read about one or two cases that have gone to trial. Why was fair use upheld or not upheld in each case? #Understand

Consider Ariel, who was working on a Web comic analysis. She created an "asset list" that included a screenshot of each Web comic's masthead as well as screenshots of different panels from the comics themselves. In thinking about these screenshots, Ariel had to keep in mind the four criteria of fair use. She was pretty certain her screenshots were OK, for several reasons:

1. The texts would be used for educational purposes—specifically, for criticism and analysis (purpose of use).

2. The comics themselves had already been published (nature of copyrighted work).

3. She was only using one image out of the entire catalog of comics each author had on his or her site (small proportion of the whole).

4. The text would primarily be available only to other people in her class (small market effect of use).

Permissions   In many cases, if you want to use part of a copyrighted text in your own multimodal project, you are supposed to request permission from the copyright owner. In some cases, this might be as simple as sending an email or a letter to a friendly author, who will reasonably grant you written permission to use the text for your project. For instance, although Ariel's plans for using screenshots of the various Web comics safely met the fair-use criteria for copyright, she also thought she would eventually use her webtext in her job portfolio, so she needed permission from the authors to use screenshots of their comics and an image of each comic's logo or masthead. The authors wrote back and granted her permission, and Ariel was able to move ahead with her project without fear of violating copyright law.

FIGURE 20.3 ▶
A Page from Ariel's Webtext Illustrating Her Use of Comic Screenshots

When Humans Are the Text

You may need a different kind of permission if you are interviewing a person about his or her personal attitudes, beliefs, experiences, etc. Most organizations (institutions of higher learning, in particular) require you to have your project approved by the local institutional review board (IRB) if the project involves research that experiments on people or asks personal questions of people, *and* if you plan on making the project public. IRBs exist to make sure that certain research—in this case, human subjects research—is conducted ethically.

For a film that she was going to show only in class (a use that is *not* considered public), Courteney needed another kind of permission: that of the actress she wanted to film. She could have requested a signed consent form from the actress or obtained vocal permission recorded on film. If people are recognizable in your footage, you need their permission.

Visit **bedfordstmartins.com/writerdesigner** to download a sample consent form.

On the other hand, getting permission from some copyright holders can be overly complicated, expensive, and potentially unnecessary (depending on whether your use of the material is fair). For instance, Courteney, an author who was composing a video-based analysis of action films and who wanted to cite scenes from *The Dark Knight* and other Hollywood movies in her project, discovered that she would have to fill out a lengthy permission form supplied by the films' production company, Warner Brothers, and include a proposal explaining her use of each clip from each Warner Brothers movie. In addition, Courteney would not have been able to use or edit any clips from these movies without first getting approval and (most likely) paying a fee. Most DIY multimodal projects (like the kind we discuss in this book) don't have a budget, so requesting permission and paying for the use of clips can raise more ethical and economic issues than it solves. That's when we encourage you to exercise your fair-use rights, transforming an asset for your project by critiquing or studying it for academic purposes, parodying it (among other appropriate fair uses), or using more permissions-friendly clips from a Creative Commons or similar search (discussed below).

Creative Commons   Confused about copyright, fair use, and permissions? Try Creative Commons, a nonprofit organization devoted to giving authors more control over how their work is used. Creative Commons (CC) also provides researchers with a massive collection of assets that are easily searchable and that can be used without worrying about strict copyright laws, ensuring fair use, or asking (and paying for) permissions. Authors can choose from six licenses, each of which is some combination of the following:

Attribution (BY): Users may copy, distribute, display, and perform the work and make derivative works based on it only if they give the author or licensor credit in the manner specified by the license.

No Derivative Works (ND): Users may copy, distribute, display, and perform only verbatim copies of the work, not derivative works based on it.

Noncommercial (NC): Users may copy, distribute, display, and perform the work and make derivative works based on it only for noncommercial purposes.

ShareAlike (SA): Users may distribute derivative works only under a license identical to the license that governs the original work.

So text licensed with an Attribution-Noncommercial (BY-NC) license can be used in your project as long as you give the original author credit. The other great thing about Creative Commons is that you can license your own work after you've completed your project. (If you use any CC assets with the ShareAlike designation, you *have* to apply a Creative Commons ShareAlike license to your project.)

Process

Visit **bedfordstmartins.com/writerdesigner** to watch this video on the kinds of licenses Creative Commons offers users. What kind of license might work best for your multimodal project? Discuss with your stakeholders which kind of license your project might need. Make a note of which license would be best for your project and why.

◀ FIGURE 20.4
Creative Commons Licenses

1. Add a "Rights" column to your list from Part 1.

2. For each asset you plan to use, designate one of the following choices in the Rights column:

   » **Get permission:** The asset is copyrighted, and thus its use requires permission. Include information for where and how to do that.

   » **Fair use:** Refer directly to the four fair-use criteria and indicate how your use of the asset qualifies as fair. Rhetorical analysis is a good method for indicating this use.

   » **CC-licensed:** Indicate which CC license this asset has and what uses the license allows.

3. If an asset needs permission, begin gathering that from the copyright holder(s).

4. For any assets you have that do not fall under fair use, try searching the Creative Commons licensed assets at http://search.creativecommons.org/ to find additional sources that might replace those copyrighted assets. Remember to look for assets that can be used commercially or can be modified, if these needs are relevant to your multimodal project. You might also consider creating your own original assets instead of using others, which we'll talk about more in the next two chapters.

Designing Your Citations

Strict citation rules such as those of the Modern Language Association (MLA) and the American Psychological Association (APA) often aren't useful when you're producing multimodal projects because those guides were created for print-based scholarship such as essays, articles, and class papers. You *might* use MLA, APA, or some other citation style in your multimodal project, but that will depend entirely on your genre and rhetorical situation.

In this book, we have only two rules for citations:

1. Provide enough information about each source so that readers can find it themselves.

2. Use a citation style that is credible within the context of the genre you've chosen to produce.

Why these two rules? Because attributing your sources shows that you care about your readers, your text, and the authors whose work you're using, which helps readers interpret and even sympathize with your argument a little more—not to mention that it helps with your credibility.

Medium: Print Cereal Box

▲ FIGURE 20.5
How to Cite a Cereal Box in MLA Style
Visit bedfordstmartins.com/writerdesigner to watch Martine Courant Rife's video about citing a cereal box in MLA format. Citation styles can be quite malleable for anyone encountering multimedia genres.

LOST DOG

Name
Male/Female
Breed
Coloring
Date last seen
Place last seen
If found, please call owner at
123-456-7890

▲ FIGURE 20.6
Finding Missing Things

Provide Enough Information for Readers It's infuriating when someone you trust shares a link to an image (say, a lolcat) on Facebook or via email without including any additional context, and the link turns out to be "404 Not Found"—i.e., a dead end. The only thing you can do in that situation is to ask your friend for more information (if you cared enough to follow up), launch an image search of the entire Internet for the correct lolcat (if you don't know which lolcat Web site it appeared on), and then sort through the 427,000 hits to find an image that you *think* is the one your friend sent you. That's very frustrating. You (and your friends) should provide enough information so that readers will be able to find your sources or will at least know that you attributed your sources well enough to give credit where credit is due. And they'll like you for that.

Here are a few basic questions to help you start documenting your credibility with appropriate credits.

» Where is the source's home?

» What is its address?

» What is its name?

» Who is its owner?

» When was it born?

(Yes, it's sort of like finding the home of a lost puppy.) Let's try asking these questions about the screenshot in Figure 20.7.

First of all, what is this asset's home and address? Let's say you ran across this image on Facebook and didn't know what it was, but you had a link you could click on so that you could read it in the context of the original site. You'd follow the link, which is the image's address (http://www.phdcomics.com/comics/archive

Works Cited, Bibliography, References, Credits?!

Different style guides call your source list different things. You may have seen the source list called a bibliography. The MLA style guide calls it a works cited list. The APA style guide calls it a references list. A film or other media project would call the source list credits. What you call your list of citations (if you even have or need a list of all the citations in your project) will depend on what genre your project is.

◀ FIGURE 20.7
**Piled Higher and
Deeper (PhD)
by Jorge Cham**

.php?comicid=405), and from there you could discover the rest of the missing information. The asset's home is the Web site the comic lives on, and that Web site is called Piled Higher and Deeper. Note that the address of a Web asset is usually *not* the same thing as the main page, which in this case would be http://www .phdcomics.com/comics.php. For the purpose of citation, the main page is like the street name of a lost puppy's home—close, but not quite enough information to get the cute little thing back to its owners. So make sure you get the specific Web address and not just the main page address.

What is the image's name? In this case, it's the comic's title. In many Web sites, the title of a text that is part of a collection will be listed at the top of the browser along with the collection's name. If the title is not listed at the top, study the page to see if you can figure out what the title is. In this image the name appears both at the top of the page and in big letters on the comic itself: "Deciphering Academese."

Now, who owns this cute little thing? On a Web site that's designed like a blog or Tumblr, the author may not be readily evident, so search for links with words like *About* or *Author*, or look for a copyright note at the bottom of the page, which is where we find Jorge Cham's name. Cham is the owner of this comic. (Note that it's perfectly acceptable these days, depending on what genre of text you're working on and what its credibility standards are, to use assets that are owned by people whose names are weird little Internet handles like famouspoundcake or s2ceball. When you don't have the author's full name, use his or her handle.)

Finally, on blog-like Web sites such as this one, each post is usually tagged with the date of publication, otherwise known as its birth date. In this case, the publication

Process

This screenshot is from a webtext (a scholarly multimedia article) published in the online journal *Kairos*. Track down the original webtext and create a citation appropriate for the genre of multimodal project you're working on.

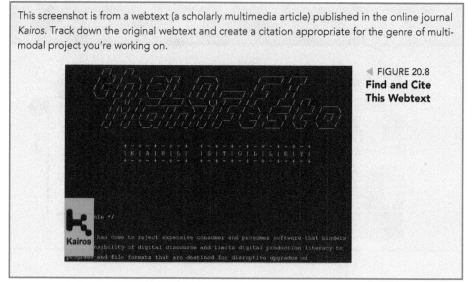

◀ FIGURE 20.8
**Find and Cite
This Webtext**

date is January 18, 2004. Now we have enough information to track down the asset again, if we need to, and we can use the name, owner, birth date, home, and address to create a citation.

Use a Credible Citation Style for Your Genre This is usually the point in the production cycle where the MLA or APA style guide or *The Chicago Manual of Style* (CMS) gets pulled out—or more likely, a Web site that has examples of these citation styles gets pulled up. But for your multimodal project, you can't assume that you'll use MLA, APA, or CMS style. Instead, you need to consider what citation styles look like *in the genre* that meets your rhetorical needs. Here's an easy example: when you go to the movies, the soundtrack credits don't appear in MLA style at the end. Readers have come to expect that the sound citations in a movie will follow the format shown in Figure 20.9. Using this style makes the citations more credible because it looks professional, and it's easily recognizable by your audience. They know what you want them to understand when you use this citation style in a movie.

Not as common with a general audience but still functioning within its own genre conventions, the DJ Edit Pack also uses its own citation practices. An edit pack is a collection of songs, usually grouped by musical genre (punk, rap, electronic, etc.), that the DJ has altered in some fashion in order to make the track more dance floor friendly. These edit packs are generally used by other DJs who are looking for new music to play or include in their own mix tapes, though occasionally fans of the DJ will listen to the packs as well. Figure 20.10 shows a screenshot of Portland-based

FEEL FLOWS
Written by
John Rieley & Carl Wilson
Performed by The Beach Boys
Courtesy of Capitol Records
Under license from EMI-Capitol
Music Special Markets

FEVER DOG
Written by Russell Hammond
Performed by Stillwater

EVERY PICTURE
TELLS A STORY
Written by
Rod Stewart & Ron Wood
Performed by Rod Stewart
Courtesy of

RIVER
Written & Performed by
Joni Mitchell
Courtesy of Reprise Records
By arrangement with
Warner Special Products

SWEET LEAF
Written by Frank Iommi,
William Ward, Terence Butler
& John Osbourne
Performed by Black Sabbath
Courtesy of Downlane Limited

SMALL TIME BLUES
Written & Performed by
Pete Droge

DJ Doc Adam's Punk Edits Vol. 1 Edit Pack. Notice the format for these citations. Each track includes the original artist, the song title, and the name of the DJ who edited the track (in this case, Doc Adam). While it's quite simple, it's the accepted convention for this genre. The point is: citation options vary as much as the genre and its features do. More likely than not, those citations look nothing like MLA-style citations. So this rule is about knowing your genre and figuring out how readers of that genre would expect citations to appear.

Punk Edits Vol.1
The Clash - Guns Of Brixton (Doc Adam Edit)
The Clash - Armagideon Time (Doc Adam Edit)
The Clash - Police & Thieves (Doc Adam Edit)
The Clash - Straight To Hell (Doc Adam Edit)
The Clash - The Magnificent Seven (Doc Adam Edit)
The Clash - This Is Radio Clash (Doc Adam Edit)
Crass - Banned From The Roxy (Doc Adam Edit)
Crass - Big A Little A (Doc Adam Edit)
Fugazi - Waiting Room (Doc Adam Edit)
Gang Of Four - At Home He's A Tourist (Doc Adam Edit)
Gang Of Four - Damaged Goods (Doc Adam Edit)
Gang Of Four - Natural Is Not In It (Doc Adam Edit)
Joy Division - Digital (Doc Adam Edit)
Joy Division - Love Will Tear Us Apart (Doc Adam Edit)
Joy Division - She Lost Control (Doc Adam Edit)
Siouxsie & The Banshees - Happy House (Doc Adam Edit)
XTC - Making Plans For Nigel (Doc Adam Edit)

Process

Visit **bedfordstmartins.com/writerdesigner** to watch the opening credits of the 1956 movie *Rock Rock Rock*. Then visit the Internet Archive (http://archive.org), where you can find over a million videos and other multimodal texts, most of which are available for download, remix, and reuse. Browse through some of the genres to see how credits have been designed historically. How are the credits for *Rock Rock Rock* effective for the movie's genre and rhetorical situation? How will the credits for your piece be different?

◀ FIGURE 20.11
***Rock Rock Rock*
Opening Credits**

write/design assignment

A Multimodal Annotated Source List, Part 3

Return to your annotated source list and decide how your references should appear in your project, based on your genre. Consider what your instructor needs from you as well as the genre conventions for citation in your particular medium. If you need additional information to cite your sources properly, collect that information now.

Next, after choosing the format in which you want to provide your citations, compose a citation for each of your sources. Remember our two rules for citations: provide enough information about each source so that readers can find it themselves, and use a citation style that is credible within the context of the genre you've chosen to produce.

Make sure to add to your annotated list as you proceed with your project.

21 PROCESS: REVISING AND DELIVERING YOUR PROJECT

CONTENTS

Drafting and Revising Your Project

Now that you have all of your assets gathered, it's time to make a rough cut of your multimodal project. A **rough cut** is one step beyond your mock-up or storyboard of your project: it's not your final draft, but you'll have your assets placed approximately where you need them in something resembling the program or technology you'll use to create your final project. Sometimes a rough cut is referred to as a

prototype. Which term you use depends on what medium you're working in: *rough cut* tends to be used with timeline-based projects such as videos or audio texts, while *prototype* is more often used with code-based projects such as Web sites and software programs. In either case, this is a stage at which you can stop, step back from your project, and see whether it's all making enough sense for you to proceed as planned. That scene seemed like a good idea in your storyboard, but does it work on video? If not, your rough cut will let you know in time for you to figure out what,

▲ FIGURE 21.1
Rough Cut of a Frog Sculpture

FIGURE 21.2 ▶
**The Stages of
Drafting,
Frog-Style**

where, and how you need to revise so that the text *does* accomplish its purpose once everything is edited together cleanly.

Planning Your Rough Cut

Rough cuts are usually missing significant elements such as background soundtracks (with audio projects), transitions and intertitles (video projects), navigation (Web sites), permanent graphics (posters), and so on. In addition, rough cuts shouldn't include tightly edited assets, because feedback on your rough cut might indicate that you need to revise your project in a different direction. If you've cut your video down to a ten-second clip and then reviewers tell you they'd like to see a little more of it, you're out of luck. You want to have enough content left in your assets to be able to add different shots or material to your revised project if your reviewers suggest such changes. The following two lists include some examples of the *roughness* we mean when we talk about rough cuts.

Static Projects (Posters, Flyers, Brochures, Statues, etc.)

» The layout (spacing, alignment, number of columns, placement of headings, etc.) has been roughly determined. A draft of the written text or dummy copy has been placed on the document.

» Visual elements (photos, illustrations, logos, etc.) have been edited for size and placed on the document.

» Fonts, text sizes, and color schemes have been selected to provide a consistent look to the document.

» The project is available in a document/page layout program (e.g., Word, InDesign, Publisher, etc.) or in printed form (to test color) but not necessarily in the final output format (e.g., a PDF file).

Interactive/Animated Projects (Videos, Audio Projects, Web Sites, Presentations, Performances, etc.)

» All major pages, slides, screens or scripts, and/or blocking and settings have been found or created.

▲ FIGURE 21.3

A Sample Rough Cut

This rough cut of a video Cheryl is making has all the static photos and animated screen captures in their correct place in the video project timeline (see the upper left-hand corner). The sources are also included in the lower right-hand corner. Cheryl still has to add titles, a voice-over, and transitions between the visuals, but this version of the video is appropriate for a rough cut review, which viewers can watch in the preview window (in the upper right-hand corner).

» Found or original multimedia assets have been edited for purpose and length:

> » graphics are cropped, compressed, and placed;
>
> » audio and video assets have been edited into smaller two- or three-minute (or two- or three-second) segments, cut down from those twenty-minute blah-blah-blahs of unnecessary footage you captured in order to get *just the right shot*;
>
> » ripped digital videos have been downloaded, and irrelevant portions have been edited out.

Are you working on a type of project that isn't listed above? If so, what kind of project is it, and what elements of the project would be useful to include in a rough cut? In what program or technology will your rough cut be viewed? #Remember #Analyze

write/design assignment

Rough Cut Feedback

Create a rough cut of your project. Have a colleague (not someone from your group) look at it to make sure nothing sticks out as odd, out of place, inaudible, nonsensical, etc. Remember, this is just a rough version of your project. The roughly edited assets should tell enough of the story or argument for your feedback loop to catch what (if anything) doesn't belong and what still may need to be added.

» Navigation/organization is in place but may not be linked yet (e.g., with a prezi, you may have the path in mind but have not yet implemented it; with audio/video, you have rough edits in a timeline-based editing program).

» The draft is available for rough cut feedback in an editing program, off-line, or in an off-site workshop location.

Moving from Rough Cut to Rough Draft

The difference between a rough cut and a **rough draft** is that in a rough draft all the assets should be finely edited and in place so that the project will work without any intervention by the author. That is, while your rough cut didn't have to work—it was a prototype of what you *hoped* would work—your rough draft should be usable in the technology and the medium that you will eventually distribute your project in.

How do you know whether your project works? Start by testing it yourself to see how easily an audience will be able to navigate and make sense of your text. You can gather useful information on how functional your project is and fix errors before the project goes to your audience. This is like proofreading an essay: the paper draft is done and you think it's ready to be turned in, but you know your teacher will catch some places where you are missing transitions or have misspellings; so you print out the paper and read it through to try to catch those issues before turning it in. Preparing and testing the rough draft of your multimodal project has the same purpose. Here are some things to check for as you move your project from a rough cut to a rough draft.

☐ All written content has been finalized, edited, and proofread.

☐ All visual and aural elements (photos, illustrations, logos, videos, audio clips, etc.) have been edited in the appropriate software to their exact lengths or sizes and converted to the correct formats and resolutions, and they have been placed in their exact locations within the project.

☐ Fonts, text sizes, and color schemes have been implemented consistently throughout the document.

Usability Testing by Any Other Name

Throughout this book, we've referred to the feedback loop as a method for checking your work with your stakeholders. But you may be familiar with other names for this process, such as *workshopping* or *usability testing*. Workshops are usually considered a process that happens within a writing class and are a valuable part of the writing, design, and revision process. But since this book focuses on real-world projects, our feedback loop is more analogous to usability testing, which is a term you'd hear in technical writing and other professional circles. Usability testing asks real users—those people who are the target audience of your project—to perform certain tasks with your materials and report on their experiences. Since we suspect that users of this book are somewhere between the writing classroom and the professional world (if not in both!), we use *feedback loop* as a nice compromise. But really these terms all mean the same thing.

- ☐ Styles (when appropriate) have been used, and style guides have been followed.
- ☐ Animations (title screens, visual transitions, object movement, etc.) have been edited, synced for appropriate duration on-screen, and placed in their final locations in the project.
- ☐ Color photocopies of all visual elements have been printed at the quality needed.
- ☐ Soundtracks or other whole-project media elements have been edited for appropriate volume, added to the timeline, and synced to the individual scenes or navigation.
- ☐ Navigation or movement within the project (e.g., prezi path, slideshow autoplay, Web menu, performance blocking, etc.) has been created and finalized.
- ☐ Nothing is broken (e.g., images are in place, links work, videos don't stall, programs don't crash, etc.).
- ☐ The project has been exported from its editing program (e.g., Word, InDesign, Publisher, Movie Maker, iMovie, Audacity, Dreamweaver, KompoZer, etc.) into the final output format (e.g., converted to a PDF, MOV, or MP3 file; moved onto a Web server; etc.).

Preparing for Rough Draft Feedback

A useful review provides feedback on an author's in-progress (but hopefully nearly completed) work. When stakeholders provide feedback, they often intuitively understand the rhetorical situation and genre expectations of a text. Sometimes, however, reviewers don't know how to evaluate a project because they are not familiar with the particular situation or genre or because they are used to working

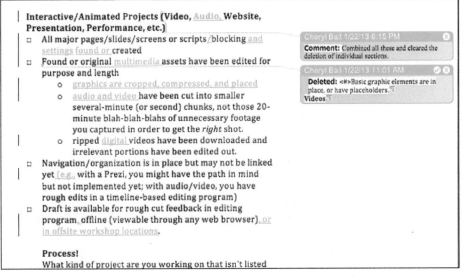

▲ FIGURE 21.4

A Rough Draft in Microsoft Word

We had plenty of rough drafts for this book—more than twenty, in fact. Each time that we made revisions (using our editors as our feedback loop), we used the Track Changes feature in Word (as shown in this example). Once our editors approved the revisions, we cleared them out (by accepting them) and continued revising *other* sections that still needed work.

How Will Readers Interact with Your Project?

As an author, you should be able to accommodate your readers interacting with whatever delivery method they might encounter your text through, as you prepare for them to give you feedback. Will they view your text on-screen? If so, what kind of screen will they view it on—computer, mobile handheld, tablet? Where will they view it? In the library, in their home office, in a classroom, on a train? Will they view it over a wireless or an Ethernet connection? Having them document this information for you will also help you troubleshoot any viewing issues.

on other kinds of projects. You can help a reader understand whether your project hits (or doesn't hit) the mark by providing them with a summary of the project's rhetorical situation; your summary should address some of the following questions:

» Who is the **intended audience** for this piece, and what rhetorical moves does the designer make to appeal to these readers/listeners/viewers/users? What suggestions do you have for further strengthening this approach or for better attending to the target audience?

» How well is the **purpose** of the project conveyed through its organization/navigation? Is there a coherent message for the audience to follow? Do the authors offer some kind of commentary (the "so what" of the argument or story)? What suggestions do you have for adding or deleting content for the sake of clarity?

» How credible do you find the **sources** used for the project's argument? Were there any sources you found problematic? If so, which ones and why, and what would you suggest be used in their place? Were there sources missing that you'd suggest for the project?

» Are the **design choices** (emphasis, contrast, organization, alignment, and proximity) used in this project appropriate? If some seemed inappropriate in relation to the rhetorical situation, what suggestions would you make for revising?

» Do the **mode and media** choices contribute to the overall purpose and meaning conveyed by the project? Are there any you would add or delete, and if so, why?

» Does the project match expected **genre conventions**? If not, does it break those conventions in productive ways that serve the text's rhetorical situation?

Prepare a summary for your reviewers, making sure that you address the questions above. Consider whether the summary should be delivered as a presentation, in writing, or in some other medium. #Analyze #Create

Providing Feedback as a Stakeholder

While you may be eager to hear commentary about your own project, providing feedback to your colleagues can be equally valuable in terms of helping you think about different and successful approaches to multimodal projects. As a reviewer of someone else's work, you have three main tasks:

1. to **read the text** from the perspective of a particular audience/rhetorical situation for which that text is intended (the summary of rhetorical situation and genre conventions is intended to assist readers with understanding this perspective),

2. to **evaluate** whether the text is successful at meeting the criteria/expectations required by that rhetorical situation, and

3. to **provide constructive feedback** to the author based on the text's (in) effectiveness.

Reading the Text   When reviewing a text, you should begin by familiarizing yourself with the rhetorical situation and genre expectations of the project. A summary or checklist like the one we recommended you create in the marginal activity on page 802 can be useful if you are unfamiliar with the genre, intended audience, or other elements of the rhetorical situation.

You may need time to figure out how the text works and why it works the way it does, and to discover whether there are elements of what the author has designed that you like (or don't like). Being an active reviewer—trying to figure out what the author's reasoning was for a particular design choice or rhetorical decision—will aid you in providing constructive feedback. In other words, don't just assume an author did it wrong.

Evaluating the Text   As you read, take notes on how and why you respond to the piece. This is where the summary of the rhetorical situation and genre conventions created by the author will serve as a touchstone for evaluating the project. As a reader, do you feel that the project meets your needs and expectations? Does it miss anywhere? For each question or comment that you pose to the author, you should be able to include discussion of "why" and "how" in your review.

Providing Constructive Feedback   In preparing your review from your reading notes, you should identify the main strengths and weaknesses of the project, summarizing your thoughts about how well the piece meets the rhetorical situation. Discuss how the piece meets (or doesn't meet) the project criteria, and provide formal and constructive feedback, including revision suggestions whenever possible. In many cases, rough draft reviews (rather than rough cut reviews) are written up and provided to the authors so that they can refer back to the review comments throughout the revision process. Here are some tips for writing a useful review:

» Use the beginning of the review to summarize the project's purpose back to the author, which helps the author see whether you understood the piece in the way that he or she intended or in a different way.

FIGURE 21.5 ▶
Feedback on a Presentation
Cheryl watched this prezi by Shawn Apostel and recorded audio of herself giving him feedback. Visit bedfordstmartins.com /WOVEN to watch the prezi, listen to the recording, and analyze Cheryl's feedback.

» Be generous in your reading, and be helpful and productive in explaining what's not working in the piece and how you think the author should revise the project. Use a tone that will help the author take in your advice rather than just be offended by it. Help the author recognize what is working so that he or she can build on those positive aspects in revising.

» The review should usually address revision suggestions in a hierarchical way, moving from the biggest issues to the smallest issues. Small issues are sometimes left out of the review if big-picture issues overwhelm the project. For example, it may not be important that a project has some grammatical errors if it's not hitting the mark as far as its overall purpose.

» Alternately, a review might be structured as a reader-response—that is, it might follow the reader's chronological progression through the text. But summaries at the beginning and end of the review are still helpful in contextualizing the reviewer's minute-by-minute commentary.

» Always explain why and how a project is or isn't working well, and make sure that your revision suggestions are clear, even if your revision ideas are more like suggestions than must-dos.

Using Feedback to Revise

Now that you have received feedback on your rough draft from your instructor, classmates, and/or stakeholders, it's time to evaluate the suggestions and make plans for revision. Try to consider *why* reviewers responded in the way that they

write/design assignment

did and whether there are changes you can make so that you get the kind of reaction you were intending. For instance, in the example we discussed in Chapter 18 (see pp. 709–10) the *Pank Magazine* cover designer had to revise some of his original design choices, based on stakeholder feedback, to achieve the rhetorical goals for his project. Remember, the reviewers had said this about the draft shown in Figure 21.6:

> The hair designs feel a bit more serious while still keeping an edgy sensibility. The second of the two feels the most polished to us, and we like that it helps to emphasize the journal name itself. I'm wondering if I can see 2 or 3 variations on the theme, leaving the image(s) as is, but playing with the typography a bit?

As the designer revised his mock-up to emphasize the name of the magazine, he aligned the image on the right and framed the logo *[Pank]* in the doll's hair. In his final cover, shown in Figure 21.7, *[Pank]* is also emphasized through the contrast between the heavy black font and the beige background. He also aligned the issue number in the curl of the bracket itself (draw an imaginary line from the top of the *n* in *no.* up to the logo and you'll see how the issue number is positioned). This helped to create proximity between the journal's name and the issue number, thus establishing a unified appearance so that the audience might more easily apprehend what they are looking at. The designer also worked to keep the cover edgy through the use of this photograph. The image creates an ethereal, eye-catching effect, and the fact that the doll seems to be reaching for the title of the magazine makes it even more appealing (and truthfully, a little creepy!).

FIGURE 21.6 ▶
***Pank Magazine
Cover Draft***
The stakeholders
wanted the designer
to work from this draft
of the *Pank* cover.

Creating a Revision Plan

After reviewing all of the feedback you've gotten, you should assess which revisions are important given your project goals, noting that sometimes reviewers have bad days, or they don't understand your rhetorical situation (because they aren't the intended audience). But don't let yourself be fooled into thinking that you are always right and that your project doesn't need any revisions. If a majority of your reviewers indicated that your font choice will give your audience the willies or that the tone of your script is condescending, they are probably right. In addition, if a majority of your reviewers didn't mention a particular problem, but one reviewer made a *really good argument* for revising and backed it up with evidence from your text and your rhetorical situation summary, it's likely that the suggestion is a good one, and you'll need to consider addressing it as well. Here are some questions to help you determine which revisions you need to make:

» What were the strengths of my draft that I should be sure to keep?

» What design choices were problematic, and how can I revise these?

» What rhetorical choices seemed out of place in my draft, and how can I better attend to my audience, purpose, context, and genre?

◀ FIGURE 21.7
Final *Pank* Cover
After revisions based
on editorial feedback.

» What multimodal elements can I add or revise to strengthen the rhetorical effect and credibility of my project?

» What are the most important changes I need to consider as I revise?

» Given the time and technology constraints of this project, what can I reasonably revise before the next due date? What else would need revision that I don't have time to complete but *should* complete, given enough time and resources?

write/design assignment

Revising Your Project

Paying close attention to the feedback you've received and the revision plan you've created, revise your rough cut into your final project. Your task is to make recommended changes and put the finishing touches on your project so that it accomplishes all of your rhetorical goals. You will want to ensure that all of the multimodal elements you've included are purposeful and support the credibility of your project and that your audience can understand and navigate your text as you intend. Then test your project by using it in a venue as close to its final publication or presentation location as possible. Tweak and revise as necessary, until you're satisfied that the text does its rhetorical work and/or you're out of time.

Putting Your Project to Work

As you work toward revising and finalizing your project, this chapter will give you some additional considerations to make sure all of your hard work pays off. You want to be sure that your final product functions effectively for its context and audience. You'll need to think about how to distribute your project—whether in print, online, or on some kind of portable media format (DVD, USB drive, etc.)—and how to ensure that clients or future users of your project can understand your rhetorical and design decisions if they plan to continue developing your materials. Throughout this chapter, we offer tips for making your project **sustainable**, so that it will endure through changes in technology and (lack of) human interaction, particularly after you have delivered your project to its stakeholders and are no longer responsible for maintaining it.

Delivering Multimodal Content

When you reviewed your technology options in Chapter 9 (pp. 178–81), you considered the possibilities for distributing your final project. Read through the following list of questions and make some final decisions about who you want to see and use your project and how you want them to be able to access it. Some of these issues may require you to do additional research, but you can easily find information about things like file formats and access restrictions through a quick Web search. These kinds of questions, which cover access and storage issues,

FIGURE 21.8 ▶
**Planning for
Down the Road**
It's good practice to
plan for the future
of your multimodal
project well before the
project is due.

will help with the sustainability of your project—an issue that most multimodal authors have to address when working on their projects.

Who Will Use Your Project?

» Should access to your project be restricted to your client or audience, or should it be available to people who may not be part of your intended audience? When you upload a video to YouTube, for example, you can set it to be viewable by any user or restrict access to just the people you share the link with.

» Do you want to be able to easily share your project with friends, family, and potential employers (and are you allowed to, based on permissions or confidentiality issues)? If you want to embed an audio or video project into a social networking site like Facebook, you'll need to think about file size and format.

How and Where Will They Use It?

» Will your audience look at a print copy of your project, an online version, or an electronic file stored in the cloud or on a CD, DVD, or USB drive? How will you get the project to them?

» Will your audience need any special software to view/use your project? For example, if you created a webtext in HTML/CSS, any Web browser will be able to display the files. If you developed an interactive animation in Flash, your audience will need to have the Flash Player plug-in installed in their Web browser. How will you make sure that your audience has this plug-in?

» Is your project platform-dependent? That is, will it run only on a Mac, or only on a PC, or only on Linux? Some programs export file types that are viewable only on a single platform. How will your audience gain access to the platform they need to view your project? Or can you create the project in multiple file types?

» What file format should you save your project in so that your audience can most easily access it? For example, if you've created an audio project, have you exported your final version as an MP3 so that it can be played on a wide variety of computers and devices?

» What resolution or compression quality should you use? If you are producing materials for print, their resolution should be a minimum of 300 PPI (pixels per

Public		folder
SS comments on WriterDesigner draft 01-08-13		shared folder
SS comments on WriterDesigner draft 11-26-12		shared folder
WriterDesigner1-18-13-CLEANED		folder
WriterDesigner1-19-13-TRIMMED		folder
WriterDesigner1-21-13-cbREV		shared folder

▲ FIGURE 21.9
Sharing Files with Dropbox
We used Dropbox to share a lot of the drafts of this book. The shared folders followed a standard naming convention we'd created. The shared folders were shared only among the three authors and our editor, whereas anyone on the Web could have accessed the "Public" folder.

▲ FIGURE 21.10
A Project Gone Viral
Daughters of Ryan Cordell of Northeastern University started the Facebook page Twogirlsandapuppy in the hopes of convincing their father to get them a puppy. Cordell never expected the page to actually get one million likes, which it did in less than twenty-four hours. The family was invited onto *Good Morning America* within the week, got a puppy (from a shelter, another form of sustainability practice), and answered thousands of pieces of fan mail. Would you be prepared to follow through like this with your multimodal project?

inch). If you're creating a video that you want to be viewable on the Web, you'll need to carefully balance image quality with file size so that users can start to watch the video as quickly as possible but still see clear images.

Preparing for the Multimodal Afterlife

Now that you've finished your multimodal project, consider what will happen once you walk away from it. Unless you've set up a *Mission: Impossible*–style self-destruct option (warn your clients if you do!), your text will continue to have a life of its own long after you've forgotten about it. This can be both good and bad.

» **Good:** Maybe your "lolcats meowing 'Happy New Year'" video that you posted to a video-sharing site goes viral, and you and your cats get invited to appear on a late-night TV show. (Well, that could be a bad thing, too.)

» **Bad:** The photo album of you dancing at a New Year's Eve party, which you unthinkingly posted to your public Facebook account to share with your friends, shows up in a Web search by the human resources department for a company where you recently interviewed for a job that you really need. And they don't hire you.

» **Worse:** You already work for the company and they fire you because somebody in the background of one of those Facebook photos was doing something not just stupid or silly but illegal, and you're now a party to that illegality.

These examples relate primarily to **privacy** issues that all digital media authors need to consider, but authors must also consider **security** issues for the afterlife of their text. In this metadata-filled, face-recognition tagging, hacker- and spam-prone age, everyone should consider privacy and security. Even Cheryl, a supposed expert in digital media, had her server hacked—during finals week, no less, with all of her syllabi and course assignments on the server!—because she hadn't bothered to keep up with the security updates to the blogging software she had installed months or, in some cases, years ago. Getting hacked is just one example of a major security breach that can take days or weeks to fix, if it can even be fixed at all without deleting everything and starting over. And once you're done with a project (particularly if it's for a client or class, and only if you really *don't* need to work on it anymore), the last thing you want to worry about is starting over. So ask yourself the following questions.

Where Are Your Project Files Located?

» If they're stored online, is that online location private (password-protected and/ or only available to a very limited group of collaborators or clients)?

  » Who do you want to continue having access to that private location? Remove/ unshare/delete any users that should no longer have access.

  » Is the location secure enough to leave the files there as a backup?

  » What will you do if that backup location stops providing the service you're using? How often will you check back to see whether the service may be discontinued? Can you set up an automatic notification?

» Is that online location public (available on the Web for any search engine to scan or a potential boss to see)?

  » Do you need to have that final draft available publicly? If not, pull it down. If you do, perhaps you're not really done with this project, and you need to make plans (vis-à-vis financial or labor resources, time management, and other things outside the scope of this book's discussion) for maintaining it.

  » Does the metadata for the project allow a level of privacy that you're comfortable with now and will be comfortable with into the future? Will you be able to update the metadata to reflect your changing privacy needs as you get older?

▲ FIGURE 21.11
Keeping Content on Facebook
Should you rely on platforms like Facebook, Picasa, YouTube, and others to keep your valuable multimedia content safe? No. Always keep backups.

How Long Are You Responsible for the Project?

» How often do you need to check into that location to make sure your privacy is being maintained?

» How often do you need to perform any upgrades or updates to the location to ensure your privacy and security? Can you set up an automatic update or arrange to be notified automatically when an update needs to be made?

» Should you copy online files (whether public or private) to an off-line location and delete the online versions?

  » Do you need to keep a copy of the files at all?

  » If so, what kind of storage device will you keep them on, and how will you ensure that you will be able to use that storage device five years from now? (Remember floppy disks? Zip disks? Probably not . . .) What is your plan for transferring your files to an upgraded storage device, or do you anticipate a time when you will stop caring about the files altogether?

Many of these questions depend on what the project is, how important it is that you and other people continue to have access to it, and what its longevity (its usefulness and rhetorical purposefulness) is expected to be. We're not all famous people who need our every digital file archived in the Library of Congress, but that doesn't mean we should just randomly delete stuff. Depending on your career path, you might need to create a portfolio of your work or refer back to an example or use an old photo in a new project. Be judicious about deleting—it should be a decision that is directly tied to the rhetorical situation of your text as well as to future, unknown rhetorical situations that are probable, given who you are and what you're likely to do with your life. Storage is cheap and getting cheaper all the time. Plus, you'll never know what you'll want to show your great-grandkids, nieces and nephews, parole officers, or cyborg pets in the future.

Take Responsibility for Your Stuff!

Yes, it might be annoying to perform regular upgrades to work we're no longer actively using, but that's the price we pay for having someone else keep copies of our stuff for us. Third-party hosting or sharing services are neither our mothers nor our guardians. They are not responsible for making sure our stuff is safe. Only banks do that (or at least we hope they do). And banks have insurance for those rare occasions when your stuff gets stolen. You don't actually get the items back; you get the monetary equivalent. But you don't get even that with free file-sharing or hosting sites or with social media sites; you only get lost projects and hacked accounts. So do the upgrades!

write/design assignment

Creating a Sustainability Plan

Use the questions on pages 808–12 to craft a sustainability plan for your project. This plan should include descriptions of where the project will reside (i.e., the storage and/or delivery medium), who will have access to it, what the access codes are (if any), and any other information relevant to the transfer of your project to your client. In other words, how will your project endure after you've completed it? For most of these questions, there is no clear-cut answer. Instead, it is a matter of weighing the pros and cons to find the solution that is best for your project's particular rhetorical situation.

Preserving Projects through Metadata

Deciding on a delivery medium for your multimodal project only fulfills part of the requirements for finalizing all of your hard work. Let's say your delivery medium is the Web, or more specifically a third-party hosting site such as Facebook, YouTube, Prezi, SoundCloud, or Wikimedia. You could just upload your project and walk away. As we discussed in the last section, you should tell your client where your project is located—but perhaps your client is not your intended audience! Maybe you've created a radio essay that you will turn in for a class project, but you also will upload it to a radio-essay Web site such as StoryCorps. So your teacher is your client, but the Web site listeners are your audience. How will your intended audience actually *find* your project? How will other people know what it is? How will a computer, which can only scan text, search for your audio file? Metadata is

◀ FIGURE 21.12
StoryCorps Web Page with Metadata
The Web page for this Studs Terkel story contains metadata in the form of a title, a recording location, credits, a description, and other data.

the answer. **Metadata** is data about data: information about a piece of content that can tell a reader who created the content, what it represents, when it was recorded, and other bits of info that make your project findable and thus usable by others.

You've probably seen keywords, tags, categories, and other metadata on media-sharing sites like Wikimedia Commons. Each media element that an author uploads to Wikimedia Commons has to include written information or data *about* the media element so that Wikimedia can help other users find that element. Without this metadata, the media element won't be easily found by, say, a user searching for the perfect audio sound effect of rain falling in Glenshaw, Pennsylvania, to include in her documentary about that tiny town.

A screenshot of the summary section of the Wikimedia Commons page for the sound effect of "Heavy rain in Glenshaw, PA" (Fig. 21.13) shows some of the metadata for this one file. The metadata includes a description of the sound effect, the date it was recorded, the source of the work, the author who created it, what the file's permissions are, where the file was recorded, and a bunch of other information further down the page. Researchers can search for the town name (if they need a specific geographic location), date (if they need a specific time period), and so on

What metadata does your delivery medium require? Which metadata do you need to create and which can you access in your project's written documentation and reuse? #Understand #Apply

FIGURE 21.13 ▶
Finding Metadata on a Wikimedia Commons Page

from either a search engine or from the Wikimedia Commons home page, where users can browse for content by topic, media type, author, copyright license, or publication source (among other options). All of this information is metadata that the file's author included when he or she uploaded the file to the Web. Additionally, supporting written material such as transcripts of audio/video files and descriptions from proposals can function as metadata for your final project. Including all of this information will help make sure that your project is sustainable.

Documenting Your Design Process for Future Users

Documentation explains how a project was created or how to use it. There are many kinds of documentation, such as white papers, reference manuals, online help files, and user guides. Providing documentation is another way to make your project sustainable, as it helps your clients or stakeholders understand how you designed your project so that they can add to or revise your work in the future. This is particularly important for a project that you know the client *will* continue to revise after you've stopped working on it. Clients will often continue working on projects after you've finished designing them, especially if you're volunteering, getting paid with one-time grant funds, or participating in a service-learning class. Projects such as newsletters, training documentation, blogs, and other serialized or continually updated texts often have a series of people working on them, which increases the likelihood that the texts will remain active and useful for the stakeholders. Providing documentation is the best way to help the next person figure out how to carry on your work. There are many ways to document your processes. In the next few sections we explain two types of documentation methods: wikis and comments. Depending on your project, you may need one or both of those methods, or you may use some other method or combination of methods to convey your processes to your client. No matter which documentation method you choose, the rhetorical considerations we've used throughout this book will be effective when considering medium, genre, or technology.

Collaborating on Wiki Documentation In Figure 21.14, you can see some of the documentation developed by a team of student writer/designers who created an online literary arts magazine called *Din*. The students who created *Din* wanted future classes of students to be able to put out new editions of the magazine. They decided to use a wiki for their documentation, which allows all registered users to add to and edit the text. This wiki contains specifics about what design elements (in relation to rhetorical choices) the design group used to distribute different social-media iterations of the magazine on a blog and on Facebook; it also hosts an archive of promotional materials and logo designs. In the future, the documentation wiki could easily be changed as needed.

☞ **Process!**

Go to *Wikipedia*, search for a term related to your project, and click that entry's "View history" tab to see what kind of changes have happened recently. How do wiki editors comment on their changes on this page?

FIGURE 21.14 ▶
**Project Documen-
tation in a Wiki**
The project docu-
mentation for *Din*
illustrates and
discusses logo and
visual design choices
(http://dinguidebook.
wikispaces.com).

Delivering Documentation through Comments   A Web site designer will
often embed comments into the HTML code to help future designers understand
the designer's thought process when creating the site. Comments do not show up
on the actual Web page but are viewable in the source code and in Web-editing
programs like Dreamweaver or KompoZer. In the comment shown in Figure 21.15,

```
1   <!DOCTYPE html PUBLIC "-//W3C//DTD XHTML 1.0 Strict//EN" "http://www.w3.org/TR/xhtml1/DTD/xhtml1-strict.dtd">
2   <html xmlns="http://www.w3.org/1999/xhtml" xml:lang="en" lang="en">
3       <head>
4           <title>Department of English at New Mexico State University</title>
5           <meta http-equiv="content-type" content="text/html; charset=iso-8859-1" />
6           <!--
7
8   NMSU CSS-targetable XHTML format template
9   ©2005 NMSU Board of Regents
10
11  Authors:     CC Chamberlin, Phillip Johnson
12  Version:     2.0
13  Date:        2005-09-01
14
15  The purpose of this document is to provide a common format for HTML
16  files so that style sheets can be distributed and updated that can be
17  applied across a wide variety of web documents.  Some extraneous tags
18  are added for future compatibility, and may not be used currently.
19  We've tried to keep the document semantically clean.
20
21  This is the starting point for a document that wants to inherit the
22  look and feel of the NMSU site without having to manually duplicate the
23  page style.  Be aware that if you hack the document structure,
24  future changes to the CSS might cause your hacks to break.  A better
25  approach would be to override the NMSU styles with your own, leaving
26  the document structure alone.
27
28  Special thanks to W3C, A List Apart, Zeldman, CSS Zen Garden, and
29  others who have provided valuable knowledge and examples over the years
30  to make web publishing as clean as it is today.  This document borrows
31  elements from many of these people/organizations.
32
33      -->
34
35          <meta name="author" content="{{ Author }}" />
36          <meta name="Keywords" content="{{ Keywords, comma-delimited }}" />
37          <meta name="Description" content="{{ Description }}" />
38          <meta name="robots" content="all" />
39          <meta name="MSSmartTagsPreventParsing" content="true" />
40
41          <!--
42              Link to the universal NMSU style sheets and the favicon. Note that
43              stylesheets group different styles together; if you need to break
44              things up beyond this, you'll have to use @import and hope that the
45              browser can deal with it.
46          -->
```

```
40    <h1 class="skip">The LO-FI Manifesto</h1>
41    <h2 class="skip">Karl Stolley, Illinois Institute of Technology</h2>
42    <!--Keep screen readers from suffering through the ASCII art with a skip link-->
43    <p class="skip">ASCII art appears below. <a href="#preamble">Skip to main content</a>.</p>
44
45    <!--The span tags on the ASCII art is a perversion of XHTML and CSS. Don't do this. Ever.-->
46    <pre title="The LO-FI Manifesto">
47         / /  / /_      ___   <span class="lo-fi">       _                            _____        </span>
48        / _/ / /__\   / _\<span class="lo-fi">/ /     /___\            /___/ / _/</span>
49       / /_ / /7 / /  __<span class="lo-fi">/ /    / / 7 /           / /     / /</span>
50      \_7 / / /_ \_   <span class="lo-fi">/ /__  / / / /____/ /    _7   _/ /</span>
51        / |/ 7 ___<span class="lo-fi">/ /____/</span>_<span class="lo-fi">\___</span>(_) / __/
52       / /\_/ /   `/ /__ \ / / / /_ 7  _\ / _7 / / /  \
53      / / 7 / / /_7 / / /7 / / / / _/ (__7 / / / / /
54     /_/ /_/ \_,_/ /_/ /_/ /_/ /_  \_7 /___/ \_7 \__/
55
56
57    + - + - + - + - +   + - + - + - + - + - + - + - +
58    | K | A | R | L |   | S | T | O | L | L | E | Y |
59    + - + - + - + - +   + - + - + - + - + - + - + - +
60
```

▲ FIGURE 21.16

Source Code Comments Can Provide Help for Future Users

The code for Karl Stolley's "Lo-Fi Manifesto" includes comments that help new designers learn how to borrow code so that they can tweak it for themselves. Visit **bedfordstmartins.com /writerdesigner** to see how that works.

the designers of New Mexico State University's Web site provide a purpose for this particular document (an HTML template that other NMSU Web designers can use to retain design consistency across university Web pages) and instructions on how to use and modify the styles provided. For non–Web-based projects, marginal comments in word-processing programs might be similarly used.

write/design assignment

Documenting Your Project

The following structure provides a rough guide that you can use to create a documentation guide for clients or for future users of your project. You can also search for other genres of documentation and analyze their structures and conventions, if your needs are greater than these questions suggest. When writing up your documentation, you should refer back to your proposal and style guide (from Chapter 9) as well as your delivery plan (from earlier in this chapter). All of these documents together will help you form a more sustainable documentation guide for your clients or stakeholders.

» **Overview:** What are the major rhetorical goals of your project?

» **Audience:** Who are the target readers/users/viewers of the project, and what design choices have you made to accommodate them?

» **Design:** What ideas guided your organization of this project? If it's a print text, presentation, or webtext, where should key elements be placed? If it's a video, audio, or animation project, what guidelines can you offer for how elements are ordered, compressed, or edited?

» **Media:** What stylistic considerations are there for images, audio, or video used in the project?

Go to a Web site that you used for your project and view its code. (The code can be found under View>Source, or you can search for instructions for finding the source code.) How did the designers of the site use HTML commenting? If they didn't use commenting, are there places where it would have been useful? #Understand

▲ FIGURE 21.17
A Flyer Advertising a Speaking Event
Design choices for this flyer include large type and contrasting colors so that it will stand out on a bulletin board.

Reporting on Your Final Project

In many classes and workplaces, you may be asked to make a presentation on your completed project. Doing so gives you a chance to show off your hard work and to talk about the many decisions and challenges you faced in creating the project. End-of-project reports can be many different genres, including presentations, written reports, white papers, technical papers, scholarly articles, news features, and less formal genres such as blog posts, reflections, and exit interviews. In any of these genres, you have an opportunity to demonstrate to your audience and stakeholders the value of what you've done and the reasoning that got you to that point. Reflecting on your research and design processes as well as on your final project also allows you to see just how much you've learned and how you might approach your next project differently to make it even stronger and more efficient.

If you are required to report on your multimodal project, keep in mind that your task is to be persuasive, not just descriptive. Help your audience understand each of the major design and rhetorical choices you've made and how those choices were appropriate to your particular rhetorical situation. For example, if your task was to create a flyer to advertise a speaking event (as in Fig. 21.17), you could point to the way you used the design choice of contrast to attract readers' attention by placing vividly colored text on a dark background. You could also discuss how this design choice was appropriate for the context because most flyers on a busy bulletin board tend to have a white background; thus this flyer is distinct and stands out. If you were asked to create an audio documentary, you could refer your audience back to the sections of your project in which you incorporated background music or specific sound effects behind your narration to help set a particular mood. No matter what your subject or mode of delivery, discussing why you made the decisions you did will help your audience understand how you attempted to navigate the rhetorical situation.

Here are some questions you should consider when reporting on your multimodal project to your stakeholders or clients:

» What were the primary ideas and intentions that guided your project?

» What were the key rhetorical choices you made?

  » What was your purpose in creating this project?

  » Who was your intended audience, and what did you do to attend to their needs or interests?

» What context did you design this project to be used in, and why?

» How did you select the genre that you used for your project?

»» What were the key design choices you made?

» How did you make use of emphasis, contrast, organization, alignment, and proximity?

» What shaped your decisions about how elements of your project were arranged, whether on paper, on-screen, or in video or audio?

»» What were your key modal choices? Which modes did you use, and why?

»» What shaped your dissemination choices for how and where you would share your project with your audience?

»» What were your most significant project challenges and successes as you planned, researched, drafted, and revised your multimodal project?

»» What would you do differently if you started over? What lessons did you learn that can be applied to future projects?

Search for different genres for presenting your final project, such as reports and white papers. How do these documents differ in terms of their genre conventions? #Understand #Evaluate

Case Study Final Reports

Phillip, a student in one of Jenny's classes, designed the "Scholarship Remixed" flyer in Figure 21.17 (page 818), and was required to write a final report for that project. In the excerpt that follows, you can see how Phillip researched the flyer genre, brainstormed by sketching initial ideas, and worked through the criteria for the assignment to consider the rhetorical situation. His report discusses his design and rhetorical choices, and reflects on his composing process to analyze what worked well and how he might improve both the flyer and his design process in the future.

Preproduction process

I started out thinking about what ideas or images the words might evoke. I gravitated toward the "Scholarship Remixed: Publishing in Virtual Spaces" title because the ideas of remixing and spaces open up lots of possibilities.

I surfed my favorite design sites to look at typefaces and color schemes. I also sketched some drawings to work out the density and hierarchy of the information and to work through a few layout ideas. I decided fairly early on this would be a typographic layout and that I wanted it to be bold in order to stand out from the clutter of a bulletin board.

Rhetorical choices

I suppose the decision to focus on producing a typographic layout is the main rhetorical choice I made. Given that the audience for this presentation is mainly English students, it seemed appropriate to focus on the words and try to find ways to make them interesting without losing readability or clarity. For me, the purpose of a flyer like this is to convince people to show up by focusing on the what, along with the where and when. Toward that end, I made sure that the time and place information is not hidden or ambiguous.

Design principles

Repetition is present in the design and is most apparent in the treatment of the photos and the accompanying text, even though the elements are not exact repeats. Colors also repeat to help unify and balance the design. Alignment is working with the various type elements on a number of levels. Proximity is most obvious in the relationship of the photos to each other and to their accompanying text.

Type

As this was always intended to be a typographic design, I spent a lot of time picking out the typefaces. I used Interstate for the bolder typeface at the top of the design, along with a few variants of News Gothic for everything else. I like the contrast between the two typefaces.

Visit **bedfordstmartins.com/writerdesigner** to see two reflective reports: Phillip's complete report, including his thoughts on the revision process, and Andrew Wasowicz's video reflection from his multimodal class.

write/design assignment

Reporting on Your Project

Analyze what kind of end-of-project report you should create to complete your project and fulfill your clients' needs. Use the questions from the Reporting on Your Final Project section (or others you and your client, boss, or instructor create) and your proposal to produce a final report on your multimodal project for your stakeholders. Your final report might include all of the major texts you've produced as part of this project (depending on the client's needs), and should most definitely include instructions on where the project itself resides or how it will be delivered (e.g., your delivery plan, with metadata) and the project's documentation/style guides. Make plans to turn in the project to your client or instructor. Then go have fun! You're done!

Credits

Art Credits for figures originally from *Writer/Designer*

5.1: Courtesy of Steve Halle; created for the English Department's Publications Unit at Illinois State University; line art by Melaina Comics; **5.2:** Courtesy of Washington State University; **6.1–6.2:** Courtesy of Angela Buchanan; **6.2a:** Courtesy of Twitter and Cheryl Ball; **6.3:** Reproduced with permission of Palgrave Macmillan; **6.4:** Maria Andersen/Prezi Inc.; **6.6:** Musicovery; **6.7:** Courtesy of Edmond Chang; **6.8:** William Maelia/Prezi Inc.; **6.9:** © Elyse Canfield; **6.10–6.11:** Courtesy of Cheryl Ball; **20.2:** Keith Aoki, James Boyle, and Jennifer Jenkins. http://web.law.duke .edu/cspd/comics; **20.3:** Courtesy of Ariel Popp; **20.4a–20.5:** Copyright Creative Commons. Made available by Creative Commons Attribution 3.0 license. http:// creativecommons.org; **20.5:** Courtesy of Martine Courant Rife; **20.6:** Photo courtesy of Jennifer Sheppard; **20.7:** "Piled Higher and Deeper" by Jorge Cham. www .phdcomics.com; **20.8:** Courtesy of Karl Stolley; **20.9:** DreamWorks/Photofest; **20.10:** Courtesy of Adam Arola; **9.1:** Courtesy of freecsstemplates.org. Made available by Creative Commons 3.0 license.; **9.2:** Courtesy of Ariel Popp; **9.3:** "Piled Higher and Deeper" by Jorge Cham. www.phdcomics.com; **9.4:** Project Bamboo; **18.1:** Courtesy of Nick Winters; **18.2:** Courtesy of Kristin Arola; **18.3:** Kenneth Chan; **18.4–18.8:** Courtesy of Courteney Dowd; **18.10–18.14:** Courtesy of Jeff Kuure, Elena Duff, and Matt Seigel; **18.15:** Copyright 2013 by Source, a Knight-Mozilla OpenNews project. Made available by Creative Commons Attribution 3.0 Unported license. http://source.mozillaopennews.org/en-US/articles/how-we -made-snow-fall; **21.1–21.2:** Biosphoto/Superstock; **21.3–21.4:** Courtesy of Cheryl Ball; **21.5:** Shawn Apostel/Prezi Inc.; **21.6–21.7:** Courtesy of Jeff Kuure, Elena Duff, and Matt Seigel; **21.8:** Shutterstock; **21.10:** Courtesy of Ryan Cordell; **21.1:** Cheryl Ball/Facebook; **21.12:** StoryCorps, www.storycorps.org; **21.13:** Wikimedia Foundation; **21.14:** Courtesy of Jen Almjeld; **21.15:** Courtesy of CC Chamberlin and Phillip Johnson; **21.16:** Courtesy of Karl Stolley; **21.17:** Courtesy of Phillip Johnson

Credits for *Writer/Designer* e-Pages

W/D E5.10–E5.16: Courtesy of Washington State University; **W/D E6.1:** Maria Andersen/Prezi Inc.; **W/D E6.3–E6.4:** Courtesy of Edmond Chang; **W/D E6.5– E6.6:** William Maelia/Prezi Inc.; **W/D E6.7–E6.8:** Courtesy of Cheryl Ball/Matt Wendling; **W/D E10.1–20.15:** Keith Aoki, James Boyle, and Jennifer Jenkins. http://web.law.duke.edu/cspd/comics; **W/D E20.17–20.18:** Creative Commons